Texas Edition · **Texas Teacher Wraparound Edition**

GLENCOE

FOUNDATIONS OF PERSONAL FITNESS

Helping You Meet the Foundations of Personal Fitness Texas Essential Knowledge and Skills (TEKS)

Contents:

Correlations:

McGraw Hill **Glencoe**

New York, New York   Columbus, Ohio   Chicago, Illinois   Peoria, Illinois   Woodland Hills, California

Texas Teacher Wraparound Edition   ISBN: 0-07-845809-9

GLENCOE
THE LEADER IN FITNESS AND HEALTH EDUCATION

Glencoe, leading the way in fitness and health education, provides programs to guide students toward personal fitness and wellness. A comprehensive approach to fitness and health is essential in motivating teens toward developing behaviors for a lifetime of personal fitness.

Designed to Help Students Get Fit and Stay Fit

With *Foundations of Personal Fitness*, students get moving and stay active. This visual program emphasizes the health-related and skill-related components of physical fitness.

Customized for Texas

Glencoe's *Foundations of Personal Fitness* textbook supports the Texas Essential Knowledge and Skills (TEKS) for Foundations of Personal Fitness. Students develop personal fitness programs with motivating activities.

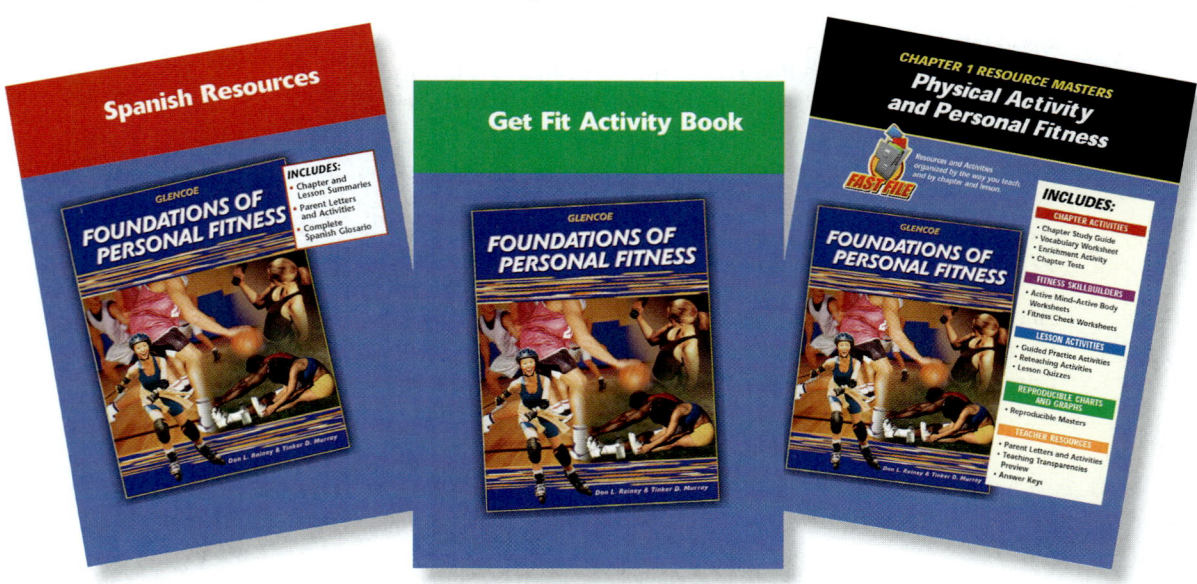

INTEGRATE YOUR FITNESS PROGRAM WITH GLENCOE's WINNING HEALTH PRODUCTS

Provide a strong foundation to improve skill-related and health-related fitness with Glencoe's *Teen Health* and *Glencoe Health*, promoting health skills development for lifelong health and wellness.

Teen Health

Give students a new approach for building health skills with Glencoe's three-book middle school series. Students model, practice, and apply what they learn while laying the foundation for building lifelong health skills.

Glencoe Health

Real-life application of health skills helps high school students apply what they learn in health class toward healthy behaviors for a lifetime. Hands-on features are integrated with technology, embedded assessment, and updated health content.

Customized, Standards-Based Program for TEXAS Teachers and Students

Glencoe's New *Foundations of Personal Fitness* program teaches the Texas Essential Knowledge and Skills (TEKS) for Foundations for Personal Fitness courses.

Any Body Can...Participate in Physical Activity

Students follow specific instruction as they learn to evaluate and improve their health-related as well as skill-related fitness in focused lessons and features.

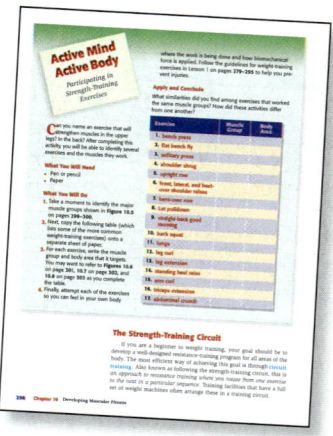
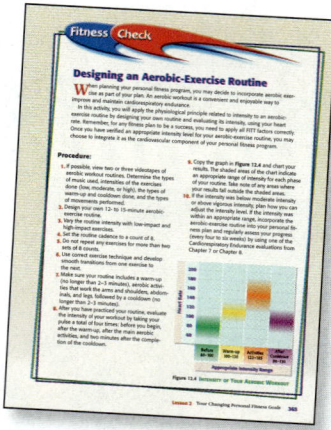

Any Body Can...Apply Fitness Principles

Features specially designed to encourage students to apply what they learn about the important principles of getting and staying fit.

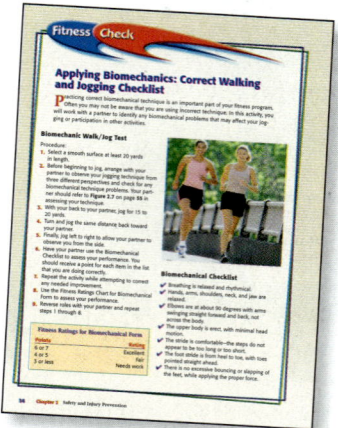
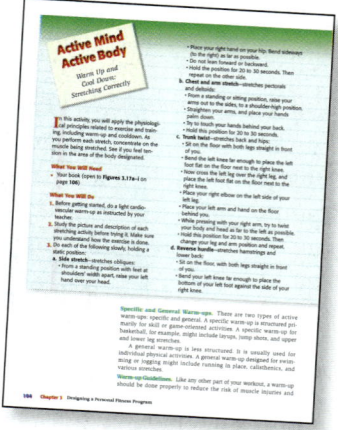
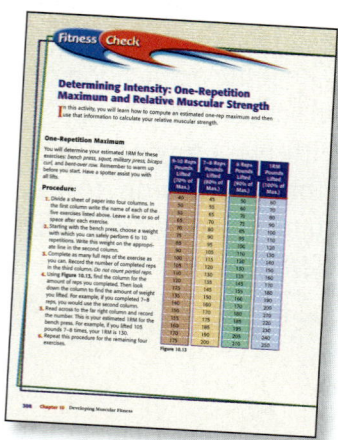

Any Body Can...Improve Daily Performance

Developing and maintaining a personal fitness program is the goal for all students, and each lesson and activity helps students in improving their daily fitness performance.

The major theme of this program emphasizes that developing and maintaining an active lifestyle is a goal that all teens can achieve. While not everyone can be a star athlete, any body can develop a successful personal fitness plan to improve their quality of life.

Promoting Wellness and Lifelong Physical Activity

Emphasize Key Concepts Using Fitness and Health Technology Options

Choose from a wide variety of options available from Glencoe's trusted Fitness and Health programs to engage students while enhancing and personalizing your fitness course for complete coverage of topics.

Fitness Video/DVD Package

Health Video Series

- Nutrition for Active Fitness
- The Human Body: Brain and Nervous System
- Warning Signs: A Look at Teenage Violence

Nutrition and Physical Activity CD-ROM

Expanded Health and Fitness Web Site

All-new Internet site combines health and fitness activities, study tools, and interactive resources.

TEXAS REPRODUCIBLE LESSON PLANS

Texas Reproducible Lesson Plans are developed especially for you, coded with TEKS correlations, making it easy for you to be sure that you have addressed each of the TEKS objectives for the Foundations of Personal Fitness for high school students. You can customize your fitness class lesson plans, choosing from a 9-week or 18-week schedule, to integrate all the concepts, activities, and resources from one convenient booklet.

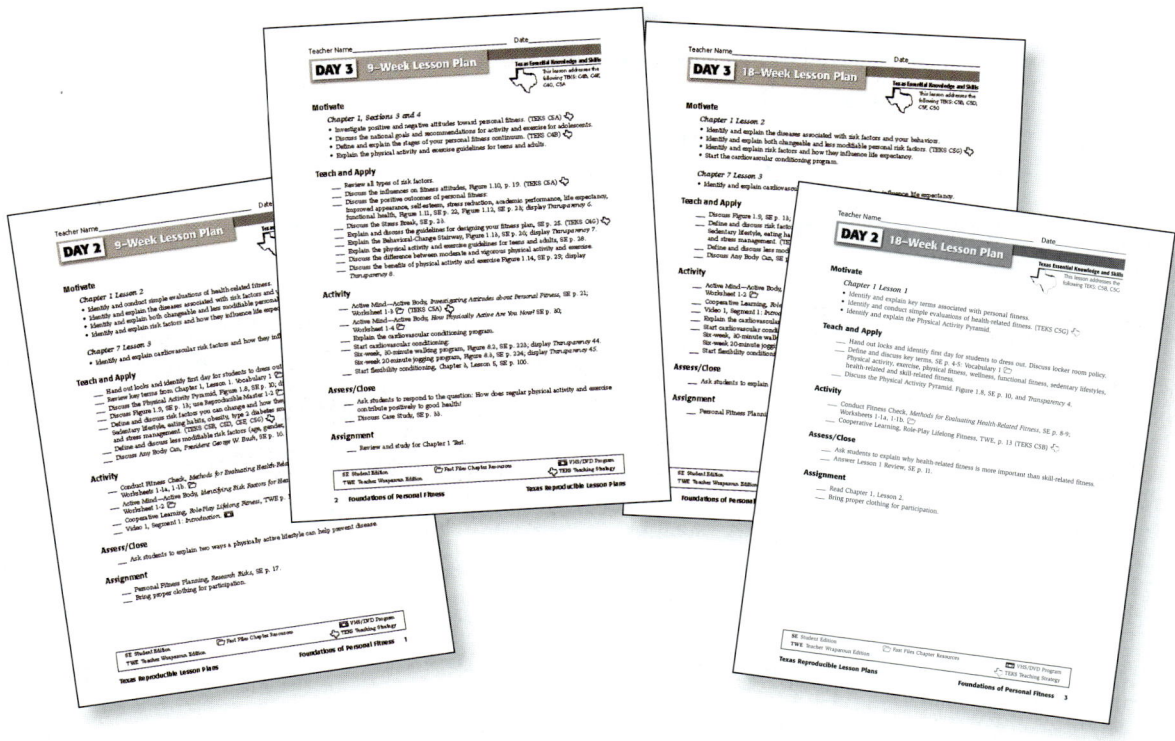

Correlations to TEKS Objectives

Correlations for the entire textbook appear in this Texas Teacher Wraparound Edition, both by Texas Essential Knowledge and Skills fitness objectives, on page TX10, and by chapters and lessons of the text on page TX13, for your quick reference. You can plan your lesson presentation, and then use the Texas Reproducible Lesson Plan sheets to record and report as you teach each TEKS objective.

Your Fitness Program to Improve Adolescent Health

Adolescents in Texas are facing the same risks that challenge young people all across America—obesity, overweight, and diabetes rates are climbing and other chronic diseases are affecting more and more people at younger ages. The Youth Risk Behavior Surveillance System (YRBSS) survey, conducted by the National Center for Chronic Disease Prevention and Health Promotion, identifies many of the health behaviors that can be improved through an effective program of physical activity and health aimed at changing these behaviors. The survey monitors major health risk behaviors that contribute to obesity, overweight, diabetes, and leading causes of death and disability among the youth of our nation. These behaviors include tobacco use, poor nutrition, and inadequate physical activity.

> **Glencoe's *Foundations of Personal Fitness* equips your students with the necessary skills to reverse these trends and improve health and fitness levels in the youth of Texas.**

Centers for Disease Control and Prevention Youth Risk Behavior Surveillance System Youth Risk Behavior Survey	2001 Texas Results
Question	**%**
Percentage of students who described themselves as slightly or very overweight	**31.2**
Percentage of students who are at risk for becoming overweight	**14.8**
Percentage of students who are overweight	**14.2**
Percentage of students who exercised to lose weight or to keep from gaining weight during the past 30 days	**59.6**
Percentage of students who ate less food, fewer calories, or foods low in fat to lose weight or to keep from gaining weight during the past 30 days	**43.1**
Percentage of students who went without eating for 24 hours or more to lose weight or to keep from gaining weight during the past 30 days	**13.9**
Percentage of students who took diet pills, powders, or liquids without a doctor's advice to lose weight or to keep from gaining weight during the past 30 days	**9.4**
Percentage of students who ate fruit one or more times during the past seven days	**82.0**

Centers for Disease Control and Prevention Youth Risk Behavior Surveillance System Youth Risk Behavior Survey **Question**	2001 Texas Results %
Percentage of students who ate green salad one or more times during the past seven days	**62.2**
Percentage of students who ate other vegetables one or more times during the past seven days	**81.3**
Percentage of students who ate five or more servings of fruits and vegetables per day during the past seven days	**19.9**
Percentage of students who drank three or more glasses of milk per day during the past seven days	**14.3**
Percentage of students who exercised or participated in physical activities for at least 20 minutes that made them sweat and breathe hard on three or more of the past seven days	**61.8**
Percentage of students who did exercises to strengthen or tone their muscles on three or more of the past seven days	**51.9**
Percentage of students who watched three or more hours of TV per day on an average school day	**44.4**
Percentage of students who attended physical education (PE) class one or more days during an average school week	**48.0**
Of students enrolled in physical education (PE) class, the percentage who exercised or played sports more than 20 minutes during an average physical education class	**85.8**
Percentage of students who played on one or more sports teams during the past 12 months	**56.7**
Percentage of students who used any tobacco during the past 30 days	**32.7**
Percentage of students who smoked cigarettes on one or more of the past 30 days	**28.4**
Percentage of students who did not participate in at least 20 minutes of vigorous physical activity on three or more of the past seven days and did not do at least 30 minutes of moderate physical activity on five or more of the past seven days	**34.3**
Percentage of students who participated in no vigorous or moderate physical activity during the past seven days	**10.8**
Percentage of students who attended physical education (PE) class daily	**32.9**

Correlation of *Foundations of Personal Fitness* to Foundations of Personal Fitness High School TEKS

TEKS	STUDENT EDITION	TEACHER EDITION
C (1) Movement. While participating in physical activity, the student applies physiological and biomechanical principles to improve health-related fitness. The student is expected to:		
(A) apply physiological principles related to exercise and training such as warm-up/cool down, overload, frequency, intensity, specificity, or progression; and	8, 82, 83, 85, 87, 89, 90, 92, 94,100, 101, 102, 104, 108, 109, 111, 158,197, 233, 236, 248, 249, 255, 267, 299, 302, 305, 307, 308, 311, 314, 319, 339, 340, 342, 343, 344, 365	78-79, 83, 84, 92, 96, 102, 104, 106, 156, 197, 221, 234, 235, 279, 281, 288, 299, 302, 306, 307, 308, 311, 319, 326, 327, 367
(B) apply biomechanical principles related to exercise and training such as force, leverage, and type of contraction	53, 54, 56, 89, 228, 247, 250, 253, 256, 276, 297, 298, 302, 303, 325, 328, 331, 341, 344	54, 55, 56, 251, 252, 253, 276, 297, 298, 300, 303, 328
C (2) Social development. During physical activity, the student develops positive self-management and social skills needed to work independently and with others. The student is expected to:		
(A) apply rules, procedures, and etiquette; and	51, 93, 255, 273, 275, 278, 279, 295, 319, 323, 328, 363	6, 213, 255, 261, 275, 278, 283
(B) recognize and resolve conflicts during physical activity.	3, 7, 11, 22, 76, 81	7, 76, 367
C (3) Physical activity and health. The student applies safety practices associated with physical activity. The student is expected to:		
(A) demonstrate safety procedures such as spotting during gymnastics and using non-skid footwear;	47, 50, 52, 69, 262, 268, 273, 276, 279, 323, 327, 349, 353,	49, 78-79, 156, 174, 197, 213, 230, 276, 297, 308
(B) describe examples and exercises that may be harmful or unsafe;	46, 51, 52, 53, 54, 60, 93, 327, 331, 338, 345, 350, 353	45, 55, 240, 276, 278, 350-351
(C) explain the relationship between fluid balance, physical activity, and environmental conditions such as loss of water and salt during exercise; and	40, 41, 42, 46, 69, 122, 125, 126, 127, 128	42, 126, 127
(D) identify the effects of substance abuse on physical performance.	61, 62, 64, 65, 67, 143, 255	6, 63, 64, 65, 66, 204

Correlation of *Foundations of Personal Fitness* to Foundations of Personal Fitness High School TEKS

TEKS	STUDENT EDITION	TEACHER EDITION
C (4) Physical activity and health. The student applies fitness principles during a personal fitness program. The student is expected to:		
(A) explain the relationship between physical fitness and health;	3, 7, 11, 29, 33, 186, 189, 210, 247, 355, 357, 359, 361, 381	10, 36, 87, 151, 154, 173, 175, 177, 186, 204, 247, 358
(B) participate in a variety of activities that develop health-related physical fitness activities including aerobic exercise to develop cardiovascular efficiency;	3, 8, 93, 109, 174, 193, 197, 198, 209, 215, 219, 221, 222, 226, 267, 298, 304, 336, 338, 347, 348, 349, 365	8, 9, 36, 38, 73, 91, 197, 213, 221, 226, 230, 232, 267, 363
(C) demonstrate the skill-related components of physical fitness such as agility, balance, coordination, power, reaction time, and speed;	71, 75, 78, 79, 80, 100, 343, 364, 367, 368	78, 79, 80, 105, 208, 209, 267, 277, 298, 334, 336, 337
(D) compare and contrast health-related and skill-related fitness;	11, 71, 73, 75, 76, 77, 81, 94, 333	77, 248, 333
(E) describe methods of evaluating health-related fitness such as Cooper's 1.5 mile run test;	3, 8-9, 11, 82, 219, 223, 224, 226, 243, 314, 373	224, 267, 373
(F) list and describe the components of exercise prescription such as overload principle, type, progression, or specificity;	5, 82, 83, 84, 89, 90, 94, 95, 96, 100, 107, 156, 233, 235, 236, 248, 249, 262, 302, 313, 340, 361, 369	83, 88, 93, 96, 97,107, 233, 248, 275, 277, 302, 313, 339, 340
(G) design and implement a personal fitness program; and	25, 111, 167, 211, 215, 226, 232, 238, 256, 315, 321, 362, 365	26, 57, 150, 238, 241, 256, 320
(H) evaluate consumer issues related to physical fitness such as marketing claims promoting fitness products and services.	18, 20, 24, 48, 49, 50, 51, 69, 143, 158, 164, 166, 180, 183, 184, 233, 235, 238, 241, 261, 265, 375, 376, 378, 379	20, 48, 50, 166, 183, 184, 229, 232, 235, 238, 240, 263, 265, 268, 373, 376, 378

Correlation of *Foundations of Personal Fitness* to Foundations of Personal Fitness High School TEKS

TEKS	STUDENT EDITION	TEACHER EDITION
C (5) Physical activity and health. The student comprehends practices that impact daily performance, physical activity, and health. The student is expected to:		
(A) investigate positive and negative attitudes toward exercise and physical activities;	18, 19, 20, 21, 24, 33, 111, 148, 355	18, 19, 20, 176, 186, 220
(B) describe physical fitness activities that can be used for stress reduction;	12, 17, 74, 102, 188, 210, 311, 340, 358	16, 74, 76, 157, 188, 311, 340, 358, 366
(C) explain how overtraining may contribute to negative health problems such as bulimia and anorexia;	95, 98, 100, 176, 177, 178, 179, 191	99, 178
(D) analyze the relationship between sound nutritional practices and physical activity;	15, 122, 128, 138, 139, 140, 141, 142, 143, 145, 158, 164, 172, 179, 381	10, 15, 17, 59, 117, 123, 154, 166, 182
(E) explain myths associated with physical activity and nutritional practices;	135, 180, 181, 182, 185, 191, 257, 259, 260, 271	181, 182, 185, 258, 259
(F) analyze methods of weight control such as diet, exercise, or combination of both; and	139, 153, 155, 156, 157, 161, 164, 165, 166, 167, 169, 186, 188, 189, 362, 372	139, 156, 161, 181, 188, 372
(G) identify changeable risk factors such as inactivity, smoking, nutrition, and stress that affect physical activity and health.	12, 13, 14, 15, 16, 17, 23, 64, 67, 137,151, 172, 175, 188, 189, 199, 200, 203, 204, 206, 210, 259, 311, 358	12, 14, 15, 58, 63, 64, 154, 186, 204, 209, 223, 340, 360

Correlation to Texas Essential Knowledge and Skills (TEKS) by Chapter and Lesson

Contents	Page #	SE	TWE
Chapter 1 Physical Activity and Personal Fitness			
Lesson 1 Physical Activity, Exercise, and Health	3–11	2B, 4A, 4B, 4D, 4E, 4F, 5G	2A, 2B, 3D, 4A, 4B, 5D, 5G
Lesson 2 Risk Factors and Your Behavior	12–17	5B, 5D, 5G	5A. 5B, 5D, 5F 5G
Lesson 3 Developing a Positive Fitness Attitude	18–24	2B, 4H, 5A, 5B, 5G	4H, 5A
Lesson 4 Guidelines for Getting Started	25–33	1A, 4A, 4G, 5A,	4A, 4G
Chapter 2 Safety and Injury Prevention			
Lesson 1 Personal Fitness Screening	35–39		4A, 4B
Lesson 2 Environmental Concerns	40–46	3B, 3C	3B, 3C
Lesson 3 Safety Gear and Clothing	47–52	1B, 2A, 3A, 3B, 4H	1B, 3A, 3B, 4H
Lesson 4 Preventing Fitness Injuries	53–60	1B, 3B, 5D	1B, 3B, 3C, 4G, 5D, 5G
Lesson 5 Avoiding Harmful Substances	61–69	3C, 3D, 4H, 5G	3D, 5G
Chapter 3 Designing a Personal Fitness Program			
Lesson 1 Health-Related and Skill-Related Fitness	71–81	1A, 2B, 4A, 4C, 4D, 5B	1A, 2B, 3A, 4B, 4C, 4D, 5B
Lesson 2 FITT and the Principle of Overload	82–89	1A, 1B, 4E, 4F, 4G	1A, 4A, 4F
Lesson 3 The Principle of Specificity	90–94	1A, 2A, 3B, 4B, 4D, 4F, 4G	1A, 4B, 4F, 4G
Lesson 4 The Principle of Progression	95–100	1A, 4A, 4F, 5C	1A, 4F, 5C
Lesson 5 Warm Up, Work Out, Cool Down	101–111	1A, 4A, 4F, 4G, 5A, 5B, 5C	1A, 4C, 4F
Chapter 4 Nutrition and Your Personal Fitness			
Lesson 1 The Importance of Nutrition	113–121	5D	5D
Lesson 2 Vitamins, Minerals, and Water	122–128	3C, 5D	3C, 5D
Lesson 3 Choosing Foods Wisely	129–137	5D, 5E, 5G	5D
Lesson 4 Nutrition for Peak Performance	138–145	3D, 4H, 5D, 5G, 5F	5F

Correlation to Texas Essential Knowledge and Skills (TEKS) by Chapter and Lesson

Correlation to Texas Essential Knowledge and Skills (TEKS) by Chapter and Lesson

Texas State Strategic Health Partnership

Glencoe/McGraw-Hill has partnered with the Texas Department of Health and is committed to the 12 goals of the Texas State Strategic Health Partnership in creating a healthier Texas for teens.

Goal A: Improve the health of all Texans by promoting healthy nutrition and safe physical activity.

Goal B: Promote healthy choices with regard to risky behaviors including, but not limited to, tobacco use, risky sexual behavior, substance abuse, and violence to reduce the disease, disability, and premature death resulting from unhealthy choices.

Goal C: Recognize mental health as a public health issue. Promote mental health and increase individual and community social connections in order to improve prevention, early detection, and treatment of mental disorders.

Goal D: Increase rates of high school graduation, adult literacy, college attendance, and other advanced education and training thereby improving socioeconomic and health status.

Goal E: Reduce health threats due to environmental and consumer hazards.

Goal F: Reduce infectious disease in Texas with a focus on increasing rates of timely immunization among Texas children and adults.

Goal G: By 2010, Texas state statute and local policy will ensure that essential public health services (emphasizing disease/injury prevention and health promotion) are available for all communities in Texas.

Goal H: By 2010, a diverse set of governmental and non-governmental partners will actively participate and collaborate to provide the services necessary to meet the public health needs of Texans.

Goal I: By 2010, Texas communities will be aware of the structure, function, and availability of the public health system.

Goal J: By 2010, the public health system workforce will have the education and training to meet evolving public health needs.

Goal K: By 2010, the Texas public health system will be operating with a flexible funding system that efficiently and effectively meets the needs of communities for all public health objectives.

Goal L: By 2010, the Texas public health system partners will be informed by, and make decisions based on, a statewide, real-time, standardized, integrated data collection and reporting system(s) for demographic, morbidity, mortality, and behavioral health indicators accessible at the local level which also protects the privacy of Texans.

Teacher Wraparound Edition

GLENCOE
FOUNDATIONS OF PERSONAL FITNESS

Any Body Can...Be Fit!

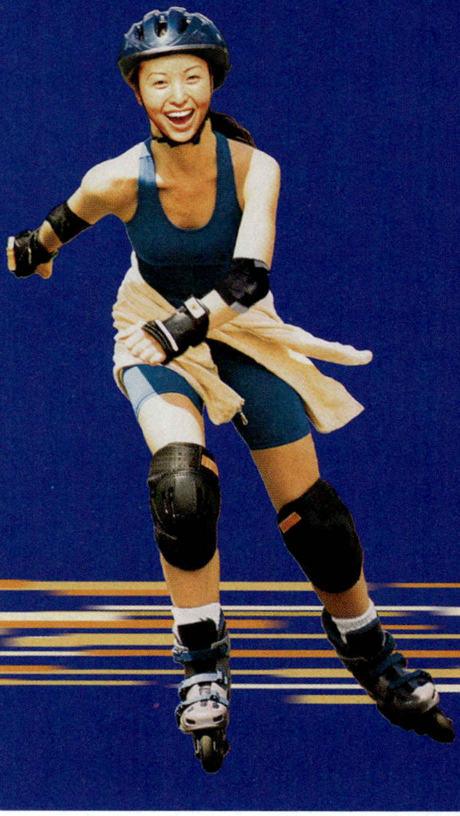

Don L. Rainey & Tinker D. Murray

New York, New York   Columbus, Ohio   Chicago, Illinois   Peoria, Illinois   Woodland Hills, California

Glencoe

Send all inquiries to:
Glencoe/McGraw-Hill
21600 Oxnard Street, Suite 500
Woodland Hills, California 91367

ISBN: 0-07-845127-2 (Student Edition)
ISBN: 0-07-845128-0 (Teacher Wraparound Edition)

Printed in the United States of America.

2 3 4 5 6 7 8 9 0 027 09 08 07 06 05

About the Authors

Don L. Rainey Don L. Rainey is a lecturer and director of the Physical Fitness and Wellness Program in the Health, Physical Education, and Recreation Department at Texas State University in San Marcos, Texas. He earned a Master of Science in Health and Physical Education at Lamar University. He was a founding member of the Texas Association for Health, Physical Education, Recreation and Dance (TAHPERD) Foundations of Personal Fitness Course Committee and taught the course at Marcus High School, where he coordinated health and physical education programs for 12 years. Don received the TAHPERD Honor Award in 1995. He has conducted over 100 workshops about the Foundations of Personal Fitness Course

for educators. He was a subcommittee member for the Governor's Commission on Physical Fitness, which developed the Fit Youth Today Program. He is also certified as a Strength and Conditioning Specialist by the National Strength and Conditioning Association (NSCA). Since 1989 he has worked with Tinker Murray to conduct and publish research in school physical education settings to promote physical activity in adolescents.

Tinker D. Murray Tinker D. Murray is a professor of Exercise and Sports Science in the Health, Physical Education, and Recreation Department at Texas State University. He earned his Ph.D. in Physical Education from Texas A&M University. He was a founding member of the Texas Association for Health, Physical Education, Recreation, and Dance (TAHPERD) Foundations of Personal Fitness Course Committee and has conducted over 60 workshops about the Foundations of Personal Fitness Course for educators. Tinker was given the TAHPERD Honor Award in 1995. He was a subcommittee member for the Governor's Commission on Physical Fitness, which developed the Fit Youth Today Program. He has been a

lecturer and examiner for the USA Track and Field Level II Coaching Certification Program since 1988. He is a fellow of the American College of Sports Medicine (ACSM) and certified as an ASCM program director. Since 1989, he has worked with Don Rainey to conduct and publish research in school physical education settings to promote physical activity in adolescents.

Physical Education Consultants

Kymm Ballard, M.S.
Physical Education Consultant
North Carolina Department of Public
    Instruction
Raleigh, North Carolina

Roberta L. Duyff, R.D., C.F.C.S.
Food and Nutrition Education Consultant
St. Louis, Missouri

D. Marian Franck, M.S., M.Ed.
Physical Education Teacher of the Year
National Association for Sport and
    Physical Education (NASPE)

Mark Giese, Ed.D.
Chair of the Health and Human
    Performance Department
Northeastern State University
Tahlequah, Oklahoma

Bonnie Mohnsen, M.A., Ph.D.
Physical Education Consultant
Cerritos, California

Scott Powers, Ph.D., Ed.D.
Professor and Director, Center for
    Exercise Science
University of Florida, Gainesville

Susannah Turney, M.S., C.A.P.E.
Adapted Physical Education Specialist
Irving Independent School District
Irving, Texas

Steven P. Van Camp, M.D.
Cardiologist, Alvarado Medical Group
Former President of American College of
    Sports Medicine
San Diego, California

Teacher Reviewers

Roy Alaniz, M.S.
Adjunct Professor, University of Texas
Curriculum Specialist
Brownsville Independent School District
Brownsville, Texas

Bill Bundy
Director of Athletics, Health, and Physical
    Education
Katy Independent School District
Katy, Texas

Nancy Duncan, M.A.
Physical Education Teacher
Fort Worth Independent School District
Fort Worth, Texas

Michael Rulon, M.A.
Health/Physical Education Teacher
Johnson Junior High School
Adjunct Faculty, Laramie County
    Community College
Cheyenne, Wyoming

Table of Contents

(Special Populations continued on XTM1–4 at the back of this book)

Physical Activity Benefits All Students

"Regular physical activity performed on a daily basis reduces the risk of developing illness or disease."

—The President's Council on Physical Activity and Sports

Promotes an Active Lifestyle

The new *Foundations of Personal Fitness* program emphasizes that physical activity is an essential part of overall health, especially during adolescence. This exciting text provides a solid foundation for learning the benefits of an active lifestyle and experiencing the positive effects of being physically fit. This comprehensive text offers:

- opportunities to learn and practice lifelong habits and healthful behaviors.

- concise, meaningful content that outlines specific ways for all students to achieve and maintain improved levels of personal fitness.

- appropriate instruction, practice opportunities, and assessments needed to design effective personal fitness programs for an active lifestyle.

Provides Strategies for Reducing Health Risks

Evidence shows that low levels of physical activity in adults are associated with increased risks of chronic diseases and premature death. Adolescent obesity and diabetes are increasing at alarming rates in the United States. National programs have responded by emphasizing the importance of physical activity as an important step toward reversing these trends. *Foundations of Personal Fitness* supports the philosophy that an active lifestyle is one of health care's best preventive strategies. Students are provided with specific information and strategies to develop and maintain personal fitness for a lifetime.

Meets Standards and Supports Learning

Developing and maintaining personal fitness begins with knowledge. The *Foundations of Personal Fitness* text is a comprehensive tool, covering all the basics related to personal fitness as identified by the National Association for Sport and Physical Education Standards. Major concepts related to physical activity and fitness are presented in a format that equips students with useful strategies to improve their fitness levels. The text helps students recognize the differences between health-related and skill-related fitness. Students will find clear explanations of biomechanics and the scientific principles of overload, specificity, and progression. Features highlight the connections between physical activity and self-esteem, stress management, and social skills, including conflict resolution and teamwork.

Emphasizes Inclusion for All Students

With *Foundations of Personal Fitness*, students from all backgrounds and all fitness and ability levels can become physically active and increase their physical fitness. Features throughout reinforce the rich content with proven evaluation methods, personal fitness ratings, and strategies for improving endurance and increasing performance. No matter what their starting point may be, students can set goals, use the assessments, and follow the steps toward developing a personal fitness program to enjoy improved fitness levels.

Any Body Can...Be Fit!

The major theme of the program is *Any Body Can...Be Fit!*—introduced and reinforced throughout the text with the initial letters of *Any Body Can*: A-B-C. The ABC concept demonstrates to students and teachers that developing and maintaining an active lifestyle is a reasonable goal that all adolescents can achieve. Students will see that while not everyone has the genetic makeup and the drive to be a successful and competitive athlete, everyone does have the ability to develop and maintain an acceptable level of physical fitness. This is accomplished in *Foundations of Personal Fitness* by

- reinforcing the recommendations of NASPE and the CDC that teens should participate in a minimum of 225 minutes of activity or exercise per week, and should be active for at least 30 minutes on five or more days per week.

- developing an appropriate fitness program and creating a plan for lifelong fitness, emphasized as an important part of the students' personal goals.

- conducting ongoing personal evaluations and assessments, which provide students and teachers with a systematic method for setting and reaching goals.

The philosophy and content of the course are based on the extensive combined personal and professional experience of the authors, who have successfully developed and implemented this course at the high school physical education level for over 20 years.

It's as simple as A-B-C.

Helping Students Master Knowledge and Skills

Relevant, Focused Lessons

Each lesson follows a strong pedagogical style, guiding students toward mastery of the content and guiding them to apply what they learn.

What You Will Do offers clear objectives, previews the contents of each lesson, and points students to key concepts as they proceed through the text.

Terms to Know are the key terms defined in the lesson. Terms are highlighted in blue throughout so students can spot the definitions.

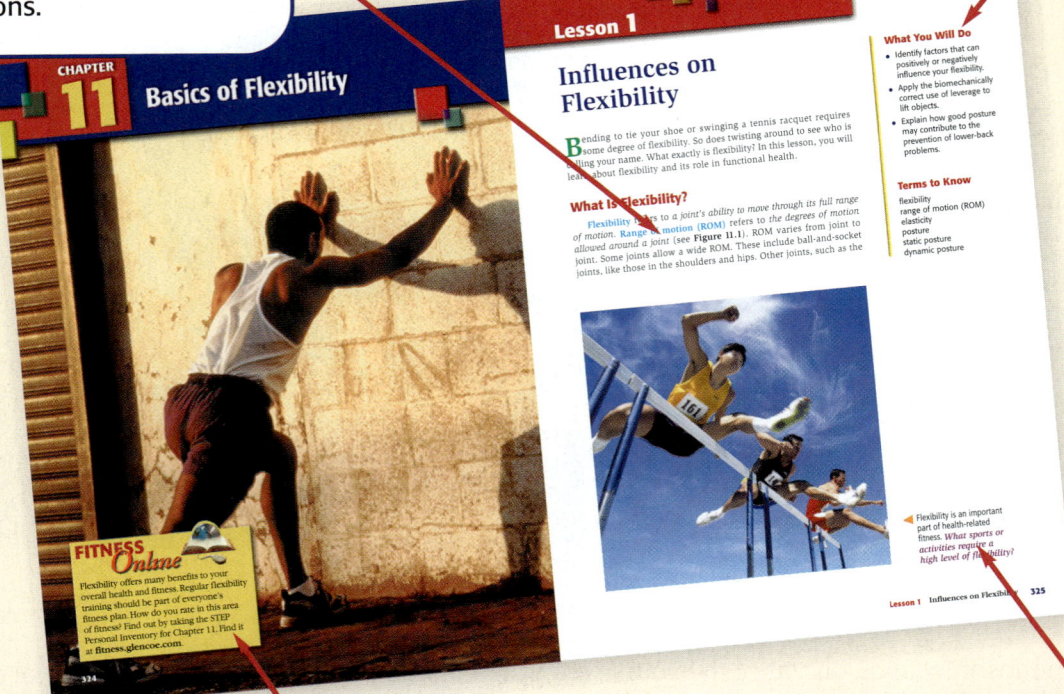

CHAPTER 11 Basics of Flexibility

FITNESS Online
Flexibility offers many benefits to your overall health and fitness. Regular flexibility training should be part of everyone's fitness plan. How do you rate in this area of fitness? Find out by taking the STEP Personal Inventory for Chapter 11. Find it at fitness.glencoe.com.

324

Lesson 1

Influences on Flexibility

Bending to tie your shoe or swinging a tennis racquet requires some degree of flexibility. So does twisting around to see who is calling your name. What exactly is flexibility? In this lesson, you will learn about flexibility and its role in functional health.

What Is Flexibility?
Flexibility refers to a joint's ability to move through its full range of motion. Range of motion (ROM) refers to the degrees of motion allowed around a joint (see Figure 11.1). ROM varies from joint to joint. Some joints allow a wide ROM. These include ball-and-socket joints, like those in the shoulders and hips. Other joints, such as the

What You Will Do
- Identify factors that can positively or negatively influence your flexibility.
- Apply the biomechanically correct use of leverage to lift objects.
- Explain how good posture may contribute to the prevention of lower-back problems.

Terms to Know
flexibility
range of motion (ROM)
elasticity
posture
static posture
dynamic posture

Flexibility is an important part of health-related fitness. What sports or activities require a high level of flexibility?

Lesson 1 Influences on Flexibility 325

The STEP evaluation in every chapter encourages students to Stop, Think, Evaluate, and Proceed with goals and strategies to develop their individual fitness programs.

Captions and discussion questions that accompany each photo provide exciting opportunities to introduce the lesson and assess students' prior knowledge and understanding of content.

Online Support

One of the many technology features in the program begins at the Chapter Opener, giving students the opportunity to examine and assess their present knowledge and to record their progress. Links to **fitness.glencoe.com** and relevant Web sites appear throughout the text.

Techniques for Student Success

Hands-on text demonstrations for use in the physical education classroom get students up and moving with tips to make the most of their training sessions.

Step-by-step instruction provides guidance and proper procedures for a variety of exercises.

Activities include specific criteria to indicate the body area and muscles to be worked, variations, and safety cautions for each movement.

Illustration Program Brings Visual Appeal

Foundations of Personal Fitness is a richly illustrated text. Charts, tables, graphs, and drawings enhance the many photos of real students doing real physical activities to create a positive attitude toward fitness.

Illustrations are strategically placed throughout to give visual appeal while clarifying concepts for visual learners.

Facts, figures, and research support the text with evidence that demonstrates to students the advantages of each activity.

Guiding Students Toward Personal Fitness

Foundations of Personal Fitness sets the standard for empowering students in their personal fitness programs. The comprehensive content is enhanced with skill-building features that let students apply the concepts as they are presented.

Fitness Check Features can be used to formally assess students' knowledge and progress in a particular area of fitness. These full-page features include directions, tips, illustrations, and Fitness Rating Charts to guide students in evaluating and establishing measurable benchmarks for improving their fitness. Separate worksheets provide space for students to record the number of repetitions they do, as well as the dates and times for each activity they perform.

Short, concise examples demonstrate to students how their mental attitudes play an important role in attaining their fitness goals in *Mind Over Matter*.

Physical activity is a great stress reliever, as showcased in the *Stress Break* features appearing throughout the text.

Factual information and statistics provided in *Fitness Facts* give evidence of the importance of physical fitness.

Enhancing Physical Activity with Facts About Fitness

Active Mind–Active Body features highlight the theme that personal fitness is both a mental and a physical activity. In addition to understanding scientific exercise principles and the components of health-related and skill-related fitness, students using the *Foundations of Personal Fitness* program are physically active. The Active Mind—Active Body feature gives students the chance to participate in physical activities while applying critical thinking skills to develop good fitness behaviors and maintain them for life.

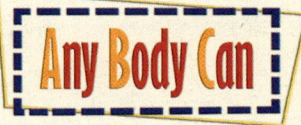
People who have accomplished outstanding performances in a variety of fitness areas are showcased in this feature. They model traits of good character while demonstrating that while not everyone is capable of superior athletic performance, everyone is capable of achieving and maintaining personal fitness.

Strategies offered in *Lifeline* encourage students to reach out to peers with positive attitudes to influence others for a lifetime of fitness.

The *Consumer Corner* builds and reinforces skills in examining and evaluating consumer fitness products and services to help students make informed decisions.

Complete Teaching Support for the Physical Educator

Use class time efficiently to present lessons and activities while keeping your students active in their physical education class. Follow the lesson cycle with strategies for the entire lesson: 1 Motivate; 2 Teach; 3 Assess; 4 Close.

Motivate

- *Getting Started* begins the lesson with a challenging discussion.
- *In This Lesson* previews lesson features.
- *Introducing Vocabulary* provides explanations that help you build students' fitness vocabulary.
- *Photo Follow-up* gives you an alternate way to capture students' interest at the start of each lesson.

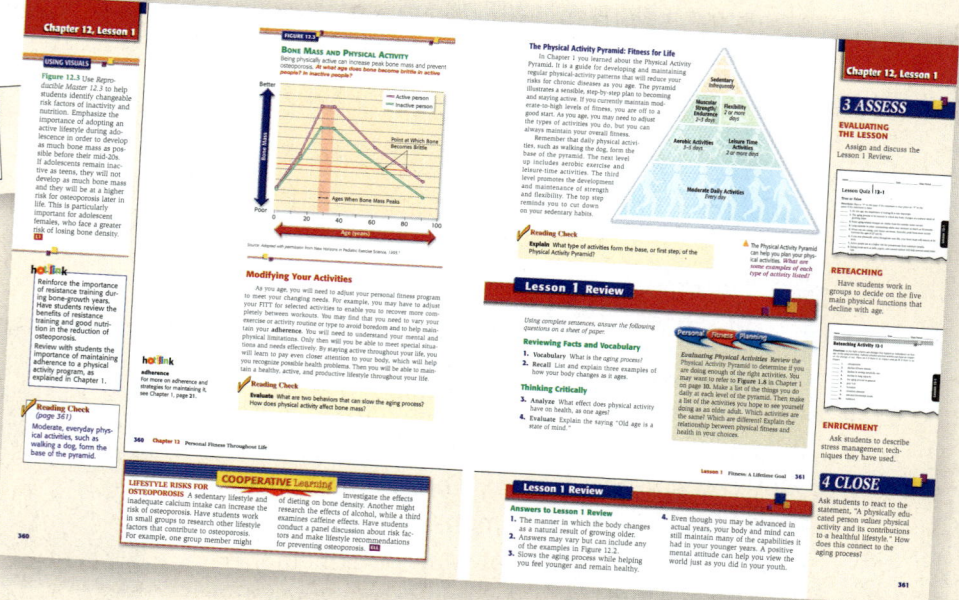

Teach

- *Discussing, Explaining, and Activity* strategies help you guide students through the content.
- *Using Visuals* provides you with relevant details, discussion points, and caption answers for each figure.

Assess

- Convenient reduced pages preview the *Resource Masters* for the lesson.
- Choose from *Reteaching* or *Enrichment* to evaluate students' grasp of key concepts.
- *Lesson Assessment* with Review Answers checks students' comprehension.

Close

- Wrap up each lesson with a culminating activity or question.

Tools to Enhance Student Learning

Every student feature is supported with teaching tips, evaluation strategies, and concluding activities to maximize student learning.

Hotlinks make cross-references to other materials, giving you opportunities to reinforce and link concepts.

Teaching Strategies support every feature in the student text with teaching tips and ideas for presenting the material.

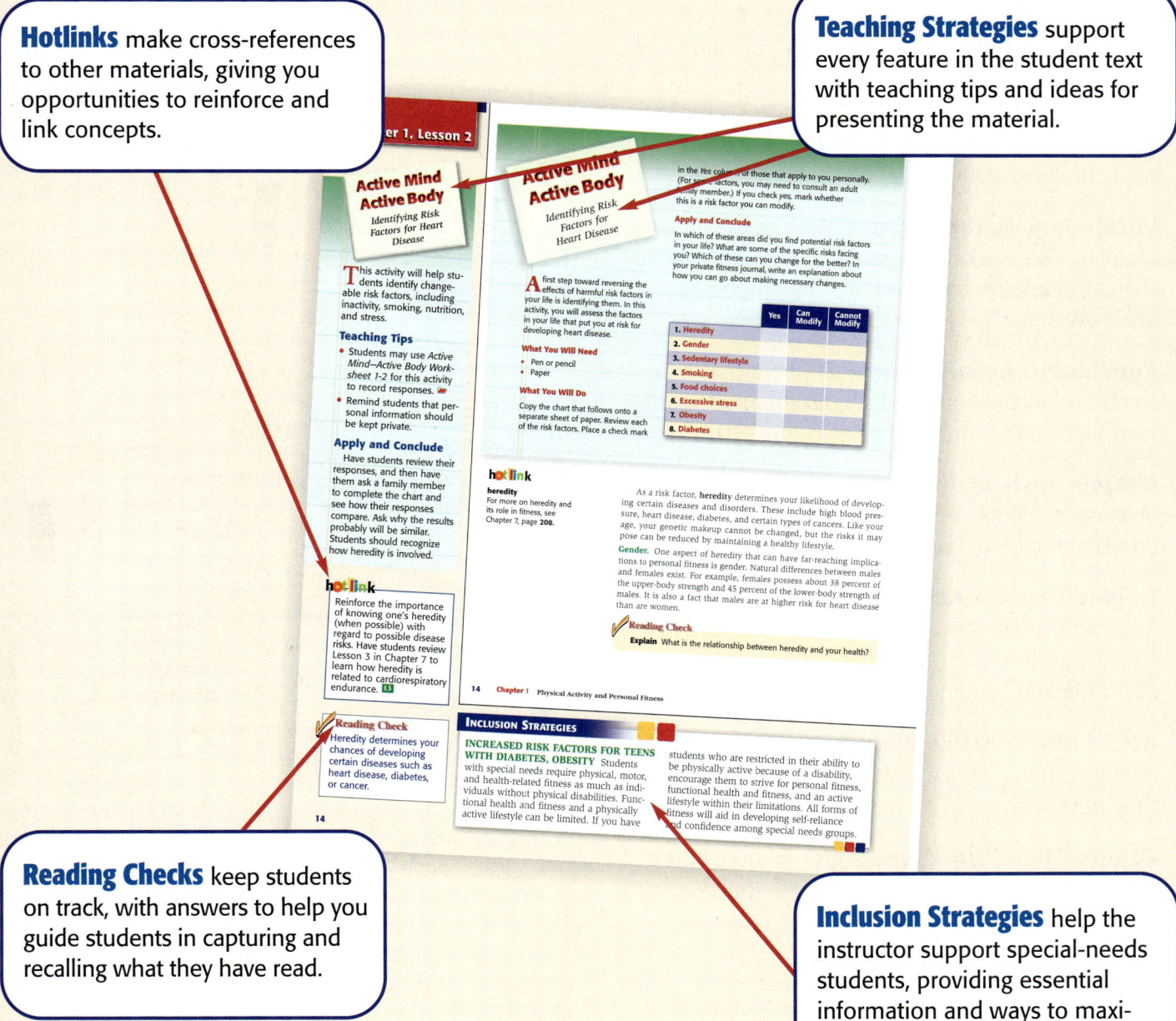

Reading Checks keep students on track, with answers to help you guide students in capturing and recalling what they have read.

Inclusion Strategies help the instructor support special-needs students, providing essential information and ways to maximize learning for all students.

Other bottom boxes include:

- Teacher / Coach Tips
- Cooperative Learning
- Myths & Realities
- Curriculum Connections
- Quotes for Life
- Technology File
- Equipment Options
- What Teens Want to Know

Chapter Resource Masters

FAST FILE

Chapter Resource Masters for each chapter include everything you need in one convenient book.

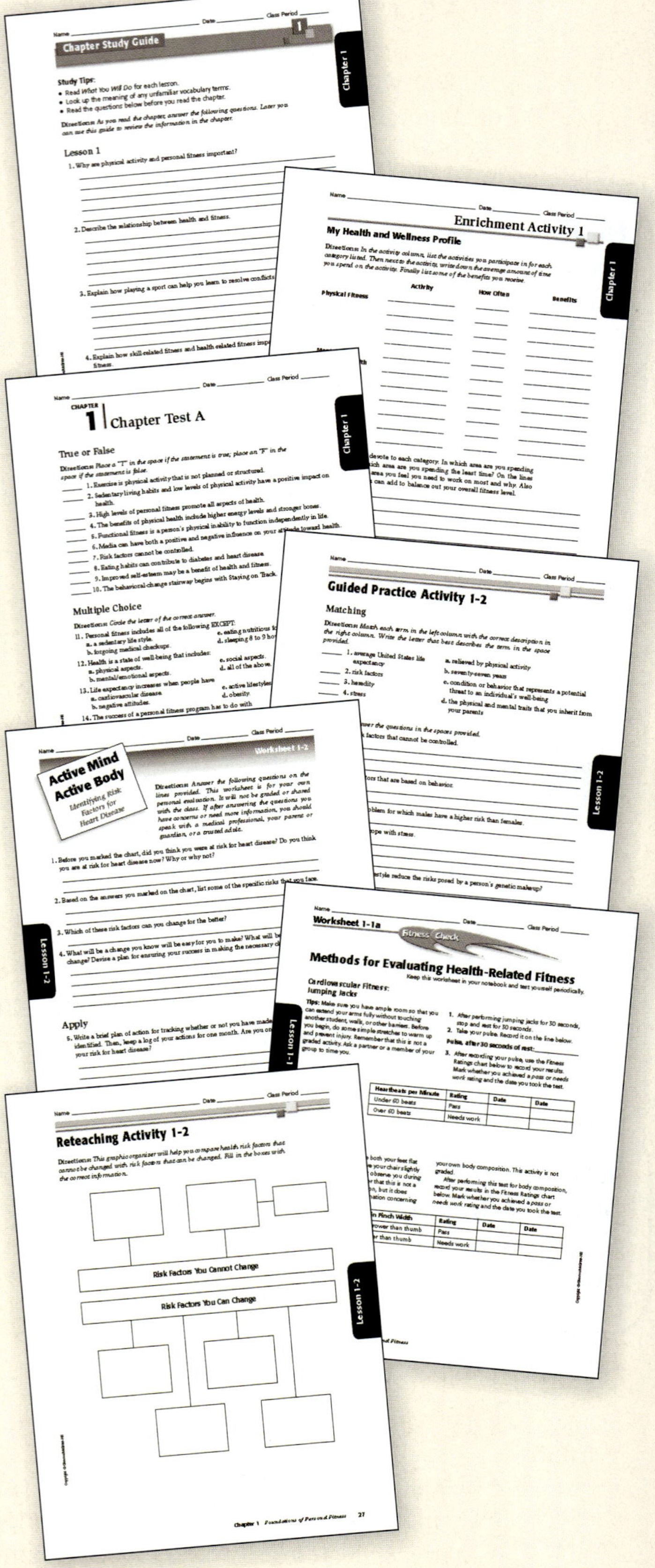

Chapter Study Guides can be used as a tool that guides students in reading and mastering the concepts of the chapter.

Vocabulary Worksheet reinforces key terms in the chapter. The worksheets include fill-in-the-blanks, matching answers, vocabulary challenges, and crossword puzzles.

Enrichment Activities expand on chapter materials to reinforce consumer skills, stress-management techniques, and more.

Chapter Tests in two formats provide comprehensive assessments. Tests include true/false, multiple-choice, matching, and short-answer questions.

Guided Practice Activities help students comprehend and retain lesson information. The activity sheets guide students to organize concepts through outlining and sentence completion.

Active Mind—Active Body Worksheets encourage students to use critical thinking and to apply what they have learned in an activity format.

Fitness Check Worksheets give students the opportunity to perform physical activities, record their results, and measure their progress.

Reteaching Activities for each lesson in the text include graphs, charts, tables, and other graphic organizers to help students review major concepts.

Lesson Quizzes A 10-question objective quiz is provided for each lesson. Quizzes can be used to review each lesson or can be compiled into a final test that covers all the lessons in the chapter.

More Teaching Resources

Reproducible Charts and Graphs

Blackline masters of the figures and activities in the student text can be used to create overhead transparencies or reproduced as handouts for students. Each of these charts, graphs, or illustrations are accompanied by an activity or discussion question to encourage class participation.

Parent Letters and Activities

These letters inform parents or guardians of the instructional program, activities, and assessment techniques to be covered in the chapter. Suggested activities are included for parents and teens to incorporate physical activity into their lives. Parent Letters in Spanish are available in the *Spanish Resources* booklet.

Teaching Transparency Preview

A brief description of teaching transparencies that go with each chapter is provided. These full-color transparencies are available in the separate *Teaching Transparencies Binder*, along with a booklet of teaching strategies and activities.

Answer Keys

A complete answer key appears at the back of each *Chapter Resource Masters* booklet. This answer key includes answers for every activity, in the order in which activities appear.

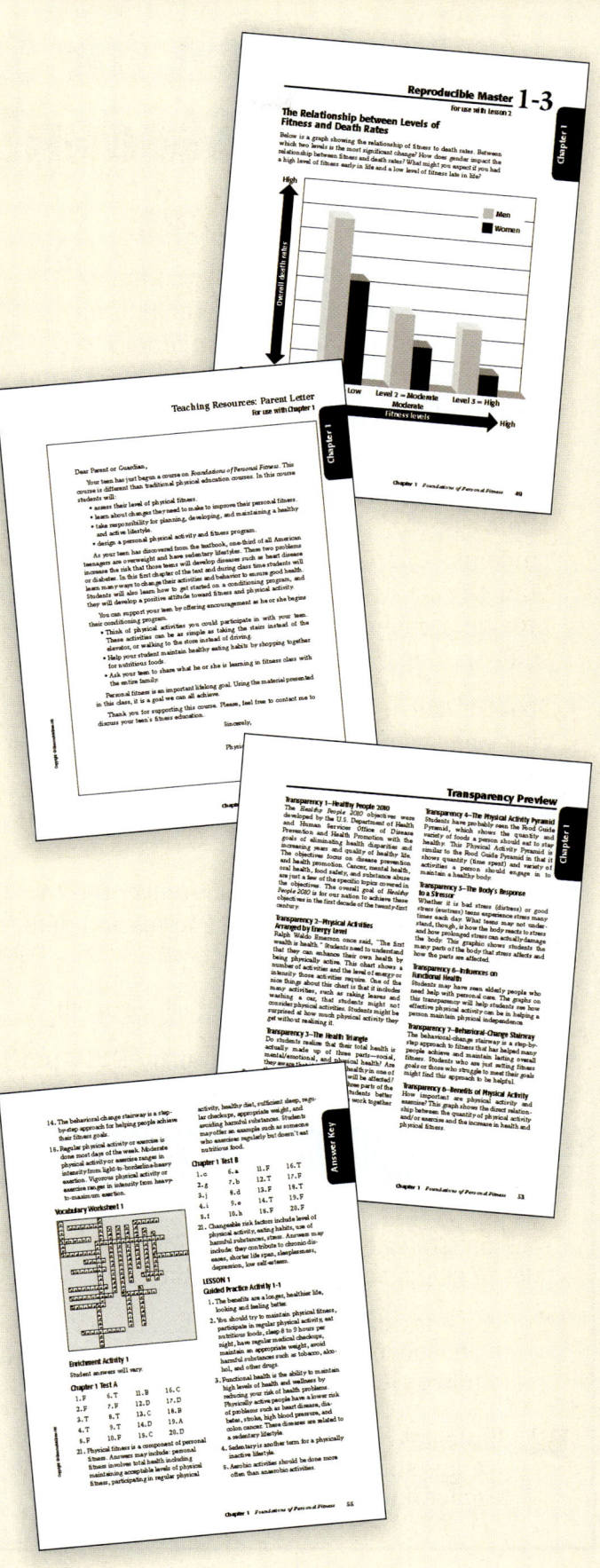

Inclusion for Spanish Speakers and Students of All Levels

Spanish Resources

- *Spanish Edition Online*—A complete Spanish version of the Student Edition available online, making *Foundations of Personal Fitness* content accessible to Spanish-speaking students.

- A new *Audio Summaries* CD-ROM, and the *Spanish Resources* booklet provide print and audio support for your Spanish-speaking students. Chapter and lesson summaries with key terms and definitions in Spanish provide a complete Spanish component for students.

- Spanish *Parent Letters and Activities* give parents and guardians a chance to be actively involved in their teens' fitness programs. An overview of each chapter and suggested activities are included.

- *Glosario* is a convenient reference for the Spanish translations of English terms and definitions.

- *PuzzleMaker* is available in English/Spanish.

- VHS videos and English/Spanish DVD programs are also available.

Spanish Resources

GLENCOE
FOUNDATIONS OF PERSONAL FITNESS
Don L. Rainey & Tinker D. Murray

INCLUDES:
- Chapter and Lesson Summaries
- Parent Letters and Activities
- Complete Spanish Glosario

Key to Ability Levels

Teaching strategies that appear throughout the chapter have been identified by one of the following codes to give teachers an idea of their suitability for students of varying learning styles and abilities.

L1 Strategies should be within the ability range of all students. Full class participation is often required. Teacher direction is usually needed.

L2 Strategies are designed for average to above-average students or for small groups. Some teacher direction is needed.

L3 Strategies are designed for students able and willing to work independently. Minimal teacher direction is needed.

ELL Strategies should be within the ability range of students learning the English language.

Options for Complete, Organized Course Presentation

Lesson Plans

Complete 9-Week and 18-Week Lesson Plans give you choices, options, and direction to be sure that all materials are utilized and appropriate instruction is maximized.

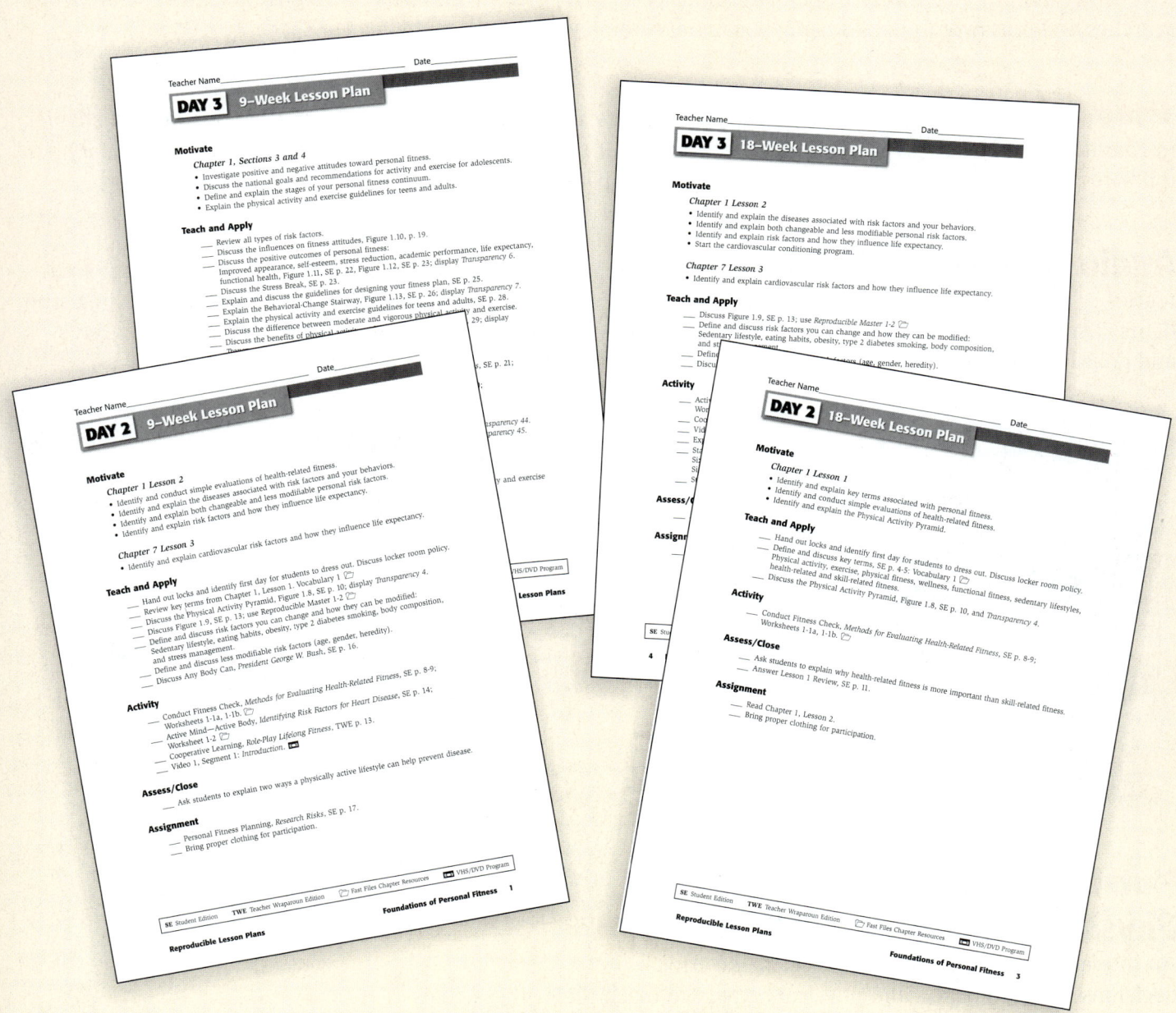

Technology Components

TeacherWorks™   Design your lesson plans with this easy-to-use tool on CD-ROM. Electronic format of all teaching resources allows you to select a pre-set plan or create your own custom lessons.

ExamView Pro Testmaker®   This computer software contains a test bank with questions in a variety of formats for each lesson and chapter. Create multiple tests from the test bank or create your own questions. Scoring is made easy with this convenient tool. All questions are provided in English and in Spanish.

PuzzleMaker   (English/Spanish) Build vocabulary skills with custom-designed puzzles. Create word searches and crossword puzzles using vocabulary from every lesson in the text.

PowerPoint®   Presentation CD-ROM A complete and concise presentation for every lesson and chapter in *Foundations of Personal Fitness* guides you and your students through key fitness concepts, vocabulary, and quick review questions for complete classroom participation.

Audio Summaries CD-ROM
(Spanish and English) Audio Summaries provide content summaries of every chapter and lesson to aid reading comprehension for both English- and Spanish-speaking students. The Spanish Resources booklet provides printed summarizes of chapters and lessons to give parents and guardians a chance to be actively involved in their teens' fitness programs.

Teaching Transparencies
64 full-color transparencies with Teaching Strategies and Activities booklet for full classroom participation.

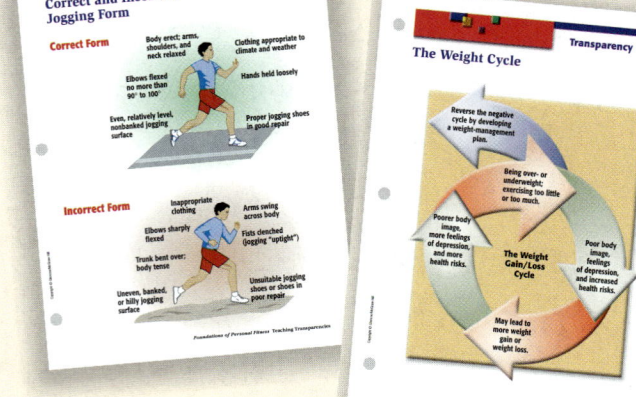

Nutrition and Physical Activity CD-ROM
An interactive program helps students make critical decisions about nutrition and physical activity to reach their fitness goals

Visit fitness.glencoe.com for Internet Support

• **Spanish Edition Online Now Available**

Full-color, illustrated, and including all charts and tables, the Spanish Edition Online for *Foundations of Personal Fitness* brings accessibility to students and parents who speak Spanish. This complete online edition, available for users of Glencoe's *Foundations of Personal Fitness* program, provides opportunities for all students to fully participate in learning important concepts and developing their personal fitness for a lifetime.

• **The new *Foundations for Personal Fitness* Web site provides essential study tools and activities for all students:**

STEP Inventory for each chapter to be used in self-evaluations

Online Fitness Journal

Web Link Exercises

Online Quizzes and eFlashcards

• **Additional tools and resources for teachers include:**

National Standards Correlations

Teacher Web Links

Fitness Logs to help students in personal fitness planning

New Exciting Video and DVD Program

With Glencoe's new Fitness Videos and DVD, you can illustrate the importance of achieving and maintaining personal fitness. Three 30-minute videocassettes, or one 90-minute DVD, are available. DVD comes in English and Spanish. A broad range of fitness topics are featured in a fast-paced, "network television" format that demonstrate that **Any Body Can** achieve personal fitness.

Video 1:
Nutrition and Body Composition

Introduce students to the fundamental concepts of nutrition and body composition. Students will learn how developing a healthful eating plan and practicing healthful behaviors, such as maintaining an appropriate body weight and avoiding harmful substances, can significantly improve their health and well-being.

Video 2:
Cardiorespiratory Endurance

Jump in to an exciting preview of the cardiovascular and respiratory systems, and the crucial role they play in developing and maintaining a fit and healthy body. Students will explore the many activities that can help boost aerobic and anaerobic performance, and discover ways to create a lifelong fitness program.

Video 3:
Muscular Fitness and Flexibility

Complete Glencoe's fitness program with a three-part video on flexibility, developing muscular fitness, and resistance training. Each segment introduces students to the fitness professionals and activities that can safely help them build stronger more flexible bodies.

Video 1	Video 2	Video 3
Segment 1: Introduction/Overview	**Segment 1:** Cardiorespiratory Endurance	**Segment 1:** Resistance Training
Segment 2: Nutrition	**Segment 2:** Developing Cardiorespiratory Endurance	**Segment 2:** Developing Muscular Fitness
Segment 3: Body Composition/ Weight & Health		**Segment 3:** Flexibility

Assessment and Evaluation for Behavioral Change

The goal of any quality fitness program is to implement changes in behaviors that result in higher levels of fitness and improved health. *Foundations of Personal Fitness* integrates assessments and evaluations into every chapter. Students learn by conducting self-assessments, setting personal goals, and evaluating progress as they build their own personal fitness programs.

Fitness Component	Fitness Check Feature	Active Mind– Active Body	Online Assessments and Other Features
Health-Related Fitness	Methods for Evaluating Health-Related Fitness *(page 8)*	Identifying Risk Factors for Heart Disease *(page 14)* What Is Your PAR-Q? *(page 37)*	STEP Inventory *(page 2)* STEP Inventory *(page 192)*
Skill-Related Fitness	Demonstrating Skill-Related Fitness *(page 78)*		STEP Inventory *(page 2)* STEP Inventory *(page 272)*
Body Composition and Weight Control	Understanding the Energy Equation *(page 142)* Measuring Body Composition *(page 162)* Exercise and Overweight *(page 174)*	Calculating Calories from a Sample Meal *(page 134)* Exercise and Calorie Expenditure *(page 156)* The Effect of Added Weight on Aerobic Performance *(page 209)*	Evaluating Nutrition *(page 121)* Analyzing Nutrition *(page 128)* STEP Inventory *(page 146)* Evaluating Your Weight *(page 152)* STEP Inventory *(page 170)*
Cardiorespiratory Endurance	Evaluating Cardiorespiratory Endurance *(page 197)*	Taking Your Resting Pulse *(page 86)* The Effect of Intensity on Heart Rate *(page 92)*	STEP Inventory *(page 192)* Participating in Aerobic Activity *(page 215)* STEP Inventory *(page 218)*

Fitness Component	Fitness Check Feature	Active Mind–Active Body	Online Assessments and Other Features
Muscular Strength	Estimating Percentage of VO_{2max} *(page 221)*	What Is in Your Weight Room? *(page 262)* Participating in Strength-Training Exercises *(page 298)*	STEP Inventory *(page 244)* Developing Muscular Strength *(page 304)*
Muscular Endurance	Evaluating Muscular Endurance *(page 267)*	Designing a Weight-Training Program *(page 320)*	STEP Inventory *(page 244)*
Flexibility	Evaluating Your Flexibility *(page 336)*	Which Activities Improve Flexibility? *(page 334)* Participating in Flexibility Activities *(page 349)*	STEP Inventory *(page 324)* Resistance Training and Flexibility *(page 335)*
Safety Procedures	Applying Biomechanics *(page 56)*	Warm Up and Cool Down: Stretching Correctly *(page 104)*	STEP Inventory *(page 34)* Investigating Safety *(page 137)*
Stress Reduction	Methods for Evaluating Health-Related Fitness *(page 8)* Exercise and Overweight *(page 174)*	Taking Your Resting Pulse *(page 86)* Practicing Passive Stretching *(page 343)*	Types of Stress *(page 23)* Varying Your Training *(page 311)* Stretching and Stress Relief *(page 340)*
Goal Setting	Designing an Aerobic Exercise Routine *(page 365)*	How Physically Active Are You Now? *(page 30)* Designing Your Personal Fitness Center *(page 238)*	STEP Inventory *(page 70)* Applying Specificity *(page 94)* Planning a Workout *(page 198)* Implementing a Plan *(page 226)* Identifying Goals *(page 260)*

Scope and Sequence

	Chapter 1 Physical Activity and Personal Fitness	Chapter 2 Safety and Injury Prevention
NASPE Standards	1, 2, 3, 4, 5, 6	1, 2, 3, 4, 5
Health-Related Fitness	Methods of evaluating (1) Components or measures (1) Diseases and risk factors (2) Attitudes toward fitness (3) Influence of physical activity on health and fitness(3) Exercise guidelines (4) Exercise and health benefits (4)	Medical screening for obesity, heart disease, diabetes, other chronic diseases (1)
Skill-Related Fitness	Components or measures (1)	
Nutrition	Nutrition as part of personal fitness (1) Practicing healthful eating habits (2) Eating habits and coping with stress (2)	Fluid balance and loss of water and salt (2)
Safety Procedures and Injury Prevention	The Health Triangle (1) The Physical Activity Pyramid (1)	Medical screenings (1) Heat-Stress index, wind-chill index (2) Guidelines for personal safety (2) Unleashed dogs (2) Facts about head injuries (3) Injury treatments and RICE (4)
Disease Prevention	Reducing risk of heart and lung diseases (2) Improving cholesterol and triglyceride levels (3)	Avoiding air pollution and risk of lung diseases (2) Substance abuse and disease (5)
Stress Management	Strategies for managing stress (2) Role of nutrition (2) Types of stress (3)	
Social Interaction and Support	Conflict resolution and friendship development (1) Peer Influence (3)	Why some people use harmful substances (5)
Behavior Management and Risk Factors	Avoiding harmful substances as a part of personal fitness (1) Role of peer influence (3) Commitment to fitness plan(3) Setting fitness goals (4) The behavioral-change stairway (4)	Climate as a risk factor (2) Choosing appropriate clothing (3) Recognizing stride irregularities (3) Safety precautions while on the move (3) Understanding and applying biomechanics (4)
Effects of Substance Abuse	Disease risks related to tobacco use (2)	Myths about substance abuse (5) Addiction (5) Effects of tobacco, alcohol, and anabolic steroids (5)
Consumer Issues and Media Awareness	Media influences (3)	Shopping for footwear (3) Purchasing a helmet (3)

Chapter 3 Designing a Personal Fitness Program	Chapter 4 Nutrition and Your Personal Fitness	Chapter 5 Your Body Composition
1, 2, 3, 4, 5, 6	2, 3, 4, 5	3, 4, 5, 6
Components or measures (1) Rating the health-related benefits of physical activities (1) Role of heredity (1) Principle of overload (2) Principle of specificity (3) Principle of progression (4) Effects of detraining (4)	Calories burned during physical activity (4) Managing the energy equation (4)	Teen body mass index (1) Body composition and functional health (1) Influences on body fat (2) Factors of resting metabolic rate (2) Body fat and skinfold tests (3) Body fat ratings (3) Maintaining a healthy weight (4)
Components or measures (1) Skill-related benefits of physical activities (1) Demonstrating skills (1) Role of heredity (1)		
	Influences on food choices (1) Nutrients for energy (1) Dietary supplements (2) *Dietary Guidelines for Americans* (3) Food Guide Pyramid (3) Pre- and post-event foods (4) Understanding the energy equation (4)	Understanding the energy equation (2) Energy needs of active and inactive teens (2) Weight control, diet, and exercise (4) Nutrient-dense foods (4)
Overtraining and health problems (4) Importance of restoration (4)	Fluid replacement and physical activity (2)	Practicing safe weight management (4)
Eating disorders—symptom of over-training	Cholesterol and heart disease (1) Keeping foods safe to eat (3) Dangers of dietary supplements (4)	Understanding overweight and obesity (1) Body composition and risk for chronic diseases (1)
Stress and stretching (1) The art of planning (5)	Avoiding caffeine (2)	Media and pressure to compete (2)
Resolving conflict and avoiding stress (1)		Watching your friends' weight (4)
Components of exercise prescription (2) Applying the FITT factors (2) Perceived exertion scale (2) Goal setting and record keeping (3) Components of a workout (5)	Daily calorie intake (1) Vitamins and minerals (2) ABCs of a healthful eating plan (3) Serving sizes for each food group (3) Calculating calories (3) Eating to optimize performance (4)	Calculations for body fat (1) Lifestyle behaviors and body composition (2) Balancing the energy equation (2) Weight and physical activity (2) Measuring body composition (3) Strategies to manage weight (4)
	Risks of performance-enhancement supplements (4)	
	Nutrition Facts panel (3) Dining out (3)	Comparing body type with media models (1)

	Chapter 6 Maintaining a Healthy Body Weight	**Chapter 7** Basics of Cardiorespiratory Endurance
NASPE Standards	1, 2, 3, 4, 5, 6	1, 2, 3, 4, 5
Health-Related Fitness	Overweight youth (1) How being overweight affects health (1) How being underweight affects health (1) Distorted body image and health (2) Healthy weight control (4)	Importance of aerobic activities (1) Benefits of aerobic activity (1) Cardiorespiratory endurance (3) Health benefits of aerobic activity (3) Advantages of interval training (4)
Skill-Related Fitness	How overweight affects exercise ability (1)	Effect of added weight on performance (3) Aerobic and anaerobic aspects of sports (4) Advantages of interval training (4)
Nutrition	Myths about weight control and nutrition (3) Myths about physical activity and nutrition (3)	Eating to keep the heart and lungs healthy (2)
Safety Procedures and Injury Prevention		Importance of medical checkups (2)
Disease Prevention	Overweight/obesity links to high blood pressure, high cholesterol, heart disease (1) Risks of cancer and other diseases(1) Underweight and risks (1) Symptoms of eating disorders (2)	Changeable risk factors (2) Risks of atherosclerosis, sudden cardiac death, stroke (2) Prevention of hypertension and emphysema (2) Lowering risk of disease through aerobic activity (3)
Stress Management	Fighting off stress-related cravings (4)	Relaxing to relieve daily stresses (2)
Social Interaction and Support	Helping an anorexic friend (2)	Recognizing signs of heart attack and cardiac arrest (2)
Behavior Management and Risk Factors	Overtraining and eating disorders (2) Analyzing fad diets (3) Methods for weight control (4) Recommendations for weight management (4)	Evaluating cardiorespiratory endurance (1) Breaking a regular routine of inactivity (1) Healthy behaviors that reduce risk of lifestyle diseases (2) Care of the circulatory and respiratory systems (2) Measuring cardiorespiratory endurance (3) Strategies for sustaining relatively high levels of fitness (3) Differentiating aerobic and anaerobic activities (4)
Effects of Substance Abuse	Risks of dietary supplements (3)	Effect of smoking on desire and ability (2) Avoiding tobacco to keep the heart and lungs healthy (2)
Consumer Issues and Media Awareness	Popular fad diets (3) Dietary supplements (3)	

Chapter 8 Developing Cardiorespiratory Endurance	**Chapter 9** Basics of Resistance Training	**Chapter 10** Developing Muscular Fitness
1, 2, 3, 4, 5, 6	1, 2, 3, 4, 5, 6	1, 2, 3, 4, 5, 6
Evaluating cardiorespiratory fitness (1) Alternative evaluations for individuals with disabilities or injuries (1) Benefits of aerobic exercises (2) Fitness facts: marathon runners (2)	Benefits of resistance training (1) Importance of relative muscular strength and endurance (1) Muscle function and effects of training (2) How and why muscles get stronger (2)	Building muscular strength and endurance (1) Fitness facts about muscle mass (2)
	Enhancing performance through resistance training (1) Fast-twitch and slow-twitch muscle fibers (2)	Weight-training exercises to develop power, balance, coordination, and speed (1)
Care of fitness equipment (4)	Role of resistance training in injury prevention (1) Treating muscle soreness (2) Precautions of equipment use (4) Appropriate clothing and footwear (4) Training accessories (4)	Safety guidelines for use of weight machines and free weights (1) Duties of a spotter (1) Using proper technique (1) Fitness facts about recovery time (3)
	Reducing risks of type 2 diabetes (1) Reducing risks of osteoporosis through resistance training (1)	
		Varying your training (3)
Becoming a fitness mentor (1)	Avoiding steroid use (2)	Weight room etiquette (1)
Measuring cardiorespiratory endurance (1) Determining maximum oxygen uptake (VO_{2max}) (1) Cardiorespiratory fitness testing (1) Develop cardiorespiratory efficiency (1) Common aerobic activity programs (2) Researching aerobic activities (2) Apply FITT to your cardiorespiratory workout (3) Determining target heart rate (3) FITT guidelines for special needs (3) Designing your personal fitness center (4)	Formula for calculating relative muscular strength (1) Types of progressive resistance-training programs (1) Factors influencing development of muscular strength (2) Myths about resistance training (3) Evaluating muscular endurance (4)	Setting resistance-training goals (1) Weight-training exercises (1) Circuit training (2) Applying overload, specificity, and progression (2) Applying FITT to resistance training (3) Determining intensity (3) Calculating training load (3) Basic resistance fitness program (4) Basic eight program with free weights (4) Programs for strength and power (4) Programs for building muscle mass (4) Personal weight-training program (4)
	Dangers of steroid use (2)	
Misleading claims in fitness advertising (3) Factors to consider when selecting fitness equipment (4) Cardiorespiratory equipment choices (4)	Fitness facility equipment checklist (4) Free weights vs. weight machines (4) Lower-cost or no-cost resistance training alternatives (4) Purchasing weight-training equipment (4)	

	Chapter 11 Basics of Flexibility	Chapter 12 Personal Fitness Throughout Life
NASPE Standards	1, 2, 3, 4, 5, 6	2, 3, 4, 5, 6
Health-Related Fitness	Factors that influence flexibility (1) Benefits of flexibility conditioning (2)	Effects of aging on health (1) Aging and physical function (1) Bone mass and physical activity (1) Health benefits of leisure-time activities (2) Careers in Health and Fitness (3)
Skill-Related Fitness		
Nutrition		Effect of exercise and nutrition on aging (1)
Safety Procedures and Injury Prevention	Measures to prevent lower-back pain (1) Proper and improper lifting (1) Fitness facts about teens and back pain (1) Proper and improper posture (1) Hyperflexibility and muscle imbalances (2) Exercises for prevention of lower-back pain (4) Hazardous stretches and their modifications (4)	Finding qualified fitness experts (3) Physical therapists and treatment for injury (3)
Disease Prevention		Types of health and fitness professionals (3)
Stress Management	Stretching and stress relief (3)	Stress and aging (1) Exercise you can enjoy (2)
Social Interaction and Support	Practicing passive stretching with a partner (3)	
Behavior Management and Risk Factors	Guidelines for staying flexible (1) Sports and activities that promote flexibility (2) Fitness facts about resistance training and flexibility (2) Evaluating your flexibility (2) Flexibility training for core stability (2) Applying FITT principles to your flexibility plan (3) Basic stretching techniques (3) Flexibility exercises for the whole body (4)	Preventing or slowing bone loss (1) Modifying a personal fitness plan with age (1) Physical Activity Pyramid (1) Leisure-time activities (2) Designing an aerobic exercise routine (2) Analyzing lifetime activities (2)
Effects of Substance Abuse		
Consumer Issues and Media Awareness		Guidelines for choosing a fitness or health expert (3) Guidelines for evaluating media ads (4) Evaluating fitness information (4) Types of health and fitness facilities (4) Choosing a fitness facility (4)

Inclusion Strategies
for Special Populations

As an educational trend, inclusion is the practice of educating all students, both disabled and nondisabled, in regular classes. In physical education, inclusion means that students with disabilities are placed in classes with their age-appropriate peers with instruction that meets their individual needs. It is a chance for teens with and without disabilities to have the opportunity to interact and work together toward common goals.

Education for All Students

The Individuals with Disabilities Education Act (IDEA), as amended in 1997, and the Americans with Disabilities Act (1990) have increased the range and coverage for individuals with disabilities. The primary purpose of these laws is to ensure that disabled people receive free and appropriate public education in the least restrictive environment. The emphasis of special education is to meet each individual's unique needs and to give disabled students equal opportunities to attain the same results, gain the same benefits, and reach the same levels of achievement as their nondisabled peers.

In order to receive special education instruction and related services, a student must be identified as having one or more disabling conditions from the 13 categories listed in IDEA. Those categories are autism, deaf-blindness, deafness, hearing impairment, mental retardation, multiple disabilities, orthopedic impairment, other health impairment, serious emotional disturbance, specific learning disability, speech or language impairment, traumatic brain injury, and visual impairment, including blindness.

Creating a Successful Environment

An inclusive environment in physical education is a place where all students have the opportunity for successful participation. It is not enough to drop disabled students into a physical education class and assume that they will develop skills. Physical educators must create an environment in their gym where all students feel safe to explore and develop their abilities, regardless of how those abilities vary among students.

Students with disabilities can be safely included and achieve success in regular physical education classes with some modifications. Each activity needs to be carefully considered for the types of modifications necessary for all students to succeed.

Often, disabled students need only a peer tutor to help them succeed in physical education classes. Some students with disabilities may need a professional assistant to accompany them to physical education class. This determination should be made on an individualized basis with input from the school's multidisciplinary team working with the special education students.

Support for Educators

Physical educators can receive help in meeting the needs of disabled students. The adapted physical education specialist assigned to a school can offer a wealth of information about working with disabled students in the general physical education setting. This specialist can offer modifications, specialized equipment, or suggestions for accommodating the special student in physical education.

If you are unsure of the nature of a student's disability, check with the school's diagnostician. If a student in your class displays several of the characteristics described and he or she has not been identified as having a disability, discuss your concerns with the diagnostician.

The information provided here and continued on pages XTM1-XTM4 at the back of this text is intended to inform general physical educators about various disabilities. It contains only suggested guidelines. Each student must be considered individually, and in many cases, a physician's written consent should be obtained.

Cardiovascular Conditions

Cardiovascular conditions include any and all diseases involving the heart or blood vessels. Disorders that are prevalent in children include congenital heart conditions and rheumatic heart disease.

The most common occurrence of cardiovascular disease in children results from rheumatic fever complications. Rheumatic fever occurs following a streptococcus infection, but the exact cause is not known. The heart is not always affected, but when it is, the mitral and aortic valves of the heart become inflamed, resulting in such severe scarring that the valves are unable to function properly.

Implications for Physical Education

Most students affected with either rheumatic or congenital cardiovascular disorders can benefit from a well-planned physical education program that allows the students to work within their capabilities. It is critical when planning a program for students with cardiac conditions to establish the intensity and tolerance level for each student's exercise routine. Restrictions for students will vary, based on the severity of their condition. Activities within a student's tolerance level can be determined by using the American Heart Association's functional classification system:

Class I (A) No significant limitations on physical activity.

Class II (B) Slight restrictions on physical activity.

Class III (C) Moderately limited physical activity. Strenuous activity is contraindicated.

Class IV (D) Severe limitations of physical activity. Unable to participate in activity without fatigue, dyspnea, and pain. These and other symptoms of cardiac insufficiency may be present even at rest.

Instructional Strategies/Accommodations

1. Any program must be first approved by a physician. Be aware of all medications that your students are taking (e.g., beta-blockers) and their effects on exercise.

2. Particular care should be given when undergoing fitness testing. Use graded exercise programs rather than the pre-test/post-test models favored in research.

3. Frequently monitor the student's pulse rate so that the level of activity can be adjusted accordingly. It is important to know what the student's resting heart rate is and to obtain a baseline measurement under a variety of situations.

4. Students with cardiac problems must be continually monitored during activity for any signs of distress (e.g., change in skin color, shortness of breath).

5. Try to design a total fitness program that does not place great demands on the cardiovascular system.

6. Exercise and activity programs should be progressive in nature. Begin with short periods of activity with frequent rest periods and progress to longer periods as the student develops tolerance.

7. Never push students who indicate that they are experiencing difficulties. Some students may need to be encouraged to stop activities when they seem fatigued.

8. Competitive activities should be avoided. Often, the emotions involved in these situations push the stress of the activity above students' tolerance level.

9. Take into consideration the personality of students when they are involved in physical activity. Some students become too competitive even in noncompetitive activities. Keep the emotional stress of participating in an activity to a minimum.

10. Modify activities with respect to pace, distances traveled, and duration of activity to reduce stress on the cardiovascular system.

11. In team sports, have students rotate positions frequently to vary the intensity of the activity.

12. Consideration must be given to weather conditions. Limit activity during hot or humid weather, which causes increased energy expenditure.

Asthma

Asthma is a chronic lung disease consisting of airway obstruction and airway inflammation. An inhaler that delivers medication directly to the lungs is often used. Some inhalers work best prior to exercise. Students with asthma are usually sensitive to weather changes, heavy exercise, body temperature changes, pollution, and cigarette smoke. Possible characteristics of an asthmatic are breathing difficulties, coughing, wheezing, and a barrel-chest appearance.

Individuals with asthma may suffer from hay fever, allergies, sinus problems, and upper respiratory infections. These problems can lead asthmatics to overuse their inhalers. Overuse causes nervousness, increased heart rate, and high blood pressure.

Implications for Physical Education

It is important that asthmatic students continue to participate in general physical education class because of the physical and psychological benefits of exercise. However, the teacher must be aware of the students' condition, limitations, and anxieties in order to adjust activity demands. If a student suffers an asthma attack during class, do the following:

- Assist the student with inhalers—allow controlled access to them during exercise.
- Use cool, wet towels on the back of the neck to assist in body temperature control.
- Make the student comfortable, monitor breathing difficulties, and seek help if needed.

Instructional Strategies/Accommodations

1. Contact students' physicians to obtain their complete medical histories. Some students with severe asthma have had surgery. Teachers need to be aware of this to avoid complications.
2. Consult with the school nurse about the prevention and management of asthma attacks.
3. Encourage participation in anaerobic activities.
4. Watch for redness in the face and fatigue.
5. Be sure to include warm-up exercises.
6. Remind students to breathe through their nose.
7. Provide activities that strengthen the abdominals, shoulder, and back muscles and that stretch the chest muscles.
8. Avoid exercises that strengthen already shortened muscles.
9. Provide instruction in relaxation training.
10. Help students avoid chalk dust by placing them away from the chalkboard.
11. Remind students to drink water continually during the class period. Fluids loosen the mucus that builds up during exercise.
12. Let students guide the level of activity at any given time, and provide alternate ways for them to be part of the class when necessary.

Cerebral Palsy

Cerebral palsy (CP) is a nonprogressive, permanent neurological condition that is the result of damage to a specific motor area of the brain. This damage affects the development of the central nervous system, and the extent of the damage and the age at which it occurs has a direct effect on the degree of neurological impairment. Cerebral palsy can occur before, during, or soon after birth (before age 5 years). About 30 percent of all cases are the result of prenatal difficulties, 60 percent occur during birth, and 10 percent occur postnatally.

General characteristics of cerebral palsy include muscular weakness, poor coordination, paralysis, and other disturbances to voluntary motor control. Often, mental retardation, seizure disorders, perceptual disorders, hearing and vision loss, and speech deficits are also present as secondary impairments.

Individuals with cerebral palsy are classified according to the amount of dysfunction and the associated motor involvement. The four basic classifications of cerebral palsy are as follows:

1. *Spastic*: Muscles are tense, contracted, and resistant to movement. This makes muscle movement jerky and uncertain. These individuals have exaggerated stretch reflexes that cause them to respond to rapid passive stretching with strong muscle contractions. Spastic CP is the most common type.
2. *Athetoid*: Characterized by involuntary movements of the body parts affected. The hands may twist and turn, and there is often facial grimacing, tongue protruding, and drooling. Because reflexes are primitive and muscles cannot be controlled, posture is unpredictable.
3. *Ataxia*: Disturbance or lack of balance and coordination. Individual may sway when standing, have trouble maintaining balance, and walk with feet spread wide to avoid falling.
4. *Mixed*: While this is the least common type, combinations of the above classifications do occur. Spasticity and athetosis are the most frequent combination.

Implications for Physical Education

A multidisciplinary approach is advised when planning physical activity for students with CP, s the psychomotor characteristics vary widely b the type of cerebral palsy, the severity of th tion, and whether secondary impairmen

Consideration must also be given to the presence of primitive reflexes and perceptual-motor deficits that may exist. Programs should focus on what the student can do and should be designed to enhance the student's functional abilities.

Instructional Strategies/Accommodations

1. Become familiar with students' complete medical condition. Obtain program recommendations for the students from physicians, occupational therapists, physical therapists, and any other member of the multidisciplinary team involved with the students.

2. Take caution during activities that involve the hip joint. Individuals with CP who use wheelchairs are at high risk for hip dislocation.

3. Allow time at the beginning and end of each class for the students to do relaxed stretching of various muscle groups.

4. When fine motor activities are part of the activity, contact the students' occupational therapists for ideas and suggestions.

5. Limit activities to those that do not require highly coordinated movements or good balance.

6. Include activities and movements that do not elicit any primitive reflexes that may be present.

7. Allow plenty of time for the students to repeat a skill or parts of a skill as many times as necessary.

8. Adjust the skill/activity requirements to each student's muscular strength and joint flexibility.

9. Mobility during activities can be greatly enhanced through the use of walkers, scooters, and other assistive devices. Contact the students' physical therapists for help with the equipment.

10. Make use of adaptive equipment such as hook-and-loop cloth fasteners, special grips, and so on that enhance the students' ability to manipulate objects. The occupational therapists can help in this area.

11. For students who also have speech deficits, use communication boards. Contact their speech therapists, who can adjust the boards to fit any activity.

12. Be aware that many students who have CP also have depth perception problems.

Spinal Cord Injuries

A spinal cord injury is a permanent condition that results when damage occurs to the spinal cord or spinal nerves. The degree of impairment depends on the site of the injury and whether the injury is partial or complete. The higher the injury, the more damage and the greater the loss of function. If the injury is partial, there is a possibility of regaining lost function. The nerves do not regenerate themselves, but as pressure from trauma and swelling is relieved, some function may be restored. If the injury is complete, it is permanent; no function will be regained since the nerves are unable to regenerate themselves.

Spinal cord injuries are classified into two basic categories:

1. *Paraplegia*: caused by injury to thoracic segments T2-T12. Impairment is in the trunk, legs, and/or pelvic region.

2. *Quadriplegia*: caused by injury to cervical segments (C1-C8) or the highest thoracic segment (T1). Impairment occurs in the arms, trunk, legs, and pelvic organs.

Implications for Physical Education

The most important consideration to make when planning an activity program for students with spinal cord injuries is to correctly assess their medical condition. The program must be planned and developed around the severity and level of injury. Realistic goals need to be established based on the student's capabilities and the skills that must be relearned.

Instructional Strategies/Accommodations

1. All activity programs need to be developed in collaboration with the medical personnel involved in the rehabilitation of students with spinal cord injuries.

2. Assess the movement capabilities of the students, and develop activities that will allow maximum participation and success.

3. Contact Disabled Sports USA for videotapes developed for individuals with various disabilities, including spinal cord injuries.

4. Focus on developing strength and endurance in the unaffected muscle groups, but watch out for muscle imbalancing.

For more information on specific disabilities, see pages XTM1-XTM4 found at the back of this Teacher Wraparound Edition.

Table of Contents

Fitness Check

Active Mind Active Body

Improving YOUR Personal Fitness
with your *Foundations of Personal Fitness textbook*

- **Why should physical activity be part of your daily routine?**
- **How can you make the most of a personal fitness program?**
- **What are the benefits of having a high level of personal fitness?**

Follow the guidelines and features below to make the most of your book.

What You Will Do
Check the objectives to preview concepts covered in the lesson.

Terms to Know
Find the terms listed at the beginning of each lesson.

Photos and Captions
Study the photos and answer the caption questions as you learn more about each fitness topic.

Lesson 1

Your Heart, Lungs, and Circulation

Josh loves to row and is a member of the school rowing team. Tina enjoys participating in a step aerobics class. Although Josh and Tina have very different interests, they have one thing in common. They both like doing aerobic activities and recognize the importance of doing them.

What are aerobic activities? How do they benefit the body? In this lesson, you will find out.

Aerobic Activities and the Body

The exercises that weightlifters do are targeted at certain muscles of the body. These include muscles of the arms, legs, chest, and back. The activities that Josh and Tina do are also targeted at a major muscle of the body. That muscle is the heart.

Aerobic activity is continuous activity that requires large amounts of oxygen. (The word *aerobic* means "with oxygen.") Like other aerobic activities, rowing and step aerobics temporarily raise the heart rate. Done regularly, aerobic activities strengthen the heart. They also strengthen another vital organ, the lungs. Aerobic activity also makes your working muscles more efficient at using oxygen. Before you can understand how aerobic activities work, you need to have some knowledge of the circulatory and respiratory systems.

What You Will Do
- Explain the importance of aerobic activity to your health and fitness.
- Recognize the role of the circulatory and respiratory systems in aerobic conditioning.
- Identify the physical benefits of aerobic activity.
- Evaluate your cardiorespiratory endurance level.

Terms to Know
aerobic activity
circulatory system
hemoglobin
stroke volume
arteries
capillaries
veins
respiratory system
diaphragm
cardiorespiratory endurance

◄ Participating in aerobic activities regularly will increase your cardiorespiratory endurance. *What are some aerobic activities that you enjoy doing?*

Lesson 1 Your Heart, Lungs, and Circulation **193**

Lesson 1 Review

Using complete sentences, answer the following questions on a sheet of paper.

Reviewing Facts and Vocabulary
1. **Vocabulary** Define *aerobic activity.*
2. **Recall** What two body systems are most immediately involved in aerobic conditioning?

Thinking Critically
3. **Analyze** What is one benefit of aerobic activity to the lungs?
4. **Synthesize** At what age do you think people should be encouraged to begin aerobic conditioning? At what age do you think people should be encouraged to stop? Explain your answers.

Personal Fitness Planning
Planning a Workout Design a walking or jogging course in or around your neighborhood that allows you to cover 2 miles in 20 to 30 minutes. When choosing your course, you should consider all safety issues and factors that will affect your intensity (hills, bridges, type of surface, and so on).

FITNESS Online

Stop...Think...Evaluate...Proceed...
Complete the **STEP Personal Inventory.** This will tell you more about your current level of personal fitness. Review what you have learned by completing **Online Vocabulary Activities** and by taking an **Online Quiz.** Design and implement your personal fitness program using the **Online Fitness Journal.**

Lesson Review
Complete the Lesson Review to check your understanding of the lesson concepts. Set your own fitness goals in the Personal Fitness Planning section of the review.

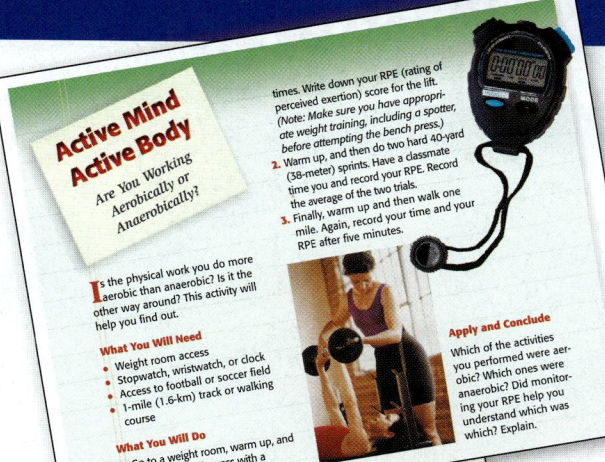

Active Mind—Active Body

Each *Active Mind—Active Body* feature provides an opportunity that lets you investigate an important concept for improving your fitness. Follow the steps under **What You Will Do** to get started, and summarize your experience in **Apply and Conclude**.

Fitness Check

Get up, get moving, and evaluate your physical fitness levels with the *Fitness Check* in each chapter. Follow the procedure for each activity and evaluate your performance by checking your Fitness Ratings.

Any Body Can

Watch for these special features, high-lighting well-known individuals whose accomplishments inspire others.

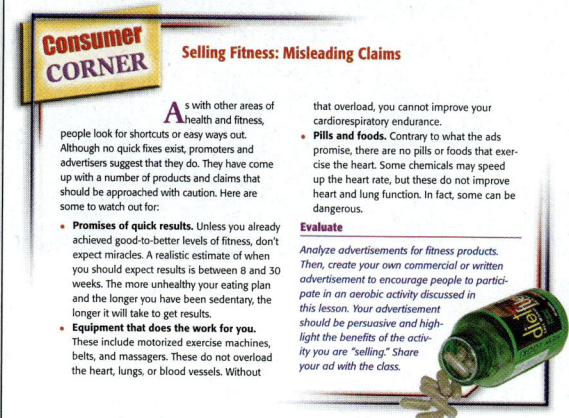

Consumer Corner

In these features, learn more about analyzing marketing claims and being a wise consumer.

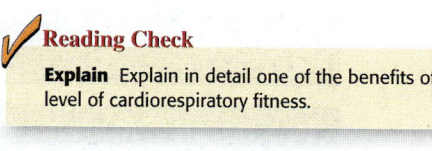

✔ **Reading Check**

Explain Explain in detail one of the benefits of maintaining a high level of cardiorespiratory fitness.

Reading Check

Stop and review what you have read by explaining key points.

CHAPTER

1 Physical Activity and Personal Fitness

CHAPTER RESOURCES

- **Chapter Study Guide 1**
- **Vocabulary Worksheet 1**
- **Enrichment Activity 1**
- **Chapter 1 Test A**
- **Chapter 1 Test B**
- **Parent Letter and Activities 1 (English/Spanish)**

FITNESS *Online*

Ask students to take the STEP Personal Inventory for Chapter 1. Have them record their responses to the statements in their notebooks. Remind students that responses are for their use only.

FITNESS *Online*

Do you play a sport or participate in some other form of physical activity? Do you eat nutritious foods? Your answers to these and related questions will give you an idea of your level of fitness. Learn more by taking the STEP Personal Inventory for Chapter 1. Find it at **fitness.glencoe.com**.

2

INCLUSION STRATEGIES

LANGUAGE DIVERSITY Use the following suggestions to help students who have difficulty with English:

- Pair English-language learners with native speakers of English who can restate key points in language that helps students comprehend important concepts.

- Direct Spanish-speaking students to the written summaries of this chapter in the *Foundations of Personal Fitness* Spanish Booklet.

- Encourage Spanish-speaking students to use the Glosario provided in the back of the student text. **ELL**

Physical Activity, Exercise, and Health

Welcome to your course on the foundations of personal fitness! This course is different from other physical education courses you have taken. Previously, they may have consisted mainly of games and sports activities. In this course you will learn the **ABC**s of total, personal fitness: **A**ny **B**ody **C**an develop a plan to become and stay physically active for life.

Throughout this course, you will face a number of challenges concerning your personal fitness. These challenges include the following:

- Assessing your level of physical fitness and progress in the course
- Learning about changes in personal habits that you may need to make
- Taking responsibility for planning, developing, and maintaining a healthy and active lifestyle
- Designing a physical-activity and fitness program that can meet your individual needs throughout your life

As you can see, there is much work to do. Let's get started.

What You Will Do

- Define the importance of physical activity and personal fitness.
- Explain the relationship between health and fitness.
- Analyze the role of fitness in recognizing and resolving conflicts effectively.
- Describe methods of evaluating health-related fitness.
- Participate in activities to evaluate your health-related fitness.

Terms to Know

physical activity
exercise
physical fitness
personal fitness
health
wellness
functional health
sedentary
self-esteem
conflicts
functional fitness
skill-related fitness
health-related fitness

There is a variety of physical activities that can benefit your personal fitness. *What type of physical activities do you enjoy?*

Physical Activity, Exercise, and Health

1 MOTIVATE

GETTING STARTED

- Ask the class to describe examples of physical activities they have performed in their past physical education class experiences.
- Distribute copies of *Guided Practice Activity 1-1* for students to use while studying this lesson.

IN THIS LESSON

- **Fitness Check**
  Methods for Evaluating Health-Related Fitness,
  page 8

INTRODUCING VOCABULARY

- Explain that the term *sedentary* is derived from the French word *sedentaire* meaning "to sit." Ask students to read the definition on page 7 and discuss the risks of a sedentary lifestyle.
- Have students use *Vocabulary Worksheet 1* or the PuzzleMaker software to practice vocabulary terms.
  ELL

Photo Follow-Up

Ask students to explain why they enjoy the physical activity they identified for the caption question.

LESSON 1 RESOURCES

Teacher Classroom Resources
- Guided Practice Activity 1-1
- Fitness Check Worksheet 1-1
- Reteaching Activity 1-1
- Lesson Quiz 1-1

Reproducible Charts and Graphs
- Reproducible Masters 1-1, 1-2

Multimedia
- Vocabulary PuzzleMaker
- Transparencies 1, 2, 3, 4

2 TEACH

Explaining

Tell students that they will learn about personal fitness in this course and that they will learn to understand, evaluate, design, and monitor their own personal fitness now and for the future. **L1**

Discussing

Have students brainstorm ways they can add more physical activity to their daily lives. Ask them what barriers keep them from being more physically active. **L1** **TEKS C5G**

Explaining

Ask students whether they have heard the term *couch potato* and what it means to them. Ask them how being a couch potato can harm their fitness. **L1**

What Is Physical Activity?

The human body is made up of many moving parts. Physical activity keeps those parts in working condition. **Physical activity** is *any movement that works the larger muscles of the body, such as arm, leg, and back muscles.* Physical activity can take several forms.

- It may be recreational, as in the case of sports, dancing, swimming, and other leisure-time activities.
- It may be incidental to some other activity, such as doing household chores, working at a part-time job, or volunteering for a neighborhood cleanup program.

Exercise is *physical activity that is planned, structured, and repetitive, and that results in improvements in fitness.* Throughout this book, you will learn about exercises that work different areas of the body, including internal organs such as the heart and lungs.

Physical activity and exercise are important to your health. Physically active people live longer, healthier lives. Physical activity and exercise add more than just years to your life; they add life to your years by making you look and feel better.

Why Are Physical Activity and Exercise Important?

Regular physical activity and exercise help keep your body physically fit. **Physical fitness** is *the body's ability to carry out daily tasks and still have enough reserve energy to respond to unexpected demands.*

Exercise is not the only way to improve physical fitness. Many forms of physical activity can provide fitness benefits. Participating in sports or action-oriented, leisure-time activities, such as dancing or ice-skating, are effective—and enjoyable—ways of staying fit. The diagram in **Figure 1.1** shows a variety of activities arranged in terms of energy level and time. Which of these activities do you enjoy doing?

Personal Fitness

Regular physical activity is central to physical fitness but, by itself, does not make a person totally fit. To achieve *total* or **personal fitness,** you should try to

- maintain acceptable levels of physical fitness.
- participate in regular physical activity.
- eat nutritious foods.
- sleep 8 to 9 hours each night.
- have regular medical checkups.
- maintain an appropriate weight.
- avoid harmful substances, such as tobacco, alcohol, and other drugs.

Physical fitness is not the same thing as personal fitness. It is only one component. Think about an all-around athlete who lives almost

Teacher-Coach Tips

Fitness Terms *Physical activity, exercise,* and *physical fitness* are terms often used by individuals interchangeably. In 1985, Dr. Carl Casperson from the Centers for Disease Control and Prevention (CDC) defined the terms separately. Physical activity and exercise are processes, while physical fitness is an outcome of either. Have students discuss these three terms in small groups and have them provide examples of each term.

FIGURE 1.1

PHYSICAL ACTIVITIES ARRANGED BY ENERGY LEVEL AND TIME

The activities at the top of the arrow take more time but are less vigorous. Those at the bottom take less time but are more vigorous.

Which type of activities could a person do daily? Which might be done weekly?

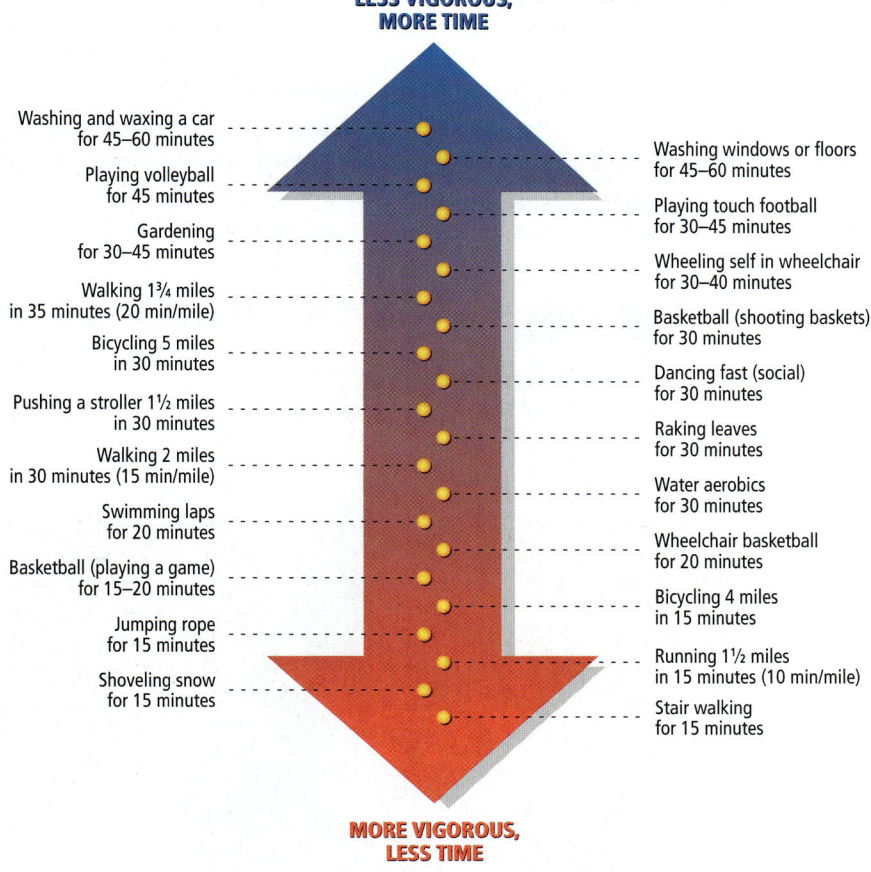

LESS VIGOROUS, MORE TIME

Washing and waxing a car for 45–60 minutes

Playing volleyball for 45 minutes

Gardening for 30–45 minutes

Walking 1¾ miles in 35 minutes (20 min/mile)

Bicycling 5 miles in 30 minutes

Pushing a stroller 1½ miles in 30 minutes

Walking 2 miles in 30 minutes (15 min/mile)

Swimming laps for 20 minutes

Basketball (playing a game) for 15–20 minutes

Jumping rope for 15 minutes

Shoveling snow for 15 minutes

Washing windows or floors for 45–60 minutes

Playing touch football for 30–45 minutes

Wheeling self in wheelchair for 30–40 minutes

Basketball (shooting baskets) for 30 minutes

Dancing fast (social) for 30 minutes

Raking leaves for 30 minutes

Water aerobics for 30 minutes

Wheelchair basketball for 20 minutes

Bicycling 4 miles in 15 minutes

Running 1½ miles in 15 minutes (10 min/mile)

Stair walking for 15 minutes

MORE VIGOROUS, LESS TIME

Source: U.S. Department of Health and Human Services, Centers for Disease Control and Prevention, 2003.[1]

entirely on high-fat food. Imagine a teen who loves aerobic dance but abuses harmful substances. Has either of these teens achieved total, personal fitness?

Reading Check

Analyze Is it possible to be physically active without exercise? Explain.

Figure 1.1 Display *Transparency 2.* Have each student make a list of the activities from Figure 1.1 that they have participated in for the last seven days. Then have students gather into groups of three or four and discuss how many in their group participated mostly in moderate or vigorous activities. *Caption answer: Those that could be done daily: more vigorous, less time. Those that could be done weekly: less vigorous, more time.* L1

Discussing

Ask students to explain the difference between physical fitness and personal fitness. *Physical fitness refers to the body's physical capabilities. Personal fitness requires one to achieve total fitness.* L1

Reading Check

A person may be very physically active and fit without exercising. For example, people in active jobs such as freight delivery workers can be fit because of their work duties and yet not participate in regular exercise.

More About . . .

PERSONAL FITNESS The recommendations for Personal Fitness on pages 4 and 5 are based on the 2003 Healthy Initiatives that can be found at **fitness.glencoe.com**. These initiatives include the following cues: Be active each day, eat a nutritious diet, get preventive health screenings, and avoid risky behaviors. At the same Web site, you can find links to numerous national/governmental health, fitness, and recreation materials.

Fitness FACTS

Ask students to discuss the two facts about endorphins. Ask them whether they have ever experienced a runner's high or good feeling during exercise. Ask them whether they have ever felt better after exercising. If so, ask them why they think this happens.

USING VISUALS

Figure 1.2 Display *Transparency 3* and have students look at Figure 1.2 to explain why this is a balanced health triangle. Have students read the caption on page 7 and discuss how participating in physical activities will benefit the health of these teens. **L1**

Critical Thinking

Ask students to identify the effects of substance abuse on physical performance. Ask: How does smoking affect a person's ability to participate in physical activities? *Tobacco use causes health problems, including respiratory infections and asthma, and damages the lungs.* Ask volunteers to investigate school rules that apply to smoking or the use of tobacco at school events. **L3** TEKS C2A1, C3D

Fitness FACTS

Physical Activity and Endorphins
- Physical activity prompts the brain to release *endorphins,* natural chemicals that make you feel calm and happy.
- Endorphins are associated with the phenomenon known as *runner's high* common among long-distance runners.

Fitness, Health, and Wellness

Fitness is an important part of maintaining your health—and health means much more than the absence of physical illness. **Health** is defined as *a combination of physical, mental/emotional, and social well-being.* The term **wellness** refers to *total health in all three areas.* Personal fitness is essential to maintaining your overall health.

Fitness and The Health Triangle

Health and wellness are sometimes represented by a triangle (see **Figure 1.2**). Personal fitness is essential to all three sides of the triangle. High levels of personal fitness promote *all* aspects of health.

Physical Health. People with high levels of personal fitness experience many benefits to their physical health. These physical benefits include

- a higher energy level.
- improved strength, flexibility, and muscle tone.

FIGURE 1.2

THE HEALTH TRIANGLE
Notice that all sides of the triangle are equal. *Is your health triangle well-balanced?*

SOCIAL

PHYSICAL

MENTAL/EMOTIONAL

---

6 Chapter 1 Physical Activity and Personal Fitness

Promoting Coordinated School Health

OBESITY AND DIABETES PREVENTION Coordinated School Health Programs involve integrating health and physical education concepts throughout the school curriculum. One major step physical educators can take to promote coordinated health programs in the school environment is by encouraging adolescents to engage in regular physical activity, which is defined as any activity or exercise performed most days of the week—preferably daily—to help them adopt lifestyle behaviors that can prevent obesity and type 2 diabetes. Teachers and administrators can be role models by participating in physical activities and avoiding the use of tobacco products.

- better heart and lung function.
- stronger bones.
- healthier weight and reduced body fat.
- improved coordination.
- more restful sleep.

These teens are engaging in behaviors that benefit their health. *Which sides of the health triangle are they focusing on?*

Another aspect of physical health is **functional health,** *the ability to maintain high levels of health and wellness by reducing your risks of developing health problems.* Physical activity is one way to maintain your functional health. Physically active people have a lower risk for physical problems that are related to a **sedentary** (SED-uhn-tayr-ee), or *physically inactive,* lifestyle. These problems include

- **heart disease.**
- high blood pressure.
- stroke.
- diabetes.
- certain forms of cancer, including colon cancer.

Mental/Emotional Health. The benefits of personal fitness go beyond physical health. Fitness also improves mental/emotional health. People who are personally fit are typically able to

- think more clearly and concentrate on work or school.
- better handle the stress and challenges of everyday life.
- experience higher **self-esteem,** or *feelings of self-confidence and personal worth.*

Social Health. Achieving personal fitness, whether it is playing on a team or working out with a partner, will also benefit your social health. Personally fit individuals are better able to

- develop and maintain friendships.
- work well as part of a group.
- effectively recognize and resolve **conflicts.** Conflicts are *struggles or disagreements.* Playing a sport especially teaches individuals how to resolve disagreements without resorting to name-calling or fighting.

Reading Check

Summarize What is the relationship between health and fitness?

heart disease
For more on heart disease and its prevention through physical activity, see Chapter 7, page **200.**

LIFELINE

Dealing with Conflicts
Volleyball, basketball, and other competitive sports are a great way to stay in shape and improve social health at the same time. When you play a game as part of a team, you also get a chance to socialize and build social skills.

Just remember that it is a game. When tempers flare, everyone loses. Should this happen, keep your cool. Talk it out, take a break, or do both. Encourage others to do the same.

hotlink

Reinforce the importance of being physically active and exercising as important ways to prevent heart disease and other health problems. Have students review Lesson 2 of Chapter 7.

LIFELINE

Dealing with Conflicts
Ask students to think of specific ways that playing sports can teach individuals to resolve disagreements and conflicts. Remind them that team sports and physical activity programs offer many opportunities for learning how to recognize and deal with conflicts. Ask students to describe ways they can recognize and resolve conflicts during physical activities. Ask: What other ways do sports help teens build character? When playing sports you can practice fairness and show respect for other players.
L3 **TEKS C2B**

Reading Check

Good health is positively associated with participation in regular physical activity or exercise.

More About . . .

MIND-BODY CONNECTION The mind-body connection has been recognized by physical educators and athletic coaches as a critical link to high performance for decades. Most sports require high degrees of mental preparation and concentration in order to optimize performance. Some examples of team sports that rely on a strong mind-body connection are football, basketball, and baseball. Have students identify and discuss other lifetime sports or physical activity skills that require a strong mind-body connection (golf and tennis, for example).

Student Edition TEKS

Page 6: C4A
Page 7: C2B, C5G

7

Fitness Check

Methods for Evaluating Health-Related Fitness

OBJECTIVES

- Test the five components of health-related fitness.
- Assess performance using Fitness Ratings Charts.

TEACHING STRATEGIES

- Have an area in the gym or hallway marked off properly before class, and make sure to conduct all tests in a safe manner.
- Demonstrate each test prior to student trials.
- You may want to create testing teams.
- It is a good idea to have students warm up prior to any test.
- Make copies and distribute *Fitness Check Worksheet 1-1* so students can record their scores. 📁
- Explain that participating in a variety of activities will help them develop health-related fitness. These are designed to introduce students to the different parts of health-related fitness. They are not tests for a grade.

TEKS C4B

Jumping Jacks

Have students perform jumping jacks at the rate of one per second. Each partner should time the other while exercising, resting, and pulse-taking for 30 seconds. Pulse may be taken at the carotid or radial artery.

8

Methods for Evaluating Health-Related Fitness

In this activity, you will participate in a variety of activities that develop health-related fitness. You will learn more about health-related fitness in Chapter 3. Before you start, be sure to warm up.

Cardiovascular Fitness: Jumping Jacks

Procedure:
1. Begin with your feet together and arms spread as in Figure 1.3a.
2. Jump, spreading your arms and legs as in Figure 1.3b.
3. Bring your arms together, hands touching, directly over your head, as in Figure 1.3c, then return to the starting position.
4. Repeat these movements for a total of thirty seconds. Once you stop, rest for an additional thirty seconds.
5. Take your pulse, as instructed by your teacher.
6. Use the Fitness Ratings Chart for Jumping Jacks to assess your performance.

Figure 1.3a   Figure 1.3b   Figure 1.3c

Fitness Ratings: Jumping Jacks	
Beats per 30 seconds	Rating
Under 60 beats	Pass
Over 60 beats	Needs work

Body Composition: Finger Pinch Test

Procedure:
1. Sit in a chair and place both feet flat on the floor.
2. Place the end of your little finger on your kneecap.
3. Spread your fingers. Extend the thumb as far up your thigh as possible.

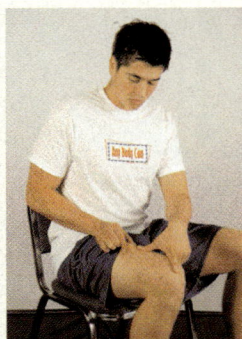

Figure 1.4

4. With your other hand, pinch a fold of skin at the end of your thumb as in Figure 1.4.
5. Use the Fitness Ratings Chart for the Finger Pinch Test to assess your current body composition. (NOTE: *Body composition* is the ratio of body fat to lean body tissues, such as muscle and bone.)

Fitness Ratings: Finger Pinch Test	
Skin Pinch Width	Rating
Narrower than thumb	Pass
Wider than thumb	Needs work

TECHNOLOGY FILE

Handhelds Make Light of Testing
Use a handheld computer to collect fitness scores (curl-up test, mile run) as students complete each test. At the end of class, transfer the data from the handheld computer (by using hot sync or active sync) to a desktop spreadsheet. Repeat the process every six weeks.

After several testing periods, instruct students to use personal data in their spreadsheets to create line graphs illustrating the changes in their performance. Print the line graphs, and have students bring them to their math classes to analyze their changes in fitness levels.

Flexibility: Zipper Stretch

Procedure:
1. Raise your right arm, bending your elbow. Reach down behind your back as far as possible.
2. At the same time, bend your left elbow and reach around your back as in **Figure 1.5**. Try to clasp your right hand. Your goal is to touch or overlap your right hand.
3. Switch arms and repeat the test. You may find that you do better on one side than the other. This is common because many individuals are more flexible on one side than the other.
4. Use the Fitness Ratings Chart for Zipper Stretch to assess your performance.

Figure 1.5

Fitness Ratings: Zipper Stretch

Ability to Touch	Rating
Touch or overlap	Pass
Inability to touch	Needs work

Muscular Strength: Push-ups

Procedure:
1. Extend your elbows and push your body up to a fully extended arm position, as in **Figure 1.6**. Keep your back straight at all times.

Figure 1.6

2. Gradually lower your body to the point where your chest just about touches the ground.
3. Repeat this motion as many times as you can.
4. Use the Fitness Ratings Chart for Push-ups to assess your performance.

Fitness Ratings: Push-ups

Number of Push-ups		Rating
Males:	5 or more	Pass
	Less than 5	Needs work
Females:	3 or more	Pass
	Less than 3	Needs work

Muscular Endurance: Wall Sit

Procedure:
1. Find a wall that you can lean back against comfortably and safely.
2. Stand 1 to $1\frac{1}{2}$ feet from the wall. Place your feet shoulder width apart.
3. Lean back against the wall so that your back is straight and your shoulder blades touch the wall.

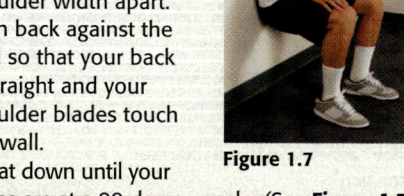

Figure 1.7

4. Squat down until your knees are at a 90-degree angle. (See **Figure 1.7**.) Try to hold this position for fifteen seconds.
5. Use the Fitness Ratings Chart for Wall Sit to assess your performance.

Fitness Ratings: Wall Sit

Time	Rating
15 seconds or more	Pass
Less than 15 seconds	Needs work

Fitness Check

Finger Pinch Test

This is not a precise test of body composition, but it can identify some concerns for carrying too much fat. Chapters 5 and 6 will provide much more information about body composition and weight control. Some students may be sensitive about this issue. Be sure to provide privacy if a student desires.

Zipper Stretch

Clarify that this flexibility activity is for the shoulder and that there are many other joints in the body that can be measured. Having good flexibility in one joint does not ensure good flexibility in other joints.

Wall Sit

Explain that this muscular endurance activity is specific to the legs and that there are many other areas of the body in which muscular endurance can be evaluated. Emphasize to students to keep their backs straight.

Push-ups

Clarify that this muscular strength activity is specific to the chest and arms and that there are many other areas of the body in which muscular strength can be evaluated. Emphasize to students to keep their backs straight.

More About . . .

EVALUATING HEALTH-RELATED FITNESS Many other tests can be used to test adolescent cardiovascular fitness, body composition, flexibility, muscular endurance, and strength. Some examples include the following:
- Cardiovascular—1.5-mile run, 20-minute steady-state jog, or 30-minute walk
- Body Composition—body mass index or skinfold measures
- Flexibility—sit-and-reach or range-of-motion tests
- Muscular endurance—curl-ups or sit-ups
- Muscular strength—pull-ups or arm hang

Student Edition TEKS

Page 8: C4B, C4E
Page 9: C4B, C4E

Discussing

Have students explain the relationship between functional health and functional fitness. Remind students that functional health involves reducing their risks for developing health problems and functional fitness involves maintaining physical independence. **L2 TEKS C4A**

HEALTHY PEOPLE 2010

Use *Transparency 1* to introduce *Healthy People 2010*. Explain that this program was developed by state health agencies, national health agencies, and professional organizations based on the results of *Healthy People 2000* objectives. See Appendix B, page 384, to read the objectives.

USING VISUALS

Figure 1.8 Display *Transparency 4* and have students analyze sound nutritional practices and physical activity by comparing this pyramid to the Food Guide Pyramid on page 28 in Chapter 4 (or use *Transparency 28*). *Caption answers will vary.* **L1 TEKS C5D**

✓ Reading Check

Skill-related fitness includes agility, power, speed, coordination, and reaction time. Health-related fitness includes cardiovascular fitness, body composition, muscular strength, muscular endurance, and flexibility.

Functional Fitness

Maintaining high levels of health and fitness yields an additional benefit: **functional fitness.** This is *a person's physical ability to function independently in life, without assistance.* Functionally fit individuals maintain high levels of health and wellness and a reduced risk of chronic problems.

Like health itself, functional fitness may be thought of as a triangle. **Figure 1.8** shows the Physical Activity Pyramid. The base of the pyramid lists physical activities that should be done daily. The second level lists goals for physical activities and exercises that should be done three to five times a week. The third level lists activities and exercises that should be done two to three times per week. The top level of the triangle highlights physical inactivity, which should occur infrequently.

FIGURE 1.8

THE PHYSICAL ACTIVITY PYRAMID

This pyramid provides guidelines for how to divide your time when doing various types of physical activity. *What physical activities do you do daily?*

Sedentary Activities
Do infrequently
Examples: watching television, talking on the phone, playing computer games, surfing the Internet

Anaerobic Activities
2–3 days *per week* (all major muscle groups)
Examples: biceps curls, push-ups, abdominal crunches, bench press, leg raises

Flexibility Activities
2 or more days *per week* (all major joints)
Examples: side lunge, side stretch, hurdler stretch, calf stretch, butterfly stretch

Aerobic Activities
3–5 days *per week* (20–60 minutes *per session*)
Examples: cycling, brisk walking, running, dancing, in-line skating, playing basketball, cross-country skiing

Moderate-Intensity Physical Activities
About 30 minutes *per day*
Examples: walking, climbing stairs, gardening or yard work, walking a dog, housecleaning

---

Curriculum CONNECTIONS

LANGUAGE ARTS Have students write a short essay addressing the following questions: What activity would you enjoy doing as a regular part of your life, now and in the future? How might your ability to perform this activity change as you grow older? How might your ability to continue this activity change as your responsibilities in life change? Would it become more difficult to continue this activity as time goes by? Ask volunteers to read their responses to the class. Have students look through newspapers and magazines to find examples of older adults who are physically active.

Healthy People 2010 and Fitness

The United States government has launched *Healthy People 2010*, an initiative designed to encourage all Americans to make health and fitness a top priority. The goal, to be achieved by the year 2010, is for all Americans to reach and sustain high levels of fitness in one or both of the following:

- **Skill-related fitness.** This is *your ability to perform success-fully in various games and sports.* It is also known as *perform-ance fitness.* There are six components, or measures, of **skill-related fitness:** *agility, balance, power, speed, coordina-tion, and reaction time.*
- **Health-related fitness.** This is *your ability to become and stay physically healthy.* There are five components of **health-related fitness:** *cardiovascular fitness, body composition, muscular strength, muscular endurance, and flexibility.*

Improving your health-related fitness will be the focus of many of the remaining chapters of this book. Each chapter will contain a "Fitness Check" that will allow you to assess your fitness level.

Reading Check

List What are the components of skill-related fitness? of health related-fitness?

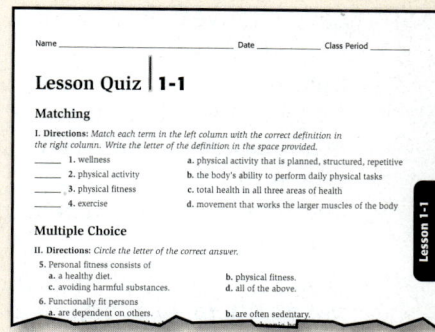

FITNESS *Online*

Go to **fitness.glencoe.com** for information about the President's Challenge for Physical fitness.

Activity Using the informa-tion provided at this site, create a plan for your school to become an Active Lifestyle Model School.

For more on **skill-** and **health-related fitness,** see Chapter 3, pages **72–76.**

Lesson 1 Review

Using complete sentences, answer the following questions on a sheet of paper.

Reviewing Facts and Vocabulary

1. **Vocabulary** What is *physical activity?* What is *physical fitness?*
2. **Recall** What is the relationship between *physical fitness* and *health?*

Thinking Critically

3. **Analyze** Explain how participating in phys-ical activity with others can help you develop skills to recognize and resolve conflicts.
4. **Synthesize** Explain why it might be possible to say that someone who does not exercise could still be physically active. Explain why it might be possible for someone to be physi-cally active without having personal fitness.

5. **Describe** Carlos is preparing to start a fitness program. Before he begins, he is eager to eval-uate how he rates in all areas of his health-related fitness. Briefly describe methods he can use to evaluate his health-related fitness in all five areas.

Personal Fitness Planning

Evaluating Physical-activity Level Make a log and record the physical activities and exercises you do for one week. Based on your log, determine whether you are currently very active, moderately active, or inactive. Write down ways you could adjust your weekly schedule to become more active than you currently are.

---

3 ASSESS

EVALUATING THE LESSON

Assign and discuss the Lesson 1 Review.

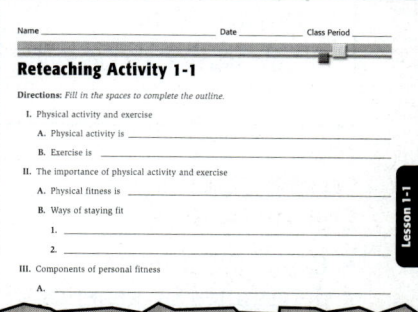

RETEACHING

Ask students to write two test questions based on the lesson content. Use them as a basis for a class discussion.

ENRICHMENT

Calculate the average score on the tests from the Fitness Check. Then have students decide how many in the class need work on improving their scores.

4 CLOSE

Divide students into small groups for five minutes, and have each group summarize the lesson to the class.

11

Lesson 1 Review

Answers to Lesson 1 Review

1. Physical activity: any movement that works the larger muscles of the body. Physical fitness: the ability to carry out daily tasks and still have energy.
2. Physical fitness is an important part of maintaining the health triangle.

3. If you learn the rules to a game, you can help others understand how to avoid conflicts.
4. Answers might include a person who works at a physically demanding job.
5. He can take the simple tests included in the Fitness Check on pages 8 and 9.

Risk Factors and Your Behavior

1 MOTIVATE

GETTING STARTED

- Ask students whether they have relatives or know of individuals who are in their 80s or 90s. Also, ask whether they think there is a relationship between quality of life as one ages and how physically active one is.

- Distribute copies of *Guided Practice Activity 1-2* for students to use while studying this lesson. 📁

IN THIS LESSON

- **Active Mind—Active Body** *Identifying Risk Factors for Heart Disease, p. 14*

- **Any Body Can** *George W. Bush, p.16*

INTRODUCING VOCABULARY

- Explain that *heredity* is determined by genetics, but some research suggests gene action in the body may be regulated negatively by a lack of physical activity.

- Have students use *Vocabulary Worksheet 1* or the PuzzleMaker software to practice vocabulary terms. **ELL** 📁 💿

PHOTO FOLLOW-UP

Caption answers: *Do not smoke, eat healthfully, control body weight, lower stress, and reduce changeable risk factors (factors you control).* **L1 TEKS C5G**

What You Will Do

- Identify changeable risk factors that affect your levels of health and personal fitness.
- Describe lifestyle choices that can improve overall levels of fitness and offset negative factors.
- Define *stress* and describe activities that you can use for stress reduction.
- Identify risk factors for developing heart disease.

Terms to Know

risk factors
heredity
stress

Risk Factors and Your Behavior

The average life expectancy in the United States is about seventy-seven years. More and more people, however, are living into their hundreds. Your life expectancy and the quality of those years will be influenced by how well you maintain your functional health and fitness.

Personal Fitness and Risk Factors

Achieving and maintaining a high level of functional health and fitness is often made more difficult by risk factors, or *conditions and behaviors that represent a potential threat to an individual's well-being.* Where personal fitness is concerned, these are factors that put you at risk for certain diseases, including heart disease, lung disease, and bone disease. **Figure 1.9** shows several of these diseases and lists the risk factors for each.

 Physical activity and exercise are ways to lower your risk of developing health problems as you age. *What other measures can you take?*

12   Chapter 1   Physical Activity and Personal Fitness

LESSON 2 RESOURCES

Teacher Classroom Resources
- 📁 Guided Practice Activity 1-2
- 📁 Active Mind—Active Body Worksheet 1-2
- 📁 Reteaching Activity 1-2
- 📁 Lesson Quiz 1-2

Reproducible Charts and Graphs
- 📁 Reproducible Master 1-3

Multimedia
- 💿 Vocabulary PuzzleMaker
- 👆 Transparency 5

FIGURE 1.9

DISEASES AND RISK FACTORS

Heredity and a sedentary lifestyle, in combination with other risk factors, increase the risk for developing all of these diseases. *Which risk factors are changeable?*

Disease	Contributing Risk Factors	Disease	Contributing Risk Factors
High Blood Pressure	• Heredity • Overweight • Sedentary lifestyle • Unhealthful eating plan	**Heart Disease**	• Diabetes • Heredity • High blood pressure • Overweight • Sedentary lifestyle • Smoking • Stress • Unhealthful eating plan
Colon Cancer	• Heredity • Sedentary lifestyle • Unhealthful eating plan		
Diabetes	• Heredity • Overweight • Sedentary lifestyle • Unhealthful eating plan	**Stroke**	• Heredity • High blood pressure • Overweight • Sedentary lifestyle • Unhealthful eating plan
Osteoporosis	• Heredity • Sedentary lifestyle • Unhealthful eating plan		

Risk Factors You Can't Modify

Some risk factors are largely beyond your control. However, it is important to be aware of how they affect you and how you can counteract their influence on your health and fitness.

Age

As we age, our chances of developing diseases such as heart disease, high blood pressure, and cancer increases. Although you cannot change your age, learning about and developing healthful habits now can make a positive difference in your levels of personal fitness throughout your life.

Heredity

To a degree, your personal fitness potential was determined before you were born. You are a product of *heredity—the sum of the physical and mental traits that you inherit from your parents.* Included are such features as eye color, hair color, and height.

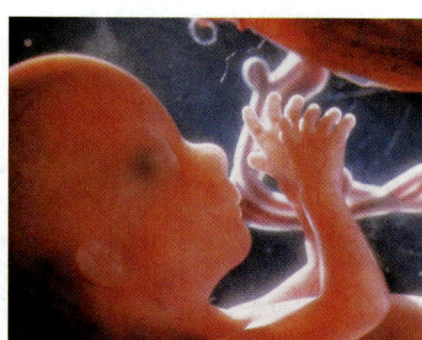

◄ Traits such as speed and power are determined before you are born. *What other traits are predetermined by heredity?*

Lesson 2   Risk Factors and Your Behavior   13

---

2 TEACH

USING VISUALS

Figure 1.9 Use the *Reproducible Master 1-3* from the TCR for Figure 1.9 to explain the table to students. Then ask: What are the contributing risk factors for diabetes? *Heredity, overweight, sedentary lifestyle, unhealthful eating plan.* Which diseases have increased risk from inactivity or having a sedentary lifestyle? *All of those listed.* Identify the changeable risk factors listed here that affect a person's health and likelihood of developing disease. **L1**
TEKS C5G

Explaining

Ask students why they think that being physically active throughout life can delay the aging process. While we cannot change our age, students will learn in Chapter 12 that a physically active lifestyle helps keep our bodies fitter and is associated with a higher quality of life during the aging process. **L1**

Photo Follow-up

Caption answer: Other inherited traits include eye color, hair color, and height.

Student Edition TEKS

Page 12: C5G
Page 13: C5G

COOPERATIVE Learning

ROLE-PLAY LIFELONG FITNESS Divide students into small groups, and have them role-play what they think they will be like when they reach the age of 65 to 70 years. Have them answer the following questions: 1) Do they think they will be physically active and healthy at that age? 2) Do they think they will have healthy habits when they are older? 3) What physical activities do they think they will be struggling to perform? Have them defend their answers based on the student text information above. **ELL**

Active Mind Active Body
Identifying Risk Factors for Heart Disease

This activity will help students identify changeable risk factors, including inactivity, smoking, nutrition, and stress. **TEKS C5G**

Teaching Tips

- Students may use *Active Mind–Active Body Worksheet 1-2* for this activity to record responses.
- Remind students that personal information should be kept private.

Apply and Conclude

Have students review their responses, and then have them ask a family member to complete the chart and see how their responses compare. Ask why the results probably will be similar. Students should recognize how heredity is involved.

hotlink

Reinforce the importance of knowing one's heredity (when possible) with regard to possible disease risks. Have students review Lesson 3 in Chapter 7 to learn how heredity is related to cardiorespiratory endurance. **L3**

Reading Check

Heredity determines your chances of developing certain diseases such as heart disease, diabetes, or cancer.

Active Mind Active Body
Identifying Risk Factors for Heart Disease

A first step toward reversing the effects of harmful risk factors in your life is identifying them. In this activity, you will assess the factors in your life that put you at risk for developing heart disease.

What You Will Need

- Pen or pencil
- Paper

What You Will Do

Copy the chart that follows onto a separate sheet of paper. Review each of the risk factors. Place a check mark in the *Yes* column of those that apply to you personally. (For some factors, you may need to consult an adult family member.) If you check *yes,* mark whether this is a risk factor you can modify.

Apply and Conclude

In which of these areas did you find potential risk factors in your life? What are some of the specific risks facing you? Which of these can you change for the better? In your private fitness journal, write an explanation about how you can go about making necessary changes.

	Yes	Can Modify	Cannot Modify
1. **Heredity**			
2. **Gender**			
3. **Sedentary lifestyle**			
4. **Smoking**			
5. **Food choices**			
6. **Excessive stress**			
7. **Obesity**			
8. **Diabetes**			

hotlink

heredity
For more on heredity and its role in fitness, see Chapter 7, page **208**.

As a risk factor, **heredity** determines your likelihood of developing certain diseases and disorders. These include high blood pressure, heart disease, diabetes, and certain types of cancers. Like your age, your genetic makeup cannot be changed, but the risks it may pose can be reduced by maintaining a healthy lifestyle.

Gender. One aspect of heredity that can have far-reaching implications to personal fitness is gender. Natural differences between males and females exist. For example, females possess about 38 percent of the upper-body strength and 45 percent of the lower-body strength of males. It is also a fact that males are at higher risk for heart disease than are women.

Reading Check

Explain What is the relationship between heredity and your health?

INCLUSION STRATEGIES

INCREASED RISK FACTORS FOR TEENS WITH DIABETES, OBESITY Students with special needs require physical, motor, and health-related fitness as much as individuals without physical disabilities. Functional health and fitness and a physically active lifestyle can be limited. If you have students who are restricted in their ability to be physically active because of a disability, encourage them to strive for personal fitness, functional health and fitness, and an active lifestyle within their limitations. All forms of fitness will aid in developing self-reliance and confidence among special needs groups.

Changeable Risk Factors

Although you cannot control risk factors such as heredity or age, you *can* lessen their impact on your health and fitness. You can reduce or eliminate some of your risks, because they stem from something you can control—your behavior.

Becoming Physically Active

One changeable risk factor for developing health problems is physical inactivity. Research has shown that adults who are sedentary develop chronic diseases at a much higher rate than do more active individuals. Choosing a physically active lifestyle is one way to reduce your risks of developing disease and to live a longer, healthier life. It is essential to maintaining your future functional health and fitness.

Practicing Healthful Eating Habits

How much food you eat—and the types of food—are considerations that greatly impact your health and fitness. For example, limiting the amount of fat intake, sodium intake, and cholesterol intake in the foods you eat can reduce your risk of developing certain diseases, including heart disease. Maintaining a healthy body weight and making nutritious, balanced food choices will also reduce your risk of becoming overweight or obese. **Obesity** is a major risk factor for developing **type 2 diabetes.** You will learn more about the connections between nutrition, body composition, and disease in later chapters.

▼ Knowing what to eat can make a difference in your health and fitness. *Do you know which foods to eat in moderation?*

Avoiding Smoking and the Use of Tobacco Products

One of the most important steps you can take to promote your health is to make a decision not to smoke or use tobacco products. Studies have shown that people who smoke for ten years or more are at far greater risk of heart and lung disease than are nonsmokers. People using smokeless tobacco, such as chewing tobacco and other products, face similar risks. These include cancer of the throat. You will learn more about harmful substances and how to avoid them in Chapter 2.

 **Reading Check**

Explain Identify two diseases that are affected by your eating plan.

hotlink

obesity
For more on obesity, see Chapter 5, page **150.**

type 2 diabetes
For more on type 2 diabetes, see Chapter 6, page **173.**

Lesson 2   Risk Factors and Your Behavior   **15**

More About . . .

NICOTINE AND SMOKING It only takes 5 to 7 seconds for nicotine to reach the brain after a person inhales tobacco smoke. In those seconds, the nicotine is absorbed into the bloodstream through the lining of the mouth and through the lungs. The smoker's blood pressure goes up; heart rate increases by up to 20 beats; oxygen supply to body tissues decreases; and blood circulation to the arms, hands, legs, and feet decreases. The first "rush" of stimulation in the brain is followed by depression and fatigue, leading the smoker to seek even more nicotine—another cigarette.

Chapter 1, Lesson 2

Critical Thinking

Ask students to use information gathered in the Active Mind—Active Body activity to identify their changeable risk factors for disease. Have them list steps they can take to control those factors for which they checked "yes." Students should be prepared to discuss the steps they can take to modify those risk factors. **L2** TEKS C5F, C5G

Photo Follow-Up

Emphasize how food choices can have positive or negative effects on health and fitness. *Caption answer: Foods that are high in fat, sodium, and cholesterol should be eaten in moderation.* **L2** TEKS C5D

Reading Check

Diseases affected by a person's eating plan are heart disease and type 2 diabetes.

hotlink

Reinforce the importance of participating regularly in physical activity and eating healthfully in order to control weight, prevent obesity, help prevent heart disease and type 2 diabetes. Have students review Chapters 5 and 6 to learn more about obesity and type 2 diabetes. **L1** TEKS C5D

Student Edition TEKS

Page 14: C5G
Page 15: C5G

15

Any Body Can

Have students review the feature on President George W. Bush. Ask them to identify the four elements of the President's Fitness Challenge described here. *Become more physically active, get preventive health screenings, choose nutritious foods, avoid alcohol, tobacco, and other drugs.* Ask students to explain how running or jogging as a regular physical activity can help Americans to meet these challenges. **L2**

Cooperative Learning

Have students work in groups of three to five and make lists of factors that make their lives stressful. Have a spokesperson from each group explain the group's responses. Then ask students as a whole why they think excessive stress may harm their functional health and fitness. **ELL** **L2** **TEKS C5B**

Discussing

Display *Transparency 5* and point out the effects of stressors on each of the body systems shown. Ask students to describe examples of stress and discuss how the effects of stress might impact their physical health and fitness. **L2**

✔ **Reading Check**
Negative effects of stress include sleepiness, depression, and other health problems.

Any Body Can

George W. Bush
The Fitness Challenge

The presidency of the United States is a job with tremendous responsibilities. You would think that with all a president has to do, the last thing on the commander in chief's mind would be personal fitness. However, George W. Bush, the forty-third president of the United States, makes time in his demanding schedule to keep fit.

George W. Bush was born on July 6, 1946, in New Haven, Connecticut. He graduated from Yale in 1968 and earned a business degree from Harvard in 1972. Bush was elected governor of Texas in 1994 and again in 1998. His leadership of this huge state paved the way for his presidency.

President Bush's life has been a model for a physically active lifestyle. In addition to participating in sports, he regularly jogs several miles and lifts weights two to three times per week. On June 20, 2002, he challenged all Americans to get healthier by becoming more physically active; by getting preventive health screenings; by choosing nutritious foods; and by avoiding alcohol, tobacco, and other drugs.

On June 22, 2002, President Bush, at age 55, set an example for all Americans by participating in a fitness challenge at Ft. McNair in Washington, D.C., where he ran 3.1 miles in under 21 minutes. That is less than 7 minutes per mile.

Not everyone can be the president. However, Any Body Can try to follow President Bush's physical activity goals.

Presentation
Working in groups, create a television commercial that promotes the four challenges George Bush has given to the American people to become healthier. Your commercial should be designed especially for a teen audience and should include visual aids and/or demonstrations, if possible.

Managing Stress in Your Life

You are probably all too aware of stress in your daily life. **Stress** is *the mind and body's response to the demands and threats of everyday life.* Stress is perfectly normal. Everyone experiences stressful moments. You may not be aware, however, that too much stress can take a toll on your health. It can lead to sleeplessness, depression, and other health problems.

Fortunately, there are strategies for coping positively with stress. These include the following recommendations:

- **Adjust your eating habits.** In particular, limit your intake of caffeine. This is a stimulant drug found in chocolate, soft drinks, some sports drinks, and coffee.

16   **Chapter 1**   **Physical Activity and Personal Fitness**

Teacher-Coach Tips

Active Lifestyles Numerous past presidents have led physically active lifestyles. Some examples include George H.W. Bush, Gerald Ford, and Teddy Roosevelt. President George H.W. Bush was an active golfer while he was in office; and he enjoyed brisk walking regularly with his wife, Barbara, and the family dog. Gerald Ford was also an avid golfer, and he was a football player during his college days at the University of Michigan. Teddy Roosevelt was an outdoorsman who rode horses and led the charge up San Juan Hill in the Spanish-American War.

- **Spend some time alone.** Taking a break and allowing yourself time to unwind can improve your mood and reduce your feelings of worry or stress. Spend time reading a favorite magazine or listening to soothing music. Writing about the concerns in your life can also be an effective way of managing stress.
- **Maintain a high level of physical activity.** Physical activity, whether it's playing a sport or working out alone is a positive outlet for stress. It allows you a way to redirect your energies and escape from stressful thoughts. Any type of exercise or physical activity can be an outlet for stress, including: weight lifting, jogging, dancing, and household chores, such as washing the car or cleaning your room.

Dealing with stress in a positive way is a challenge that will arise periodically throughout your life. It is important to redirect your energy, keep a positive outlook, and seek out support, if necessary. To help you understand and handle stress, the chapters to come will present coping strategies geared to the specific chapter topic. You will find these under the heading "Stress Break" in the margins.

Reading Check

Identify What are the negative effects of stress?

Lesson 2 Review

Using complete sentences, answer the following questions on a sheet of paper.

Reviewing Facts and Vocabulary

1. **Vocabulary** What are *risk factors*?
2. **Vocabulary** What is *stress*?
3. **Recall** Name three changeable risk factors that can impact your functional health.

Thinking Critically

4. **Analyze** Todd has a family history of heart disease on both sides of his family. Because he is male, his risk of developing heart disease is higher than if he were female. Todd believes there is no point in worrying about this as a teen because, as he ages, he will develop heart disease, no matter what. What advice would you give Todd?

5. **Extend** Many people have their own ways of coping with stress, such as listening to music, speaking with a close friend, or doing something physically active. List physical activities that you have used in the past or could use in the future to reduce stress in your life. Share your list with your classmates.

Personal Fitness Planning

Researching Risks Visit **fitness.glencoe.com** to learn more about the specific health risk factors for developing type 2 diabetes. Evaluate the health risk factors of a close relative of yours and determine if that person is at low, medium, or high risk for type 2 diabetes.

Lesson 2 Review

Answers to Lesson 2 Review

1. Risk factors are conditions or behaviors that represent a potential threat to an individual's well-being.
2. Stress is the mind and body's response to the demands and threats of everyday life, and is perfectly normal.
3. Three changeable risk factors are: becoming physically active, avoiding smoking and the use of tobacco products, and practicing healthful eating habits.
4. Answers will vary; some risk factors can be eliminated by controlling behavior.
5. Answers will vary.

3 ASSESS

EVALUATING THE LESSON

Assign and discuss the Lesson 2 Review.

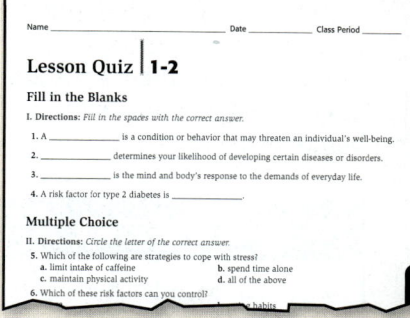

RETEACHING

Ask students to explain two ways a physically active lifestyle can help prevent the risk of disease.

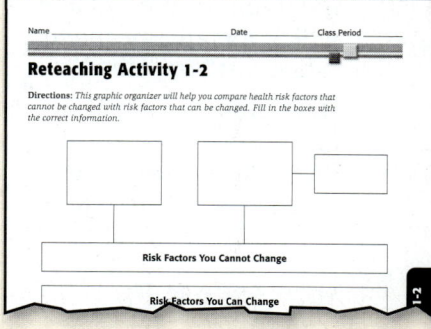

ENRICHMENT

Have students work in groups of 3 or 4 to create slogans that will encourage teens to reduce one of the changeable risk factors.
TEKS C5D, C5G

4 CLOSE

Ask students to respond to the following question: Is there anything in life more valuable than your health? Describe the quality of life without good health.

17

Developing a Positive Fitness Attitude

■ *1 MOTIVATE*

GETTING STARTED

Ask students to identify two examples of how peer influences and their attitudes affect their physical activity behaviors.

IN THIS LESSON

- **Active Mind—Active Body** *Investigating Attitudes about Personal Fitness,* p. 21

INTRODUCING VOCABULARY

- Explain that *adherence* is the noun form of *adhere,* which literally means to "stick fast" or "cling."
- Have students use *Vocabulary Worksheet 1* or the PuzzleMaker software to practice vocabulary terms. **ELL** 🗀 💿

Photo Follow-Up

Allow time for class discussion to investigate students' positive and negative attitudes regarding exercise, physical activity, and fitness. Ask: What choices do you make that reflect your attitudes about physical activity? *Caption answers will vary. Encourage volunteers to describe ways they incorporate physical activity into their day.* **L2** TEKS C5A

What You Will Do

- Investigate positive and negative attitudes toward personal fitness.
- Evaluate the role of peer influence in the decisions you make.
- Evaluate consumer issues, including marketing claims in the media, in your attitude toward fitness.
- Identify the benefits of adhering to a commitment to personal fitness.

Terms to Know

attitude
peers
media
commitment
adherence
self-concept

Developing a Positive Fitness Attitude

The secretary of the U.S. Department of Health and Human Services has called physical activity "a passport to good health for all Americans." Similar endorsements have been made for other lifestyle behaviors that promote wellness. However, current government statistics reveal that about a third of all teens nationwide are sedentary. Not surprisingly, the same percentage of American youth is overweight.

Your Attitudes

Although people might be aware of the importance of personal fitness, some find it difficult to develop and maintain a personally fit lifestyle for themselves.

One reason for this is attitude. Attitude is *your mindset or outlook toward a given topic or subject.* Your attitudes, especially during adolescence, play a major role in the decisions you make.

Your personal beliefs shape your attitudes about physical activity. Your beliefs about physical activity will change as you age and your

▶ Your attitudes and choices about how you spend your free time will affect your health and fitness levels. *Do you make physical activity and exercise part of your daily routine?*

18   Chapter 1   Physical Activity and Personal Fitness

LESSON 3 RESOURCES

Teacher Classroom Resources
🗀 Guided Practice Activity 1-3
🗀 Active Mind—Active Body Worksheet 1-3
🗀 Reteaching Activity 1-3
🗀 Lesson Quiz 1-3

Reproducible Charts and Graphs
🗀 Reproducible Masters 1-4, 1-5, 1-6

Multimedia
💿 Vocabulary PuzzleMaker
⚡ Transparency 6

knowledge about physical activity increases. The following are some common attitudes toward the subject of personal fitness. How many of these are familiar to you? How many have you expressed yourself?

- Exercise is boring.
- I'll start watching what I eat when I get to be an adult.
- I'm too busy for sports right now.
- I don't have time for breakfast in the morning.
- Exercise doesn't work.
- Sleep is for babies.
- I don't want to hurt myself.
- Physical activity is strictly for "athletes."
- I'm too tired to exercise today; I'll start tomorrow.
- I only need about 4 hours of sleep a night to function fully the next day.
- There has to be an easier way to get in shape!

In the "Active Mind—Active Body" activity on page **21,** you'll explore other attitudes that affect personal fitness.

Peer Influence

Where do negative attitudes like these come from? One source may be your **peers.** Peers are *people the same age who share a common range of interests and beliefs.* As a teen, your peers include your friends, classmates, and other students you see at school and around the community. Peer influence is the effect these individuals' words and actions have on your attitudes and behaviors. As shown in **Figure 1.10,** this influence can be either direct or indirect, positive or negative.

FIGURE 1.10

EXAMPLES OF PEER INFLUENCE
Peer influence can be positive or negative. *Can you think of another example of each type of peer influence?*

	Positive	Negative
Direct	Volunteering time at a nursing home based on encouragement from a friend who thinks you would be great at it	Accepting a dare to do something physically dangerous
Indirect	Developing good study habits because you see your friends studying hard	Adopting an unhealthful habit, such as smoking, because other people are doing it

Chapter 1, Lesson 3

2 TEACH

LIFELINE

Positive Peer Influence
You may know other teens that have a negative attitude about behaviors and habits that promote good health. They might even encourage you to engage in behaviors that harm your health.

Remember, just as your peers influence you, you also influence them.

Think about the kind of friend you are and your attitudes. Know that a positive outlook will not only benefit you, but it has the power to positively influence others.

LIFELINE

Positive Peer Influence
Have students investigate the attitudes of a person they know who is physically active daily. Have them ask the person why he or she participates in regular physical activity and to describe that person's positive attitude. Also, have them ask how peers have positively influenced the person to be physically active. **L2**
TEKS C5A1

USING VISUALS

Figure 1.10 Using *Reproducible Master 1-4,* have students read the examples and discuss answers to the caption. Positive examples might include a student becoming physically active because a teacher or coach provides a positive role model or the student becomes a positive role model and encourages a family member to become physically active. Negative examples might include students becoming turned off to physical activity because a teacher or coach has used exercise as punishment or students themselves become negative role models and discourage others from becoming physically active. **L1 TEKS C5A1**

COOPERATIVE Learning

ATTITUDES SURVEY
Divide students into three groups, and have them design a survey using the list of attitudes at the top of this page. Have them give the survey to adults including family members, teachers, or friends to determine their attitudes about personal fitness. Each student should contact three adults and have them answer the questionnaires by agreeing or disagreeing with each statement. Remind students to respect privacy and keep survey results anonymous. Have students share and discuss their findings briefly in class. **ELL**

Student Edition TEKS
Page 18: C4H
Page 19: C5A

Photo Follow-Up

Ask students whether they have ever seen other ads that suggest a person can get fit or lose weight easily without being physically active or participating in regular exercise. Ask them to evaluate how accurate they think these ads are. How do these types of ads influence a person's attitude toward becoming more physically active?
L2 TEKS C4H

✓ **Reading Check**
Advertisements may foster negative attitudes and inaccurate information.

Activity

Have students make a list of reasons they have made a commitment to activities that they enjoy doing, such as regularly visiting with family, hanging out with friends, or attending religious services. Then have them investigate their attitudes toward exercise by listing reasons they think they should make a commitment to become physically active. **L1** TEKS C5A

Activity

Have students complete the following activity. Make two lists of the aspects of your own physical appearance that you a) like and want to maintain and b) dislike and would like to change. Include such items as muscle tone, body size, weight, and body fat. How many items on your "like" list can be maintained by physical activity or exercise? How many items on your "dislike" list can be enhanced by physical activity and exercise? **L1**

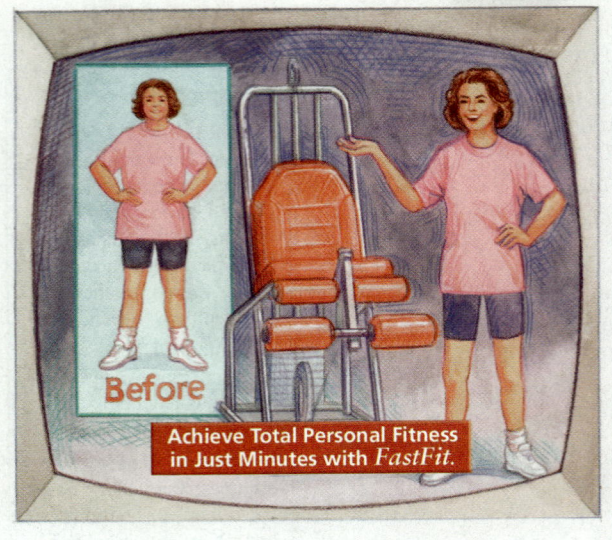

Achieve Total Personal Fitness in Just Minutes with *FastFit*.

Before

▶ Ads for some products suggest that achieving fitness should be fast and easy. *How can such messages contribute to a negative attitude about fitness?*

The Media

Another source that may promote negative attitudes about physical activity is the media. The term media is used to denote *the collective forms of mass communication found within society at any given time.* The media today include TV, radio, the movies, books, newspapers, magazines, music, and the Internet. Advertisements found on these sources are also examples of media.

Although these media can provide positive messages, many foster negative attitudes and inaccurate information. Take for example an advertisement for a belt that claims to tone the abdominal muscles without any kind of workout, or another for a pill that promises to burn fat. Ads like these reinforce the attitudes that exercise is too difficult and that there must be an easy shortcut to fitness.

✓ **Reading Check**
Explain How can an advertisement that is selling a fitness product lead to a negative attitude about fitness?

A Commitment to Change

As a teen, you may not feel the necessity of developing your personal fitness. The health risks of sedentary living may seem years away. You may be telling yourself that there will be plenty of time to "turn things around."

The truth, however, is that your adult years are just around the corner. There is no time like the present to make a commitment to personal fitness. A commitment is *a pledge or promise.* By making a commitment to fitness, you are making a promise to develop and maintain positive fitness behaviors.

Begin by examining your attitudes toward each of the lifestyle factors that promote fitness. The self-inventory in the "Active Mind—Active Body" activity on page **21** will help you explore some of your attitudes. Be honest with yourself and take your answers seriously. If your attitudes are negative, make the commitment to work at changing them. If your attitudes are positive, you have already taken a step in the right direction.

In the next lesson, you will learn how to put your positive thoughts and attitudes into action. You will learn how to launch and maintain a program that will keep you fit for life.

Myths & Realities

Myth 1 It is easy to burn 1,000 calories per hour using home exercise equipment.

Fact 1 You burn 1 calorie per minute sitting quietly at rest. To burn 1,000 calories per hour, you would have to burn an additional 12.3 calories per minute during exercise (to burn 1,000/hour) —a very intense workout.

Myth 2 You can lose 10–20 pounds per week and keep the weight off by using various weight loss products.

Fact 2 These types of ads are false and potentially dangerous. Excessive rapid weight loss is mostly due to dehydration, which can lead to medical problems.

Adherence

Adherence refers to *the ability to stick to a plan of action.* If you adhere to a fitness program, you will succeed. Sometimes, people who start personal fitness programs fail to adhere to them. Many of the reasons for this were explained earlier in this lesson. By developing an awareness of negative attitudes, you can increase your chances for succeeding in a fitness program. Remember, to be a healthy individual, it is your responsibility to develop your personal fitness.

 **Reading Check**

Compare What is the difference between commitment and adherence?

✓ **Reading Check**
Commitment is a pledge or promise to do something, whereas adherence refers to how well you can stick to your pledge.

Active Mind Active Body

Investigating Attitudes about Personal Fitness

Evaluating your attitudes is the first step toward changing those that are negative. This activity will help you do that.

What You Will Need
- Pen or pencil
- Paper

What You Will Do

The 20 statements that follow are designed to evaluate your current attitudes about fitness-related lifestyle factors. Copy the statements onto a separate sheet of paper. After each statement, write a number from 1 through 5, where 5 means "strongly agree" and 1 means "strongly disagree." Be as truthful as you can. There will be no grade assigned to this activity.

Apply and Conclude

Did you respond honestly to every statement? Which positive attitudes do you currently have toward your fitness? What areas, if any, do you need to improve?

1. I don't have time to exercise.
2. I eat breakfast every day.
3. I am not very athletic.
4. I seldom weigh myself.
5. I have always enjoyed participating in physical activities and exercise.
6. I enjoy physical education classes.
7. I have a moderate-to-high level of health and physical fitness.
8. I get 8 to 9 hours of sleep every night.
9. I take the stairs instead of the elevator or escalator whenever possible.
10. I like team games and sports.
11. I like to lift weights.
12. I enjoy eating healthful snacks.
13. I like to engage in physical activities with friends.
14. Exercising twice a week is all I need to do to stay in shape.
15. I prefer to ride rather than walk, even to go short distances.
16. Learning about personal fitness will be valuable to me later in life.
17. I find physical education classes boring.
18. I eat three balanced meals every day.
19. I have trouble sleeping.
20. I spend more than 25 hours a week watching TV.

Lesson 3 Developing a Positive Fitness Attitude **21**

Active Mind Active Body

Investigating Attitudes About Personal Fitness

This activity will help students become more aware of their attitudes about personal fitness. Explain that this information is private and will not be graded. **TEKS C5A**

Teaching Tips

- Encourage students to evaluate their attitudes at the beginning of this course.
- Distribute the *Active Mind–Active Body Worksheet 1-3*, and ask students to respond to each question honestly and thoughtfully. 📂
- Save the surveys, and return them to students at the end of the course to see whether their attitudes have changed.

Apply and Conclude

After students have completed the survey, discuss the importance of evaluating their attitudes. Ask volunteers to give examples of how students may improve their personal fitness.

Student Edition TEKS

Page 20: C4H
Page 21: C5A

More About . . .

ATTITUDES ABOUT PERSONAL FITNESS Have students review each response in the Active Mind—Active Body above and explain how they answered each question. Ask them why they strongly agreed (5), strongly disagreed (1), or didn't know for sure (3). Then ask them to determine how much influence their peers and the media had in their decisions. Have them share their findings with a partner to determine how the influence of peers and the media impact the decisions teens make about personal fitness.

Discussing

Share the following with students. Recent studies show that teens who are physically active as compared to inactive teens actually do better in the classroom in terms of academic performance. Physical educators have referred to this as "brain research," and scientists are just now starting to understand how physical activity and exercise help improve academic performance. **L1**

Source: California Department of Education Physical Fitness Testing Study, 2002.

USING VISUALS

Figure 1.11 Use *Reproducible Master 1-6* to discuss with students the ways in which regular participation in physical activity and exercise can enhance a teen's self-esteem. Examples might include impact on physical self-concept, personality, body image, acquired competence, or personal fitness level. **L1**

FITNESS *Online*

Encourage students at the beginning of this course to make a commitment toward increasing physical activity by starting their personal online Fitness Journal at **fitness.glencoe.com**.

Student Edition TEKS

Page 22: C2B

Mind OVER Matter

Fitness and Your Social Health

Remember that physical fitness is essential to all sides of the health triangle. When you are personally healthy and fit, you have a positive self-image that allows you to work well with others. Describe one example when a person who has a high level of personal health can be helpful in recognizing a conflict in a team sport before it develops into a major conflict.

Benefits of Personal Fitness

During your teen years, you will experience periods of growth and many physical changes. As discussed in Lesson 1, regular physical activity or exercise, combined with a sound nutrition plan, will provide many benefits to your physical health as you grow and change. In the remaining sections of this lesson, you will take a closer look at some other benefits related to mental/emotional health, as well as your overall functional fitness throughout life.

Enhancement of Self-Esteem

Most people agree that self-esteem is a powerful force within each individual. It enables people to cope better with the basic challenges of life. Healthy, fit people are more likely to experience feelings of happiness and higher self-esteem. They also have a more positive **self-concept.** This is *the view you have of yourself.* Simply put, people who are fit, healthy, and feel good about their health and physical appearance are more likely to live an enjoyable, productive life. **Figure 1.11** shows some of the more important factors affecting your self-esteem and your physical self-concept.

FIGURE 1.11

FACTORS INFLUENCING SELF-ESTEEM
Put yourself in the circle at the center of this diagram. *How do you regard yourself in each of these areas?*

Self-Esteem

Intelligent thinking · Emotional centeredness · Finances · Honors · Accomplishments · Family status · Friends · Social acceptance · Physical self-concept · Personality · Appearance (body image) · Acquired competence · Inborn talent · Physical fitness and condition

---

More About . . .

COMMITMENT TO CHANGE There are many behavioral strategies and models that have been designed to encourage adolescents to make healthy decisions and to adopt positive attitudes and behaviors toward personal fitness. One model that can be used by students is the STAR Model. The model includes: Stop and think about their behaviors and actions, Think about the possible positive options, Act and perform, and Review their actions and possible consequences. Students may find the STAR model is an effective strategy in making a commitment to improve personal fitness.

FIGURE 1.12

THE INFLUENCE OF PHYSICAL ACTIVITY ON FUNCTIONAL HEALTH AND FITNESS

Physical activity improves functional fitness. *Where does your current level of activity fall on this graph? What changes, if any, do you need to make?*

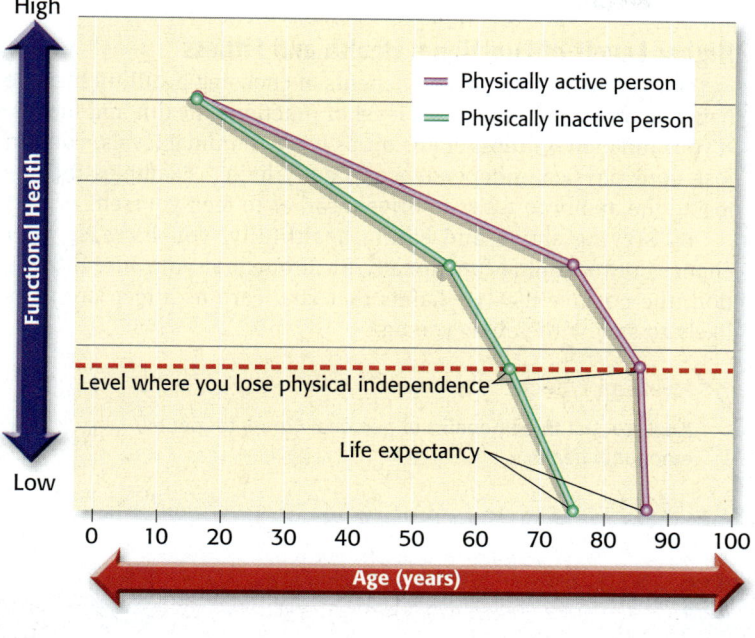

Chapter 1, Lesson 3

STRESS BREAK
Types of Stress

Not all stress is negative. Technically speaking, there is *good stress* and *bad stress*. Bad stress, also known as "distress," can increase your risk for chronic disease.

By contrast, positive stress—or "eustress" is enjoyable. It is the kind of stress that accompanies scoring high on a difficult exam, winning an important game, or being elected class president.

You can increase the amount of eustress, simultaneously decreasing the amount of distress, by making physical activity a lifelong habit.

STRESS BREAK

Have students make a list of things in their current daily schedules that are examples of distress and eustress. Have two or three volunteers share their results with the class. Have them describe what types of physical fitness activities can help reduce stress. **TEKS C5B**

hotlink

Reinforce the importance of understanding that high levels of cholesterol and/or triglycerides can increase the risk of disease. Have students review Lesson 1 in Chapter 4 to learn more about cholesterol.

USING VISUALS

Figure 1.12 Use *Transparency 6* to discuss the graph with students. Ask them where on the graph they would fall based on their current levels of physical activity.

Stress Reduction

As noted earlier in this chapter, managing stress is part of maintaining a healthy lifestyle. One of the benefits of personal fitness is stress reduction. Regular physical activity or exercise is an effective stress reducer. For example, regular physical activity lowers blood pressure and can reduce hormone levels that cause stress.

Improvements in Academic and Physical Performance

Regular participation in physical activity, exercise, or both has been shown to enhance performance in school. Teens who are physically active often have enhanced concentration spans, have higher energy levels, and miss fewer days of school.

Increased Life Expectancy

Physical activity and exercise increase muscular strength and endurance. Researchers have discovered that an active lifestyle also improves blood **cholesterol** and **triglyceride** levels. As you will see in

hotlink

For more on **cholesterol** and **triglycerides**, see Chapter 4, pages **119–120**.

Reading Check
(page 24)

Benefits include: self-esteem, stress reduction, improvements in academic and physical performance, increased life expectancy, higher levels of functional health and fitness.

Lesson 3 Developing a Positive Fitness Attitude   **23**

Curriculum CONNECTIONS

ACADEMICS AND PHYSICAL ACTIVITY A large-scale study in California, done in 2003, revealed that 5th, 6th, and 7th graders who had higher fitness levels showed better academic scores in reading and math than those students with lower fitness levels. The study included over 900,000 total students.

Students were evaluated for personal fitness by using measures of cardiorespiratory fitness, body composition, strength, and flexibility. This study provides strong evidence that the physical wellness of students has a direct impact on their ability to achieve academically in other curriculum areas.

Student Edition TEKS

Page 23: C5B, C5G
Page 24: C4H, C5A

3 ASSESS

EVALUATING THE LESSON

Assign and discuss the Lesson 3 Review.

Name _____ Date _____ Class Period _____

Lesson Quiz | 1-3

Matching

I. Directions: *Match each term in the left column with the correct definition in the right column. Write the letter of the definition in the space provided.*

_____ 1. attitude   a. pledge or promise
_____ 2. commitment   b. the view you have of yourself
_____ 3. self-concept   c. mind set or outlook toward a given topic or subject
_____ 4. adherence   d. ability to stick to a plan of action

Multiple Choice

II. Directions: *Circle the letter of the correct answer.*

5. Which of the following play a role in the decisions people make?
   a. attitude   b. peer influence
   c. media   d. all of the above
6. Personal fitness includes all of the following EXCEPT:

RETEACHING

Ask students to summarize the benefits of being physically active versus living a sedentary lifestyle.

Name _____ Date _____ Class Period _____

Reteaching Activity 1-3

Directions: *Complete the activities described in the shaded boxes.*

1. Identify and explain two influences on your attitude toward personal fitness.

2. List and describe two things that will help you change your attitude and behavior toward personal fitness.

ENRICHMENT

Have students work in teams to come up with an idea for an advertisement to encourage teens to adhere to their fitness plans.

4 CLOSE

Ask: How does regular physical activity or exercise contribute positively to good health?

Chapter 4, these are substances in the blood that increase a person's risk of cardiovascular disease.

Physically active people are also less likely to smoke or begin smoking. Thus, physical activity and exercise decrease disease risks and increase life expectancy. **Figure 1.12** compares the aging process of a physically active person with a physically inactive person. The physically inactive person has a shorter life expectancy than the physically active person.

Higher Levels of Functional Health and Fitness

One of the most important benefits of choosing healthful lifestyle habits is that it increases your level of functional health and fitness. If your functional-fitness status drops below minimal levels, you can lose your physical independence in daily living. Examples include losing the ability to walk, to drive a car, or to feed yourself.

By staying active and eating healthfully, you increase your chances of remaining functionally fit throughout your life. In addition, the positive lifestyle habits that you learn as a teen are more likely to stay with you as you age.

 Reading Check

Analyze List three benefits of personal fitness to mental/emotional health.

Lesson 3 Review

Using complete sentences, answer the following questions on a sheet of paper.

Reviewing Facts and Vocabulary

1. **Recall** Explain how your attitudes affect your level of fitness.
2. **Vocabulary** What are *peers*? What is *peer influence*?
3. **Recall** What is a *commitment*?

Thinking Critically

4. **Evaluate** Sean is a straight-A student. He does not participate in any type of physical activity regularly. Between the academic demands of school and the stress he feels meeting those demands, he says he has no time for exercise. What advice would you give him about the relationship among physical activity, stress, and academic performance?
5. **Analyze** Kevin believes that physical activity is the only lifestyle behavior anyone needs to follow. He tells his friends, "If you work out, you can eat anything you want." Assess Kevin's attitude toward total personal fitness.

Personal Fitness Planning

Evaluating Claims For the next week, take note of any advertisements you see for fitness products. Evaluate which of these consumer issues fosters a negative attitude toward physical activity and which emphasizes a positive attitude toward physical fitness. Be prepared to share your findings with your class.

Lesson 3 Review

Answers to Lesson 3 Review

1. Your attitudes help determine whether you will or will not engage in regular physical activity or exercise.
2. Peers share a common range of interests. Peer influence is the effect peers have on your attitudes and behaviors.
3. Commitment is a pledge or promise such as having positive attitudes and behaviors about physical activity.
4. Regular physical activity reduces stress, which can affect academic performance.
5. Kevin should eat right, get enough sleep, and have regular medical checkups.

Guidelines for Getting Started

Don't put off 'til tomorrow what you can do today. Have you heard this saying? It makes a good motto for someone who has made a commitment to become and stay personally fit. Is that someone you? If so, it is time to get started.

In this lesson, you will take your first steps toward developing an effective program of fitness. The chapters ahead will provide details you will need to put your plan into action.

Setting Fitness Goals

As discussed in Lesson 3, sticking to your fitness plan is essential to becoming personally fit. The following guidelines will help you design a plan that enables you to stick with your commitment.

- Make a contract with yourself to show your commitment to improving your personal fitness.
- Make a list of goals that are both reasonable and specific.
- Make a schedule of your fitness activities that fits in with your other obligations and responsibilities.
- Be patient: begin slowly and progress gradually.
- Enjoy it. Make it a social experience by participating with others in a variety of activities that you like doing.

► Designing a fitness plan involves careful planning. *Why do you think it is important to write down your goals?*

What You Will Do

- Design a personal fitness program by using specific guidelines.
- Define different levels of physical activity.
- Evaluate your current level of physical activity.

Terms to Know

behavioral-change stairway
regular physical activity
    or exercise
moderate physical activity
    or exercise
vigorous physical activity
    or exercise

Lesson 4   Guidelines for Getting Started   **25**

Guidelines for Getting Started

1 MOTIVATE

GETTING STARTED

- Have students describe three factors they think are important to consider when developing a fitness plan.
- Distribute copies of *Guided Practice Activity 1-4* for students to use while studying this lesson. 📁

IN THIS LESSON

- **Active Mind—Active Body** *How Physically Active Are You Now?* p. 30

INTRODUCING VOCABULARY

- Explain to students that there is some controversy in the sports medicine research literature as to whether *moderate* or *vigorous* physical activity or exercise is needed to help reduce one's health risks for disease. Therefore, it is important to understand both terms.
- Have students use *Vocabulary Worksheet 1* or the PuzzleMaker software to practice vocabulary terms. ELL 📁 💿

Photo Follow-Up

Caption answers will vary but should include that planning can help you meet your commitments successfully.

LESSON 4 RESOURCES

Teacher Classroom Resources
📁 Guided Practice Activity 1-4
📁 Active Mind—Active Body Worksheet 1-4
📁 Reteaching Activity 1-4
📁 Lesson Quiz 1-4

Multimedia
💿 Vocabulary PuzzleMaker
⬇ Transparencies 7, 8

2 TEACH

Activity

Ask students to identify one or two initial fitness goals that they wish to accomplish. Have them make a plan for accomplishing these goals. **L2**

Reading Check

Make a list of reasonable and specific goals; make a schedule.

Photo Follow-up

Discuss with students the goals of the teen in the photo on page 27. *Caption answer: She might start by setting short-term goals such as learning to swim efficiently. Then she might try to gradually swim non-stop for 5 minutes, then for 10 minutes, and up to 30 minutes over a period of six to eight weeks.* **L2**

Activity

Ask students to help you develop a personal fitness plan for yourself (the teacher). Give them two or three goals you want to achieve (getting stronger, losing weight, maintaining weight, walking/jogging more, for example), and ask students where and how you should start a physical activity program. **L2** **TEKS C4G**

Choosing Your Physical Activities

When designing your fitness program, choose activities that will be both effective and safe. As you begin your program, the activities you choose should be of moderate intensity. While you want to challenge yourself, it is important that you do not take on more than you can physically handle. Activities should be low-impact and lower weight-bearing, such as walking or lap swimming. Choose a variety of activities and consider safety. Avoid activities that can cause injury or personal harm.

Reading Check

Explain What written steps should you take when planning your fitness program?

The Behavioral-Change Stairway

One approach that has helped many people achieve and maintain lasting overall fitness is the **behavioral-change stairway**. This is *a step-by-step approach for helping people achieve their fitness goals.* The steps in this approach are shown in **Figure 1.13.** By taking fitness one step at a time, anyone—including you—can reach your fitness objectives.

Beginning to Climb. It may surprise you to learn that one of the hardest legs of the upward journey is the first. Moving from Step 1 (not thinking about fitness) to Step 2 (beginning to think about fitness) requires conscious effort. This is why making a contract with yourself can be very helpful.

FIGURE 1.13

BEHAVIORAL-CHANGE STAIRWAY

Improving fitness happens one step at a time. *What step on the behavioral-change stairway are you currently at in regard to personal fitness?*

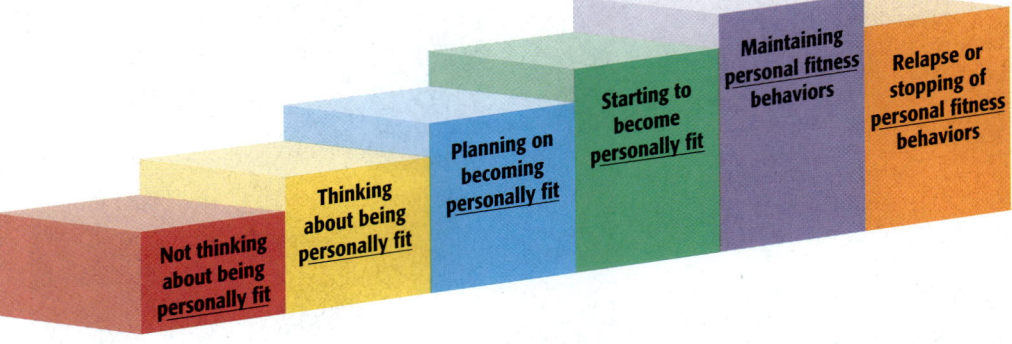

Not thinking about being personally fit

Thinking about being personally fit

Planning on becoming personally fit

Starting to become personally fit

Maintaining personal fitness behaviors

Relapse or stopping of personal fitness behaviors

Source: U.S. Department of Health and Human Services, Centers for Disease Control and Prevention, 1999.[2]

More About . . .

THE BEHAVIORAL-CHANGE STAIRWAY The following questionnaire can be used to help determine where individuals are at on the behavioral-change stairway (or their motivational readiness). The following questions should be answered with a "yes" or "no" response.

1. I am currently active.
2. I intend to become more physically active in six months.
3. I currently engage in regular physical activity. (see page 28 for definitions)
4. I have been regularly active for the past six months.

◄ Achieving goals involves making a realistic plan. *How can this teen achieve her goal of swimming one mile nonstop? Why is having a plan of action helpful?*

USING VISUALS

Figure 1.13 Display *Transparency 7* to explain the Behavioral-Change Stairway. Ask students to rate where their family members or friends are on the behavioral stairway with regard to physical activity and exercise. Have them discuss why they think their family or friends are at that particular stage and how they might become more active. **L1**

Explaining

Explain to students that the Behavioral-Change Stairway is based on the psychological theory called the *Transtheoretical Model of Behavioral Change*. This model has been used successfully to help identify where people are in terms of changing behaviors (such as smoking, losing weight, and becoming more physically active) and how to help them achieve healthy maintenance by "staying on top." **L3** TEKS C4G

Once you have reached Step 2, you need to think "actively." Assess your current behaviors, taking note of which need the most work. Be on the lookout at this stage for any negative attitudes that may still be holding you back.

Planning Your Journey. At Step 3, you develop your game plan, including setting goals and a realistic schedule. Begin by asking yourself, "What is my goal?" Then devise a regular schedule of activity to follow. Allow a reasonable time for achieving your goal. Consider Martha's goal: to be able to swim one mile nonstop. To achieve this goal, she will need to start slowly, maybe doing five minutes at first, then adding a few minutes more in each following session. By exercising patience as well as her muscles, Martha will eventually reach her fitness objective.

Staying on Track. Step 4 of the journey is the point where some people begin to slide back. Once you have developed a plan for your program, make up your mind to stick with it. You may have "off" days; everyone does. However, if you can stick with your routine until it becomes habit, you will be well on your way to success.

Lesson 4 Guidelines for Getting Started **27**

To score the questionnaire on page 26 to determine an individual's motivational readiness, use the following guide:

Answers to 1 and 2: No, No, score: *not thinking about fitness.*

Answers to 1 and 2: No, Yes, score: *beginning to climb and planning your journey.*

Answers to 1 and 3: Yes, No, score: *beginning to climb and planning your journey.*

Answers to 1, 3, and 4: Yes, Yes, and No, score: *staying on track.*

Answers to 1, 3, and 4: Yes, Yes, and Yes, score: *staying on top.*

Source: Marcos, B. & Lewis, B., Research Digest, 2003

Student Edition TEKS

Page 26: C4G

Cooperative Learning

Divide students into small groups, and have them discuss why someone might relapse or fall off the Behavioral-Change Stairway. Explain that each individual probably interrupts their physical activity or exercise routine during holiday seasons, illness, or as a result of other personal responsibilities. The important step to remember is to know how to get started again successfully. **L2** **ELL**

✓ **Reading Check**

In Step 4, individuals will begin to see success by staying physically active or with exercise. However, they will not become consistent until they reach Step 5 (usually six months), which is also called the "maintenance phase" of the behavioral change.

Critical Thinking

Have students determine whether they meet the recommendations for total minutes of physical activity and exercise per week (225 minutes) and whether they get five days of moderate intense activities per week and three days of vigorous activities per week. Remind them that these are reasonable and obtainable goals for teens in planning a physical activity and exercise program. **L2**

hotlink

frequency and intensity
For more on frequency and intensity, see Chapter 3, pages **84–87**.

Staying at the Top. Once you have reached Step 5, your goal should be to stay there. This might involve trying new activities and including a friend or family member. Make physical activity or exercise a social experience as well as a physical one.

Don't worry if you have an occasional relapse. That's normal. If you do, just be sure to get back into a regular routine as soon as possible. Most important of all, engage in physical activities and exercises that you like to do. Vary your routine by doing different activities on different days. Be creative.

✓ **Reading Check**

Identify Briefly summarize what happens at Step 4 and Step 5 of the behavioral-change stairway.

Physical Activity and Exercise Guidelines

As you will discover in this program, a relationship exists between the amount of energy you burn in performing an exercise or activity and the benefits you receive. **Figure 1.14** shows the relationship between the level of physical activity and the amount of benefits to your health and fitness. In general, the harder you work, the greater the rewards to your health and fitness.

In order to compare activities and exercises in terms of the energy they require, fitness experts have devised three ratings. These are *regular, moderate,* and *vigorous.* You will come across these terms frequently throughout this program.

Note that the definition of the terms depends on two factors: **frequency** (how often an activity or exercise is done) and **intensity** (how much energy is expended). As a teen, you should strive to do a minimum of 225 minutes of activity or exercise per week. Adults should do a minimum of 150 minutes per week.

Regular Physical Activity or Exercise

Regular physical activity or exercise is *any activity or exercise performed most days of the week, preferably daily.* Such activity may also be done

- 5 or more days of the week if moderately intense activities are done.
- 3 or more days per week if vigorous activities are done.

Moderate Physical Activity or Exercise

Moderate physical activity or exercise is *any activity or exercise that ranges in intensity from light-to-borderline-heavy exertion.* Examples of such activities and exercises are walking briskly, mowing the lawn, dancing, swimming, and cycling on level terrain. To achieve moderate intensity, any of these activities or exercises must:

QUOTES FOR LIFE

"Those who think they have not time for bodily exercise will sooner or later have to find time for illness."

—**Edward Stanley**
Earl of Derby, 1873

FIGURE 1.14

BENEFITS OF PHYSICAL ACTIVITY AND EXERCISE

This graph shows the effect that physical activity and exercise have on health and fitness. *What is the relationship between physical fitness and health as explained in this graph?*

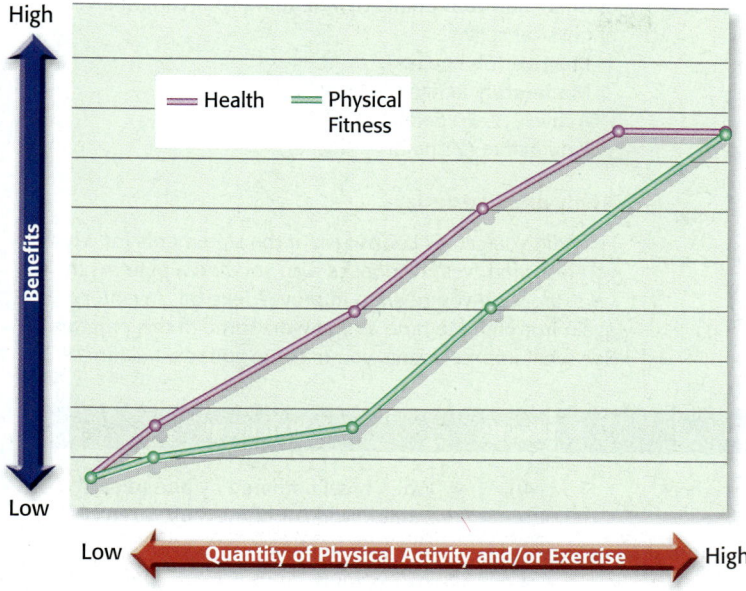

Figure 1.14 Display *Transparency 8* on the Benefits of Physical Activity and Exercise. Ask students how much physical activity or exercise they should get to maintain good health. They should note that just a little helps to improve one's health. Ask them how much physical activity and exercise are needed to achieve higher-level fitness goals. Explain that there is a minimal threshold required to achieve weight reduction, for example, or improved cardiorespiratory fitness. These goals require increased physical activity or exercise. Students should also recognize that too much physical activity or exercise can have negative effects on health or higher-level fitness goals. **L2**

- Reach a rating of perceived exertion of 11 through 14. As you will see in Chapter 3, **rating of perceived exertion (RPE)** is a measure of how hard you *feel* you are working during physical activity or exercise.
- Burn 3.5 to 7 calories per minute. You will learn more about the relationship between calories and activities in Chapter 5.

Vigorous Physical Activity or Exercise

Vigorous physical activity or exercise is *any activity or exercise that ranges in intensity from heavy-to-maximum exertion.* Examples of such activities and exercises are jogging, shoveling snow, high-impact aerobic dance, swimming continuous laps, and cycling uphill. In a later chapter you will learn other strategies for determining the intensity level of an exercise or activity. To achieve vigorous intensity, any of these activities or exercises must

- reach a rating of perceived exertion of 15 or higher.
- burn more than 7 calories per minute.

hotlink

rating of perceived exertion (RPE)
For more on the RPE scale, see Chapter 7, page **209.**

hotlink

Explain to students the recommendations for the frequency and intensity of regular physical activity and exercise. Students should understand they can easily rate the intensity of activity or exercise by using the RPE scale. Have students review Lesson 2 in Chapter 3 and Lesson 4 in Chapter 7 to learn more about frequency, intensity, and RPE.

TECHNOLOGY FILE

Pedometers: Measuring Daily Physical Activity

Provide students with pedometers to wear during various physical activities (walking, basketball, softball). After each activity session, have students enter the number of steps taken using a single database with fields for "Activity," "Time," and "Steps." After compiling entries from numerous activities, have them use database formulas to calculate the average number of steps taken per minute for each type of activity. Instruct students to use this information to create a personal physical activity plan that results in 12,000–13,000 steps per day.

Student Edition TEKS
Page 28: C1A
Page 29: C4A

Active Mind Active Body

How Physically Active Are You Now?

Explain to students that this activity will not be graded. Tell them that the purpose of the activity is to help them determine where they are located in the range between inactive and very active.

Teaching Tips

- Distribute the *Active Mind—Active Body Worksheet 1-4.* 📁
- When discussing the results in class, be sure to do so in a general way.
- Be sure students realize that anything fewer than 12 points means that they need to become more active.
- Have students keep their worksheets and do the activity again at the end of the course to see whether they have increased their activity level.

Apply and Conclude

Ask students who scored over 12 points whether they also met the recommendations for regular physical activity and exercise on page 28. If not, they may need to increase their physical activity levels.

Student Edition TEKS

Page 30: C4B
Page 31: C4G

Active Mind Active Body

How Physically Active Are You Now?

This activity will help you determine your current activity level.

What You Will Need

- Pen or pencil
- Paper

What You Will Do

Respond to the statements that follow. For each "yes" response, write the point value shown. When you have finished, add your points to determine your current level of physical activity:

Inactive (0–5 points)
Moderately active (6–11 points)
Active (12–20 points)
Very active (21 points or higher)

Apply and Conclude

How did you score? Look again at the statements for which you recorded "yes" responses. Can you find a pattern? In what areas do you need to improve? Take this inventory again from time to time as you work through this program. See what improvements you make to your overall fitness.

Points	Statement
1	1. I usually walk to and from school and work.
1	2. I usually take the stairs rather than use elevators or escalators.
	3. My typical daily physical activity is best described as:
0	a. Light (such as walking to class, sitting in class, or sitting at home).
4	b. Moderate (such as fast walking).
9	c. Vigorous (such as playing football, volleyball, basketball, or working out in the gym).
1	4. I spend a few hours each week in light leisure activity (such as walking or slow cycling).
1	5. I hike or bicycle at a moderate pace once a week or more on the average.
1	6. At least once a week, I participate for an hour or more in vigorous dancing, such as aerobic or folk dancing.
2	7. I play racquetball or tennis at least once a week.
1	8. I often walk for exercise or recreation.

Points	Statement
1	9. When I feel bothered by pressures at school, work, or home, I use exercise as a way to relax.
3	10. Two or more times a week I perform calisthenic exercises (sit-ups, push-ups, and so on) for at least 10 minutes per session.
2	11. I regularly participate in yoga or perform stretching exercises.
4	12. Twice a week or more, I engage in weight training for at least 30 minutes.
	13. I participate in active recreational sports such as volleyball, baseball, or softball:
2	a. about once a week.
4	b. about twice a week.
7	c. three times a week or more.
	14. I participate in vigorous fitness activities like jogging or swimming for a minimum of 20 minutes per session:
3	a. about once a week.
5	b. about twice a week.
10	c. three times a week or more.

Source: **Health: Making Life Choices,** 2nd Edition, 2000. Activity adapted from Russell Pate (University of South Carolina, Department of Exercise Science).[3]

30 **Chapter 1** Physical Activity and Personal Fitness

COOPERATIVE Learning

BARRIERS TO PHYSICAL ACTIVITY Have students list and compare their answers with other students to the Active Mind—Active Body activity on this page. Divide students into small groups, and have them brainstorm about barriers that keep them from being physically active. Also, have groups list and share with the class ways in which they can reduce or remove these barriers and increase their opportunities to become more physically active. **ELL**

Jump Starting Your Personal Fitness Program

In this course you will participate in a conditioning program that will allow you to experience the benefits of physical activity and regular exercise in a positive way. The conditioning program will focus on health-related fitness components, including a cardiovascular component (such as walking, jogging, cycling, or aerobic dance), a muscular strength and endurance component (such as weight lifting or calisthenics), and a flexibility component (for example, stretching or range-of-motion activities). You will learn more about each of these components of fitness as you read this text.

It is important for you to get started *now* on your personal-conditioning program. That way you can begin to assess your fitness levels accurately and safely in the "Fitness Check" activities in each chapter. It is also important that you follow the personal-conditioning program for several weeks prior to your physical evaluations. Doing so will help you improve your levels of physical fitness.

Begin your conditioning program at a low-to-moderate level. Gradually increase this level over a period of several weeks to reduce injury risk. When you first start your program, it will be difficult to include all the fitness components at one time. It is best to start with the cardiovascular and flexibility components. Add the muscular-strength and endurance components later. Remember to be patient when you first start your program. This will help you move successfully through the behavioral-change stairway to a lifetime of personal fitness.

Lesson 4 Review

Using complete sentences, answer the following questions on a sheet of paper.

Reviewing Facts and Vocabulary

1. **Vocabulary** What is the *behavioral-change stairway?*
2. **Recall** Between which two steps does the behavioral-change stairway descend? Explain.
3. **Recall** How often should teens perform regular physical activity?

Thinking Critically

4. **Extend** Two friends, Wanda and Kay, are both 15. Wanda is just beginning the behavioral-change stairway. Kay is at Step 5. What can Kay do to motivate her friend to maintain a commitment to physical activity and exercise?

5. **Evaluate** Using the recommended days per week and recommended intensity levels for a person beginning a fitness program, how many days per week should a beginner participate in physical activity or exercise?

Personal Fitness Planning

Designing and Implementing a Program
Using the guidelines listed at the beginning of this lesson, write out a plan for your personal fitness program. Include a contract, a list of goals, and a schedule. You should also make a list of ways to motivate yourself to move toward the maintenance stage of the behavioral-change stairway and a list of the reasons why you might fall into the relapse stage.

Lesson 4 Review

Answers to Lesson 4 Review

1. A step-by-step approach for helping individuals achieve their fitness goals.
2. Maintaining fitness behaviors, and relapse.
3. Teens should perform five or more days a week of moderate, and three or more days of vigorous, physical activity.
4. Answers will vary; Kay can explain to Wanda that, if she can adhere to her program for the next few weeks, she will begin to experience positive benefits.
5. Start slowly and work at moderate levels up to five or more days per week.

3 ASSESS

EVALUATING THE LESSON

Assign and discuss the Lesson 4 Review.

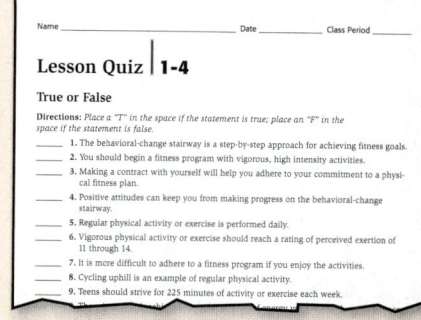

RETEACHING

Ask students to write two test questions based on the lesson content.

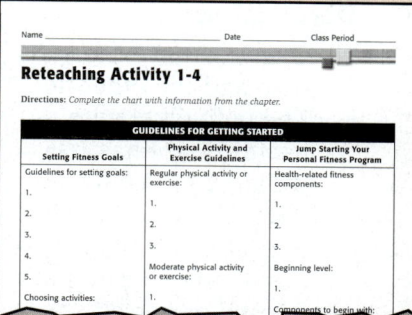

ENRICHMENT

Ask students to explain the relationship between where their family members are on the stairway and their weekly physical activity level.

4 CLOSE

Have students design a one-page outline of a starter personal fitness program based on the information included in this lesson.

CHAPTER 1 Review

CHECKING COMPREHENSION

- Assign and discuss the chapter review.
- Use the Puzzlemaker CD-ROM to review vocabulary. 💿

CHAPTER 1 REVIEW ANSWERS

1. False	6. False
2. False	7. True
3. False	8. False
4. True	9. False
5. True	10. True

Multiple Choice

11. d	16. c
12. a	17. c
13. b	18. c
14. d	19. a
15. b	20. b

Discussion

21. One may have heart disease and the other not. The individual with heart disease has less wellness but could still have his or her functional health and fitness and is still able to care for himself or herself.

22. Even though there is a history of heart disease in the family, it is possible to reduce the chances of heart disease. This can be done by becoming physically active daily; eating a nutritious diet; getting preventive screenings; and making healthy choices including avoiding tobacco, alcohol, and other drugs.

Student Edition TEKS

Page 33: C4A

TRUE/FALSE

On a sheet of paper, write the numbers 1–10. Write True or False for each statement below.

1. The only way to develop fitness is to become an athlete.
2. Personal fitness is another name for physical fitness.
3. The fitness behaviors that you develop as a young adult will have little effect on you and your health as an adult.
4. Heredity is one risk factor that can threaten your health.
5. You can lessen the impact risk factors have on your health and fitness through the behaviors you choose.
6. The foods you eat have little to do with the possibility of developing heart disease.
7. Your peers can have a positive or negative influence on your attitudes.
8. Making a commitment to keep fit is lying to yourself.
9. Adherence is another word for commitment.
10. The *Healthy People 2010* objectives are designed to encourage all Americans to develop and maintain healthy, active lifestyles.

MULTIPLE CHOICE

On a sheet of paper, write the letter of the word or phrase that best completes each statement.

11. Physical fitness affects
    a. physical health.
    b. social health.
    c. mental and emotional health.
    d. all of the above.
12. People who are personally fit do all of the following EXCEPT
    a. lose at least 20 pounds.
    b. eat healthfully.
    c. get adequate rest.
    d. avoid tobacco.

13. People who lead sedentary lifestyles
    a. live longer.
    b. are inactive.
    c. experience less stress.
    d. make great athletes.
14. Which of the following is a changeable risk factor?
    a. Age
    b. Gender
    c. Genetics
    d. Stress
15. A major risk factor for developing diabetes is
    a. smoking.
    b. obesity.
    c. gender.
    d. stress.
16. The average life expectancy for adults in the United States today is about ___ years.
    a. seventy-five
    b. seventy
    c. seventy-seven
    d. eighty-seven
17. The media includes all of the following EXCEPT
    a. the Internet.
    b. movies.
    c. peers and classmates.
    d. music.
18. Peer influence in your life can be all of the following EXCEPT
    a. direct.
    b. negative.
    c. from a teacher.
    d. from a classmate.
19. When starting a fitness program, your best advice is to
    a. take it slow at first.
    b. stop if you don't see results.
    c. look for shortcuts.
    d. do without food.
20. *Healthy People 2010* seeks to get all Americans to do each of the following EXCEPT
    a. become physically active.
    b. take turns exercising.
    c. get regular health screenings.
    d. avoid tobacco.

23. Personal fitness is one aspect of health, but it does influence your overall health. Maintaining personal fitness is essential to physical, mental/emotional, and social health.

Vocabulary

24. c	28. e
25. g	29. d
26. b	30. f
27. a	

Critical Thinking

31. As you develop your personal fitness, you may work with partners or teammates. This results in new friendships. Working in a group develops cooperation and conflict resolution skills.

DISCUSSION

Using complete sentences, answer the following questions on a sheet of paper.

21. **Evaluate** Explain how two 75-year-old adults could both have their functional health but at the same time differ in terms of their functional-fitness levels. Give examples.
22. **Analyze** Explain how a person can adjust his or her lifestyle and behaviors to reduce his or her risk for early death due to heredity.
23. **Discuss** What is the relationship between personal fitness and health?

VOCABULARY

On a sheet of paper, write the letter of the term in Column B that best fits the definition in Column A.

Column A	Column B
24. Conditions and behaviors that represent a potential threat to an individual's well-being.	a. wellness
25. The mind and body's response to the demands and threats of daily life.	b. physical fitness c. risk factors d. sedentary e. commitment f. media g. stress
26. The body's ability to carry out daily tasks and still have enough reserve energy to respond to unexpected demands.	
27. Total health.	
28. Pledge or promise.	
29. Inactive.	
30. The collective forms of mass communication found within society at any given time.	

CRITICAL THINKING

Using complete sentences, answer the following questions on a sheet of paper.

31. **Extend** How can developing your personal fitness benefit your social health?
32. **Compare and Contrast** What advantages does a physically fit person have over a person with a low level of physical fitness on a day-to-day basis? Explain your answer.

33. **Evaluate** A friend who doubts that a physically active lifestyle can improve your academic performance points to a player on the school football team, who is an average student. Explain the flaw in your friend's reasoning.

CASE STUDY

RAUL CUTS CLASS

Raul is a junior who avoids physical education classes. Since his first days in middle school, he has managed to develop a bag of tricks that allows him to sit out more days than he participates. His problems with physical education are that:

- He dislikes other students making fun of his inability to pass fitness tests.
- He is overweight and finds it embarrassing to be seen in gym shorts and a T-shirt.
- There is a history of heart trouble in his family. Raul thinks he heard somewhere that there is a connection between heart attacks and working out.

HERE IS YOUR ASSIGNMENT:

Assume that you are Raul's friend. Write a letter to Raul trying to convince him not only to attend physical education class this semester but also to work hard during this class to get himself into shape. Use information from this chapter to support your case.

KEYS TO HELP YOU

- Consider Raul's lifestyle and behaviors.
- Consider Raul's attitudes and beliefs.
- Consider Raul's self-esteem.
- Consider Raul's health risks.
- Consider the potential benefits of physical activity for Raul's overall health.

Critical Thinking (continued)

32. Physically fit individuals are more likely to have positive self-esteem, be better able to cope with stresses in their lives, have higher energy levels, be healthier, miss fewer days of school because of illness, have better muscular strength and endurance, and better enjoy life.
33. Physically active people have more energy, better attention spans, sleep better, and miss less school because of illness. There is also recent evidence that being more fit can improve math and reading scores.

EVALUATE

Name _____ Date _____ Class Period _____

CHAPTER 1 | Chapter Test A

True or False

Directions: *Place a "T" in the space if the statement is true; place an "F" in the space if the statement is false.*

_____ 1. Exercise is physical activity that is not planned or structured.
_____ 2. Sedentary living habits and low levels of physical activity have a positive impact on health.
_____ 3. High levels of personal fitness promote all aspects of health.
_____ 4. The benefits of physical health include higher energy levels and stronger bones.
_____ 5. Functional fitness is a person's physical inability to function independently in life.
_____ 6. Media can have both a positive and negative influence on your attitude toward health.
_____ 7. Risk factors cannot be controlled.
_____ 8. Eating habits can contribute to diabetes and heart disease.
_____ 9. Improved self-esteem may be a benefit of health and fitness.
_____ 10. The behavioral-change stairway begins with Staying on Track.

ENRICHMENT

Name _____ Date _____ Class Period _____

Enrichment Activity 1

My Health and Wellness Profile

Directions: *In the activity column, list the activities you participate in for each category listed. Then next to the activity, write down the average amount of time you spend on the activity. Finally list some of the benefits you receive.*

	Activity	How Often	Benefits
Physical Fitness			
Mental and Emotional Health			

CASE STUDY

ANSWERS

- Assessment of Raul's health risk factors
- Positive peer influence.
- Completion of the Active Mind—Active Body activities to determine his attitudes and current participation in physical activity.
- Use of the Behavioral-Change Stairway
- Advice about how much physical activity Raul should strive for as an initial goal.

CHAPTER 2 Safety and Injury Prevention

CHAPTER RESOURCES

- **Chapter Study Guide 2**
- **Vocabulary Worksheet 2**
- **Enrichment Activity 2**
- **Chapter 2 Test A**
- **Chapter 2 Test B**
- **Parent Letter and Activities 2 (English/Spanish)**

FITNESS *Online*

Ask students to take the STEP Personal Inventory for Chapter 2. Have them record their responses to the statements in their notebooks. Remind students that responses are private and for their use only.

FITNESS *Online*

Do you consider yourself a safe and careful person? Do you know how to avoid injury when playing sports or taking part in physical activity? Answer these and similar questions by taking the STEP Personal Inventory for Chapter 2. Find it at **fitness.glencoe.com**.

34

INCLUSION STRATEGIES

LANGUAGE DIVERSITY *Use the following suggestions to help students who have difficulty with English:*

- Pair English-language learners with native speakers of English who can restate key points in language that helps students comprehend important concepts.

- Direct Spanish-speaking students to the written summaries of this chapter in the *Foundations of Personal Fitness* Spanish Booklet.

- Encourage Spanish-speaking students to use the Glosario provided in the back of the student text. **ELL**

Personal Fitness Screening

After being sedentary for years, April decided to take up tennis. Some of her friends already played tennis, so she asked them for advice on getting started. One suggestion, which came as a surprise, was to have a medical screening. "What's a medical screening?" April asked. "What does it have to do with tennis?"

Do you know the answer to April's questions? After reading this lesson, you will.

Medical Screening

A *medical screening* is *a basic assessment of a person's overall health and personal fitness*. It includes a physical examination and may be performed by a doctor, nurse, or other health care professional.

A medical screening measures, among other things, the individual's physical readiness to take part in strenuous activity. It also tests for previously undetected medical problems that may be aggravated by vigorous activity.

What You Will Do

- Define medical screenings and identify who needs them.
- Identify the types of information gathered during a medical screening.
- Describe the role your medical history plays in your overall levels of fitness.

Terms to Know

medical screening
obesity
chronic disease
asthma
hernia
medical history

► A medical screening is an important step in personal fitness planning. *Why do you think it is important to have a medical screening before beginning a new sport or fitness program?*

Personal Fitness Screening

1 MOTIVATE

GETTING STARTED

- Ask students: What medical screening tests do you think teens need before starting a physical activity or exercise program? Why do you think these tests are important?
- Distribute copies of *Guided Practice Activity 2-1* for students to use while studying this lesson. ☞

IN THIS LESSON

- **Active Mind— Active Body** *What Is Your PAR-Q? page 37*

INTRODUCING VOCABULARY

- Explain that the term *screen* pertains to an act of protecting, guarding, or shielding. A *medical screening* is an attempt to determine whether a person is fit for participation in physical activities.
- Have students use *Vocabulary Worksheet 2* or the PuzzleMaker software to practice terms for this lesson. ELL ☞ ◉

LESSON 1 RESOURCES

Teacher Classroom Resources
☞ Guided Practice Activity 2-1
☞ Active Mind—Active Body Worksheet 2-1
☞ Reteaching Activity 2-1
☞ Lesson Quiz 2-1

Multimedia
◉ Vocabulary PuzzleMaker

2 TEACH

Activity

Have students list reasons why a teen would need to see a physician. Ask students to think about their last visit to their physician. Ask volunteers to describe what types of tests they had done at the physician's office. What kinds of information did the tests provide? **L1**

✓ Reading Check

Anyone considering starting a vigorous physical activity program should have a medical screening, especially those with poor lifestyle habits, people over 60, people who are overweight, and people with a known chronic disease. **TEKS C4A**

USING VISUALS

Figure 2.1 Using the Medical Screen Timetable, discuss the relationship between a person's age and the frequency of medical screening sessions needed. *Caption answer: As you age, you should decrease the amount of time between medical screenings.* **L2**

---

hotlink

heart disease
For more on heart disease, see Chapter 7, page 200.

diabetes
For more on diabetes, see Chapter 6, page 173.

Fitness FACTS

Obesity
- 60 percent of American adults are overweight or obese.
- Over 80 percent of people with diabetes are overweight or obese.
- High blood pressure is twice as common in obese adults than in those who are at a healthy weight.

Source: The Surgeon General's Call to Action to Prevent and Decrease Overweight and Obesity, 2001.[1]

Who Should Have a Medical Screening?

In general, everyone should have a medical screening before starting a program of vigorous physical activity. Such an examination is especially important for people who fit one or more of the following descriptions:

- **People with poor lifestyle habits.** This includes people who have been physically inactive.
- **People over 40.** Middle-aged and older adults need to be particularly mindful of the importance of medical screenings.
- **People who are overweight or suffer from obesity.** Obesity is *a medical condition in which a person's ratio of body fat to lean muscle mass is excessively high.* Obesity and overweight are major health problems in the United States today.
- **People with a known chronic disease.** A chronic disease is a disease *that is ongoing.* One such disease that affects a person's ability to perform physically demanding activities is asthma (AZ-muh). This is *a disease in which the small airways of the lungs become narrowed, making it difficult to breathe.* Two other chronic illnesses are **heart disease** and **diabetes.**

In addition to an initial medical screening, everyone is advised to have a periodic follow-up evaluation. There are no absolute guidelines for how often this needs to occur. The chart in **Figure 2.1** gives some basic recommendations, based on age.

✓ Reading Check

Identify Who should have a medical screening?

FIGURE 2.1

MEDICAL SCREEN TIMETABLE

The necessity of a medical screening varies with age. *What trend do you notice in the frequency of visits as a person gets older?*

Age		Frequency of Screening
6 to 15	→	Every 3 years
16 to 34	→	Every 2 years
35 to 59	→	Once a year
60 and up	→	Twice a year

TECHNOLOGY FILE

Blood Pressure Monitor

Set up a testing location in the learning environment where students can measure their own blood pressure using a digital electronic blood pressure device and test their lung capacity using a spirometer. Ask students to visit the testing location once each month and to record their findings. Then, instruct students to research the meaning of their initial findings and any significant changes that occur throughout the year. Based on their research, have students describe what they can do to improve or maintain their personal health.

Active Mind Active Body

What Is Your PAR-Q?

Preparation for any program of physical activity should include the use of a Physical Activity Readiness Questionnaire, or PAR-Q. Answering these questions correctly will help you understand your own readiness for beginning a program of physical activity. In this activity you may want to answer these questions along with your parents or guardian to ensure correct answers.

What You Will Need

- Pen or pencil
- Paper
- PAR-Questionnaire (page **38**)

What You Will Do

1. On a separate sheet of paper, answer as many of the seven PAR-Q questions as you can. Leave a blank for any questions you are unable to answer.
2. Discuss the questions you were unable to answer with a parent or other adult in the home. Complete the questionnaire.
3. Discuss the PAR-Q answers with your physical education teacher.
4. Design a modified program of exercise or physical activity with the guidance of your physician and physical education instructor.

Apply and Conclude

Based on the answers of the PAR-Q, how ready are you to begin a physical-activity program? What modifications, if any, should you consider for your physical-activity program? Will you need special equipment?

What Happens During a Medical Screening?

A medical screening may consist of just a few tests or a full medical examination. The following are some of the tests and measurements that might be performed:

- A complete blood count, or CBC. This is a test in which a sample of blood is drawn. The sample is then sent to a laboratory where it is tested for possible indicators of diseases and disorders.
- Your height and weight.
- An examination of your eyes, ears, nose, and throat.
- Your **blood pressure.** Blood pressure is the force of the blood in the blood vessels of the body.
- An examination of your lungs to make sure they are clear.
- An examination of your heart to make sure the heartbeat is regular and normal.
- For males, a test for hernia, *a condition that occurs when muscle fibers from the intestine protrude through the wall of the abdomen.* Hernias are painful and often require surgery. People with hernias are advised not to lift weights or participate in other activities that may aggravate the condition.

hot link

blood pressure For more on blood pressure, see Chapter 7, page **206.**

Lesson 1 Personal Fitness Screening **37**

COOPERATIVE Learning

HEALTH RISK APPRAISALS Questionnaires are often used to determine one's health risks prior to beginning exercise programs. These instruments are called health risk appraisals. Ask students to work in small groups to develop a health risk appraisal that is more detailed than the PAR-Q. Have them design one for a teen who has multiple health risk factors and one for a middle-aged adult. Ask them to explain how and why the two appraisals would probably be different. Encourage English-language learners to work with partners. **L2** **ELL**

Active Mind Active Body

What Is Your PAR-Q?

This activity will help students understand how to complete a simple questionnaire that can help them screen for their health risks prior to beginning a physical activity or exercise program.

Teaching Tips

- Have students complete the *Active Mind–Active Body Worksheet 2-1* for this activity. Tell them that this information is private and will not be graded.
- If students answer yes to any of the seven PAR-Q questions, they should follow up with their physician, parents, and you to make sure it is safe to start their personal fitness program.
- Follow the directions based on the students' answers, and make sure the form is signed for your files.

Apply and Conclude

Ask students to explain how the PAR-Q provides a quick and easy way of conducting a simple medical screening prior to beginning a personal fitness program. Discuss the limitations of the PAR-Q, and explain why some individuals may need more detailed medical screening prior to beginning a personal fitness program.

Photo Follow-Up

Ask students whether they have ever filled out a form like the PAR-Q. Emphasize the importance of determining an individual's health status prior to starting a personal fitness program. Discuss with students the legal issues that might arise if professional personal trainers do not give their clients a PAR-Q before starting a personal fitness program. **L1**

Discussing

Sudden death, rare in young athletes, is often caused by "enlarged heart" syndrome. Enlarged heart syndrome is usually due to one's heredity. The PAR-Q is not designed to screen for enlarged heart syndrome, and the most common method by which it can be identified is with a detailed medical screening where a physician listens to the heart and performs a special test called an echocardiogram. This type of screening provides an image of the heart that helps identify it as enlarged. **L2**

Critical Thinking

Have interested students make a list of the medical screening tests that they think middle school or high school athletes should undergo prior to participating in competitive athletics. Have them analyze what is done at their school and how much it costs to conduct the tests. Have them then discuss how cost-effective they think a detailed medical screening would be for every athlete that is trying out for sports. **L3**

PAR - Q & YOU
(Physical Activity Readiness—Questionnaire)

(A Questionnaire for People Aged 15 to 69)

Regular physical activity is fun and healthy, and increasingly more people are starting to become more active every day. Being more active is very safe for most people. However, some people should check with their doctor before they start becoming much more physically active.

If you are planning to become much more physically active than you are now, start by answering the seven questions in the box below. If you are between the ages of 15 and 69, the PAR-Q will tell you if you should check with your doctor before you start.

Common sense is your best guide when you answer these questions. Please read the questions carefully and answer each one honestly: check YES or NO.

YES	NO	
☐	☐	1. Has your doctor ever said that you have a heart condition and that you should only do physical activity recommended by a doctor?
☐	☐	2. Do you feel pain in your chest when you do physical activity?
☐	☐	3. In the past month, have you had chest pain when you were not doing physical activity?
☐	☐	4. Do you lose your balance because of dizziness or do you ever lose consciousness?
☐	☐	5. Do you have a bone or joint problem that could be made worse by a change in your physical activity?
☐	☐	6. Is your doctor currently prescribing drugs (for example, water pills) for your blood pressure or heart condition?
☐	☐	7. Do you know of any other reason why you should not do physical activity?

NOTE: If the PAR-Q is being given to a person before he or she participates in a physical activity program or a fitness appraisal, this section may be used for legal or administrative purposes.

I have read, understood, and completed this questionnaire. Any questions I had were answered to my full satisfaction.

NAME _____ DATE _____

DATE _____ WITNESS _____

SIGNATURE _____

WITNESS _____

SIGNATURE OF PAR...

If you answered

YES to one or more questions

Talk with your doctor by phone or in person BEFORE you start becoming much more physically active or BEFORE you have a fitness appraisal. Tell your doctor about the PAR-Q and which questions you answered YES to.

- You may be able to do any activity you want—as long as you start slowly and build up gradually. Or, you may need to restrict your activities to those which are safe for you. Talk with your doctor about the kinds of activities you wish to participate in and follow his/her advice.
- Find out which community programs are safe and helpful for you.

NO to all questions

If you answered NO honestly to all PAR-Q questions, you can be reasonably sure that you can

- start becoming much more physically active–begin slowly and build up gradually. This is the safest and easiest way to go.
- take part in a fitness appraisal–this is an excellent way to determine your basic fitness so that you can plan the best way for you to live actively.

DELAY BECOMING MUCH MORE ACTIVE:

- if you are not feeling well because of a temporary illness such as a cold or a fever—wait until you feel better; or
- if you have other medical conditions, talk to your doctor

Please note: If your health changes so that you then answer YES to any of the above questions, tell your fitness or health professional. Ask whether you should change your physical activity plan.

Source: Canada's Physical Activity Guide to Healthy Active Living, 2002.[2]

▲ The PAR-Q helps you assess your readiness for beginning a program of physical activity.

Myths & Realities

Myth 1 If an individual looks lean and muscular, it is safe for that person to begin a personal fitness program. He or she does not need to complete a PAR-Q.

Fact 1 A person who looks healthy may actually have health problems such as high blood pressure, diabetes, or a hernia. These conditions make it risky to start a personal fitness program without proper medical attention. Every individual should at least complete a PAR-Q prior to starting a fitness program.

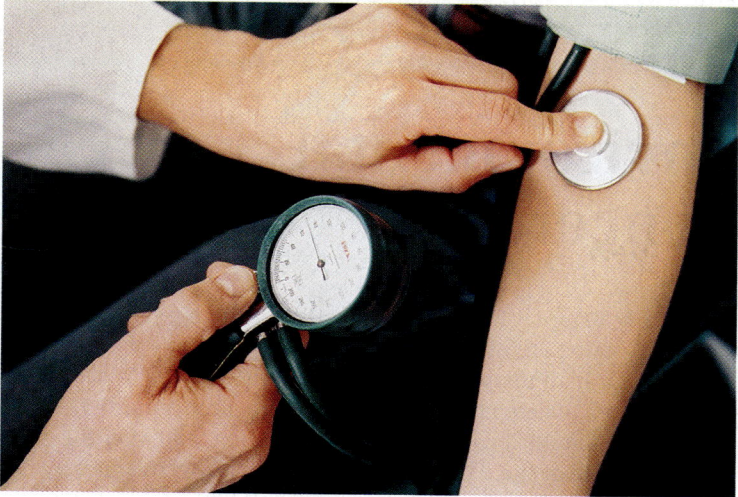

During a medical screening, your health care provider will check your blood pressure. *What other tests might he or she perform?*

Your Medical History. A medical screening carried out by a physician usually includes an update of your **medical history,** *a record of past health problems and illnesses.* The doctor will ask about any medications you may be taking. He or she will also ask about the health of other members of your family. This will help determine whether you are at risk of diseases relating to **heredity.**

hotlink

heredity For more on heredity, see Chapter 1, page 13.

✔ **Reading Check**

Summarize Name five tests that might be done during a medical screening.

Lesson 1 Review

Using complete sentences, answer the following questions on a sheet of paper.

Reviewing Facts and Vocabulary

1. **Vocabulary** Define *medical screening.*
2. **Recall** What are some diseases that make a complete medical screening necessary before beginning a fitness program?

Thinking Critically

3. **Recall** How is your medical history a factor in your overall levels of fitness?
4. **Extend** Seth has never had a medical screening before, and feels a little nervous. How

would you explain to Seth what is involved, to put his mind at ease?

Personal Fitness Planning

Evaluating Health Review your results for the PAR-Q, then take the survey home to help your family or friends to determine their readiness for physical activity. What differences did you notice among the responses? If the answers to the questions were *Yes* on the questionnaire, how should these individuals prepare for physical activity?

Lesson 1 Personal Fitness Screening **39**

Lesson 1 Review

Answers to Lesson 1 Review

1. Basic assessment of a person's overall health and personal fitness.
2. Asthma, heart disease, and diabetes.
3. Your medical history is a record of your past health problems and illnesses.
4. Answers will vary, but Seth will probably feel more comfortable knowing about his medical history and screening than if he remains uninformed and afraid of how safe it is for him to be physically active.

Chapter 2, Lesson 1

3 ASSESS

EVALUATING THE LESSON

Assign and discuss the Lesson 1 review.

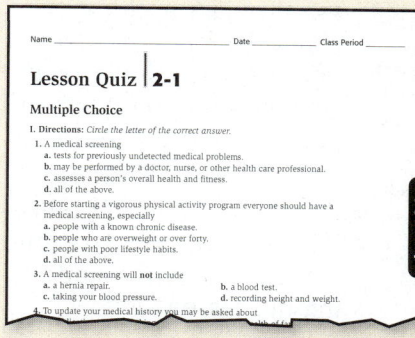

Lesson Quiz 2-1

RETEACHING

Ask students to write two test questions based on the lesson content. Use them as a basis for a class discussion.

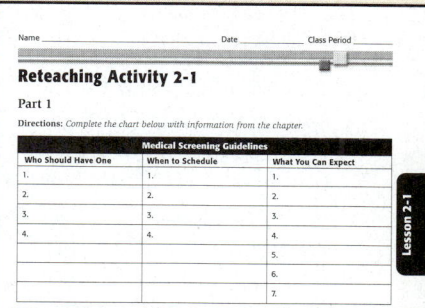

Reteaching Activity 2-1

ENRICHMENT

Have students make posters highlighting why medical screenings are important. Posters should provide clear details.

4 CLOSE

Ask students whether they think their answers on the PAR-Q are different from members of their family. Have them explain why.

39

Environmental Concerns

1 MOTIVATE

GETTING STARTED

- Before you begin roll call, ask the class to think about the following question: How can you protect yourself from injury when performing activities in cold or hot weather?

- Distribute copies of *Guided Practice Activity 2-2* for students to use while studying this lesson. 📁

IN THIS LESSON

- **Fitness Facts,** *page 42*
- **Lifeline,** *page 43*

INTRODUCING VOCABULARY

- Ask volunteers to define *hydro*, the Latin root of two vocabulary words in this lesson. *Hydrate means to supply water in order to restore or maintain fluid balance.* Ask students how many times a day they replace the fluids that may have been lost (*dehydration*). What are the fluids they use to *rehydrate*?

- Have students use *Vocabulary Worksheet 2* or the PuzzleMaker software to practice terms for this lesson. 📁 ELL

Photo Follow-up

Emphasize the importance of being aware of the weather conditions in your area. *Caption answer: Maintaining fluid balance and adapting to the heat.*

What You Will Do

- Explain how environmental conditions can influence the safety of your fitness program.
- Describe the relationship among fluid balance, physical activity, and loss of water and salt.
- Plan a program of physical activity to reduce environmental risks.

Terms to Know

fluid balance
dehydration
heat cramps
heat exhaustion
heatstroke
acclimatization
rehydrate
heat-stress index
hypothermia
frostbite
wind-chill factor

Environmental Concerns

It is early Saturday morning on the day of the big race. Tony has been planning and training for months now. Today's weather forecast calls for high temperatures and humidity. Most of Tony's training has been in cooler temperatures with low humidity. What precautions should Tony consider before, during, and after the race? What are some of the dangers of being physically active in very hot or very cold weather? In this lesson, you will find out.

Environmental Conditions and Physical Activity

Climate is a potential risk factor in personal health and fitness. This is especially true for people who are physically active or play sports on days when the temperature reaches extreme highs or lows. Does this mean you should avoid physical activity on such days? Not necessarily. As long as you use common sense and follow a few simple rules, most activities can be carried out safely.

 Physical activity in hot weather can lead to dehydration and heat-related injury. *What precautions should you take when exercising on a hot day?*

LESSON 2 RESOURCES

Teacher Classroom Resources
📁 Guided Practice Activity 2-2
📁 Reteaching Activity 2-2
📁 Lesson Quiz 2-2

Reproducible Charts and Graphs
📁 Reproducible Master 2-1

Multimedia
💿 Vocabulary PuzzleMaker
👆 Transparency 9

Extreme Heat and Fluid Balance

During physical activity, your body produces heat. This causes your body temperature to rise above normal. To prevent overheating, your body perspires. The sweat you produce evaporates on your skin. This, in turn, cools your body.

Hot and humid weather can cause you to perspire too much and affect your fluid balance. This is *the body's ability to balance the amounts of fluid taken in with the amounts lost through perspiration or excretion.* In extreme heat, you perspire so heavily that your body loses too much water and important body chemicals such as salt. This is called dehydration, or *body fluid loss,* and it can put you at risk of several heat-related injuries.

Heat Cramps. Heat cramps are *muscle spasms resulting from the loss of large amounts of salt and water through perspiration.* These contractions are due, at least in part, to the loss of sodium caused by dehydration. Heat cramps are the mildest form of heat injury. They can be minimized by drinking plenty of fluids before and during physical activity. This will help you to maintain a normal body fluid balance.

Heat Exhaustion. Heat exhaustion is *an overheating of the body resulting in cold, clammy skin and symptoms of shock.* Other symptoms of heat exhaustion include weakness, headache, rapid pulse, stomach discomfort, dizziness, and heavy sweating. Body weight may drop due to loss of water. Individuals who display these symptoms should stop physical activity immediately and get to a cool, dry place and drink plenty of fluids. They should not resume physical activity for a day or two, or until they have returned to their normal body weight.

Heatstroke. The most serious of the heat-related injuries is heatstroke, *a condition in which the body can no longer rid itself of heat through perspiration.* Its symptoms include a very high body temperature, rapid pulse, and loss of consciousness. The skin becomes hot and dry to the touch. Heatstroke requires immediate medical attention. If you suspect someone is suffering from heatstroke, call 911. Move the person to a cool place and sponge him or her with cold water until help arrives.

 hot link

fluid balance For more on your body's fluid balance and how to maintain it, see Chapter 4, page 125.

▼ Learning to recognize the symptoms of heat-related injury during physical activity and exercise is important. *What are the symptoms of heat cramps? Heat exhaustion? Heatstroke?*

✓ **Reading Check**

List Name some common symptoms of the three heat-related illnesses described.

2 TEACH

Discussing

Ask students whether they sweat during physical activity or exercise in very cold conditions. For example, have them compare conditions for someone running outside for 20 minutes in International Falls, Minnesota (the icebox of the United States), during January versus Dallas, Texas, in July. **L1**

Photo Follow-Up

Ask students whether they have experienced any symptoms of heat problems mentioned in the text. How does the equipment being worn by this athlete increase his chances of experiencing heat injury? **L1**

✓ **Reading Check**

Heat Cramps: muscle spasms and heavy sweating.
Heat Exhaustion: elevated body temperature, cold clammy skin, and symptoms of shock.
Heatstroke: very high temperature, rapid pulse, dry hot skin, and loss of consciousness.

More About . . .

HOT WEATHER HEALTH RISKS Scientists have developed a heat index that combines heat and humidity values to assess risks of prolonged activity in various conditions. For example, 90 degrees + 60 percent humidity = a heat index of 100, the apparent temperature; 100 degrees + 60 percent humidity = a heat index of 132. A heat index of 80 to 90 means fatigue is possible; 90 to 105 indicates that heat cramps and heat exhaustion are possible; 105 to 130 signifies that heat cramps and heat exhaustion are likely and heatstroke is possible; 130 or above indicates that heatstroke is likely.

Student Edition TEKS
Page 40: C3C

Figure 2.2 Divide the class into groups of three, and have each group fill up three 1-liter bottles with water. Then have each member of the group hold up the filled water bottles to experience the potential amount of weight lost as sweat (water) in one hour during vigorous exercise. Have the class weigh the three liters of water to see how much temporary weight loss can occur during exercise.
L2 **ELL** **TEKS C3C**

Fitness FACTS

Explain to students why they should drink fluids often and not just when they feel thirsty. Ask volunteers to explain the relationship between fluid balance, physical activity, and loss of water and salt during exercise. Ask what steps they should take to be certain to avoid loss of these essential nutrients.
TEKS C3C

Discussing

Ask students to discuss why some professional football teams conduct summer preseason drills in northern states, where it is cool, while other teams work out in southern states, where it is much warmer. Explain why it is not unusual to see a team acclimatized to the heat in early season games perform much better than a team that is not acclimatized. **L2**

Fitness FACTS

Thirst and Fluid Balance
- The body's thirst mechanism may lag behind the body's actual need for fluid, so replace fluids even when you are not feeling thirsty.
- The thirst mechanism diminishes with age, making dehydration a serious health risk for older adults.

FIGURE 2.2

MAINTAINING WATER BALANCE
Think about how much water there is in a 1.5 liter bottle of water. In an hour-long workout, your body can sweat the equivalent of 2 bottles this size. *How can you avoid dehydration?*

How to Avoid Heat-Related Injury

Although heat-related injury is a serious concern, you can avoid such injury and still enjoy physical activity on hot days. When exercising in the heat, gradually increase the intensity of your activity. The following are some other strategies for preventing heat-related injuries.

Acclimatization. Acclimatization is *the process of allowing your body to adapt slowly to weather conditions.* You can become acclimatized to working out in the heat after five to ten days. The first few physical-activity or exercise sessions should be light. They should also be brief, lasting no more than twenty minutes.

Fluid Intake. During physical activity in hot weather, your body can lose up to 3 liters of water per hour through perspiration. (See **Figure 2.2**.) To prevent dehydration, you need to **rehydrate**—*restore lost water*—by drinking plenty of fluids before, during, and after physical activity. Here are some guidelines:

- **Before.** Consume between $1\frac{1}{2}$ and $2\frac{1}{2}$ cups of cool water or sports drink 10 to 20 minutes *before* exercising in the heat. (1 cup = 8 ounces.)
- **During.** During physical activity in the heat, attempt to match fluid loss with fluid intake, approximately $1\frac{1}{2}$ cups to $3\frac{1}{4}$ cups (12 to 36 ounces) of water every hour.
- **After.** Drink 2 cups of water or sports drink for every pound lost. It may take up to 12 hours to achieve complete fluid replacement after strenuous exercise in the heat.

For most situations, water works as well as any beverage in preventing dehydration. You can also choose one of the many sports drinks on the market. Avoid beverages that are carbonated and/or

More About . . .

HYPONATREMIA Sometimes, drinking too much water can be bad for you. For example, hyponatremia is a disorder that results when an individual drinks too much water (or retains it) and their blood sodium drops below normal. In extreme cases individuals have symptoms of confusion, seizure, and coma. Individuals who participate in endurance events such as marathons and triathlons appear to be at increased risk, particularly if participants take 6–8 hours to complete the event and they consume large amounts of water without replacing much needed electrolytes (sodium, potassium, that contain caffeine. Such beverages are absorbed at a much slower rate than plain water. Caffeine, in addition, may slow rehydration.

Clothing. When choosing clothing for sports or activities in the heat, choose lightweight material. Cotton fabrics are best, since they absorb moisture rapidly and promote evaporation and cooling. Garments should be loose-fitting and light in color. Tight clothes do not allow air to circulate between the skin and the clothing. Dark clothing absorbs heat. Wearing a brimmed hat or cap can provide protection from the sun. Sunscreen should be used on all areas of exposed skin.

Setting Limits. One of the most important safeguards against heat-related injury is learning to use the *heat-stress index.* This is *a scientific measure of the combined effects of heat and humidity on the body.* Take a moment to examine the chart in **Figure 2.3.** Observe that a reading of 105 degrees or higher places you at high risk of injury. You can reduce this risk by limiting strenuous outdoor activity or exercise when the heat-stress index is in the red zone. In general, try to exercise during the cooler parts of the day, such as early morning or evening.

LIFELINE

Increasing Awareness of Heatstroke
People experiencing heat-stroke are too sick to take care of themselves. That is why recognizing symptoms in others can save a life.

If you take part in a hot-weather activity or team sport, make sure others are aware of the dangers of heatstroke. Get permission to post a list of the symptoms in your school locker room.

LIFELINE

Increasing Awareness of Heatstroke
Have students review the specific symptoms and dangers of heatstroke on page 41. Ask: What are the signs and symptoms of heatstroke? How should it be treated?

Critical Thinking
Have the class give the main reason why light-colored clothing is better suited for physical activities in the sun with high temperatures. Explain how dark colors absorb sunlight and create greater heat. Ask students what they might wear on a trip to the desert in summer. **L2**

USING VISUALS

Figure 2.3 Use *Transparency 9* for Figure 2.3 to discuss the heat-stress index with students. Ask them to find the heat stress index for an air temperature of 85 degrees and 60 percent relative humidity and for an air temperature of 100 degrees and 40 percent relative humidity. Then have them calculate the difference. **L2**

FIGURE 2.3

HEAT-STRESS INDEX
Using the heat-stress index chart can help you avoid heat-related injury. *What would the heat-stress index be if it were 90 degrees and the humidity were 70 percent?*

Relative Humidity	Air Temperature (°F)										
	70°	75°	80°	85°	90°	95°	100°	105°	110°	115°	120°
0%	64	69	73	78	83	87	91	95	99	103	107
10%	65	70	75	80	85	90	95	100	105	111	116
20%	66	72	77	82	87	93	99	105	112	120	130
30%	67	73	78	84	90	96	104	113	123	135	148
40%	68	74	79	86	93	101	110	123	137	151	
50%	69	75	81	88	96	107	120	135	150		
60%	70	76	82	90	100	114	132	149			
70%	70	77	85	93	106	124	144				
80%	71	78	86	97	113	136					
90%	72	80	91	108							

Low Risk 90 or Less	Medium Risk 91 to 105	Higher Risk 106 to 130	Probable Injury 131 or More

RISK OF HEAT INJURY

and magnesium). Some research indicates that females may be at greater risk for hyponatremia because of hormonal differences. To prevent hyponatremia, individuals should regularly drink fluids but should not rely solely on water (expressly in endurance events greater than 2–3 hours in duration), should not restrict salt intake, and should weigh themselves to monitor hydration. (Individuals should have a stable weight if they are drinking enough.) If you ever have the beginning of symptoms for hyponatremia, stop your physical activity, and seek medical help immediately.

Student Edition TEKS
Page 43: C3B

Discussing

Ask the class whether any students have ever gone snow skiing. What types of clothing did they wear? What were the weather conditions? Was it colder standing still or when they were skiing? Why? What did it feel like when riding the ski lift back up the mountain and the wind was blowing hard? **L1**

USING VISUALS

Figure 2.4 Discuss the wind-chill index shown in Figure 2.4. Ask students to calculate the wind-chill factor in the caption and then calculate the wind chill if it were 35 degrees Fahrenheit and the wind was blowing at 40 mph. *Caption answer: The wind chill would be 29 (increased risk).* **L2**

Explaining

Tell students that recent studies have shown that just one or two severe sunburns during childhood or adolescence greatly increases a person's chances of developing skin cancer in adulthood. Emphasize that the risk of skin cancer can be reduced by applying sunscreen frequently. Have students research to learn about the UV index and how they can use it to help prevent sunburn when participating in outdoor activities. **L1**

Physical Activity in Extreme Cold

When you are physically active or exercise in cold weather, you are at risk of **hypothermia**, *a condition in which your body temperature drops below normal.* Hypothermia can also result from long exposure in windy or rainy weather. When hypothermia occurs, body temperature becomes dangerously low. The brain cannot function at a low temperature, and body systems may cease to function properly. Hypothermia can lead to death. A person with hypothermia may act disoriented and lose motor control. Seek medical help as soon as possible.

In extremely cold conditions you also significantly increase your risk of **frostbite**, *tissue damage from freezing.* It occurs most often on the head, face, feet and hands. If you notice a lack of feeling in your toes, fingers, nose, or ears while exercising in cold weather, go indoors to warm up.

When you plan to exercise or be physically active in cold weather, pay attention to weather forecasts. Note in particular the **wind-chill factor.** This is *the combined influence of wind and temperature on the body* (see **Figure 2.4**). Avoid spending extended periods outdoors when the wind-chill factor is below −22 degrees. When you do go

FIGURE 2.4

WIND-CHILL INDEX

The wind-chill index will help you determine if it is unsafe to exercise outdoors. *If it were 15 degrees Fahrenheit and the wind were blowing at 30 mph, what would the wind-chill factor be?*

Wind Speed (mph)	Air Temperature (°F)														
Calm	40°	35°	30°	25°	20°	15°	10°	5°	0°	−5°	−10°	−15°	−20°	−25°	−30°
5	37	33	27	21	16	12	6	1	−5	−11	−15	−20	−26	−31	−35
10	28	21	16	9	4	−2	−9	−15	−21	−27	−33	−38	−46	−52	−58
15	22	16	11	1	−5	−11	−18	−25	−36	−40	−45	−51	−58	−65	−70
20	18	12	3	−4	−10	−17	−25	−32	−39	−46	−53	−60	−67	−76	−81
25	16	7	0	−7	−15	−22	−29	−37	−44	−52	−59	−67	−74	−83	−89
30	13	5	−2	−11	−18	−26	−33	−41	−48	−56	−63	−70	−79	−87	−94
35	11	3	−4	−13	−20	−27	−35	−43	−49	−60	−67	−72	−82	−90	−96
40	10	1	−6	−15	−21	−29	−37	−45	−53	−62	−69	−76	−85	−94	−101

Low Risk Warmer than −21	Increasing Risk −22 to −67	High Risk Colder than −67

RISK OF FROSTBITE

EQUIPMENT OPTIONS

SAFETY AND FITNESS EQUIPMENT

Manufacturers of fitness equipment today make a major effort to provide safe equipment. Although most fitness equipment is safe, physical education teachers still need to review their equipment needs and investigate the safety of a piece of equipment prior to purchase. A major emphasis in today's market is protective head gear for cyclists and in-line skaters. Helmets for cyclists are made from a range of materials and must meet ANSI or SNELL standards to ensure the quality necessary to protect a person from injury. Physical education out, wear warm, loose-fitting clothing in layers. These layers will help trap warm air as it leaves the body. Protect your extremities—your hands, feet, head, and ears—from extreme cold. These are the places where much of your body heat is lost.

Chapter 2, Lesson 2

 Reading Check

Compare In what ways are the risks of exercising in extreme heat similar to those of exercising in extreme cold?

Other Outdoor Environmental Concerns

Weather-related concerns are important when participating in outdoor sports and activities. However, other potential environmental factors can also pose a risk.

Air Pollution

Air quality is an important factor to consider when participating in outdoor physical activity. Gases and particles emitted from factories, motor vehicles, and other sources can worsen air quality. Exercising outdoors when air quality is poor increases the amount of pollutants that enter the body, increasing the risk of **lung diseases.** Carbon monoxide is a particularly harmful gas because it absorbs into the blood more readily than does oxygen.

However, there are several steps you can take to reduce the health risks associated with air pollution. First, pay attention to daily media reports of the air quality index, which reports local air quality. During periods of poor air quality, limit or avoid outdoor exercise. In addition, identify the areas and times of day that have less motor vehicle traffic. Finally, find suitable indoor physical activity and exercise opportunities as an alternative to outdoor activities on days when air quality is poor.

Altitude

Do you live in a mountainous or other high-altitude region? High altitudes begin at about 5,000 feet above sea level. The air at higher altitudes is thinner than at lower altitudes. Less oxygen is available to the heart and lungs. This can reduce your ability to exercise or perform strenuous work. It can also cause you to tire more quickly than you would at sea level.

If you move from a low altitude to a high altitude, gradually increase the amount you exercise over a period of days. If possible, change altitude slowly over several hours. Drink plenty of water, because dehydration is more likely to occur at high altitudes.

▼ Air pollution can make physical activity and exercise hazardous. *What steps can you take to reduce your risks from air pollution?*

 **hotlink**

lung diseases For more on respiratory problems and their causes, see Chapter 7, page 203.

Lesson 2 Environmental Concerns **45**

 Reading Check

Both can cause serious problems if you do not take precautions. Wear proper clothing and check the weather conditions before exercising in extreme temperatures. **TEKS C3B**

Discussing

Ask students to identify and describe outdoor environmental hazards such as air quality, sunlight, ozone levels, automobiles, etc. How could exercising in these situations be hazardous to their health? **L3 TEKS C3B**

Photo Follow-Up

Have students identify areas in their community that would be hazardous and those that might provide safer environments. Check the air quality index reports, limit outdoor exercise during periods of poor air quality, avoid areas that have high traffic volume, or participate in indoor physical activities on those days. **L2**

Critical Thinking

Ask students to share any experiences they might have had while exercising in high altitudes, such as hiking or snow skiing in the mountains. What was the effect on their breathing? Ask for an explanation. **L3**

 Reading Check
(page 46)

Environmental factors include air pollution, altitude, crime, and encountering unleashed dogs.

---

teachers may want to suggest protective clothing for runners during cold weather periods. Advancements in materials and fabrics for running apparel have produced lightweight clothes that act as an insulation against cold, are waterproof, and remain flexible. This clothing is lighter than traditional cotton sweat suits. Remind students to look at manufacturers' labels and compare materials and prices when considering any purchase.

3 ASSESS

EVALUATING THE LESSON

Assign and discuss the Lesson 2 Review.

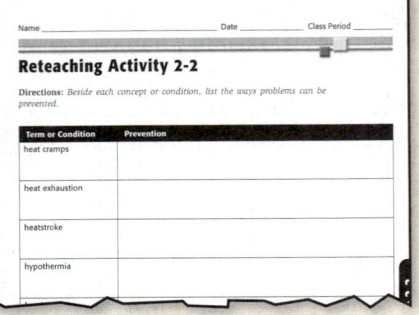

Name _____ Date _____ Class Period _____

Lesson Quiz | 2-2

True or False

Directions: *Place a "T" in the space if the statement is true; place an "F" in the space if the statement is false.*

_____ 1. It is not possible to exercise safely when temperatures are extremely high or extremely low.
_____ 2. Heat, physical activity, and perspiration can affect fluid balance in the body.
_____ 3. Heat-related illnesses from least to most severe are heat cramps, heatstroke, heat exhaustion.
_____ 4. To prevent heat-related illness you should acclimate, stay hydrated, wear appropriate clothing, and set limits.
_____ 5. The heat-stress index shows the combined effects of heat and humidity on the body.
_____ 6. Hypothermia, frostbite, and wind-chill are cold-related injuries.
_____ 7. Air quality refers to pollen in the air and is not a health risk.
_____ 8. Some effects of high altitude include fatigue and dehydration.
_____ 9. When you let others know where you plan to exercise and when you expect to return, you will protect your personal safety.

RETEACHING

Ask students to summarize the most important environmental concerns discussed in this lesson.

Name _____ Date _____ Class Period _____

Reteaching Activity 2-2

Directions: *Beside each concept or condition, list the ways problems can be prevented.*

Term or Condition	Prevention
heat cramps	
heat exhaustion	
heatstroke	
hypothermia	

ENRICHMENT

Let students work together in groups to compile a list of safe exercise practices during hot or cold weather and a list of areas in the community that might be safe areas to exercise.

4 CLOSE

Have the class discuss specific safety and weather considerations in your area.

▲ Jogging with a partner is one way of maintaining safety while exercising. *What other actions can you take?*

Personal Safety

It is important to protect your personal safety when participating in physical activities. You can reduce the risk of becoming a victim of crime by developing an awareness of risk factors. Here are some guidelines to keep in mind.

- Take time to examine and plan your outdoor routes.
- Exercise in well-lit areas.
- Exercise with friends, especially at night.
- Wear reflective clothing.
- Avoid exercising in high-crime neighborhoods.
- Avoid isolated trails or paths.
- Always let someone know where you are going. Make sure to say when you expect to return as well.

Unleashed Dogs

As you exercise outdoors, be alert for dogs not on leashes. If you encounter a dog, do not unnecessarily frighten or threaten it. If confronted by a dog that appears vicious, it may be best to face it and yell, "Bad dog! Stop!" Then walk slowly away—never run.

✓ **Reading Check**

List What are the environmental factors that can put your physical and personal safety at risk?

Lesson 2 Review

Using complete sentences, answer the following questions on a sheet of paper.

Reviewing Facts and Vocabulary

1. **Vocabulary** Define *frostbite*.
2. **Recall** How can you prevent dehydration?

Thinking Critically

3. **Explain** How can environmental conditions affect your body's fluid balance? Explain what causes loss of water and salt during exercise.
4. **Synthesize** Before exercising, what precautions should you take to reduce risks in each of the following areas: *hot weather, cold weather, pollution, crime?*

Personal Fitness Planning

Analyzing Risks Make a list of all the places you were physically active or exercised during the past thirty days. Identify any of the environmental concerns discussed in this lesson that were factors in the success of your workout or game. Tell how you will avoid these in the future. Identify other activities you could do that might be safer.

46 **Chapter 2** Safety and Injury Prevention

Lesson 2 Review

Answers to Lesson 2 Review

1. Drink plenty of fluids before, during, and after physical activity.
2. *Frostbite* is tissue damage from freezing.
3. Extreme heat can cause you to perspire. Your body loses water and salt through perspiration.
4. During hot weather, drink plenty of water, wear light clothing, and pay attention to the heat-stress index. In extremely cold weather, avoid extended periods of activity outdoors. Limit outdoor exercise during periods of poor air quality. Protect yourself from crime while exercising.

Safety Gear and Clothing

It was the first day of school. At the end of fourth-period physical education class, students were given a checklist of items they would need to buy. "Two pairs of cotton socks—why cotton?" Elias asked his friend. "Socks are socks."

Contrary to what Elias believes, when it comes to physical activity, not all clothing choices are equal. Neither is all safety equipment, such as protective headgear. In this lesson, you will learn how to make informed purchases in both areas.

Clothing

Clothing does not need to be expensive to be effective for physical activity and exercise. It does, however, need to be suited to the particular activity or exercise. If you will be doing a lot of stretching or bending, such as aerobic dance, you will want material that is not too tight and that allows you to move comfortably. If you will be doing a rugged activity such as rock climbing, you will want fabrics with durability.

For outdoor activities, choose a fabric that breathes, while absorbing perspiration. Cotton does both. New state-of-the-art fabrics are lightweight, highly breathable, and can provide warmth for a variety of temperatures. You may also want to consider fabrics that are wind and water-resistant.

Another prime consideration in choosing any sportswear or active wear is comfort. Select clothing that fits well but that stretches so you can move freely.

▶ Choosing appropriate clothing for physical activities can ensure comfort and reduce the risk of injury. *What type of clothing is appropriate for outdoor activities?*

What You Will Do

- Identify appropriate clothing for your personal fitness program.
- Demonstrate the basics of choosing appropriate, nonskid footwear.
- Explain how to reduce your risk of activity-related injury.

Terms to Know

pronation
supination
toe box

LESSON 3 RESOURCES

Teacher Classroom Resources
- Guided Practice Activity 2-3
- Active Mind—Active Body Worksheet 2-3
- Reteaching Activity 2-3
- Lesson Quiz 2-3

Reproducible Charts and Graphs
- Reproducible Master 2-3

Multimedia
- Vocabulary PuzzleMaker
- Transparency 10

Safety Gear and Clothing

1 MOTIVATE

GETTING STARTED

- Before you begin roll call, ask the class to think about the following question: *Is trendy, or fashionable clothing always effective for the exercise environment?*
- Distribute copies of *Guided Practice Activity 2-3* for students to use while studying this lesson. 📁

IN THIS LESSON

- **Consumer Corner** *Smart Shoe Shopping*, page 50
- **Active Mind—Active Body** *Wet Foot Test*, page 51

INTRODUCING VOCABULARY

- Explain to students that the words *supine* and *pronate* both come from Latin and refer to the positioning of the foot: up, forward (*supine*) or inward, downward (*pronate*).
- Have students use *Vocabulary Worksheet 2* or the PuzzleMaker software to practice terms for this lesson. ELL 📁 💿

Photo Follow-Up

Use the photo to generate input from the class about specific activities that are common to your area or state that require additional safety equipment. L1

Figure 2.5 Use *Transparency 10* to begin a discussion about what features students should look for in a good personal fitness shoe. Ask students why one type of shoe, such as for basketball, would probably have different features than a shoe for golf or jogging. **L2**

Quick Demo

Bring a variety of different types of shoes to class to promote discussion on shoe construction. You may even collect shoes from the past to show how exercise shoes have greatly improved over the years. For this demonstration, cut the shoes in half to show how the soles and interior of the different shoes are constructed. You may want to show how the bottoms of shoes wear out. Have students inspect the bottoms of their shoes to check for wear patterns. Shoes that have excessive wear can increase the risk of injury. **L1**

Discussing

Guide students in ways to evaluate consumer issues related to fitness. Ask how they would analyze marketing claims promoting fitness products. Ask students to identify appropriate places to find someone knowledgeable about footwear. Consider inviting someone who knows about shoe construction to your class to do a guest lecture. **L2 TEKS C4H**

Footwear

The starting point for most fitness activities is footwear. No matter what type of training you're interested in, you should always choose nonskid footwear. A nonskid shoe can significantly reduce your risk for injuries.

When shopping for footwear, think about the activities you will be doing. For example, if you are going to play basketball, select a shoe specifically designed for that sport. To give ankle support, you should consider getting a high-top shoe. If you will be doing a variety of activities, consider all-purpose cross-training shoes. **Figure 2.5** shows the features you should look for in an exercise shoe.

FIGURE 2.5

FEATURES OF AN EXERCISE SHOE
Learning the parts of a shoe can help you make a more informed choice.

High-top versus low-top exercise shoes

High-top exercise shoe
Provides ankle support and excellent cushioning

Low-top exercise shoe
Provides better flexibility for all-around movement

Parts of a proper exercise shoe

Upper
Flexibility and comfort are necessary for workouts

Toe Box
The part of the shoe that surrounds the toes

Sockliner
Provides cushioning and reduces heat buildup inside shoe

Heel cushion
Cushions and protects the foot from impact shock

Forefoot cushion
Cushions the metatarsal heads from impact shock

Midsole
Cups and supports the foot during lateral movement and provides arch support

Outsole
Made of abrasion-resistant rubber, with toe wrap

"A sound mind in a sound body is a short but full description of a happy state in this world."

—John Locke
Essayist, 1632–1704

FIGURE 2.6

Chapter 2, Lesson 3

TYPES OF FEET AND ARCHES

Not everyone has the same shape of foot or type of arch. *Which foot most resembles yours? Which tread is more like your own?*

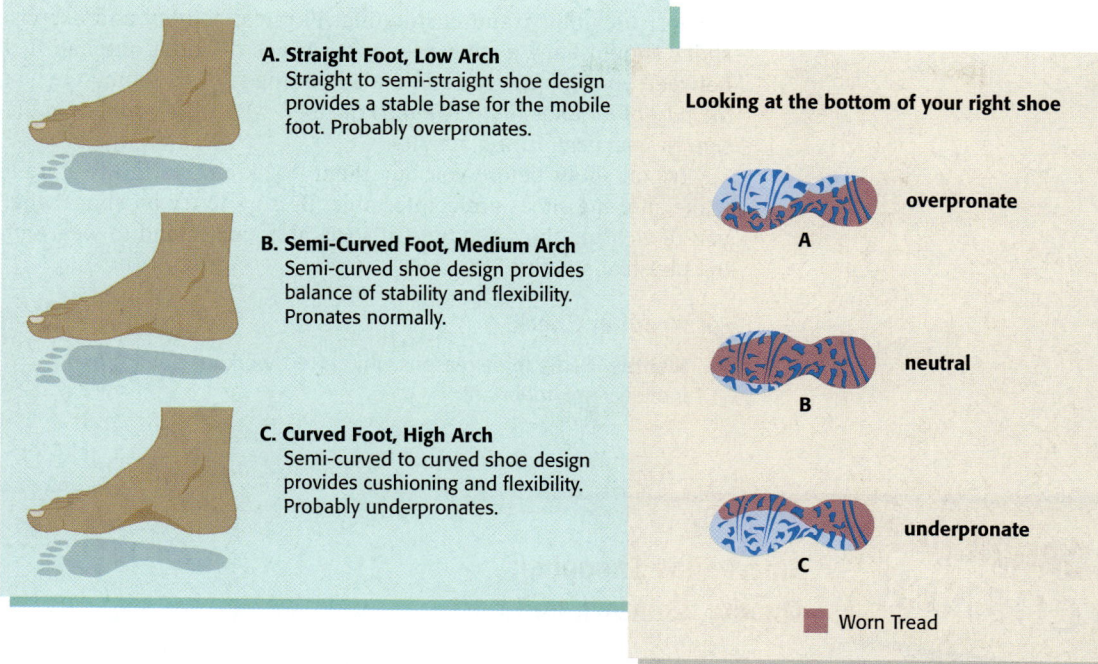

A. Straight Foot, Low Arch
Straight to semi-straight shoe design provides a stable base for the mobile foot. Probably overpronates.

B. Semi-Curved Foot, Medium Arch
Semi-curved shoe design provides balance of stability and flexibility. Pronates normally.

C. Curved Foot, High Arch
Semi-curved to curved shoe design provides cushioning and flexibility. Probably underpronates.

Looking at the bottom of your right shoe

overpronate
A

neutral
B

underpronate
C

■ Worn Tread

Stride Irregularities

One factor you need to consider when shopping for shoes is stride irregularities, such as overpronation and underpronation. **Pronation** is *the normal motion of the foot as you walk or run, from the outside of the heel striking the ground through the normal inward roll of the foot.* In normal pronation, the body's weight is distributed evenly over the surface of the foot. In overpronation, the motion of the foot rolls inward too far. This may cause pain to the inside of the knees or legs.

Supination is *the normal outward roll of the foot as it hits the ground.* Too much supination, or underpronation, causes the weight to shift to the outside of the foot. This can cause soreness and injury to the outside of your knees and thighs.

Figure 2.6 shows the profiles of a foot that pronates normally, along with those that over- and underpronate. It also shows the amount of shoe wear that occurs in each situation.

If you stride normally, an average shoe without special features should work for you. If you tend to overpronate, you may need a shoe that provides greater stability. If you underpronate, you may need a shoe that has greater cushioning and flexibility.

Lesson 3 Safety Gear and Clothing **49**

INCLUSION STRATEGIES

ASSISTIVE DEVICES Certain factors must be considered when including students with disabilities in fitness programming. The disability may make displaying correct biomechanics impossible. A student's walking pattern can be greatly impaired, yet he or she can still benefit from a fitness program that includes walking. The student may need some form of assistance in order to ambulate, such as a prosthesis, AFOs (ankle-foot orthotics), a walker, forearm crutches, or a wheelchair. Evaluation of the student's biomechanics should take ambulation aids into consideration.

Quick Demo

Show your students how the shoe and foot look when overpronation occurs (excessive inward rotation).Then demonstrate how supination looks (excessive outward rotation of the foot). Lastly, demonstrate the proper biomechanics of the foot strike: heel strike, then the rotation of weight to the ball of the foot, and finally through the big toe without excessive rotation of the foot from side to side. You might wish to have student volunteers assist with this demonstration. **L1**
TEKS C1B

USING VISUALS

Figure 2.6 Use this figure and the Active Mind—Active Body activity on page 51 to help students determine the type of shoe that best meets their needs for proper foot support. Point out to students the picture of overpronation and the risk involved in this biomechanical technique. **L1**

Activity

Ask volunteers to prepare a demonstration for the class on the importance of applying safety procedures by using nonskid footwear. Have them emphasize safety concerns and show examples of how a nonskid shoe can enhance performance. **L3**
TEKS C3A

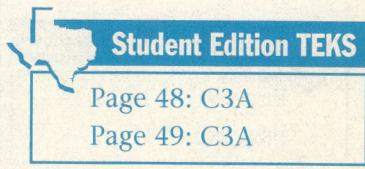

Student Edition TEKS

Page 48: C3A
Page 49: C3A

✓ **Reading Check**

Choosing correct clothing and footwear for workouts reduces the chance of injury, and improves performance, comfort, and proper support.

Consumer CORNER

Smart Shoe Shopping

Ask students whether they ever had a pair of shoes that were too big or too small for them. Ask volunteers to explain why they bought shoes that did not fit. What mistakes did they make? *(Didn't try them on? Didn't walk around in them in the store? Tried them on with socks that were too thick?)* Remind students that, if they do have more than one pair of shoes, they will get better wear out of them by alternating pairs worn each day.
L1 **TEKS C4H**

Quick Demo

Demonstrate to students how to put on their socks and shoes properly to prevent blisters or improper wear of shoes. Make sure socks do not have wrinkles and laces are properly tightened. **L1**

Student Edition TEKS

Page 51: C2A, C3A
Page 52: C4H

Buying Shoes

Before you buy shoes for physical activity or exercise, it's wise to visit a local sporting goods store. Seek the advice of a knowledgeable salesperson. You might also ask your physical education instructor for advice.

The best shoe for you is one that fits you and provides proper support, flexibility, and cushioning. Physical-activity and exercise shoes should have a snug heel and a space of about one half-inch between your longest toe and the end of the shoe. A roomy toe box, *the part of the shoe that surrounds the toes,* will allow proper circulation in your feet during activity.

Try on shoes before you buy them. Walk around in the store to make sure the shoes are comfortable. Be sure to try on shoes when you're wearing the same type of socks that you intend to wear during physical activity.

✓ **Reading Check**

Identify Name three reasons why correct workout clothing and footwear are important.

Consumer CORNER

Smart Shoe Shopping: Quality, Comfort, and Cost

You can spend anywhere from $25 to $150 for a pair of exercise shoes. If you plan to be physically active—and hopefully you do—you need to purchase a pair of quality shoes. Here are some tips for making a smart purchase:

- **Look for quality.** When it comes to shoes, be sure not to compromise on comfort and fit. A quality pair of shoes will last longer than an inexpensive brand.
- **Choose nonskid footwear.** The soles of your shoes should be nonskid, especially for activities such as skateboarding, weight lifting, and basketball.
- **Choose comfortable shoes over shoes that look good.** If you feel you must have the latest shoe from companies with well-known names, don't settle for a poor fit because of its look.
- **Know when to replace shoes.** Knowing when to replace your shoes is as important

as any other shopping consideration. Once an exercise shoe starts to lose its sole and support, it should no longer be used for fitness activities. Such a shoe could cause injuries to your feet and joints.

- **Have a spare pair.** If possible, you may want to have a second pair of exercise shoes and alternate their use. This will give one pair time to dry out and regain its cushioning effect. This strategy will provide you with the support you need and can extend the life of your shoes significantly.

Comparison Shopping

Compare prices for a single brand and style of exercise shoe online or in print resources. Which stores or Web sites appear to have the best prices?

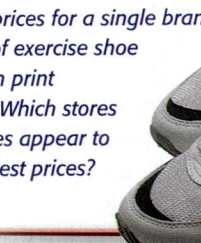

50 **Chapter 2** Safety and Injury Prevention

Teacher-Coach Tips

Preventing Injuries It is not unusual for students to experience minor injuries in their personal fitness programs (see Lesson 4, "Preventing Fitness Injuries.") You can help students minimize their risk for injury and help them recover sooner by encouraging them to change their shoes regularly when they begin to wear out. Inform students to replace their shoes when excessive outer sole wear occurs and/or shoes begin to lose their cushioning effects. Replacing shoes can become expensive, but it's better to pay a little to prevent minor injuries than to have to relapse due to a preventable injury.

Active Mind Active Body

Wet Foot Test

Choosing the right shoe for the right activity begins with knowing the shape of your foot, specifically your arch. Does your foot have a low arch, semi-curved arch, or curved arch? Finding out is easy. In this activity you examine the shape of your arch and become better able to choose the footwear you need.

What You Will Need
- Bucket or pan of water
- Paper (colored preferred) and pencil

What You Will Do
1. Place the bottom of either foot into the water.
2. Lightly press your wet foot on the colored paper.
3. Trace the outline of the water impression on the paper.
4. Examine the shape to determine your arch category.

Apply and Conclude

Refer back to **Figure 2.6** on page **49** to compare your arch impression. What type of arch do you have?

- Straight feet (Type A) leave an imprint that is oval shaped.
- Semi-curved feet (Type B) show the forefoot and the heel connected by a band about 2 inches wide or more.
- Curved feet (Type C) have a narrow band connecting the forefoot and heel.

Have you been using the correct type of footwear? How will knowing the shape of your arch influence you the next time you purchase a pair of exercise shoes?

Safety Equipment

If you participate in an activity such as bicycling, skateboarding, downhill skiing, snowboarding, or in-line skating, you should always wear protective equipment. The most important piece of equipment you can buy is a safety helmet. Statistics show that the likelihood of head injury is reduced 85 percent when a helmet is worn. When skateboarding or in-line skating, wear helmets, light gloves, elbow pads, knee pads, and wrist guards.

Helmet Specifics

A protective helmet should have a foam liner inside to absorb impact to the head in case of a fall. Choose a helmet that meets the standards set by either the American National Standards Institute (ANSI) or the Snell Memorial Foundation. Make sure the helmet has a snug but comfortable fit. Finally, the helmet should have a chin strap and buckle, so it will stay securely fastened. Other safety precautions might include the following.

Mind OVER Matter

Etiquette and Safety

There are many ways you can use your understanding of fitness principles to avoid injury to yourself or others. Give four examples where you can apply etiquette during physical activity. Explain how thinking of the other person can help you prevent injuries at the gym or during certain sports and games.

Active Mind Active Body

Wet Foot Test

Display Transparency 10, and distribute *Active Mind–Active Body Worksheet 2-3* with this activity. Have students perform the Wet Foot Test to determine their foot shape. Use Figure 2.6 to give specific directions. 📁

Teaching Tips
- Make sure students do this activity on a safe, nonslippery surface.
- Have towels available for cleanup after the activity.
- Provide a bucket or pail of water for students to wet their feet.

Apply and Conclude

Ask students how the information they have gathered from the Wet Foot Test will help them choose their next pair of shoes.

Fitness FACTS

Discuss the Fitness Facts on page 52. Explain that *Healthy People 2010* increases use of helmets to at least 79 percent of motorcyclists and increases requirements for bicycle helmet use.

More About . . .

INJURIES TO THE NERVOUS SYSTEM
Emphasize the importance of safety equipment by discussing damage to the central nervous system. Concussion occurs when the brain absorbs external forces and collides with the cranium, causing the brain to bruise. Symptoms include loss of memory, disorientation, loss of balance, blurred vision, and unconsciousness. Research efforts are helping recovery possibilities for those with spinal cord injury. The late actor Christopher Reeve, who had been completely paralyzed from the neck down, raised public awareness of the need for further research.

3 ASSESS

EVALUATING THE LESSON

Assign and discuss the Lesson 3 Review.

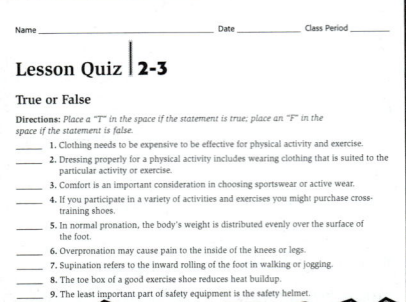

Name _____ Date _____ Class Period _____

Lesson Quiz | 2-3

True or False

Directions: *Place a "T" in the space if the statement is true; place an "F" in the space if the statement is false.*

_____ 1. Clothing needs to be expensive to be effective for physical activity and exercise.

_____ 2. Dressing properly for a physical activity includes wearing clothing that is suited to the particular activity or exercise.

_____ 3. Comfort is an important consideration in choosing sportswear or active wear.

_____ 4. If you participate in a variety of activities and exercises you might purchase cross-training shoes.

_____ 5. In normal pronation, the body's weight is distributed evenly over the surface of the foot.

_____ 6. Overpronation may cause pain to the inside of the knees or legs.

_____ 7. Supination refers to the inward rolling of the foot in walking or jogging.

_____ 8. The toe box of a good exercise shoe reduces heat buildup.

_____ 9. The least important part of safety equipment is the safety helmet.

RETEACHING

- Have students list three important environmental risk factors they can control to avoid injury.

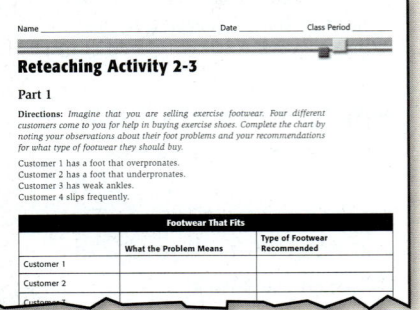

Name _____ Date _____ Class Period _____

Reteaching Activity 2-3

Part 1

Directions: *Imagine that you are selling exercise footwear. Four different customers come to you for help in buying exercise shoes. Complete the chart by noting your observations about their foot problems and your recommendations for what type of footwear they should buy.*

Customer 1 has a foot that overpronates.
Customer 2 has a foot that underpronates.
Customer 3 has weak ankles.
Customer 4 slips frequently.

Footwear That Fits		
	What the Problem Means	Type of Footwear Recommended
Customer 1		
Customer 2		

ENRICHMENT

Have students work together in groups to compile a list of safety considerations to remember when choosing exercise equipment. Have groups develop a presentation for the class.

4 CLOSE

Ask how many students have purchased new exercise shoes. Ask those who have whether the shoes helped them perform better. Why?

52

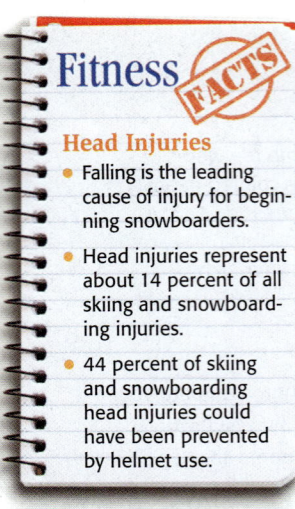

Fitness FACTS

Head Injuries

- Falling is the leading cause of injury for beginning snowboarders.
- Head injuries represent about 14 percent of all skiing and snowboarding injuries.
- 44 percent of skiing and snowboarding head injuries could have been prevented by helmet use.

Sources: Healthlink. Medical College of Wisconsin, 2001. U.S. Consumer Product Safety Commission, 1999.[3,4]

- Take extra care around pedestrians and vehicles.
- Always control your speed.
- Pay close attention to the pavement for holes or obstructions.
- If you do fall, prepare your body for the blow by curling up into a ball and rolling as you hit the ground. This will help reduce the chance of serious injury.
- Replace your helmet if it has any damage.

▶ Most head injuries could be avoided if riders wore proper head gear. *What features should you look for when choosing a helmet?*

Lesson 3 Review

Using complete sentences, answer the following questions on a sheet of paper.

Reviewing Facts and Vocabulary

1. **Vocabulary** Define *pronation* and *supination*.
2. **Recall** Give two reasons for wearing a safety helmet while skateboarding, cycling, and snowboarding.

Thinking Critically

3. **Extend** Name a sport that might require a clothing fabric that easily stretches. What sport would demand durability in a fabric?
4. **Analyze** Why is nonskid footwear important for safe physical activity?
5. **Synthesize** Alex and Calvin play one-on-one basketball on a regular basis. Alex has been complaining about the discomfort of his shoes for some time. Calvin has recently read about pronation and other concerns associated with purchasing shoes. What advice could Calvin give to Alex about purchasing new shoes?

Personal Fitness Planning

Evaluating Equipment Take time to evaluate all of your workout clothing and equipment. Are the soles of your shoes wearing out? Has the cushion support of your shoes diminished? Are there any cracks in your helmet or tears in the chin strap? Make a note of any problems. If possible, make arrangements to replace damaged shoes or other equipment.

Lesson 3 Review

Answers to Lesson 3 Review

1. *Pronation* is the normal motion of the foot as you walk or run. *Supination* is the normal outward roll of the foot.
2. A helmet protects against head injury.
3. Aerobic dancing or running requires clothing made of flexible fabric. Outdoor activities and contact sports may require durability in a fabric.
4. Nonskid footwear is needed to protect from injury during physical activities.
5. Answers will vary, but should include tips from the Consumer Corner, page 50.

Preventing Fitness Injuries

Charlie has been jogging regularly now for three months. He has not experienced any soreness since the early weeks of his fitness program. However, recently he has been experiencing a slight pain in his lower back. He is curious about the cause of this injury. He is concerned about whether continued exercise will cause serious back problems.

Do you know the potential causes of minor back pain? Do you know what treatments Charlie might consider? After reading this lesson, you will learn how to avoid common fitness-related injuries.

 Understanding biomechanics can help you avoid fitness-related injury or soreness. *Have you ever experienced soreness after a workout? What action did you take to relieve the discomfort?*

What You Will Do

- Apply the biomechanical principle of force to walking and jogging.
- Describe examples of unsafe walking/jogging technique.
- Identify common fitness-related injuries.
- Explain how to treat and prevent common fitness injuries.

Terms to Know

biomechanics
tendons
ligaments
cartilage
shinsplint
strain
sprain
RICE
stress fracture

Lesson 4 **Preventing Fitness Injuries** **53**

LESSON 4 RESOURCES

Teacher Classroom Resources
- Guided Practice Activity 2-4
- Fitness Check Worksheet 2-4
- Reteaching Activity 2-4
- Lesson Quiz 2-4

Multimedia
- Vocabulary PuzzleMaker
- Transparencies 11, 12, 13

Preventing Fitness Injuries

1 MOTIVATE

GETTING STARTED

- Before you begin roll call, ask the class to think about the following question: *Why do you think some people have developed incorrect running and walking styles?*
- Distribute copies of *Guided Practice Activity 2-4* for students to use while studying this lesson.

IN THIS LESSON

- **Fitness Check** *Applying Biomechanics: Correct Walking and Jogging Checklist, page 56.*

INTRODUCING VOCABULARY

- Explain that the term *biomechanics* refers to living organisms (*bio*) and how forces, actions, and constructions of materials can impact that organism (*mechanics*).
- Have students use *Vocabulary Worksheet 2* or the PuzzleMaker software to practice terms for this lesson. **ELL**

Photo Follow-up

Review the opening paragraph and photo on this page to introduce the concept of biomechanics. Have volunteers share their response to the caption question. **L1**

2 TEACH

Explaining

The human body is moving all the time. A person will take millions of steps and perform millions of movements throughout his or her lifetime. Tell students that in this lesson they will learn the importance of using correct biomechanics to reduce the chance of injury. **L1 TEKS C1B**

 Reading Check

Your foot should land on the heel as it strikes the ground, with toes pointing straight ahead. Then you should apply the proper amount of force as you push off on the ball of the foot. **TEKS C1B1**

Biomechanics

Charlie's back pain relates to **biomechanics.** Biomechanics is both *the study and the application of principles of physics to human motion.*

The laws of biomechanics dictate that when you jog slowly, your foot strikes the ground with a force that is three to five times your body weight. This activity places tremendous force and stress on the feet, lower legs, knees, upper legs, hips, and back. By understanding and reacting to these principles, you can minimize this stress and the injuries that can result. This holds true not only for jogging but also for in-line skating, tennis, and many other recreational sports.

The following suggestions will help you walk and jog safely and efficiently from a biomechanical standpoint.

- Start slowly. Follow the recommendations for efficient, gentle walking and jogging shown in **Figure 2.7.**
- Breathe deeply through your nose and mouth, rather than through your nose only.
- Relax your fingers, hands, arms, shoulders, neck, and jaw.
- Bend your arms at the elbows at an angle of about 90 degrees.
- Swing your arms straight forward and back instead of across your body.
- Stand upright.
- Hold your head up, and minimize your head motion.
- Develop a smooth, even stride that feels natural and comfortable to you.
- When your foot strikes the ground, it should land on the heel.
- Try to point your toes straight ahead as your heel strikes the ground. Push off on the ball of your foot.
- Do not pound noisily as you walk or jog.
- Avoid slapping your feet and excessive bouncing.
- Try to walk or jog on a soft surface, such as a dirt road, track, or grassy area, as compared to a concrete or asphalt surface.
- Avoid hilly surfaces, because they can place unusual stress on your muscles and joints.

Use the "Fitness Check" activity on page **56** to evaluate your walking and jogging form. This information will help you prevent injuries and may improve your form. Correct biomechanical form is important for all physical activities that place stress on the body. In Chapter 11, you will learn more about biomechanics and how to apply biomechanically correct form to daily activities such as lifting.

Reading Check

Explain Describe the biomechanically correct way your foot should strike the ground when jogging.

Curriculum CONNECTIONS

BIOLOGY, CHEMISTRY, AND PHYSICS A general understanding of science is helpful for anyone interested in studying exercise science, sports medicine, and personal fitness. Physical activity and exercise are similar to medicine: They can be prescribed for people, and in the right dosage, they can have positive effects. However, too much physical activity or exercise can cause negative effects such as overtraining, injuries, or addiction. Ask students to choose one area—biology, chemistry, or physics—and research to find the relationship between this science and personal fitness.

FIGURE 2.7

CORRECT AND INCORRECT JOGGING FORM

For effective, gentle jogging, start slowly and follow the mechanics illustrated by the top runner. *How could the bottom runner correct his form?*

Correct Form

Body erect; arms, shoulders, and neck relaxed

Clothing appropriate to climate and weather

Elbows flexed no more than 90° to 100°

Hands held loosely

Even, relatively level, nonbanked jogging surface

Proper jogging shoes in good repair

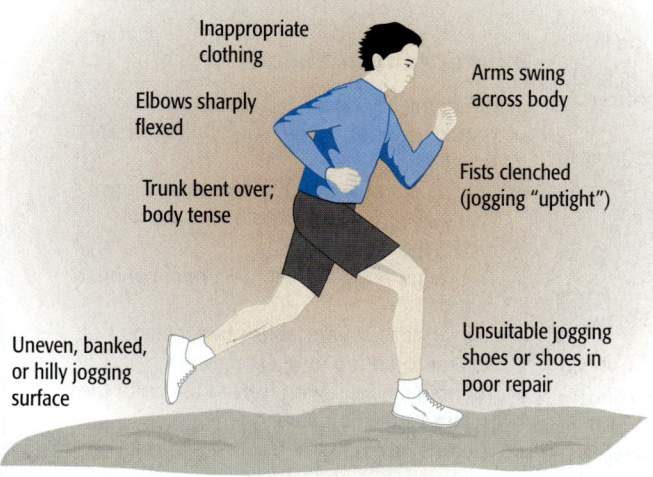

Incorrect Form

Inappropriate clothing

Elbows sharply flexed

Arms swing across body

Trunk bent over; body tense

Fists clenched (jogging "uptight")

Uneven, banked, or hilly jogging surface

Unsuitable jogging shoes or shoes in poor repair

USING VISUALS

Figure 2.7 Display *Transparency 11* to illustrate correct and incorrect jogging form. Ask students to give examples that are harmful. Have they ever seen someone walking or jogging whose actions looked inefficient or who had a lot of wasted motion? Have them explain how the figure demonstrates ways to apply biomechanical principles related to training such as force, leverage, and type of contraction while walking or jogging for exercise and training. Ask them what factors they saw that could be corrected. *Caption answer: The neck, shoulders, arms, hands, and jaw should be relaxed. The arms should bend at 90 degrees and swing forward and back. The trunk should be erect and not bent over or tensed. Jogging should take place on a soft, even surface.* **L1**
TEKS C3B, C1B1,2,3, C3B1

Quick Demo

After discussing Figure 2.7, demonstrate each of the correct biomechanics for jogging. Break down each part, and explain why they are important. Include in your demonstration what the incorrect technique looks like. Demonstrate proper walking technique for students who prefer to use walking as an alternative to jogging. **L1** **TEKS C1B, C3B**

Student Edition TEKS

Page 54: C1B
Page 55: C1B, C3B

TECHNOLOGY FILE

Digital Video Analysis of Jogging

Instruct students to videotape one another using a digital video camera. Then, have students transfer the images to a computer. Using the seven-point checklist on page 56, have students analyze their own jogging performance and make suggestions for improvement. This process is repeated after several weeks. However, this time students compare their initial jogging performance to their current performance by viewing the two side-by-side on the computer monitor. Have them note their improvements along with the need for additional practice.

Applying Biomechanics: Correct Walking and Jogging Checklist

OBJECTIVE

To identify any incorrect biomechanical form for jogging or walking and apply the correct technique.

TEACHING STRATEGIES

- Distribute *Fitness Check Worksheet 2-4* and have students record their scores. 📁

- Have students work with partners to analyze their partners' walking and jogging technique.

- If a student needs improvement, have that student repeat the activity until he or she is doing it correctly.

- Once students have evaluated their partner, students should switch roles and repeat the process.

Discussing

At the completion of the Fitness Check, be sure students understand how to apply biomechanical principles when jogging or running. Excessive force causes stress to joints, feet, hips, and back, and can result in injury. Ask: Did the newly corrected technique feel strange? Was it difficult to correct? Were you aware you had been performing the technique incorrectly? **L1**
TEKS C1B1,2

Applying Biomechanics: Correct Walking and Jogging Checklist

Practicing correct biomechanical technique is an important part of your fitness program. Often you may not be aware that you are using incorrect technique. In this activity, you will work with a partner to identify any biomechanical problems that may affect your jogging or participation in other activities.

Biomechanic Walk/Jog Test

Procedure:
1. Select a smooth surface at least 20 yards in length.
2. Before beginning to jog, arrange with your partner to observe your jogging technique from three different perspectives and check for any biomechanical technique problems. Your partner should refer to **Figure 2.7** on page **55** in assessing your technique.
3. With your back to your partner, jog for 15 to 20 yards.
4. Turn and jog the same distance back toward your partner.
5. Finally, jog left to right to allow your partner to observe you from the side.
6. Have your partner use the Biomechanical Checklist to assess your performance. You should receive a point for each item in the list that you are doing correctly.
7. Repeat the activity while attempting to correct any needed improvement.
8. Use the Fitness Ratings Chart for Biomechanical Form to assess your performance.
9. Reverse roles with your partner and repeat steps 1 through 8.

Fitness Ratings for Biomechanical Form

Points	Rating
6 or 7	Excellent
4 or 5	Fair
3 or less	Needs work

Biomechanical Checklist

- ✔ Breathing is relaxed and rhythmical.
- ✔ Hands, arms, shoulders, neck, and jaw are relaxed.
- ✔ Elbows are at about 90 degrees with arms swinging straight forward and back, not across the body.
- ✔ The upper body is erect, with minimal head motion.
- ✔ The stride is comfortable—the steps do not appear to be too long or too short.
- ✔ The foot stride is from heel to toe, with toes pointed straight ahead.
- ✔ There is no excessive bouncing or slapping of the feet, while applying the proper force.

COOPERATIVE Learning

INJURY AND TREATMENT OPTIONS Have students work in small groups or as a class for this activity. Provide one index card for each student. On half of the cards, write an injury or exercise-related problem, such as a sprained ankle. (Write a different injury on each card.) On the rest of the cards, write a first-aid treatment or action such as RICE (rest, ice, compression, elevation). (Write a different treatment on each card.) Distribute one card to each student. Students with injury or exercise-related problems on their cards should role-play,

Common Fitness Injuries and Treatment

When people are active and in motion, injuries can happen. Luckily, most of the injuries you encounter in keeping fit will probably be minor. However, you should always pay close attention to any injury. Seek medical attention if the injury interferes with your ability to perform daily tasks or take part in your fitness program for more than a few days. The most common types of fitness injuries are to the skin, muscles, connective tissue, and bones.

Skin Injuries

Common skin injuries include cuts, scrapes, bruises, and blisters. Minor cuts and scrapes usually heal in a few days if you keep them clean. Apply antiseptic medicine to the injured area, and cover the injury with a bandage. Most minor bruises will not need treatment and will disappear in a week.

Blisters are usually caused by excessive friction between the skin and another surface. Foot blisters are common when you first start physical conditioning. They can be prevented by gradually breaking in your shoes and wearing socks that fit well. If you get a blister, treat it as you would a cut or scrape, and do not let it dry out.

Muscle Injuries

One of the most common muscle injuries is a muscle cramp. These are painful spasms that can occur during physical activity or exercise. Muscle cramps may be associated with dehydration or an imbalance of **minerals** in the body. A cramp in the side or sides of your abdomen is often referred to as a side stitch. These are commonly experienced during vigorous activities that involve running.

You can avoid most muscle cramps by making sure you follow a proper warm-up and cooldown routine, and stay hydrated. If you experience a muscle cramp, it is best to stretch the muscle and firmly massage the area. You may also want to apply moist heat to the affected area. If the cramp does not go away, you should see a doctor or health care provider.

Connective Tissue Injuries

Other common fitness-related injuries involve connective tissue. Connective tissue is the soft material that helps hold bones and joints of the body in place. There are three types of connective tissues, as shown in **Figure 2.8** on page **59**. *Tendons* are *bands of connective tissue that connect muscles to bones.* *Ligaments* are *bands of tissue that connect bone to bone and limit the movement of joints.* *Cartilage* is *tissue that surrounds the ends of bones at a joint to prevent the bones from rubbing against each other.*

Inflammation of a tendon or muscle in the leg is known as a *shinsplint.* A shinsplint is often the result of overuse. Improper footwear, running or jogging on hard surfaces, or incorrect jogging form can also cause shinsplints.

Exercise for Life

Physical activity, as you have seen, can improve your appearance and make you feel better. You should try, therefore, to fit workouts into your daily routine.

If you have a busy schedule, don't worry. Deal with your priorities and, as soon as possible, get back to your workout routine.

Taking time off from your routine may be good. You may find that after a break you are more relaxed and enjoy your workout even more.

minerals
For more about minerals and their role in physical activity, see Chapter 4, page **125**.

Exercise for Life

Remind students that keeping a daily log will help them implement their daily fitness programs. When they do take a break from their routine, keeping track of their progress as they begin again can be beneficial because they can see improvements. **L3** TEKS C4G

Discussing

Ask students whether they have experienced minor skin injuries such as cuts, scrapes, bruises, and blisters. What are the main causes for these injuries, and what kinds of treatment have they used in the past? **L2**

Activity

Display *Transparency 12* and ask volunteers to identify and describe each of the three types of connective tissue shown. Ask students to name a type of injury that affects these tissues. *(shinsplint, strain, or sprain)* **L2**

hotlink

Remind students that the body does not manufacture minerals but that they are essential for development and repair of injuries to muscle and connective tissue. Have students review Chapter 4 on minerals and other nutrients.

one at a time, situations in which the injuries could occur. Students with first-aid treatments on their cards should offer the solutions/treatments given on their cards if they fit the situations. Encourage discussion as students analyze possible solutions and treatments. Then have students work in teams to draw conclusions about possible outcomes if no action or improper action is taken in each of the injury situations. **ELL**

Student Edition TEKS
Page 56: C1B

Quick Demo

Obtain the first-aid kit from the training room or nurse's office to show the kinds of medicine and supplies that can be used to treat minor injuries. Show items such as tape, bandages, wraps, and ointments. Discuss how sanitation is important to prevent infection. **L1**

Photo Follow-Up

Display *Transparency 13* and have students identify the steps in the RICE formula. Explain that, while RICE is good for many forms of athletic injuries, it is not beneficial for cramps that have been caused by overuse or dehydration. Rehydrating with water and electrolyte solutions, stretching, and massaging can be very beneficial. *Caption answer: Use stretching and massage to treat cramps. See page 58 for more information.* **L1**
TEKS C3C

Discussing

Stress the point with students that inactivity is a changeable risk factor and that it is far more hazardous to their long-term health to be inactive than to face the risk of injury they might incur by being active. **L1**
TEKS C5G

✓ **Reading Check**
The RICE procedure should be used as a first-aid measure to reduce swelling after an injury.

A pull or rip in a muscle or tendon is a **strain.** Strains may result from insufficient warm-up, lack of flexibility, or overuse. Strains are painful and often result in bruising and swelling of the injured area. Never immediately apply heat to a strain. Doing so can cause additional swelling and slow the recovery process.

A tear of a ligament is called a **sprain.** They result from a sudden twisting force to a joint, such as the wrist or ankle. Like strains, they result in pain and swelling, and may be minor or severe. However, sprains are a more serious injury and should be evaluated by a health care professional for proper care.

Treatment for Connective Tissue Injuries

If you are uncertain about any pain or injury you experience during or after physical activity or exercise, it is always best to seek medical attention as soon as possible. In the event of a strain or sprain, you should immediately use the **RICE** formula. This is *a first-aid procedure for strains and sprains that become swollen.* The letters in RICE correspond to each step of the formula.

- *R*est the injured area.
- *I*ce the area to reduce swelling. (Do not apply ice directly to the skin. Use an ice pack or ice wrapped in a towel.)
- *C*ompress the area by wrapping it in an elastic bandage.
- *E*levate, or raise, the body part.

▶ The RICE formula is used to relieve muscle strains. *What is the proper treatment for muscle cramps?*

More About . . .

BUILDING STRONGER BONES Recent studies have shown that young people should get calcium from a number of sources, not just dairy products. In fact, some studies have shown that diets high in animal protein have an adverse effect on calcium absorption. Calcium absorption from milk is approximately 30 percent, while absorption from vegetables—such as Brussels sprouts, mustard greens, turnip greens, kale, green beans and some other leafy green vegetables—range between 40 to 64 percent. Getting regular exercise and vitamin D from sunlight is also recommended.

FIGURE 2.8

A JOINT AND ITS CONNECTIVE TISSUE

Connective tissue can be injured by overuse. *What types of injuries can occur to these tissues? What should you do for each type of injury?*

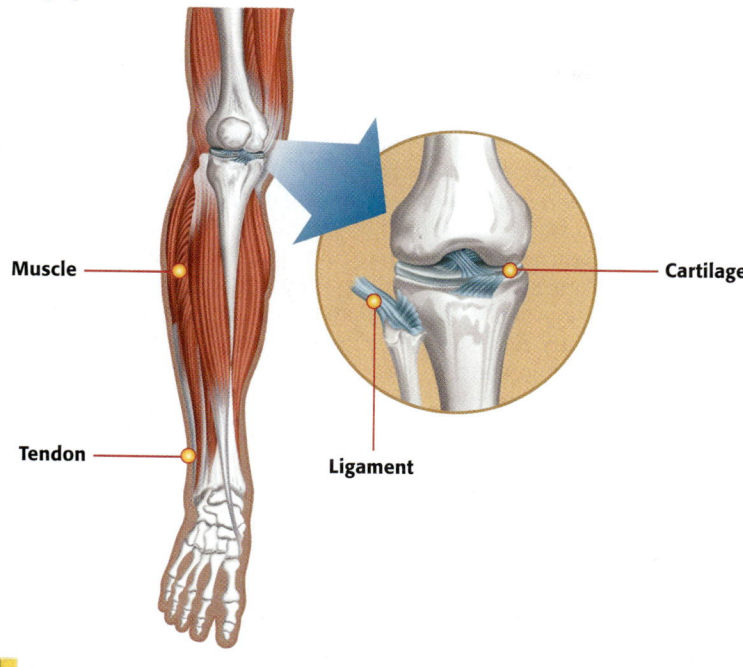

Muscle

Cartilage

Tendon

Ligament

USING VISUALS

Figure 2.8 Display *Transparency 12* again and review with students where injuries to muscles, tendons, or ligaments can occur. Ask students whether they have ever experienced shinsplints. Some students may have developed shinsplints since they started a walking or jogging program. Tell them that shinsplints usually go away after six to eight weeks of conditioning. **L1**

Injuries to Bones

Injuries to bones are serious and require medical care. A **stress fracture,** one such injury, is *a break in the bone caused by overuse.* Your doctor may not be able to diagnose a stress fracture until several weeks after it occurs. Stress fractures start as a small crack in a bone. There is usually pain above and below the crack in the bone, and it is very tender to touch. Over time (four to six weeks), the stress fracture will worsen. At that time it can often be detected through X-ray examination.

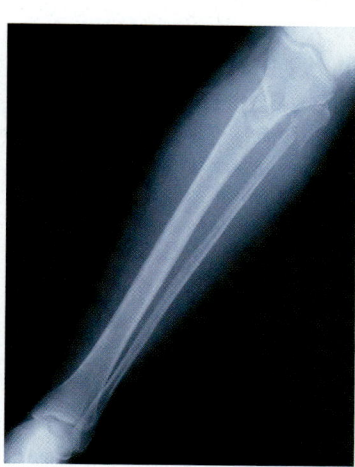

◄ An X ray might be necessary in order to detect a stress fracture. *What causes a stress fracture?*

Photo Follow-Up

Remind students that fractures such as the one shown here can be avoided by keeping bones strong through good nutrition and proper physical conditioning. Use this opportunity to help students analyze the relationship between sound nutritional practices and physical activity. Have students refer to Chapter 4 to identify nutrients that improve bone density. *Caption answer: Pain above and below a cracked bone may indicate a stress fracture.* **L1** **TEKS C5D**

ULTRASOUND AND X-RAY TECHNOLOGIES

Doctors who suspect injuries or damage to bones and tissues order various tests. Many of these tests are administered by licensed technicians. For example, a patient may be sent for ultrasound, a procedure that uses ultrasonic sound waves that create a visual image of an internal organ or structure. An ultrasound technologist needs a license and special training from a trade school or medical teaching college. X rays can produce cross-section images of the body when multiple scans are taken from several different angles and enhanced by computer.

Student Edition TEKS

Page 58: C3B
Page 59: C5D

3 ASSESS

EVALUATING THE LESSON

Assign and discuss the Lesson 4 Review.

Name _____ Date _____ Class Period _____

Lesson Quiz | **2-4**

Fill in the Blanks

Directions: *Fill in the blanks with the correct answers.*

1. _____ is the study and application of principles of physics to human motion.
2. The most common types of fitness injuries are to skin, muscles, _____, and bones.
3. A _____ is a band of tissue that connects muscle to bone.
4. A _____ connects bone to bone and limits the movement of joints.
5. _____ surrounds the ends of bones at a joint.
6. Inflammation of a tendon or muscle in the leg is known as a _____.
7. A pull or a rip in a muscle or tendon is a _____.
8. When a ligament tears it is called a _____.
9. The letters _____ correspond to the steps in a first-aid procedure for swollen strains and sprains.

RETEACHING

Have students work in groups to list and discuss ways to protect muscles and bones from injury.

Name _____ Date _____ Class Period _____

Reteaching Activity 2-4

Directions: *Each of the phrases below refers to one of the injuries listed in the box. Write the letter of the injury in the space next to the correct answer.*

a. skin injury
b. muscle cramp
c. connective tissue injury
d. blisters
e. shinsplint
f. strain
g. sprain
h. stress fracture
i. back injury

1. Can occur due to incorrect biomechanics _____
2. Caused by excessive friction between the skin and another surface _____
3. One of the most common types of fitness injuries _____

ENRICHMENT

Have interested students contact a family doctor or orthopedic clinic and ask about the type of treatment recommended for shinsplints. What type of footwear is recommended to avoid shinsplints?

---

4 CLOSE

Ask volunteers to explain two ways to prevent common fitness injuries.

---

hotlink

warm-up For more on warm-up, see Chapter 3, page 102.

cooldown For more on cooldown, see Chapter 3, page 108.

FITT For more on FITT, see Chapter 3, page 83.

Preventing Injuries

While it is important for you to become physically active, it is equally important to take proper caution and avoid injury. To prevent or safely treat common injuries, follow these guidelines.

- Pay attention to your body. If you feel unusually sore or fatigued, postpone activity or exercise until you feel better.
- Include a proper **warm-up** and **cooldown** in your personal fitness program. You'll learn about warm-ups and cooldowns in the next chapter.
- Monitor the frequency, intensity, time, and type (**FITT**) of your exercise closely. Progress slowly but steadily.
- If you run or walk along busy streets, always face oncoming traffic.
- Wear reflective clothing during night physical activities or exercise, such as walking or jogging.
- Use proper safety equipment for activities with a higher injury risk, such as skateboarding, snowboarding, in-line skating, and cycling.
- Always seek out proper medical advice when you have an injury.

 Reading Check

Explain Tell how RICE can be used to treat muscles, connective tissue, and bone injuries.

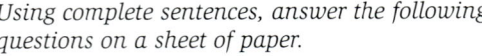
Lesson 4 Review

Using complete sentences, answer the following questions on a sheet of paper.

Reviewing Facts and Vocabulary

1. **Vocabulary** Define *biomechanics*.
2. **Vocabulary** What do the letters in *RICE* stand for?
3. **Recall** What are the three types of connective tissue? What are two common connective tissue injuries?

Thinking Critically

4. **Summarize** Describe examples of unsafe walking/jogging techniques.

5. **Extend** During his morning run, Ian got a muscle cramp. What are two steps he can take to minimize the risk of this happening again?

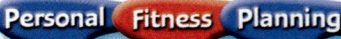 **Personal Fitness Planning**

Investigating Fitness Plan a visit to your school's or a local athletic training facility. Interview any of the trainers about the variety of athletic injuries and treatments they administer regularly. Discuss with them the equipment used to treat injuries. Make note of the treatments used on the most common injuries.

Lesson 4 Review

Answers to Lesson 4 Review

1. *Biomechanics* is the application of principles of physics to human motion.
2. Rest; Ice; Compress; Elevate.
3. Three types of connective tissue are tendons, ligaments, and cartilage. Injuries include shinsplints, strains, and sprains.

4. Answers may include: running with tense head, arms, shoulders, or neck; unsuitable shoes; jerky or uneven stride; running on hilly, uneven surfaces.
5. By following proper warm-up and cooldown routines, and staying hydrated, he can avoid muscle cramps.

Avoiding Harmful Substances

Each year, more people die in the United States from smoking cigarettes than from motor vehicle crashes, murders, and fires combined. Smoking diminishes a person's lung capacity, making it harder for the person to take part in physical activity. Over the long run, smoking severely compromises a person's functional health and fitness.

Why then do people choose to smoke? In this lesson, you will find some answers to that question. You will also find some compelling reasons to avoid using tobacco, alcohol, and other illegal drugs.

Why Some People Use Harmful Substances

Smoking can have serious health consequences. The consequences of using alcohol and illegal drugs, as you will see, are similarly grave. Considering these facts, why do you think so many people take such extreme risks?

◀ While some people may find reasons to abuse harmful substances, many more find reasons to avoid them. *How many reasons can you think of to avoid harmful substances?*

What You Will Do

- Explain common myths about substance abuse.
- Identify the effects of substance abuse such as alcohol, tobacco, and other drugs on physical performance.

Terms to Know

substance abuse
addiction
smokeless tobacco
anabolic steroids

Lesson 5 Avoiding Harmful Substances **61**

---

1 MOTIVATE

GETTING STARTED

- Ask students to identify three harmful effects that can result from the use of tobacco, alcohol, or other drugs.
- Distribute copies of *Guided Practice Activity 2-5* for students to use while studying this lesson.

IN THIS LESSON

- **Active Mind— Active Body** *Myths About Substance Abuse,* page 62

INTRODUCING VOCABULARY

- Discuss with students the differences between the definitions of the terms *use* (to consume or take regularly) and *abuse* (to put to a wrong or improper use).
- Have students use *Vocabulary Worksheet 2* or PuzzleMaker software to practice terms for this lesson. ELL 📁 💿

Photo Follow-Up

Ask: How are these teens demonstrating their commitment to remain drug free? *Caption answer: Students may mention health risks, legal consequences, or social consequences.*

LESSON 5 RESOURCES

Teacher Classroom Resources
- 📂 Guided Practice Activity 2–5
- 📂 Active Mind—Active Body Worksheet 2–5
- 📂 Reteaching Activity 2–5
- 📂 Lesson Quiz 2–5

Reproducible Charts and Graphs
- 📂 Reproducible Masters 2-4, 2-5, 2-6, 2-7, 2-8

Multimedia
- 💿 Vocabulary PuzzleMaker
- 🖐 Transparency 14

Active Mind Active Body

Myths About Substance Abuse

This activity will help students recognize the risk of substance abuse.

Teaching Tips

- Have students use *Active Mind–Active Body Worksheet 2-5* as they review each myth. 📁

- Ask students to discuss what influences might cause teens to believe smoking is glamorous.

- Explain to students that an addictive drug can have both psychological and physiological effects on the body. Psychological dependence causes a person to believe a drug is needed in order to function. Physiological dependence is a condition in which the user has a chemical need for the drug.

Apply and Conclude

Encourage students to survey family members and friends regarding their beliefs about substance abuse. Allow time for class discussion.

hotlink

Ask students to give examples of ways peers can have a positive influence on a teen's decision to avoid harmful substances.

Active Mind Active Body

Myths About Substance Abuse

It is important that you have a clear understanding about the myths associated with harmful substance abuse. Review the following myths. See if you already understand why they are myths. Then complete the follow-up activity provided.

What You Will Need

- Pen or pencil
- Paper

What You Will Do

- Review each of the three myths shown.

- List the reasons(s) why you believe each is a myth.
- Discuss your answers with your physical education teacher.
- Complete the follow-up activity provided.

Myth #1: Smoking is glamorous.
Reality: Smoking can speed up the aging process, making a person look older than he or she is. It also decreases your physical working ability.

Myth #2: If an alcoholic really wanted to control his or her drinking, he or she could.
Reality: Alcohol is an addictive drug. If used habitually, it can lead to the disease of alcoholism, which may require professional intervention.

Myth #3: Steroid use is an easy, painless way to become stronger.
Reality: Steroids alone will not make a person stronger. A person must also work out in order to make strength gains. In addition, there are many dangerous side effects that can accompany steroid use. These include a tendency to become violent ("roid rage"), to lose hair, and to gain unwanted hair.

Apply and Conclude

Conduct a survey to see how many people believe one or more of the myths presented here. Present the results to your class.

hotlink

peer influence For more on peer influence during the teen years, see Chapter 1, page 19.

One reason commonly cited by people is **peer influence.** Peer influence is the effect people your own age have on your thoughts and actions. Many teens claim to use these substances because they *believe* others their age are doing so. In many cases, this assumption is incorrect.

Another reason given is that smoking and drinking are viewed as cool. However, there is nothing cool about taking risks with your health and future.

Athletes who choose to take performance-enhancing drugs such as anabolic steroids claim they do so to excel at sports. As you will see, steroid use is very dangerous. This is why it is banned from professional sports.

As you may realize, a number of myths surround the use of these substances. How many of these myths are you aware of? Find out by completing the "Active Mind—Active Body" activity on this page.

More About . . .

STEROID ABUSE Since the late 1950s, both athletes and nonathletes have used anabolic steroids illegally to improve athletic ability and physical appearance. The serious side effects of steroid use have been well documented, including risk of cancer, heart disease, and sterility. According to recent studies, adolescent steroid users are also more likely to use other drugs and to share needles, increasing the risk of HIV infection. Preventive measures should start by the beginning of middle school. Examples include peer counseling and presentations by physicians, coaches, athletes, and school nurses.

Substance Abuse and Its Effects

Substance abuse is *any unnecessary or improper use of chemical substances for nonmedical purposes.* This includes alcohol, nicotine, illegal drugs, and over-the-counter medications. Alcohol, which is classified as a drug, is an abusable substance. Since it is illegal for teens to drink, consuming any amount of alcohol also constitutes a crime. It is also illegal in most localities for teens to buy cigarettes, which contain *nicotine,* a powerful stimulant drug. Any time a person uses a chemical substance or drug for recreation or any other purpose than the one intended, he or she is guilty of substance abuse.

When a person abuses harmful substances, he or she risks the possibility of damaging or ruining his or her functional health and fitness. The habitual use of many drugs and other harmful substances can lead to **addiction**—*physical and mental dependence.* This causes the body and mind to crave more and more of the substance.

In the remaining sections of this chapter, you will take a closer look at the health risks associated with the use of tobacco, alcohol, and steroids.

Tobacco

Cigarettes contain over 40 poisonous chemicals. Among these are the poisons arsenic and cyanide, and the gas carbon monoxide. It should be noted that smoking cigarettes is harmful not only to the smoker but to others who breathe in the smoke. Some of the health problems caused by this secondhand smoke are the same as those associated with inhaling directly.

Smoking interferes with the normal working of the lungs. Habitual smokers are three times more likely than nonsmokers to experience shortness of breath during exercise or physical activity. Smokers are also more prone to coughs and lung infections, which can hamper daily routine, including work or school.

Tobacco contains a stimulant drug, nicotine. This causes the hearts of smokers and other tobacco users to beat faster. Nicotine is also powerfully addictive, making it difficult for smokers to quit when they want to. The graphic in **Figure 2.9** on page **64** shows some other effects of smoking on the body.

▶ Substance abuse can take a toll on the emotional and physical health of the user as well as the user's family and friends. *What are some other dangers of substance abuse?*

Lesson 5   Avoiding Harmful Substances   **63**

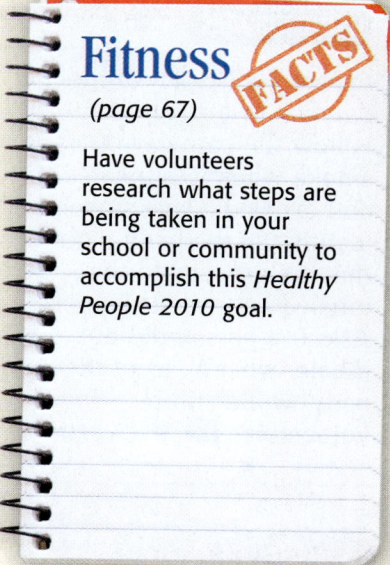

Fitness FACTS
(page 67)

Have volunteers research what steps are being taken in your school or community to accomplish this *Healthy People 2010* goal.

Activity

Have volunteers interview adults who do not smoke. Ask them to find out whether the adult ever smoked; if so, when and how the adult quit; if not, why the adult chose not to smoke; when and where the adult felt most pressured to smoke; how the adult feels now about smoking and smokers. Have students share their findings.
L3 TEKS C5G

Photo Follow-up

Remind students that individuals who choose to abuse drugs lose their interest in healthy activities and have little time for friends and family members who value a drug-free lifestyle. *Caption answer: In addition to health risks, addiction, and social consequences, illegal drug use carries legal consequences that can affect a teen's future.*
L1 TEKS C3D, C5G

Student Edition TEKS

Page 62: C3D, C5G
Page 63: C3D, C5G

COOPERATIVE Learning

ALCOHOL AND THE MEDIA Divide the class into small groups. Provide a selection of popular magazines, and have groups determine which ones have the most advertisements for alcohol. Ask them to draw conclusions about the way alcohol is advertised and the people likely to read the magazine. What is the target audience? Have groups discuss the following: Are the people in the ads having fun? Do they seem sophisticated or not? Are they portrayed as athletic? Have groups discuss other possible destructive behaviors often promoted in the media. **ELL**

USING VISUALS

Figure 2.9 Display *Transparency 14* for Figure 2.9. Follow the pathway of smoke when it is inhaled and exhaled. Have students identify all the body parts that are exposed to the inhaled and exhaled smoke. Ask: If a person did not inhale, what areas of the body would still be vulnerable? **L2** **TEKS C3D**

Explaining

Tell students what happens to the body when a person uses tobacco. Ask: Why is smoking identified as a changeable risk factor affecting physical activity and health? Explain that, after about 30 minutes, the tobacco user wants more. The constriction of the blood vessels causes a mild high. When the vessels return to normal, there is a sensation of restlessness and irritation. This causes a cycle of use that becomes habitual. The frequent use builds up an addiction to nicotine. **L1** **TEKS C3D, C5G**

Critical Thinking

Have students identify the effects of substance abuse on physical performance. Ask: What is the reason a person with heart disease is told to avoid the use of tobacco? Why does the heart have to work harder in a smoker than in a non-smoker? What happens to the heart when it works overtime? **L2** **TEKS C3D**

FIGURE 2.9

EFFECTS OF TOBACCO USE
Tobacco use seriously damages the respiratory system. *What other body systems are negatively affected by tobacco use?*

Nervous System
Short-term Effects: Changes take place in brain chemistry. Withdrawal symptoms (nervousness, shakes, headaches) may occur as soon as 30 minutes after the last cigarette. The heart rate and blood pressure increase.
Long-term Effects: There is an increased risk of stroke due to decreased flow of oxygen to the brain.

Respiratory System
Short-term Effects: User has bad breath, shortness of breath, reduced energy, coughing, and more phlegm (mucus). Colds and flu are more frequent. Allergies and asthma problems increase. Bronchitis and other serious respiratory illnesses increase.
Long-term Effects: Risk of lung cancer, emphysema, and other lung diseases increases.

Circulatory System
Short-term Effects: Heart rate is increased. Energy is reduced because less oxygen gets to body tissues.
Long-term Effects: Blood vessels are weakened and narrowed. Cholesterol levels increase. Blood vessels are clogged due to fatty buildup. Oxygen flow to heart is reduced. Risk of heart disease and stroke is greater.

Digestive System
Short-term Effects: User has upset stomach, bad breath, stained teeth, dulled taste buds, and tooth decay.
Long-term Effects: Risk of cancer of the mouth and throat, gum and tooth disease, stomach ulcers, and bladder cancer increases.

Smokeless Tobacco. One form of tobacco that has been popular among some athletes, and especially baseball players, is **smokeless tobacco.** This is *tobacco that is sniffed through the nose or chewed.* Although the use of this product has declined among athletes, who have become aware of its dangers, its teen users still number in the millions. The following are some of the facts about smokeless tobacco.

- It releases 10 times the amount of cancer-causing substances into the bloodstream than cigarettes do.
- Long-term use of smokeless tobacco can lead to an elevated heart rate and high blood pressure.
- It causes cancer of the mouth, lips, and gums.

Promoting Coordinated School Health

ALCOHOL RESISTANCE What role does the school play in helping students resist alcohol abuse? In recovering from addiction and other alcohol-related problems? In dealing with alcohol-related problems at home? What role can the school play in supporting teachers and other school staff with alcohol problems? Is there an appropriate role for the school health system in educating and helping other members of the community? These are questions to be considered and resolved in the development of a coordinated school health program.

Alcohol

Alcohol is a depressant drug. This means that it slows down the central nervous system, impairing vision, reaction time, and coordination. It also affects the function of internal organs, such as the stomach and kidneys. This may result in nausea, vomiting, and dehydration.

One of the most serious short-term dangers of using alcohol is impaired judgment, often increasing risk-taking behaviors. Combined with slowed reaction time, this factor makes drinking and any physical activity a dangerous combination.

Long-term drinking increases the risk for high blood pressure, heart rhythm disorders, heart muscle disorders, and stroke. It is also associated with the development of many cancers and liver disease. In teens, alcohol use can interfere with growth and development. The graphic in **Figure 2.10** shows some other effects of alcohol on the body.

FIGURE 2.10

EFFECTS OF ALCOHOL USE ON THE BODY
Alcohol has both short- and long-term effects on the body.
What organs are damaged by long-term alcohol use?

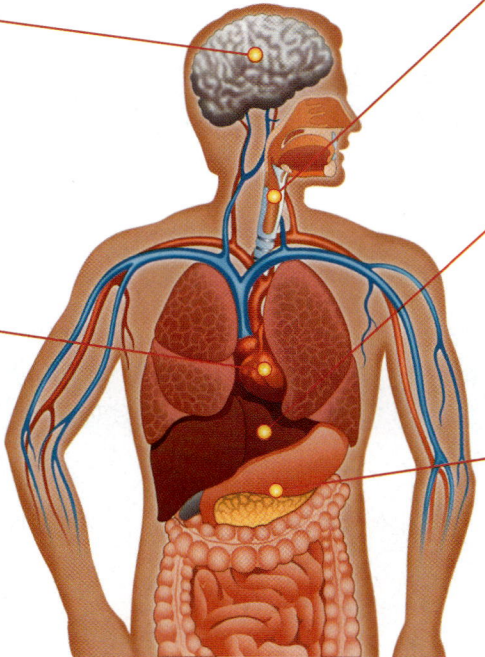

Brain and Nervous System
Short-term Effects: Speech is slurred and vision is blurred. Drinker has difficulty walking.

Long-term Effects: Brain cells, many of which cannot be replaced, are destroyed. Damage occurs to nerves through the body, resulting in numbness in the hands and feet.

Heart and Blood Vessels
Short-term Effects: Perspiration increases and skin becomes flushed.

Long-term Effects: High blood pressure and damage to the heart muscle is common. Blood vessels harden and become less flexible.

Mouth and Esophagus
Short-term Effects: Tongue, gums, and throat are affected. Breath smells of alcohol.

Long-term Effects: Damage occurs to tissues of the esophagus, resulting in possible bleeding.

Liver
Short-term Effects: Liver changes alcohol into water and carbon dioxide.

Long-term Effects: Liver is damaged, possibly resulting in **cirrhosis** (suh-ROH-sis), scarring and destruction of the liver.

Stomach and Pancreas
Short-term Effects: Stomach acids increase, which often results in nausea and vomiting.

Long-term Effects: Irritation occurs in the stomach lining, causing open sores called ulcers. Pancreas becomes inflamed.

USING VISUALS

Figure 2.10 Refer to Figure 2.10, and discuss the effects of alcohol use on the body. Discuss each body system, and ask students to consider: How would this effect change your life? Identify the effects on physical performance. **L1**
TEKS C3D, C5G

Activity

Help students discuss why avoiding alcohol demonstrates responsibility as well as respect for themselves and others. Let them brainstorm a list of possible pledges about staying alcohol free during sporting events, homecoming, and other events. Have students write and sign their own pledges. **L1**

Cooperative Learning

Ask interested students to work in groups to learn about the particular physical effects of alcohol on teens. You may suggest they research information from the library, newspaper, or magazine articles. Have them summarize their findings and share information with the rest of the class. Ask: What do you consider the most serious danger of teen alcohol consumption? Why? **L2** **ELL** **TEKS C3D, C5G**

COOPERATIVE Learning

ALCOHOL'S FAR-REACHING EFFECTS Let students work in groups to review the effects of alcohol on the body. Then ask group members to brainstorm responses to the following questions: How would these physical effects impact the mental and emotional health of the person abusing alcohol? How would they affect that person's social health? How would the health of that person's family members and friends likely be affected? Ask volunteers to prepare a presentation to the class to explain their answers. **ELL**

Student Edition TEKS

Page 64: C3D, C5G
Page 65: C3D, C5G

USING VISUALS

Figure 2.11 Ask students to use information in the figure to identify the effects of substance abuse on physical performance. What are the effects of steroids on the body? Explain to students that a typical reason to take steroids is to get bigger, stronger, or faster. Explain that, in addition to the effects listed in the figure, steroid use during adolescence can result in permanent stunting of growth. This is due to steroids causing the premature closure of the epiphyseal plates at the ends of long bones where growth occurs. **L1**
TEKS C3D

Discussing

Emphasize that steroid use in competitive sports is banned and drug testing is carried out to enforce this ban. Ask students to recall news items they have seen regarding athletes' use of steroids during the Olympics or other sports events. Remind students that losing a medal or being disqualified from competition is a small penalty compared with the health risks involved with steroid use. **L1**

Reading Check

Students should cite any of the health risks listed in the table in Figure 2.11.

Anabolic Steroids

Anabolic steroids are *chemicals similar in structure to the male hormone testosterone.* Steroids are used as a medicine to treat specific chronic diseases. All other uses of steroids are illegal and dangerous. Anabolic steroids are taken as pills or by injection, using syringes and needles. If needles are shared or contaminated, anabolic steroid users run a serious risk of exposure to disease-causing bacteria and viruses, including the HIV virus that causes AIDS. The federal Anabolic Steroids Act of 1990 made illegal manufacture, distribution, possession, and use of anabolic steroids a crime in all states. There is no valid medical reason for a healthy person to use steroids. This is why nonmedical use of anabolic steroids is a crime, punishable by law.

Effects of Steroid Use. Athletes sometimes use steroids in an attempt to increase weight, strength, and muscle mass. Others might use them to boost confidence and aggressiveness. However, steroid use has harmful effects on a person's physical, mental, and social health.

FIGURE 2.11

EFFECTS OF ANABOLIC STEROIDS
Anabolic steroids have serious effects for both males and females.
Which of the effects listed are the most threatening to your physical health?

Males	Females
• Lower sperm count	• Infertility (inability to have children)
• Smaller testicles	• Deeper voice
• Increased risk of testicle or prostate cancer	• More facial hair
• Larger breasts	• Smaller breasts

Both Males and Females	
• Hair loss or baldness	• Acne
• Sleeping problems	• Upset stomach
• Rapid weight gain	• Difficulty urinating

More About . . .

STEROID RISKS Side effects of and reactions to anabolic steroid use include cancer of the liver and other organs, heart disease, high blood pressure, high blood cholesterol, depression, hostility, mood swings, suicidal tendencies, baldness, and acne; testicular atrophy, impotence, and breast enlargement in males; and deepening voice, more facial hair, smaller breasts, and infertility in females. If injectable anabolic steroids are abused, there is the additional risk of HIV infection and AIDS from sharing contaminated needles.

Although steroids might increase muscle size, the tendons and ligaments that attach those muscles to the bones are not made stronger by steroid use. This imbalance between muscles and their connective tissues can result in serious injury that can take a long time to heal and can end an athlete's career. Steroids also have serious physical effects on other body systems. These are shown in **Figure 2.11.**

People who are on anabolic steroids can have wide mood swings. Happy one minute, users can suddenly feel angry and bad-tempered. Some users become impulsive and try dangerous stunts. Others get depressed and may contemplate—or commit—suicide. Both males and females can become much more aggressive on anabolic steroids. Bursts of anger called "roid rage" can result in violence; users risk harming themselves and others and may face arrest and jail time. Athletes who test positive for steroids can face exclusion from an event, expulsion from the team, monetary fines, and possibly jail time. All steroid use other than that prescribed by a doctor or physician has serious consequences to a person's health and fitness.

✔ **Reading Check**

Summarize What is one physical risk associated with using anabolic steroids?

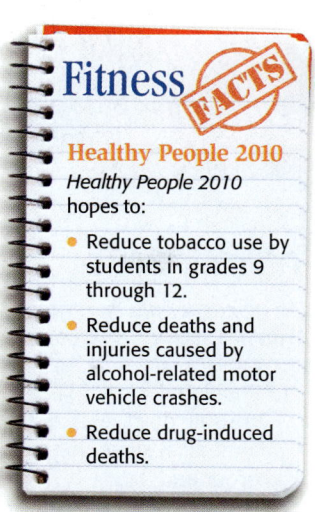

Fitness FACTS

Healthy People 2010

Healthy People 2010 hopes to:

- Reduce tobacco use by students in grades 9 through 12.
- Reduce deaths and injuries caused by alcohol-related motor vehicle crashes.
- Reduce drug-induced deaths.

Source: Modified from the National Healthy People 2010 Objectives as measured by the National Youth Risk Behavior Survey, 2001.[5]

Lesson 5 Review

Using complete sentences, answer the following questions on a sheet of paper.

Reviewing Facts and Vocabulary

1. **Vocabulary** What is *addiction*?
2. **Recall** How can addiction to a substance negatively affect your functional health and fitness?
3. **Recall** Name three harmful effects of smokeless tobacco.

Thinking Critically

4. **Evaluate** Choose one substance detailed in the lesson and identify how it is harmful to physical performance.

5. **Extend** Johnny and Harrell are both age 15. They have both heard that by taking anabolic steroids and lifting weights they can increase their muscle mass more quickly than by just using weights. What advice can you give them about using anabolic steroids?

Personal Fitness Planning

Understanding Risks Research the negative effects of alcohol, tobacco, or a particular drug. Explain how the substance affects overall health, including physical performance, emotional health, and social relationships. Share your report with the class.

Lesson 5 Avoiding Harmful Substances **67**

Lesson 5 Review

Answers to Lesson 5 Review

1. Physical and mental dependence.
2. Addiction causes the user to crave more and more of a harmful substance.
3. Smokeless tobacco can cause increased heart rate, high blood pressure, and cancer of mouth, lips, and gums.

4. Tobacco causes shortness of breath, lung infections, cancer; alcohol use impairs judgment; increases blood pressure, risk of heart damage, stroke, cancers, and liver disease; steroid use causes mood swings, depression, and risk of HIV.
5. Answers will vary.

3 ASSESS

EVALUATING THE LESSON

Assign and discuss the Lesson 5 Review.

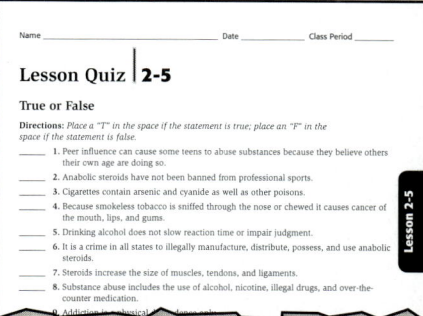

Name _____ Date _____ Class Period _____

Lesson Quiz | 2-5

True or False

Directions: *Place a "T" in the space if the statement is true; place an "F" in the space if the statement is false.*

_____ 1. Peer influence can cause some teens to abuse substances because they believe others their own age are doing so.
_____ 2. Anabolic steroids have not been banned from professional sports.
_____ 3. Cigarettes contain arsenic and cyanide as well as other poisons.
_____ 4. Because smokeless tobacco is sniffed through the nose or chewed it causes cancer of the mouth, lips, and gums.
_____ 5. Drinking alcohol does not slow reaction time or impair judgment.
_____ 6. It is a crime in all states to illegally manufacture, distribute, possess, and use anabolic steroids.
_____ 7. Steroids increase the size of muscles, tendons, and ligaments.
_____ 8. Substance abuse includes the use of alcohol, nicotine, illegal drugs, and over-the-counter medication.

RETEACHING

Ask students to explain why avoiding smoking and the use of tobacco is a risk factor that can be controlled.

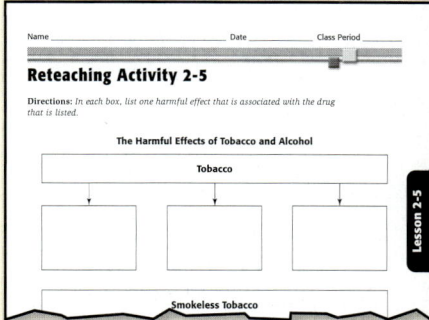

Name _____ Date _____ Class Period _____

Reteaching Activity 2-5

Directions: *In each box, list one harmful effect that is associated with the drug that is listed.*

The Harmful Effects of Tobacco and Alcohol

Tobacco

Smokeless Tobacco

ENRICHMENT

Have interested students create posters sharing drug abuse awareness and emphasizing the risks to health and fitness. Have them share their posters with younger students.

4 CLOSE

Ask students to identify the value of being committed to a drug-free life.

CHECKING COMPREHENSION

- Assign and discuss the Chapter 2 review.
- Use the PuzzleMaker CD-ROM to review vocabulary. 💿

CHAPTER 2 REVIEW ANSWERS

True/False

1. True   5. True
2. False   6. False
3. True   7. True
4. True   8. False

Multiple Choice

9. d   14. d
10. d   15. b
11. a   16. b
12. c   17. a
13. c

Discussion

18. It is important to consider the air temperature and the amount of humidity in the air to calculate the heat index. This is helpful when trying to avoid heat injuries because it can be 85 degrees and 90 percent humidity and this can create a higher heat risk primarily due to the increased humidity.

19. Air pollution and altitude are two non-weather environmental concerns students should be aware of. To avoid exposure to pollution, find suitable indoor or alternative outdoor activities.

20. Answers may vary but might include: Visit a sporting goods store and get expert advice. Take the Wet Foot Test to determine your foot type. Select a specific shoe for

TRUE OR FALSE

On a sheet of paper, write the numbers 1–8. Write True or False for each statement below.

1. People with poor lifestyle habits or known chronic diseases are strongly advised to have a medical screening before starting an exercise program.
2. In cold weather, exercise clothing should be made of a heavy material and be tight fitting to help prevent heat loss.
3. Carbon monoxide, a dangerous pollutant, is more readily absorbed by the bloodstream than oxygen.
4. It is always a good idea to try on exercise shoes with socks before you purchase them.
5. RICE stands for rest, ice, compression, and elevation.
6. Shinsplints are a type of safety equipment that should be worn to protect injury to the knees and ankles.
7. The regular use of many drugs and other harmful substances can lead to physical and mental dependence.
8. Smokeless tobacco is a less harmful tobacco product than cigarettes.

MULTIPLE CHOICE

On a sheet of paper, write the letter of the word or phrase that best completes each statement.

9. Of the following, the one that is NOT an example of a chronic disease is
   a. heart disease.   c. diabetes.
   b. asthma.   d. common cold.
10. Of the following, all are questions that might be asked during a medical history EXCEPT
    a. what medications you may be taking.
    b. what health problems and illnesses you have had.
    c. what health problems and illnesses members of your family have had.
    d. how fast you are able to run.

11. The biological reason for perspiration during physical activity in hot weather is
    a. it cools down the body.
    b. it removes harmful chemicals that build up in the body during intense activity.
    c. it enables you to play better.
    d. none of the above.
12. Anyone exercising in extreme cold conditions is exposed to all of the following health risks EXCEPT
    a. frostbite.
    b. hypothermia.
    c. wind-chill factor.
    d. none of the above.
13. Of the following, the one that is NOT a guideline for exercising in high altitudes is
    a. drink plenty of fluids.
    b. gradually change altitude.
    c. eat meals more often to prevent altitude sickness.
    d. gradually increase exercise over a period of time.
14. An important consideration when purchasing a new pair of athletic shoes is
    a. the shape of your foot.
    b. proper support.
    c. nonskid sole.
    d. all of the above.
15. All of the following are things to look for when selecting a protective helmet EXCEPT
    a. a foam liner inside to absorb blows to the head in case of a fall.
    b. a racing stripe that shows other bikers or skaters that you mean business.
    c. a snug but comfortable fit.
    d. a chin strap and buckle so that the helmet will stay securely fastened.
16. All of the following are aspects of good biomechanical technique EXCEPT
    a. breathing deeply through your nose and mouth.
    b. keeping your arms straight down at your sides.
    c. standing nearly erect, with your head up.
    d. choosing a soft surface, such as a dirt road or grassy area as opposed to concrete or asphalt.
17. Of the following, the one that is NOT a connective body tissue is
    a. shinsplint.   c. ligament.
    b. cartilage.   d. tendon.

your needs (jogging, basketball, sports, etc.). Try on the shoes before you buy them to ensure a proper fit. Make sure the shoe has a roomy toe box that fits your foot type.

Vocabulary

21. d   24. f
22. c   25. b
23. a   26. e

DISCUSSION

Using complete sentences, answer the following questions on a sheet of paper.

18. **Explain** Tell why it is important to know the air temperature and the amount of humidity in the air when exercising or taking part in a vigorous physical activity.

19. **Identify** List two possible non-weather-related dangers of your exercise environment. Give two safety recommendations for each.

20. **Summarize** Tell what you should consider and do before you buy a pair of physical-activity or athletic shoes.

VOCABULARY

On a sheet of paper, write the letter of the term in Column B that best fits the definition in Column A.

Column A	Column B
21. The normal motion of the foot as you walk or run.	a. chronic disease
	b. hypothermia
22. A tear of a ligament.	c. sprain
23. Ongoing, as in a disease that continues for an extended time.	d. pronation
	e. addiction
24. The study of the principles of physics applied to human motion.	f. biomechanics
25. A drop in body temperature to below normal.	
26. A physical or mental dependence.	

CRITICAL THINKING

Using complete sentences, answer the following questions on a sheet of paper.

27. **Analyze** What are the steps involved in administering the RICE treatment to injuries?

28. **Synthesize** Most serious fitness injuries can be prevented by the use of safety equipment. Give reasons why people, especially teens, may be reluctant to use safety equipment.

29. **Explain** Detail the importance of using replacement fluids during and after vigorous exercise in the heat. Tell which fluids to use and which to avoid, giving reasons in each case.

CASE STUDY

CASE STUDY—DAVID'S FITNESS PROGRAM

David is an unfit, overweight fifteen-year-old who has lived all his life in Minnesota. His family recently moved to central Texas. David has never been very athletic or physically active, and he has not paid much attention to his health or personal fitness.

Now that he has moved to a warmer climate, he would like to make some changes in his fitness habits. His goals are to lose 20 pounds and to become more physically fit overall.

David has no experience with personal fitness programs and knows little about them. He does realize that he needs the help of someone knowledgeable in designing and implementing his fitness program. He needs someone like you!

HERE IS YOUR ASSIGNMENT:

Assume that you are David's neighbor and that he has asked you to help him plan his new physically active lifestyle. Organize a list of things David should consider and do before beginning a moderate to vigorous fitness program.

KEYS TO HELP YOU

- Consider David's current medical status.
- List the concerns David must deal with as he changes from his previous environment to his new environment.
- Consider David's needs and desires.

Critical Thinking

27. Rest the injured area; Ice the area to reduce swelling (Do not apply ice directly to the skin. Use an ice pack or ice in a towel.) Compress the area by wrapping it in an elastic bandage; Elevate, or raise, the body part.

28. Answers will vary, but students should include specific examples such as appearance, convenience, or peer pressure that may cause teens to be reluctant to use safety equipment.

29. Answers will vary but should include a discussion of restoring lost water and electrolytes before, during, and after physical activity or exercise.

EVALUATE

Name _____ Date _____ Class Period _____

CHAPTER
2 | Chapter Test A

True or False

Directions: Place a "T" in the space if the statement is true; place an "F" in the space if the statement is false.

_____ 1. If you have a chronic disease, medical screenings are not necessary to start an exercise program.
_____ 2. As a general guideline, the frequency of medical screenings should increase as a person ages.
_____ 3. Heatstroke is not life threatening.
_____ 4. Dehydration includes loss of body fluid and loss of body chemicals.
_____ 5. Applying the laws of biomechanics to physical activity can minimize stress and injuries.
_____ 6. Preventing injuries includes overlooking body cues such as soreness or fatigue.
_____ 7. When peers are minors they do not exert much peer influence.
_____ 8. Tobacco is the only substance that damages functional health.
_____ 9. Alcohol impairs judgment and slows reaction time.

ENRICHMENT

Name _____ Date _____ Class Period _____
Enrichment Activity 2

Smart Gear Checklist

Directions: Place a checkmark next to each characteristic listed in the left column that you should consider when shopping for fitness clothing, footwear, or a helmet. (Note: Some characteristics fit more than one category.)

Guidelines: This item should	Clothing	Footwear	Helmet
stretch			
be suited to your activity			
be nonskid			
have a roomy toe box			
be fitted for stride irregularities			
have a foam liner			
meet the standards of the American National Standards Institute or the Snell Memorial Foundation			
be considered your most important fitness			

CASE STUDY

ANSWERS

David needs to start slowly and set reasonable goals. He should evaluate his health status before beginning a program by completing the health screening questionnaire in this chapter. He will have to acclimatize to the warm Texas climate. David would improve adherence to his fitness program by making a contract with himself, being patient, developing a regular schedule, participating in physical activities with friends or family, and developing a progress chart to record his improvements.

CHAPTER 3

Lesson 1 Health-Related and Skill-Related Fitness

Lesson 2 FITT and the Principle of Overload

Lesson 3 The Principle of Specificity

Lesson 4 The Principle of Progression

Lesson 5 Warm Up, Work Out, Cool Down

CHAPTER RESOURCES

- Chapter Study Guide 3
- Vocabulary Worksheet 3
- Enrichment Activity 3
- Chapter 3 Test A
- Chapter 3 Test B
- Parent Letter and Activities 3 (English/Spanish)

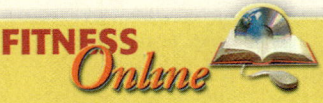

FITNESS Online

Ask students to take the STEP Personal Inventory for Chapter 3. Have them record their responses to the statements in their notebooks. Remind students that responses are for their use only.

CHAPTER 3 Designing a Personal Fitness Program

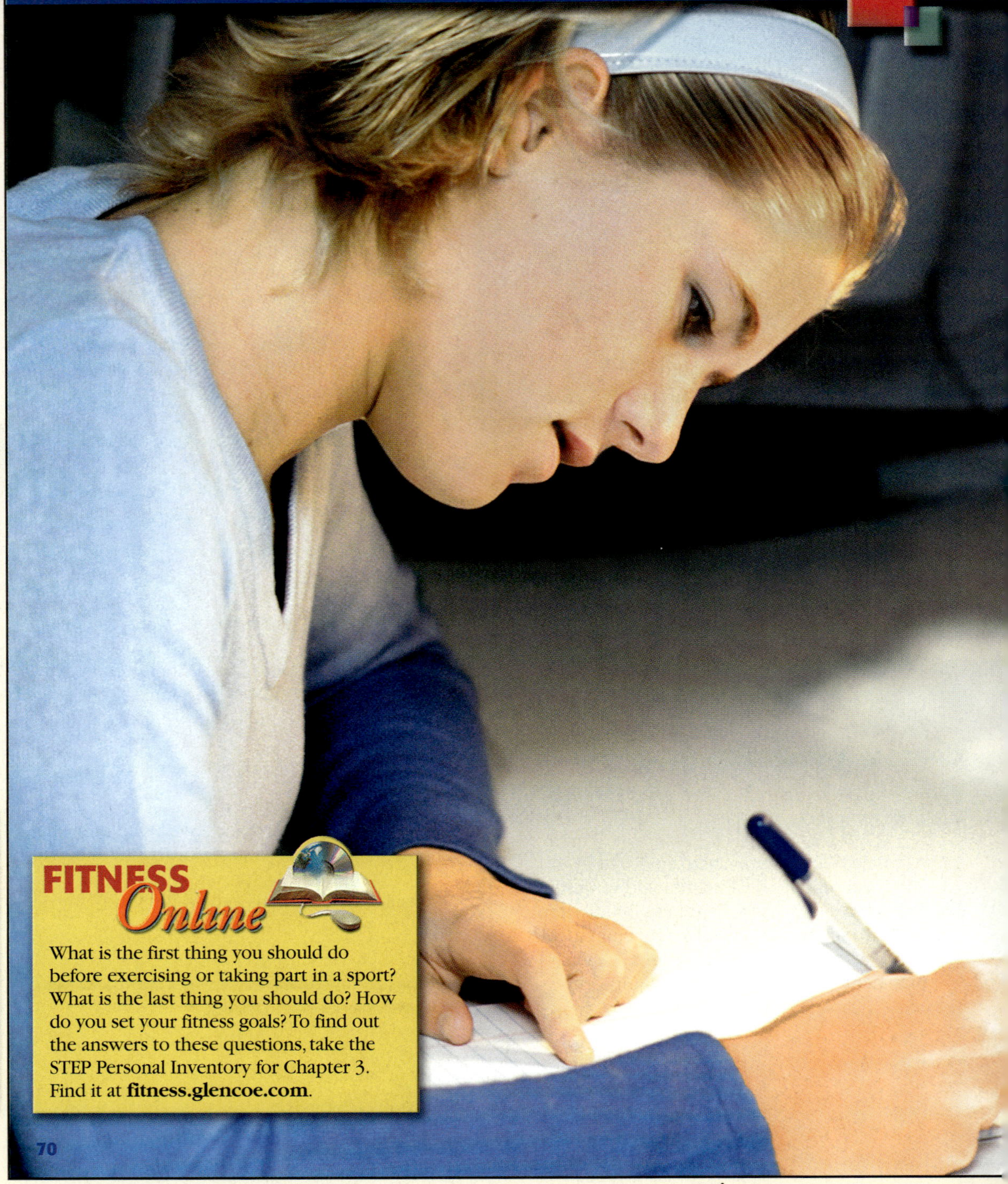

FITNESS Online

What is the first thing you should do before exercising or taking part in a sport? What is the last thing you should do? How do you set your fitness goals? To find out the answers to these questions, take the STEP Personal Inventory for Chapter 3. Find it at **fitness.glencoe.com**.

70

INCLUSION STRATEGIES

LANGUAGE DIVERSITY *Use the following suggestions to help students who have difficulty with English:*

- Pair English-language learners with native speakers of English who can restate key points in language that helps students comprehend important concepts.
- Direct Spanish-speaking students to the written summaries of this chapter in the *Foundations of Personal Fitness* Spanish Resources Booklet.
- Encourage Spanish-speaking students to use the Glosario provided in the back of the student text. ELL

Health-Related and Skill-Related Fitness

Jack is on the school track team. His dream is to become an Olympic sprinter. The team coach believes Jack has real potential. "You just have to be willing to work hard," the coach has told him.

Jack is not sure what the coach means. How, he wonders, can a person work at becoming a better runner? Is it possible to increase your speed? After reading this lesson, you will know the answers to Jack's questions.

Health-Related Fitness vs. Skill-Related Fitness

As you learned in Chapter 1, total physical fitness includes both of the following:

- **Health-related fitness.** This is your ability to become and stay physically healthy.
- **Skill-related fitness.** This is your ability to maintain high levels of performance on the playing field.

While your level of skill-related fitness is reflected in how well you perform a physical activity, your level of health-related fitness provides a measure of your physical health. Improving in one area may lead to improvements in the other.

◀ It is possible to improve both your health-related and skill-related fitness. *How do you think participating in a sport, such as track, can help you develop both health- and skill-related fitness?*

What You Will Do

- Identify the specific components of health-related and skill-related fitness.
- Compare and contrast health-related and skill-related fitness.
- Analyze factors that influence your health-related and skill-related fitness.
- Demonstrate the skill-related components of fitness.

Terms to Know

energy cost
agility
balance
coordination
speed
power
reaction time

Health-Related and Skill-Related Fitness

1 MOTIVATE

GETTING STARTED

- Ask the class to describe the difference between health-related and skill-related activities based on what they learned in Chapter 1.
- Distribute copies of *Guided Practice Activity 3-1* for students to use while studying this lesson. 📁

IN THIS LESSON

- **Fitness Check** *Demonstrating Skill-Related Fitness, p. 78*

INTRODUCING VOCABULARY

- Explain to students that the term *energy cost* refers to how many calories a person uses in doing a physical activity and how efficient the person is at performing the activity.
- Have students use *Vocabulary Worksheet 3* or the PuzzleMaker software to practice vocabulary terms for this lesson. ELL 📁 💿

Photo Follow-up

Point out to students that the coach and teen in this photo can work on ways to improve this runner's performance by being aware of his health- and skill-related fitness. *Caption answer: Answers will vary but should include improvements in cardiorespiratory fitness (health-related) and speed and power for skill-related fitness.*

LESSON 1 RESOURCES

Teacher Classroom Resources
📁 Guided Practice Activity 3-1
📁 Fitness Check Worksheet 3-1
📁 Reteaching Activity 3-1
📁 Lesson Quiz 3-1

Reproducible Charts and Graphs
📁 Reproducible Master 3-1
Multimedia
💿 Vocabulary PuzzleMaker
🖱 Transparencies 15, 16, 17

hotlink

Reinforce to students that cardiorespiratory endurance is one of the most important health-related components they can develop and maintain throughout life. Have students review Chapters 1 and 7 for more information about these topics.

✓ Reading Check

Five components of health-related fitness are cardiovascular fitness, body composition, muscular strength, muscular endurance, and flexibility. **TEKS C4C**

Discussing

Ask students which of the following activities requires the most skill to promote cardiovascular fitness: brisk walking, hiking, jogging, dancing, skipping rope, rowing, swimming, or skating. (*Dancing, skipping rope, and skating require more skill than the other activities.*) **L1**

Explaining

Display *Transparency 15* and discuss with students each component of health-related fitness shown. Ask students to identify which elements of fitness they are able to incorporate into their daily physical activities. **L1**

Health-Related Fitness

There are five components, or measures, of health-related fitness. These are:

- **Body composition.** This is the relative percentage of body fat to lean body tissue, including water, bone, muscle, and connective tissue.
- **Cardiovascular fitness.** This is the ability of your body to work continuously for extended periods of time. Because this involves your lungs as well as your heart and vessels, cardiovascular fitness is sometimes called **cardiorespiratory endurance.**
- **Muscular strength.** This refers to the maximum amount of force a muscle or muscle group can exert against an opposing force.
- **Muscular endurance.** This refers to the ability of the same muscle or muscle group to contract for an extended period of time without undue fatigue.
- **Flexibility.** This is the ability to move a body part through a full range of motion.

Levels of **health-related fitness** for any given component vary from person to person. These differences are due partly to heredity and partly to other, external factors. Some people, for example, are born with greater muscular strength, others with greater flexibility. As you will see, however, it is possible to improve in all of these areas.

✓ Reading Check

List Name the five components of health-related fitness.

Body Composition. For most people, the most critical factor in **body composition** is body fat. While some body fat is important, too much can impair your functional health and increase your risks for chronic disease. By the same token, too little body fat—being too lean—can also be problematic.

hotlink

cardiorespiratory endurance
For more on cardiorespiratory endurance, see Chapter 7, page **198.**

body composition
For more on measuring body composition, see Chapter 5, page **162.**

By adopting a physically active lifestyle, you can help control your percentage of body fat. When you engage in physical activities or exercise, you burn or expend energy. The source of this energy is found in calories from the foods you eat. Calories that are not expended are stored by the body as fat.

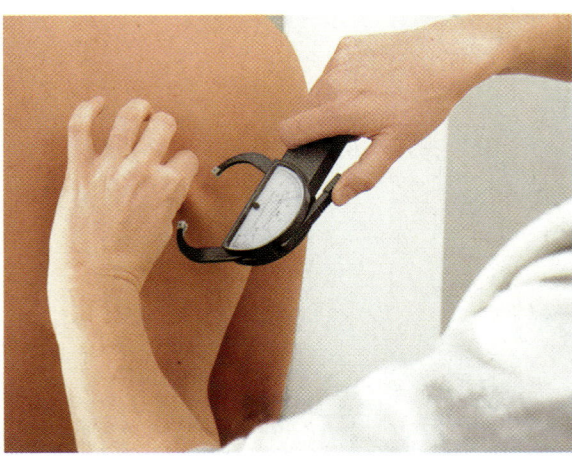

◀ One method for determining body composition is to measure a skin fold with a tool called a caliper. Males should carry 7 to 19 percent body fat, females 12 to 24 percent.

More About . . .

HEALTH-RELATED FITNESS In the 1980s, most health and fitness experts considered cardiovascular fitness to be the most important health-related fitness component because heart disease was the number one cause of death for adults during the 1960s and 1970s. While heart disease is still the leading cause of death in adults today, the incidence of obesity and type 2 diabetes is increasing rapidly. Thus, many health and fitness experts now feel that the health-related component of body composition is just as important as cardiovascular fitness.

◀ Swimming laps is an excellent activity for increasing your muscular endurance. *What other component of health-related fitness does swimming improve?*

Photo Follow-up

Ask students to describe the advantages of swimming laps. *Caption answer: Answers should include cardiovascular fitness, body composition, muscular strength, and flexibility.*

hotlink

Reinforce to students that body composition, calisthenics, and muscular endurance are important concepts to understand when they are learning to improve their health-related fitness. Have students review Chapters 5 and 9 for more information about these topics. **TEKS C4B**

✔ **Reading Check**

Muscular strength is partly determined by factors such as age, gender, and heredity. You can increase muscular strength through weight training and calisthenics. Muscular endurance is increased through repetitive exercises such as sit-ups and push-ups.

Cardiovascular Fitness. Cardiovascular fitness, or cardiorespiratory endurance, is a function of how well your heart and lungs do their job. Moderate to high levels of cardiovascular fitness have been shown to increase life expectancy, reduce the risk of cardiovascular disease, and improve functional health.

A number of activities and exercises promote cardiovascular fitness. These include brisk walking, hiking, jogging, dancing, skipping rope, rowing, swimming, and skating.

Muscular Strength. Muscular strength is partly determined by factors beyond your control. These include age, gender, and heredity. Individual levels of muscular strength can be increased, however, through weight training, **calisthenics,** or similar exercises. Work that requires heavy lifting will also lead to gains in muscular strength.

A moderate to high level of muscular strength improves functional health and fitness. It also helps reduce your risk for muscle, bone, and joint injuries. In addition, muscular strength contributes to more efficient movement and reduces your energy cost. Energy cost is *the amount of energy needed to perform different physical activities or exercises.*

Muscular Endurance. Like muscular strength, **muscular endurance** helps you move more efficiently. The higher your level of muscular endurance, the lower your energy cost. You are thus able to do more physical work without tiring.

Exercises such as sit-ups and push-ups can increase muscular endurance. So can work that requires repetitive heavy lifting. You will learn more about muscular endurance in Chapters 9 and 10.

hotlink

calisthenics
For more on calisthenics, see Chapter 9, page **266.**

muscular endurance
For more on measuring muscular endurance, see Chapter 9, page **267.**

✔ **Reading Check**

Compare Explain the difference between muscular strength and muscular endurance.

COOPERATIVE Learning

CALISTHENICS Have  students work in small groups to make a list of calisthenic exercises that they have done in physical education classes. Then have one member of each group demonstrate two of those calisthenic exercises. Finally, have the class review the hot link in Chapter 9 for calisthenics and compare their list of exercises to the newer recommendations. Students should discuss how calisthenics can help develop muscular strength and muscular endurance. **ELL**

Student Edition TEKS

Page 72: C4D
Page 73: C4D

Photo Follow-up

Ask students to describe in their own words how flexibility is important to a gymnast. *Caption answer: Answers may vary but might include physical activities such as cheerleading, skateboarding, and in-line skating.*

Discussing

Display *Transparency 16* on Skill-Related Fitness. Discuss the basic components of skill-related fitness and determine which sports require them. **L1**

Emphasize the importance of flexibility in improving and maintaining efficient physical movement. Refer students to Chapter 11 to review information about flexibility.

Stress and Stretching

Have students discuss the muscle tension and stiffness that can result from sitting for long periods. Have them work in small groups to design a two- to three-minute stretching routine that can be done to ease those symptoms. Have groups describe physical fitness activities that can reduce stress, and share their programs with the class. **TEKS C5B**

Student Edition TEKS

Page 74: C4D, C5B
Page 75: C4D

▶ Flexibility enhances your performance in sports as well as helps you maintain a high level of functional fitness. *In addition to gymnastics, what other sports require a high level of flexibility?*

flexibility
For more on flexibility and exercises that can improve it, see Chapter 11, page **334**.

Stress and Stretching

It is not uncommon for people who sit most of the day to have headaches and neck aches. Do you suffer from either of these problems? They are caused by muscle stress. Messages from your body include clenched teeth and rigid shoulders.

Through basic stretching exercises, you can avoid muscle stress. Moving your shoulders in a circular motion will stretch the muscles, easing the tension.

Flexibility. A moderate to high level of **flexibility** is central to efficient physical movement. It can also

- help reduce your risk for muscle and bone injuries.
- improve performance fitness.
- reduce some types of muscle soreness following physical activity or exercise.
- improve functional health and fitness.

You can achieve moderate to high levels of flexibility through stretching activities, some of which are provided in Chapter 11.

Skill-Related Fitness

Why are some individuals capable of outstanding physical performance? How can a track star high jump seven feet? What enables the Olympic weight lifter to lift massive amounts of weight? Why aren't all people capable of such physical feats? The answer to these questions can be summed up in one term: *skill-related fitness.*

As noted in Chapter 1, another name for skill-related fitness is *performance fitness.* Skill-related fitness has six components, or measures. These are *agility, balance, coordination, speed, power,* and *reaction time.* Highly skilled athletes generally excel in most, and sometimes all six, areas.

Like health-related fitness, skill-related fitness can enhance your ability to complete daily chores and other physical tasks unrelated to exercise. Unlike health-related fitness, skill-related fitness will not necessarily reduce lifestyle-related health risks.

INCLUSION STRATEGIES

SKILL-RELATED FITNESS The six skill-related components of fitness are a concern for individuals with disabilities. Low motor skill fitness levels can be a result of conditions that may inhibit efficient movement. Maintaining balance and center of gravity is difficult for students who have disabilities that affect posture. Students who have loss of hearing or vision rely on other sensory input to sustain balance while performing activities that require coordination. Any nervous system damage will affect coordination. Speed, agility, and reaction time also involve central nervous system function.

Agility. What do skilled football running backs have in common with successful soccer players? The answer is **agility.** This is *the ability to change and control the direction and position of the body while maintaining a constant, rapid motion.* Other skill-related components of fitness, such as speed and coordination, may influence your level of agility. Sports that require a high level of agility include football, soccer, basketball, baseball, and softball.

Balance. This is *the ability to control or stabilize the body while standing or moving.* A simple act such as walking requires a great deal of balance. The gymnast, golfer, and ice skater all need high degrees of balance. Balance helps you maintain control while coordinating your movements.

Balance in sports depends in large measure on biomechanics. As explained in Chapter 2, biomechanics is the application of principles of physics to human motion. Often, redistributing body weight will result in improved balance and, hence, performance in a sport. For example, many golfers are able to improve their swing by shifting their body weight so that the weight is evenly distributed. Basketball players can improve their defensive plays by widening their stance. This provides a wider base of support and lowers the center of gravity to improve balance and overall performance.

Coordination. This is *the ability to use the senses to determine and direct the movement of your limbs and head.* Gymnastics, cheerleading, and juggling demand a high level of coordination.

Coordination requires using a combination of different muscle groups at once. This ability can be sharpened with practice. Other components of skill-related fitness, such as speed, reaction time, and agility, may influence your level of coordination. Like balance, coordination can be improved by widening the base of support and lowering your center of gravity.

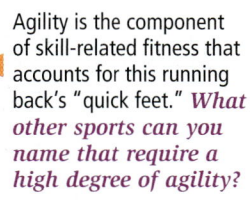

Agility is the component of skill-related fitness that accounts for this running back's "quick feet." *What other sports can you name that require a high degree of agility?*

Fitness FACTS

Athletic Records
- The most home runs in a U.S. baseball career is 755, hit by Hank Aaron.
- The longest field goal kicked in NFL history is 63 yards, a record held jointly by Tom Dempsey and Jason Elam.
- The most points scored in an NBA game is 100, by Wilt Chamberlain.

Fitness FACTS

Ask students whether they have ever seen an athlete break a record, either in person or on television. Ask: Why do people tend to get excited when they see someone set a new athletic record? Does this excitement encourage you to participate in physical activities or discourage you? Why?

Activity

Using *Transparency 17,* have students work in teams of two to assess their fitness levels by performing the tests listed. Have each team member record his or her partner's results and then switch so each has a turn to perform the tests. `L2`

Explaining

Ask students whether they think coordination improves as a person grows from the age of 10 or 11. If so, ask them if they think that growth and development help improve coordination. (*Growth and development do indeed improve coordination. Students who develop early usually improve coordination earlier.*) `L1`

Photo Follow-up

Ask students to describe some of the specific advantages of agility in various activities and sports. *Caption answers might include physical activities such as basketball, dancing, or soccer.*

Lesson 1   Health-Related and Skill-Related Fitness   75

Curriculum CONNECTIONS

LITERATURE Courage, self-reliance, endurance, physical skills, and survival are frequent themes in literature for adolescents. Many of these books are award-winning classics (some of which have been made into blockbuster movies) that portray youth in conflict or in overwhelming situations surrounded by seemingly insurmountable challenges. In many of these classics, skill-related and health-related fitness have a lot to do with the characters' survival. Have students identify two of their favorite books that highlight skill-related and/or health-related fitness themes.

Photo Follow-up

Photo Follow-up

Ask a volunteer to point out the ways in which the teen in this photo is demonstrating speed and power. *Caption answer: Answers may vary but might include physical activities such as boxing, sprinting, and power lifting.*

STRESS BREAK

Ask students whether they have ever experienced conflict or stress while participating in or observing sports or competitive games. Then ask them how they avoided or could have resolved the stress in a positive way. **TEKS C2B, C5B**

✓ Reading Check

Answers will vary but might include football, basketball, soccer, dancing, cheerleading, or any other sport that requires a high level of agility, balance, coordination, speed, power, or reaction time.

Activity

Have students role-play a situation where they recognize and resolve a conflict during physical activity at school. Ask for two volunteers to imagine a disagreement during a game. Have them demonstrate the character traits of respect, rights, and responsibility to resolve the conflict. **TEKS C2B**

▶ This athlete possesses extraordinary levels of speed and power.

STRESS BREAK

Resolve Conflicts, Avoid Stress

Physical activity is a positive way to reduce stress. Games and sports, however, involve challenges and competition that can *cause* stress and lead to conflicts with your peers.

One effective way to resolve conflicts on the playing field is to follow the R's:

• **Respect** Show respect for others on and off the field.
• **Rights** Remember other people's rights.
• **Responsibility** Take responsibility for your own actions and role in the conflict.

Speed. This is *the ability to move your body, or parts of it, swiftly.* Foot speed is usually measured over a short and straight distance, usually less than 200 meters. Other speed evaluations might include hand or arm speed. The baseball pitcher, boxer, sprinter, and volleyball spiker all require specific kinds of speed.

Although speed is largely determined by heredity, speed can be increased. Building muscular strength, for example, can lead to speed gains.

Power. This is *the ability to move the body parts swiftly while simultaneously applying the maximum force of your muscles.* Power is thus a function of both speed and muscular strength. The long jump, power lifting, and swimming all require high levels of power. Increasing muscular strength will lead to improvements in power. Proper biomechanics can also enhance power by improving your balance, coordination, and speed.

Reaction Time. This is *the ability to react or respond quickly to what you hear, see, or feel.* The quicker your response, the better your reaction time.

Good reaction time is important to sprinters and swimmers, who must react to starts. The tennis player, boxer, and hockey goalie all require quick reaction times as well. Factors such as decreased motivation and increased fatigue can slow your reaction time. Finding ways to stay motivated and practicing regularly will improve your reaction time.

Some activities and sports mainly benefit skill-related fitness, while others might be more beneficial to health-related fitness. Some, like volleyball and cross-country skiing, benefit both areas of fitness. **Figure 3.1** lists several activities, each followed by an *S* if its benefits are mainly skill-related, an *H* if its benefits are health-related, or a *B* if it is beneficial for both. The chart also ranks each activity according to the individual components of skill- and health-related fitness.

✓ Reading Check

Extend Name a sport or activity that requires at least three components of skill-related fitness.

TECHNOLOGY FILE

Recording Reaction Times in a Spreadsheet

The "reaction time" test involves dropping a 30-cm ruler in front of subjects with their thumbs and index fingers on either side of the zero mark on the ruler, about 1 cm apart. Ask students to test reaction time of family members and friends and then collect additional data on their height, age, and gender. Have students record the data in a spreadsheet and create scattergraphs using the spreadsheet Chart function. Ask students to compare the reaction time scores to the other variables and to look for relationships (i.e., height and reaction times).

FIGURE 3.1

BENEFITS OF PHYSICAL ACTIVITIES
Which of these sports or activities are you currently involved in?
How do they compare in each of the 11 areas of skill- and health-related fitness?

Activity or Sport	Skill-Related Fitness						Health-Related Fitness				
	A	B	R	P	S	C	CF	F	MS	ME	BC
Archery *S*	1	3	1	1	3	4	1	2	3	1	1
Backpacking *H*	2	2	1	2	2	2	3	3	2	4	3
Ballet *B*	4	4	2	3	2	4	3	4	4	3	3
Baseball *S*	3	3	4	4	3	4	1	3	3	1	1
Basketball *B*	4	3	4	4	3	4	3	3	3	3	3
Bicycling *H*	1	4	2	1	2	2	4	2	2	4	3
Canoeing *B*	1	3	2	3	3	3	2	2	3	3	2
Circuit training *H*	2	2	1	3	3	2	2	3	3	4	3
Dance, aerobic *H*	3	2	2	1	1	4	4	3	2	3	4
Dance, social *H*	3	2	2	1	2	3	2	2	2	2	2
Fitness calisthenics *H*	3	2	1	2	2	2	1	4	2	3	2
Football *S*	4	3	4	4	4	3	2	2	4	2	2
Golf (walking) *B*	2	2	1	3	1	4	2	4	2	1	4
Gymnastics *B*	4	4	3	4	2	4	2	4	4	4	4
Handball *H*	4	2	3	3	3	4	4	3	2	3	3
Hiking *H*	2	2	1	2	1	2	3	2	2	4	3
Interval training *H*	2	2	1	1	2	2	4	1	3	3	4
Jogging *H*	1	2	1	1	1	2	4	1	2	3	4
Judo *S*	4	3	4	4	4	4	1	4	2	2	3
Karate *S*	4	3	4	4	4	4	1	4	4	2	3
Racquetball *B*	4	2	3	2	3	4	4	2	2	3	3
Rope jumping *H*	3	2	2	2	2	3	3	2	2	3	3
Rowing *H*	3	2	1	4	2	4	4	2	2	4	4
Skating, ice *B*	3	4	2	2	3	4	3	2	2	3	4
Skating, in-line *B*	3	4	1	2	3	4	3	2	1	3	4
Skiing, cross-country *B*	3	2	1	4	2	4	4	3	2	3	4
Skiing, downhill *B*	4	4	3	3	3	4	2	3	3	2	3
Soccer *B*	4	2	3	3	3	4	4	2	2	3	4
Softball (fast pitch) *S*	3	2	4	3	3	4	3	2	3	1	1
Softball (slow pitch) *S*	2	2	3	3	3	4	2	1	3	1	1
Surfing *B*	4	4	3	3	2	4	2	3	2	3	4
Swimming *H*	3	2	1	2	2	4	4	3	2	3	4
Tennis *B*	3	2	3	3	3	4	4	2	3	3	3
Volleyball *B*	3	2	3	2	3	4	3	2	3	2	3
Walking *H*	1	2	1	1	1	2	3	1	1	2	3
Weight training *H*	2	3	1	2	1	3	1	3	4	3	4

Legend

S = Skill-Related Fitness	2 = Fair	P = Power	MS = Muscular Strength
H = Health-Related Fitness	1 = Low	S = Strength	ME = Muscular Endurance
B = Both of the Above	A = Agility	C = Coordination	BC = Body Composition
4 = Excellent	B = Balance	CF = Cardiovascular Fitness	
3 = Good	R = Reaction Time	F = Flexibility	

Figure 3.1 Use this figure to let students compare health-related and skill-related fitness activities. Have students choose three of the activities or sports listed in Figure 3.1 in which they either have participated in themselves or might want to participate. Have them rate their current skill-related fitness and health-related fitness compared with the levels required in the figure. Then have them make a list of the skill-related and/or health-related fitness items they think they would need to improve in order to successfully participate in the activities and sports they chose. **TEKS C4D**

Activity

Substances that may enhance strength and power are sometimes used by athletes to increase their performance. Have interested students research the dangers of performance-enhancing drugs. Ask: In addition to steroids, what are some other substances used by athletes to improve their strength and endurance? What are the health risks of using these substances? Have volunteers present their findings to the class. **L3**

Enrichment

Creating Individual Fitness Tests When you feel that students have a thorough understanding of the different components of fitness, have them create their own tests for measuring the components of both skill-related and health-related fitness. Students may use the Fitness Checks as background information to help them create their own tests. Have the class select the best test for measuring each component. Then have each student complete those tests, keeping their own scores. Once all testing has been completed, have students devise class norms based on the test results.

Student Edition TEKS

Page 76: C4D, C5B
Page 77: C4D

Demonstrating Skill-Related Fitness

OBJECTIVES

- Test the six components of skill-related fitness.
- Assess performance using Fitness Ratings Charts.

TEACHING STRATEGIES

Explain to the class that this activity is meant only to introduce them to the different parts of skill-related fitness. It is not a test for a grade, nor is it a play activity. The activities should be conducted safely and responsibly. Encourage students to have fun but also to be serious about understanding the concepts.

Divide the class into pairs. Demonstrate each of the activities to be performed. Provide a safe environment for conducting all activities. **TEKS C4C**

Distribute *Fitness Check Worksheet 3-1*. Have students record results on the Fitness Ratings Chart to assess performance. ☞

Demonstrating Agility: Picking Up Lines

This activity requires some warm-up first. **TEKS C1A**

- Use tape or markers to prepare the course.
- Try to avoid a slick surface and use nonskid footwear. **TEKS C3A**
- Have partners count out five seconds.
- Have students record results on the Fitness Ratings Chart to assess performance.

Demonstrating Skill-Related Fitness

In this activity, you will do six tests, one for each of the six skill-related fitness components. As you progress through later chapters, you may want to retake one or more of these tests to assess your progress.

Demonstrating Agility: Picking Up Lines

Procedure:
1. Mark off two parallel lines 5 feet apart.
2. Start at one line. Run to the other line and bend over to touch the line with your hand, as in **Figure 3.2**.
3. Reverse your direction and return to the start, again bending over to touch the line.
4. Repeat steps 2 and 3. Do not stop running until you have completed two full circuits.
5. Use the Fitness Ratings Chart for Picking Up Lines to assess your performance.

Fitness Ratings: Picking Up Lines

Time	Rating
Under 5 seconds	Pass
Over 5 seconds	Needs work

Figure 3.2

Demonstrating Balance: Blind One-Leg Stand

Procedure:
1. Stand on one foot.
2. Gently pull your other leg up and back. Do not pull back in a way that puts stress on your knee. Do not wobble or hop. Close your eyes (see **Figure 3.3**).
3. Try to hold this position for ten seconds.
4. Use the Fitness Ratings Chart for the Blind One-Leg Stand to assess your performance.

Fitness Ratings: Blind One-Leg Stand

Time	Rating
10 seconds or more	Pass
Under 10 seconds	Needs work

Figure 3.3

More About . . .

AGILITY TESTS There are many other ways to measure the skill-related component of agility besides "Picking Up Lines." One popular test that personal fitness instructors have used for many years requires the student to run as fast as possible on a flat surface for 30 feet up and back, then run two figure-8 patterns, and finish by repeating the first step. If a teen can complete the agility course in less than 16.7 seconds for males or less than 18.4 seconds for females, he or she is considered to be in the range of good to better in skill-related fitness levels.
Source: Cureton, T.K., *Physical Fitness of Athletes*, University of Illinois Press, 1951.

Demonstrating Coordination: Foot-and-Ball Volley

Procedure:

1. For this activity you will need a ball at least the size of a tennis ball or bigger.
2. Drop the ball over your dominant foot, as shown in see **Figure 3.4.** (Your dominant foot is the one you usually kick with.)
3. Try to bounce the ball off your foot three consecutive times.
4. Now try it with your other foot.
5. Use the Fitness Ratings Chart for Foot-and-Ball Volley to assess your performance.

Figure 3.4

Fitness Ratings: Foot-and-Ball Volley

Number of Bounces	Rating
3 bounces or more	Pass
Under 3 bounces	Needs work

Demonstrating Power: Standing Long Jump

Procedure:

1. Lie on the floor.
2. Have a partner mark off two lines, one at the top of your head and one at your feet.
3. Stand up. Starting at either line, jump as far as you can toward the other line. (See **Figure 3.5.**)
4. Use the Fitness Ratings Chart for the Standing Long Jump to assess your performance.

Fitness Ratings: Standing Long Jump

Jump Height	Rating
Jump your height or greater	Pass
Jump less than your height	Needs work

Figure 3.5

continued on next page

Lesson 1 Health-Related and Skill-Related Fitness   79

Balance: Blind One-Leg Stand

- Make sure students are clear of any wall or obstacle they might hit if they fall.
- Have partners count aloud to ten.
- Students may attempt the activity more than once.

Demonstrating Coordination: Foot and Ball Volley

- Use a tennis ball or a soft rubber ball that is slightly bigger.
- Try to avoid a slick surface and use nonskid footwear. **TEKS C3A**
- Kicks should not be hard. Students should be properly spaced to avoid being hit with a ball.
- Explain to students that this is a test of foot-eye coordination.

Demonstrating Power: Standing Long Jump

- The activity area should be a smooth, nonslip surface. Students should wear shoes with a nonskid sole. **TEKS C3A**
- Have students use their arms as well as their legs to propel their bodies.
- Partners should observe and mark the distance of the jumps. Repeated attempts are allowed.

SPEED TESTS There are many ways to measure the skill-related component of speed besides the "Push and Clap" test. Two popular speed tests are the 40-yard and 50-yard dash. The 40-yard dash is a sport-specific test often used in football training, and the 50-yard dash is used to evaluate speed. For football players the 40-yard dash score varies by position. For example, a good high school wide receiver can probably run the 40 in around 4.6 seconds. For the 50-yard dash, norms have been developed for students to evaluate their speed based on gender and age.

Student Edition TEKS

Page 78: C4C
Page 79: C4C

Demonstrating Speed: Push and Clap

- This activity is intended to introduce the concept of push-up and hand speed.

- Have students perform this activity on a mat.

- This activity will require adequate upper body strength, so encourage students by telling them that one clap is good and two claps is great.

Demonstrating Reaction Time: Hand Slap

- Many students are familiar with this activity.

- Match students equally by body size and gender as much as possible.

- Be sure to remind students that this activity involves only a light touch; it is not intended for hitting someone hard. This is a test to demonstrate speed. **TEKS C3A**

Demonstrating Speed: Push and Clap

Procedure:
1. Lie face down on the floor in a push-up position.
2. Place your hands on the floor so that they line up alongside your chest.
3. Push your body up in the air. Try to clap your hands twice before returning to the floor, as in **Figure 3.6**. Use a mat if one is available.
4. Use the Fitness Ratings Chart for Push and Clap to assess your performance.

Fitness Ratings: Push and Clap	
Number of Completions	**Rating**
1 completion	Pass
No completions	Needs work

Figure 3.6

Demonstrating Reaction Time: Hand Slap

Procedure:
1. Stand facing a partner.
2. Have your partner place his or her hands palms up. Place your hands palms down over your partner's hands. Allow 4 inches of space between your hands and your partner's.
3. Your partner will quickly attempt to touch the top of your hands as in **Figure 3.7**. Try to remove your hands before they are touched.
4. Use the Fitness Ratings Chart for Hand Slap to assess your performance.

Fitness Ratings: Hand Slap	
Result	**Rating**
Do not touch	Pass
Touch	Needs work

Figure 3.7

Myths & Realities

Myth 1   Good athletes are born, so if you don't have the best genes, you will not be able to compete at high levels of performance or competition.

Fact 1   While genes play an important role in high-level performance (they can account for up to 30 to 50 percent of a person's ability to perform, depending on the sport), training is still key. You can have all the best genes, but if you don't train hard, you won't be able to outperform a person who has less of a genetic advantage but who does train hard.

Health-Related Fitness, Skill-Related Fitness, and You

According to some estimates, heredity may account for as much as 70 percent of your skill-related fitness and 40 percent of your health-related fitness. Does this mean that only people born with the gift of speed or strength can achieve high levels of fitness in these areas? Not necessarily. Low levels of fitness do not have to be permanent. Any of these 11 components can be nurtured and developed. One key is practice.

Practice is important for anyone who wants to improve his or her skills and performance in a specific game or sport. Agility, coordination, and power, in particular, are skill-related components that can be improved through practice. Often, one skill-related ability requires the use of other skill-related components. For this reason, working to improve one skill may lead to benefits in other areas.

Health-related fitness can be improved by participating in many physical activities that are not necessarily related to sports or games. In fact, some of the most popular physical activities, such as swimming, bicycling, hiking, and jogging, are not sports- or game-related.

In the lessons and chapters to come, you will learn exercises and activities that will lead to improvements in your health-related and skill-related fitness. Whether you make these behaviors a part of your lifestyle is up to you. The next step is yours.

Hidden Benefits
Among the benefits of developing your health-related and skill-related fitness is your improved ability to demonstrate positive self-management and social skills needed to work with others. Think of an example when you have had an opportunity to recognize a potential conflict during a game, sport, or physical activity. Explain how you were able to apply positive behaviors and find a way to resolve the conflict so that you and your teammates could continue playing or participating in an activity.

Lesson 1 Review

Using complete sentences, answer the following questions on a sheet of paper.

Reviewing Facts and Vocabulary

1. **Recall** What physical activities require a high level of balance, coordination, and speed? Why?

2. **Vocabulary** List and define each of the five health-related fitness components.

Thinking Critically

3. **Compare and Contrast** What is the difference between health-related and skill-related fitness?

4. **Evaluation** Clint and Ellen are both 15. Clint is interested in developing his skill-related fitness, particularly his speed and agility. Ellen is interested in developing her health-related fitness, particularly her muscular endurance. Make a list of hints and tips you can give Clint and Ellen to help them meet their initial goals.

Personal Fitness Planning

Assessing Progress Make a chart of your Fitness Ratings on the "Fitness Check" activities in Chapters 1 and 3. In which health-related and skill-related activities do you perform well? Which are your weaker areas? Make a list and plan to improve in as many of those areas as possible.

Lesson 1 Review

Answers to Lesson 1 Review

1. Answers will vary but should include examples from pages 75–76.
2. Answers should include specific descriptions from page 72.
3. Health-related fitness is your ability to become and stay physically healthy, and skill-related fitness is your ability to maintain high levels of performance on the field of play.
4. Answers will vary, but Clint might practice sport-specific drills; Ellen might practice strengthening exercises.

3 ASSESS

EVALUATING THE LESSON

Assign and discuss the Lesson 1 Review.

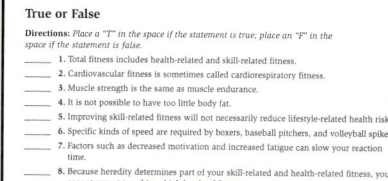

RETEACHING

Have students describe an example of ways to improve their health- or skill-related fitness.

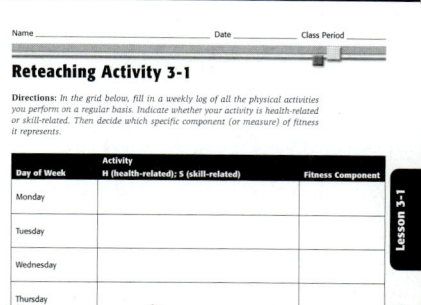

ENRICHMENT

Have students conduct a survey of three or four school athletes. The athletes are to rate the six components of skill-related fitness in terms of their importance in succeeding at the sport.

4 CLOSE

Ask students to identify which of the Fitness Check tests they performed best and why they did well.

FITT and the
Principle of Overload

1 MOTIVATE

GETTING STARTED

- Ask students if they have ever seen or used the concepts of frequency, intensity, time, and type as they relate to physical activity and exercise.
- Distribute copies of *Guided Practice Activity 3-2* for students to use while studying this lesson. 📁

IN THIS LESSON

- **Active Mind—Active Body** *Taking Your Resting Pulse, p. 86*

INTRODUCING VOCABULARY

- Explain to students that the term *exercise prescription* refers to the concept that exercise can be prescribed in a similar manner as medicine. Too little exercise will not be of much benefit, and too much exercise can be harmful to your personal fitness. Thus, an accurate exercise prescription can help a person acquire personal fitness more effectively.
- Have students use *Vocabulary Worksheet 3* or the PuzzleMaker software to practice vocabulary terms for this lesson. ELL 📁 💿

What You Will Do

- List the components of exercise prescription.
- Describe the overload principle and how it applies to a fitness program.
- Apply the physiological principles of frequency, intensity, time, and type to a fitness program.
- Describe methods of evaluating levels of intensity in a workout.

Terms to Know

exercise prescription
overload principle
frequency
cardiovascular conditioning
intensity
heart rate
perceived exertion
talk test
time
type

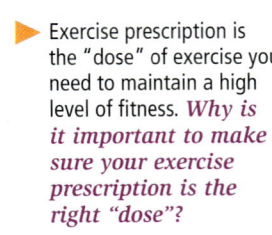
▶ Exercise prescription is the "dose" of exercise you need to maintain a high level of fitness. *Why is it important to make sure your exercise prescription is the right "dose"?*

FITT and the Principle of Overload

Has a doctor ever prescribed a medication for you? Such medications come with a recommended dose on the label. A dose is the amount a person needs to receive the medication's benefit.

Did you know that physical activity and exercise are also dose-related? Unlike medications, these fitness behaviors never require a doctor's prescription. *You* control the dose. In so doing, you also control the benefits.

82   Chapter 3 Designing a Personal Fitness Program

LESSON 2 RESOURCES

Teacher Classroom Resources
📁 Guided Practice Activity 3-2
📁 Active Mind—Active Body Worksheet 3-2
📁 Reteaching Activity 3-2
📁 Lesson Quiz 3-2

Reproducible Charts and Graphs
📁 Reproducible Masters 3-2, 3-3, 3-4
Multimedia
💿 Vocabulary PuzzleMaker
🖱 Transparencies 18, 19

Your Exercise Prescription

In order to be effective, a medical prescription must be exact. It must include the name of the medicine, the dose needed, and how often the medicine should be taken. The same information needs to be present in an **exercise prescription.** This is *a breakdown of how often you need to work, how hard, the length of time per session, and the type of activity or exercise performed.* As shown in **Figure 3.8,** these factors of exercise prescription are often referred to as FITT: *frequency, intensity, time,* and *type.*

Like medications, exercise prescriptions are governed by three scientific principles: the overload principle, the specificity principle, and the progression principle. The **overload principle** states that *in order to improve your level of fitness, you must increase the amount of regular activity or exercise that you normally do.* You will learn more about the principles of specificity and progression in Lessons 3 and 4.

These principles are applied to an exercise program by adjusting any or all of the FITT factors in your prescription. These are:

- *frequency*—how often you work.
- *intensity*—how hard you work.
- *time*—the length of time, or duration, that you work.
- *type*—the specific type or mode of activity you choose.

✔ Reading Check

Summarize List and describe the components of exercise prescription.

FIGURE 3.8

THE PARTS OF FITT

FITT stands for frequency, intensity, time, and type of activity. *How can each of these aspects of working out be adjusted to suit your goals and experience level?*

Frequency	Intensity	Time/Duration	Type

Lesson 2 FITT and the Principle of Overload **83**

More About . . .

EXERCISE PRESCRIPTION The American College of Sports Medicine (ACSM) published *The Guidelines for Exercise Testing and Exercise Prescription* in the 1970s. This guide, now in its sixth printing, provides detailed information about how adolescents and adults can achieve lifetime personal fitness. The ACSM notes that exercise prescription is both an art and a science. This is because instructors and students need to understand how to apply scientific principles for sound physical activity and exercise programs, as well as understanding what actually works for each individual.

2 TEACH

Explaining

Ask students whether they or anyone they know has used the FITT formula in order to set up an exercise program. Then ask them whether they or their acquaintances were successful at applying all parts of the FITT formula. Then have them describe overload as a component of an exercise prescription. Ask for examples of how they can apply this physiological principle to their fitness program. **L1**
TEKS C1A3, C4F5

USING VISUALS

Figure 3.8 Display *Transparency 18* to explain the FITT formula to students. Have students design a one-day exercise program by using the examples in the FITT formula table. Ask them to write their program on a sheet of paper and exchange it with a fellow classmate. Then have students discuss for two to three minutes the programs their partners designed.

✔ Reading Check

Exercise prescription includes frequency, intensity, time, type, and the overload principle.
TEKS C4F

Student Edition TEKS

Page 82: C1A, C4F
Page 83: C4F

USING VISUALS

Figure 3.9 Introduce the concept of frequency using information provided in the figure. Display *Reproducible Master 3-2* to discuss ways that students can apply these physiological principles to exercise and training. How is frequency adjusted for fitness level? Review the overload principle and ask students to give a specific example. ☞ **TEKS C1A4**

Caption answer: Answers will depend on which stage students are at in their personal fitness program: beginner, average, or fit.

Activity

Have students list their current specific fitness goals and their current perceived or measured levels of fitness. Then have them add the other priorities and responsibilities in their daily lives. Discuss strategies for incorporating physical activities into their routines. This assignment should take only five to ten minutes of class time. Remember, students should be physically active for most of the class period. **L1**

✔ **Reading Check**

When exercise frequency is limited, progress will be limited.

FIGURE 3.9

FREQUENCY OF EXERCISES FOR VARYING FITNESS LEVELS

The frequency of your activity depends largely on your fitness level.
Based on this chart and your current level of activity, how often should you exercise in order to reach overload?

Type of Activity	Frequency for Beginners	Frequency for Those of Average- to High-Fitness Levels
Cardiovascular conditioning	3–5 days per week	4–6 days per week
Weight training	2–3 days per week	3–5 days per week

Frequency

Frequency refers to *the number of times per week you engage in physical activity or exercise.* Exercise that is infrequent results in limited progress. Exercising too often can increase the possibility of injury.

How frequently do you need to do a particular activity or exercise in order to achieve overload? The answer to that question will depend on the intensity of your workouts, how much time you invest in each, and the type of activity you do. Other considerations include:

- **Your specific fitness goals.** Do you want to raise your levels of health-related fitness? Do you want to improve your performance on the playing field? One basic goal that should be part of every teen's fitness program is **cardiovascular conditioning.** This consists of *exercises or activities that improve the efficiency of the heart, lungs, blood, and blood vessels.*
- **Your current level of fitness.** Are you currently inactive? Do you regularly play sports or take part in other physical activities? The chart in **Figure 3.9** shows suggested ranges of workout frequency for people at different fitness levels.
- **Other priorities and responsibilities in your daily life.** As a teen, one of your chief responsibilities is school—getting an education. You probably also have after-school activities. Maybe you hold down a part-time job. You will want to set a frequency for exercising that fits in with your other priorities and obligations.

✔ **Reading Check**

Explain What is the result if exercise frequency is limited?

INCLUSION STRATEGIES

SPECIAL NEEDS AND MAXIMUM HEART RATE When active muscle mass is limited by paralysis, amputation, or muscular dystrophies, the individual will normally have a lower MHR (maximum heart rate). Any student with central nervous system damage (such as cerebral palsy or minimal brain damage) will have a lower MHR, as will students on certain medications. These students should be encouraged to "underwork" or modify their FITT by starting with a lower intensity than average and increasing their frequency of training more slowly.

Intensity

Intensity refers to *the difficulty or exertion level of your physical activity or exercise.* If the intensity is too low, progress is limited. If you work too hard, you fatigue quickly and increase your risk for injury.

How intense your workouts are will depend partly on the other three factors in the FITT formula: *frequency, time,* and *type.* Several additional methods can help you determine your intensity needs. These are explained in the sections that follow. The "Active Mind—Active Body" in Lesson 3 will help you to understand how increasing intensity affects your heart rate.

Percentage of Maximum Heart Rate. For cardiovascular conditioning, a reliable measure of intensity is a percentage of your maximum heart rate. The term **heart rate** refers to *the number of times your heart beats per minute.* Another name for heart rate is pulse. You will learn how to take your pulse in the "Active Mind—Active Body" activity on page **86.**

To compute your *maximum heart rate,* subtract your age from the number 220. (If you are currently 15, for example, your maximum heart rate is 205 beats per minute.) Once you know your maximum heart rate, you can refer to the chart in **Figure 3.10** for conditioning guidelines. As with the other components of exercise prescription, you need to take into account your current level of fitness. Beginners should work at a lower level of intensity than those with average-to-high fitness levels.

FIGURE 3.10

INTENSITY OF EXERCISES FOR VARYING FITNESS LEVELS

Your heart rate can help you determine the intensity of your workout. *Using your maximum heart rate, how many times should your heart beat per minute if you are 16 years old and just beginning cardiovascular training?*

Type of Activity	Intensity for Beginners	Intensity for Those of Average- to High-Fitness Levels
Cardiovascular conditioning	60 to 70 percent maximum heart rate	70 to 90 percent maximum heart rate
Weight training	60 to 70 percent maximum strength	70 to 90 percent maximum strength

Activity

Have students set a goal to increase their aerobic activity level in order to improve their cardiorespiratory endurance. To achieve results, students should work within their maximum-heart-rate range. Encourage them to keep a log of their activities and to assess their resting heart rates each week. After six weeks, have students graph their resting heart rates. If the number has decreased, they have achieved their goal. **L1**

Discussing

Have students calculate the maximum heart rate of their family members. Ask them what happens to maximum heart rate as one ages. (*It goes down.*) **L1**

USING VISUALS

Figure 3.10 Discuss with students the importance of understanding intensity for varying levels of fitness.
Caption answer: Between 124 and 142 beats per minute for cardiorespiratory training and 102 and 119 pounds for weight lifting.

What Teens *Want* to Know

How accurate is the *220 minus age* equation? While this equation is used by fitness instructors around the world to predict maximum heart rate (MHR), the equation is not perfect, as is true with most predictions. It has an error margin of plus or minus 10 beats per minute. This means that if you are 15 years old and have a predicted MHR of 205 beats per minute, you can feel confident that your true MHR is between 195 and 215 beats per minute. The only true way to determine MHR is to test the person's physical limits; for example, by running on a treadmill while measuring heart rate.

Student Edition TEKS

Page 84: C4F
Page 85: C1A

Active Mind Active Body

Taking Your Resting Pulse

Pair students and have them work with partners for this activity. Distribute *Active Mind–Active Body Worksheet 3-2* for students to record their results. 📁

Teaching Tips

- Another easy way for students to determine their heart rate is to count their pulse for six seconds and then add a zero to the number they get. This is the same as multiplying the number by 10.

- Encourage students to take their pulse rate for 15, 30, and 60 seconds to see whether they are getting consistent results and have mastered the concepts.

Apply and Conclude

Students should get similar results for readings at the carotid and radial pulses. However, they may find it easier to take the carotid pulse because it is usually easier to find than the radial pulse. Explain that if they take their pulse when they first wake up, it will be lower than later in the day, when they are more alert. Taking their pulse upon waking will give them an accurate resting heart rate.

Active Mind Active Body

Taking Your Resting Pulse

As noted, your heart rate, or pulse, can help you figure out your intensity needs for physical activity or exercise. In this activity, you will learn how to measure your heart rate.

What You Will Need

- Pen or pencil
- Paper
- Stopwatch, wristwatch, or clock

What You Will Do

1. Using two fingers on one hand, find the carotid (kuh-ROT-id) pulse on *one side* of your throat. Do *not* use your thumb, which has a pulse of its own.
2. *Press lightly* until you feel a slight throbbing sensation.
3. Using a clock or watch, count the number of throbs, or beats, in six seconds.
4. Record the number of beats. Add a zero to get your heart rate for one minute.
5. Now find your radial pulse on the thumb side of your wrist.
6. Repeat steps 3 and 4.

Apply and Conclude

What reading did you get for your carotid pulse? Was it the same as for your radial pulse? Try taking a partner's pulse. To get your true resting pulse, you will need to perform one of these techniques the instant you wake up in the morning. Why would taking your pulse then make a difference?

hotlink

RPE
For more on using the RPE scale, see Chapter 7, page **209**.

Perceived Exertion. Another method of determining intensity is using perceived exertion. This is *a measure of how hard you feel you are working during physical activity or exercise.* This rating is usually used to determine intensity of cardiorespiratory workouts. **Ratings of perceived exertion (RPE)** are based on your awareness of specific body "cues." These cues include how hard you are breathing, your heart rate, your body temperature, and any muscle or skeletal discomfort.

The perceived exertion scale in **Figure 3.11** assigns numerical values to different levels of perceived exertion. Notice that the range is from 6 ("no exertion at all") to 20 ("maximum exertion"). What rating would you assign to yourself at this moment?

Talk Test. A fourth method for monitoring your intensity uses the perceived exertion scale. It is also used in cardiorespiratory evaluations. This method is the talk test. It is *a measure of your ability to carry on a conversation while engaged in physical activity or exercise.* For example, if you are able to talk with some slight effort during a workout, your RPE is probably between 11 and 16 (light to vigorous). This is an appropriate intensity level for your fitness program.

TECHNOLOGY FILE

Pulse Monitors

Pulse rates (or heart rates) can be measured with other, higher-tech options. These options include telemetry systems that use an elastic chest strap transmitter and a radio receiver that looks like a wristwatch. Telemetry system monitors transmit the frequency of a person's heart rate from the transmitter to the receiver. Other less expensive (but less accurate) heart rate monitors include pulse bars that the student holds with both hands, or finger-attached pulse monitors that clip to the end of a student's finger.

If talking is very difficult or impossible, you are overdoing it. If you are able to talk effortlessly, you are not working hard enough to derive benefits.

Percentage of Maximum Strength. For weight training, a useful gauge of intensity is a percentage of your **maximum strength.** *Maximum strength* is a measure of how much weight you can lift one time for a given exercise. Suppose, for example, that for a particular exercise you were able to lift 100 pounds just once. Then your maximum strength for that exercise would be 100.

Once you know your maximum strength, you can use the guidelines in **Figure 3.10** (on page 85) to determine a recommended intensity.

hot link

maximum strength
For more on maximum strength, see Chapter 10, page **308**.

hot link

It is important for students to understand the concept of maximum strength, as it is often used to set exercise prescriptions for weight lifting. Have students review Chapter 10 for more on maximum strength.

FIGURE 3.11

PERCEIVED EXERTION SCALE
This scale reflects how hard a person feels he or she has worked during physical activity or exercise.

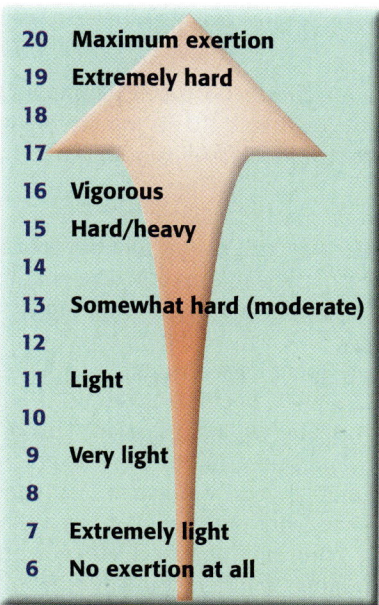

20	**Maximum exertion**
19	**Extremely hard**
18	
17	
16	**Vigorous**
15	**Hard/heavy**
14	
13	**Somewhat hard (moderate)**
12	
11	**Light**
10	
9	**Very light**
8	
7	**Extremely light**
6	**No exertion at all**

Source: Borg's Perceived Exertion and Pain Scales, 2002[1]

✔ **Reading Check**

Identify What are the three methods for evaluating intensity that are used in cardiorespiratory conditioning?

USING VISUALS

Figure 3.11 Use *Transparency 19* to explain the Perceived Exertion Scale. Have students determine how they usually feel on the RPE scale when they engage in physical activities and regular exercise. Ask them to explain the relationship between physical fitness and health. Ask students why they do not need to work at the levels of 17–20 very often. *(RPEs of 17–20 are usually associated with high-intensity or maximal exercise. These levels of exertion are not required for average levels of personal fitness but may sometimes be required for athletes seeking peak performance.)* **TEKS C4A**

✔ **Reading Check**

Any one of the following criteria can be used to evaluate intensity: FITT, percentage of maximum heart rate, perceived exertion, talk test, and percentage of maximum strength.

Student Edition TEKS

Page 87: C1A

More About . . .

PERCEIVED EXERTION SCALE Dr. Gunnar Borg developed the Perceived Exertion Scale in the 1970s as an alternative way to help people monitor their exercise intensity. Dr. Borg originally tested several young adults in their early 20s riding stationary cycles at different intensities while he measured their heart rates and RPE responses. Based on the data he collected, he determined that a strong relationship existed between the heart rate responses and the RPE responses of the subjects. Therefore, he was able to use the scale effectively as an optional way to measure exercise intensity.

USING VISUALS

Figure 3.12 Have students examine the information in the chart and determine which column applies to their personal fitness level. *Caption answer: Exercise sessions should be 20 to 30 minutes for beginning cardiovascular training and 45 minutes to one hour for the experienced weight lifter.*

Activity

Have students list the components of their exercise prescription. How will they incorporate warm-up and cooldown? Have them record the total amount of time they spent doing continuous physical activity and exercise during the past three days. Then ask them if they met the guidelines in Figure 3.12. Finally, ask them why or why not. Have students apply the FITT principle to determine where they need improvement. **L1 TEKS CF4**

Reading Check

Type is a component of FITT that refers to the particular type or kind of physical activity or exercise chosen. **TEKS CF4**

Student Edition TEKS

Page 89: C1A, C4F, C4G

FIGURE 3.12

EXERCISE TIME BASED ON FITNESS LEVEL

Based on this chart, how long should your exercise sessions last if you are just beginning cardiovascular conditioning? How long should sessions last if you are an experienced weight lifter?

Type of Activity	Time for Beginners	Time for Those of Average- to High-Fitness Levels
Cardiovascular conditioning	20–30 minutes	35 minutes to 1 hour
Weight training	20–30 minutes	45 minutes to 1 hour

Time

Time refers to *the duration of a single workout, usually measured in minutes or hours.* A workout that is too brief may result in limited progress. A workout that goes on too long will increase your risk for injuries.

Once again, your specific goals, current fitness level, frequency, intensity, time, and type will play a role in determining how much time to devote to a particular workout. The goal of weight loss, for example, is best accomplished by working longer at a lower intensity. Weight-training time will be determined by the number of exercises done and time spent between sets.

As **Figure 3.12** shows, beginning exercisers should do 20 to 30 minutes of cardiovascular work per session. This pace will allow you to progress slowly and safely and to increase gradually.

You may accumulate your minutes in one, continuous workout, or you may choose to work out in two or three shorter intervals per day. For example, you may choose to take a brisk walk for ten minutes in the morning, another in the afternoon, and again in the evening.

If you already have an average-to-high fitness level, you may find that the length of your workouts needs to be longer. One way to gradually increase your time is by alternating days with longer workouts (45 minutes to 1 hour) with days having shorter workouts (20 to 30 minutes).

The beginning weight trainer should spend 20 to 30 minutes per workout. How does this compare with the time needs of individuals with average to high fitness levels?

What Teens *Want* to Know

Can I get fitness benefits by working out for shorter periods of time? Yes, you can get fitness benefits (especially as a beginner) with three ten-minute sessions of exercise per day. According to most experts, however, people will benefit more as they improve their fitness levels if they work continuously for longer (e.g., 20 to 60 minutes). As an individual's fitness improves, fitness goals change, and more work is required to achieve those goals. For beginning exercisers or those rehabilitating from injury or surgery, short periods several times a day is an effective plan.

Type of Activity

The final component of the FITT formula is *type.* Type refers to *the particular type of physical activity or exercise you choose to do.* As a teen, you should be physically active on a daily basis. You should also engage in three or more sessions per week of activities that last at least 20 minutes and require moderate-to-vigorous levels of exertion. However, the choice and type of activity you participate in are up to you.

You should consider your personal fitness goals when choosing your activities. For example, if your goal is to improve your cardiovascular fitness, you should select activities that rate highly in that area, such as swimming, jogging, or cycling. Reviewing **Figure 3.1** in Lesson 1 can provide you with suggestions about the types of activities you may want to include in your program, depending on your personal goals.

The type of activity and the particular activity you do should be guided by several considerations. These include:

- What you enjoy doing
- How much time you have for the activity
- How much money you can afford to spend on needed equipment

 **Reading Check**

Describe What does *type* refer to in an exercise prescription?

Lesson 2 Review

Using complete sentences, answer the following questions on a sheet of paper.

Reviewing Facts and Vocabulary

1. **Vocabulary** What is an *exercise prescription*?
2. **Vocabulary** Describe *overload principle.*
3. **Recall** What is the talk test? How and when should you use it?

Thinking Critically

4. **Compare and Contrast** What is the difference between frequency and time in a fitness program?
5. **Evaluation** Mike and Bill are both age 15. Mike is beginning a cardiovascular training program. Bill, who runs every day, wants to increase his cardiovascular fitness level. What tips can you give Mike and Bill about how long they need to work to improve or maintain their cardiovascular fitness levels?

Personal Fitness Planning

Applying Physiological Principles Review the plans you made in Lesson 1 to improve your performance in health-related and skill-related activities. Schedule a fitness workout for yourself to practice some of your weaker activities over the next month. How would you apply overload, frequency, intensity, time, and type to your plan?

Lesson 2 FITT and the Principle of Overload   **89**

3 ASSESS

EVALUATING THE LESSON

Assign and discuss the Lesson 2 Review.

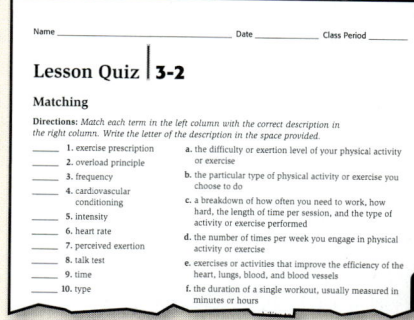

RETEACHING

Ask students to briefly explain how the FITT principle applies to fitness levels.

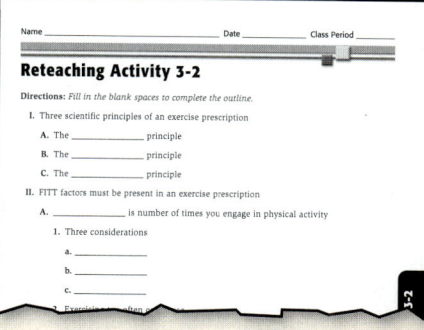

ENRICHMENT

Have students keep a personal fitness training log that records the FITT of their physical activity and exercise for four weeks. Ask them to review and assess their progress.

4 CLOSE

Ask students how the FITT for active athletes might compare to the FITT for most other individuals.

Lesson 2 Review

Answers to Lesson 2 Review

1. See definition on page 83.
2. See definition on page 83.
3. The talk test is the ability to carry on a conversation during physical activity.
4. Frequency is how often you work out; time is the length of time or duration.
5. Answers will vary but should include suggestions for frequency, intensity, time, and types of activities.

The Principle of Specificity

1 MOTIVATE

GETTING STARTED

- Ask students if they have specific changes they would like to make in their personal fitness profiles. Then ask what specific physical activities or exercises they would need to do to make those changes happen.

- Distribute copies of *Guided Practice Activity 3-3* for students to use while studying this lesson. 📁

IN THIS LESSON

- **Active Mind—Active Body** *The Effect of Intensity on Heart Rate, p. 92*

INTRODUCING VOCABULARY

- Explain to students that *short-term goals* refers to the idea that setting small, attainable goals will help them adhere to a regular physical activity or exercise program, which in turn will help them meet their long-term goals.

- Have students use *Vocabulary Worksheet 3* or the PuzzleMaker software to practice vocabulary terms for this lesson. ⒺⓁⓁ 📁 💿

What You Will Do

- Describe the specificity principle and how it applies to a fitness program.
- Design goals for your fitness program.

Terms to Know

specificity principle
short-term goals
long-term goals

▼ Targeting specific areas can help you achieve your overall goal. *What specific area of your personal fitness would you like to target?*

The Principle of Specificity

Sophia wanted to improve her overall grade point average. She came up with a plan that focused specifically on improving her grades in English and then biology, her two weakest areas. After a few months of concentrated effort in those classes, Sophia succeeded.

In the last lesson you learned about the principle of overload in exercise prescription. Sophia's story is an example of another important component of any plan: *specificity*. Not only did she work harder, she worked harder in specific areas that would help her reach her goal.

Specificity and Fitness

The specificity principle states that *overloading a particular component will lead to fitness improvements in that component alone.* Every exercise or physical activity works at least one component. For example, cardiovascular conditioning works a component, the heart muscle.

Any component or muscle that is not involved in the exercise or activity will remain unchanged. If you lift weights, for example, muscles that are not required to help move the weights will not become stronger.

Specificity and Change

The specific improvements that result from conditioning or training depend on the activity or exercise in which you engage. Suppose, for example, your goal is to become a better in-line skater. You will get the best results by focusing on conditioning and skill while you actually skate. Other activities, such as cycling on a regular basis, may lead to some improvements. However, these changes will not be as noticeable as they would be if your conditioning were *specific* to in-line skating.

To apply the specificity principle effectively, you need to evaluate your personal fitness goals and design a plan that will target specific areas of your fitness.

90　**Chapter 3**　Designing a Personal Fitness Program

LESSON 3 RESOURCES

Teacher Classroom Resources
- 📁 Guided Practice Activity 3-3
- 📁 Active Mind—Active Body Worksheet 3-3
- 📁 Reteaching Activity 3-3
- 📁 Lesson Quiz 3-3

Multimedia
- 💿 Vocabulary PuzzleMaker

Goal Setting

Setting goals is essential to the success of any effort. Some goals are short-term goals. These are *goals that can be accomplished relatively easily and quickly.* Other goals are long-term goals. They are *goals that are more complex and require considerable time and planning.* Fitness goals require both short-term and long-term planning. The **behavioral-change stairway,** discussed in Chapter 1, is a good strategy for achieving your fitness goals.

Note that high-performance goals require more specific and detailed fitness plans than those for moderate levels of fitness and health. Consider Rita's goal: to take a 50-mile mountain-bike trip. Rita's short-term preparation includes mountain-bike riding on hilly courses. She is also doing a good deal of cardiovascular conditioning. This is because she understands that her long-term goal requires more cardiorespiratory fitness than strength and flexibility fitness.

Whatever fitness goal you choose for yourself, it should follow at least the minimum recommendations for teens spelled out in *Healthy People 2010.* You should also keep these recommendations in mind.

- Keep your goals simple, specific, and realistic.
- List ways that will help you reach your goals.
- Seek help from others (friends, family, and teachers) who can help you achieve your goals.
- Be flexible in case you need to reevaluate your progress.
- Keep records to monitor your progress.
- Be positive. Avoid being negative about yourself.
- Reward yourself in a healthy way as you achieve your goals.

Special Situations

Your personal fitness program should be designed to optimize your health and well-being. This means that you should be prepared to adjust your personal fitness plan and/or activities as the need arises. Two situations that require such adjustments are injury and illness. Imagine, for example, that while jogging to improve cardiovascular fitness you twisted your ankle. You would probably have to stop jogging until your leg healed. In the meantime, you could engage in other activities such as rowing. This would enable you to adhere to your conditioning goals without placing added stress on your leg.

▶ The variety of physical activities that can be part of a personal fitness program is virtually limitless. *Which physical activities do you enjoy doing?*

behavioral-change stairway
For more on the steps of the behavioral change stairway, see Chapter 1, page **26.**

FITNESS Online
Keeping track of your personal fitness program is easy at **fitness.glencoe.com.**
Activity Set your personal fitness goals and record your progress in Glencoe's Online Fitness Journal.

---

2 TEACH

Explaining

Ask students to list one short-term and one long-term goal that corresponds to their step on the behavioral-change stairway to fitness. Have them explain and discuss how they think their goals will help them succeed in adopting a physically active lifestyle. **L1**

hotlink

Explain that the behavioral-change stairway is a useful guide for students wanting to adopt a physically active lifestyle. The behavioral-change stairway can help them adjust their short- and long-term goals to reflect their changing attitudes and behaviors.

FITNESS Online

The Online Fitness Journal in the Student Activities Section at **fitness.glencoe.com** allows students to update their personal fitness programs and submit progress to teachers electronically. **TEKS C4G**

Photo Follow-up

Ask students to discuss what type of benefits the teens in the photo are getting. Ask: Which new physical activities would you like to try? Why?

Student Edition TEKS
Page 90: C4F, C4G
Page 91: C4G

More About . . .

THE INTERACTION OF THE BEHAVIORAL-CHANGE STAIRWAY AND GOAL SETTING The Centers for Disease Control and Prevention (CDC) has developed informational booklets on goal setting to help individuals who are at different levels of progress on the behavioral-change stairway achieve success at adopting physically active lifestyles. The CDC five-step process includes Step 1, Thinking About Getting Fit; Step 2, The Benefits of Getting Fit; Step 3, Preparing to Become Physically Fit; Step 4, Feeling Good About Being Fit; and Step 5, Staying Fit for Good.

Active Mind Active Body
The Effect of Intensity on Heart Rate

Discuss with students what happens to the pulse following vigorous exercise. Tell them this activity will demonstrate the effects of exercise on heart rate.

Teaching Tips

- Distribute *Active Mind–Active Body Worksheet 3-3* and have students do the activity. 📁
- Pair students up and have them work in teams for this activity.
- Use the graph in Figure 3.13 to summarize the effects that different kinds of exercises have on heart rate.
- Ask a volunteer to read the definition of intensity on page 85. Ask students to apply the physiological principle related to intensity as they explain the effect of exercise on heart rate. Discuss why heart rate varies from one activity to another. **TEKS C1A**

Apply and Conclude

After completing the steps of this activity, have students work in groups to discuss the questions in Apply and Conclude. Ask the groups to compile their answers and take turns sharing with the class.

Active Mind Active Body
The Effect of Intensity on Heart Rate

Imagine taking your pulse after completing moderate to vigorous physical activity. Would you expect this measurement to differ from your resting pulse rate? Why? In this activity, you'll find out.

What You Will Need

- Pen or pencil
- Paper
- Stopwatch, wristwatch, or clock

What You Will Do

1. Sit or lie down and remain still and quiet for five minutes. Then record your pulse. Note that this is an estimate of your resting pulse.
2. Now perform each of the following activities in the order shown. Allow one to two minutes of recovery time between each activity. After each, record your pulse:

   a. Stand in place for two minutes.
   b. Walk around the track for one minute.
   c. Jog slowly around the track for one minute.
   d. Bound, jump, or hop around the track for forty seconds.
   e. Do thirty jumping jacks.
   f. Sprint for forty seconds. (As you run, be careful and leave space between you and your classmates.)
   g. Walk around the track for three minutes.
   h. Sit and stretch in place for two minutes.

3. Copy the following graph from **Figure 3.13** onto a separate sheet of paper. Make a dot to indicate the heart beats per minute for each activity. (Steps *g* and *h* both correspond to *Recovery*.) Then connect the dots with a thin line.

Apply and Conclude

Which activity generated the highest pulse? The lowest pulse? Which activity was the easiest? The most difficult? What is the relationship between pulse and intensity? Which of these activities would be the best choice for a daily 20-minute cardiovascular training session? Why?

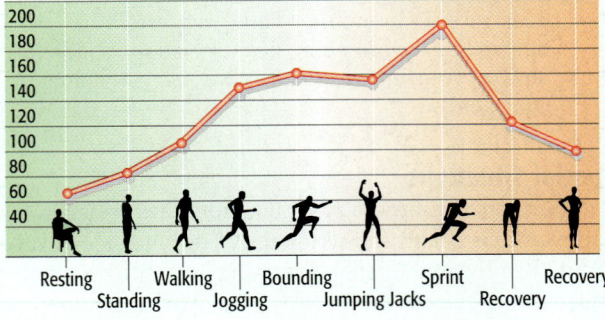

Sample Effects of Different Exercises on Your Heart Rate

Resting — Standing — Walking — Jogging — Bounding — Jumping Jacks — Sprint — Recovery — Recovery

Figure 3.13

Choosing Activities

As you plan the steps for meeting your goals, the types of activities you choose are especially important. You need to consider several factors when selecting physical activities for your fitness program.

- **Where you live.** You will most likely reach your fitness goals if you have a local and convenient place to participate in physical activities. For example, if cycling is part of your fitness plan, make sure you have a location that is safe and easy to access.
- **Time and place.** Schedule your program into your daily routine in a way that suits your needs and personality. Do not plan on jogging at 6:00 A.M. if you are not a morning person. The more thought you put into designing a schedule that

EQUIPMENT OPTIONS

TIMERS To measure the skill-related components of speed, power, and reaction time, teachers and coaches often use a stopwatch. More precise equipment options are now available. For example, speed guns and laser-barrier timers can measure speed (time) over 40 yards, which could be useful in a specific football-skill test. Power and reaction time can be tested with electronic timers that measure down to the thousandths of a second. These "high-tech" devices provide the precision required to evaluate individual scores for those trying to achieve higher levels of skill performance.

Any Body Can

Marion Jones

On the Fast Track

What must it feel like to win an Olympic gold medal, or even a bronze? Just ask Marion Jones. She's won both. In fact, she's won several of each!

Marion Jones was born on October 12, 1975, in Los Angeles, California. She was an excellent basketball player in high school, averaging 22.8 points per game during her senior year. Her first love, though, was track. She won several state competitions before graduating.

Marion entered the University of North Carolina in 1993. During her freshman year, she won the 100-meter dash and long jump in the ACC Conference Track Meet.

Marion burst onto the world track-and-field scene in 1998 and was named *Track and Field's* Athlete of the Year. Her best times were 10.65 seconds in the 100 meters, 21.62 in the 200 meters, and 50.36 in the 400 meters.

In the 2000 Olympic games, Marion represented the U.S. track team. She claimed three gold medals—one each for the 100 meters, 200 meters, and 4×400 meters relay. She won bronze medals in the long jump and 4×100 meters relay. She was named Athlete of the Year by the Associated Press, ESPN, and the International Amateur Athletic Federation (IAAF).

Marion Jones has become an international hero. Although not everyone has the talent and athletic resilience of Marion Jones, anyone can learn to develop his or her levels of health- and skill-related fitness. It's true: Any Body Can!

Research

Marion Jones has excelled in many track-and-field events as well as in basketball. Learn about another international figure, using print or online resources, who has excelled in different sports or physical activities. Share your findings with your physical education classmates.

Any Body Can

It is important to point out that women have only been able to participate in organized school sports since Title IX was passed in 1972. Great athletes such as Marion Jones have benefited from the opportunities that resulted from this law. Students should also recognize that Jones is a gifted individual who has trained very hard for over 10 years to become a world-class athlete. Finally, they should recognize that Jones is a role model for anyone hoping to make a commitment to a lifetime of personal fitness.

---

works with your weekly routine, the easier it will be to accomplish your goals.

- **Personal safety.** Always consider your personal safety. If you exercise outdoors, such as running, make sure you choose a safe, well-lit area. Use appropriate safety equipment and procedures for all activities. Avoiding injury is important to keeping your fitness plan on track.
- **Comprehensive planning.** Try to participate in activities that benefit all five areas of health-related fitness. You may want to focus on different aspects of health-related fitness, but it is important to consider all five areas as you vary your activities.

Participating regularly in various physical activities is the short-term goal that will help you achieve your long-term fitness goals. Choosing and scheduling these activities wisely will make your fitness program more effective.

LIFELINE

Applying Rules

When choosing physical activities that you would like to try, be sure you apply rules, procedures, and etiquette appropriately. For example, find out about rules and procedures that should be followed when using local facilities such as public basketball or tennis courts. Discuss your findings with the class.

✔ Reading Check
(page 94)

Records such as personal goals, days, time, distance and intensity of workouts, and other details can be included.

Activity

Ask students to describe how specificity can be effective as a component of an exercise prescription.

TEKS C4F

Lesson 3 The Principle of Specificity   **93**

More About . . .

MARION JONES Marion Jones is recognized as a star Olympic athlete and a media star. However, she is also a person of high character. She has faced athletic and personal adversity during her life and has prevailed to become a champion on and off the field. Marion injured her knee and back in competitions, yet was able to make successful comebacks to regain her world-class form. Marion is charismatic, well spoken, and enthusiastic. She is credited with attracting renewed attention to U.S. track and field.

Student Edition TEKS

Page 92: C1A, C2A, C4G
Page 93: C3B, C4B

3 ASSESS

EVALUATING THE LESSON

Assign and discuss the Lesson 3 Review.

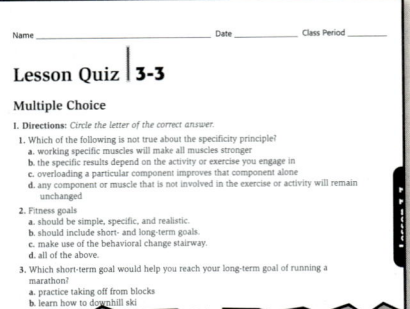

RETEACHING

Ask students to work in teams to describe the concept of specificity.

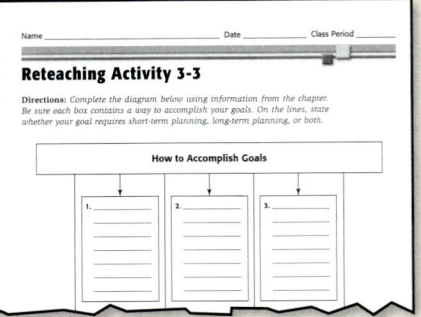

ENRICHMENT

Have students design a training log for physical activities or exercise routines with their top three short-term and long-term personal fitness goals.

4 CLOSE

Have students do research to find published examples of physical-activity logs and exercise logs.

Record Keeping

Record keeping is just as important to the beginning exerciser as it is to the high-performance athlete. Keeping records is critical to reaching your goals safely. It is convenient to keep records in a notebook or notepad. Your record-keeping book should include the following:

- Your goals (for example, to lose weight, get stronger, reduce stress, or run a marathon)
- The days you exercise
- Time, distance, and intensity (heart rate, amount of weight lifted on hard and easy days)
- Environmental conditions (temperature, smog, or humidity)
- Different routes you may have taken
- Places you exercised
- Specific activities or exercises you did
- Any injuries
- Foods and liquids consumed
- Weight loss or gain
- Progress

 Reading Check

Identify List three items that should be included in your fitness record-keeping notebook.

Lesson 3 Review

Using complete sentences, answer the following questions on a sheet of paper.

Reviewing Facts and Vocabulary

1. **Vocabulary** Describe the *specificity principle.* What is its role in a personal fitness plan?

2. **Recall** List four factors to consider when setting personal fitness goals.

3. **Recall** How can record keeping contribute positively to your personal fitness program?

Thinking Critically

4. **Compare and Contrast** What is the relationship between the type of physical activity and exercise and your personal fitness?

5. **Extend** Jody and Megan are both age 15. Jody has been participating in her personal fitness program for 6 months. She is in the maintenance stage of the behavioral change stairway. Megan is just planning to start her program. What tips can Jody give Megan to develop a record-keeping book that will help Megan reach the maintenance stage of the behavioral change stairway? Develop a log sheet that Megan might use to record her fitness progress.

Personal Fitness Planning

Applying Specificity Review the fitness plan that you designed in Lesson 1. Explain how you can apply the specificity principle to your plan. Also, adjust your plan so that you can remain active in case any of these situations arise: injuries, illnesses, a condition that requires taking medication.

Lesson 3 Review

Answers to Lesson 3 Review

1. See definition on page 90. To succeed, you must apply the specificity principle to your personal fitness plan.

2. Answers will vary but might include keeping the plan simple, specific, realistic, flexible, and positive.

3. Record keeping helps you determine whether you are meeting your personal fitness goals and any changes needed.

4. The type of physical activities or exercise you choose to participate in will affect specific results.

5. Answers and logs will vary.

The Principle of Progression

So far you have learned about two scientific principles, overload and specificity, involved in exercise prescription. They govern fitness behaviors and outcomes. In this lesson, you will learn about a third principle: *progression.*

Progression

Have you learned to play a musical instrument or speak a second language? When acquiring any new skill, you start slowly, beginning with the basics. When you are ready, you progress to more advanced levels.

This same rule applies to fitness conditioning. It is known as the **progression principle.** The principle holds that *as your fitness levels increase, so do the factors in your FITT.* The work gets harder as you progress, and *you* are the best judge of when you are ready to move forward. You make this decision by "listening" to your body. You analyze how you feel as you adapt to new challenges.

It is important to note that you should never increase all the factors in your FITT at once. Neither should you increase any one factor too fast or too soon. If you do, you risk an **overuse injury.** This is a muscular injury that results from overloading your muscles beyond a healthful point.

What You Will Do

- Describe the progression principle and how it applies to your fitness plan.
- Recognize the relationship between progression and trainability.
- Explain how overtraining and detraining contribute to negative health problems.
- Identify ways of optimizing your recovery from physical activity or exercise.

Terms to Know

progression principle
overuse injury
trainability
training plateau
detraining
cross-training
overtraining
fatigue
insomnia
restoration

▶ The progression principle states that as your fitness levels increase, so do the factors in your FITT. *How should you decide when to increase the factors in your FITT?*

Lesson 4   The Principle of Progression   95

The Principle of Progression

1 MOTIVATE

GETTING STARTED

- Ask students how long it takes to learn a new skill and to move from the beginning stage to the intermediate and advanced stages of skill acquisition.
- Distribute copies of *Guided Practice Activity 3-4* for students to use while studying this lesson. 📂

IN THIS LESSON

- **Lifeline** *Getting Help for a Friend, p. 98*

INTRODUCING VOCABULARY

- Explain to students that the term *plateau* refers to a leveling-off period. People often experience a "plateau effect" when learning new skills or when trying to improve their personal fitness.
- Have students use *Vocabulary Worksheet 3* or the PuzzleMaker software to practice vocabulary terms for this lesson. ELL 📂 ◎

Photo Follow-up

Ask a volunteer to describe the scene in this photo. *Caption answer: Students should base their decisions on tracking their success and progress.*

Student Edition TEKS
Page 94: C1A, C4F, C5C
Page 95: C1A, C4F, C5C

2 TEACH

Figure 3.14 Display *Transparency 20* and explain to students that Figure 3.14 illustrates the time changes that can occur with conditioning and that they relate to movement along the behavioral-change stairway. Have students answer the caption question. *Caption answer: Students should note that the graph shows rapid progress followed by a plateauing of improvement in the maintenance stage.*

✓ Reading Check

The stages of progression are an initial stage, an improvement stage, and a maintenance stage. Progression can be listed as a component of an exercise prescription.
TEKS C1A7, C4F

FIGURE 3.14

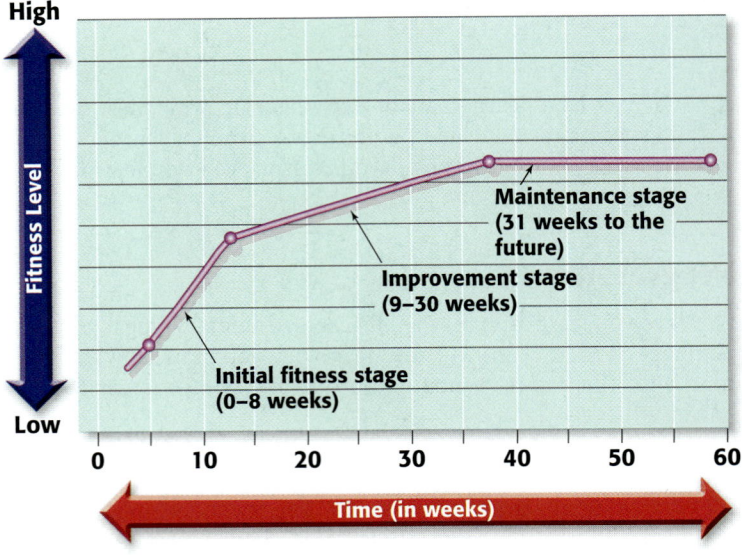

TYPICAL PROGRESS CHART
Progress in your fitness plan usually occurs in stages. *What factors do you think might affect the estimated time frames shown in this graph? What happens to the direction of the progress line at the various stages?*

Fitness Level — High / Low

Maintenance stage (31 weeks to the future)

Improvement stage (9–30 weeks)

Initial fitness stage (0–8 weeks)

Time (in weeks) — 0 10 20 30 40 50 60

Stages of Progression

Progression in a personal fitness program usually occurs in three stages. Corresponding roughly to the steps of the behavioral-change stairway, these include:

- An initial stage
- An improvement stage
- A maintenance stage

Figure 3.14 shows how a person might typically advance through the stages of progression. The time frames shown are approximate. These will vary from person to person and program to program. Note how rapidly this person improved in the initial stage. This indicates that he or she probably was inactive at the start. Note also that as the program moves forward in time, the rate of improvement tends to slow. By the maintenance stage, the person's FITT levels off completely. It is important at this stage to continue your program to keep your FITT at this level.

✓ Reading Check

Summarize List and describe the stages of progression in a personal fitness program or exercise prescription.

COOPERATIVE Learning

PROGRESSION STAGES Divide the class into small work groups and have them discuss the three stages of progression illustrated in Figure 3.14. Ask each group to make a list of the challenges a person might face. Have one person from each group share that group's results. Possible challenges: Initial Stage—starting too fast, changing FITT too fast, and expecting results too soon; Improvement Stage—changing FITT, hitting a plateau, and expecting results too soon; Maintenance Stage—boredom, injury, or overtraining.

Factors Affecting Progression. Remember that everyone's body and levels of fitness are different. Your rate of progress will depend on several factors:
- Your initial fitness level (the lower you start, the more quickly you usually improve)
- Your heredity
- The rate at which you overload your body or change your FITT
- Your specific goals (health or performance)

One additional factor that influences your rate of progression is your **trainability.** Trainability is *the rate at which an individual's fitness levels increase during fitness training,* discussed in the next section.

Trainability

Do you consider yourself a "quick study"? Do you tend to learn new physical skills quickly? Do you think of yourself as athletic? Your answers may be a clue to your trainability. Trainability is determined, to a large extent, by heredity. Heredity determines why "natural athletes" usually improve more quickly than nonathletes and enables an athlete to train at higher skill levels. **Figure 3.15** illustrates the trainability of five teens participating in the same conditioning program.

FIGURE 3.15

DIFFERENCES IN TRAINABILITY AMONG INDIVIDUALS
Different people train at different rates. *What is the difference in trainability for each of the individuals?*

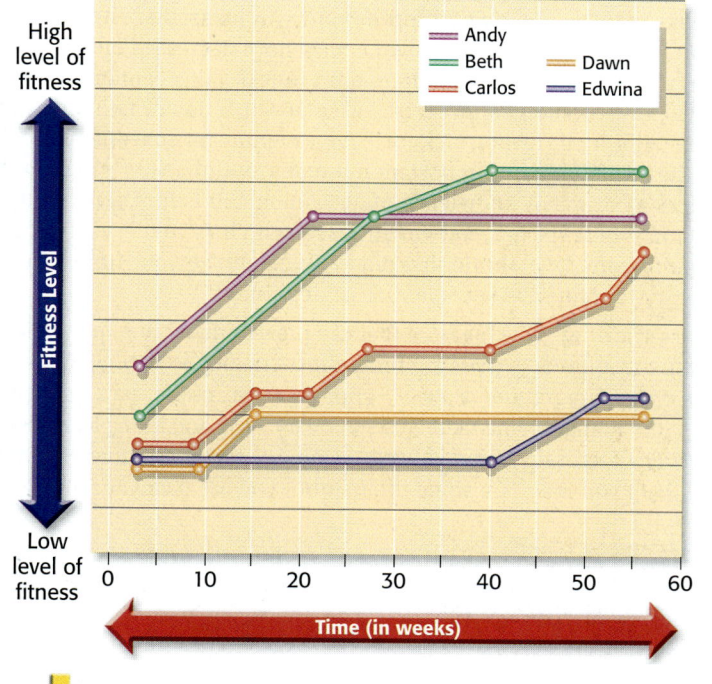

Discussing

Have each student work with a partner to discuss how they should change their progression based on their current personal fitness levels and goals. **L2**

USING VISUALS

Figure 3.15 Point out to students that Figure 3.15 illustrates how people respond differently to personal fitness conditioning, even if the FITT is the same for everyone. Have students answer the caption question, then ask them to determine which line on the graph best represents their trainability.

Activity

Encourage a discussion of the progression principle by displaying *Transparency 21.* Ask them to work in small groups to identify an example of how changes in fitness levels will show different stages of change over the course of several weeks. Have groups share their findings with the class. Ask for volunteers to describe how progression, as a component of an exercise prescription, contributes to the increase in fitness levels. **L2**
TEKS C4F

More About . . .

TRAINABILITY Dr. Claude Brochard, a French-Canadian exercise scientist, is responsible for much of what we know about the trainability of individuals. Exercise experts once thought that the $VO_{2\,max}$ (the maximal cardiorespiratory ability) of an individual was 90 percent genetically determined. However, Dr. Brochard has shown that it is only 30 to 40 percent genetically determined, which means that training and other factors have a large influence on how we perform physically.

Student Edition TEKS
Page 96: C4F
Page 97: C1A

Activity

Have students imagine that they have to complete 20 days of bed rest, during which they can't get up for any reason. Ask them to explain how they would feel when they are finally able to get up and move about. Explain to students that bed rest is an extreme example of detraining and has been used to determine the physical effects of space flight on astronauts, who are subjected to zero gravity.

✓ Reading Check

Cross-training can be called a remedy for detraining because it will help a person maintain a reasonable level of personal fitness.

LIFELINE

Getting Help for a Friend

Not only can overtraining lead to serious health problems, it can also be a symptom of an even larger problem—an eating disorder. If someone you know displays any signs of overtraining, he or she may need professional help.

Begin by speaking with the person. Explain the health risks. If you don't seem to be getting through, share your concerns with a trusted adult.

Take a moment to study this graph. Which teen makes the most improvement over the course of a year? Which teen makes the least progress? Which would you describe as the least trainable?

Find the line on the graph corresponding to Andy's trainability. Notice that Andy improved rapidly for about twenty weeks, then leveled off. This leveling off is known as a **training plateau.** A training plateau is *a period of time during training when little, if any, fitness improvement occurs.* Plateaus are a natural part of training. Everyone experiences them at one time or another. Some people feel tempted to quit during plateaus. It is important to fight off this temptation and adhere to your fitness plan.

Detraining

Some people lose the battle of will when training plateaus occur and stop training altogether. These people will experience a phenomenon known as *detraining.* **Detraining** can be defined as *the loss of functional fitness that occurs when one stops fitness conditioning.* Some detraining will occur during relapses on the behavioral-change stairway. These relapses, as noted earlier, can arise from a number of causes, including illness and injury. In general, the longer the period of detraining, the greater the loss of fitness gains.

Take the case of Janean. Janean was forced to spend a month in bed as the result of an illness. Prior to her relapse, Janean was able to jog two miles in twenty minutes. Once she was back on her feet, she found it hard to jog one mile nonstop, let alone two miles in twenty minutes.

It is important to recognize that detraining affects different fitness modes at different rates. For example, if you detrain for four weeks, you may notice a drop in your cardiovascular fitness level. Your levels of strength, meanwhile, may have decreased only slightly. You should also realize that long-term fitness gains cannot be lost in a day, or two, or even three. It is wise to skip a day or two if you are unusually tired, feeling sick, or have a significant schedule conflict. At the same time, it is important not to discontinue your program for weeks at a time. A knowledge of detraining will help you *maintain* a reasonable level of personal fitness—which is much easier than *obtaining* the level in the first place. To maximize your fitness benefits, try to minimize your periods of detraining.

Cross-training. One measure that can prevent detraining, particularly if you are injured, is **cross-training.** Cross-training is *varying your exercise or activity routine or type.* Suppose, for example, you hurt your shoulder lifting weights. Riding a stationary cycle and lifting leg weights provides a cross-training solution. Doing these alternative exercises will help you maintain some fitness until you are past your injury.

✓ Reading Check

Infer In what way can cross-training be called a remedy for detraining for an individual with a training-related injury?

More About . . .

DETRAINING Dr. Edward Coyle from the University of Texas conducted one of the best studies to date about cardiorespiratory detraining. He showed that subjects who were highly fit (in cardiorespiratory levels) initially and who then detrained for 84 days, lost about half of their cardiorespiratory levels within 10 days. He called this the "half-life of cardiorespiratory fitness," which means that after a period of detraining (in this case, 10 days), you lose half of what you gained with training. If you cross-train, however, you can at least hold on to some of your fitness levels.

Overtraining and Health Problems

Look at the graph in **Figure 3.15** on page **97**. Note that the graph stops at about 56 weeks. If it were to continue, you would find Carlos's line dropping sharply over the next month. The reason for this sudden dip was an overuse injury resulting from *overtraining, exercising, or being active to a point where it begins to have negative effects.* Among these effects are abnormal levels of physical and mental stress or "burnout." Overtraining is also a leading cause of overuse injuries, as in Carlos's case.

Overtraining has a number of well-defined effects on health. Many of these are serious health problems. They include:

- Chronic *fatigue—the feeling of being tired all the time*
- *Insomnia,* or *sleeplessness*
- Constant muscle soreness
- Rapid weight loss
- Loss of appetite
- Elevated resting heart rate
- Elevated blood pressure
- Weakened immune system
- In females, absence of menstrual cycles, and possible infertility.

Overtraining itself can be a symptom of another serious health problem, **eating disorders,** such as bulimia and anorexia nervosa. Although an eating disorder is considered a psychological illness, people with bulimia or anorexia nervosa are likely to overtrain in an effort to fulfill their unhealthy desire to stay thin.

Sometimes people who overtrain suffer from an unhealthy physical and psychological dependence on exercise, often referred to as exercise addiction. These people exhibit all the classic signs of addiction. To them, exercise is more important than family, friends, work, or other commitments. They will exercise with excessive frequency and for extended periods of time, even if they are exhausted or injured. They become nervous and irritable if they are unable to work out.

Recovery from chronic overtraining can take weeks or months. People who are addicted to exercise may even require special counseling in order to recover.

▶ Working hard is good, but be careful not to overtrain. *What are some risks of trying to do too much too soon?*

Lesson 4   **The Principle of Progression**   **99**

hot link

eating disorders
For more on eating disorders, see Chapter 6, page **176.**

Chapter 3, Lesson 4

LIFELINE

Getting Help for a Friend
Ask students to describe the symptoms of a person who is overtraining. Ask them to explain how overtraining may contribute to negative health problems such as bulimia and anorexia. Explain that individuals who suffer from chronic overtraining (training all the time) and eating disorders need professional treatment and sometimes counseling to overcome their health problems.
TEKS C5C

Photo Follow-up

Ask students whether they know of someone who has overtrained and experienced an injury. Then reinforce to them that a common sign of overtraining is injury.

hot link

Remind students that nutrition plays an important role in fitness and that eating disorders can be very dangerous to their health. Have them review Chapter 6 to learn more about eating disorders.

✓ **Reading Check**
(page 100)
Factors include age, experience, environment, rest, nutrition, and fluids.

OVERTRAINING AND RESTORATION Exercise scientists have described overtraining as "overreaching" or training too hard, and not allowing the body enough time to adapt to the increasing FITT factors that the individual places upon his or her body. Overtraining may actually have two phases, an acute (short-term) phase and a chronic (long-term) phase. Acute overtraining is so intense physically that if athletes continued, they would be mentally and physically exhausted. Athletes who experience chronic overtraining often quit physical activity and become inactive adults.

Student Edition TEKS

Page 98: C5C
Page 99: C4A, C5C

99

3 ASSESS

EVALUATING THE LESSON

Assign and discuss the Lesson 4 Review.

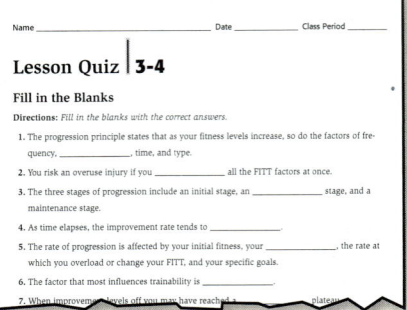

RETEACHING

Ask students to explain the difference between detraining and overtraining.

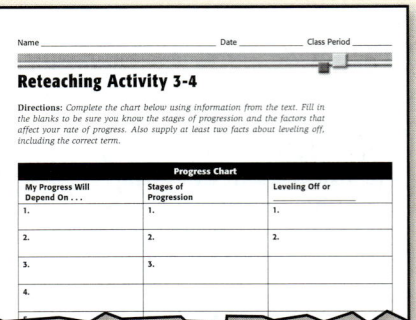

ENRICHMENT

Have students list and discuss the factors associated with restoration they have considered in their personal fitness planning and which ones they practice regularly.

4 CLOSE

Invite an athlete who has had to detrain after an injury to speak to the class about how long it took to lose his or her healthy fitness level.

Restoration

Restoration refers to *ways in which you can optimize your recovery from physical activity or exercise.* The speed at which you recover depends upon your FITT. If you exercise daily, you will need to recover more quickly than you would if you worked out every other day. The same is true of working at very high versus lower levels of intensity. One of the most common conditioning mistakes is not allowing ample recovery time after physical activity or exercise.

Restoration is influenced by several factors. These include the following:

- **Age.** The older you are the slower you tend to recover.
- **Experience.** As a rule, the more experienced you are, the quicker you recover.
- **Environment.** The more extreme the environmental conditions, the slower the recovery.
- **Amount of rest.** Getting 8 to 10 hours of sleep a night will hasten recovery. Any less will lead to a slower recovery.
- **Nutrition, including fluids.** What you eat and drink is an important aspect of fitness training. You will learn more about how to make sound nutritional choices in Chapter 4.

 Reading Check

Identify Name four factors that affect the speed at which an individual recovers from physical activity or exercise.

Lesson 4 Review

Using complete sentences, answer the following questions on a sheet of paper.

Reviewing Facts and Vocabulary

1. **Vocabulary** Describe the *progression principle.* Why is it important to your personal fitness program?

2. **Recall** What is a *training plateau?* What effect do plateaus have on an individual's fitness conditioning?

3. **Recall** Why do some individuals progress in their fitness level at faster rates than others?

Thinking Critically

4. **Explain** List the negative health problems associated with overtraining. What serious illness is associated with overtraining?

5. **Evaluate** Lisa and Debra are 14. Six weeks ago both girls started doing exactly the same conditioning. Lisa, however, has improved much faster than Debra. What factors might explain this difference? What tips can you give Debra to help her stay motivated?

 **Personal Fitness Planning**

Identifying Risks Find out how overtraining contributes to negative health problems. Talk with an athlete on a school team. Ask if he or she has ever overtrained. If the answer is yes, ask if any of the symptoms described in the lesson were present. How did the person optimize recovery from exercise? Share your findings with the class.

Lesson 4 Review

Answers to Lesson 4 Review

1. See definition on page 95. You need to understand progression, or you may change your FITT and be injured.

2. A plateau is when the improvements in trainability level off. Some people want to quit when they experience a plateau.

3. Individuals improve at different rates due to the "trainability" principle.

4. Answers will vary but should include problems listed on page 99.

5. Answers will vary.

Lesson 5

Warm Up, Work Out, Cool Down

It was the first day of baseball practice, and Sean was excited. He couldn't wait to get out on the field and catch some flies. He was slightly annoyed, therefore, when the coach ordered the team to do two laps of the field. "Why do we have to run? I want to play ball," Sean grumbled to his teammate as they ran.

Sean didn't realize that running laps was a standard preliminary part of any workout: the warm-up. In this lesson, you will learn about the warm-up and other components of a complete workout.

What You Will Do

- Apply the physiological principles of warm-up and cooldown to a fitness program.
- Analyze the importance of warming up and types of warm-up in exercise and training.
- Analyze the importance of cooling down and phases of a cooldown in exercise and training.

Terms to Know

warm-up
active warm-up
passive warm-up
blood pooling
cardiovascular cooldown
stretching cooldown

◀ A warm-up is one part of a complete workout.
Why do you think warming up is important prior to doing vigorous activity?

Lesson 5 Warm Up, Work Out, Cool Down **101**

Warm Up, Work Out, Cool Down

1 MOTIVATE

GETTING STARTED

- Ask students what they think the components of a complete workout are.
- Distribute copies of *Guided Practice Activity 3-5* for students to use while studying this lesson. 🗁

IN THIS LESSON

- **Active Mind—Active Body** *Warm-up: Stretching Correctly, p. 104*

INTRODUCING VOCABULARY

- Have students read the definition of *blood pooling* found on page 108. Explain that the term describes the physiological effect of not performing a proper cooldown after physical activity or exercise. **TEKS C1A**
- Have students use *Vocabulary Worksheet 3* or the PuzzleMaker software to practice vocabulary terms for this lesson. **ELL** 🗁 💿

Photo Follow-up

Caption answer: A warm-up increases blood flow to the working muscles and increases body temperature so that the person can begin exercising more effectively.

📖 LESSON 5 RESOURCES

Teacher Classroom Resources
- 🗁 Guided Practice Activity 3-5
- 🗁 Active Mind—Active Body Worksheet 3-5
- 🗁 Reteaching Activity 3-5
- 🗁 Lesson Quiz 3-5

Reproducible Charts and Graphs
- 🗁 Reproducible Masters 3-5, 3-6, 3-7

Multimedia
- ◎ Vocabulary PuzzleMaker
- ⬇ Transparencies 22, 23, 24

2 TEACH

Figure 3.16 Have students study Figure 3.16 and consider the question as they analyze and apply the physiological principles they are learning about warm-up and cooldown as components of a complete workout. Ask a volunteer to explain the purpose of a warm-up and how warm-ups affect the heart and muscles before a workout.
Caption answer: Students should mention that each workout should include all three components but that the components may vary, depending on the person's FITT. TEKS C1A1, C1A2

Discussing

Ask students if they do better in physical activities or exercise if they warm up first. Most will say they feel or do better after a warm-up. Explain that even though scientists promote the benefits of regular warm-ups, warming up may or may not prevent injuries—a lot depends on the type and intensity of the exercise. L1
TEKS C1A1

STRESS BREAK

Have students make a list of ways that they deal with daily stress in their lives. After they have read the Stress Break feature on this page, have them explain how their list might change.

FIGURE 3.16

COMPONENTS OF A COMPLETE WORKOUT

This chart contains components of one possible routine. *Is this workout similar to your own? How does yours differ?*

Component	Type of Activity	Time (in minutes)
Warm-up	Cardiovascular, stretch, low-level calisthenics, walking	10
Workout	*Cardiovascular Conditioning:* Walk, jog/run, swim, bike, cross-country ski, dance, stair step, in-line skating	20–50
	Muscular conditioning: Calisthenics, weight training	15–30
Cooldown	Walking, stretching	5–10

Components of a Complete Workout

A complete workout includes three main components: a warm-up, the workout itself, and a cooldown. **Figure 3.16** shows one possible approach to a complete workout. Note that the workout begins with a warm-up and ends with a cooldown. In the sections that follow, you will learn more about each of these components. You will also learn safe and healthy reasons for making them part of your workout routines.

The Warm-up

The **warm-up** is *a portion of a complete workout that consists of a variety of low-intensity activities that prepare the body for physical work.* A warm-up should always precede any moderate-to-vigorous activity. Unfortunately, many people warm up too quickly, or not at all. A well-designed warm-up will help you participate in a safe, successful, and enjoyable workout.

Why Warm Up? There are physiological principles related to the warm-up. The primary purpose of any warm-up is to raise your heart rate gradually before physical activity or exercise. This gradual increase causes a slight rise in muscle temperature. This in turn enables your muscles to work safely and more efficiently. In fact, your whole body benefits. Muscles, bones, and nerves perform better when the body temperature is slightly increased. Evidence suggests that warming up helps minimize physical-activity and exercise injuries. It may reduce some of the symptoms of muscle soreness.

STRESS BREAK

The Art of Planning

Your feelings about yourself—and what you believe others think about you—can influence the amount of positive and negative stress in your life. By organizing your daily routine, you can greatly improve your ability to deal with stress. Here are some tips:

- Plan your days in advance.
- Remember that fitness doesn't happen overnight.
- Set achievable goals.

INCLUSION STRATEGIES

WARM-UP EXERCISES Any warm-up exercises done by students with physical challenges should be based on their actual workout programs but fewer in number and lower in intensity. Any workout program should be based on information gathered from health professionals and should include assessments of the beginning level of fitness. Similarly, cooldown exercises should be at lower intensity. Cooldown for students with disabilities may need to be longer. Some students with low levels of cardiovascular fitness may exhibit high levels of muscular strength and endurance.

Types of Warm-ups. There are two main methods of warming up, active and passive. An *active warm-up raises body temperature by actively working the body systems centering on the muscles, skeleton, heart, and lungs.* An active warm-up will have two phases:

- **A cardiovascular phase.** This phase is designed to gradually increase your heart rate and body temperature. A cardiovascular warm-up can include jogging slowly around a track, running in place or on a treadmill, or stationary cycling at low resistance.
- **A muscular-skeletal phase.** This phase is designed to loosen up the muscles and connective tissues. A muscular-skeletal warm-up is usually performed by doing static body stretches. These are stretches that are done slowly, smoothly, and in a sustained fashion. You will learn more about stretching in Chapter 11. You will also get some stretching practice in the "Active Mind—Active Body" activity on page **104**.

In contrast to the active warm-up, a *passive warm-up raises the body temperature through the use of outside heat sources.* These include blankets, hot baths, saunas, or skin creams. Obviously, the active warm-up is a far more effective way of preparing your body for physical work.

✓ **Reading Check**

Describe What types of physical activities might be included in each phase of the active warm-up?

◀ An active warm-up consists of a cardiovascular phase and a muscular-skeletal phase. *What phase of the warm-up are these athletes performing?*

Photo Follow-up

Explain to students that stretching is a normal part of a warm-up but that recent studies suggest it is best done after a 5- to 15-minute cardiovascular warm-up.

Discussing

Ask students what types of static stretches they already know how to do. Have one or two students demonstrate what they know, and compare them with the Active Mind—Active Body stretches on page 104. **L2**

✓ **Reading Check**

A cardiovascular phase (jog, run, stationary cycle) and a static stretching phase.

Myths & Realities

Myth 1 Stretching prevents injuries.

Fact 1 Fitness experts recommend stretching before physical activity to help prevent injuries. Research suggests it's beneficial to do most stretching during the cooldown.

Myth 2 You do not need to do a cardiovascular warm-up before lifting weights.

Fact 2 Recent research has shown that doing 10 to 15 minutes of cardiovascular warm-up prior to weight lifting allows people to lift more weight and to fatigue less quickly.

Student Edition TEKS

Page 102: C1A, C4G
Page 103: C1A

Active Mind Active Body

Warm Up and Cool Down: Stretching Correctly

Before you have students do the warm-up stretches in the Active Mind–Active Body activity on these two pages, spread out the class and demonstrate each stretch. Let students practice each stretch as you move through the group to critique students.

Teaching Tips

- Explain that a muscle-skeletal phase is a critical part of every warm-up and cooldown. Have students apply these physiological principles related to exercise and training as they practice warm-up and cooldown stretches. **TEKS C1A1,2**

- Have students stretch to the point that they feel a slight discomfort but not to the point of pain during the stretch.

- Do not allow students to bounce (do ballistic stretching) during stretches.

- Be sure to allow enough time to observe each student performing the stretches.

Active Mind Active Body

Warm Up and Cool Down: Stretching Correctly

In this activity, you will apply the physiological principles related to exercise and training, including warm-up and cooldown. As you perform each stretch, concentrate on the muscle being stretched. See if you feel tension in the area of the body designated.

What You Will Need

- Your book (open to **Figures 3.17a–i** on page **106**)

What You Will Do

1. Before getting started, do a light cardiovascular warm-up as instructed by your teacher.
2. Study the picture and description of each stretching activity before trying it. Make sure you understand how the exercise is done.
3. Do each of the following slowly, holding a static position:
   a. **Side stretch**—stretches obliques:
      • From a standing position with feet at shoulders' width apart, raise your left hand over your head.
      • Place your right hand on your hip. Bend sideways (to the right) as far as possible.
      • Do not lean forward or backward.
      • Hold the position for 20 to 30 seconds. Then repeat on the other side.
   b. **Chest and arm stretch**—stretches pectorals and deltoids:
      • From a standing or sitting position, raise your arms out to the sides, to a shoulder-high position.
      • Straighten your arms, and place your hands palm down.
      • Try to touch your hands behind your back.
      • Hold this position for 20 to 30 seconds.
   c. **Trunk twist**—stretches back and hips:
      • Sit on the floor with both legs straight in front of you.
      • Bend the left knee far enough to place the left foot flat on the floor next to the right knee.
      • Now cross the left leg over the right leg, and place the left foot flat on the floor next to the right knee.
      • Place your right elbow on the left side of your left leg.
      • Place your left arm and hand on the floor behind you.
      • While pressing with your right arm, try to twist your body and head as far to the left as possible.
      • Hold this position for 20 to 30 seconds. Then change your leg and arm position and repeat.
   d. **Reverse hurdle**—stretches hamstrings and lower back:
      • Sit on the floor, with both legs straight in front of you.
      • Bend your left knee far enough to place the bottom of your left foot against the side of your right knee.

Specific and General Warm-ups. There are two types of active warm-ups: specific and general. A specific warm-up is structured primarily for skill or game-oriented activities. A specific warm-up for basketball, for example, might include layups, jump shots, and upper and lower leg stretches.

A general warm-up is less structured. It is usually used for individual physical activities. A general warm-up designed for swimming or jogging might include running in place, calisthenics, and various stretches.

Warm-up Guidelines. Like any other part of your workout, a warm-up should be done properly to reduce the risk of muscle injuries and

104 **Chapter 3** Designing a Personal Fitness Program

More About . . .

HEALTHY PEOPLE 2010 Goals for Muscular Strength, Muscular Endurance, and Flexibility: Increase the proportion of adults who perform physical activities that enhance muscular strength and endurance; Increase the proportion of adults who perform physical activities that enhance and maintain flexibility; Increase the proportion of the nation's public and private schools that require daily physical education for all students; and, Increase the proportion of adolescents who participate in daily school physical education.

- Reach for your right ankle with both hands.
- Gently pull your body forward while trying to touch your head to your knee.
- Hold this position for 20 to 30 seconds. Then change your leg and arm position and repeat.

e. **"Yes," "no," "maybe"**—stretches head and neck:
- Tilt your head slightly back. Then bring your head forward and touch your chin to your chest. Return to normal. This is the "yes" stretch.
- Slowly turn your head as far to the right as possible, then back to the left as far as possible. Return to normal. This is the "no" stretch.
- Now pull both of your shoulders up toward your ears. Return to normal. This is the "maybe" stretch.
- Avoid using one continuous, circular motion for these stretches.
- Hold each position for 20 to 30 seconds.

f. **Side lunge**—stretches inner thigh and groin:
- From a standing position, step to the left with your left foot and leg.
- Bend your right knee, and balance most of your weight on your right leg.
- Keep your left leg straight out to the side.
- Balance yourself with one or both hands touching the floor.
- Hold this position for 20 to 30 seconds. Then change legs and repeat.

g. **Forward lunge**—stretches hip flexors:
- From a standing position, step directly to the front with your left leg.
- Bend your left knee to a 90-degree angle while keeping your right leg back and straight. Your right foot should be on its toes.

- Be sure not to let your left knee extend past your left foot.
- Balance yourself with one or both hands on the floor.
- Hold this position for 20 to 30 seconds. Then change legs and repeat.

h. **Butterfly**—stretches groin:
- From a sitting position, bend both knees, and place the bottoms of both feet against each other.
- Lean forward, and place both hands on your feet.
- Slowly pull the heels of your feet toward your body.
- You may lean forward slightly.
- Try to keep your knees out and down.
- Hold this position for 20 to 30 seconds.

i. **Calf stretch**—stretches gastrocnemius:
- From a standing position, face a wall. Place your feet 3 feet from the wall.
- Step forward with your left foot, and support your weight by placing your hands on the wall.
- Your right foot should remain in its position and should stay flat on the floor as you lean forward.
- There should be no weight on your left foot.
- Hold this position for 20 to 30 seconds. Then change legs and repeat.

Apply and Conclude

Were you able to isolate the muscle being stretched? Take note of any stretches you will need to retry. Practice these exercises as part of your warm-up and cooldown.

soreness. There are specific guidelines you can follow to make sure your warm-up is safe and effective.

- Remember to do a cardiovascular and muscular-skeletal phase in every warm-up.
- Start slowly, and gradually increase intensity.
- Warm up for five to fifteen minutes in temperate weather. When it is cold, you may want to take more time to warm up.
- Design a specific warm-up intended for your exercises or physical activities.
- Make your warm-up intensity high enough to produce an increase in heart and breathing rates and a light sweat.

Lesson 5   Warm Up, Work Out, Cool Down   105

Active Mind Active Body

- Distribute the *Active Mind—Active Body Worksheet 3-5* for students to record their warm-up stretches. 📁

Apply and Conclude

Students should learn to stretch safely and with proper technique. They should incorporate these stretches into the warm-up and cooldown sections of their personal fitness workouts.

Activity

Remind students that applying warm-up and cooldown can improve performance. Ask them to note their improvement as they demonstrate the skill-related components of physical fitness that they practiced on page 78. They should consider agility, balance, coordination, speed, and reaction time when evaluating their performance.
TEKS C4C1,2,3,5,6

Promoting Coordinated School Health

ROLE MODELS Teachers, administrators, coaches, and other staff members can be important role models for students. So can adult family members and other members of the community. Because physical activity and exercise relate to all three components of health—physical, mental/emotional, and social—physical education classes and athletic periods and competitions provide good opportunities for adults to model appropriate choices and behaviors. Take the time to interact with students and show them that you live a physically active lifestyle. Encourage students to invite parents, guardians, or other adult family members to observe the physical activity programs.

Student Edition TEKS

Page 104: C1A
Page 105: C1A

Figure 3.17 Ask students which of the stretches they like best. Which ones are the easiest for them to complete? Which are the hardest? Encourage students to explain why they prefer certain stretches.

Activity

Divide students into small groups or teams of two to four students. Using *Transparency 22* as a guide, assign each group one of the recommended warm-up stretches shown in Figure 3.17. Ask them to apply physiological principles related to exercise and training when they choose warm-up stretches for their sessions. Have each team develop a stretching warm-up session that includes three stretches, five stretches, and as many as 10 stretches. Be sure stretches include a wide range of muscles stretched. Encourage students to share their warm-up session plans with classmates. **L2**

TEKS C1A1

FIGURE 3.17

RECOMMENDED WARM-UP STRETCHES
These stretches can help you meet flexibility goals safely.

Figure 3.17a

Figure 3.17b

Figure 3.17c

Figure 3.17d

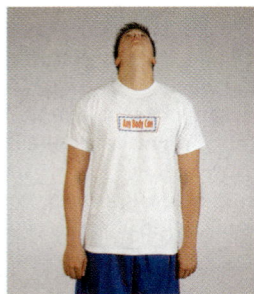 

Figure 3.17e

Figure 3.17f

Figure 3.17g

Figure 3.17h

Figure 3.17i

COOPERATIVE Learning

WARM-UP STRETCHING Have students work in small groups to discuss warm-up stretches. Then have them make a list of sports that they think would require only a minimal warm-up compared with sports that would require a much more extensive warm-up. Have each group list the stretches they would recommend for a light warm-up versus an extensive warm-up. Finally, have one student from each group report their results to the rest of the class. **ELL**

FIGURE 3.18

SAMPLE FITNESS PRESCRIPTION FOR A TEEN

This is an example of a fitness prescription. *Does your exercise prescription look similar to this one? How does it differ?*

Frequency	3–5 days per week
Intensity	Moderate to vigorous and continuous, if possible
Time	Accumulate 20–60 minutes on each session
Type	Walk-hike, run-jog, bike, cross-country ski, dance, skip rope, row, stair climb, swim, in-line skate, endurance games
Resistance-Weight Training	8–10 exercises, 2–3 times per week
Flexibility	Include warm-up and cooldown stretches

The Workout

The workout phase of your fitness program is the period of time that you should spend daily, or almost daily, in physical activity or exercise. A well-designed workout phase should be based on scientific exercise principles. It should also be tailored to your personal fitness goals and experience level.

Figure 3.18 shows details of a sample "fitness prescription" designed for a teen. You might want to use this prescription in designing your workout. Note that the chart shows you how to combine the modes of your conditioning with FITT.

▶ A well-designed weight-training program can benefit everyone—young and old, male and female alike. *What are some other examples of exercise workouts you have learned about?*

Lesson 5   Warm Up, Work Out, Cool Down   **107**

Photo Follow-up

Ask students what type of warm-up the female should do before lifting weights. *Caption answer: She should do both a cardiovascular warm-up and a static stretching one.*

USING VISUALS

Figure 3.18 Display *Transparency 23*. Explain to students that this is an example of a fitness prescription. Ask: Does your current personal fitness prescription look like this? Why or why not? *Caption answers will vary, but students should express an understanding of the components listed in the fitness prescription.*

Activity

After students have examined figure 3.18, ask them to apply what they learned in Lessons 2, 3, and 4 of this chapter to an exercise prescription. Have them create a chart with two columns. Have them list in one column the components of exercise prescription including overload principle, type, progression, and specificity. In the other column, have them describe each component listed. **TEKS C4F**

More About . . .

PLANNING AND STRESS LEVELS The ability to plan and get organized has been recognized by sports psychologists as the key to reducing competitive stress in athletic competition. Planning and organization can help reduce stress in everyday life as well. Students, athletes, teachers, and coaches should all take a moment once in a while to analyze why they are experiencing extra stresses or "burnout." Sports psychologists have also reported that burnout is related to being unorganized and operating without a detailed plan based on short- and long-term goals.

Student Edition TEKS

Page 107: C1A, C4G

Photo Follow-up

Ask students why a cooldown is just as important as the warm-up phase of a workout. *Answer: The cardiovascular component (walking, slow jogging, standing in place and moving your feet up and down) and the static stretching phase.*

Reading Check

The cooldown will help you avoid blood pooling in the lower body, which can cause dizziness and faintness.

USING VISUALS

Figure 3.19 Ask students to imagine that an athlete at a track meet or a student in physical education class ran a lap around a track as fast as possible. What would happen if the runner sat down immediately and then stood up five minutes later? Many students will note that the person might faint or get dizzy. This reaction would be caused by the blood pooling that results from not doing an effective cooldown. Using *Transparency 24*, discuss with students the physiological effects of blood pooling.

The Cooldown

The cooldown portion of your routine is every bit as important as the warm-up. Yet, as with warming up, many people cool down too quickly or not at all. A well-designed cooldown after every workout will ensure a safe and more effective recovery.

The cooldown also follows physiological principles. The main job of the cooldown is the opposite of that of the warm-up: It is to lower your heart rate gradually. This gradual decrease will help you prevent **blood pooling** in the lower body. This is *a condition in which blood collects in the large veins of the legs and lower body* (see **Figure 3.19**).

Blood pooling can cause you to become dizzy and feel faint. That is because less blood is being pumped to your heart and brain. Blood pooling typically results from stopping abruptly at the end of an exercise or physical-activity session. Cooling down will prevent this.

Reading Check

Summarize Why is it necessary to cool down after participating in moderate to vigorous activity?

FIGURE 3.19

BLOOD POOLING

(a) Blood may pool around the one-way valves in the leg if you do not keep your legs moving during recovery. (b) During a proper cooldown, the muscles contract against the leg veins. Blood is squeezed back toward the heart.

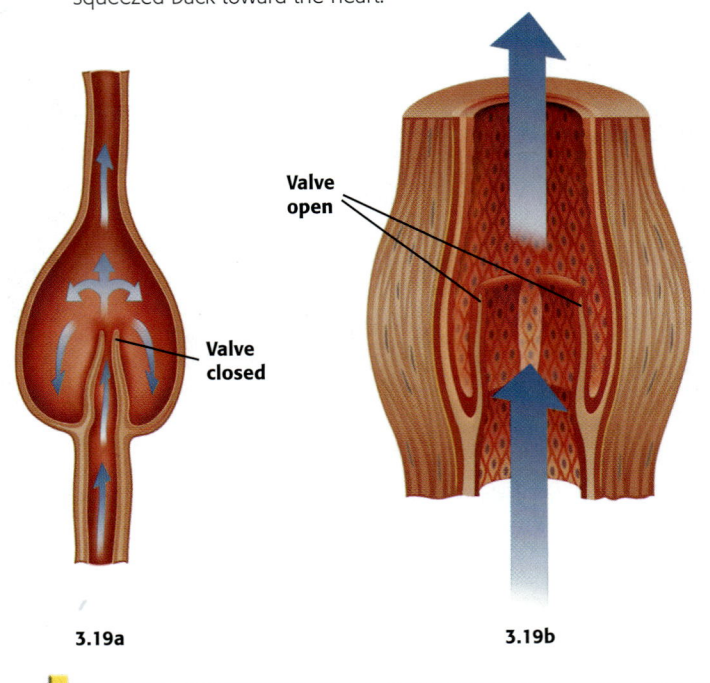

Valve open

Valve closed

3.19a

3.19b

Teacher-Coach Tips

Blood Pooling Prevention Blood pooling following exercise can be prevented by cooling down properly. Blood pooling can also occur after sitting or standing at rest for long periods of time. Have you ever been sitting or lying comfortably at home and the doorbell or the telephone rings and you jump up suddenly? Did you suddenly feel dizzy? The dizziness is caused because much of the blood in the body pools in the legs when we are at rest, and when we change positions suddenly, it takes a few moments for the heart to pump blood to the brain.

Parts of the Cooldown. Like the warm-up, the cooldown has two phases. These are, in the order in which they should occur:

- **The cardiovascular cooldown.** A cardiovascular cooldown *consists of moving about slowly and continuously for three to five minutes following physical activity or exercise.* Variations include walking, standing in place and moving your feet up and down, or jogging slowly.
- **The stretching cooldown.** The stretching cooldown *involves three to five minutes of stretching.* This will minimize stiffness and muscle soreness. Cooldown stretches should use the same static stretching exercises you use to warm up.

▼ Cooldown is just as important as warm-up. Always be sure to include a cooldown in each workout session. *What are the elements of a proper cooldown?*

Lesson 5 Review

Using complete sentences, answer the following questions on a sheet of paper.

Reviewing Facts and Vocabulary

1. **Vocabulary** What is a *warm-up?* Why is it important?
2. **Recall** Name the two phases of an *active warm-up.*
3. **Recall** Name the two phases of a *cooldown.*

Thinking Critically

4. **Compare and Contrast** How do warm-up and cooldown activities differ? What common traits do the two share?
5. **Synthesize** Troy and Scott are both 16. Troy plans to try out for the basketball team. Scott wants to try out for football. What tips can you give each teen as to the specific types of warm-ups they should do in preparation for a workout in their sport?

Personal Fitness Planning

Applying Physiological Principles of Warm-up and Cooldown Design and apply a specific active warm-up or cooldown program for playing softball, volleyball, or another sport of your choice. Begin by thinking about or researching which body parts are used most often in the sport. Then write, draw, or demonstrate the kinds of stretches and activities that are involved in your warm-up.

Lesson 5 Warm Up, Work Out, Cool Down **109**

3 ASSESS

EVALUATING THE LESSON

Assign and discuss the Lesson 5 Review.

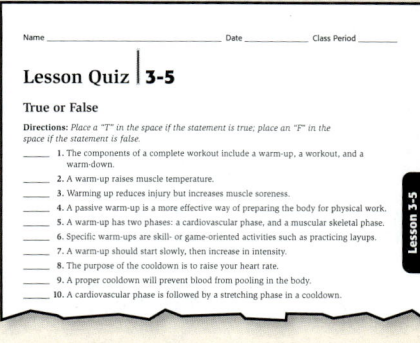

RETEACHING

Ask students to create a sentence using three vocabulary terms from the lesson.

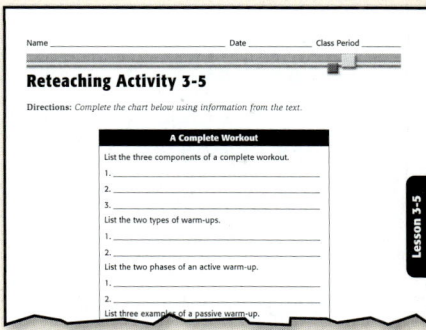

ENRICHMENT

Have students attend an athletic sport competition and determine whether the teams did a cardiovascular and static warm-up and cooldown.

4 CLOSE

Reinforce to students that their workout should include all the components in Figure 3.18.

Lesson 5 Review

Answers to Lesson 5 Review

1. See definition on page 102. A warm-up is important to prepare your body properly before physical activity and exercise.
2. Cardiovascular and static stretching.
3. Cardiovascular and static stretching (same as active warm-up).
4. Many of the activities in warm-ups and cooldowns are the same, but the goals of warming up and cooling down are different.
5. They should talk with the coach and observe other athletes.

CHAPTER 3 Review

CHECKING COMPREHENSION

- Assign and discuss the chapter review.
- Use the PuzzleMaker CD-ROM to review vocabulary.

CHAPTER 3 REVIEW ANSWERS

True/False

1. False	**6.** False
2. True	**7.** True
3. False	**8.** True
4. False	**9.** True
5. True	**10.** False

Multiple Choice

11. a	**16.** c
12. d	**17.** a
13. b	**18.** d
14. d	**19.** a
15. b	**20.** d

Discussion

21. If you exercise at a heart rate of 60–90 percent of your maximum heart rate, you will have an RPE scale rating of between 13 (somewhat hard) and 16 (vigorous).

22. Detraining signs include loss of strength, a drop in cardiovascular fitness, dizziness, and fainting.

23. The FITT represents frequency, intensity, time, and type. All of these factors must be considered together to optimize the progression of an individual's physical-activity or exercise prescription.

Student Edition TEKS

Page 109: C1A, C4A
Page 111: C1A

TRUE OR FALSE

On a sheet of paper, write the numbers 1–10. Write True or False for each statement below.

1. Another name for skill-related fitness is cardiovascular fitness.
2. Power is a measure of performance fitness.
3. The three factors that can be adjusted to achieve overload are frequency, intensity, and type.
4. The number of times per week you engage in physical activity or exercise is known as time.
5. The principle of specificity states that overloading a particular muscle will lead to fitness improvements in that muscle alone.
6. Once you have developed a fitness plan, you should never alter it, even if you are injured.
7. If you work your muscles beyond a safe and reasonable point, you risk overuse injury.
8. Heredity is a factor that will affect your rate of progression.
9. Moderate to vigorous exercise sessions should always include a warm-up phase and a cool-down phase.
10. Blood pooling can be prevented by sitting down and relaxing after vigorous exercise.

MULTIPLE CHOICE

On a sheet of paper, write the letter of the word or phrase that best completes each statement.

11. The overload principle involves an increase in
    a. physical activity or exercise above what you normally do.
    b. the improvement you would normally expect.
    c. the changes that occur in your body.
    d. the negative effects that occur in your body.
12. Your exercise intensity is affected by your
    a. level of fitness.
    b. fitness goals.
    c. length of each workout session.
    d. all of the above.

13. Of the following, the piece of information that would NOT be recorded in personal fitness record book is
    a. a list of the foods you have eaten.
    b. the amount of progress made by a competitor.
    c. your goals.
    d. any changes in your body weight.
14. Potential differences in physical-fitness improvement between two people training the same way for the same length of time is due to
    a. overload.
    b. specificity.
    c. progression.
    d. trainability.
15. The principle which states that the factors in your FITT change as your fitness levels increase is
    a. specificity.
    b. progression.
    c. overload.
    d. mode.
16. All of the following are symptoms of overtraining EXCEPT
    a. constant muscle soreness.
    b. mental burnout.
    c. high performance.
    d. chronic fatigue.
17. A term that refers to optimizing your recovery from physical activity or exercise is
    a. restoration.
    b. detraining.
    c. overload.
    d. intensity.
18. All of the following are examples of active warm-up EXCEPT
    a. jogging slowly around a track.
    b. stationary cycling at low resistance.
    c. pitching in the bullpen.
    d. sitting in a sauna.
19. Of the following, the activity that would NOT be a specific warm-up for basketball is
    a. jumping jacks.
    b. layups.
    c. passing drills.
    d. free-throw shooting.
20. Blood pooling results from
    a. overtraining.
    b. detraining.
    c. failing to warm up properly.
    d. failing to cool down properly.

Vocabulary

24. c	**28.** a
25. b	**29.** f
26. d	**30.** e
27. g	

Critical Thinking

31. Answers may vary but might include: When you change your FITT, you can either overload the body for continued improvements in fitness, keep it the same for maintenance purposes, or decrease it to recover from an event such as an illness.

DISCUSSION

Using complete sentences, answer the following questions on a sheet of paper.

21. **Explain** Describe how the perceived exertion scale and your heart rate can be used to determine your exercise intensity needs.
22. **Identify** List some common signs of detraining. Tell how to avoid detraining.
23. **Describe** Explain the relationship between the four FITT factors.

VOCABULARY

On a sheet of paper, write the letter of the term in Column B that best fits the definition in Column A.

Column A

24. Frequency, intensity, time, and type.
25. The need to increase the amount of activity or exercise above what you normally do to improve your fitness level.
26. The kind of activity or exercise you do.
27. A loss of functional fitness resulting from a stoppage in fitness conditioning.
28. A condition in which blood collects in the large veins of the legs and lower body.
29. Your ability to use the five senses to determine and direct the movement of your limbs and head.
30. The amount of energy needed to perform different physical activities or exercises.

Column B

a. blood pooling
b. overload principle
c. FITT
d. type
e. energy cost
f. coordination
g. detraining

CRITICAL THINKING

Using complete sentences, answer the following questions on a sheet of paper.

31. **Explain** How can you influence your personal fitness progression by changing your FITT? Explain your answer.

32. **Evaluate** If a friend tells you that she started an exercise program to improve her physical fitness but quit after two weeks because she didn't see any improvements, what would you tell her?
33. **Synthesize** What advice can you give someone you know who becomes frantic over missing a single workout? Explain your answer.

CASE STUDY

GARY'S PERSONAL EXERCISE

Gary is a sixteen-year-old who has just transferred to your high school. He played soccer and baseball when he was younger but has since been sedentary. Although Gary likes athletics, he doesn't want to play sports in high school. He is interested in improving his health and personal fitness but hasn't had much experience with working out on his own.

Gary thinks that his personal fitness levels are about average, but he has noticed that he tires more easily than he did when he played sports. He doesn't have much energy left by the end of the school day. His goals are to lose 5 to 10 pounds, to improve his cardiovascular fitness levels, and to begin a regular weight-lifting program. Gary could use your personal fitness expertise.

HERE IS YOUR ASSIGNMENT:

Design a beginning physical-activity and exercise plan for Gary. Prepare a detailed two-week warm-up, workout, and cooldown program. Try to be as specific as possible when choosing activities and exercises. Use your knowledge and imagination to create a safe and effective personal-fitness program.

KEYS TO HELP YOU

The following tips may help you design Gary's program:
- Consider his history of personal activity and exercise.
- Consider his current fitness level.
- Consider his needs and goals.

Chapter 3 Review 111

32. Answers may vary but might include: She didn't stay with the program long enough to see the benefits. She wasn't successful because she probably worked too hard and too soon. She may have unrealistic expectations. She can improve her chances for success by learning more about personal fitness.
33. Encourage the person to lighten up a bit about their physical activity and exercise program. Explain that he or she will not lose any significant fitness by missing a day or two of conditioning. In fact, doing too much physical activity and exercise can have negative effects.

EVALUATE

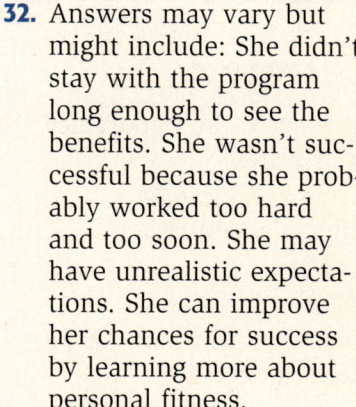

ENRICHMENT

CASE STUDY

ANSWERS

Answers may vary but might include: Have Gary use the material in Figures 3.8, 3.9, 3.10, 3.11, 3.12, 3.14, 3.15, 3.16, 3.17, and 3.18 in Chapter 3 to help him design his personal fitness program.

CHAPTER 4 Nutrition and Your Personal Fitness

CHAPTER RESOURCES

- Chapter Study Guide 4
- Vocabulary Worksheet 4
- Enrichment Activity 4
- Chapter 4 Test A
- Chapter 4 Test B
- Parent Letter and Activities 4 (English/Spanish)

FITNESS Online

Ask students to take the STEP Personal Inventory for Chapter 4. Have them record their responses to the statements in their notebooks. Remind students that responses are private and for their use only.

FITNESS Online

Do you eat breakfast every day? Do you know how many calories you take in? Your answers to these questions provide information about your current level of health. Learn more by taking the STEP Personal Inventory for Chapter 4. Find it at **fitness.glencoe.com**.

112

INCLUSION STRATEGIES

LANGUAGE DIVERSITY *Use the following suggestions to help students who have difficulty with English:*

- Pair English-language learners with native speakers of English who can restate key points in language that helps students comprehend important concepts.

- Direct Spanish-speaking students to the written summaries of this chapter in the *Foundations of Personal Fitness* Spanish Resources Booklet.

- Encourage Spanish-speaking students to use the Glosario provided in the back of the student text. **ELL**

The Importance of Nutrition

Personal fitness requires a lifestyle that includes physical activity and several other positive lifestyle choices. One of those choices is healthful eating.

What does healthful eating mean to you? Does it mean living entirely on so-called "health foods" such as wheat grass? Does healthful eating mean saying goodbye forever to pizza, burgers, and candy bars? You may be relieved to find out that the answer to both of these questions is no.

Healthful Eating

From a scientific perspective, healthful eating means taking in the appropriate amounts of **nutrients** each day. Nutrients are *substances in food that your body needs for energy, proper growth, body maintenance, and functioning.* There are six classes of nutrients: carbohydrates, proteins, fats, vitamins, minerals, and water. Nutrient needs vary with age, gender, health, and activity level. *The study of food and how your body uses the substances in food* is known as **nutrition.**

In this lesson you will learn more about the importance of good nutrition. You will also see that there is room in a healthful eating plan for all your favorite foods.

A first step toward developing healthful eating habits is to examine the factors that influence your food choices.

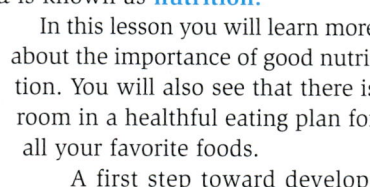

◀ Good nutrition involves eating a variety of healthful foods, including plenty of fruits and vegetables. *What are your favorite fruits and vegetables?*

What You Will Do

- Identify factors that influence your food choices.
- Explain the role of carbohydrates, proteins, and fats in your eating plan.
- Identify the recommended daily amounts of carbohydrates, proteins, and fats.

Terms to Know

nutrients
nutrition
culture
carbohydrates
proteins
fats
calorie
adipose tissue
dietary fiber
amino acids
vegetarian
saturated fatty acids
trans fatty acids
unsaturated fatty acids
cholesterol
LDL
HDL

113

The Importance of Nutrition

1 MOTIVATE

GETTING STARTED

- Ask students how healthy eating is important to their personal fitness based on what they learned about functional health and fitness in Chapter 1.

- Distribute copies of *Guided Practice Activity 4-1* for students to use while studying this lesson. 📁

INTRODUCING VOCABULARY

- Review with students the list of vocabulary terms for this lesson. Ask them to identify two terms that are unfamiliar to them, and have volunteers look up the definitions of those terms in the Glossary/ Glosario. Ask the volunteers to read the definitions aloud to the class.

- Have students use *Vocabulary Worksheet 4* or the PuzzleMaker software to practice vocabulary terms for this lesson. ELL 📁 💿

Photo Follow-up

Emphasize to students the importance of making healthy food choices by including fruits and vegetables in their daily eating plans.

LESSON 1 RESOURCES

Teacher Classroom Resources
📁 Guided Practice Activity 4-1
📁 Reteaching Activity 4-1
📁 Lesson Quiz 4-1

Reproducible Charts and Graphs
💿 Reproducible Masters 4-1, 4-2, 4-3

Multimedia
💿 Vocabulary PuzzleMaker
🔦 Transparency 25

Student Edition TEKS
Page 113: C5D

2 TEACH

Discussing

Ask students to identify what factors influence their food choices. Students should realize that all the bulleted points on this page influence their food choice behaviors. Stress the difference between appetite and hunger. **L1**

Photo Follow-up

Answers to the photo caption will vary but should relate to the discussion of peer influence in Chapter 1.

Activity

Ask students to interview one person to find out what factors influence his or her food choices. Have students compare their interview responses to the factors listed on this page. Ask: Are there any other factors that influence food choices? **L3**

✔ **Reading Check**
> Hunger is a physical need, and appetite is a desire rather than a need.

▶ Friends and peers can influence your food choices. *Give one example of how friends have a positive influence on your food choices and one example of how they might have a negative influence.*

Influences on Your Food Choices

Have you ever asked yourself why you choose to eat the foods you do? Several factors play a role in your food choices. These include:

- **Hunger.** Hunger is a natural, inborn drive that protects you from starvation. It is a physical need that drives you to eat.
- **Appetite.** Appetite is a personal desire, rather than a need, to eat. Appetite is psychological, not physical.
- **Culture.** *The shared customs, traditions, and beliefs of a particular group* make up a person's **culture.** Cultural or ethnic background may influence food choices. For example, rice is a staple in many Asian cultures.
- **Family and friends.** You may choose certain foods because you have grown up eating them. Friends and peers may also influence many teens' food choices.
- **Emotions.** Have you ever eaten just because you were bored? Have you ever been too upset to eat? Your feelings can have an enormous impact on your food choices.
- **Convenience and cost.** Due to busy schedules, many people, including teens, select foods that are easy to prepare and eat. For example, you may choose to buy foods from a vending machine because they can be eaten quickly. Cost is also a consideration for many people. For example, its low cost may make it easier to choose fast food.
- **Advertising.** Food advertising is a multibillion-dollar industry. Think about the food ads you have seen recently on TV. What products were these ads promoting? What eating decisions have you made based on food ads?

✔**Reading Check**

Compare What is the difference between hunger and appetite?

COOPERATIVE Learning

FOOD CHOICES Our environment has a strong influence on our food choices. For example, our access to food at home, school, and restaurants affects how and what we choose to eat. Discuss with students how their environment affects what they see and hear, including food advertising; what their peers consume; and the convenience and cost of food. Then have students form small groups to develop a list of ways they can change their environments to have more positive influences on food choices. Have each group report their findings. **ELL**

Nutrients for Energy

What do running, taking a test, and sleeping all have in common? All these activities require energy. Even when you are asleep, your heart and lungs are hard at work, pumping blood and taking in air. Proper nutrition is necessary for your body to function at its best.

In a way, your body is like a car. Both need fuel in order to run. Your body's fuel comes from the energy sources in the foods you eat. There are three such energy sources, all of which are nutrients. They are carbohydrates, proteins, and fats.

- **Carbohydrates** are *the starches and sugars found in food.* They are the body's chief source of energy.
- **Proteins** are *nutrients that help build, maintain, and repair body tissues.* They also serve, when necessary, as a secondary source of energy.
- **Fats** *supply a concentrated form of energy and help transport other nutrients to locations in the body where they are needed.*

Your body's energy needs are measured in calories. A **calorie** is *the amount of energy needed to raise the temperature of 1 kilogram (about a quart) of water 1 degree Celsius.* You expend calories with everything you do.

It is important to note that your levels of physical activity and exercise have a direct bearing on your energy needs. As your activity level increases, so does your body's demand for more calories. **Figure 4.1** contains some general guidelines for daily calorie intake.

FIGURE 4.1

DAILY CALORIE INTAKE
Calorie intake depends on gender, age, and level of activity. *How many calories should you consume daily?*

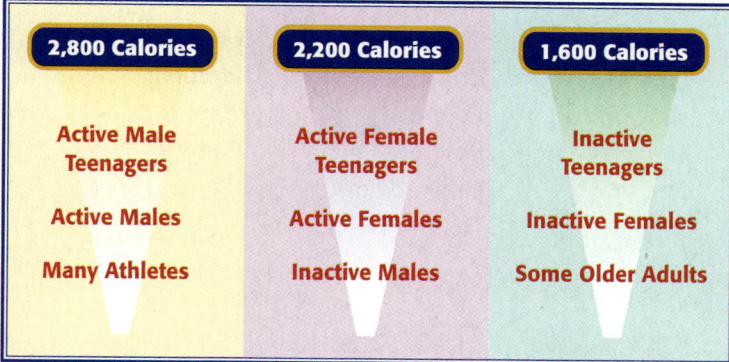

2,800 Calories	2,200 Calories	1,600 Calories
Active Male Teenagers	Active Female Teenagers	Inactive Teenagers
Active Males	Active Females	Inactive Females
Many Athletes	Inactive Males	Some Older Adults

Source: USDA, 2002.[1]

Fitness FACTS

Nutrients and Exercise

- Walking a mile burns about the same number of calories—100—as jogging a mile. Jogging permits you to finish sooner.
- One pound of fat has 3,500 calories.
- You can lose up to 3 liters of water through perspiration in one hour.

Cross-Curriculum Activity

Math Have students calculate how many calories they would need to maintain their energy needs while sitting at rest for 24 hours, based on a rate of approximately 1 to 1.5 calories burned per minute. *Answers will vary but should be between 1,440 calories and 2,160 calories.*

USING VISUALS

Figure 4.1 Distribute *Reproducible Master 4-1.* Have students answer the caption question based on their individual gender and activity level. Then ask students why they might need to consume more than the recommended number of calories shown. One reason might be that they are exercising for high performance and burning more than 2,800 calories per day.

More About . . .

PHYSICAL ACTIVITY AND CALORIES Physical activity can account for 15 to 30 percent of your total daily caloric expenditure, depending on how active you are at school, at work, and during your leisure time. Remind students that they burn 1 to 1.5 calories per minute just sitting at rest. Moderate physical activity helps them burn about 3 to 6 calories per minute, and vigorous physical activity helps burn over 7 calories per minute. By integrating moderate and vigorous physical activity into their lifestyles, students can learn to achieve a healthy body weight that can be maintained into adulthood.

Student Edition TEKS
Page 115: C5D

Critical Thinking

Have students list all the simple and complex carbohydrates they have eaten in the past 24 hours. Ask them to determine whether they are meeting the recommended amounts (45 to 65 percent) of carbohydrates in their diet. Have them explain why or why not. **L1**

USING VISUALS

Figure 4.2 Display *Transparency 25* and discuss the variety of available carbohydrate sources. Have students answer the figure caption. *Caption answer: 4 calories of energy.* Then ask them how many calories they would consume if they ate 70 grams of carbohydrates. *280 calories* Reinforce that this method is used by nutritionists to compute how much energy (or how many calories) we get from foods.

Carbohydrates

Gram for gram, carbohydrates are more energy efficient than fat because they require less oxygen to be converted into energy. One gram of carbohydrates provides 4 calories of energy. Carbohydrates come mainly from plant sources of food and are classified as either simple or complex.

- **Simple carbohydrates.** These are sugars; they are found mostly in fruits, candy, cookies, and soda. Simple carbohydrates are absorbed quickly into the bloodstream and provide a quick form of energy.
- **Complex carbohydrates.** These are starches; they are found in certain vegetables such as corn and potatoes, as well as breads, cereals, pasta, rice, and dry beans. Complex carbohydrates are broken down more slowly by your body than simple carbohydrates and supply more vitamins. Thus, they are a better source of sustained energy than simple carbohydrates for endurance sports and activities such as running.

Between 45 to 65 percent of the calories you consume daily should come from carbohydrates, mostly complex carbohydrates. **Figure 4.2** lists carbohydrates from the various food groups.

FIGURE 4.2

SOURCES OF CARBOHYDRATES
Carbohydrates can be found in foods from many of the food groups. *How much energy does one gram of carbohydrate provide?*

Grains Group	Fruit Group	Vegetable Group	Milk Group
Bagels	Apples	Broccoli	Frozen yogurt
Breads	Bananas	Carrots	Milk (2% or skim)
Cereals	Fruit juices	Corn	Pudding
Crackers	Nectarines	Peppers	Yogurt
English muffins	Oranges	Potatoes	Cheese
Graham crackers	Pears	Green beans	
Pasta noodles		Tomatoes	
Popcorn			
Pretzels			
Rice			

More About . . .

COMPLEX CARBOHYDRATES AND WHOLE GRAINS Found in whole grains, complex carbohydrates are the common food for people worldwide. Some species of grains include:

- Wheat—domesticated nearly 9,000 years ago in the Near East; now the world's most cultivated plant.
- Rice—domesticated in Southeast Asia; now used more than any other grain.
- Corn—domesticated in the Americas; now used chiefly to feed livestock.
- Sorghum, barley, rye, oats, and millet—significant food crops worldwide.

Carbohydrates in the Body

Before your body can use carbohydrates for energy, it must convert them to a simple sugar known as glucose. Excess glucose is also stored in the liver and muscles as a starchlike substance known as glycogen (GLY-kuh-jun). The body can convert glycogen back to glucose when more energy is needed. If a person takes in more carbohydrates than his or her body can use immediately for energy or store as glycogen, the excess glucose is stored as **adipose tissue,** or *body fat.*

People who engage in ultra-endurance training or competition lasting two hours or longer often deplete their glycogen stores. With careful training and eating practices, these athletes can make their bodies store more glycogen so that they have additional energy stores for prolonged physical performance. People who are regularly glycogen-depleted are at higher risk for overtraining and poor physical performance. To maintain normal glucose and glycogen levels, you must regularly replenish your carbohydrate stores.

Dietary Fiber

Dietary fiber is *a special subclass of complex carbohydrates that has several functions, including aiding the body in digestion.* Fiber is not digestible in humans and thus provides no calories.

Certain types of fiber may help reduce the risk of heart disease by lowering levels of cholesterol in the blood. Some types of fiber have also been useful in controlling diabetes by reducing blood glucose levels. For teens ages 14 to 18, the recommended amount of fiber is 38 grams per day for males and 36 grams per day for females.

Fiber-rich foods include whole-grain products, vegetables, and many fruits. These foods help you to feel full and satisfied while being low in calories. Fiber is best consumed in foods rather than supplements. Fiber-rich foods have many nutrients that supplements do not have.

These foods are good sources of dietary fiber. *Which of these foods are a part of your eating plan?*

 **Reading Check**

Explain What is the recommended daily amount of fiber for female teens? for Male teens?

Protein

Muscles are made up of 29 percent protein and 70 percent water. Protein is also a component of bones, connective tissues, skin, blood, and vital organs. Your body needs protein to grow, repair, and maintain itself. Daily living exposes body tissues to wear and tear. The proteins in the foods you eat help repair and maintain these body tissues. Protein helps fight disease, since parts of the immune system are also composed of protein. Protein also supplies your body energy in the form of calories.

Lesson 1 The Importance of Nutrition **117**

Explaining

Help students analyze the relationship between sound nutritional practices and physical activity. Explain that glycogen can be stored in limited amounts in the liver and the skeletal muscles.

The body can store about 2,000 calories of glycogen, which means that if walking or jogging 1 mile burns 100 calories, a person can store enough carbohydrate energy to walk approximately 20 miles. Ask a volunteer to explain how replenishing carbohydrates regularly is important during physical activity. **L1** **TEKS C5D**

Quick Demo

Remind students that they need 20 to 35 grams of fiber daily for good health. Have students read the labels of several breakfast-cereal boxes that you bring to class. Then have them calculate how many servings of the cereal they would have to eat to meet their daily needs for dietary fiber. **L2**

Photo Follow-up

Have students answer the photo figure caption. *Caption answers will vary.* Then ask them why they eat these foods and why they should be included in their eating plan.

Reading Check

Recommended fiber intake for teen females=36 grams; for teen males=38 grams.

Student Edition TEKS

Page 117: C5D

What Teens Want to Know

How can I decide which media messages are accurate and which carry misinformation? One way is to follow the United States Department of Agriculture's Dietary Reference Intake (DRI) Guidelines. For example, many people believe that if a little bit of something is good for you, then more is even better. When it comes to nutrition, however, that is usually not true. For example, if a 14- to 18-year-old teen doubles his or her recommended daily consumption of dietary fiber to 76 grams per day, he or she might not digest foods as well and might not absorb nutrients from foods as easily.

Critical Thinking

Ask students to record their food choices for a five-day period. Then have them count how many servings of complete proteins and incomplete proteins they consumed during that period. Explain that incomplete proteins lack all of the essential amino acids. (Some students will have consumed very few complete proteins.)

L3

USING VISUALS

Figure 4.3 Distribute *Reproducible Master 4-2* and have students answer the figure caption. *Caption answer: 56 grams of protein.* Then ask them to calculate how many grams of protein they would consume if they ate one serving each of the food items listed in the figure. *Answer: 161 grams.* Finally, have them calculate the energy they would get from 161 grams of protein. *Answer: 644 calories.*

The building blocks of proteins are called **amino** (uh-MEE-noh) **acids.** There are 22 different amino acids; your body can manufacture all but nine. These nine are called *essential amino acids* because you must get them from the foods you eat.

The total amount of protein in your eating plan should be between 10 and 35 percent of the calories you consume daily. In the United States, most people consume an adequate amount of protein with little effort. Be aware that if you eat more protein than you need, it will be stored as body fat if you already consume enough calories from carbohydrates and fat. **Figure 4.3** features a list of lean and low-fat foods that are high in protein and also gives examples of serving sizes.

Proteins can only do their job if you consume enough carbohydrates and fat to meet your energy needs. If you do not, the body will use protein for energy, rather than for growth, and for building and repairing cells and tissues.

Complete and Incomplete Proteins

There are two types of proteins found in foods: complete and incomplete. *Complete proteins* contain all nine essential amino acids. Animal products such as meats and dairy products are sources of complete proteins. With the exception of soybeans, plant foods contain *incomplete proteins*—that is, they lack one or more of the essential amino acids. This information is especially important for **vegetarians,** *individuals who eliminate meat, fish, and poultry from their eating plans.* If you are a vegetarian, make sure you eat a variety

FIGURE 4.3

PROTEIN IN VARIOUS FOODS
How many grams of protein would there be in taco filling that contains one serving of turkey and one serving of black beans?

Protein in Various Foods

Food	Protein (grams)	Serving Size
Turkey, roasted, diced	41	3 ounces
Cottage cheese, 2% fat	31	½ cup
Tuna, canned, water packed	30	3 ounces
Lean pork rib, roasted, boneless	21	3 ounces
Yogurt, plain, low-fat	12	8 ounces (1 cup)
Black beans, dry, cooked	15	½ cup
Eggs, hard-cooked	6	1 egg
Peanut butter	5	2 tablespoons

Teacher-Coach Tips

Vegetarian Diets Consuming enough complete protein may be a challenge for some vegetarians. Unless they combine foods carefully, their meals will not provide the protein they need. Three equations help create vegetarian meals with complete protein:

- Legumes + Grains = Complete Protein
- Legumes + Nuts or Seeds = Complete Protein
- Any Plant Protein + Eggs or Dairy Products = Complete Protein

of plant-based foods and dairy products to ensure an adequate intake of complete proteins. Vegans (VEE-guhnz), vegetarians who also eliminate eggs and dairy products from their eating plans, need special nutritional guidance from a health professional to meet their protein needs.

✓ **Reading Check**

Compare What is the difference between complete and incomplete proteins?

Fats

Fats, or lipids, are another type of nutrient that provides energy. At nine calories per gram, fats supply more than twice the energy of a gram of carbohydrate or protein. Fats also

- transport and absorb vitamins A, D, E, and K.
- help regulate the hormone **testosterone,** which is used to build body tissues.
- enhance the flavor and texture of foods.
- help satisfy hunger because they take longer to digest.

Fats can be stored in the body as *triglycerides* (try-GLIS-uhr-idz) and used as energy for exercise or physical activity, especially for periods of exertion that last 30 minutes or longer.

Considering all the positive properties of fats, you may wonder why fats have such a bad reputation. Here's why: Eating too many fats is linked to many serious health problems, including heart disease and certain cancers. In addition, most fat that is not used by the body for energy is stored as adipose tissue. Excess body fat may lead to unhealthful weight gain and obesity, which increases the risk of health conditions such as type 2 diabetes.

Types of Fat

Fats are a mixture of different types of fatty acids, which can be classified into three basic types.

- **Saturated fatty acids** are *fats that come mainly from animal fats, including butter and lard, and are often solid at room temperature.* Fatty meats, cheese, ice cream, and whole milk contain saturated fats. Some oils, like palm oil and coconut oil, are also high in saturated fats.
- **Trans fatty acids** are *fats that are formed when certain oils are processed into solids.* Margarine and shortening are two examples of foods high in trans fats. The presence of trans fats in processed foods can often be identified by the words *partially hydrogenated* in the list of ingredients. Nutrition Facts panels may also contain information on trans fats.
- **Unsaturated fatty acids** are *fats that are usually liquid at room temperature and come mainly from plant sources.* Unsaturated fats include corn oil, soybean oil, olive oil, sunflower oil, and some fish oils.

Lesson 1 The Importance of Nutrition **119**

testosterone
For more on testosterone and its role in building muscles, see Chapter 9, page **257.**

---

hot link

Point out that fats help regulate the role that testosterone plays in muscle development. Have students review Chapter 9 for more about this topic.

✓ **Reading Check**

Complete proteins contain all nine essential amino acids required for growth and development. Incomplete proteins must be combined to ensure proper protein consumption.

Critical Thinking

Ask students whether it is healthy for a person to cut all fat out of his or her eating plan. If not, why not?

Answer: Among other functions, fats transport vitamins in the bloodstream, provide energy, and are needed for healthy skin. **L3**

More About . . .

TRANS FATTY ACIDS Hydrogenation, the process of adding missing hydrogen atoms to unsaturated fats, makes these fats more saturated and firmer in texture. Margarine, for example, is a hydrogenated form of vegetable oil. The fats that result from hydrogenation are called trans fatty acids. Many foods containing these fats are advertised as being more healthful than foods containing saturated fat, but recent studies indicate that trans fatty acids may present as great a health risk as the saturated fats they replace. Ask students to research more about trans fatty acids and report their findings.

Student Edition TEKS

Page 118: C5D
Page 119: C5D

USING VISUALS

Figure 4.4 Use *Reproducible Master 4-3* to discuss fat intake. Have students answer the caption question. *Caption answer: Answers will vary based on gender and activity level.* Then have them pair off, ask their partners the same questions, and calculate the number of calories from fat they would advise, based on their partners' daily nutritional needs. 📁

Activity

Have the school nurse attend class and bring a standard blood analysis that has been processed and includes measures of total cholesterol, LDL cholesterol, and HDL cholesterol. Then have the nurse lead a class discussion about normal levels for each type of cholesterol. *Total cholesterol: <200 mg/dl or lower is best; HDL: >60 mg/dl lowers risk for heart disease and diabetes, but HDL >40 mg/dl is best; LDL: 100-129 mg/dl is optimal.* L2

Source: *American Heart Association*

✔ Reading Check

Saturated fats and trans fats increase cholesterol levels.

FIGURE 4.4

WHAT IS YOUR UPPER LIMIT ON FAT?

How many calories do you consume? How many grams from fat a day are recommended, based on your calorie intake? How many grams of fat do you consume?

Total Daily Calories	Recommended Daily Intake of Saturated and Trans Fat	Recommended Daily Intake of Total Fat
1,600	18 grams or less	53 grams
2,000	20 grams or less	65 grams
2,200	24 grams or less	73 grams
2,500	25 grams or less	80 grams
2,800	31 grams or less	93 grams

Cholesterol

Saturated fats and trans fats typically contain cholesterol. **Cholesterol** is *a fatlike substance that is produced in the liver and circulates in the blood.* Cholesterol is found only in foods of animal origin. Your body needs some cholesterol for certain processes. For example, cholesterol is used in the production of cell membranes and certain hormones. Your body can manufacture all the cholesterol it needs. Cholesterol can also be obtained from food, such as egg yolks, meat, and high-fat milk products.

High levels of cholesterol in the blood have been linked to an increased risk of heart disease, because excess cholesterol is deposited in the arteries. An eating plan that is high in saturated fats or trans fats raises blood cholesterol levels. Thus, it's important to limit intake of foods that contain these types of fatty acids. In addition, the American Heart Association recommends limiting dietary cholesterol to less than 300 milligrams per day.

Cholesterol in the Blood. Cholesterol circulates through the bloodstream in special fat-protein "packages" called lipoproteins (LY-poh-PROH-teenz). There are two major types of lipoproteins.

- **Low-density lipoprotein (LDL)** is *a type of compound that carries cholesterol from the liver to areas of the body where it is needed.* When too much LDL cholesterol is circulating in the blood, the excess amounts can build up inside arteries—blood vessels that carry blood away from the heart. This buildup increases the risk of heart disease or stroke. Thus, LDL cholesterol is sometimes referred to as "bad" cholesterol.

More About . . .

CHOLESTEROL Lipoproteins are molecules made by the liver that transport cholesterol in the blood. The cholesterol carried by low-density lipoproteins (LDLs) tends to build up in arteries. The higher the level of LDLs in the blood, the greater the risk of heart disease. High-density lipoproteins (HDLs) carry excess blood cholesterol back to the liver, where it can be eliminated. Thus, HDL cholesterol helps prevent buildup in the blood vessels. Limit intake of saturated fats and dietary cholesterol, both of which raise LDL levels. Increase physical activity and manage weight to elevate HDL levels.

- **High-density lipoprotein (HDL)** is *a type of compound that picks up excess cholesterol and returns it to the liver.* Because it carries excess cholesterol to the liver before it can do any harm, HDL cholesterol is sometimes called "good" cholesterol.

Fat and Daily Calories

Fats should make up about 20 to 30 percent of your daily calories. Because of the link between excess consumption of saturated fats and an increased risk of heart disease, you need to keep your intake of saturated fats as low as possible. The chart in **Figure 4.4** provides some general guidelines for relative amounts of fats in your eating plan. Here are two other recommendations for reducing your fat intake.

- Limit your use of solid fats, such as butter, hard margarines, lard, and partially hydrogenated shortenings. Use vegetable oils as a substitute.
- Choose fat-free or low-fat dairy products, cooked dry beans and peas, fish, and lean meats and poultry.

Eating less fat overall may promote weight loss if calorie intake is less, too. However, restricting fat consumption to less than 20 percent of daily calories may be difficult to maintain over the long term and may not be healthful.

 Reading Check

Evaluate Which types of fat increase blood cholesterol level?

Lesson 1 Review

Using complete sentences, answer the following questions on a sheet of paper.

Reviewing Facts and Vocabulary

1. **Vocabulary** What is *nutrition?*
2. **Vocabulary** List two categories of *carbohydrates.* Name two foods that are a good source of each type.
3. **Recall** What are the three types of fatty acids? Which two raise blood cholesterol levels?

Thinking Critically

4. **Analyze** Maya is considering following a vegetarian eating plan. However, she has heard that vegetarians do not get enough protein in their diets. What advice would you give her about proteins and vegetarianism?

5. **Compare and Contrast** What is the difference between saturated and unsaturated fatty acids? Between HDL cholesterol and LDL cholesterol?

Personal Fitness Planning

Evaluating Nutrition Make a list of your food choices over the past week. How many times did you eat fast foods or snack foods that contain saturated or trans fats? List four to five ways you can reduce the amount of foods you consume that contain saturated and/or trans fats. If you do not consume a lot of foods with saturated and/or trans fats, how would you advise a person who is trying to cut back on such foods?

Lesson 1 The Importance of Nutrition **121**

Lesson 1 Review

Answers to Lesson 1 Review

1. The study of food and how your body uses the substances in food.
2. Two types of carbohydrates are *simple* and *complete*. Examples will vary.
3. Saturated, trans fats, unsaturated fats; saturated, trans fats raise cholesterol.

4. Maya should eat a variety of plant-based foods and dairy products, and seek special nutritional guidance.
5. Saturated fats are solid at room temperature and come mainly from animal sources, while unsaturated fats are usually liquid and come from plant sources.

---

3 ASSESS

EVALUATING THE LESSON

Assign and discuss the Lesson 1 Review.

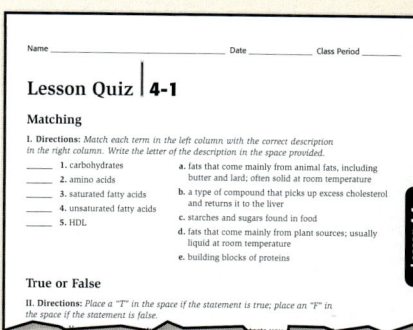

RETEACHING

Ask students to identify three nutrients that provide energy and summarize the role and importance of those nutrients to physical activity.

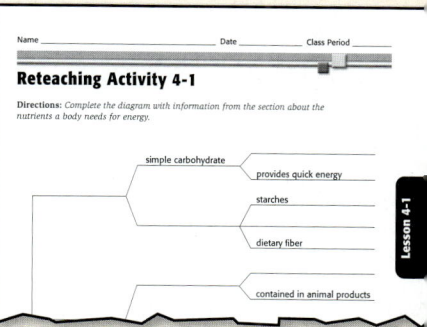

ENRICHMENT

Have students develop a flash-card calories game using photos from magazines. Have them identify the calories and grams of fat in each serving, using a nutrition analyzer.

4 CLOSE

Have students list three foods with high nutritional value and three with lower nutritional value.

Vitamins, Minerals, and Water

Lesson 2

1 MOTIVATE

GETTING STARTED

- Ask students whether they feel they need to take vitamin and mineral supplements to meet their daily nutritional needs. If they do, ask why they think so. Inform them that it is not necessary to take vitamin supplements if they learn to eat wisely.

- Distribute copies of *Guided Practice Activity 4-2* for students to use while studying this lesson. 📁

IN THIS LESSON

- **Stress Break,** *p. 127*

INTRODUCING VOCABULARY

- Point out that the term *dietary supplements* refers to products that are not standardized, so there is no assurance of their potency or purity. The Food and Drug Administration (FDA) requires only that manufacturers ensure product safety and that certain information appear on dietary supplement labels.

- Have students use *Vocabulary Worksheet 4* or the PuzzleMaker software to practice vocabulary terms for this lesson. 🅴🅻🅻 📁 ◎

What You Will Do

- Identify the two categories of vitamins and foods that provide them.
- List and describe the major minerals and their role in nutrition.
- Analyze the relationship between sound nutritional practices and physical activity.
- Explain the relationship between fluid balance and physical activity.
- Identify the importance of water to your body's functioning.

Terms to Know

vitamins
antioxidants
minerals
phytonutrients
dietary supplement

Vitamins, Minerals, and Water

Have you ever heard it said that good things come in small packages? This saying certainly applies to the nutrients known as vitamins and minerals. In this lesson, you will learn what these substances do for the body. You will also learn about another important nutrient, water.

Micronutrients

Because vitamins and minerals are nutrients needed in tiny amounts, they are known as micronutrients. Although you need only small amounts of these, they have very important functions. They help your body convert and release energy as well as protect your body's cells from certain types of damage.

 You can get many of the vitamins your body needs from food sources instead of supplements. *What nutrients do these food sources provide?*

LESSON 2 RESOURCES

Teacher Classroom Resources
📁 Guided Practice Activity 4-2
📁 Reteaching Activity 4-2
📁 Lesson Quiz 4-2

Reproducible Charts and Graphs
📁 Reproducible Master 4-4

Multimedia
◎ Vocabulary PuzzleMaker
✋ Transparencies 26, 27

FIGURE 4.5

FAT-SOLUBLE VITAMINS

A variety of foods can provide you with the appropriate vitamins.

Which of the foods listed are a part of your regular eating plan?

Vitamin/Amount Needed Each Day	Function	Food Source
A Teen female: 800 mcg Teen male: 1,000 mcg	helps maintain skin tissue, strengthens tooth enamel, promotes use of calcium and phosphorous in bone formation, promotes cell growth, keeps eyes moist, helps eyes adjust to darkness, may aid in cancer prevention	milk and other dairy products, green vegetables, carrots, deep-orange fruits, liver
D Teen female: 5 mcg Teen male: 5 mcg	promotes absorption and use of calcium and phosphorous, essential for normal bone and tooth development	fortified milk, eggs, fortified breakfast cereals, sardines, salmon, beef, margarine; also produced in skin exposed to sun's ultraviolet rays
E Teen female: 8 mg Teen male: 10 mg	may help in oxygen transport, may slow the effects of aging, may protect against destruction of red blood cells	present in vegetable oils, nuts, seeds, whole grain breads and cereals, dark green leafy vegetables, dry beans, and peas
K Teen female: 55 mcg Teen male: 65 mcg	essential for blood clotting, assists in regulating blood calcium level	spinach, broccoli, eggs, liver, cabbage, tomatoes

Vitamins

Vitamins are *micronutrients that help control body processes and help your body release energy to do work.* Because vitamins do not contain calories, they don't provide your body with energy.

Vitamins may be classified as fat-soluble or water-soluble.

- **Fat-soluble vitamins,** carried by fat in food and in your body, can be stored in the body. The fat-soluble vitamins are vitamins A, D, E, and K. A list of fat-soluble vitamins and food sources for each may be found in **Figure 4.5.**
- **Water-soluble vitamins** are not stored in your body. They need to be replaced daily by eating nutritious foods. Vitamin C and the B complex vitamins (thiamin, riboflavin, niacin, folate, B_6, and B_{12}) are among these important vitamins. A complete list of water-soluble vitamins and food sources for each may be found in **Figure 4.6.**

 **Reading Check**

Compare How do fat-soluble and water-soluble vitamins differ?

Promoting Coordinated School Health

NUTRITION AT SCHOOL The school cafeteria has become a major focus of many coordinated school health programs that include helping students and teachers learn more about healthy eating. Many states are currently passing legislation that limits the availability of so-called "junk foods" in school cafeterias and vending machines. Have students interview the manager of the school cafeteria and ask how he or she is adjusting the food menus to meet the newer *Dietary Guidelines.* Have students evaluate the foods and beverages in the school vending machines, and ask them to make recommendations for possible alternative selections.

Chapter 4, Lesson 2

2 TEACH

USING VISUALS

Figure 4.5 Have students answer the figure caption. *Caption answers will vary, but students should emphasize that all the foods listed can and should be part of a healthy eating plan.* Have students do research on vitamin E and ask them to explain why it is considered an antioxidant vitamin. (*Because it helps transport oxygen and may slow the effects of aging.*)

Explaining

Explain to students that foods containing water-soluble vitamins need to be cooked carefully so that the vitamins are not destroyed by heat or lost through steam or in cooking water. To conserve water-soluble vitamins in food:

- Cook fruits and vegetables quickly, or steam them.
- Cover food during cooking. **L1**

Discussing

Help students analyze the relationship between sound nutritional practices and physical activity. Have them examine Figures 4.5, 4.6, and 4.7 to identify the functions of vitamins and minerals in the body and how these functions are important for physical activities. **TEKS C5D**

Student Edition TEKS

Page 122: C3C, C5D

FIGURE 4.6

WATER-SOLUBLE VITAMINS

Many foods are a good source of more than one vitamin. *Name one food that is a good source of Vitamins B₂, Niacin, and B₁₂.*

Vitamin/Amount Needed Each Day	Function	Food Source
C (ascorbic acid) Teen female: 60 mg Teen male: 60 mg	protects against infection, helps form connective tissue, helps heal wounds, maintains elasticity and strength of blood vessels, promotes healthy teeth and gums	citrus fruits, cantaloupe, tomatoes, cabbage, broccoli, potatoes, peppers
B₁ (thiamine) Teen female: 1.1 mg Teen male: 1.5 mg	converts glucose into energy or fat, contributes to good appetite	whole-grain or enriched cereals, liver, yeast, nuts, legumes, wheat germ
B₂ (riboflavin) Teen female: 1.3 mg Teen male: 1.8 mg	essential for producing energy from carbohydrates, fats, and proteins; helps keep skin healthy	milk, cheese, spinach, eggs, beef liver
Niacin Teen female: 15 mg Teen male: 20 mg	important for maintenance of all body tissues; helps in energy production; needed by body to utilize carbohydrates, to synthesize body fat, and for cell respiration	milk, eggs, poultry, beef, legumes, peanut butter, whole grains, enriched and fortified grain products
B₆ Teen female: 1.5 mg Teen male: 2.0 mg	essential for amino acid and carbohydrate metabolism, helps turn the amino acid tryptophan into serotonin (a messenger to the brain) and niacin	wheat bran and wheat germ, liver, meat, whole grains, fish, vegetables
Folic Acid Teen female: 180 mcg Teen male: 200 mcg	necessary for production of genetic material and normal red blood cells, reduces risk of birth defects	nuts and other legumes, orange juice, green vegetables, folic acid-enriched breads and rolls, liver
B₁₂ Teen female: 2.0 mcg Teen male: 2.0 mcg	necessary for production of red blood cells and for normal growth	animal products such as meat, fish, poultry, eggs, milk, and other dairy foods; some fortified foods

Figure 4.6 Use *Transparency 26* to review the sources of vitamins shown in Figures 4.5 (on page 123) and Figure 4.6. Ask for volunteers to read aloud the recommended daily amount of each vitamin, the vitamin's role in the body, and food sources of each vitamin. Have students answer the figure caption. *Caption answer: Milk and eggs are a good source of these vitamins.*

Activity

Ask students to examine the ingredients in several bottles of vitamin supplements. They can find these at home or at a pharmacy or grocery. Students should list supplements that contain more than the recommended daily amount of vitamins and note whether the vitamins are fat soluble or water soluble. Students will find that supplements often contain extra amounts of water-soluble vitamins, because those vitamins cannot be stored in the body and will be eliminated. Supplements containing extra amounts of fat-soluble vitamins stay in the body, and too much of them can be toxic. **L3**

Antioxidants. Some vitamins and minerals exhibit antioxidant (an-tee-OKS-uh-duhnt) properties. Antioxidants are *substances that protect body cells, including those of the immune system, from damage.* Cells can be damaged by by-products of cell energy production and by environmental factors, such as cigarette smoke and air pollution. Antioxidants protect cells from injury, thereby reducing the risk of cancer, heart disease, and premature aging. Vitamins C and E are both antioxidants.

Reading Check

(page 123)
Fat-soluble vitamins are stored in body fat, and water-soluble vitamins are not stored in the body.

More About . . .

VITAMIN SUPPLEMENTS People who eat a balanced diet do not normally need vitamin supplementation. Americans who feel that they don't eat the way they should, however, often choose to supplement their diets with daily multivitamins. It takes several days or weeks to become vitamin-deficient; therefore, most experts recommend that people wanting to supplement their diets use a simple, low-cost multivitamin. It's always a good idea to seek medical advice when using vitamin supplements because excess vitamin supplementation can cause serious side effects in some individuals.

Minerals

Minerals are *substances that the body cannot manufacture but that are needed for forming healthy bones and teeth and for regulating many vital body processes.* Like vitamins, minerals do not supply your body with energy. **Figure 4.7** lists several minerals, their key roles, and food sources for each.

Four minerals are addressed in detail here: calcium, potassium, sodium, and iron. The first three work as *electrolytes* because their electrical charges help maintain normal heart rhythm and control the body's fluid balance. **Fluid balance** is the body's ability to balance the amount of fluid taken in and the amount lost through perspiration or excretion. There is a direct relationship between fluid balance and performance during physical activity. Proper fluid balance prevents dehydration.

During vigorous physical activity or exercise, electrolyte levels can drop dangerously low if a person perspires heavily. Low potassium levels, in particular, can lead to muscle cramps or difficulties in the conduction of nerve impulses. You can avoid these problems through proper hydration. In some circumstances, athletes may benefit from consuming sports drinks that replenish electrolytes.

hotlink

fluid balance
For more on fluid balance, see Chapter 2, page **41**.

FIGURE 4.7

MINERALS: KEY ROLES AND SOURCES

Minerals help your body function. *Which of the foods listed in the column on the right do you enjoy eating?*

Mineral/Amount Needed Each Day	Function	Food Source
Calcium Teen female: 1,300 mg Teen male: 1,300 mg	building material of bones and teeth (skeleton contains about 99% of body calcium), regulation of body functions (heart muscle contraction, blood clotting)	dairy products; leafy vegetables; canned fish with soft, edible bones; tofu processed with calcium sulfate
Phosphorus Teen female: 1,250 mg Teen male: 1,250 mg	combines with calcium to give rigidity to bones and teeth, essential in cell metabolism, helps maintain proper acid-base balance of blood	milk and most other dairy foods, peas, beans, liver, meat, fish, poultry, eggs, broccoli, whole grains
Magnesium Teen female: 360 mg Teen male: 410 mg	enzyme activator related to carbohydrate metabolism, aids in bone growth and muscle contraction	whole grains, milk, dark green leafy vegetables, legumes, nuts
Iron Teen female: 15 mg Teen male: 12 mg	part of the red blood cells' oxygen and carbon dioxide transport system, important for use of energy in cells and for resistance to infection	meat, shellfish, poultry, legumes, peanuts, dried fruits, egg yolks, liver, fortified breakfast cereal, enriched rice

---

Chapter 4, Lesson 2

USING VISUALS

Figure 4.7 Display *Transparency 27* and introduce the minerals chart to students. Have them answer the figure caption. *Caption answers will vary, but students should note that all the foods listed can and should be part of a healthy eating plan.* Ask students if they know which disease is associated with the lack or loss of calcium that comes with aging (*osteoporosis*, or "brittle bone disease").

Explaining

Explain to students that three main factors contribute to the risk of developing osteoporosis: loss or lack of calcium, inactivity, and low estrogen (hormone) levels. It is very important during the teen years, especially for females, to consume enough calcium and to be physically active. These steps will increase bone mass, which will help prevent osteoporosis later in life. **L1**

QUOTES FOR LIFE

"More people die in the United States of too much food than of too little."

John Kenneth Galbraith
Economist, "The Affluent Society" (1908 –

Student Edition TEKS

Page 124: C5D
Page 125: C5D

Photo Follow-up

Ask students to answer the photo caption question. *Caption answers: Fluid balance involves the body's ability to balance the amounts of fluid taken in with the amounts lost through perspiration or exertion. Answers for how to avoid dehydration will vary but should be based on the information in Chapter 2 about proper hydration and environmental concerns.*

Reinforce to students that hypertension is the major risk factor related to stroke and that it is important for them to prevent the development of hypertension. For those with high blood pressure, one way to control hypertension is to limit sodium. Have students review Chapter 7 for more about this topic.

✓ Reading Check

Electrolytes help control the body's fluid balance to prevent dehydration. **TEKS C3C**

Activity

Ask students to find an illustration or information about perspiration from their science class. Have them use this information to explain the relationship between physical activity and loss of salt during exercise. Have them present their explanation to the class. **TEKS C3C**

▲ Calcium, potassium, and sodium help maintain the body's fluid balance. *What is fluid balance? How can you avoid dehydration during physical activity?*

hypertension
For more on hypertension, see Chapter 7, page **203**.

Calcium. Calcium helps build and maintain strong bones. It is particularly important to consume calcium during your teen years and young adulthood. During the teen years, bones continue to become more dense. After the age of 25, your body is no longer able to add to bone density and calcium stores on its own. Calcium must be replaced regularly since bones are constantly being maintained and repaired. Your muscles also use calcium when they contract. Eating calcium-rich foods, such as dairy products, dark green, leafy vegetables, and canned fish with soft, edible bones, is the best way to get the calcium you need. Taking calcium supplements is another way to make sure you are getting enough calcium. Weight-bearing and weight-lifting exercises can also help maintain and strengthen bones.

Potassium. Potassium aids in normal muscle contractions and in the sending of nerve impulses that control the movement of muscles. Bananas, many dried fruits, and many fruit juices are good sources of potassium.

Sodium. Sodium helps maintain the fluid balance inside and outside cells and helps in the transmission of nerve impulses. Many foods you eat are likely to contain sodium, which is one of the two minerals in table salt—*sodium chloride.* People with **hypertension,** or high blood pressure, need to monitor their sodium intake. Since hypertension is often hereditary, you may be at risk if a parent or grandparent has this health problem. See the *Dietary Guidelines* for specific suggestions on reducing your sodium intake.

Iron. Iron is part of the hemoglobin in red blood cells. Hemoglobin carries oxygen from the lungs to all cells throughout the body. Meats are good sources of this mineral. Because vegetarians do not eat meat, they are at higher risk for iron deficiencies. If you are vegetarian, you need to eat plant foods that contain iron, such as legumes (beans), peanuts, and dried fruits. Iron from plant sources is absorbed better if consumed with a Vitamin-C rich food.

✓ Reading Check

Explain What is the role of electrolytes in maintaining fluid balance?

Water

Between 60 and 70 percent of your body weight is water. Water is an essential nutrient for life. Without it, death would occur in six to seven days.

Water helps regulate body temperature, carries nutrients to cells, aids in digestion and elimination, and is important for many chemical reactions in your body. You need to consume a total of

Teacher-Coach Tips

Sodium and Fluids The National Athletic Trainer's Association has published a position statement on fluid replacement for athletes in the *Journal of Athletic Training* that provided updated recommendations for sodium supplementation for optimal fluid replacement. Experts now recommend that 0.3 to 0.7 grams of salt may need to be added to replacement fluids under specific conditions: if there is inadequate access to meals or if meals have not been eaten; if an athletic event has lasted longer than 4 hours; or if the initial days (the first 5 to 10 days) of training are occurring in hot weather.

64 ounces (8 cups) of water or other fluids daily to maintain normal fluid balance. Certain foods, such as fruits, vegetables, and soup, are also sources of water.

As explained in Chapter 2, drinking adequate fluids is critical when exercising and perspiring heavily. It is often difficult to "catch up" on your fluid balance if you wait until you are thirsty before you begin to rehydrate. Instead, hydrate before, during, and after physical activity or exercise. **Figure 4.8** lists some general guidelines for drinking water or other fluids when you are active. Although water is often the most convenient fluid, you may prefer a sports drink for the taste.

Phytonutrients

Literally meaning "plant nutrients," **phytonutrients** are *health-promoting substances found in plant foods.* According to current estimates, a simple plant-based food may contain several hundred phytonutrients. So far, scientists have been able to isolate only a few.

Some phytonutrients are antioxidants. One well-known example is *beta carotene* (BAY-tuh KAR-uh-teen). This phytonutrient gives certain fruits and vegetables their bright orange color. Carrots and cantaloupe are good sources of beta carotene.

Lutein (LOO-tee-en) is a phytonutrient that may protect against blindness. Lutein is found in yellow-orange fruits such as mangoes, peaches, tangerines, and yellow and red bell peppers. It is also found in green leafy vegetables such as kale, spinach, and collard greens.

✓ Reading Check

Identify What are two examples of phytonutrients?

FIGURE 4.8

FLUID REPLACEMENT AND PHYSICAL ACTIVITY
Drinking water before, during, and after physical activity is essential. Explain the relationship to water and salt loss.

Before	During	After
Drink 10 to 14 ounces of water one to two hours before the activity or exercise.	Drink ½ cup (4 ounces) of cold water every fifteen minutes.	Drink 2 cups (16 ounces) of cold water for every pound of weight loss.

Source: Play Hard, Eat Right: A Parent's Guide to Sports Nutrition for Children, 1998.[2]

More About . . .

CAFFEINE Caffeine stimulates the central nervous system and is considered a controlled drug in athletic competition such as the Olympics. Excess caffeine (the equivalent of four to seven cups of coffee, an illegal dosage level) has been used by athletes to mask fatigue in short events such as sprints and longer events such as the 10,000-meter run. The side effects from caffeine, however, which can include insomnia, nervousness, headaches, and dehydration—not to mention possible disqualification—are hardly worth it.

STRESS BREAK
Avoid Rehydrating with Caffeine
When it comes to rehydrating, not all beverages are created equal. Cola or other drinks containing caffeine can give you a quick lift—but they can also give you the jitters. Caffeine is a stimulant. It may increase your heart rate and can cause headaches, upset stomach, nervousness, sleeplessness, and irritability. Play it smart. Play it safe. Avoid caffeine.

STRESS BREAK
Have students read and discuss the Stress Break feature. Ask students how often they rehydrate by drinking caffeinated beverages. Have volunteers describe the effects they experienced. Explain that the diuretic effect of carbonated sodas actually causes excess fluid excretion and could lead to dehydration.

USING VISUALS

Figure 4.8 Discuss the importance of fluid replacement using *Reproducible Master 4-4*. Ask students to explain the relationship between physical activity, fluid balance, and environmental conditions, such as water loss during exercise. Have students interview members of their school football defensive line concerning two-a-day summer workouts. How much weight does the player lose during a practice session? How much fluid will they need to drink for rehydration? 📂 **TEKS C3C**

✓ Reading Check
Lutein, found in kale, spinach, and collard greens, is an example of a phytonutrient; Beta carotene, found in carrots and cantaloupe.

Student Edition TEKS
Page 126: C3C, C5D
Page 127: C3C, C5D

3 ASSESS

EVALUATING THE LESSON

Assign and discuss the Lesson 2 Review.

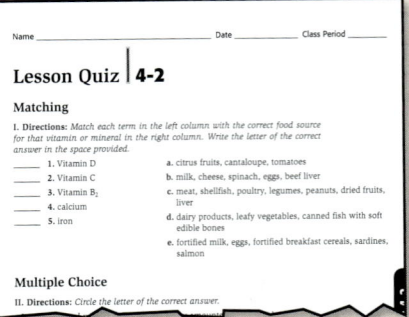

RETEACHING

Ask students to summarize three main points about ways vitamins, minerals, and water benefit physical fitness.

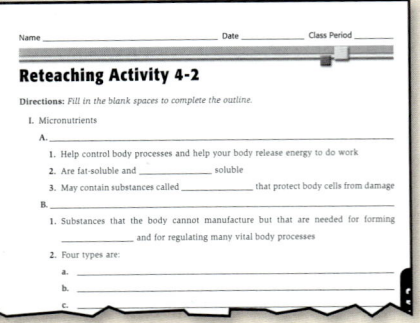

ENRICHMENT

Ask students to interview someone outside their immediate family about whether they think they get all the vitamins and minerals they need in their normal diet.

4 CLOSE

Divide the class into teams and have teams create lists of facts about each vitamin or mineral.

Dietary Supplements

A **dietary supplement** is *a nonfood form of one or more nutrients*. Vitamins and minerals have long been available in supplement form. More recently, herbs and other substances that claim to enhance health or improve certain health conditions are also sold as supplements.

People with special dietary needs may be advised by health care professionals to use dietary supplements. One such group is pregnant females, who need extra amounts of iron and the B vitamin folate. Older adults and people who get little exposure to sunlight may need a Vitamin D supplement if they do not consume enough Vitamin D-fortified milk or spend enough time in sunlight. Vegans are often counseled to take Vitamin B_{12} supplements because this vitamin is found only in animal foods.

While taking dietary supplements may be useful in certain cases, it is no substitute for eating healthfully. In addition, taking supplements may increase the likelihood of getting too much of a particular nutrient or other substance. For example, fat-soluble vitamins are stored in the body and can build up to toxic levels if taken in large amounts. Always seek advice from a health care provider before taking any dietary supplement.

In Chapter 6, you will explore another group of dietary supplements—those marketed as aids to weight loss or weight gain.

Reading Check

Explain Who might be advised to take a dietary supplement?

Lesson 2 Review

Using complete sentences, answer the following questions on a sheet of paper.

Reviewing Facts and Vocabulary

1. **Vocabulary** What are *vitamins*? Name three fat-soluble and three water-soluble vitamins.
2. **Recall** Describe the importance of water to health.

Thinking Critically

3. **Synthesize** Explain the relationship between physical performance and proper intake of each of the following: calcium, potassium, and sodium.
4. **Analyze** After her early morning workout, Allie is always in a rush and doesn't properly

rehydrate. What would you tell Allie about the importance of water to convince her to hydrate before, during, and after her workout?

Personal Fitness Planning

Analyzing Nutrition Keep a fluid log for three days. Note each time you consume a beverage, including the amount in ounces consumed. Also write down any food sources of water that you consume. Determine whether you are meeting your needs for this nutrient. If not, plan how you can go about doing so.

Lesson 2 Review

Answers to Lesson 2 Review

1. Vitamins are micronutrients that help control body processes and help your body release energy to do work. Examples from Figures 4.5, 4.6.
2. Water is essential for life. Without it, death would occur in six to seven days.
3. Calcium, potassium, and sodium regulate important bodily functions. Calcium is important for strong bones.
4. Remind Allie that if she is dehydrated before she works out, she is at risk for heat injuries, and she may perform at lower levels.

Choosing Foods Wisely

What foods do you enjoy eating? Which nutrients do these foods provide? When it comes to making food choices, both these questions are important.

You already know the answer to the first question. In this lesson, you will learn more about the answer to the second.

The Foods You Eat

The good news is that foods that are good for you can also taste good. Do you eat any of the foods in the photo on this page? These and other popular foods have high nutrient content. The sections that follow will introduce easy-to-use tools to determine if your food choices are nutritious. These are the *Dietary Guidelines for Americans,* Food Guide Pyramid, and Nutrition Facts panel on food labels.

Dietary Guidelines for Americans: Aim, Build, Choose

The U.S. Department of Agriculture and the Department of Health and Human Services has released the *Dietary Guidelines for Americans.* These guidelines spell out in simple language the healthy-eating and active-living needs for all Americans as a whole, including teens.

This document identifies ten main guidelines for healthy eating and living. These ten guidelines are shown in **Figure 4.9.** Note that they are categorized into three groups, under the headings *Aim for Fitness,* *Build a Healthy Base,* and *Choose Sensibly.* These ABCs of good health make it even easier to eat healthfully and maintain an active lifestyle.

▶ The Food Guide Pyramid can help you determine a balanced eating plan for yourself. *To what food groups do each of the foods pictured belong?*

What You Will Do

- Identify the *Dietary Guidelines for Americans.*
- Identify the role of the Food Guide Pyramid and the Nutrition Facts panel in a healthful eating plan.
- Analyze a meal by calculating its percentage of calories that come from the various food groups.
- Explain how to develop healthful eating habits.
- Identify ways to keep food safe.

Terms to Know

Food Guide Pyramid
Dietary Reference Intakes (DRIs)
Nutrition Facts panel
foodborne illnesses
cross-contamination

Choosing Foods Wisely

1 MOTIVATE

GETTING STARTED

- Ask students to explain in their own words the concept of the ABCs of nutrition. Finally, ask them what ABC stands for.
- Distribute copies of *Guided Practice Activity 4-3* for students to use while studying this lesson. 📁

IN THIS LESSON

- **Active Mind—Active Body** *Calculating Calories from a Sample Meal, p. 134*
- **Consumer Corner,** *Dining Out: A Word to the Wise, p. 136*

INTRODUCING VOCABULARY

- Explain that *Dietary Reference Intakes (DRI)* is a newer term that replaced the older term *Recommended Daily Allowance (RDA).* The DRI is set by the United States Department of Agriculture (USDA).
- Have students use *Vocabulary Worksheet 4* or the PuzzleMaker software to practice vocabulary terms for this lesson. ELL 📁 💿

Photo Follow-up

Ask students to answer the photo caption question. *Caption answers may vary but should include the Fruit group, the Grains group, and the Milk group listed in the Food Guide Pyramid.*

LESSON 3 RESOURCES

Teacher Classroom Resources
- 📁 Guided Practice Activity 4-3
- 📁 Active Mind—Active Body Worksheet 4-3
- 📁 Reteaching Activity 4-3
- 📁 Lesson Quiz 4-3

Reproducible Charts and Graphs
- 📁 Reproducible Masters 4-5, 4-6

Multimedia
- 💿 Vocabulary PuzzleMaker
- 🖱 Transparencies 28, 29, 30

2 TEACH

USING VISUALS

Figure 4.9 Use *Reproducible Master 4-5* to help students comprehend and retain the concept of building a healthy base by having them develop a chart or concept map. Have them review the main ideas presented in the *Build a Healthy Base* section of Figure 4.9 and include these in the form of a chart or concept map. Have students answer the figure caption.

Caption answers will vary but should indicate that students recognize they should follow the ABCs of nutrition to maintain their health and fitness. 📁

FITNESS *Online*

Encourage students to work with a partner to develop meal plans that include recommended serving sizes and a variety of healthy foods.

Cooperative Learning

Ask students to make a list of their favorite foods. Then have them form small groups in which each student shares his or her list with the group. Have each group identify where the foods fit into the Food Guide Pyramid and how frequently the foods should be eaten. Finally, have each group share its results with the rest of the class. **ELL** **L2**

FITNESS *Online*

Find out more about making healthful food choices at **fitness.glencoe.com**.

Activity Use the Food Guide Pyramid and serving size recommendations to create a healthful meal plan.

FIGURE 4.9

DIETARY GUIDELINES FOR AMERICANS

These guidelines can help you design a healthful eating plan.
Which of these guidelines do you already follow?

AIM FOR FITNESS	➤ Aim for a healthy weight. ➤ Be physically active each day.
BUILD A HEALTHY BASE	➤ **Let the Food Guide Pyramid guide your food choices.** ➤ **Choose a variety of grains daily, especially whole grains.** ➤ **Choose a variety of fruits and vegetables daily.** ➤ **Keep food safe to eat.**
CHOOSE SENSIBLY	➤ **Choose a diet that is low in saturated fat and cholesterol and moderate in total fat.** ➤ **Choose beverages and foods to moderate your intake of sugars.** ➤ **Choose and prepare foods with less salt.** ➤ **Avoid alcoholic beverages.**

The Food Guide Pyramid

Under the heading, "Build a Healthy Base," the *Dietary Guidelines for Americans* refers to the Food Guide Pyramid, a *visual guide to help make healthful food choices* (see **Figure 4.10**). You have probably seen it many times on cereal boxes, bread wrappers, and other food products. It shows a range of servings for the different food groups you need to eat each day to achieve and maintain good health.

The recommendations in the Food Guide Pyramid are based on Dietary Reference Intakes (DRI). Determined by nutrition and health experts, DRIs are *daily nutrient recommendations for healthy people of both genders and different age groups.*

What Is a Serving?

Take a moment to study **Figure 4.10**. Notice the Pyramid's structure. Observe that a range of servings accompanies each of the five food groups. The size of a serving and the number of servings varies from food to food and from group to group. **Figure 4.11** on page **132** gives examples of amounts of food that count as one serving within each group.

The base of the Pyramid—the Bread, Cereal, Rice, and Pasta (Grains) Group—is the largest. This means that most of your daily servings should come from this group.

You may have noticed that no specific serving range is given for the foods at the tip of the Pyramid—Fats, Oils, and Sweets. These

---

More About . . .

THE FOOD GUIDE PYRAMID The USDA Food Guide Pyramid was first introduced in 1992, and the major recommendation at that time was that people should avoid fats but eat plenty of carbohydrate-rich foods, such as bread, cereal, rice, and pasta. The goal was to reduce the consumption of saturated fat, which raises cholesterol levels. In a recent research review article in *Scientific American*, Professors Walter Willet and Emir Stampfer at the Harvard School of Public Health reported that many nutritionists are recommending a new food pyramid that encourages the consumption foods should be consumed sparingly. An occasional soda, handful of chips, or piece of candy is fine but avoid eating too much of these types of foods too often.

For good nutrition, try to stay within serving ranges for each of the food groups. Eat at least the minimum number of servings to get enough nutrients. Be creative. A strawberry smoothie made from ½ cup of fresh strawberries, a cup of plain yogurt, and crushed ice makes a refreshing drink. It also gives you one serving from the Fruit Group and one from the Milk, Yogurt, and Cheese Group.

✔ **Reading Check**

Describe From which food group should most of your daily servings come?

✔ **Reading Check**
Most servings should come from the Bread, Cereal, Rice, and Pasta (Grains) Group.

FIGURE 4.10

THE FOOD GUIDE PYRAMID

This Pyramid is referred to in the *Dietary Guidelines for Americans.*
Have you seen this pyramid before? Where? Have you ever examined the information it contains? What does it tell you?

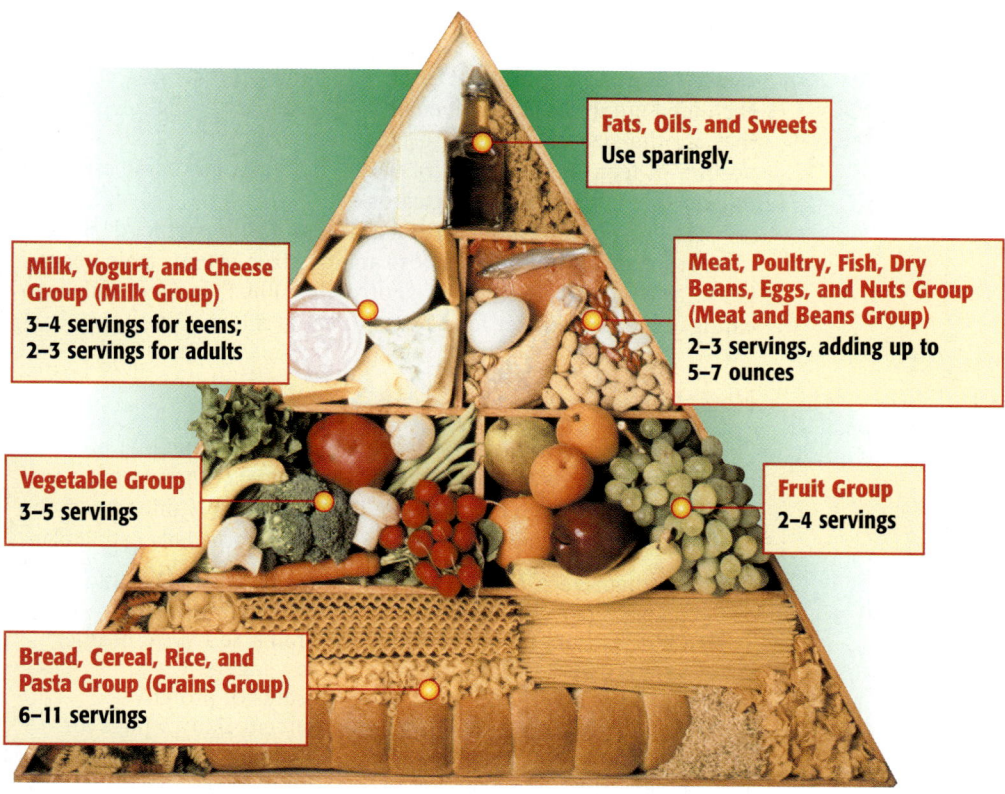

Fats, Oils, and Sweets
Use sparingly.

Milk, Yogurt, and Cheese Group (Milk Group)
3–4 servings for teens;
2–3 servings for adults

Meat, Poultry, Fish, Dry Beans, Eggs, and Nuts Group (Meat and Beans Group)
2–3 servings, adding up to 5–7 ounces

Vegetable Group
3–5 servings

Fruit Group
2–4 servings

Bread, Cereal, Rice, and Pasta Group (Grains Group)
6–11 servings

USING VISUALS

Figure 4.10 Display *Transparency 28* and discuss each of the food groups shown and why they are positioned on the pyramid as they are. Have students answer the figure caption. *Caption answers will vary, but you should remind students that the pyramid is an effective visual aid that represents the Dietary Guidelines for Americans.*

Activity

Ask students to list the meals and snacks they have eaten in the last 24 hours. Then have them draw a pyramid that represents their food choices and compare it with the Food Guide Pyramid in Figure 4.10. Have students share their drawings with classmates. Ask which pictures most resemble the Food Guide Pyramid. Ask: Does your pyramid resemble the Food Guide Pyramid, or do you need to work on developing healthier nutritional habits? **L1**

Lesson 3 **Choosing Foods Wisely**   **131**

---

of healthy fats and whole-grain foods but discourages the use of refined carbohydrates, butter, and red meat. The rationale for this revision is based on the fact that since the introduction of the original Food Guide Pyramid, the number of Americans who are overweight, obese, or afflicted with type 2 diabetes has increased dramatically. Have students learn more about the proposed new food pyramid by reading the article ("Rebuilding the Food Pyramid," *Scientific American*, December 17, 2002).

Student Edition TEKS
Page 130: C5D, C5G

Figure 4.11 Introduce *Transparency 29* and have students answer the figure caption. *Caption answers: 3–5 servings of 1/2 cup cooked or raw vegetables, adding up to 1 1/2 to 2 1/2 cups from the vegetable group.* Ask: How many servings should you have from the Fats, Oils, and Sweets Group? *Use sparingly.* From the Vegetable Group? *3–5 servings.* From the Milk, Yogurt, and Cheese Group? *3–4 servings.* From the Fruit Group? *2–4 servings.*

Critical Thinking

Discuss with students the differences in the number of servings from the major groups:

• How do you think age, gender, and activity levels affect the recommended number of servings?

• Do you think all the members of a soccer team should have the same number of servings from each group? Why or why not? **L1**

Cooperative Learning

Have each student bring two or three labels from canned food items to class. Divide the class into small groups and have them analyze how many servings are in each can, relative to a 2,000-calorie daily eating plan. **ELL** **L2**

FIGURE 4.11

SERVING SIZES FOR EACH FOOD GROUP

Serving sizes for food groups vary. *How many cups of cooked or raw vegetables meet the recommended serving size?*

Grains Group	Vegetable Group	Fruit Group	Milk Group	Meat and Beans Group
• 1 slice bread • 1 tortilla • ½ small bagel • 1 cup dry cereal • ½ cup cooked cereal, rice, or pasta	• 1 cup raw leafy vegetables • ½ cup cooked or raw vegetables • ¾ cup vegetable juice	• 1 medium apple, orange, pear, or banana • ½ cup chopped, cooked, or canned fruit • ¾ cup fruit juice	• 1 cup milk or yogurt • 1.5 oz. natural cheese, such as Swiss • 2 oz. processed cheese	• 2–3 oz. cooked lean meat, fish, or poultry **Equivalents of 1 oz. of meat:** • ½ cup cooked dry beans/tofu • 1 egg • 2 tbsp. peanut butter • ⅓ cup nuts

Controlling Portion Size. Figure 4.11 shows the serving sizes for each food group. Learn to "eyeball"—to recognize by sight—portions that are the size of Pyramid servings. For example, a 2- to 3-ounce portion of lean meat or poultry would be about the same size and thickness as a deck of playing cards.

Many restaurants often serve extra-large portions of food. To control portion size, you might choose an appetizer as your main course. Learn also to pay attention to your body. When you feel full, stop eating. Take the leftover food home to eat at a later meal.

Nutrition Facts

All food product labels have a **Nutrition Facts panel** that provides *a thumbnail analysis of a food's calories and nutrient content for one serving* (see **Figure 4.12**). The *% Daily Value (%DV)* column shows the nutrients in one serving of the food to a 2,000-calorie daily eating plan.

• Serving size
• Calories per serving
• Calories from fat per serving
• Grams and %DV of total fat
• Grams and %DV of saturated fat
• Milligrams and %DV of cholesterol
• Milligrams and %DV of sodium

• Grams and %DV of total carbohydrate
• Grams and %DV of fiber and sugars
• Grams of protein
• Percent Daily Values for vitamins and minerals found in the food

What Teens Want to Know

How are portion sizes changing? A study in the *Journal of the American Medical Association* revealed that fast food restaurants have increased portion sizes. Between 1977 and 1996, food portion sizes increased both inside and outside the home for all categories except pizza (which was just cut into smaller slices). Hamburgers have gotten bigger by 1.3 ounces, French fries by half an ounce, Mexican food by 1.7 ounces, and soft drinks by 6.8 ounces. Many experts blame these larger portions for the increasing number of overweight and obese Americans.

By reading Nutrition Facts panels, you can compare different food products, make wise choices, and get an idea of what and how much you are consuming. Food labeling can help you balance your calorie intake and expenditure if you pay attention to serving sizes and know how much you're really eating.

 Reading Check

Summarize Identify two pieces of information found on a food label's Nutrition Facts panel.

FIGURE 4.12

NUTRITION FACTS PANEL
Reading the Nutrition Facts panel gives you valuable information about the food you eat. *What nutrients does this food provide and in what amounts?*

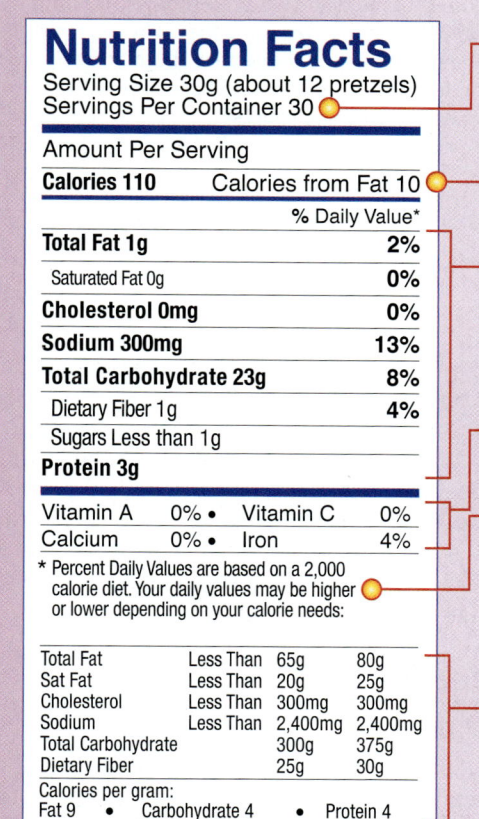

Nutrition Facts
Serving Size 30g (about 12 pretzels)
Servings Per Container 30

Amount Per Serving	
Calories 110	Calories from Fat 10

	% Daily Value*
Total Fat 1g	**2%**
Saturated Fat 0g	**0%**
Cholesterol 0mg	**0%**
Sodium 300mg	**13%**
Total Carbohydrate 23g	**8%**
Dietary Fiber 1g	**4%**
Sugars Less than 1g	
Protein 3g	

Vitamin A	0%	•	Vitamin C	0%
Calcium	0%	•	Iron	4%

* Percent Daily Values are based on a 2,000 calorie diet. Your daily values may be higher or lower depending on your calorie needs:

Total Fat	Less Than	65g	80g
Sat Fat	Less Than	20g	25g
Cholesterol	Less Than	300mg	300mg
Sodium	Less Than	2,400mg	2,400mg
Total Carbohydrate		300g	375g
Dietary Fiber		25g	30g

Calories per gram:
Fat 9 • Carbohydrate 4 • Protein 4

Serving Size and Servings Per Container
- Nutrient and calorie content is calculated according to serving size. The serving size on the label may differ from sizes in the Food Guide Pyramid. The number of servings in the package is also listed.

Calories and Calories from Fat
- The number of calories in one serving and how many of these calories come from fat is given here.

Nutrients (Top section)
- The amounts of total fat, saturated fat, cholesterol, and sodium per serving are listed in either grams (g) or milligrams (mg).
- The amounts of total carbohydrates, dietary fiber, sugars, and protein per serving are given.

Nutrients (Bottom section)
- Major vitamins and minerals are listed with their Percent Daily Values.

Percent Daily Value
- This section tells you how much the nutrients in one serving contribute to your total daily eating plan. The general guideline is that 20% or more of a nutrient is a lot and 5% or less isn't very much. Choose foods that are high in fiber, vitamins, and minerals and low in fat, cholesterol, and sodium.

The Footnote (Lower part of Nutrition Facts Panel)
- This information is the same from product to product. It contains recommendations about the amounts of certain nutrients that should be eaten each day.

Activity
Using one label from a canned food item from the previous *Cooperative Learning* activity, have students list the values on the can for each of the bulleted items shown at the bottom of page 132. **L2**

✓ **Reading Check**
Answers may vary but should include information from Figure 4.12 on this page.

USING VISUALS

Figure 4.12 Have students examine the Nutrition Facts panel and answer the caption question. Use *Transparency 30* to discuss each part of the label. *Caption answer: Fat, 1g; Cholesterol, 0mg; Sodium, 300mg; Total Carbohydrate, 23g; Dietary Fiber, 1g; Sugars, less than 1g; Protein, 3g; Vitamin A, 0%; Vitamin C, 0%; Calcium, 0%; Iron, 4%.*

Discussing
Ask students to share their own experiences with using Nutrition Facts panels on food packages:
- Do you check these panels in the store before purchasing a product? If so, what do you look for? If not, why not?
- Do you check these panels at home before eating a particular food? Why or why not?
- For whom do you think these panels are designed? How effective do you think they are? **L1**

INCLUSION STRATEGIES

UNDERSTANDING NUTRITION LABELS
One of the keys to helping monitor caloric intake and, therefore, weight control, is to be aware of the food that is being consumed by the individual. This involves the ability to read labels and analyze nutritional qualities of food in the diet. This may be a difficult task for students with cognitive disabilities who may have difficulty reading and/or processing information. The student's special education teacher is a good resource, and he or she can provide the physical education teacher with information on the student's ability level in this area.

Active Mind Active Body
Calculating Calories from a Sample Meal

This activity will help students become more aware of the number of calories they are consuming in their daily diet. It will also help them calculate their daily caloric intake. Make sure they understand that they will be graded not on their food choices for this activity, but on their effort, participation, and general understanding of concepts.

Teaching Tips
- Encourage students who may need help with math calculations to pair up with a partner.
- Distribute the *Active Mind–Active Body Worksheet 4-3* so students can record their caloric intake. 📁
- You may want students to do a dietary recall for one day during the week and then another day from the weekend, since it is typical for people to have different eating behaviors on the weekends due to variations in daily routines.

Apply and Conclude
After students have completed the activity, discuss the importance of evaluating their caloric intake. Provide discussion time and ask volunteers to give examples of ways students can improve their intake of carbohydrates, proteins, and fats.
TEKS C5D

Active Mind Active Body
Calculating Calories from a Sample Meal

In this activity, you will calculate the percentage of the calories you eat in a day that come from carbohydrate, protein, and fat. Understanding how much of each nutrient you consume is important for developing healthful eating habits.

What You Will Need
- Pen or pencil
- Paper
- Calculator (optional)

What You Will Do
1. List the food that you eat on a particular day. Add up the grams of carbohydrate, protein, and fat that you consume in the food you eat that day.
2. Calculate the number of calories in your food choices for that day. Use the following equivalents to determine calories:
   - 1 gram of carbohydrate = 4 calories
   - 1 gram of protein = 4 calories
   - 1 gram of fat = 9 calories)
3. Calculate what percentage of these calories comes from carbohydrate, protein, and fat. *Hint:* Divide the number of calories for each nutrient by the total number of calories from all the nutrients, then move the decimal point two places to the right.

Apply and Conclude
How many calories for the day are from carbohydrate? from protein? from fat? What percentages are they? Do you recall what percentage of your total daily calories should come from carbohydrate, protein, and fat? What are some ways to reduce fat calories in meals and snacks?

Developing Healthful Eating Habits
Whatever your food preferences might be, any food that supplies calories and nutrients can be part of a healthful eating plan. Good nutrition comes from an eating plan that has *variety, moderation,* and *balance.* Also remember that nutrition guidelines apply to all of your food choices all the time—even when snacking or dining out. However, healthful eating does not mean eliminating certain foods, or eating one particular kind of food all the time. By being aware of your serving sizes and nutrient needs, and with a little planning, you can eat the foods you like and have a healthy eating plan.

The Importance of Breakfast
Many nutritionists agree that breakfast is the most important meal of the day. Your body uses energy even while you sleep, and you need to replenish your body's energy supply once you wake up. A healthy breakfast can improve your physical and mental performance throughout the day. Eating breakfast is also important for maintaining a healthy weight. People who do not eat breakfast may have a tendency to overeat later in the day.

TECHNOLOGY FILE
Spreadsheet Analysis of Energy Expenditure
Have students open a computer spreadsheet and enter "vigorous" in cell B1 and "moderate" in cell C1. Then, have students enter "per energy expenditure" in cell A2, "Exercise Time" in A3, "Days Per Week" in A4, and "Total Caloric Expenditure" in A5. Finally, have students enter "8" in cell B2, "6" in cell C2, "=B2*B3*B4" in B5, and "=C2*C3*C4" in C5. Students can now forecast their total caloric expenditure by inputting different exercise times (in minutes) in column B and days per week in column C.

If you do not enjoy typical breakfast foods like cereal or eggs, try eating foods you like, even if they are not traditional breakfast foods. Just make sure you get enough Vitamin C from citrus fruit or juice. You may also want to include a high-fiber cereal, and get some calcium by having a serving of milk, cheese, or yogurt.

Snacking

Some people may believe that part of healthful eating means eliminating snacks. In reality, snacking is fine as long as you choose healthful snacks. Potato chips, soft drinks, and candy contain too many calories and not enough nutrients. They may also be high in fat, added sugars, or salt.

Try to plan your snacks and choose wisely. Healthful snacks can provide the extra energy you need during the growth years and provide nutrients that you might not have been able to eat at other meals. When choosing snacks, select whole-grain products, fruits, and vegetables. Also look for healthier alternatives offered by many companies, such as potato chips that are baked instead of fried. **Figure 4.13** lists the nutrition information for some sensible snacks. You will learn more about a healthful eating plan in Chapters 5 and 6.

Reading Check

Summarize Why is it important to eat breakfast?

FIGURE 4.13

NUTRITIOUS SNACKS

A healthful eating plan includes nutritious snacks. *What healthful snacks do you enjoy? Explain the myth associated with snacking.*

Food	Food Group	Total Calories per Serving	Calories from Fat
Air-popped popcorn, 3 cups (plain)	Grains	23	0
Apple, 1 medium	Fruit	80	0
Bagel, $\frac{1}{2}$ half (small, 2 oz.)	Grains	83	10
Bread stick, 1	Grains	42	6
Frozen juice bar, 4 oz.	Fruit	75	0
Skim milk, 1 cup	Milk	90	0
Sugar-free gelatin ($\frac{1}{2}$ cup) with $\frac{1}{2}$ cup sliced banana	Fruit	76	0
Graham cracker squares, 3	Grains	80	15
Pretzel sticks, 50 small	Grains	60	9
Fat-free, sugar-free yogurt, 6 oz.	Milk	86	0

Discussing

Ask students whether they eat breakfast on a regular basis, and ask them to discuss why or why not. Reinforce the information from the text that highlights the importance of eating breakfast regularly. **L1**

Reading Check

Breakfast replenishes the body's energy supply and can improve physical and mental performance throughout the day.

USING VISUALS

Figure 4.13 Discuss the breakdown of calories from the snacks shown in *Reproducible Master 4-6.* Have students make a snack chart over a 3-day period, showing the snack they chose, where they got it, the time, how they were feeling (hungry, sad, angry, for example), and what they were doing (watching TV, talking on the phone). Then have them rate their snack as *healthy* or *not healthy.* *Caption answers will vary but should follow the guidelines in the paragraph about snacking.*

More About . . .

WISE NUTRITIONAL CHOICES In November 2000, the newsletter of the American Institute for Cancer Research (AICR) suggested a four-step process to change the American way of eating. In Step 1, we realize that the typical American meal is heavy on meat, fish, and poultry (8–10 ounces). In Step 2, we feature more moderate servings of meat (4–6 ounces). In Step 3, we reduce meat to a modest 3-ounce serving. In Step 4, we introduce more vegetables, hearty grains, vitamins, minerals, and phytochemicals. In Step 4, meat appears only as a condiment or flavoring.

Student Edition TEKS

Page 135: C5E

Activity

Work with the class to have students develop their ideal menu for school cafeteria lunches. Encourage them to include optional choices that are low-fat, low in sugar, and low in salt. **L2**

Cooperative Learning

Divide the class into small groups and have each group arrange a schedule (over the next week or two) so they can visit a local restaurant. The groups should pose the following questions to the manager of the restaurant they visit: What local agency regulates your food preparation and certifies that you are meeting health standards for safe food preparation? How do you train your employees to prepare foods and keep them safe? Have students report their results to the class. **ELL** **L3**

✔ **Reading Check**

Four steps for safe food-handling are: clean, separate, cook, and chill.

136

Consumer CORNER

Dining Out: A Word to the Wise

More Americans are eating meals away from home than ever before. As a wise consumer, you can make smart choices and eat healthfully when you dine out. Here are some tips for eating wisely when dining out.

- **Pay attention to how your food is prepared.** For example, have your chicken grilled instead of fried. If possible, minimize use of high-fat sauces, sour cream, and butter.
- **Choose healthful side dishes.** For example, order a salad instead of french fries with your meal.
- **Watch portion sizes.** Ordering extra-large portions at fast-food restaurants may seem like a good value, but it probably provides more calories than necessary.

- **Estimate servings.** If you are served a large portion, try to estimate the true number of servings in that portion. Eat the equivalent of one serving, and take the rest home for a later meal.
- **Drink healthful beverages.** Choose low-fat milk or water instead of high-sugar soft drinks.

Investigate

Try implementing one or more of these suggestions the next time you dine out, either at a sit-down or fast-food restaurant. Report to classmates on the success of your efforts.

Keeping Food Safe to Eat

Eating healthfully means more than just choosing foods that meet your nutrient and calorie needs. It also means eating foods that have been handled and prepared safely. Otherwise, there is a risk of food-borne illness—*illness that results from consuming food contaminated with disease-causing organisms, the poisons they produce, or chemical contaminants.* You should discard any food that you suspect has spoiled. Never taste it to check. Remember: When in doubt, throw it out.

Anyone who handles food should use the following guidelines to help keep foods safe to eat.

- **Clean.** Wash your hands, cutting boards, and countertops with hot, soapy water before and after food preparation and after handling raw meat, poultry, or fish. This prevents cross-contamination, *the spreading of bacteria or other pathogens from one food to another.* Use cutting boards made of non-porous materials, such as plastic or glass, for preparing foods. Remember to wash fruits and vegetables before you eat them.
- **Separate.** Separate raw, cooked, and ready-to-eat foods while shopping, preparing, or storing. Use a separate cutting board for raw meats.

COOPERATIVE Learning

FOOD SAFETY Have students form small groups and discuss ways they can follow food safety rules. Ask them to analyze the following behaviors related to foodborne illness that are common among Americans, and have them determine whether members in their group practice these behaviors: 50 percent of Americans eat raw or undercooked eggs; 23 percent of Americans eat undercooked hamburger; 28 percent of Americans leave perishable foods unrefrigerated for more than two hours. Then have each group report their findings. **ELL**

- **Cook.** Cook foods to a safe temperature: 160°F for ground beef, 170°F for roasts and poultry, and 145°F for fish. The juices of meat or poultry should run clear when properly cooked. Fish should be opaque and flake easily with a fork. Avoid eating dishes that contain raw or partially cooked eggs.
- **Chill.** Refrigerate perishable foods promptly. Foods should be at room temperature no longer than two hours—one hour on a warm day. Cold foods should be refrigerated at 40°F or less and frozen foods should be kept at 0°F. Defrost frozen foods in the refrigerator or microwave, or by running them under cold water—never on the kitchen counter.

▲ Handling and preparing food safely will prevent foodborne illness. *What are some tips to follow to keep food safe to eat?*

✔ **Reading Check**

Identify What are four tips for handling food safely?

EVALUATING THE LESSON

Assign and discuss the Lesson 3 Review.

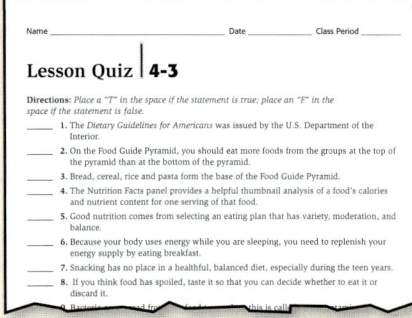

RETEACHING

Ask students to list three changes they can make to improve their eating plans, based on content.

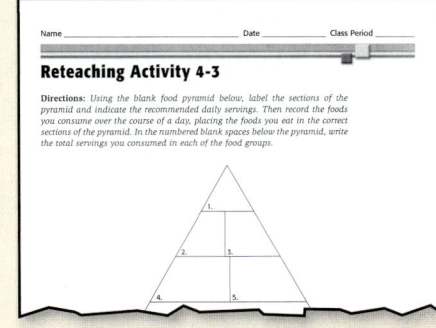

ENRICHMENT

Have students conduct research on current studies that focus on the effects of dietary fat on health. Ask volunteers to share their results.

Lesson 3 Review

Using complete sentences, answer the following questions on a sheet of paper.

Reviewing Facts and Vocabulary

1. **Vocabulary** What is the *Food Guide Pyramid*?
2. **Recall** Why is eating breakfast important to your health?
3. **Recall** List three practices that can help prevent foodborne illness.

Thinking Critically

4. **Analyze** For lunch, Shauna had a turkey sandwich on whole-wheat bread, a glass of tomato juice, and a peach. Identify the group in the Food Guide Pyramid to which each food belongs. Then tell how many Pyramid servings of each Shauna had. What could she add to her lunch for more nutrition?

5. **Evaluate** Most restaurants do not list serving size and nutrition information on their menus. What can you do to make sure you maintain a healthy eating plan, even when dining out?

Personal Fitness Planning

Investigating Safety Inspect your kitchen at home. Write a list of ways you can help make the kitchen safer in terms of food preparation. In addition, check your refrigerator for any foods that might be spoiled or outdated. Share the results with your family members. Help them become aware of the dangers of foodborne illness and ways to prevent it.

Lesson 3 Choosing Foods Wisely **137**

Lesson 3 Review

Answers to Lesson 3 Review

1. A visual guide for the *Dietary Guidelines for Americans*.
2. Breakfast helps replenish your body's energy supply and can improve your physical and mental performance.
3. Clean, separate, cook, and chill.

4. Answers should include the use of the Food Guide Pyramid and references to serving sizes from pages 131–132.
5. Pay attention to how the food is prepared, choose healthy side dishes, watch portion sizes, estimate servings, and drink healthful beverages.

Have students review the Food Guide Pyramid and recommend changes for future versions of the Pyramid.

Lesson 4

1 MOTIVATE

GETTING STARTED

- Ask volunteers to list strategies that help improve performance in physical activities. Remind students that nutrition also plays an important role.
- Distribute copies of *Guided Practice Activity 4-4* for students to use while studying this lesson. 📁

IN THIS LESSON

- **Fitness Check** *Understanding the Energy Equation, p. 142*

INTRODUCING VOCABULARY

- Emphasize to students that three of the vocabulary terms for this lesson—*ephedrine, creatine, and androstenedione*—are harmful substances that carry serious health risks. Students will learn more about these dangerous substances later in the lesson.
- Have students use *Vocabulary Worksheet 4* or the PuzzleMaker software to practice vocabulary terms for this lesson. ELL 📁 ⦿

What You Will Do

- Apply sound nutritional practices to physical activity and performance.
- Analyze the effects of performance-enhancing supplements on health and physical performance.

Terms to Know

pre-event meal
ephedrine
creatine
androstenedione

Nutrition for Peak Performance

Do you play a sport or participate in a competitive recreational activity? If so, you need to pay extra attention to what you eat before, during, and after physical activity. This lesson will provide some information about proper nutrition and physical activity.

Food for Performance Fitness

As noted in Chapter 1, athletics, sports, and competitive recreational activities all demand high levels of performance—or skill-related—fitness. One key factor to achieving high performance fitness levels is appropriate physical training. Another equally important factor is eating wisely to optimize your performance.

When you play hard, your body provides you with the energy you need by burning calories. **Figure 4.14** shows the relationship between physical activity and energy expenditure.

▶ Carbohydrates can be an important source of energy before participating in a sporting event. *What foods are valuable sources of complex carbohydrates?*

LESSON 4 RESOURCES

Teacher Classroom Resources
📁 Guided Practice Activity 4-4
📁 Fitness Check Worksheet 4-4
📁 Reteaching Activity 4-4
📁 Lesson Quiz 4-4

Multimedia
⦿ Vocabulary PuzzleMaker
⬇ Transparencies 31, 32

FIGURE 4.14

CALORIES BURNED DURING PHYSICAL ACTIVITY

Analyze exercise as a method of weight control. Approximately how many calories would you burn in an hour of cycling?

Activity	Calories Burned in 30 minutes	Time to Burn 230 Calories
• Aerobics	211	33 minutes
• Bicycling 10–12 mph	158	44 minutes
• Frisbee	106	66 minutes
• Gardening	176	39 minutes
• Running at 6.7 mph, 9 min/mile	387	18 minutes
• Skateboarding	176	39 minutes
• Stretching (hatha yoga)	140	49 minutes
• Tennis doubles	211	33 minutes
• Walking at 4 mph	140	49 minutes
• Weight lifting (vigorous)	211	33 minutes

Pre-Event Meals

Proper sports nutrition begins *before* the competitive event. Eating the right variety and amounts of foods ensures a steady supply of energy during the event. It's important to choose foods wisely, not only on the day of the event but also in the days and weeks leading up to it.

Your pre-event meal is *the last full meal consumed prior to a practice session or the competitive event itself.* The pre-event meal should be eaten within one to three hours before the practice or event. This allows time for the food to fully digest. Eating any closer to the time of the event can result in nausea or stomach cramps.

The pre-event meal should consist primarily of foods high in complex carbohydrates. These include pasta, whole-grain breads, and rice. Foods high in protein or fat take longer to digest. Foods such as candy bars and other foods with simple carbohydrates do not supply energy right away. For endurance sports, a small sugar snack or drink may be acceptable. However, too much sugar may affect how fast your body replaces fluids. This can slow your performance. **Figure 4.15** on page **140** lists foods that might be part of an effective pre-event meal.

Reading Check

Explain What nutrient is most important to a pre-event meal?

More About . . .

FOOD FOR PERFORMANCE FITNESS Some teen athletes think they need to consume dietary supplements—including vitamins, minerals, amino acids, and herbal supplements—to improve their performance and health. However, teens should use caution because dietary supplements are not regulated by the Food and Drug Administration in the way that medications are. Some dietary supplements may contain ingredients that can produce positive tests for banned substances and cause serious health risks. Anyone considering using them should consult with a physician before doing so.

---

2 TEACH

Discussing

Ask students if they have ever competed in athletics, sports, or competitive recreational activities. Then ask whether they changed their dietary behaviors when they participated. Finally, ask why or why not.

USING VISUALS

Figure 4.14 Display *Transparency 31* to discuss how much time must be spent in various physical activities to burn a certain amount of calories. Have students use the information in Figure 4.14 to analyze exercise as a method of weight control. Estimate how many calories they would burn in an hour while participating in a physical activity of their choosing. **TEKS C5F**

Reading Check

Complex carbohydrates are most important to consume in a pre-event meal.

Student Edition TEKS

Page 138: C3D, C5F

rehydrate
For more on proper ways to rehydrate before, during, and after exercise, see Chapter 2, page **42**.

restoration
For more on restoration and factors that influence recovery, see Chapter 3, page **100**.

FIGURE 4.15

PRE-EVENT FOODS

Your pre-event meal supplies your body with enough energy for the event. *What main source of energy does each of these foods provide?*

1 to 2 Hours Before
- Fruit or vegetable juice
- Fresh fruit (low fiber, such as plums, melon, cherries, or peaches)

2 to 3 Hours Before
- Fruit or vegetable juice
- Fresh fruit
- Breads, bagels, English muffins (no margarine or cream cheese)

3 or More Hours Before
- Fruit or vegetable juice
- Fresh fruit
- Breads, bagels, English muffins
- Low-fat yogurt
- Baked potato
- Peanut butter, lean meat, low-fat cheese
- Cereal with low-fat milk (2%)
- Pasta with tomato sauce

Source: Play Hard, Eat Right: A Parent's Guide to Sports Nutrition for Children, 1998.[3]

Foods During Day-Long Events

Some competitions are day-long events or a series of events that span several hours, for example, track meets, basketball tournaments, and wrestling meets. When participating in this type of event, you need to eat at intervals during the day to renew energy. You also need to prevent dehydration, which will have a negative effect on your performance and may be dangerous to your health.

The best advice is to choose foods that have complex carbohydrates, such as bread, cereals, and pasta. Also include vegetables and fruit. Avoid simple sugars such as soft drinks, cookies, and candy. Make sure also to **rehydrate** throughout the day. Drink plenty of fluids to replace those lost through perspiration.

Post-Event Eating: Restoration

Following a high-intensity workout or competition, you need to eat foods that will promote **restoration.** Doing so is especially important if you plan to train or compete again the next day or shortly thereafter.

Myths & Realities

Myth 1 Sports drinks are needed only for exercise lasting more than one hour.

Fact 1 Sports drinks can be beneficial in activities that last one hour or less, especially if the exercise is intense or occurs in hot, humid conditions.

Myth 2 The ideal ratio of nutrients for those interested in high performance is 40 percent carbohydrates, 30 percent protein, and 30 percent fat.

Fact 2 Research suggests that those interested in high performance should consume a diet with 55–65 percent carbohydrates, 12–15 percent protein, and 25–30 percent fat.

Sources: American College of Sports Medicine, the American Dietetic Association

Foods rich in complex carbohydrates and protein are the best choice for optimizing recovery. These foods will renew your glucose level and your glycogen stores. You also need to replace fluids lost in the form of perspiration during physical activity.

There are three phases to post-event eating:

- **Phase 1: Drink Fluids.** Rehydrating with water or sports drinks should begin immediately after the event for proper restoration and continue for several hours until normal body weight is regained.
- **Phase 2: Have a Snack.** This should occur as soon after the event as possible, within the first 30 minutes. This phase consists of consuming a snack or beverage to begin the restoration process. The chart in **Figure 4.16** shows some possible food choices for this phase of recovery. A good guideline is to consume 1.2 to 1.5 grams of carbohydrate per kilogram of body weight and between 0.3 and 0.5 grams of protein per kilogram of body weight. For example, a 154-pound—or 70-kg—male (154/2.2 = 70) would need to consume between 84 and 105 grams of carbohydrates and 21 and 35 grams of protein.
- **Phase 3: Eat a Meal.** This should occur two hours after competition. This phase consists of a full meal, rich in carbohydrates. Small amounts of protein and fat can be added to the post-event meal for calories and taste.

✓ Reading Check

Summarize What are the three phases of restoration?

POST-EVENT FOODS
Explain how eating foods like these after an event makes it possible to work out or compete again the next day.

Food	Carbohydrate (in grams)	Protein (g)
Medium bagel	50	7.5
Cranberry-apple juice (1 cup)	43	0.1
Fruit yogurt (1 cup)	40	9.9
Large banana	40	1.3
Apple juice (1 cup)	30	0.1
Orange juice (1 cup)	28	1.7
Pretzels (10)	23	5.5

Source: Play Hard, Eat Right: A Parent's Guide to Sports Nutrition for Children, *1998.*[3]

More About . . .

RESTORATION EATING In 1986, John Ivy from the University of Texas at Austin reported research on optimal recovery strategies after high-intensity exercise by using restoration phases. His first reports were challenged by the sports medicine community, but Dr. Ivy was able to duplicate his research findings recently (2003) using even more sophisticated techniques than before. His original strategies for optimal recovery from high-intensity exercise are now considered a favorable alternative for those who might choose illegal or dangerous supplements to do the same job.

Explaining

Explain to students that the three main goals for optimal recovery following intense exercise are:

1. rehydration
2. replenishment of carbohydrate stores (glycogen)
3. repair of muscle tissue
L1

✓ Reading Check

Drink fluids after the event, have a snack as soon as possible, and eat a meal two hours after the event.

USING VISUALS

Figure 4.16 Using the portion of *Transparency 32* that displays post-event foods, discuss with students the importance of providing the body with proper nutrients and fluids to recover from the stresses of high-intensity workouts and competition.
Caption answer: The foods in this table are high in carbohydrates, which aid the body in the restoration process.

Student Edition TEKS

Page 140: C5D, C5G
Page 141: C5D, C5G

Understanding the Energy Equation

OBJECTIVES

- Determine how many calories are burned during the exercise that students perform.
- Determine how many calories are required to balance the number of calories burned.

TEACHING STRATEGIES

- Lead students through a 5- to 10-minute warm-up.
- Review the definitions of *moderate* and *vigorous intensity* from Chapters 1 and 3. Tell students that RPE will be the best indicator of intensity.
- Distribute copies of *Fitness Check Worksheet 4-4* so students can record their scores. 📁
- Explain that this activity is designed to introduce the energy-balance equation that compares caloric intake against caloric expenditure. Students will not be tested for a grade on their choice of activities.

Estimating Calories Expended

Review students' plans and use two or three as examples to demonstrate options for optimizing restoration after moderate to intense exercise.

Student Edition TEKS

Page 142: C5D
Page 143: C3D, C4H, C5D

Fitness Check

Understanding the Energy Equation

To maintain weight, the calories you take in from food must equal the calories you burn. The equation of calories consumed relative to calories burned varies from person to person. In this test, you will perform a 20-minute walk/jog evaluation to learn more about energy intake and energy demands.

Before you attempt this activity, perform a warm-up. Practice the test before you try it. Allow 5 to 10 minutes to cool down after taking the test. *If you feel dizzy or become overheated at any point during the test, stop immediately.*

Following your warm-up, begin walking or jogging. Try to reach a moderate-to-vigorous level of intensity that you know you can maintain for 20 minutes. If you are not used to walking or jogging, make sure you choose a pace that will keep you at a moderate intensity for the 20-minute duration. Review the guidelines for determining intensity level on pages **28–29,** Chapter 1, and for using the Borg scale on page **87,** Chapter 3.

Estimating Calories Expended

1. Determine if you have walked/jogged at a moderate-to-vigorous level. Then estimate how many calories you burned in 20 minutes by using the following guide:

Intensity Level	Average Calories Burned
Moderate intensity for 20 minutes	120 calories
Vigorous intensity for 20 minutes	160 calories

2. Now estimate how many calories you would have burned if you had kept walking/jogging for two hours and record that total.
3. Once you have that estimate, develop an eating plan for how to replace that same number of calories with nutrient-rich foods. Then make a plan to optimize your recovery if you had to walk or jog for two hours the next day.

More About . . .

FOOD FOR PERFORMANCE FITNESS Highly competitive school or recreational teen athletes need to consume more calories. For example, healthy teens should consume between 2,200 and 2,800 calories, depending on gender and activity level. The following list provides some estimates for average caloric-intake needs for high performance: *Cyclists*—7,000 to 9,000 calories per day; *Boxers*—3,500 to 5,000 calories per day; *Basketball players*—3,500 to 5,000 calories per day; *Track and field athletes*—3,500 to 6,000 calories per day; *Swimmers*—3,500 to 6,000 calories per day.

Risks of Supplements

Dietary supplements are dangerous if used to enhance athletic performance. These include:

- **Ephedrine.** Also called ephedra or ma huang, ephedrine (eh-FED-ruhn) is *a compound that increases the rate at which the body converts calories to energy.* It increases resting heart rate and body temperature. Ephedrine may lead to heat-related injury, heart problems, and even death.
- **Creatine.** Creatine (KREE-uh-teen) is *a supplement that increases muscle size while enhancing the body's ability to use protein.* It is especially risky for teens because the long-term effects on growth and development are unknown.
- **Androstenedione.** Androstenedione (an-DROS-tuh-NED-ee-ohn) is *a chemical agent that aids the body in its production of testosterone.* Like anabolic steroids, this chemical promotes muscle growth. Its use may increase the risk of heart disease.

These supplements involve serious health risks for adults and teens. In addition, they may give the user an unfair advantage over fellow competitors. Athletes who choose to use such substances are putting their health and their athletic careers at risk.

✔ Reading Check

Discuss Why should a person avoid performance-enhancing supplements?

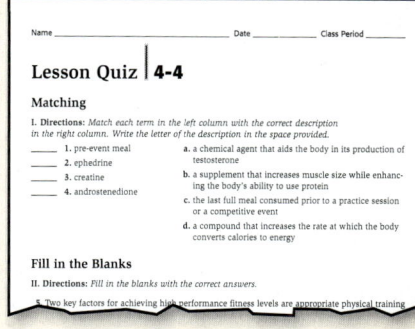

FITNESS Online

Learn more about the harmful effects of dietary supplements and other substances at **fitness.glencoe.com**.

Activity Identify other dangerous supplements and their effects on health and fitness. Create an electronic slide show on the risks of using these substances.

Lesson 4 Review

Using complete sentences, answer the following questions on a sheet of paper.

Reviewing Facts and Vocabulary

1. **Vocabulary** What is a *pre-event meal?*
2. **Recall** Describe the three phases of post-event restoration through food.

Thinking Critically

3. **Compare and Contrast** Compare any two of the performance-enhancing supplements in terms of (a) what they claim to do and (b) their effect on health and physical performance.
4. **Analyze** Kim is on the school track team. Kim is not concerned about her pre- and post-event meals. Pretend you are Kim's coach and advise her about what she should eat before and after the event. Explain to Kim the relationship between sound nutritional practices and physical activity.

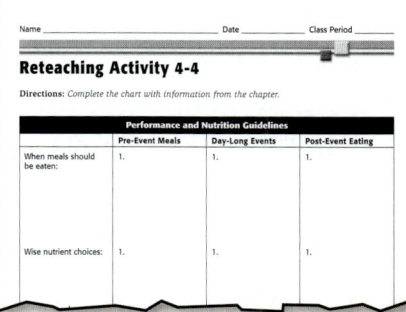

Personal Fitness Planning

Evaluating Products Visit a local pharmacy, food supplement store, or health food store. Review the labels on various herbal or food supplements the store carries. List any claims on product labels about improving personal fitness performance. Then access reliable print and online resources to evaluate the validity of these claims. Share your findings with the class.

Lesson 4 Nutrition for Peak Performance **143**

Lesson 4 Review

Answers to Lesson 4 Review

1. The pre-event meal is the last full meal consumed before a practice session or the competitive event itself.
2. Post-event phases are: drink fluids, have a snack, eat a meal.
3. Answers will vary but should include comparisons of ephedrine, creatine, or androstenedione.
4. Kim could chart her performance and compare the results for when she does not pay attention to her pre- and post-event meals with the results for when she does follow recommendations.

3 ASSESS

EVALUATING THE LESSON

Assign and discuss the Lesson 4 Review.

Name _____ Date _____ Class Period _____

Lesson Quiz 4-4

Matching

I. Directions: *Match each term in the left column with the correct description in the right column. Write the letter of the description in the space provided.*

_____ 1. pre-event meal
_____ 2. ephedrine
_____ 3. creatine
_____ 4. androstenedione

a. a chemical agent that aids the body in its production of testosterone
b. a supplement that increases muscle size while enhancing the body's ability to use protein
c. the last full meal consumed prior to a practice session or a competitive event
d. a compound that increases the rate at which the body converts calories to energy

Fill in the Blanks

II. Directions: *Fill in the blanks with the correct answers.*

5. Two key factors for achieving high performance fitness levels are appropriate physical training

RETEACHING

Have students explain the reasons for choosing certain pre- and post-event foods.

Name _____ Date _____ Class Period _____

Reteaching Activity 4-4

Directions: *Complete the chart with information from the chapter.*

Performance and Nutrition Guidelines			
	Pre-Event Meals	Day-Long Events	Post-Event Eating
When meals should be eaten:	1.	1.	1.
Wise nutrient choices:	1.	1.	1.

ENRICHMENT

Have students research how world-class athletes recover from high intensity daily workouts. Ask them to submit an optimal plan for recovery for the athlete.

4 CLOSE

Ask students to consider what they have learned about nutrition for peak performance and list ways to improve their eating plans.

CHECKING COMPREHENSION

- Assign and discuss the chapter review.
- Use the Puzzlemaker CD-ROM to review vocabulary.

CHAPTER 4 REVIEW ANSWERS

True/False

1. True	6. True
2. False	7. True
3. False	8. True
4. False	9. False
5. False	10. True

Multiple Choice

11. b	16. c
12. a	17. d
13. c	18. c
14. b	19. c
15. b	20. c

Discussion

21. Answers may vary but might include hunger, appetite, culture, family and friends, emotions, convenience, and advertising.
22. Answers may vary but might include: clean, separate, cook, and chill.
23. Answers may vary but might include: primarily follow the guideline for pre-event meals.

Vocabulary

24. f	28. b
25. d	29. a
26. g	30. e
27. c	

TRUE/FALSE

On a sheet of paper, write the numbers 1–10. Write True or False for each statement.

1. Nutrient needs vary with age, gender, and activity level.
2. Hunger is a personal desire, rather than a need, to eat.
3. Dietary fiber is easily digestible and is high in calories.
4. Of your total calories, 20 to 35 percent should come from fat.
5. Vitamin K is an example of a water-soluble vitamin.
6. Antioxidants may help protect against cancer, atherosclerosis, overtraining, and premature aging.
7. DRIs are daily nutrient recommendations for healthy people of both genders and different age groups.
8. An example of the size of one serving of fruit is one medium apple.
9. If you are eating to compete, you should consume simple carbohydrates for quick energy right before the contest.
10. Taking the supplement ephedrine before engaging in intense physical activity may increase the risk for heat-related injuries.

MULTIPLE CHOICE

On a sheet of paper, write the letter of the word or phrase that best completes each statement.

11. Before your body can use carbohydrates for energy, it must convert them to
    a. fiber.
    b. glucose.
    c. fats.
    d. electrolytes.
12. Candy bars, cookies, and soft drinks all contain a category of nutrients known as
    a. simple carbohydrates.
    b. fiber.
    c. complex carbohydrates.
    d. fat.
13. Of the following, cholesterol is found only in
    a. plant foods.
    b. soft drinks.
    c. meats.
    d. corn and olive oil.
14. Of the following, the vitamin that is NOT fat soluble is
    a. Vitamin A.
    b. Vitamin C.
    c. Vitamin D.
    d. Vitamin E.
15. Of the following, the mineral that does not function as an electrolyte is
    a. sodium.
    b. iron.
    c. calcium.
    d. potassium.
16. The number of daily servings of fruit recommended by the Food Guide Pyramid is
    a. 2–3.   c. 2–4.
    b. 3–5.   d. none of the above.
17. The following are all tips for controlling portion sizes when dining out EXCEPT
    a. choosing an appetizer as your main course.
    b. ordering regular-size portions rather than bigger value sizes.
    c. noticing when you begin to feel full, then not eating any more.
    d. ordering more than you think you can eat.
18. A Nutrition Facts panel on a food label will contain all of the following information EXCEPT
    a. serving size.
    b. total grams of protein.
    c. the number of servings of vegetables you should eat daily.
    d. Percent Daily Values for some vitamins.
19. A pre-event meal should be eaten
    a. within 30 minutes of the competition.
    b. every day for several weeks leading up to the competition.
    c. 1 to 3 hours before the competition.
    d. none of the above.
20. Use by competitive athletes of performance-enhancing supplements such as ephedrine and creatine is
    a. legal.
    b. unfair.
    c. dangerous.
    d. all of the above.

DISCUSSION

Using complete sentences, answer the following questions on a sheet of paper.

21. **Discuss** Identify which factors identified in Lesson 1 have the greatest influence on your food choices. Be specific.
22. **Summarize** Make a checklist that could be used to evaluate food safety practices in any home or professional kitchen.
23. **Extend** If you were to train and compete in a 10-kilometer walk/run in your community, how could you modify your nutrition plan to optimize your performance?

VOCABULARY EXPERIENCE

On a sheet of paper, write the letter of the term in Column B that best fits the definition in Column A.

Column A

24. Fats that are formed when certain oils are processed into solids.
25. A nonfood form of one or more nutrients.
26. A fatlike substance that is produced in the liver and circulates in the blood.
27. A special subclass of complex carbohydrates that aids the body in digestion.
28. A natural inborn drive that protects you from starvation.
29. Substances that protect body cells from damage.
30. A personal desire, rather than a need, to eat.

Column B

a. antioxidant
b. hunger
c. dietary fiber
d. dietary supplement
e. appetite
f. trans fatty acids
g. cholesterol

CRITICAL THINKING

Using complete sentences, answer the following questions on a sheet of paper.

31. **Compare** What is the difference between water-soluble and fat-soluble vitamins?
32. **Explain** Why is it especially important for a physically active person to make sure that he or she is getting enough potassium?

33. **Compare** Compare your eating habits with those of a family member. Which one of you is making wiser food choices? Explain your answer.

CASE STUDY

JAVIER'S WEIGHT GOALS

Javier is an active fifteen-year-old male who is interested in gaining muscle mass. He has started lifting weights two times a week, but he knows that he also needs to create a nutritious and balanced eating plan in order to help him reach his goal safely and effectively. His current dietary habits include skipping breakfast, eating a light lunch, and having a large dinner. He doesn't snack between meals. Javier needs the help of someone knowledgeable about designing and implementing a fitness program that includes nutritional advice—someone like you!

HERE IS YOUR ASSIGNMENT:

Assume you are Javier's friend, and that he asks you for some assistance with his plans for gaining muscle by adjusting his nutrition and physical-activity routine. Make a list of things Javier should consider and do before beginning his program. Then list the recommendations you would give to Javier for the first two weeks of his program.

KEYS TO HELP YOU

- Consider Javier's current eating plan and nutrition habits.
- Decide how he should evaluate his current eating plan.
- Think about his needs and goals. For example, how should he go about changing his eating habits?
- Develop a reasonable eating plan for Javier.

Critical Thinking

31. Fat-soluble vitamins are carried by fat in food and stored in the body, whereas water-soluble vitamins are not stored in the body.
32. Potassium helps regulate fluid balance; low levels of potassium can lead to muscle cramps and can affect the functioning of the nervous system.
33. Answers will vary but should demonstrate an understanding of the importance of making healthful food choices.

EVALUATE

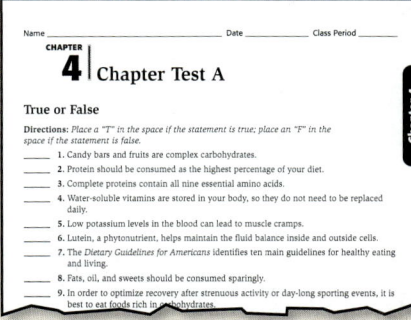

ENRICHMENT

CASE STUDY

ANSWERS

Answers will vary but might include use of the Food Guide Pyramid and use of the ABCs of nutrition. He should also use the information in Chapter 3 to help develop a beginning exercise training program.

CHAPTER 5

CHAPTER RESOURCES

- **Chapter Study Guide 5**
- **Vocabulary Worksheet 5**
- **Enrichment Activity 5**
- **Chapter 5 Test A**
- **Chapter 5 Test B**
- **Parent Letter and Activities 5 (English/Spanish)**

FITNESS *Online*

Ask students to take the STEP Personal Inventory for Chapter 5. Have them record their responses to the statements in their notebooks. Remind students that responses are private and for their use only.

CHAPTER 5 — Your Body Composition

FITNESS *Online*

How often do you weigh yourself? Have you ever had your body composition measured to estimate your percentage of body fat? These questions can help you understand the importance of body composition. Complete the STEP Personal Inventory for Chapter 5. Find it at **fitness.glencoe.com**.

146

INCLUSION STRATEGIES

LANGUAGE DIVERSITY *Use the following suggestions to help students who have difficulty with English:*

- Pair English-language learners with native speakers of English who can restate key points in language that helps students comprehend important concepts.

- Direct Spanish-speaking students to the written summaries of this chapter in the *Foundations of Personal Fitness* Spanish Booklet.

- Encourage Spanish-speaking students to use the Glosario provided in the back of the student text. **ELL**

The Basics of Body Composition

There is no single ideal body weight or body type for everyone. Instead, there is an appropriate range of body weights that will help you to maintain your functional health and fitness. To understand the relationship among your weight, body composition, and health, you need to consider many factors. You will explore these factors throughout this chapter.

Your Body Type

If you look around your school, you will notice people of all sizes and shapes, or *body types*. Body type is determined by a number of characteristics. These include bone size, muscle size, muscle mass, and percentage of body fat. There are three general body types.

- **Ectomorph.** The ectomorph body type is *characterized by a low percentage of body fat, small bone size, and a small amount of muscle mass and size.* Ectomorphs exhibit a lean appearance, often with long, slender arms and legs.
- **Mesomorph.** The mesomorph body type is *characterized by a low-to-medium percentage of body fat, medium-to-large bone size, and a large amount of muscle mass and size.* Mesomorphs appear muscular and well-proportioned.
- **Endomorph.** The endomorph body type is *characterized by a high percentage of body fat, large bone size, and a small amount of muscle mass and size.* Endomorphs generally have a round face, short neck, and wide hips.

What You Will Do

- Identify various body types.
- Analyze how your body composition can influence your functional health and fitness.
- Determine your BMI.

Terms to Know

ectomorph
mesomorph
endomorph
lean body weight
body mass index (BMI)
body composition
overweight
essential fat
excessive leanness
overfat

▶ The three basic body types are ectomorph, mesomorph, and endomorph. *What is the name for the body type shown in the picture?*

Lesson 1   The Basics of Body Composition   147

LESSON 1 RESOURCES

Teacher Classroom Resources
📁 Guided Practice Activity 5-1
📁 Reteaching Activity 5-1
📁 Lesson Quiz 5-1

Reproducible Charts and Graphs
📁 Reproducible Masters 5-1, 5-2, 5-3

Multimedia
◎ Vocabulary PuzzleMaker
🖱 Transparency 33

The Basics of Body Composition

1 MOTIVATE

GETTING STARTED

- Ask students to identify their favorite media star. Then ask students whether they think that person is physically active or exercises regularly. Finally, ask why students have this opinion.
- Distribute copies of *Guided Practice Activity 5-1* for students to use while studying this lesson. 📁

IN THIS LESSON

- **Mind Over Matter** *One Size Does Not Fit All, p. 148*

INTRODUCING VOCABULARY

- Tell students that *body mass index* (BMI) refers to the relationship between weight and height and is one method used by the Centers for Disease Control and Prevention (CDC) to determine how many Americans are considered to be overweight.
- Have students use *Vocabulary Worksheet 5* or the PuzzleMaker software to practice vocabulary terms for this lesson. ELL 📁 ◎

Photo Follow-up

Discuss with students the body types listed on page 148. *Caption answer: ectomorph. She has a lean appearance with long, slender arms and legs.*

2 TEACH

Discussing

Ask students what body type they think they have. Then ask what determines body type. *Their heredity and behaviors.* **L1**

USING VISUALS

Figure 5.1 Distribute *Reproducible Master 5-1.* **Caption answers may vary but will probably be yes, due to their heredity.** 📁

Mind OVER Matter

One Size Does Not Fit All

Have students read the *Mind Over Matter* feature. Explain to students that while heredity plays a major role in determining body type, they can still have an important impact on how they look and feel by practicing good nutrition and personal fitness behaviors now and as adults.

Explaining

Explain that one way to determine body type is to measure the circumference of the wrist at the styloid process of the radius and ulna. The wrist circumference for endomorph body types for females is >6 inches and >7.5 inches for males. Ectomorph body types are characterized as having wrist circumferences of <5.5 inches for females and <6.5 inches for males.

Mind OVER Matter

One Size Does Not Fit All

As a teen, you may feel inadequate because you don't look like one of the many models you see on television or in magazines.

Remember, however, that body type is hereditary. Models have been born with a body type that can't be achieved solely through any kind of eating plan or exercise.

Learn to accept your body type. It is part of who you are, like your hair color or eye color. It is part of your unique identity. Focus on exercise and eating habits as a way of maintaining your functional health and fitness—not a way to change who you are.

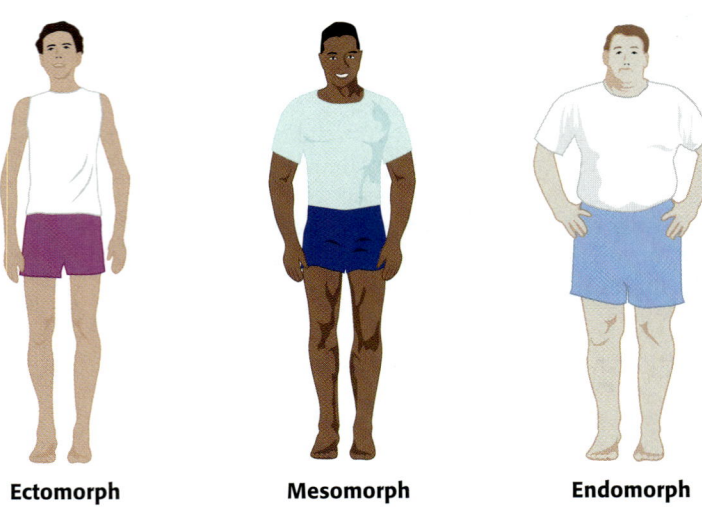

FIGURE 5.1

BODY TYPES: ECTOMORPH, MESOMORPH, AND ENDOMORPH

Body type is determined by heredity. *Do you have the same body type as someone else in your family?*

Ectomorph **Mesomorph** **Endomorph**

Figure 5.1 illustrates these three different body types. Body type is determined by heredity. Nevertheless, you still have some ability to control your body weight and composition as you age.

Your Body Weight

While your overall body type is determined by heredity, one aspect you can control is your weight. Although there is no one ideal weight, there are healthy ranges for each individual. These ranges are determined by several factors, including gender, age, height, body type, growth rate, metabolic rate, and activity level. For example, teens need more calories than adults because they are still growing. Active people need more calories than sedentary people because they burn more energy.

Many people place too much importance on weight. Weight by itself is not an accurate indicator of health. It tells you little about how lean or fat you are. In reality, when you compare two people of the same size, one may simply weigh more because he or she has more lean body weight than the other person. **Lean body weight** is *the combined weight of bone, muscle, and connective tissue.*

INCLUSION STRATEGIES

SELF-ESTEEM AND DISABILITIES

Students with disabilities often experience difficulty with self-esteem because their physical appearance may be affected by their conditions. These students may not physically fit within norms, thus making it awkward to discuss body composition.

Endomorphic students may have difficulty with endurance activities. Mesomorphic students have high energy levels and may be hyperactive. Ectomorphs may do well with endurance activities. A student's body type tends to have a direct effect on postural deviations and alignment.

Body Mass Index

One way to determine if your weight is within a healthy range is by using **Body Mass Index (BMI).** This is *a way to assess body size in relation to your height and weight.* **Figure 5.2** explains how to determine your BMI. Because BMI for teens varies according to age and gender, different charts are used for males and females. Adults also use a different chart for determining BMI. Notice that many different ratios of height and weight can be healthy. There is no single size and shape that's healthy for everyone.

 **Reading Check**

Summarize How can a person determine if his or her weight is within a healthy range?

Explaining

Explain to students that they can increase their lean muscle mass by performing resistance (weight) training on a regular basis. Have students see Chapters 9 and 10 for more on resistance training. **L1**

✓ **Reading Check**
BMI can be used to assess a person's healthy weight range.

FIGURE 5.2

TEEN BODY MASS INDEX
BMI is a useful tool when evaluating your body weight.
What is your BMI?

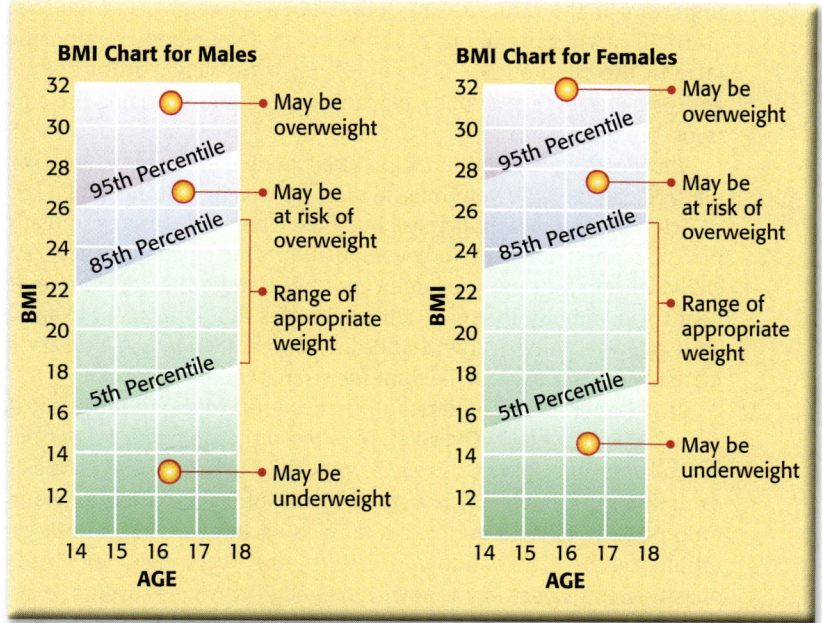

USING VISUALS

Figure 5.2 Distribute *Reproducible Master 5-2.* Begin by guiding students in how to use the BMI chart. Have students answer the figure caption. *Caption answers will vary based on students' height and weight. Have students use the chart to determine if they fall below the 5th percentile (excessively lean), above the 85th percentile (at risk for overweight), or above the 95th percentile (overweight). Explain that this information will be used later in Chapter 6.* 📁

Lesson 1 The Basics of Body Composition **149**

Teacher-Coach Tips

Athletes and Body Composition Many teen athletes have BMIs that exceed the 95th percentile for age and gender. These athletes are not necessarily overweight by the CDC standards, because they have high levels of lean muscle mass that makes them heavier. If you have students who regularly participate in vigorous activity, you can help them maintain or improve their body composition. First monitor their body composition. If it is too high or too low, encourage them to safely adjust the energy intake and energy expenditure equation to remain within the healthy range.

Student Edition TEKS
Page 148: C5A

hotlink

obesity
For more information on obesity, see Chapter 2, page **36.**

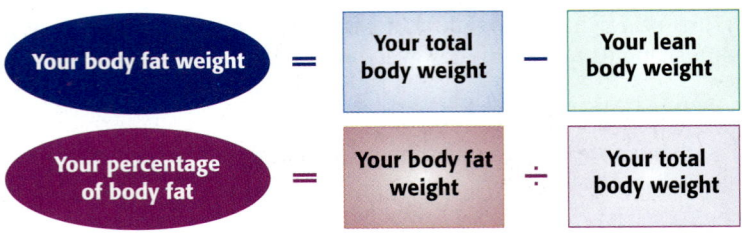

FIGURE 5.3

CALCULATIONS FOR BODY FAT

Lean body weight and body weight from fat are more relevant to understanding your health than total body weight. *Which tissues are included in lean body weight?*

Your body fat weight = Your total body weight − Your lean body weight

Your percentage of body fat = Your body fat weight ÷ Your total body weight

Body Composition

Understanding **body composition,** *the relative percentage in your body of fat to lean body tissue, including water, bone, and muscle,* is important to understanding a person's overall health. Particularly important is the ratio of lean body weight to weight from body fat. You will learn more about how to evaluate your body composition later in the chapter. For now, note that your weight from body fat and your percentage of body fat can be calculated by using the equations in **Figure 5.3**.

Physical activity and nutrition affect body composition. For example, you can increase your muscle mass by weight training, and a high-calorie eating plan will increase body fat. The nutrients in your eating plan also influence your body composition. During adolescence, especially, certain nutrients become very important to the development of healthy, lean body tissues, such as muscles and bones. For example, zinc aids the body's growth and development. Iron is necessary for increasing muscles, and calcium for strengthening bones.

It is important to understand that amount of body fat is not the same as body weight. **Overweight** is *a condition in which a person is heavier than the standard weight range for his or her height.* **Obesity,** as defined in Chapter 2, is a medical condition in which a person's ratio of body fat to lean muscle mass is excessively high. Both conditions can be high-risk to your health, and overweight may lead to obesity. Being overweight, however, is not always the result of excess body fat, as is the case with some body builders. They may exceed the appropriate weight range due to their excess muscle tissue.

Body Fat

When asked which aspect of body type they would most like to change, most people mention body fat. However, eliminating body fat entirely is not possible, or desirable. Everyone needs some body

More About . . .

BMI Body mass index, or BMI, is used by the CDC to determine the number of overweight or obese in America. For youth, those below the 5th percentile for BMI are considered underweight, those greater than the 85th percentile are considered at risk for being overweight, and those greater than the 95th percentile are considered overweight. Adults are considered underweight if they are below a BMI of 18.5, overweight if they are over a BMI of 25, obese if they are over a BMI of 30, and morbidly obese or at high risk for chronic disease if they are over a BMI of 40.

fat. **Essential fat** is *the minimum amount of body fat necessary for good health.* It is necessary for several reasons. Essential fat

- insulates your body against the cold.
- cushions your internal organs, protecting them from injury.
- provides you with a valuable source of stored energy. This enables you to meet your body's need for fuel.

While there are no hard-and-fast guidelines on how much body fat teens need, various measures may be used to determine whether a person's body composition is *within normal limits* for good health. You may reasonably assume the following:

- Teen males need 7 to 19 percent body fat.
- Teen females need 12 to 24 percent body fat.

Body Composition and Your Functional Health and Fitness

Body composition has an impact on your overall health, as shown in **Figure 5.4.** If you carry too little body fat, you are excessively lean. **Excessive leanness** may be defined as *having a percentage of body fat that is below the acceptable range for your age and gender.* Being **overfat** means *carrying too much body fat for your age and gender.*

FIGURE 5.4

BODY COMPOSITION AND RISK FOR CHRONIC DISEASES

According to this graph, people with a high percentage of body fat are at the greatest risk for chronic diseases. ***Which group is at second greatest risk?***

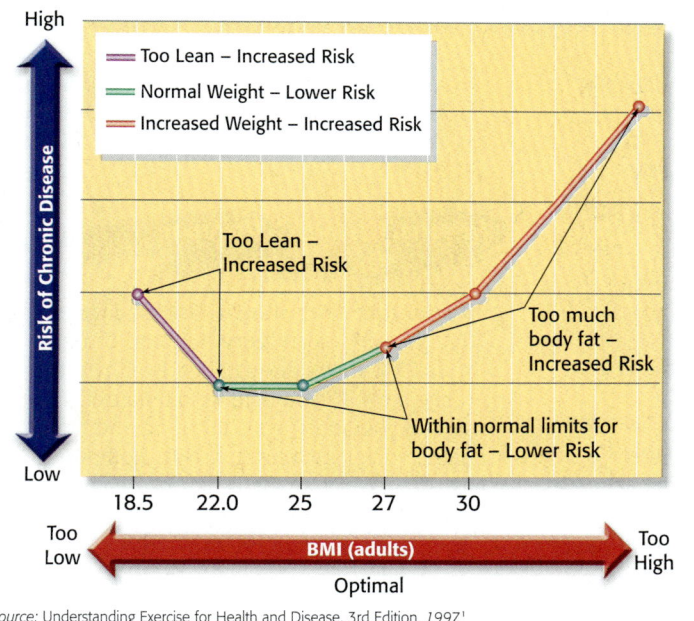

Source: Understanding Exercise for Health and Disease, 3rd Edition, 1997.[1]

OVERWEIGHT More American teens and adults are considered to be overweight than ever before. Many of the health problems in the United States result from dietary excess. People eat for a variety of reasons, only one of which is hunger. The sight or smell of food can be tempting, and social functions often involve food. Have students make a list of what they have eaten for the past 24 hours, the time they ate, and their reasons for eating. Have them speculate about how their reasons for eating might differ if food were scarce or hard to obtain.

Explaining

Explain to students that the term *WNL* (within normal limits) is often used in the health and fitness fields to emphasize that a range of normal values exists for many common health/fitness measures. For example, point out that there is not just one value, but a range, for percentage of body fat. **L1**

✓ **Reading Check**
(page 152)

A healthy range of body fat for teen females is 12 to 24 percent, for males a healthy range is 7 to 19 percent.

USING VISUALS

Figure 5.4 Display *Transparency 33* while discussing Figure 5.4. Ask students to use this information to explain the relationship between physical fitness and health. Point out that the shape of the graph illustrates the "J" relationship between increased functional health and fitness and the percentage of body fat a person has. Be sure to explain that if individuals are 20 to 30 pounds lighter *or* heavier than normal, they may be at higher risk for chronic disease later in life. ***Caption answer: Individuals at second greatest risk are those who are too lean.*** **TEKS C4A**

Student Edition TEKS

Page 151: C5G

3 ASSESS

EVALUATING THE LESSON

Assign and discuss the Lesson 1 Review.

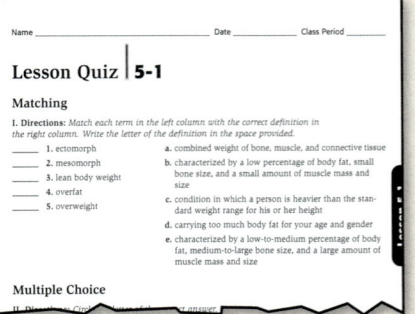

RETEACHING

Have students work in teams to discuss why body composition is important to a person's overall health.

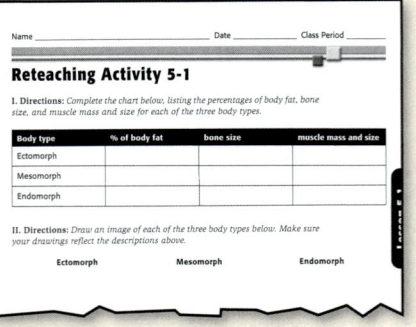

ENRICHMENT

Have students write a paragraph explaining why it is harmful to functional health and fitness to be overweight.

4 CLOSE

Ask students why they think many people are obsessed with being thin. Ask them how this affects eating behaviors.

Teen males are considered to be overfat and at risk for overweight when their body fat is greater than 20 percent. They are considered overweight when their body fat exceeds 25 percent. Teen males are excessively lean if their body fat is less than 7 percent.

Teen females are considered to be overfat and at risk for overweight when their body fat is greater than 25 percent. They are considered overweight when their body fat exceeds 32 percent. Excessive leanness for teen females is less than 12 percent body fat.

Overfat and excessive leanness place your functional health and fitness at risk for developing chronic diseases. In Figure 5.4 on page **151,** notice the *J* shape of the curve. This shape emphasizes the two population groups with the greatest risks for developing health problems. These are:

- People who weigh the least and are excessively lean
- People who weigh the most and have too much body fat

You will learn more about the risks associated with unhealthy weight and body composition in Chapter 6.

 Reading Check

Compare What is considered a healthy range for percentage of body fat for a female teen? for a male teen?

Lesson 1 Review

Using complete sentences, answer the following questions on a sheet of paper.

Reviewing Facts and Vocabulary

1. **Vocabulary** Define *Body Mass Index (BMI)*.
2. **Recall** Identify the three basic body types.
3. **Recall** Why is essential fat necessary for the health and functioning of your body?

Thinking Critically

4. **Compare** What is the difference between overweight and obesity? Is it possible for a person to be overweight, but not at risk for obesity? Explain.
5. **Extend** Jerry is 16 years old and has a BMI of 28. He is concerned because his family has a history of obesity. What advice can you give Jerry about whether he is at risk for being overweight?

Personal Fitness Planning

Evaluating Your Weight Use the formula for figuring BMI (see **Figure 5.2**) and compute your BMI. If you are within a healthy weight range, how do you plan to maintain it? How should you adjust your nutrition and fitness habits to ensure a healthy body composition as you become an adult? If you are not within a healthy weight range, what goals can you set for achieving a healthy weight?

Lesson 1 Review

Answers to Lesson 1 Review

1. Body mass index is a way to assess body size in relation to height, weight.
2. Ectomorph, mesomorph, endomorph.
3. Essential fat helps insulate your body and cushion internal organs, and it provides a source of stored energy.
4. Overweight is a condition in which a person is heavier than the standard weight range for his or her height, whereas obesity is when a person's ratio of body fat to lean muscle is extremely high.
5. Jerry needs to develop a plan to reduce his risk for obesity.

Influences on Your Body Composition

Body type, it was noted in Lesson 1, is determined by heredity. In this lesson you will learn about other factors that play a role in body size and shape. You will also learn which of them you can control and which you cannot.

Influences on Body Fat

After infancy, your teen years are the most dramatic growth period in your life. During these years, your body is rapidly transforming itself into an adult.

There is a common link between infancy and adolescence. They are the only times when the body develops new fat cells. The number of fat cells your body adds during adolescence depends in part on body type. Ectomorphs will acquire fewer new fat cells than mesomorphs or endomorphs. Endomorphs will acquire more new fat cells than mesomorphs or ectomorphs. This change is a fact of life—a fact of who you are. There is nothing you can do to change it. However, body fat percentage is both a function of the size of your body's fat cells as well as the *number.* Obese people, in other words, may have more fat cells than people who are within normal limits. Obese people also have larger fat cells.

Although you cannot control the number of fat cells in your body, you can control their size. The next section will discuss ways that can help.

▶ During the teen years, your body develops new fat cells. *What determines how many fat cells your body develops?*

What You Will Do

- Identify influences on amount of body fat.
- Analyze the role of energy balance in maintaining body weight and body composition.
- Describe the importance of metabolism to the energy equation.
- Identify the role of exercise as a method of weight control.
- Calculate the calories expended during various physical activities.

Terms to Know

calorie intake
calorie expenditure
metabolism
resting metabolic rate (RMR)

Influences on Your Body Composition

1 MOTIVATE

GETTING STARTED

- Ask: How do you think diet and exercise affect the number and size of fat cells? Tell students that in this lesson they will learn what influences fat cells and body composition.
- Distribute copies of *Guided Practice Activity 5-2* for students to use while studying this lesson. 📁

IN THIS LESSON

- **Active Mind—Active Body** *Exercise and Calorie Expenditure,* p. 156

INTRODUCING VOCABULARY

- Explain to students that the term *resting metabolic rate* (RMR) is similar to the term *basal metabolic rate* (BMR), which is how much energy you expend during rest in standard laboratory conditions.
- Have students use *Vocabulary Worksheet 5* or the PuzzleMaker software to practice vocabulary terms for this lesson. **ELL** 📁 ◎

Photo Follow-up

Emphasize that it's the size of fat cells, not the number, that determines percentage of body fat. *Caption answer: Heredity determines how many fat cells a person develops.*

LESSON 2 RESOURCES

Teacher Classroom Resources
- 📁 Guided Practice Activity 5-2
- 📁 Active Mind—Active Body Worksheet 5-2
- 📁 Reteaching Activity 5-2
- 📁 Lesson Quiz 5-2

Reproducible Charts and Graphs
- 📁 Reproducible Master 5-4

Multimedia
- ◎ Vocabulary PuzzleMaker
- ⬇ Transparencies 34, 35

2 TEACH

Explaining

Explain to students that their lifestyle and personal fitness behaviors can have a major influence on their body composition. Display *Transparency 34* and discuss calories used during activities.
L1 TEKS C4A

USING VISUALS

Figure 5.5 Be sure students understand the energy equation. Use examples in Figure 5.5 to evaluate the number of calories in foods they eat. *Caption answer: Fat provides 9 calories per gram.*

Quick Demo

To help students understand the units used in measuring calorie intake, demonstrate to them the size and weight of 1 gram. Borrow a gram weight scale from the school science department to demonstrate gram weight. Have students measure the gram weight of their watches or common items in the classroom, such as paper clips. **L2**

✓ Reading Check

Eating patterns and activity level are two changeable risk factors that affect body fat. **TEKS C5D**

Lifestyle Behaviors

Have you ever heard the saying, "You are what you eat?" There is some truth to this saying. Your body composition, in other words, is partly a function of your eating patterns. If you take in more calories from food than your body needs, the extra calories will be stored as fat. This stored fat will, in turn, increase the size of your fat cells.

Another lifestyle behavior that affects your body composition is activity level. The more physically active you are, the more calories you burn as fuel. The opposite, of course, is also true.

By eating healthfully and maintaining an active lifestyle, you can help control your body composition now and as you get older.

✓ Reading Check

Identify What are two lifestyle behaviors that can affect body fat?

The Energy Equation

The question of what percentage of your body weight is from fat comes down ultimately to energy balance. Do you recall reading about calories and energy in Chapter 4? To manage your weight and stay healthy, your body needs to maintain an energy balance. This means that it needs to expend, or use up, the energy taken in from food each day.

Energy balance is determined by **calorie intake,** *the total number of calories you take in from food*, and **calorie expenditure,** *the total number of calories you burn or expend.* If you take in fewer calories from food than you expend over a period of weeks or months, you will lower your percentage of body fat. The reverse is also true.

Calorie Intake

As explained in Chapter 4, three of the six nutrient classes provide calories—carbohydrates, proteins, and fats. **Figure 5.5** shows the number of calories supplied by each type. If you know the number of grams of these nutrients in the foods you eat, you can calculate the amount of calories you consume at meals and snacks. You can then use this information to determine if your daily calorie intake is appropriate for your energy needs.

Even if you have a healthy body composition as a teen, it will be necessary to adjust your eating habits and level of physical activity as you become an adult. This will help you maintain a proper energy balance as your body's needs change. The Daily Calorie Intake chart in **Figure 4.1** on page 115 shows estimates of calories needed by any given individual based on age and activity level. Remember that less active teens and adults require fewer calories than those who are physically active.

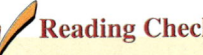

FIGURE 5.5

CALORIES PER GRAM OF NUTRIENT

All of these nutrients provide energy. *Which nutrient provides the most calories per gram? Which provides the most energy per gram?*

Nutrient	Calories per Gram
Carbohydrate	4
Protein	4
Fat	9

More About . . .

THE ENERGY BALANCE EQUATION Students will learn about a variety of influences that affect the energy balance equation. Here is another way to think about balancing the energy equation in order to burn 1 pound of fat (or 3,500 calories) in one week: Reduce one's energy intake by about 200 to 300 calories per day, while increasing caloric expenditure by about 200 to 300 calories. A person following this plan daily for seven days can lose 3,500 calories—1 pound of fat. This strategy can be safe, effective, and easy to adhere to because it does not require major lifestyle changes.

Calorie Expenditure and Metabolism

The process by which the body converts calories from food to energy is known as **metabolism**. Metabolism is an ongoing process. It occurs even when you are at rest. The rate at which the body uses energy varies from person to person and during different physical activities. Your **resting metabolic rate (RMR)** is *the amount of calories you expend for body processes while at rest.* Your calorie expenditure is determined by your RMR and how physically active you are each day.

Your RMR represents the energy needed for involuntary body activities. Among these are heartbeat, blood circulation, and breathing. For most young adults, such activities require between 1 to 1.5 calories per minute. You need to consume between 1,400 and 1,800 calories just to keep your body functioning.

Your Resting Metabolic Rate (RMR). Your RMR is shaped by several factors. These include:

- **Gender.** Males on average have higher RMRs than females, as illustrated in **Figure 5.6.** This is because male teens typically have a higher proportion of muscle mass to fat than do female teens. Muscle burns more calories than body fat.

FIGURE 5.6

YOUR METABOLIC RATE AS YOU AGE

Metabolic rate depends on several factors, including age and gender.
Describe the difference in the trends between male and female RMR.

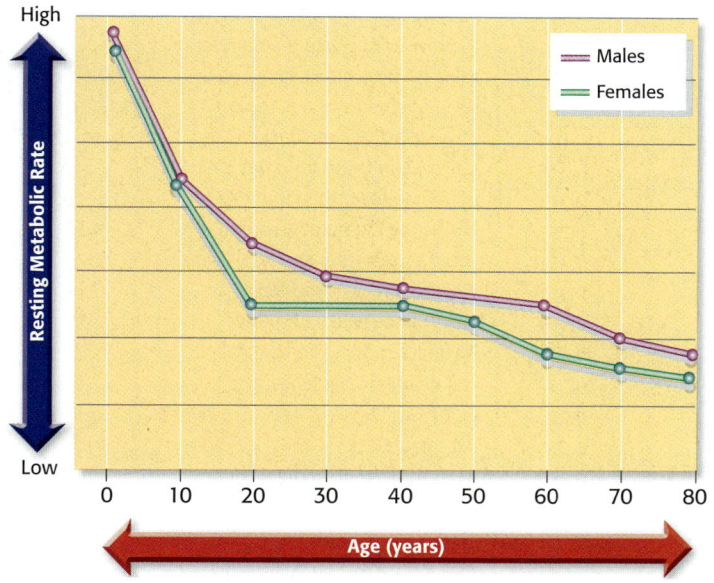

Source: Exercise Physiology, Nutrition, and Human Performance, 5th Edition, *2001.*[2]

Discussing

Ask students why their diets may need to change as they age and their caloric intake decreases. Have them discuss this with family members who may be in their 30s, 40s, or 50s. Students should recognize that their RMR will decrease with age. Females usually experience a greater decrease than males because of differences in muscle mass. Therefore, people need to stay physically active as they get older and manage their caloric intake to control body weight and body composition. **L2**

USING VISUALS

Figure 5.6 Use *Transparency 35* to discuss the chart on Your Metabolic Rate as You Age. *Caption answer: On average, the RMR of females as they age is lower than that of males. Students should note, however, that other factors besides aging can also influence their RMR, such as eating habits and physical activity or exercise.*

What Teens *Want* to Know

Which is the better way to lose weight? Diet (reducing energy intake) only, exercise only, or the combination of diet and exercise? Research suggests that it may depend on how long a person follows one method versus another. Dr. John Foreyt of the Baylor College of Medicine in Houston, Texas, studied three groups of individuals (diet only, exercise only, and diet and exercise together) for two years to determine how successful each group was with weight loss. He found that the diet and exercise group lost more weight in the first year compared with the other two groups.

Student Edition TEKS

Page 155: C5F

Active Mind Active Body
Exercise and Calorie Expenditure

This activity will help students understand how participating in physical activity at different intensity levels and durations will help them burn calories and control their body weight and body composition. **TEKS C4A**

Teaching Tips

- Be sure that students wear proper exercise attire and demonstrate safety procedures by using nonskid footwear. **TEKS C3A**
- Distribute *Active Mind–Active Body Worksheet 5-2* for students to record results. 📁
- Remind students to warm up properly before they complete the two activities. **TEKS C1A**
- Have students compare their results with partners to see whether they might require more or less caloric expenditure.

Apply and Conclude

After completing the activity, have students analyze exercise as a method of weight control. Then have them describe one method that combines diet and exercise and compare its effectiveness to exercise alone. **TEKS C5F**

Student Edition TEKS

Page 156: C5F
Page 157: C5F

Active Mind Active Body
Exercise and Calorie Expenditure

In this activity, you will determine the effect exercise and physical activity have on energy balance by determining the caloric expenditure for certain physical activities. This will help you analyze how exercise and physical activities you enjoy can influence your personal energy balance and affect body weight and composition.

What You Will Need

- Pen or pencil
- Paper
- Calculator (optional)

What You Will Do

1. Review **Figure 5.7** below. Select two physical activities or exercises that you do somewhat regularly.
2. Calculate and record how many calories you would expend for one week if you did each exercise or activity three times a week for the following durations:
   - 20 minutes
   - 40 minutes
   - 60 minutes

Apply and Conclude

What was the largest calorie expenditure you recorded? For what activity did you record this number?

Energy Demands of Activities

Activity	Cal/Lb/Min	Calculating Calories Expended
Aerobic dance (vigorous)	0.062	*Cal/Lb/Min* means *Calories per pound* of body weight *per minute.* In order to calculate the number of calories you would expend after several minutes of a particular physical activity, multiply the *Cal/Lb/Min* factor from this chart by your weight. Then multiply your answer by the number of minutes you spend on the activity. For example, if you weigh 142 pounds, and you spend 30 minutes doing aerobic dance, you would do the following: 0.062 Cal/Lb/Min × 142 = 8.8 calories per minute 8.8 Cal/Min × 30 = 264 calories expended
Basketball (vigorous, full court)	0.097	
Bicycling (13 mph)	0.045	
Bicycling (19 mph)	0.076	
Canoeing (flat water, moderate pace)	0.045	
Cross-country skiing (8 mph)	0.104	
Golf (carrying clubs)	0.045	
Handball	0.078	
Horseback riding (trot)	0.052	
Rowing (vigorous)	0.097	
Running (5 mph)	0.061	
Running (7.5 mph)	0.094	
Running (10 mph)	0.114	
Soccer	0.097	
Swimming (20 ypm)	0.032	
Swimming (45 ypm)	0.058	
Tennis (beginner)	0.032	
Walking (3.5 mph)	0.035	

Figure 5.7

Source: Nutrition Concerns for the Endurance Athlete.[3]

Myths & Realities

Myth 1 Participating in weight (or resistance) training does not significantly increase your energy expenditure.

Fact 1 Weight (or resistance) training does in fact significantly increase energy expenditure when movements that involve the larger muscle groups are included. Weight training also increases energy expenditure during recovery from exercise and can increase your resting metabolic rate, which means you expend more calories even at rest if you include weight training in your fitness program.

- **Age.** RMR decreases with age. As people grow older, they need fewer calories to meet their daily energy needs. If they fail to reduce their calorie intake or increase their energy expenditure levels, they will see a weight and fat gain.
- **Heredity.** Some people inherit much higher RMRs than others. This may explain, at least in part, why some people have an easier time losing weight than others.
- **Eating habits.** Your eating habits can stimulate or slow your RMR. For example, when you eat regularly (three to six small meals) throughout the day, you stimulate your RMR more often. This is because the act of digestion itself requires energy. However, if you eat only one meal per day (as many busy people do), your RMR may be slower. This can promote weight gain and increase your body fat.
- **Eliminating calories.** Restricting the number of calories taken in slows down your RMR. Suppose you reduced your daily calorie intake to 500 calories, which is well below daily recommendations. Over the course of several days, your RMR would drop as much as 50 to 75 percent. This would produce negative results. You probably would be tired, hungry all the time, and your energy would be low.
- **Physical activity and exercise.** Participation in regular physical activity or exercise stimulates metabolic rate. This is true not only during physical activity but also for a short while afterward. Thus, regular exercise or physical activity can increase your RMR.

Weight Control and Physical Activity

Obviously, the more physically active you are, the more calories you will burn. Yet, as with RMR, the number of calories you burn through physical activity will vary with respect to several factors. These include:

- **The number, size, and weight of body parts that you work.** If you work with your legs (by walking, for example), you will burn more calories than you would working your arms (by lifting weights, for example). The reason is simple: The leg muscles are larger than the arm muscles. The larger the muscle mass, the more energy needed to work it.
- **The intensity of your workout.** The more physically demanding, or intense, your workout is, the more calories you will burn. This is because harder work requires more fuel.
- **The duration, or time, of your activities.** If you engage in daily physical activities, you will burn more calories than someone who is sedentary. For example, Molly and her friend Nelda in **Figure 5.8** (page **158**) have the same RMR. Nelda burns more calories because she is physically active.

Reading Check

Explain Describe the relationship between expending calories and physical activity or exercise.

STRESS BREAK

Attractive vs. Healthy

Some teens feel pressure to compete with the media's idea of what is attractive. Don't get caught up in these unrealistic images.

Just because someone looks thin or muscular does not mean he or she is healthy. Some people who *look* attractive may use fad diets, diet pills, or other risky practices to keep up their image.

Know what are healthful and reasonable goals for your body composition. After all, working toward a healthy, fit body will make you feel good about yourself.

STRESS BREAK

Have students read the *Stress Break* feature on this page. Remind students that during adolescence, their bodies are growing and developing rapidly. Many teens grow several inches during a school semester and their bodies may change dramatically in appearance. Encourage students to recognize that the stresses that accompany these growth and development patterns are normal and will subside somewhat as they reach maturity. Ask students to describe one healthy physical activity they can practice to reduce stress. **TEKS C5B**

Reading Check
The more physically active you are, the more calories you will burn.

USING VISUALS

Figure 5.8 Introduce the figure on page 158 using *Reproducible Master 5-4*, and have students compare the daily energy needs of Nelda and Molly. Ask students to consider both the RMR and the energy used in physical activities to explain their answers to the question. *Caption answers might include differences in RMR, energy intake, or energy expenditure.* ☞

TECHNOLOGY FILE

Spreadsheet Caloric Analysis

Students may use the spreadsheet they created in Chapter 4. Enter "Caloric Intake" in cell A6, "Caloric Difference" in cell A7, "Weekly Weight Change" in cell A8, and "Yearly Weight Change" in cell A9. Then enter "=B5+C5" in cell D6, "=D6–D5" in cell D7, "=d7/3500" in cell D8, and "=D8*365" in cell D9. Students can then forecast their total caloric intake (calculated in cell D6) along with their total caloric expenditure (cells B3, B4, C3, C4) in order to determine their potential weight loss or gain on a weekly and yearly basis.

3 ASSESS

EVALUATING THE LESSON

Assign and discuss the Lesson 2 Review.

RETEACHING

Have students explain the relationship between calorie intake and expenditure in maintaining body weight.

ENRICHMENT

Ask students to debate which factors have the most influence on body composition.

4 CLOSE

Ask students what advice they might give to people interested in modifying or controlling their body weight and body composition.

FIGURE 5.8

ENERGY EXPENDITURE OF AN ACTIVE TEEN VERSUS AN INACTIVE TEEN

The chart shows a typical breakdown of the total energy needs of two different teens. *Why does Nelda burn 500 calories more than Molly? How many more calories will she burn in a week's time?*

Daily Energy Needs	Nelda (Active)	Molly (Sedentary)
Energy for RMR	1,600 calories	1,600 calories
Energy for physical activity	600 calories	100 calories
Total energy needs	2,200 calories	1,700 calories

Lesson 2 Review

Using complete sentences, answer the following questions on a sheet of paper.

Reviewing Facts and Vocabulary

1. **Vocabulary** What is *metabolism?*
2. **Recall** Explain the relationship among calorie intake, calorie expenditure, and amount of body fat.
3. **Recall** What are three factors that influence the amount of calories expended during physical activity or exercise?

Thinking Critically

4. **Synthesize** Marcus eats five small meals a day and gets at least 60 minutes of physical activity a day. Natasha eats two large meals a day and does not participate in regular physical activity. Which one most likely has the highest RMR? Explain your answer.

5. **Analyze** For exercise, Martin runs 60 minutes each day. His friend Jamel lifts weights for 45 minutes each day. Which teen expends more calories through these physical activities? Explain.

Personal Fitness Planning

Investigating Claims Some fitness equipment manufacturers claim that if you work out with their product you can easily burn 1,000 calories per hour. Using **Figure 5.7**, apply the physiological principles related to exercise. Calculate the type and intensity of activity a person would need to do to burn 1,000 calories in an hour. Do you think these claims are valid? Why or why not?

Lesson 2 Review

Answers to Lesson 2 Review

1. The process by which your body converts calories from foods to energy.
2. One needs to match caloric intake with caloric expenditure in order to maintain a certain percentage of body fat.
3. The number and size of muscles worked, the weight of the body parts moved, intensity, and duration.
4. Marcus probably has a higher BMI because he is male, eats frequently, and exercises regularly.
5. Martin expends more calories because running uses larger leg muscles.

Evaluating Your Body Composition

In this lesson, you will learn about several ways to measure body composition. You will also learn how to perform some of these methods.

It is important to be aware that every method of measuring body composition has some degree of inaccuracy built in. If your body fat measurement is borderline for any test, you should consult a health care professional. You may need to make adjustments to your calorie intake and expenditure.

Body Circumference

Body fat is stored differently in males and females. In males, body fat accumulates primarily around the waist. In females, it gravitates toward the hips. The body-circumference test accounts for these differences by having separate procedures for males and females.

The body-circumference tests measure **girth.** This is *the distance around a body part.* For all of these tests, you will need a cloth tape measure and a ruler.

What You Will Do

- Analyze methods of measuring body composition.
- Define ranges of healthy body fat percentages for teens.
- Identify tools that are used in computing body composition.

Terms to Know

girth
calipers

▶ Measuring body circumference is one way to evaluate body composition. *Why is body circumference measured differently in males and females?*

Lesson 3   Evaluating Your Body Composition   **159**

1 MOTIVATE

GETTING STARTED

- Ask students whether they have ever had their body composition measured. If so, what techniques were used? Ask what techniques they think could be used to calculate body composition.
- Distribute copies of *Guided Practice Activity 5-3* for students to use while studying this lesson. ☞

IN THIS LESSON

- **Fitness Check**
  Measuring Body Composition, p. 162

INTRODUCING VOCABULARY

- Have students read the definition for the vocabulary term *calipers* on page 161. Ask for a volunteer to explain what "adipose tissue" refers to in this definition. *Adipose tissue is connective tissue in which fat is stored, often between the skin and muscles.*
- Have students use *Vocabulary Worksheet 5* or the PuzzleMaker software to practice vocabulary terms. **ELL** ☞ ◉

Photo Follow-up

Point out the proper method for taking measurements for body composition. *Caption answer: Because males and females store body fat differently.*

LESSON 3 RESOURCES

Teacher Classroom Resources
- Guided Practice Activity 5-3
- Fitness Check Worksheet 5-3
- Reteaching Activity 5-3
- Lesson Quiz 5-3

Reproducible Charts and Graphs
- Reproducible Masters 5-5, 5-6

Multimedia
- ◉ Vocabulary PuzzleMaker
- ⚓ Transparencies 36, 37

2 TEACH

Discussing

Discuss with students that body circumference measures are a quick and easy way to estimate body composition, but they carry greater chance for error than other methods. However, the U.S. Navy does consider measures of neck and abdomen girth as accurate enough to determine body composition for their personnel. **L1**

USING VISUALS

Figure 5.9 Distribute *Reproducible Master 5-5*. Ask students to take time to make accurate body circumference measures. Remind them that following the instructions is important. Then have them assess their percentages of body fat using information in Figure 5.10. *Caption answer: For males, you need to measure weight in pounds and the girth at the waistline; for females, you need to measure height and the girth of the hips.* 👉

✔ **Reading Check**

Underwater weighing, bioelectrical impedance, and DEXA or MRI scans.

Student Edition TEKS

Page 158: C1A

Body-Circumference Test for Males

For males, the body-circumference test has two steps. First, measure your weight in pounds. Then, measure your girth at the waistline.

Before weighing yourself, you should remove your shoes and dress in your exercise clothing. Measure your waist circumference with the tape measure pulled snugly, but not too tightly. Measure to the nearest half-inch. Once you have obtained your measurements, use the chart in **Figure 5.9** to help you determine your percentage of body fat. Using a ruler, connect the points from your body weight to your waist circumference. The point where the ruler crosses the scale in the center column is your approximate percentage of body fat.

Body-Circumference Test for Females

Females can estimate their percentage of body fat by measuring their height and the girth of their hips at the widest point. First, remove your shoes. Compute your height to the nearest half-inch. The hip circumference measurement should be taken with the tape measure pulled snugly, but not too tightly, and to the nearest half-inch.

Once you have obtained your measurements, you can use **Figure 5.9** to determine your percentage of body fat. Using a ruler, connect the points from your body height to your hip circumference. The point where the ruler intersects the scale in the center column is your approximate percentage of body fat.

FIGURE 5.9

BODY-FAT PERCENTAGE FROM CIRCUMFERENCE TESTS: MALE AND FEMALE

Body-fat percentages are calculated differently for males and females. *How are the two tests different?*

Males

Body Weight (pounds)	Percent of Body Fat	Waist (inches)

| 120, 140, 160, 180, 200, 220, 240, 260 | 40, 30, 25, 20, 15, 10, 5 | 45, 40, 35, 30, 25 |

Females

Hip (inches)	Percent of Body Fat	Height (inches)

| 32, 34, 36, 38, 40, 42 | 10, 14, 18, 22, 26, 30, 34, 38, 42 | 72, 70, 68, 66, 64, 62, 60, 58, 56 |

EQUIPMENT OPTIONS

BODY COMPOSITION EQUIPMENT The various methods for determining body composition require the teacher or coach to use a variety of equipment items to help students understand the concept of body composition measurement. To measure BMI, you will need a standard-quality height and weight scale like that found in the school nurse's office. To measure body circumferences, you will need several flexible measurement tapes. To measure skinfolds, you'll need at least several pairs of plastic calipers that cost $10 to $15. More expensive calipers can cost $250 to $300 and are

FIGURE 5.10

BODY-FAT RATINGS

Use your percentage of body fat to determine your health rating.

Where on this chart do you fall? What changes, if any, do you need to make to your body composition?

% Fat (Males)	% Fat (Females)	Fitness Rating and Evaluation
25% or more	30% or more	Overfat – Too high *(A person in this range is at higher risk for chronic diseases.)*
20–24%	25–29%	Borderline High – Possible health risks *(A person in this range needs to lose weight.)*
10–19%	15–24%	Healthy – Most desirable level
7–9%	12–14%	Healthy Lean – Acceptable level
6% or less	11% or less	Too Lean – Possible health risks *(Acceptable only for a competitive endurance athlete)*

Evaluating Body Circumference

Once you have determined your percentage of body fat, you can use **Figure 5.10** to evaluate your body fat score. As mentioned in Lesson 1, males should carry 7 to 20 percent body fat. Females should carry 12 to 25 percent body fat. If you do not score in the *acceptable-to-most-desirable* health zones, try to improve your body composition.

Skinfold Measures

Another method used to evaluate body composition is skinfold measurement. The finger pinch test featured in the "Fitness Check" on page **8** is an example of a simplified skinfold test. More accurate skinfold measurements are made using **calipers.** This is *a tweezerlike device used to pinch a fold of skin surrounding adipose tissue.* The resulting fold is measured in millimeters.

A skinfold test is a good indicator of body composition because 50 percent of all body fat is between the muscles and skin, as shown in **Figure 5.11.** The other 50 percent is inside the body.

For adolescents, two skinfold measurements are typically taken: the back of the upper arm (triceps) and the inside of the calf at its widest part. See **Figure 5.13** on page **163** for percentages.

✔ Reading Check

Summarize What are the medical evaluations that can be used to measure body composition?

FIGURE 5.11

SKINFOLD TEST

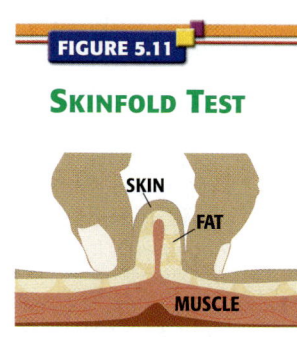

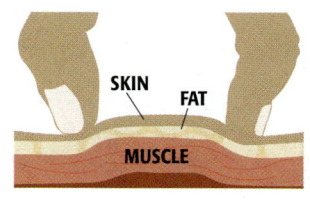

slightly more accurate. These can be useful for students to compare measurement tools. The cost varies for medical equipment and equipment for laboratory evaluations of body composition: underwater weighing—$10,000 to $15,000; bioelectrical impedance measuring devices—$3,000 to $6,000 (less expensive models predict body composition percentages based on BMI measures, which are less accurate); DEXA and MRI machines—$40,000 to $1,000,000.

USING VISUALS

Figure 5.10 Use *Reproducible Master 5-6* to explain that measuring the percentage of body fat can provide important health information. Point out that the Fitness Ratings and Evaluation column shows possible health risks for both males and females. *Caption answers will vary, based on students' measurements, but strategies might include adjusting caloric intake and caloric expenditure.* 📂

USING VISUALS

Figure 5.11 Display *Transparency 36* on Body Fat Measurements. Guide students in learning how to assess one another's body composition, but remind them to respect each person's privacy and not share the body composition results with others in class.

Activity

Ask volunteers to investigate the various medical or laboratory evaluations available. Ask volunteers to learn more about how underwater weighing or bioelectrical impedance actually works. They may ask science teachers about the principles involved with either of these techniques. Allow class time for volunteers to share their findings. **L3**

Student Edition TEKS

Page 161: C5F

Fitness Check

Measuring Body Composition

OBJECTIVES

- Students will learn to measure, practice, and evaluate taking skinfolds as a way of determining body composition.

TEACHING STRATEGIES

- Have students observe you performing the measures on a student volunteer (secure the volunteer before class).

- Students may also benefit from watching an instructional video that demonstrates the skinfold technique.

- Distribute copies of *Fitness Check Worksheet 5-3* so students can record their results. ☞

- Plastic (economical) skinfold calipers are suitable for this activity. However, if more expensive calipers are available, you may want to demonstrate the same skinfolds with the more expensive calipers and compare the results.

USING VISUALS

Figure 5.13 Use the chart, on page 163, *Transparency 37*, and student measurement results to help screen individuals who are in the "very low" and "very high" subcategories, as these individuals may be at high risk for eating disorders and excessive exercise behaviors.

Measuring Body Composition

For your personal fitness assessments, skinfold evaluations of body composition are adequately reliable. In this activity, you and a partner will take turns performing a skinfold test on each other. Use a separate sheet of paper to record all calculations.

Procedure:

1. Use your left hand to grasp each skinfold. Avoid grasping the muscle or pinching too tightly.

2. For the triceps, use your thumb and index finger to pick up a skinfold in the middle of your partner's right arm exactly halfway between the shoulder and the elbow. Have your partner keep his or her arm relaxed at the side of the body. (See **Figure 5.12a.**)

3. For the calf, have your partner stand up and place his or her right foot on a bench or chair. Use your thumb and index finger to pick up a skinfold in the middle of the inside part of the lower leg at its widest part. (See **Figure 5.12b.**)

4. With your right hand, place the opened calipers one-half inch below the skinfold grasp and directly below the pinch, with the scale of the calipers visible.

5. Close the calipers on the skinfold. Hold it for two to three seconds. Read and record the measurement to the nearest millimeter. Repeat this step two more times.

6. Use the middle of the three readings as your skinfold score. (For example, if the three readings are 18, 16, and 15 mm, use 16 as your score.)

7. Add up your triceps and calf skinfold scores as follows:
   triceps (mm) + calf (mm) = sum of skinfolds
   Use **Figure 5.13** to determine your percentage of body fat. Read straight down from the sum of skinfolds to the "% fat" reading.

8. Calculate your body-fat weight by multiplying your weight by your percentage of body fat:
   weight × % body fat = body-fat weight

9. Calculate your lean body weight by subtracting your fat weight from your weight:
   weight − body-fat weight = lean body weight

10. For females, determine your ideal minimum weight by dividing your lean weight by 0.76. Determine your ideal maximum weight by dividing your lean body weight by 0.88.

11. For males, determine your ideal minimum weight by dividing your lean body weight by 0.81. Determine your ideal maximum weight by dividing your lean body weight by 0.93.

12. Refer to **Figure 5.10** on page 161 to evaluate your body-fat score. If you did not score within a healthy zone, try to improve your body composition by getting closer to your healthy body weight range.

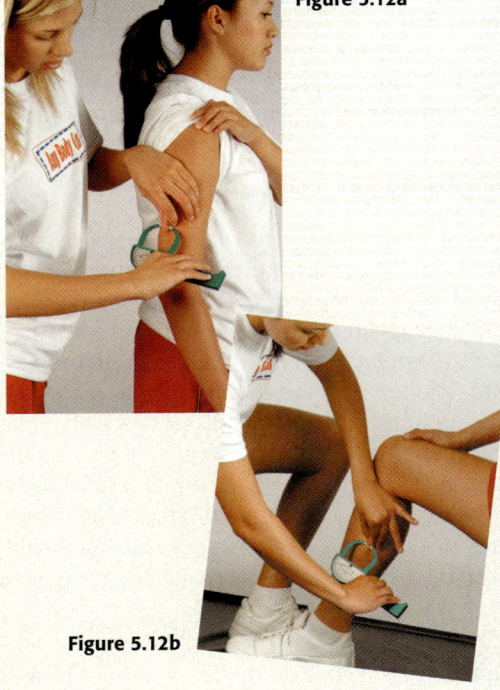

Figure 5.12a

Figure 5.12b

More About . . .

BEST MEASURES OF BODY COMPOSITION

The best method for measuring body composition depends on the following factors: accuracy, cost, and ease of measurement. One way to determine the accuracy of a body composition test is to consider the margin of error for each method. The following is a list of the error margin of each body composition test and the DEXA or MRI methods: body circumference measures: ± 3–6 percent; BMI: ± 6 percent; skinfolds: 3 percent; bioelectrical impedance: 3–6 percent; underwater weighing: 1–3 percent.

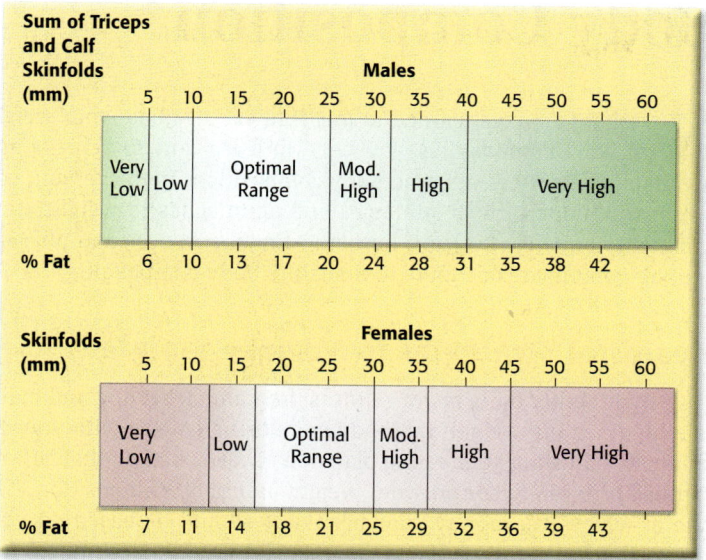

FIGURE 5.13

SKINFOLD MEASUREMENTS AND BODY-FAT PERCENTAGES

Skinfold measurements are one way to measure body composition.

Why is this a good indicator of percentage of body fat?

3 ASSESS

EVALUATING THE LESSON

Assign and discuss the Lesson 3 Review.

RETEACHING

Ask students to explain how body circumference tests are used.

ENRICHMENT

Have students write a paragraph answering the following: What do you think you'll need to do in the future to obtain or maintain a desirable level of body composition?

Lesson 3 Review

Using complete sentences, answer the following questions on a sheet of paper.

Reviewing Facts and Vocabulary

1. **Recall** Name two approaches for measuring body composition.

2. **Vocabulary** What are *calipers* used for?

3. **Recall** What is a healthy body-fat percentage for teen males? For teen females?

Thinking Critically

4. **Analyze** Emma wants to evaluate her body composition using the body-circumference test. Explain the procedure she should follow, including what she will need to evaluate her body-fat percentage.

5. **Evaluate** Harry had his skinfolds measured. The sum of his folds was 20. What would you tell Harry about his current level of health with respect to body-fat percentage?

Personal Fitness Planning

Evaluating Body Composition Using the body-circumference test described in this lesson, measure your body composition. Compare the results with your results from the "Fitness Check." Did you get the same results each time? What might account for the difference? Write a paragraph about how body composition impacts your personal fitness plan.

Lesson 3 Evaluating Your Body Composition **163**

---

4 CLOSE

Have students compare their own results for body circumference and for skinfold measures. Be sure students keep their results private.

Lesson 3 Review

Answers to Lesson 3 Review

1. Any two: body circumferences, skinfold, underwater weighing, bioelectrical impedance, and MRIs.

2. Measuring percentage of body fat.

3. Males, 7–20%; females, 12–25%.

4. She can have her skinfolds measured, and follow procedures in the fitness check.

5. Harry should maintain or lower his current body composition by adjusting his energy input and increasing his expenditure.

Maintaining a Healthy Body Composition

1 MOTIVATE

GETTING STARTED

- Ask students whether they have tried to control their body weight in the past. If so, what strategies have they used? What strategies have they observed in others?
- Distribute copies of *Guided Practice Activity 5-4* for students to use while studying this lesson. ☞

IN THIS LESSON

- **Lifeline** *Watching Your Friends' Weight, p. 165*
- **Consumer Corner** *Practicing Safe Weight Management, p. 166*

INTRODUCING VOCABULARY

- Explain to students that the term *nutrient-dense foods* refers to the Food Guide Pyramid and *Dietary Guidelines for Americans* they learned about in Chapter 4.
- Have students use *Vocabulary Worksheet 5* or the PuzzleMaker software to practice vocabulary terms. **ELL** ☞ ◎

Photo Follow-up

Emphasize the importance of participating in physical activity on a daily basis. *Caption answers should include increases energy expenditure.* **TEKS C5F**

What You Will Do

- Identify strategies to manage weight.
- Explain the role of nutrition and physical activity in weight management.
- Analyze diet, exercise, physical activity, and a combination of both as methods of weight control.
- Evaluate consumer issues related to physical fitness such as choosing services for weight management.

Terms to Know

nutrient-dense foods

Maintaining a Healthy Body Composition

Now that you have learned to measure and evaluate your weight and body composition, you need to learn how to achieve and maintain a healthy weight and body composition. In this lesson, you will learn about various strategies and approaches to weight management. You will also learn how nutritional practices and physical activity combined contribute to a healthy body composition.

Healthful Strategies to Manage Weight

As with other parts of your fitness program, achieving and maintaining a healthy weight and body composition starts with you. By gradually adjusting your eating plan and physical-activity habits, you can begin to safely control your weight and body composition. The rate at which you modify your behaviors should be based on your personal fitness goals and your changing levels of body composition.

Do you recall the behavioral-change stairway in Chapter 1? It is a step-by-step procedure for achieving personal fitness goals. This stairway can be used to improve your eating habits and help you manage your body weight. Some other guidelines that can help you include:

- **Evaluate your needs.** Ask a health care professional to help you target your appropriate weight and identify your goals.
- **Be realistic.** For long-term success, a person should lose no more than 1 to 2 pounds per week for safe, effective results. If the goal is to gain weight, it's best to gain slowly—no more than $\frac{1}{2}$ pound per week.

◀ Physical activity is a necessary component of maintaining body composition. *How does physical activity help a person maintain a healthy body composition?*

164 Chapter 5 Your Body Composition

LESSON 4 RESOURCES

Teacher Classroom Resources
- ☞ Guided Practice Activity 5-4
- ☞ Reteaching Activity 5-4
- ☞ Lesson Quiz 5-4

Multimedia
- ◎ Vocabulary PuzzleMaker

- **Design a personal plan.** Develop a plan in writing that includes healthful eating and regular physical activity.
- **Become physically active.** You should try to get 60 minutes per day of physical activity or exercise, or a minimum of 225 minutes per week. Engage in physical activities that are right for your goals. For example, aerobic exercise can help you burn calories and lose fat weight while activities like weight training can help you gain muscle mass and increase your RMR.
- **Keep track of your progress.** Monitor your body weight and body composition regularly (every three months).

Nutrition and Physical Activity

Where do you fit into the big picture? Are you happy with your current body composition? Do you want—or need—to make changes to your weight or body composition? To effectively do this, you need to understand the relationship between your eating plan and level of physical activity, and how each can be used to control weight and body composition.

Weight Control, Diet, and Exercise

To lose a pound of fat, you could reduce your calorie intake in your diet by 3,500 calories, or expend 3,500 more calories in physical activity. However, focusing on only one side of this energy equation is not healthful.

The best approach to weight loss or weight gain is a combination approach. The healthiest and most effective method is to combine a healthful eating plan with a program of regular physical activity or exercise.

Weight Loss. To lose weight, adjust your eating plan to reduce calorie intake while increasing calorie expenditure through physical activity or exercise.

When reducing calorie intake, be sure you are still getting the proper nutrients. Eat at regular intervals and get at least 1,700 to 1,800 calories per day to meet your daily needs. Use the Food Guide Pyramid and *Dietary Guidelines for Americans* to help you. Eat a variety of low-calorie nutrient-dense foods. These are *foods that are high in nutrients as compared with their calorie content.* These include vegetables, fruits, and whole-grain products. Remember to drink at least eight glasses of water daily to maintain your body's proper function.

In addition to proper nutrition, engage in physical activities or exercises that cause you to work for a longer period of time (45 to 60 minutes) at moderate-to-vigorous intensity. Those exercises are the most effective at burning fat and excess calories. This dual approach of diet and exercise enables you to build lean muscle mass and lower your percentage of body fat.

LIFELINE

Watching Your Friends' Weight

Weight management is a science. Like any branch of science, it requires professional guidance. Simply skipping meals to drop some pounds is a dangerous practice.

Without energy from food to fuel the brain, concentration becomes difficult. If you know of friends who are taking personal weight loss into their own hands, urge them to seek professional help. Help them help themselves.

2 TEACH

Discussing

Remind students that good weight control programs are based on the principles of the behavioral-change stairway they learned about in Chapter 1. Ask for a volunteer to summarize what he or she recalls about the behavioral-change stairway. *The behavioral-change stairway is a step-by-step approach for helping people achieve their fitness goals.*
L1

Photo Follow-up

Have students answer the photo caption on page 167. *Caption answers will vary but might include: Advice from parents and professionals will help to ensure that the program is safe and effective.*

LIFELINE

Watching Your Friends' Weight

Tell students that excessive caloric restriction can lower blood sugar levels (causing hypoglycemia) and can also reduce the ability to concentrate. Long-term caloric restriction has negative effects on normal growth and development and can stimulate behaviors that lead to eating disorders. Have students encourage the friend to talk with parents, guardians, or a trusted adult.

More About . . .

BEHAVIORAL-CHANGE STAIRWAY AND GOAL SETTING The CDC has developed informational booklets on goal setting to help individuals at different levels of progress on the behavioral-change stairway succeed at achieving and maintaining a healthy body composition. The CDC five-step process is as follows: Step 1, think about controlling your body composition; Step 2, realize the benefits of a healthy body composition; Step 3, prepare to control your weight; Step 4, feel good about managing your body composition; and Step 5, maintain a healthy body composition.

Student Edition TEKS

Page 164: C5D, C4H, C5F
Page 165: C5F, C5G

Discussing

Explain that most dietary pills for weight loss contain caffeine, ephedra, or other stimulants that can cause dangerous side effects. **L1** **TEKS C3D**

Consumer CORNER

Have volunteers evaluate consumer issues and identify media examples of weight loss products or procedures they may have heard about that could potentially cause health risks. **TEKS C4H**

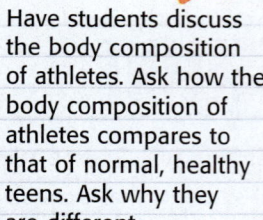

Fitness FACTS

Have students discuss the body composition of athletes. Ask how the body composition of athletes compares to that of normal, healthy teens. Ask why they are different.

✓ Reading Check

Nutrient-dense foods are high in nutrients and lower in calories. **TEKS C5D**

(from page 167)
Increased energy level and self-esteem, and decreased stress levels and risk for disease.

Consumer CORNER — Practicing Safe Weight Management

Excessive weight loss over a short period of time can be a serious health concern. People who have a serious weight problem and are considering a diet plan that promises extreme, rapid weight loss should talk to their doctor or other health professional. As with any health issue, strict weight-loss programs like these must be followed only under the direction of a physician or other health care professional. Keep in mind that many unqualified individuals claim to have a wealth of knowledge about weight-loss procedures when they do not.

Do not accept the opinion of someone who is not professionally trained and qualified in nutrition and weight control. This can create unnecessary health risks, as well as a good way to get "ripped off." The best way to control your body weight and body composition is to speak to your doctor or other health care professional for advice. They can help you devise a plan that combines both exercise and diet to help you achieve total, personal fitness.

Interview

Speak to a doctor or other health care professional to evaluate how he or she would advise teen patients who are concerned with weight management and body composition. Ask about other qualified, licensed professionals who are good resources for advice about nutrition and weight management. Share your findings with your physical education classmates and your teacher.

"I Lost 100 Pounds Easy! Eating My Favorite Foods!!! This is the Greatest Diet Ever!"

Users Have Dropped Over 2 Million Pounds! TRY IT NOW!!

Fitness FACTS

Body Composition and Athletes

- Male marathon runners may have about 3.3% body fat; female runners about 10%.
- Male swimmers have about 6.8% body fat, female swimmers about 18.6%.
- Male gymnasts have about 4.6% body fat, females about 14%.

Source: Exercise Physiology: Energy, Nutrition, and Human Performance, 2001.⁴

Weight Gain. If the goal is weight gain, a person should consume more calories and maintain his or her physical-activity level. Increase calorie intake by increasing complex carbohydrates, such as breads, pasta, and potatoes. Eat more than the minimum number of servings from each food group and choose healthy snacks.

It is healthiest for a person to gain weight slowly and steadily. This adds less body fat and more lean muscle. Also, a supervised resistance-training program will help a person gain weight by adding muscle mass without adding unwanted fat.

Weight Maintenance. If you are within an appropriate weight range and have a healthy body composition, you want to maintain it. If you maintain a healthful eating plan with the same amount of calorie intake, as well as continue to maintain a moderate level of physical activity, you will maintain your weight and body composition.

✓ Reading Check

Summarize Why are nutrient-dense foods necessary if a person is trying to lose weight?

Teacher-Coach Tips

Female Athletic Triad Many athletes, especially females, strive to have low percentages of body fat in order to improve their athletic performances. This can result in eating disorders or exercising too much. These factors can be particularly dangerous for females, who can develop an increased risk for osteoporosis, decreased estrogen levels, and irregular menstruation. This phenomenon has been labeled the "female athletic triad," involving three factors: disordered eating, menstrual dysfunction, and osteoporosis. To avoid this problem, these athletes should be monitored by a health professional.

Benefits of Achieving Your Goals

You will need to be persistent and patient in working toward your goals. Keep in mind that while you are young and growing, your body composition can change fairly quickly. As you get older, however, you may not experience much change for at least three to six months. When choosing types of activities, keep in mind that aerobic exercise can help you burn calories and lose body fat, while activities like weight training can help you gain muscle mass and increase you RMR.

Maintaining a healthy weight and body composition through proper nutrition and exercise has several benefits. It will

- increase your energy.
- increase your self-esteem.
- reduce your stress levels.
- reduce your risk for developing diseases.

The combination of diet and physical activity will help you look and feel your best.

 Reading Check

List What are the benefits of achieving your weight maintenance goals?

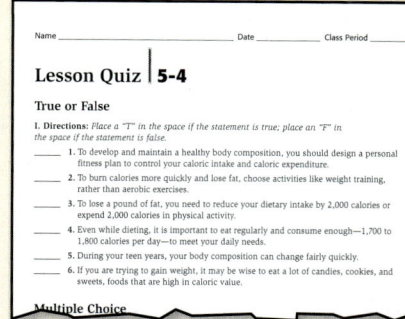
▲ Teens should always seek the advice of their parents and a health care professional when planning their weight maintenance program. *How will this help them in achieving their goals?*

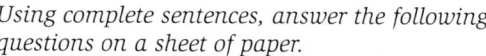
Lesson 4 Review

Using complete sentences, answer the following questions on a sheet of paper.

Reviewing Facts and Vocabulary

1. **Vocabulary** Define *nutrient-dense foods*.
2. **Recall** How many calories must you burn beyond what you consume to lose a pound of fat?
3. **Recall** What type of physical activity is effective for a person who needs to gain weight?

Thinking Critically

4. **Analyze** Explain why combining diet and exercise as a method of weight control is healthier and more effective than relying on diet or exercise alone.
5. **Evaluation** Tristan's goal is to gain 10 pounds over the next three months. He has

adjusted his eating plan accordingly, but has decided to greatly reduce his level of physical activity. Explain why it is important for Tristan to maintain his physical activity.

Personal Fitness Planning

Designing a Program Write a personal fitness plan to improve or maintain your body composition (depending upon your personal needs). Set a realistic goal for you to accomplish in the next month. Consider how your diet and exercise combined will help you achieve that goal. Include your eating plan and your physical-activity program. Explain how each will help you improve or maintain your body composition.

---

3 ASSESS

EVALUATING THE LESSON

Assign and discuss the Lesson 4 Review.

Name _____ Date _____ Class Period _____

Lesson Quiz | 5-4

True or False

I. **Directions:** *Place a "T" in the space if the statement is true; place an "F" in the space if the statement is false.*

_____ 1. To develop and maintain a healthy body composition, you should design a personal fitness plan to control your caloric intake and caloric expenditure.
_____ 2. To burn calories more quickly and lose fat, choose activities like weight training, rather than aerobic exercises.
_____ 3. To lose a pound of fat, you need to reduce your dietary intake by 2,000 calories or expend 2,000 calories in physical activity.
_____ 4. Even while dieting, it is important to eat regularly and consume enough—1,700 to 1,800 calories per day—to meet your daily needs.
_____ 5. During your teen years, your body composition can change fairly quickly.
_____ 6. If you are trying to gain weight, it may be wise to eat a lot of candies, cookies, and sweets, foods that are high in caloric value.

Multiple Choice

RETEACHING

Ask each student to name one healthful strategy for managing weight.

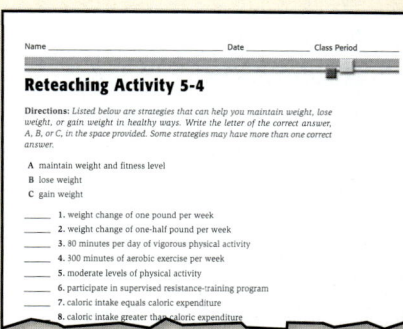
Name _____ Date _____ Class Period _____

Reteaching Activity 5-4

Directions: Listed below are strategies that can help you maintain weight, lose weight, or gain weight in healthy ways. Write the letter of the correct answer, A, B, or C, in the space provided. Some strategies may have more than one correct answer.

A maintain weight and fitness level
B lose weight
C gain weight

_____ 1. weight change of one pound per week
_____ 2. weight change of one-half pound per week
_____ 3. 80 minutes per day of vigorous physical activity
_____ 4. 300 minutes of aerobic exercise per week
_____ 5. moderate levels of physical activity
_____ 6. participate in supervised resistance-training program
_____ 7. caloric intake equals caloric expenditure
_____ 8. caloric intake greater than caloric expenditure

ENRICHMENT

Assign students to summarize newspaper or magazine articles on issues related to controlling body composition.

4 CLOSE

Have students write a one-page strategic plan outlining their personal weight management goals.

Lesson 4 Review

Answers to Lesson 4 Review

1. Nutrient-dense foods are those that are high in nutrients, rather than calories.
2. 3,500 calories.
3. Resistance training will help a person gain weight.
4. By dieting only, you will lose fat weight

as well as lean mass. By exercising only, you can lose fat weight but you must burn 3,500 calories per pound of fat loss.
5. Tristan should add weight training to his program because he will add lean muscle while improving body composition and improving cardiorespiratory functions.

CHECKING COMPREHENSION

- Assign and discuss the chapter review.
- Use the PuzzleMaker software to review vocabulary. ☉

CHAPTER 5 REVIEW ANSWERS

True/False

1. True	6. True
2. False	7. False
3. True	8. False
4. False	9. True
5. False	10. True

Multiple Choice

11. b	16. b
12. c	17. a
13. d	18. d
14. b	19. a
15. c	20. a

Discussion

21. Answers will vary but might include heredity, gender, age, RMR, caloric intake, and caloric expenditure.
22. Answers will vary but might include body circumferences, skinfolds, bioelectrical impedance, underwater weighing, and MRIs.
23. Answers will vary but should include: Use the energy balance equation to guide you with your goals.

Vocabulary

24. b
25. e
26. d
27. a
28. c
29. f

TRUE/FALSE

On a sheet of paper, write the numbers 1–10. Write True or False for each statement.

1. Your body type is determined by your genetic makeup.
2. Lean body weight equals body-fat weight divided by total body weight.
3. The graph showing the relationship between body weight and the risk for developing chronic diseases is J shaped.
4. There are no risks associated with excessive leanness.
5. The size of your fat cells will not increase after your teen years.
6. The energy balance includes energy input and energy expenditure.
7. RMR increases as you age and is higher for females than males.
8. Adopting a diet of less than 1,000 calories is a good way to lose weight.
9. One pound of fat is equivalent to 3,500 calories.
10. Teens should try to accumulate at least 225 minutes of physical activity and exercise per week.

MULTIPLE CHOICE

On a separate sheet of paper, write the letter of the word or phrase that best completes each statement.

11. What is the minimum recommended amount of essential fat for teen males?
    a. 1 percent
    b. 7 percent
    c. 12 percent
    d. 18 percent
12. What is the minimum recommended amount of essential fat for teen females?
    a. 1 percent
    b. 7 percent
    c. 12 percent
    d. 18 percent

13. Your body composition is influenced by which of the following?
    a. Genetics
    b. Age
    c. Gender
    d. All of the above
14. Your RMR is not influenced by which of the following?
    a. Age
    b. Height
    c. Gender
    d. Physical-activity level
15. If you want to lose weight, your eating plan should include
    a. mainly carbohydrates.
    b. mainly protein.
    c. nutrient-dense foods.
    d. vitamin-rich foods.
16. What percentage of your body fat is between your muscles and skin?
    a. 25 percent
    b. 50 percent
    c. 75 percent
    d. 100 percent
17. The body composition evaluation method of underwater weighing is based on what concept?
    a. Fat floats
    b. Fat sinks
    c. Fat neither sinks nor floats
    d. None of the above
18. What type of physical activity is especially important for you to include in your personal-fitness program if you are trying to lose body fat, but gain weight?
    a. Flexibility
    b. Plyometric
    c. Aerobic
    d. Weight-training
19. If you want to gain weight, how much in pounds per week would be healthful?
    a. $\frac{1}{2}$
    b. 1
    c. 2
    d. 5
20. If you want to lose weight, how many pounds per week maximum would be healthful?
    a. 1 to 2
    b. 3 to 5
    c. 5 to 7
    d. 10

Critical Thinking

30. Answers may vary but should include: Body weight by itself does not take into consideration lean body mass, which is what helps a person carry less body fat than someone with a lower lean body mass.
31. Answers may vary but might include: speed up—regular exercise and eating more small meals per day; slow down—restricting calories to 500 per day.

DISCUSSION

Using complete sentences, answer the following questions on a sheet of paper.

21. **Identify** List and describe five factors that influence your body composition.
22. **Identify** List and describe three methods to evaluate your body composition.
23. **Explain** Tell how you can safely reduce your body weight, increase your body weight, or maintain your body weight.

VOCABULARY

On a sheet of paper, write the letter of the term in Column B that best fits the definition in Column A.

Column A	Column B
24. The process by which the body converts calories from food to energy.	a. calorie intake
25. The combined weight of bone, muscle, and connective tissue.	b. metabolism c. calorie expenditure
26. The minimum amount of body fat necessary for good health.	d. essential fat e. lean body weight
27. The total number of calories you take in from food.	f. resting metabolic rate
28. The total number of calories you burn or expend.	
29. The amount of calories you need and expend for body processes while at rest.	

CRITICAL THINKING

Using complete sentences, answer the following questions on a sheet of paper.

30. **Analyze** Why is body weight alone not an accurate indicator of total body composition? Explain your answer.
31. **Identify** What behaviors will slow down or speed up your resting metabolic rate?

32. **Evaluate** Analyze each of the following as methods of weight control: diet, exercise, and a combination of diet and exercise.

CASE STUDY

JACKIE'S ACTIVITY LEVEL

Jackie is a sixteen-year-old inactive female who has 32 percent body fat and would like to lose 20 pounds. However, she is unsure about how to lose the weight healthfully, reduce her body fat to 25 percent, and begin a regular physical activity or exercise program. Therefore, Jackie needs the help of someone knowledgeable about designing and implementing fitness programs—someone like you!

HERE IS YOUR ASSIGNMENT:

Assume you are Jackie's friend. She asks you for some assistance with her plans for improving her body composition. Make a list of things Jackie should consider and do before beginning a program to improve her body composition. Then list the recommendations that you would give to Jackie for the first two weeks of her program. Use the following keys to help you:

KEYS TO HELP YOU

- Consider Jackie's current body composition and percentage of body fat.
- Think about how her current body composition could be evaluated.
- Analyze her needs and goals. (For example, how should she go about improving her body composition?)
- Consider the importance of energy balance as you advise Jackie about her eating habits (calorie intake) and her level of physical activity (energy expenditure).

32. Answers will vary but might include: Reducing caloric intake can help you lose weight. However, you will lose not only fat weight, but also lean weight. Increasing energy expenditure by exercising more often will help you lose weight, but this by itself is not very effective. By combining safe changes in caloric intake and expenditure, individuals can expect the most effective results. **TEKS C5F**

EVALUATE

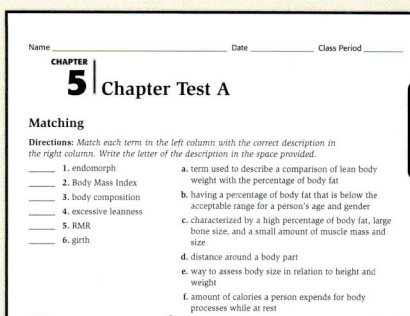

ENRICHMENT

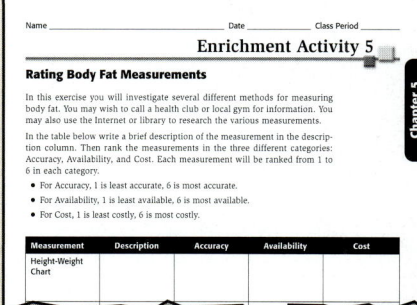

CASE STUDY

ANSWERS

Answers will vary but might include: Advise Jackie to talk with her parents and a health professional to help her with her goals. Have her study the energy balance equation and develop a weight management plan that includes safe changes in energy intake and energy expenditure to reach her goal in improving her body composition.

Student Edition TEKS

Page 169: C5F

CHAPTER

6 Maintaining a Healthy Body Weight

CHAPTER RESOURCES

- Chapter Study Guide 6
- Vocabulary Worksheet 6
- Enrichment Activity 6
- Chapter 6 Test A
- Chapter 6 Test B
- Parent Letter and Activities 6 (English/Spanish)

FITNESS Online

Ask students to take the STEP Personal Inventory for Chapter 6. Have them record their responses to the statements in their notebooks. Remind students that responses are private and for their use only.

FITNESS Online

Do you consider your eating habits healthful? Do you know whether your weight is within a healthful range? Your answers reveal much about your current levels of fitness. Find out more by taking the STEP Personal Inventory for Chapter 6. Find it at **fitness.glencoe.com**.

170

INCLUSION STRATEGIES

LANGUAGE DIVERSITY *Use the following suggestions to help students who have difficulty with English:*

- Pair English-language learners with native speakers of English who can restate key points in language that helps students comprehend important concepts.

- Direct Spanish-speaking students to the written summaries of this chapter in the *Foundations of Personal Fitness* Spanish Resources Booklet.

- Encourage Spanish-speaking students to use the Glosario provided in the back of the student text. ELL

Body Weight and Health Risks

In previous chapters, you read about the importance of being physically active and eating right. Both, as you have seen, can positively affect body composition. In this chapter, you will learn how to maintain a healthful body weight throughout your life. You will also learn how doing so relates to your functional health and fitness.

Overweight and Youth

In the last several decades, the number of teens in this country who are overweight has nearly tripled, as shown in **Figure 6.1**. This trend has become a major concern among health professionals.

As you learned in Chapter 5, overweight is a condition in which a person is heavier than the standard weight range for his or her height. This means a person with a **Body Mass Index (BMI)** that is above the 85th percentile for his or her age group is considered *at risk for overweight*. A person with a BMI above the 95th percentile for his or her age group is considered *overweight*. Remember that BMI changes with age.

Developing a healthy eating plan as a teen will reduce your risk of becoming overweight as you age. *How might learning to cook help you maintain a healthy eating plan?*

What You Will Do

- Identify health risks related to overweight and underweight.
- Identify impaired glucose tolerance and its role in diabetes.
- Evaluate the effect of overweight on physical activity.

Terms to Know

excessive weight disabilities
sleep apnea
impaired glucose tolerance (IGT)
insulin
underweight

 **hotlink**

Body Mass Index
For more on body mass index (BMI) and how to evaluate it, see Chapter 5, page **149**.

Lesson 1   **Body Weight and Health Risks**   **171**

LESSON 1 RESOURCES

Teacher Classroom Resources
- Guided Practice Activity 6-1
- Fitness Check Worksheet 6-1
- Reteaching Activity 6-1
- Lesson Quiz 6-1

Reproducible Charts and Graphs
- Reproducible Master 6-1

Multimedia
- Vocabulary PuzzleMaker

---

1 MOTIVATE

GETTING STARTED

- Ask students whether they think more teens are overweight today than five years ago. Then ask them why they think this is a national trend. (Remind students that this is a sensitive topic. Discussion should be thoughtful and considerate of others.)
- Distribute copies of *Guided Practice Activity 6-1* for students to use while studying this lesson. ☞

IN THIS LESSON

- **Fitness Check**
  Exercise and Overweight, p. 174

INTRODUCING VOCABULARY

- Explain to students that the term *insulin* refers to a hormone that helps muscle cells metabolize glucose. Getting regular physical activity helps muscles to use glucose more effectively.
- Have students use *Vocabulary Worksheet 6* or the PuzzleMaker software to practice vocabulary terms. **ELL** ☞ ◎

Photo Follow-Up

Have students brainstorm about where they might learn to cook healthful meals. *Caption answer: Students may have more success if they cooked their own food.*

2 TEACH

FITNESS Online

Help students recognize the seriousness of problems related to obesity by investigating Web Links at Glencoe's Fitness Web site. Encourage students to find ways to make positive changes regarding obesity issues in your school or community.

Fitness FACTS

Ask students to discuss each of the three facts about overweight teens. Ask them to discuss why there has been such a large increase in the number of youths who are considered overweight. Have the class make recommendations for ways to reverse this trend.

USING VISUALS

Figure 6.1 Begin by displaying *Reproducible Master 6-1*. *Caption answer: In 1970 the number of overweight teens was 4.6 percent, and today it is 14 percent, so there has been a 9.4-percent total increase.* Ask students to create a graph to predict the trend in the chart for the next 10 years. Have them justify their answers. ☞

FITNESS Online

Learn more about the problems of obesity and what can be done at **fitness.glencoe.com**.

Activity Investigate the research, prevention, and treatment efforts being made, and find out how you and your classmates can participate in advocacy efforts.

Fitness FACTS

Overweight Teens
- About 14 percent of teens today are overweight.
- Overweight adolescents have a 70% chance of becoming overweight or obese adults.
- In the last 20 years, the number of overweight children and adolescents has nearly tripled.

Source: The Surgeon General's Call to Action to Prevent and Decrease Overweight and Obesity.[2]

FIGURE 6.1

PERCENTAGE OF AMERICAN YOUTH WHO WERE OVERWEIGHT, BY AGE

The number of overweight teens has greatly increased over the past 40 years. *What percentage of teens (ages 12–17) were overweight in 1970? By how much has that percentage risen in recent years?*

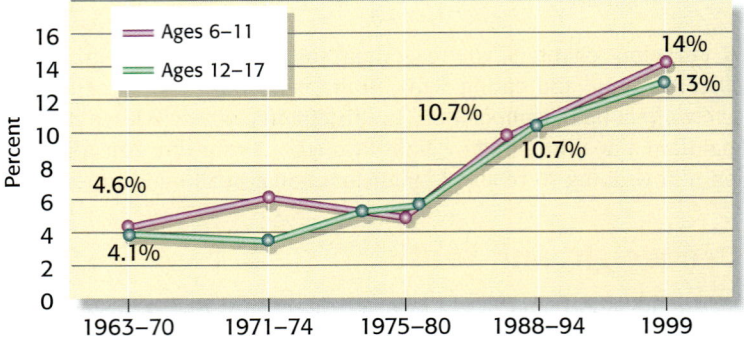

Source: Centers for Disease Control and Prevention, 2003[1]

The Effect of Overweight on Health

Being overweight can affect a person's self-esteem and quality of life. This is especially true during the teen years. Adolescence is a time when the individual undergoes dramatic physical and social growth. Overweight can interfere with these natural and necessary growth processes.

Teens who are seriously overweight often have trouble taking part in physical games and activities. This can make these teens feel cut off from their peers. Simple everyday tasks such as walking up a flight of stairs become a physical challenge. Being overweight or at risk for overweight in adolescence can also prevent a person from developing positive eating and physical-activity patterns for his or her future functional health and fitness.

However, as you learned in Chapter 5, you can achieve and maintain a healthy weight and body composition. A healthy body allows you to stay physically active and enjoy the benefits personal fitness offers your physical, social, and emotional health.

Physical Health Risks

Being excessively overweight is linked with a number of chronic physical diseases and conditions. Overweight increases the risk of high blood pressure and high blood cholesterol. It also increases the risks of heart disease and some cancers.

172   Chapter 6   Maintaining a Healthy Body Weight

More About . . .

THE COST OF OVERWEIGHT AND OBESITY IN AMERICA Health care costs for overweight and obese adults have been estimated to be $93 billion per year. This is a staggering amount of money when one considers that it represents up to 9 percent annually of all medical spending. The cost of treating overweight adults now rivals costs associated with smokers. This has prompted many government agencies such as the CDC to encourage all Americans to learn to control their body weight by becoming more physically active and eating healthier.

Some conditions are grouped together under the heading **excessive weight disabilities.** This term refers to *health problems and diseases linked to or resulting directly from long-term overweight or obesity.* These disabilities include:

- **Breathing difficulties.** Accumulations of internal body fat may press against the **diaphragm.** This is the primary muscle involved in breathing. Even light physical activity may cause shortness of breath. Overweight people with asthma are at higher risk for more frequent and more severe attacks of this disease. They also may suffer from **sleep apnea,** *a condition in which a person stops breathing during sleep, due to obstructed or reduced air passages.* Individuals with sleep apnea often snore, wake up, and interrupt their normal restful sleeping patterns. Untreated, sleep apnea can cause high blood pressure and other cardiovascular diseases, memory problems, weight gain, and headaches.
- **Bone and joint problems.** Extra weight can put stress on the bones and joints. This, in turn, diminishes range of motion. It can also cause muscle aches.

Impaired Glucose Tolerance and Diabetes

Another especially serious condition related to overweight is **impaired glucose tolerance (IGT).** This is *a disorder in which blood glucose levels become elevated.* As noted in Chapter 4, carbohydrates from food are converted by the body into glucose, a simple sugar. This sugar is converted, in turn, into energy. The chemical in the body that is responsible for this process is **insulin,** *a hormone produced by the pancreas.* Often in people with IGT, the pancreas produces too little insulin to convert the glucose, which is then stored in the blood.

IGT is a major risk factor for type 2 diabetes. People with this disease develop infections more easily than healthy individuals. Other symptoms include blurred vision, nausea, muscle weakness, and fatigue.

At one time, IGT and type 2 diabetes were exclusively adult illnesses. With the rise of overweight in children and teens, however, childhood cases of these conditions are becoming more common. Teens with type 2 diabetes must remain under strict medical supervision and follow a restricted eating plan. Daily finger-stick tests to check blood glucose levels may become necessary. So may periodic injections of insulin. In short, diabetes can affect a teen's quality of life during adolescence.

Reading Check

Explain What are excessive weight disabilities?

hotlink

diaphragm
For more on the diaphragm and its functions, see Chapter 7, page **194.**

▼ Some people with type 2 diabetes must have regular insulin injections to help their bodies turn glucose into energy. *What are the symptoms of type 2 diabetes?*

hotlink

Remind students that the diaphragm is important to the process of inhalation and exhalation. Have students review Chapter 7 for more about this topic.

Photo Follow-up

Ask students whether they know of anyone who has type 2 diabetes. Discuss the challenges diabetics face every day. Then have students answer the photo caption. *Caption answer: blurred vision, nausea, muscle weakness, and fatigue.*

Reading Check

Disabilities associated with excessive weight include breathing difficulties, bone and joint stress, and other health problems linked to overweight or obesity.
TEKS C4A

Discussing

Ask students to consider how the wide availability of fast food and high-calorie snacks might be a factor in the increase of type 2 diabetes in children. **L2**

INCLUSION STRATEGIES

MANAGING DIABETES If you have a student with diabetes, take note of the time of the class in relation to when the student has lunch. The class should be within two hours of eating. Avoid psychological stress caused by competitive activities. Stress may influence the student's metabolic rate, which in turn changes blood sugar levels. Encourage the student to exercise with a partner who knows signs of hyperglycemia (when daily exercise volume is suddenly reduced without increasing insulin levels) or hypoglycemia (occurs when delaying meals, exercising, or too much insulin lowers blood sugar).

Student Edition TEKS

Page 172: C5D, C5G
Page 173: C5D, C5G

Exercise and Overweight

OBJECTIVES

- Recognize the effects of being overweight on exercise responses.
- Evaluate changes in bio-mechanics with or without excess weight.

TEACHING STRATEGIES

1. This activity requires a warm-up.
2. Have students work in pairs for this activity.
3. Demonstrate each of the activities to be performed.
4. Observe students to make sure they perform the activities safely. Be sure they avoid working on slick surfaces, and have them demonstrate safety procedures by wearing nonskid footwear. Students with back or joint problems should be cautioned not to perform this activity. **TEKS C3A**
5. Make copies of *Fitness Check Worksheet 6-1* in the TCR. Have students record their results to evaluate performance. 📁

✓ Reading Check

Teens who are underweight may be at greater risk for infections from cold viruses or other pathogens.

Fitness Check

Exercise and Overweight

In this activity you will revisit two exercises from earlier Fitness Checks. This will permit you to experience what it would be like to exercise if you weighed more.

1. Insert schoolbooks into an empty backpack. Place the weighted pack on a scale. Aim for a total weight of 10 pounds, adding and subtracting books of different sizes as necessary.

Figure 6.2

2. Review the procedure for jumping jacks in **Figure 6.2**. Perform the exercise. Meanwhile, a partner should videotape your performance.
3. Next strap on the weighted backpack. Repeat the jumping jacks exercise, again while your partner videotapes your performance. (Note: If the weight feels too heavy, try subtracting five pounds. It is important that you avoid injuring yourself.)
4. Review the procedure for the Blind One-Leg Stand in **Figure 6.3**. Perform this exercise twice—once with and once without—the weighted backpack. Again your partner should videotape your performance.
5. Switch roles with your partner. Tape your partner performing the two exercises with and without the weighted backpack.
6. When each of you has completed all exercises described, review the videotapes. Determine whether your movement biomechanics changed while doing the tests with and without excess weight.

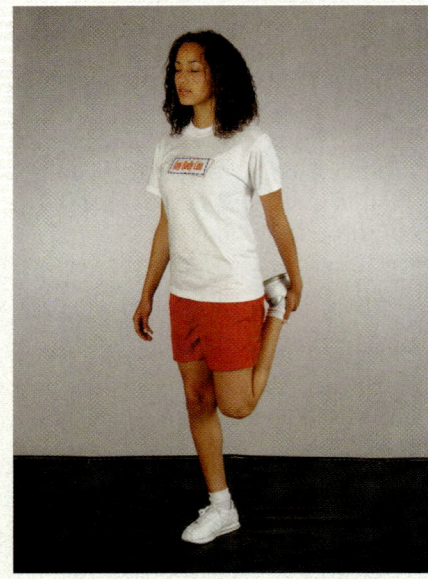

Figure 6.3

Curriculum CONNECTIONS

FAMILY AND CONSUMER SCIENCES Team up with a food and nutrition class to discuss nutrient-dense vs. empty-calorie foods.

LANGUAGE ARTS Encourage students to write letters to their favorite athletes, asking about their training diets and pre-competition meals. Students may need to write outlines to help organize their ideas. Instruct students to develop drafts and proofread for errors before completing their final drafts. **ELL**

Underweight

In the face of the overweight epidemic, it is easy to lose sight of the reverse problem—being excessively lean, or underweight. **Underweight** may be defined as *having a Body Mass Index (BMI) that is below the 5th percentile for one's age.* Teens who are underweight usually have insufficient body fat. Since this fat stores protective nutrients, these teens are at greater risk of infection from cold viruses and other pathogens.

In addition, underweight teens may be undernourished. This means they fail to take in enough essential nutrients on a regular basis to ensure normal growth and body function. They also are not providing their bodies with a proper energy reserve, causing fatigue and irritability. Underweight teens also are at greater risk of anemia, a disease linked to a lack of iron. Undernourished female teens may experience irregular menstrual cycles. The risk of developing osteoporosis later in life also increases.

Underweight teens should eat three to four meals a day, consisting of nutrient-dense, high-calorie foods. They should also begin a resistance-training program to increase lean body weight.

 **Reading Check**

Identify What are the health risks of being underweight?

Lesson 1 Review

Using complete sentences, answer the following questions on a sheet of paper.

Reviewing Facts and Vocabulary

1. **Recall** List and describe two health problems related to overweight.
2. **Vocabulary** What is *sleep apnea?*
3. **Vocabulary** Define *underweight.*

Thinking Critically

4. **Compare and Contrast** What is the relationship between impaired glucose tolerance and type 2 diabetes?
5. **Synthesize** Mackenzie is 16 years old and is underweight. What are some of the health problems Mackenzie might experience due to her low BMI?

Personal Fitness Planning

Assessing Lifestyle Assess your current level of fitness in the area of nutrition and body weight. How does your eating plan and level of physical activity impact your ability to perform daily tasks? Do you generally feel healthy and energetic, or are there changes you would like to make? If so, make a list of changes you might make to your current behaviors, including your eating plan and daily physical activity, in order to improve your overall feeling of physical health.

Lesson 1 Body Weight and Health Risks **175**

Lesson 1 Review

Answers to Lesson 1 Review

1. High blood pressure, high cholesterol, heart disease, and certain cancers.
2. A condition in which a person stops breathing during sleep, due to obstructed or reduced air passages.
3. Underweight is having a BMI less than the 5th percentile for your age and gender.
4. Impaired glucose tolerance (IGT) is a major risk factor for type 2 diabetes.
5. She is at greater risk for infection, and may be undernourished.

---

3 ASSESS

EVALUATING THE LESSON

Assign and discuss the Lesson 1 Review.

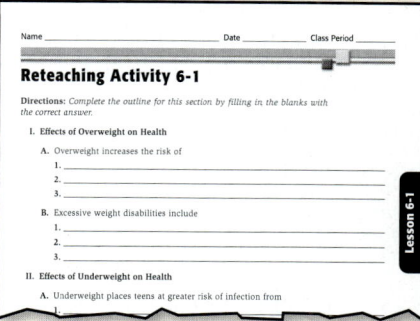

RETEACHING

Ask students to name and describe diseases associated with obesity.

ENRICHMENT

Have students interview doctors, nurses, or patients about the challenges faced by diabetics trying to manage their disease.

4 CLOSE

Ask volunteers to describe specific ways that maintaining a healthy weight can benefit physical, mental/emotional, and social health.
TEKS C4A

Body Image and Weight Control

1 MOTIVATE

GETTING STARTED

- Ask volunteers to brain-storm possible reasons why some people develop eating disorders.
- Distribute copies of *Guided Practice Activity 6-2* for students to use while studying this lesson. 📁

IN THIS LESSON

- **Lifeline** *Helping an Anorexic Friend, p. 177*

INTRODUCING VOCABULARY

- Emphasize to students that the term *body image* is related to mental/emotional health as well as the physical aspects of health.
- Have students use *Vocabulary Worksheet 6* or the PuzzleMaker software to practice vocabulary terms for this lesson. **ELL** 📁 💿

Photo Follow-up

Encourage students to investigate positive and negative attitudes toward exercise and physical activities. Ask students why they think some people do not have a positive body image. Then ask them how a person can begin to change their perception to a more positive self image. *Caption answer: A distorted body image can lead to health problems.* **TEKS C5A**

What You Will Do

- Identify the symptoms and risks of eating disorders.
- Explain how to help a friend who may have an eating disorder.
- Explain how overtraining contributes to eating disorders.

Terms to Know

body image
eating disorders
anorexia nervosa
bulimia nervosa
exercise bulimia
binge eating disorder
bigorexia

Lesson 2

Body Image and Weight Control

Have you ever glimpsed your reflection in a funhouse mirror? These mirrors are curved in a way that purposely distorts your image. *The way you see your body* is called your **body image.** Some people do not need a special mirror to have a distorted body image. They already see themselves as too fat or too thin. A distorted body image can lead to serious health risks.

Eating Disorders

Sometimes, a person's concerns about weight can become an obsession. Some teens develop **eating disorders.** These are *psychological illnesses that cause people to undereat, overeat, or practice other dangerous nutrition-related behaviors.* Although the exact causes of eating disorders are unknown, they are typically driven by mental or emotional factors, such as poor body image, social and family pressures, and perfectionism. Teens with a family history of weight problems, depression, or substance abuse may be at higher risk for developing an eating disorder.

People with these disorders wrongly view themselves as too heavy, too thin, or not bulked-up enough. To "correct" their perceived limitations, they will eat in an unhealthful manner that also disrupts their energy balance. This is particularly dangerous for a person whose body is still growing and developing.

▶ Body image is the way you see your body. *Why is it important to have a positive body image?*

LESSON 2 RESOURCES

Teacher Classroom Resources
📁 Guided Practice Activity 6-2
📁 Reteaching Activity 6-2
📁 Lesson Quiz 6-2

Multimedia
💿 Vocabulary PuzzleMaker

Anorexia Nervosa

Anorexia (an-uh-REK-see-uh) **nervosa** is *an eating disorder in which a person abnormally restricts his or her calorie intake.* More females than males suffer from anorexia, though the number of male cases is on the rise. People with this disorder have a fear of becoming fat or gaining weight. This belief persists even after the person becomes dangerously underweight.

People with anorexia can develop serious malnutrition. The loss of body fat can cause female anorectics to stop menstruating and can lead to sterility. Anorexia also causes reduced bone density, low body temperature, low blood pressure, slowed metabolism, and reduction in organ size. Anorexia can also lead to serious heart problems. In extreme cases, the disease can result in death.

Some common indicators of a person with anorexia include:

- Sudden, massive weight loss
- Lying about having eaten
- Denying feeling hungry
- Consuming minimal amounts of food in front of others
- Preoccupation with food, calories, and weight
- Signs of **exercise addiction**
- Withdrawing from social activities
- Belief that he or she is overweight

 Reading Check

Identify List three serious health risks of anorexia.

Bulimia Nervosa

Bulimia (boo-LEEM-ee-uh) **nervosa** is *an eating disorder in which people overeat and then force themselves to purge the food afterward.* This cycle is also called "bingeing and purging." The most common method for purging is self-induced vomiting. Laxatives may also be used. Excessive physical activity is another method used to purge food. **Exercise bulimia** is *an eating disorder in which people purge calories by exercising excessively.* These people will miss out on important events and appointments in order to work out, will work out even if they are sick or injured, and do not allow any days for recovery.

Like anorexia, bulimia has little to do with weight, calories, or being "thin." It is symptomatic, rather, of underlying turmoil or emotional problems. Unlike anorectics, bulimics often have normal body composition. This makes it harder to identify someone suffering with bulimia.

Bulimia can cause serious, negative long-term health effects. Health risks of bulimia include dehydration, osteoporosis, kidney damage, and irregular heartbeat. Frequent vomiting damages tissues of the stomach, esophagus, and mouth. It also erodes tooth enamel and leads to tooth decay. The use of laxatives interferes with proper digestion, causing nutrient deficiencies.

exercise addiction
For more on exercise addiction and the dangers of overtraining, see Chapter 3, page **99**.

Helping an Anorexic Friend
People with anorexia may not know—or believe—that they need help. They will often refuse efforts to help them and deny they have a problem. You can still help a friend you suspect of being anorexic. If you know someone with several of the symptoms noted, talk to a trusted adult. Let him or her know your friend may be sick.

---

2 TEACH

Explaining

Explain that while it may be easy for anyone to recognize the symptoms of various eating disorders, successful treatment of these disorders almost always requires professional medical intervention. It is important to encourage a person with symptoms to talk with parents, guardians, a trusted adult and to consult his or her physician. **L1**

hotlink

Emphasize that developing an exercise addiction can lead to potential health problems. Have students review Chapter 3 for more about this topic.

LIFELINE

Helping an Anorexic Friend
Have students read the margin feature. Then have them draft an outline listing the specific points they could use to tell a trusted adult that a friend has an eating disorder or distorted body image.

Reading Check
Serious health effects include (any three) malnutrition, menstrual problems, sterility, reduced bone density, low body temperature, low blood pressure, slowed metabolism, reduction in organ size, or heart problems. **TEKS C4A**

Enrichment

Inform Others about Eating Disorders Eating disorders are a serious problem in the United States, especially among teen girls. Discuss with students why this is the case. Ask students how society and culture have influenced people in such a way as to pressure them into developing eating disorders. Have students write a letter to the school or local newspaper that highlights the dangers of disordered eating. Ask them to include the following points: the seriousness of eating disorders, the life-threatening nature of eating disorders, and how to help those trapped by these disorders.

Reading Check
Health risks of bulimia include dehydration, osteoporosis, kidney damage, and irregular heartbeat.

Discussing
Ask students whether they would assume that an individual suffering from bigorexia might have an exercise addiction. **L2**

hotlink
Reinforce the negative side effects of performance-enhancing supplements. Have students review Chapter 4.

Reading Check
People with binge eating disorder eat more rapidly than normal, and people with bigorexia believe they are underweight.

Photo Follow-up
Have students read the photo caption on page 179 and discuss how competitive athletes should deal with the issue of overtraining. *Caption answer: Overtraining is exercising to the point at which negative effects occur. An eating disorder is often the result of overtraining because a person becomes obsessed with training and may not match caloric intake needs with energy expenditure.* **TEKS C5C**

Student Edition TEKS
Page 172: C5D, C5G
Page 173: C5D, C5G

Many of the signs and symptoms of bulimia are the same as those for anorexia. Additional signs include:

- Malnutrition
- Excessive concerns about weight
- Eating large amounts of food without weight gain
- Use of laxatives and diuretics
- Visiting the bathroom immediately after meals. This is often a sign that the person is planning to induce vomiting.
- Practicing strict weight-loss programs followed by eating binges
- Excessive exercise

Reading Check
Identify What are the long-term health risks of bulimia?

Binge Eating Disorder
Binge eating disorder is *an eating disorder where individuals eat more rapidly than normal until they cannot eat any more.* Binge eaters do not engage in purging, like bulimics. Yet, they have a poor body image. Binge eaters often have feelings of guilt, depression, lack of control, and frustration. Binge eaters may not necessarily become obese, but their habits can be addictive.

Bigorexia
Although it is not an eating disorder in the strict sense, **bigorexia** (by-guh-REK-see-uh) is a serious health condition nevertheless. Also known as "reverse anorexia," bigorexia is *a disorder in which an individual falsely believes he or she is underweight or undersized.* Bigorexia is more common in male rather than female teens. This disorder is closely associated with exercise addiction. Symptoms and signs of bigorexia include:

hotlink
supplements
For more on the dangers of performance-enhancing supplements, see Chapter 4, page **143**.

- Lifting excessive amounts of weight, even when not in sports training
- Using performance-enhancing **supplements**
- Checking their appearance in the mirror frequently
- Feeling ashamed to show their bodies in public, even when fully clothed

Reading Check
Compare Discuss the difference between binge eating disorder and bigorexia.

Overtraining and Eating Disorders
Teens who engage in competitive athletics or in high levels of recreational competition may find that they can perform best when they are very lean. In certain cases, an athlete's desire to stay thin may result

What Teens *Want* to Know
What makes some people have a negative self image? Individuals with eating disorders or body image disorders often suffer from negative perfectionism. They are never satisfied with how they look or how they perform. Instead of focusing on the positive aspects of their eating habits or physical condition, they criticize themselves, which often upsets them further. Negative perfectionists often tell themselves that they are just "never good enough." It is important to seek professional help if one develops extreme negative perfection habits that include eating disorders.

in overtraining, which has serious health risks, including insomnia, weight loss, weakened immune system, and infertility (in women).

If an athlete's desire to perform well becomes an obsession and is combined with certain other factors, such as poor body image, social and family pressures, or depression, he or she may not only be overtraining but may also have an eating disorder. A person with an eating disorder may overtrain, causing weight problems and health risks.

Help for Eating Disorders

People with eating disorders need professional help. If you believe a friend has an eating disorder, discuss the problem with a trusted adult, such as a parent, a counselor, or a teacher. Also speak to your friend and encourage him or her to seek professional help.

✓ Reading Check

Identify What are the health risks of overtraining?

⚠ Some competitive athletes may overtrain in an effort to perform well. *How is overtraining different from an eating disorder?*

Lesson 2 Review

Using complete sentences, answer the following questions on a sheet of paper.

Reviewing Facts and Vocabulary

1. **Vocabulary** Define *anorexia nervosa*.
2. **Recall** List three signs of *bulimia*.
3. **Recall** What are the symptoms of *bigorexia*?

Thinking Critically

4. **Evaluate** Explain the relationship between eating disorders and overtraining. How can overtraining contribute to eating disorders?
5. **Synthesize** Harrison is 16 years old and he hopes to have a massive body like those of the wrestlers he sees on television. He is 5 feet, 8 inches tall and weighs 145 pounds. He has begun drinking protein shakes and lifting weights every day. What disorder does he place himself at risk for if he tries to accomplish his goals? What advice would you give him?

Personal Fitness Planning

Analyzing Influences Although eating disorders are caused by a complex set of psychological and emotional factors, many believe that media images of thin and super-fit models and celebrities place added pressure on teens to be thin. Evaluate the degree to which images on television and in magazines impact your body image. Write a paragraph describing how you and other teens can avoid this pressure and have a positive body image.

Lesson 2   Body Image and Weight Control   **179**

Lesson 2 Review

Answers to Lesson 2 Review

1. An eating disorder in which a person abnormally restricts caloric intake.
2. Malnutrition, reduced bone density, low blood pressure, low body temperature.
3. Symptoms include using performance-enhancing supplements, checking appearance constantly.
4. Individuals often overtrain, which can lead to stress, depression, and eating disorders.
5. Harrison should share his personal fitness goals with his teacher and family.

3 ASSESS

EVALUATING THE LESSON

Assign and discuss the Lesson 2 Review.

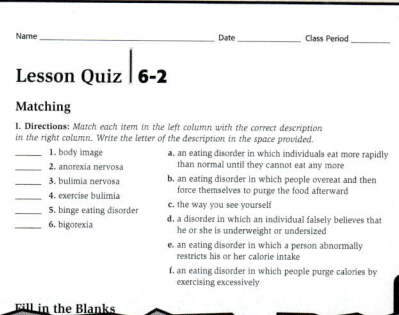

RETEACHING

Have students identify the health risks associated with overtraining.

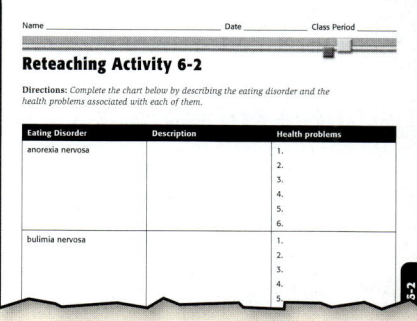

ENRICHMENT

Have students work in small groups to come up with slogans for a public service announcement to promote healthy body image.

4 CLOSE

Have students identify a sports celebrity, famous model, or musician who has suffered from an eating disorder. Have students discuss their findings.

GETTING STARTED

- Ask students to identify and discuss with the class any myths about nutrition, physical activity, or exercise that they can recall.

- Distribute copies of *Guided Practice Activity 6-3* for students to use while studying this lesson. 📁

IN THIS LESSON

- **Active Mind—Active Body,** *Analyzing Fad Diets,* p. 183

- **Consumer Corner** *Dietary Supplements,* p. 184

INTRODUCING VOCABULARY

- Ask students to describe the meaning of the term *fad* in *fad diet. Answer: A* fad *is a practice followed for a period of time with exaggerated enthusiasm.*

- Have students use *Vocabulary Worksheet 6* or the PuzzleMaker software to practice vocabulary terms for this lesson. ELL 📁 💿

Photo Follow-up

Discuss with students their answers to the photo caption question. Ask students why they think people would be tempted to use these products.

What You Will Do

- Explain myths associated with physical activity and nutrition.
- Identify fad diets and risky weight-loss strategies.
- Evaluate consumer issues related to the safety of dietary supplements.

Terms to Know

fad diets

hotlink

RMR
For more on RMR, see Chapter 5, page **155.**

◀ Often, weight-loss products promote false ideas about health and fitness in an effort to sell their products. *What are some false claims you have seen on packages of weight-loss products?*

Nutrition Myths and Fad Diets

In our society, learning to achieve and maintain a healthy body weight is often complicated by misinformation about nutrition and physical fitness. In this lesson, you will explore several common myths associated with physical activity and nutrition, as well as identify fad diets and other risky weight-loss strategies.

Myths about Nutrition

With all of the information in the media about health and fitness, it is difficult to separate myth from reality. Many people lack the appropriate knowledge and expertise about fitness to know what is fact and what is fiction. The following section will help to clarify the truth behind several common myths about physical activity and nutrition.

Weight Control and Nutrition

Myth. *It is best to eat only one or two meals per day to control your body weight and composition.*

Fact. For most teens, it is best to eat several (three to five) smaller meals and snacks per day to control body weight and composition. Eating several small meals will also help you maintain a higher **Resting Metabolic Rate (RMR),** allowing your body to burn more calories through involuntary functions such as breathing and digestion. Eating more often also helps curb hunger and prevents overeating when you do get hungry.

LESSON 3 RESOURCES

Teacher Classroom Resources
📁 Guided Practice Activity 6-3
📁 Active Mind—Active Body Worksheet 6-3
📁 Reteaching Activity 6-3
📁 Lesson Quiz 6-3

Reproducible Charts and Graphs
📁 Reproducible Master 6-2

Multimedia
💿 Vocabulary PuzzleMaker

Myth. *It is reasonable to lose 10 to 20 pounds in one week.*

Fact. While some people can lose this much weight in one week, they usually lose mostly water weight, causing severe dehydration, and put themselves at risk for health problems because they are not eating enough calories or are exercising too much.

Myth. *Consuming large amounts of protein and lifting weights are the best ways to increase the size of your muscles and your muscular strength.*

Fact. Lifting weights is an excellent activity to help you increase the size of your muscles and your muscular strength. However, extra **protein** is not needed in your diet to increase the size of your muscles or your muscular strength. You can get all the protein you need by following the ABCs of nutrition.

Myth. *Consuming extra vitamins and minerals will help you feel better and perform better during exercise.*

Fact. **Vitamins and minerals** cannot give you extra energy because they do not supply your body with calories. Also, taking large amounts of vitamin and mineral supplements can cause health risks. You will learn more about dietary supplements later in this lesson.

Myth. *Vegetarianism is much healthier and better for exercise performance than a diet that includes animal sources.*

Fact. Vegetarians can be healthy and perform well during exercise. However, those who decide to become vegetarians may initially not get all the nutrients, vitamins, and minerals they need unless they eat a variety of foods, such as fruits, vegetables, leafy greens, whole grains, nuts, seeds, legumes, dairy foods, and eggs.

▲ Although protein powders and drinks are sold as supplements, it is not necessary to consume extra protein to build muscle mass. *What is the best way to build muscle mass?*

hot link

protein
For more on protein, see Chapter 4, page **117**.

vitamins and minerals
For more on vitamins and minerals, see Chapter 4, pages **123** and **125**.

Reading Check

Discuss Explain one myth associated with weight control and nutrition.

Physical Activity and Nutrition

Myth. *The best way to control your weight and body composition is by adjusting your exercise levels.*

Fact. While adjusting the amount of exercise you do will affect your weight, it is healthiest to combine exercise with a healthful eating plan for effective long-term weight control. This requires you to combine the ABCs of sound nutrition and to become physically active.

Myth. *It is easy to lose one pound of fat by burning 3,500 calories through exercise.*

Fact. Yes, you can burn 3,500 calories by exercising, but you must work at very high intensities. Even to burn 1,000 calories in one hour, you would have to run 8 to 10 miles in one hour, or cycle 25 to 30 miles in one hour. A more reasonable goal is to burn 400–600 calories in an hour by performing moderate-to-vigorous physical activity.

2 TEACH

Photo Follow-up

Help students identify the types of protein drinks or powders available to consumers. ***Caption answer: Lifting weights and following the ABCs of nutrition are the best ways to build muscle mass.***

Activity

Divide the class into five groups. Assign each group one of the myths and facts on this page. Allow a few minutes for each group to read and discuss its myth and fact. Ask each group to assign a spokesperson to read the fact section aloud to the class and analyze why sound nutritional practices and diet are the best choice for weight control. L2 TEKS C5E

hot link

Stress the importance of relationships between RMR, protein, vitamins, and minerals and how they influence weight control and nutrition. Have students review Chapters 4 and 5 for more about these topics.

Reading Check

Answers will vary but should include facts from the text on these pages.

Teacher-Coach Tips

Athletes and Body Weight Body weight is important in many sports. In football, for example, extra weight is an advantage, whereas sports such as wrestling have weight restrictions. An athlete's weight should be within his or her healthy weight range and should remain stable. Crash dieting or taking sweat baths before a weigh-in are unhealthy; they result in fatigue, dehydration, muscle loss, and poor performance. Athletes who need extra weight should begin a slow, steady program of weight gain. Building extra muscle mass takes time and dedication to a regular exercise program.

Student Edition TEKS

Page 180: C4H, C5E
Page 181: C5E

Discussing

Ask for a volunteer to explain why eating sweets does not give the body energy it can use during a workout. *Foods high in sugar can lower glucose levels and cause tiredness.* Remind students about importance of pre-event meals, following the ABCs of nutrition, and avoiding foods high in sugar prior to exercise.

 **hotlink**

Review with students the important concepts of pre-event meals and rehydration in order to distinguish myth from fact with regard to physical activity and nutrition. Have students review Chapters 2 and 4 for more about these topics.

Explaining

Tell students that most people regain weight lost on fad diets or other quick weight-loss methods. Often, dieters gain back more weight than they had lost as soon as they return to their regular eating habits. Stress the importance of eating for optimal health. **L1**

✓ **Reading Check**

Answers will vary but should include facts from this page that explain myths associated with physical activity and nutrition. **TEKS C5D**

 **hotlink**

pre-event meals
For more on pre-event meals, see Chapter 4, page **139**.

rehydration
For more on rehydration, see Chapter 2, page **42**.

Myth. *Foods high in sugar, like candy bars and sodas, are good sources for quick energy if eaten 30 minutes before exercise.*

Fact. The energy you need for exercise comes from **pre-event meals** you have consumed the day or days before. Foods high in sugar consumed right before exercise can lower your glucose levels and leave you feeling tired.

Myth. *The best fluid you can drink after exercise to replace the fluids you have lost by sweating is water.*

Fact. The best fluid for your needs depends upon on how long you work, how dehydrated you were before you began exercise, how hard you work, and how quickly you need to recover before you exercise again. Sometimes sport drinks may actually be better than water for fast **rehydration.**

 **Reading Check**

Discuss Explain one myth associated with physical activity and nutrition.

Fad Diets

Many of the common misconceptions about nutrition and weight come from **fad diets.** These are *weight-loss plans that are popular for only a short time.* As their name implies, fad diets come and go. Information on them suddenly appears in the media and vanishes almost as quickly. Some popular fad diets that have appeared in recent years are listed in **Figure 6.4.**

FIGURE 6.4

SOME POPULAR FAD DIETS

Fad diets do not lead to healthy or effective weight loss.
What are some other fad diets you have heard of?

Diet	Claims	Health Risks and Problems
Liquid diets featuring fruit drinks	Simple to follow, rapid weight loss	Weight is quickly regained once normal eating habits are resumed
High-fiber diets	Rapid weight loss	Poor digestion, upset stomach, malnutrition
Fasting	Rapid weight loss; "detoxifies" body	Weight is quickly regained once normal eating habits are resumed

---

Promoting Coordinated School Health

THE TEAM Under the coordinated school health program, each campus would have a site-based decision-making committee comprised of teachers, campus staff, parents, community members, and business representatives. In addition to academic performance objectives, plans related to students' physical and psychological needs must also be addressed. Schools might already have a dropout prevention committee working together with school/community drug-prevention committees. These committees can also focus on the effects of students' health on their academic performance.

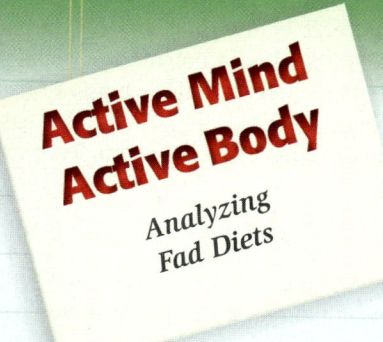

Active Mind Active Body

Analyzing Fad Diets

Understanding and evaluating marketing claims for fad diets are important skills. They can help you recognize false or misleading claims about weight-loss products or methods.

What You Will Need
- Pen or pencil
- Paper

What You Will Do
1. Working as a group, you and several classmates should each choose a different form of media, such as television programming (including the news), TV advertising (including infomercials), magazines, and so on.
2. For one week, each group member is to monitor his or her chosen medium. The group member should record the number of times he or she encounters information concerning weight-loss programs or products. Each member should take notes regarding
   a. the date on which the information appeared.
   b. the medium in which it appeared.
   c. the name of the diet or product.
   d. a brief description of the advertisement or program.
3. At the end of the week, the group should compile its findings. These are to be shared with the class in a round-table discussion.

Apply and Conclude

Which products or diets were featured in more than one medium? What claims were made about each product? What does this suggest about that particular product or diet? Was there any information about the product or diet that seemed to be left out (how it works, for example)? Which of the claims for a product or diet seemed to be the most misleading?

Although the theories behind fad diets often differ, the majority of them are based on faulty science. Some fad diets focus on one essential nutrient, excluding or ignoring others. Other fad diets assign some perceived fat-burning power to a single food, such as grapefruit or cabbage. Most of these strategies advocate taking in fewer daily calories than needed for proper energy and health. You may be aware of some of these, but others may be more difficult to identify. Be aware of any weight-loss plan or product that

- centers on eating one food.
- claims you can eat whatever you want.
- requires the purchase of a weight-loss aid, such as a supplement, appetite suppressant, or books and videos.
- does not include making changes to behavior and habits.

No matter what the angle, all fad diets have one thing in common. All place the unsuspecting consumer at risk of malnutrition or other health problems.

TECHNOLOGY FILE

Software Analysis of Fad Diets
Ask students to select one fad diet as the topic for a research project. As part of the assignment, have students enter typical breakfast, lunch, and dinner menus for the fad diet into a nutritional-analysis program. Instruct students to use the software analysis to support the position that fad diets are not nutritionally sound. In addition, have them compare the fad diet analysis to the "meal design project" analysis and their own personal diet analysis. Using this information, have students reflect on the changes they need to make to their diets.

Active Mind Active Body

Analyzing Fad Diets

This activity will guide students in understanding and analyzing advertisements for fad diets.

Teaching Tips
- Have students use *Active Mind—Active Body Worksheet 6-3* from the TCR to record their information.
- Remind students in each group to divide and share the work equally.
- Have students bring to class examples of the products they have chosen, if possible.

Apply and Conclude
After students have completed the activity, discuss with them the importance of becoming a responsible health- and fitness-product consumer. Emphasize to students that they can be consumer mentors and set an example for others who may be influenced by misleading advertisements. **TEKS C4H**

USING VISUALS

Figure 6.4 Have students identify three popular fad diets and evaluate their claims in class. **TEKS C4H**

Student Edition TEKS

Page 182: C4H, C5E
Page 183: C4H

Consumer CORNER

Dietary Supplements

Have students read the *Consumer Corner* feature and then have them complete the Analyze section at the end of the feature. Ask them to evaluate dietary supplements and explain how this consumer issue is related to physical activity concerns. Ask: What are some of the possible health effects of using herbal supplements? Allow class time for two or three student volunteers to share the results of their investigation with the class.
TEKS C5D

High-Protein Diets

One popular diet in recent years is one that involves an eating plan that is high in protein and eliminates carbohydrates. Some people also take protein supplements to increase muscle mass. However, these practices can be dangerous.

Following a high protein diet can have a negative impact on your physical performance. Such diets:

- increase the risk of dehydration, because they place extra stress on the kidneys.
- increase the risk of calcium loss from bone over time. This can eventually lead to osteoporosis, a disorder characterized by brittle bones.
- will not provide an adequate amount of carbohydrates, including fiber.

Consumer CORNER

Dietary Supplements

Dietary supplements may sound like an easy and safe way to lose weight or improve performance. However, they may not deliver what their ads promise, and they may pose a serious risk to your health.

Unlike other medicines and drugs, dietary supplements do not need approval from the Food and Drug Administration (FDA), and the FDA does not study the safety or effectiveness of the products before they are sold to consumers. The manufacturers themselves are responsible for accurately reporting the ingredients and testing the safety of their products. The FDA only studies supplements if there are reports of injury or illness. The FDA also does not regulate the advertising claims made by the manufacturers.

Many of the ingredients in dietary supplements marketed for weight loss have harmful effects. Some herbal supplements may have health effects, including dizziness, jitters, irregular sleeping patterns, and nausea. Even common supplements containing caffeine or protein can be harmful if taken in large doses.

Although they may seem like a convenient method of controlling weight, dietary supplements are not guaranteed to be effective or safe. Just because they are available for sale in many stores does not mean they are effective. If you have questions about weight loss and dietary supplements, ask your health care professional.

Analyze

With a partner, research more about dietary supplements and the role and responsibilities of the FDA. Find out why the FDA does not currently regulate dietary supplements, and establish a list of pros and cons regarding FDA regulation of dietary supplements.

Enrichment

Analyzing Diet Claims Have students bring in a description of a type of diet plan (from a media source) and an advertisement for some type of weight loss plan (the more unusual the better). Then have them analyze two of the plans and identify the positive and negative aspects of each plan. Ask students to focus on the following in their analysis: (1) claims made; (2) common denominators; (3) positive effects; (4) negative effects, especially if a drug is involved; (5) nutritional value; and (6) whether exercise is recommended as part of the plan.

Diet Pills

Many products claim to "burn" or "flush" fat from the body. Science has yet to devise such a medicine that is both safe and effective. Diet pills may help control the appetite, but they can have very serious side effects. Some cause drowsiness. Others may produce nervousness or anxiety. Some diet pills may even lead to addiction.

Risks of Dietary Supplements

As you learned in Chapter 4, a dietary supplement is a nonfood form of one or more nutrients. In an effort to avoid consuming too many calories, some people may try to get all the appropriate nutrients and vitamins from dietary supplements, or they may use dietary supplements as a method of suppressing their appetites and shedding unwanted pounds.

However, a person needs a healthful plan to meet the body's demands for nutrients. Also, as mentioned in Chapter 4, some vitamins can build up to toxic levels in the body if a person takes them in large amounts. Some supplements are marketed as "all-natural" weight-loss remedies, but they are not necessarily safe. A product's being natural is no guarantee against harm. For example, the leaves of the senna plant are a powerful laxative. Anyone who drinks senna tea in the hopes of purging weight should be aware of the potential health risks.

Fitness FACTS

Dieting
- Dieting without physical activity rarely works. Some 95 percent of all dieters regain the lost weight and more within 1 to 5 years.
- Dieting can force your body into starvation mode and slow your metabolism.

Lesson 3 Review

Using complete sentences, answer the following questions on a sheet of paper.

Reviewing Facts and Vocabulary

1. **Vocabulary** What are *fad diets*?
2. **Recall** What are the risks of a high-protein diet?
3. **Recall** List one myth associated with nutrition and weight control and one associated with nutrition and physical activity.

Thinking Critically

4. **Evaluate** Choose a fad diet discussed in this lesson. Explain why it is an ineffective method of weight loss and how it might put a person's health at risk.

5. **Analyze** Anna has recently started taking dietary supplements because she does not want to worry about counting calories in her eating plan. What are the risks associated with such a plan? What advice would you give her?

Personal Fitness Planning

Evaluating Information Make a list of any misconceptions you had about nutrition and fitness before reading this chapter. Write a paragraph explaining what you have learned and how understanding the realities behind these myths will impact your personal fitness plan in terms of your eating plan and physical activity.

3 ASSESS

EVALUATING THE LESSON

Assign and discuss the Lesson 3 Review.

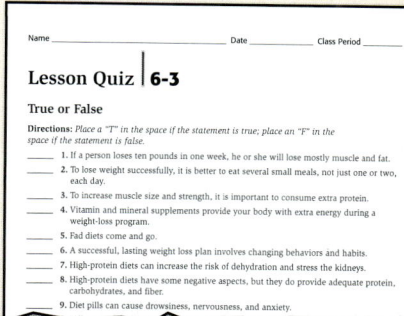

RETEACHING

Ask students to summarize and outline the dangers of fad dieting.

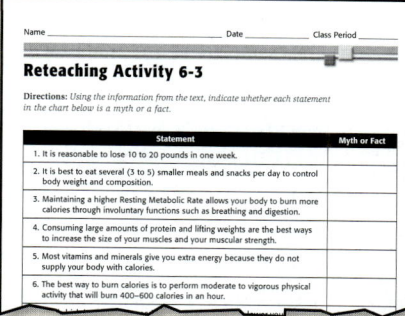

ENRICHMENT

Have students share the list of myths from this lesson with a relative and record how many myths the person thinks are really facts. Ask them to report the results back to the class. **TEKS C5E**

4 CLOSE

Have students interview other teachers, coaches, administrators, school staff, or students about their opinions on fad diets.

Lesson 3 Review

Answers to Lesson 3 Review

1. Fad diets are weight loss plans that are popular for a short time.
2. Risks include dehydration; calcium loss, which can lead to osteoporosis; and an inadequate amount of carbohydrate, including fiber.
3. Answers may vary but should include one each from pages 180-182.
4. Fad diets may produce quick weight loss but cannot be maintained, do not lead to permanent weight loss, and do not provide proper nutrients.
5. She may develop an eating disorder.

Methods for Weight Control

![MOTIVATE icon] **1 MOTIVATE**

GETTING STARTED

- Ask students whether they have ever thought about making a plan to maintain a healthy weight. If so, ask them to explain what their plan includes.
- Distribute copies of *Guided Practice Activity 6-4* for students to use while studying this lesson. 📁

IN THIS LESSON

- **Stress Break** *Eating Under Pressure, p. 188*

INTRODUCING VOCABULARY

- Explain to students that the word *cycling* in the vocabulary term *weight cycling* refers to a continuous series of events that repeat in the same order. Ask students how this might apply to a person's eating habits.
- Have students use *Vocabulary Worksheet 6* or the PuzzleMaker software to practice vocabulary terms. ELL 📁 💿

Photo Follow-up

Encourage students to recall the health risks associated with body weight and body image they learned about in previous lessons. *Caption answer: Improves body image, functional health, and functional fitness.* **TEKS C4A; C5A; C5G**

Lesson 4

What You Will Do

- Explain how positive behaviors can lead to healthy weight management.
- Describe how nutrition and physical activity affect weight control.
- Identify the steps in a healthy weight-management plan.

Terms to Know

weight cycling

Methods for Weight Control

In the last three lessons you have examined the many risks associated with body weight, body image, and myths about nutrition. However, achieving and maintaining a healthy weight should not put your health at risk. No matter what your current weight, everyone can achieve their fitness goals by making positive choices and practicing healthful behaviors.

By working with a health care professional to evaluate your current body composition and adjust your eating and physical activity habits, you can achieve and maintain a body weight and body composition that is best for you. This lesson will offer safe guidelines for achieving your goals.

▶ Managing your weight in a healthy way will have a positive impact on your health and personal fitness. *How can maintaining a healthy weight benefit your mental and physical health?*

186   Chapter 6   Maintaining a Healthy Body Weight

 **LESSON 4 RESOURCES**

Teacher Classroom Resources
- 📁 Guided Practice Activity 6-4
- 📁 Reteaching Activity 6-4
- 📁 Lesson Quiz 6-4

Multimedia
- 💿 Vocabulary PuzzleMaker
- 🔦 Transparencies 38, 39

FIGURE 6.5

THE WEIGHT CYCLE

Positive fitness behaviors can help reverse the negative effects associated with weight problems. *What type of positive behaviors will help reverse this cycle?*

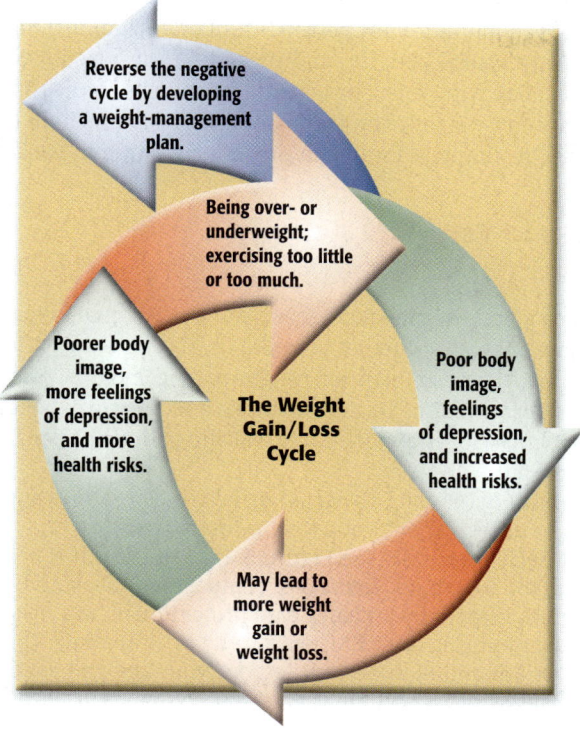

Reverse the negative cycle by developing a weight-management plan.

Being over- or underweight; exercising too little or too much.

Poorer body image, more feelings of depression, and more health risks.

The Weight Gain/Loss Cycle

Poor body image, feelings of depression, and increased health risks.

May lead to more weight gain or weight loss.

Achieving and Maintaining a Healthful Weight

A first step toward making behavioral changes that will lead to a more healthful weight is understanding the effect of unhealthful weight gain or weight loss. This cycle is illustrated in **Figure 6.5.** Take a moment to study this diagram. Notice that the arrows that point in a clockwise direction represent a cycle. Too much or too little weight, for example, can lead to a low self-image, or even depression. This in turn can lead to decreased levels of personal fitness and increased disease risks.

Now note the blue arrow containing the sentence "Reverse the negative cycle by developing a weight-management plan." This arrow points counter-clockwise. This shows that the cycle can be broken—that you can turn your behavior around.

Whether you adopt healthful behaviors and maintain a healthful weight is up to you. In this lesson, you will learn about ways of healthfully changing your weight and your overall level of personal fitness.

Lesson 4 Methods for Weight Control **187**

2 TEACH

USING VISUALS

Figure 6.5 Ask students to examine the Weight Cycle illustrated in Figure 6.5 (*Transparency 38*) and answer the caption question. *Caption answers should include: Use the ABCs of nutrition and combine them with regular physical activity and exercise.* Then ask students how this figure might relate to other personal fitness behaviors, including controlling blood pressure and blood glucose.

Critical Thinking

Ask students to react to the following statement and have them explain how it relates to the concept of the weight cycle illustrated in Figure 6.5: "If you keep doing what you're doing, you'll keep getting what you've been getting." **L2**

HEALTHY PEOPLE 2010

Healthy People 2010

One of the *Healthy People 2010* Goals is to reduce the percentage of children and adolescents who are overweight or obese. The goal for the year 2010 is to have no more than 5 percent of children and adolescents be overweight or obese. Today, 11 to 14 percent of youth are overweight or obese. Refer students to Appendix B, page 384, to read the goals of *Healthy People 2010*.

STRESS BREAK
Eating Under Pressure

Have students read the *Stress Break* feature. Then have them describe ways that physical activity or exercise helps relieve stress. Ask students why they think changes in their stress levels following physical activity or exercise are due to changes in their hormone levels. Explain to them that the stimulus of regular physical activity or exercise has a significant effect on our hormone levels. **TEKS C5B**

Activity

Explain to students that the tips listed on this page regarding diet and physical activity for weight control are behavioral in nature. Ask students to use this information to write a paragraph analyzing methods of weight control that combine diet and exercise. **L2 TEKS C5F**

✔ Reading Check
You should re-evaluate and set new short-term goals every three months until you reach your goal.

Figure 6.6 Display *Transparency 39* and have students determine which weight management plan they should be following. Then ask them to answer the caption question. *Caption answers will vary but should include the recommendations listed on this page.* **TEKS C5F**

STRESS BREAK
Eating under Pressure

Do you find yourself eating more when you feel stressed? You may not realize that this response to stress is physical as much as it is psychological.

Scientists have discovered that under stress, the brain releases a hormone called *cortisol*. This hormone increases your appetite, particularly for foods high in fat and carbohydrates. The final result can be unwanted pounds.

However, physical activity will help you fight off stress-related cravings. Physical activity releases beta endorphins, a group of chemicals that will counter the effects of cortisol and other stress hormones.

Next time you feel stressed, instead of reaching for a bag of chips, reach for your running shoes.

Healthy Weight Control

To manage your body weight, it is wise for you to develop a personal plan based on the guidelines listed below. It is important to be patient and consistent as you work to achieve your goals. This will help you avoid weight cycling, *the cycle of losing, regaining, losing and regaining weight.* To keep your weight within a healthy range, you need to monitor your personal fitness, including your BMI, eating plan, physical activity, and personal-fitness goals. You should always check with your physician or health care professional before you start any weight-control program. He or she will do a complete checkup, testing you for health problems relating to weight.

Diet and Physical Activity for Weight Control

Once you determine your goals, you can begin to follow a weight-management plan. Whether your BMI is high, low, or within the normal range, the basic plan for weight management is essentially the same, with variations in calorie intake and energy expenditure. The following list offers a guide for a realistic and healthy plan for managing weight.

- Check with your physician or health care professional if you are unsure about your weight-loss goals.
- Check your BMI (see **Figure 5.2**, page **149**). If it is too high or too low, have your body composition measured with skinfold calipers by a health care professional. You need to set a goal to bring your BMI within the healthy range (between the 5th and 85th percentiles) for your age and gender.
- Use the ABCs and the Food Guide Pyramid for healthy eating.
- Adjust calorie intake and energy expenditure, depending upon your needs. **Figure 6.6** offers specific guidance, based on BMI.
- Work 30 to 60 minutes per day of moderate-to-vigorous physical activity, or a minimum of 225–300 minutes per week for long-term success.
- Allow plenty of time (20–30 weeks) for long-term results.
- Retest body composition every three months.
- Keep a log of your progress and re-evaluate how your plan is working every three months.
- Reward yourself in a positive way as you meet your goals.
- Continue to make new short-term weight-loss goals every three months until you achieve your goal.

Your ultimate goal, in any case, should be to make permanent, positive changes in your eating habits. This approach will work far better than a series of short-term changes that can not be sustained.

✔ Reading Check
Explain How often should you evaluate your progress and make new goals?

TECHNOLOGY FILE

Spreadsheet-Assisted Meal Design
Students can use spreadsheet software to develop a one-week personal nutrition plan. Have students enter "Item" in cell B1, "Quantity" in C1, and "Cost" in D1. Then, have them enter "Day 1" in A2, "Day 2" in A22, "Day 3" in A42, "Day 3" in A62, "Day 4" in A82, "Day 5" in A52, "Day 6" in A102, and "Day 7" in A122. Finally, have students enter "=sum (D2:D142)" in D143 for the total cost for seven days. Once students have planned all the menus, have them enter their food choices, quantities, and costs into the spreadsheet for the week to calculate the cost.

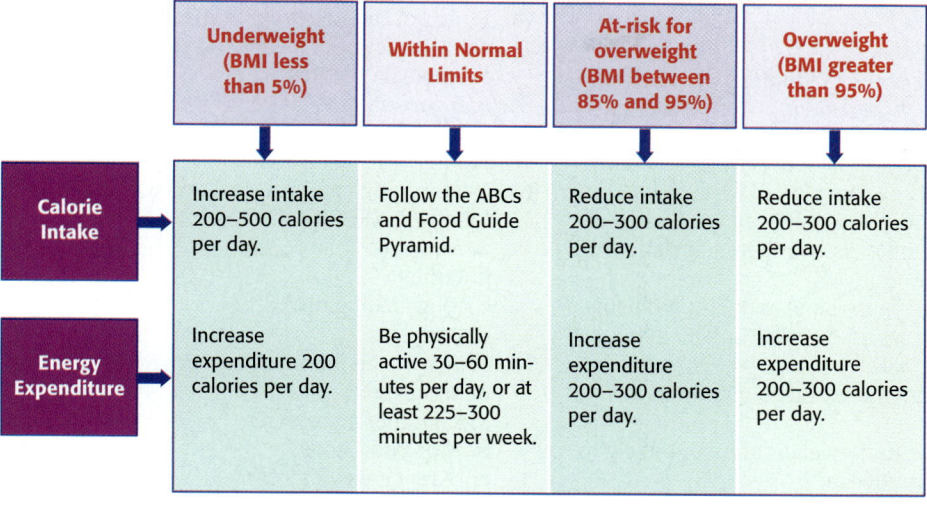

FIGURE 6.6

RECOMMENDATIONS FOR WEIGHT MANAGEMENT

To properly change or maintain body weight, it is best to adjust both calorie intake and energy expenditure. *What are some other important steps in a weight-management plan?*

	Underweight (BMI less than 5%)	Within Normal Limits	At-risk for overweight (BMI between 85% and 95%)	Overweight (BMI greater than 95%)
Calorie Intake	Increase intake 200–500 calories per day.	Follow the ABCs and Food Guide Pyramid.	Reduce intake 200–300 calories per day.	Reduce intake 200–300 calories per day.
Energy Expenditure	Increase expenditure 200 calories per day.	Be physically active 30–60 minutes per day, or at least 225–300 minutes per week.	Increase expenditure 200–300 calories per day.	Increase expenditure 200–300 calories per day.

Lesson 4 Review

Using complete sentences, answer the following questions on a sheet of paper.

Reviewing Facts and Vocabulary

1. **Vocabulary** What is *weight cycling?*
2. **Recall** Explain how unhealthful weight loss or weight gain can lead to further weight loss or weight gain.
3. **Recall** What is the first step in determining your weight goals?

Thinking Critically

4. **Analyze** Analyze methods of a weight control plan that includes diet and exercise.

5. **Evaluation** Dave is 16 years old. He has a BMI of 16 and 6 percent body fat. He wants to gain weight, but he is not sure what to do. What positive advice can you give him to gain weight in a healthful way?

Personal Fitness Planning

Designing a Plan Based on the information in this lesson, create a plan that states your goal for improving or maintaining your weight. For each step presented in this lesson, write a sentence or two explaining how and when you will implement each one.

Lesson 4 Methods for Weight Control **189**

3 ASSESS

EVALUATING THE LESSON

Assign and discuss the Lesson 4 Review.

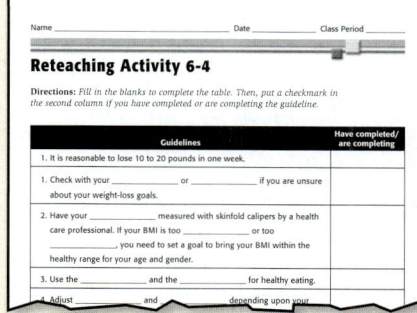

Name _____ Date _____ Class Period _____

Lesson Quiz | **6-4**

Fill in the Blanks

I. Directions: *Fill in the blanks with the correct answers.*

1. By adjusting your eating and _____ habits, you can achieve and maintain a healthy body weight and composition.
2. Too much or too little weight can lead to a _____, and it can lead to depression.
3. If you are patient and consistent as you work to achieve your weight goals, you will be able to avoid _____.
4. Before you begin any weight-loss or weight-gain program, you should consult with a _____ professional.
5. You should use the ABCs and the _____ to help you choose nutritious, healthful foods.
6. To maintain or change your body weight, you should adjust both your _____ and your energy expenditure.

RETEACHING

Ask volunteers to list the most important concepts they have learned for maintaining a healthful weight.

Name _____ Date _____ Class Period _____

Reteaching Activity 6-4

Directions: *Fill in the blanks to complete the table. Then, put a checkmark in the second column if you have completed or are completing the guideline.*

Guidelines	Have completed/ are completing
1. It is reasonable to lose 10 to 20 pounds in one week.	
1. Check with your _____ or _____ if you are unsure about your weight-loss goals.	
2. Have your _____ measured with skinfold calipers by a health care professional. If your BMI is too _____ or too _____, you need to set a goal to bring your BMI within the healthy range for your age and gender.	
3. Use the _____ and the _____ for healthy eating.	
4. Adjust _____ and _____ depending upon your	

ENRICHMENT

Have students identify a friend or family member who has expressed an interest in developing a weight management plan. Then have students help the person develop their plan.

4 CLOSE

Have students develop a one-page individual weight management plan for the next six months.

189

Lesson 4 Review

Answers to Lesson 4 Review

1. Weight cycling refers to losing, regaining, losing, and regaining weight.
2. Weighing too much or too little can lead to decreased levels of personal fitness and increased disease risks.
3. Check with your physician.
4. Use the ABCs and the Food Guide Pyramid for healthy eating, and work up to 30 to 60 minutes per day of moderate to vigorous physical activity.
5. Have Dave use Figure 6.6 as a guide and encourage him to set reasonable goals.

CHECKING COMPREHENSION

- Assign and discuss the chapter review.
- Use the PuzzleMaker software CD-ROM to review vocabulary. 💿

CHAPTER 6 REVIEW ANSWERS

True/False

1. False	6. True
2. True	7. False
3. True	8. False
4. False	9. False
5. False	10. True

Multiple Choice

11. c	16. a
12. b	17. b
13. d	18. c
14. c	19. d
15. c	20. a

Discussion

21. Any three: lowered self-esteem, negative growth and development effects, breathing difficulties, and bone and joint problems.
22. Overtraining is often associated with obsessive behavior, which can also lead to disordered eating. **TEKS C5C**
23. They increase the risk of malnutrition and health problems.

Vocabulary

24. c
25. e
26. b
27. f
28. d
29. a

TRUE/FALSE

On a sheet of paper, write the numbers 1–10. Write True or False for each statement.

1. A person whose BMI is between the 85th and 95th percentiles is considered overweight.
2. A person whose BMI is between the 85th and 95th percentiles is considered at risk for overweight.
3. Overweight can cause bone and joint problems.
4. Anorexia is an eating disorder in which an individual overeats.
5. Bigorexia occurs more in teen girls than in boys.
6. People who are underweight are more likely to get colds and influenza.
7. Fad diets are usually effective at helping you maintain weight loss over the long term.
8. To build muscle mass, it is necessary to consume large amounts of protein.
9. Eating foods high in sugar will provide your body with the energy it needs to perform well during exercise.
10. Teens should get 60 minutes a day or at least 225 minutes per week of moderate-to-vigorous physical activity.

MULTIPLE CHOICE

On a sheet of paper, write the letter of the word or phrase that best completes each statement.

11. A person with a BMI higher than the 95th percentile is
    a. within normal limits.
    b. underweight.
    c. overweight.
    d. at risk for overweight.
12. A person with a BMI lower than the 5th percentile is
    a. within normal limits.
    b. underweight.
    c. overweight.
    d. at risk for overweight.

13. Which of the following is not linked to obesity?
    a. Asthma
    b. Type 2 diabetes
    c. Bone and joint problems
    d. Anorexia nervosa
14. Which of the following terms is associated with the act of bingeing and purging?
    a. Anorexia nervosa
    b. Bigorexia
    c. Bulimia
    d. Binge eating disorder
15. Overtraining can be associated with all of the following EXCEPT:
    a. Anorexia
    b. Bulimia
    c. Binge eating disorder
    d. Bigorexia
16. Which of the following is not a symptom of anorexia?
    a. High blood pressure
    b. Poor body image
    c. Massive weight loss
    d. Excessive exercise
17. Bigorexia is also known as
    a. binge eating disorder.
    b. reverse anorexia.
    c. overtraining.
    d. weight cycling.
18. All of the following are examples of risky weight-loss strategies, EXCEPT
    a. high-protein diets.
    b. surgical procedures.
    c. the *Dietary Guidelines for Americans.*
    d. fasting.
19. The first step in any teen weight-control program is to
    a. reduce energy intake.
    b. increase energy intake.
    c. get 225 minutes of weekly physical activity.
    d. check with your physician if you are unsure about your weight-loss goals.
20. How often should you check your body composition during a weight-control program?
    a. Every 3 months
    b. Every 6–8 weeks
    c. Every 3 weeks
    d. Every 1–2 weeks

DISCUSSION

Using complete sentences, answer the following questions on a sheet of paper.

21. Identify What are three health risks associated with being overweight?

22. Explain How can overtraining contribute to an eating disorder?

23. Evaluate Why should you avoid fad diets?

VOCABULARY

On a sheet of paper, write the letter of the term in Column B that best fits the definition in Column A.

Column A

24. Health problems and diseases linked to or resulting directly from long-term overweight or obesity.

25. A disorder in which an individual falsely believes he or she is underweight or undersized.

26. Disorder in which blood glucose levels become elevated.

27. Weight-loss plans that are popular for only a short time.

28. Psychological illnesses that cause people to undereat, overeat, or practice other dangerous nutrition-related behaviors.

29. Hormone produced by the pancreas that helps convert carbohydrates into glucose.

Column B

a. insulin
b. impaired glucose tolerance
c. excessive weight disabilities
d. eating disorders
e. bigorexia
f. fad diets

CRITICAL THINKING

Using complete sentences, answer the following questions on a sheet of paper.

30. Analyze Why do you think the number of overweight teens has increased significantly over the past 25 years? Explain.

31. Evaluate You suspect a friend may have an eating disorder. What should you do?

32. Describe Explain one myth associated with physical activity and nutrition.

CASE STUDY

LOSING WEIGHT

Sandy is a 15-year-old active female. She participates in aerobic dance classes for 30 minutes, five times a week. However, even though she is physically active, she feels like she is overweight and has been thinking of going on a high-protein diet to lose more weight. She snacks on a candy bar or soda before dance class. Otherwise, she typically eats two meals a day.

HERE IS YOUR ASSIGNMENT:

Assume you are Sandy's friend, and she asks you for some assistance with her plans for losing weight. Make a list of things Sandy should consider and do before beginning her program. Then list the recommendations you would give Sandy for the first two weeks of her program. Use the following keys to help you:

KEYS TO HELP YOU

- Consider Sandy's current lifestyle habits and choices.
- List the possible health risks associated with her current eating habits.
- List the possible health risks associated with her future plan of a "high-protein" diet.
- Decide how she should evaluate her current diet.
- Think about her needs and goals. For example, how should she go about changing her diet?
- Determine a reasonable plan to give Sandy that covers the concepts of risky weight-loss strategies and recommended teen weight-control programs.

CHAPTER 6
REVIEW

Critical Thinking

30. Answers will vary but might include decreases in physical activity, increases in caloric intake, increased consumption of fast-foods, and increased consumption of foods high in fat.

31. Answers will vary, but students should use the information in the Lifeline feature on page 177.

32. Answers will vary but should relate to those listed on page 182.

EVALUATE

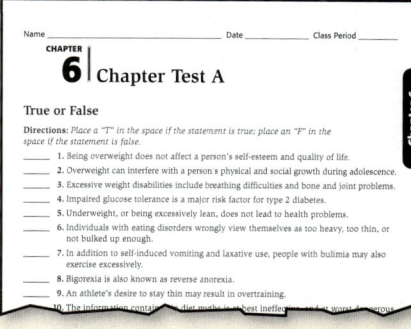

ENRICHMENT

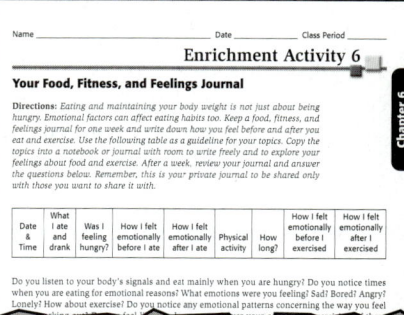

CASE STUDY

ANSWERS

Answers will vary, but Sandy should follow the recommendations listed on page 188 and choose a plan illustrated in Figure 6.6. She should continue her exercise program but work at using the ABCs of nutrition more effectively.

Student Edition TEKS

Page 189: C5F, C5G
Page 191: C5C, C5G

191

CHAPTER 7

Basics of Cardiorespiratory Endurance

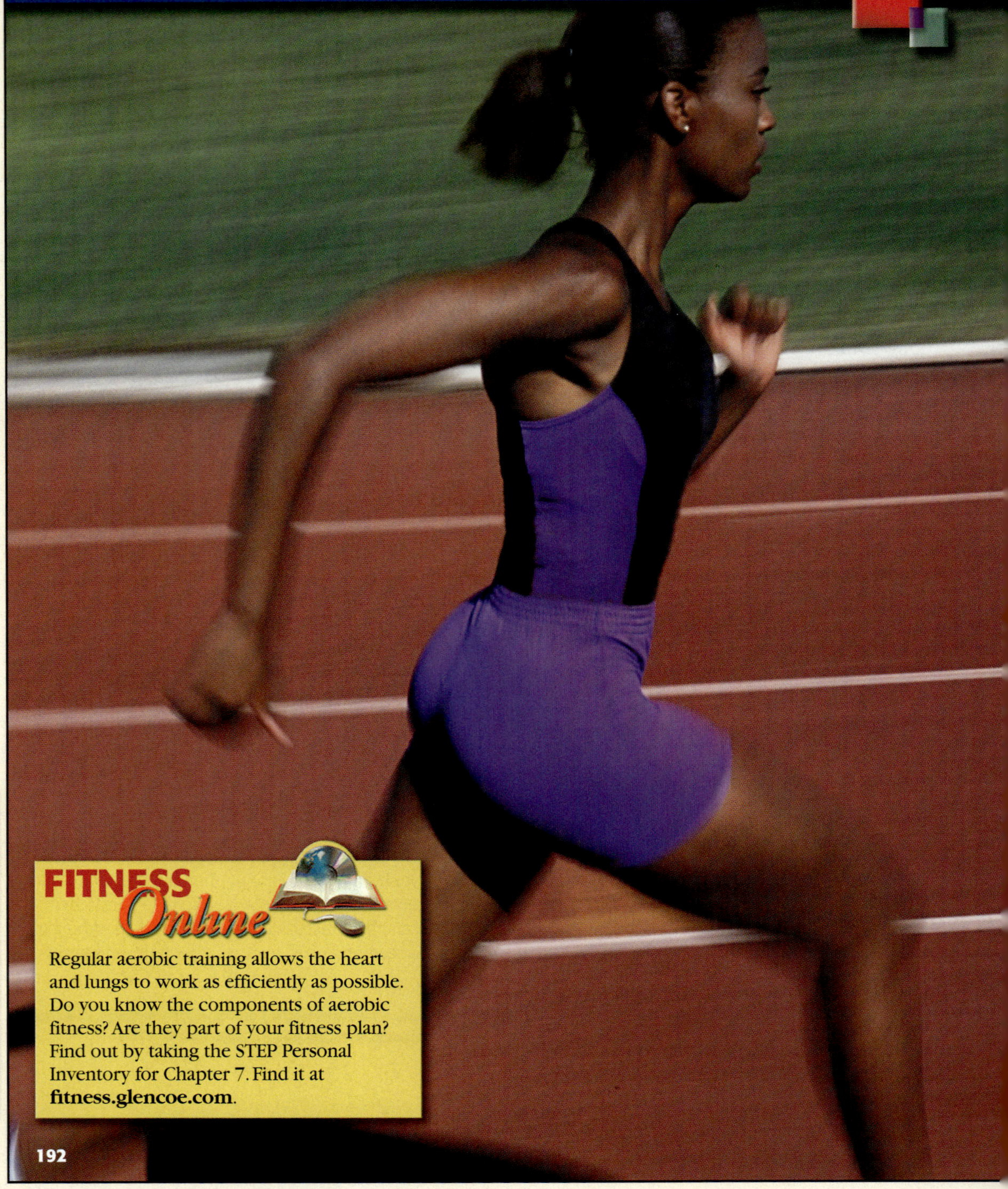

FITNESS Online

Regular aerobic training allows the heart and lungs to work as efficiently as possible. Do you know the components of aerobic fitness? Are they part of your fitness plan? Find out by taking the STEP Personal Inventory for Chapter 7. Find it at **fitness.glencoe.com**.

CHAPTER 7

Lesson 1 Your Heart, Lungs, and Circulation

Lesson 2 Problems and Care of Your Heart and Lungs

Lesson 3 Influences on Cardiorespiratory Endurance

Lesson 4 Aerobic vs. Anaerobic Physical Activities

CHAPTER RESOURCES

- Chapter Study Guide 7
- Vocabulary Worksheet 7
- Enrichment Activity 7
- Chapter 7 Test A
- Chapter 7 Test B
- Parent Letter and Activities 7 (English/Spanish)

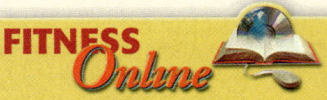

FITNESS Online

Ask students to take the STEP Personal Inventory for Chapter 7. Have them record their responses to the statements in their notebooks. Remind students that responses are private and for their use only.

INCLUSION STRATEGIES

LANGUAGE DIVERSITY *Use the following suggestions to help students who have difficulty with English:*

- Pair English-language learners with native speakers of English who can restate key points in language that helps students comprehend important concepts.
- Direct Spanish-speaking students to the written summaries of this chapter in the *Foundations of Personal Fitness* Spanish Resources Booklet.
- Encourage Spanish-speaking students to use the Glosario provided in the back of the student text. ELL

Your Heart, Lungs, and Circulation

Josh loves to row and is a member of the school rowing team. Tina enjoys participating in a step aerobics class. Although Josh and Tina have very different interests, they have one thing in common. They both like doing aerobic activities and recognize the importance of doing them.

What are aerobic activities? How do they benefit the body? In this lesson, you will find out.

Aerobic Activities and the Body

The exercises that weightlifters do are targeted at certain muscles of the body. These include muscles of the arms, legs, chest, and back. The activities that Josh and Tina do are also targeted at a major muscle of the body. That muscle is the heart.

Aerobic activity is continuous activity that requires large amounts of oxygen. (The word *aerobic* means "with oxygen.") Like other aerobic activities, rowing and step aerobics temporarily raise the heart rate. Done regularly, aerobic activities strengthen the heart. They also strengthen another vital organ, the lungs. Aerobic activity also makes your working muscles more efficient at using oxygen. Before you can understand how aerobic activities work, you need to have some knowledge of the circulatory and respiratory systems.

What You Will Do

- Explain the importance of aerobic activity to your health and fitness.
- Recognize the role of the circulatory and respiratory systems in aerobic conditioning.
- Identify the physical benefits of aerobic activity.
- Evaluate your cardiorespiratory endurance level.

Terms to Know

aerobic activity
circulatory system
hemoglobin
stroke volume
arteries
capillaries
veins
respiratory system
diaphragm
cardiorespiratory endurance

◄ Participating in aerobic activities regularly will increase your cardiorespiratory endurance. *What are some aerobic activities that you enjoy doing?*

Lesson 1 Your Heart, Lungs, and Circulation **193**

1 MOTIVATE

GETTING STARTED

- Ask the following: *What role do your heart and lungs play in circulation?*
- Distribute copies of *Guided Practice Activity 7-1* for students to use while studying this lesson. 📁

IN THIS LESSON

- **Fitness Check** *Evaluating Cardiorespiratory Endurance, page 197*

INTRODUCING VOCABULARY

- Explain that the term *circulatory* comes from the Latin root *circus,* which means circle. Explain the circular nature of the blood's movement through the body.
- Have students use *Vocabulary Worksheet 7* or the PuzzleMaker software to practice vocabulary terms for this lesson. **ELL** 📁 💿

Photo Follow-up

Discuss with students the benefits of aerobic activities. *Caption answers will vary. Encourage students to share their responses.*

LESSON 1 RESOURCES

Teacher Classroom Resources
- 📁 Guided Practice Activity 7-1
- 📁 Fitness Check Worksheet 7-1
- 📁 Reteaching Activity 7-1
- 📁 Lesson Quiz 7-1

Multimedia
- 🔧 Transparencies 40, 41
- 💿 Vocabulary PuzzleMaker

Student Edition TEKS
Page 193: C4A, C4B

2 TEACH

Explaining

Explain to students that every muscle and organ depends upon oxygen to function. The heart and lungs work together to meet the body's need for oxygen. Aerobic activity conditions the heart and lungs to function efficiently. **L1**

Quick Demo

To demonstrate how much blood the heart pumps in a minute, take two one-liter bottles and fill one with water. Pour the water from one bottle to the other at the rate of five times per minute. **L1**

Activity

Students can simulate the work a heart does by squeezing a tennis ball 72 times in one minute. The force needed to squeeze the tennis ball is about the same as the force needed to squeeze blood from the heart, which the heart does about 72 times a minute. **L1**

> **✓ Reading Check**
>
> The heart pumps the blood, the blood carries oxygen, and the vessels deliver the blood. It provides oxygenated blood to the body.

Your Circulatory System

The **circulatory system** *consists of the heart, blood, and blood vessels.* This system is also sometimes called the *cardiovascular system.* This system is responsible for circulating blood throughout the body.

The Heart

Figure 7.1 shows the heart, the main organ of the circulatory system. It is a muscle about the size and shape of your fist. The right side of the heart pumps blood to the lungs. There, the blood picks up oxygen and rids itself of carbon dioxide. The left side of the heart pumps oxygen-rich blood to the rest of the body. **Hemoglobin** is *an iron rich compound in the blood that helps carry the oxygen.* The oxygen helps your cells produce the energy you need to meet the demands of daily life.

The heart beats at different rates depending upon whether your body is at rest or at work. When resting, the heart beats an average of 72 times per minute. During strenuous physical activity, your heart rate—or *pulse*—increases, sometimes to twice or more its resting rate. *The amount of blood pumped per beat of the heart,* or **stroke volume,** also increases. This is because your working muscles demand more blood to supply them with oxygen and other nutrients.

The Blood Vessels

Blood is carried to and from the heart via a network of blood vessels. There are three types of vessels. *Vessels that carry blood from the heart to the major extremities—such as the arms, legs, and head—are known as* **arteries.** Smaller blood vessels called **capillaries** (KAP-uh-LAYR-eez) *deliver oxygen and other nutrients to individual cells.* **Veins** *deliver the blood back to the heart.* There it receives a fresh supply of oxygen and begins its journey again.

> **✓ Reading Check**
>
> **Explain** What are the main parts of the circulatory system and what is the function of each?

Your Respiratory System

The oxygen that your blood carries comes from the air around you. It is introduced into your body by means of your **respiratory** (REH-spir-uh-tor-ee) **system.** This is *the body system that exchanges gases between your body and the environment.*

The principal organ of your respiratory system is your lungs. Your lungs exchange oxygen and carbon dioxide. This process is known as *respiration.*

Unlike the heart, the lungs are not a muscle. Rather, they get their power from the **diaphragm,** *a muscle found between the chest cavity and abdomen,* as well as the intercostal muscles around the ribs

---

More About . . .

THE HEART The heart is a muscle that responds to an increase in anaerobic and aerobic activity. An increase in aerobic activity makes the muscle stronger and more efficient. The ventricles are made up of the stronger muscles of the heart. They force blood out of the heart to all parts of the body. Because the heart is a muscle, it requires nutrients, oxygen, and removal of wastes. It has its own system of veins and arteries to do the job efficiently. It responds to hormones by accelerating or decelerating its beating. Control of the beating mechanism is within the medulla of the brain.

FIGURE 7.1

THE HEART

Your heart pumps about 5 liters of blood every minute when your body is at rest. During high levels of aerobic activity, the heart pumps 4 to 5 times as much blood. *Compute the number of liters of blood the heart pumps during 5 minutes of vigorous physical activity.*

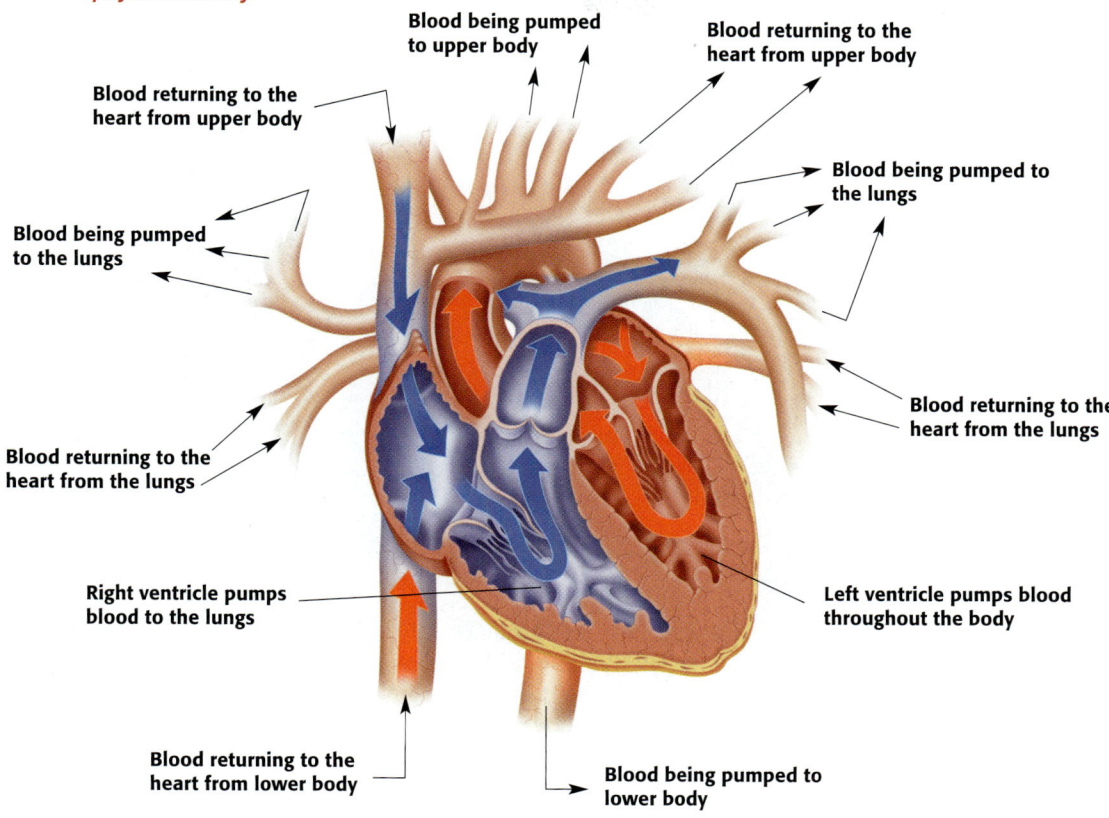

Blood being pumped to upper body

Blood returning to the heart from upper body

Blood returning to the heart from upper body

Blood being pumped to the lungs

Blood being pumped to the lungs

Blood returning to the heart from the lungs

Blood returning to the heart from the lungs

Right ventricle pumps blood to the lungs

Left ventricle pumps blood throughout the body

Blood returning to the heart from lower body

Blood being pumped to lower body

and the abdominal muscles in the lower stomach area. As shown in **Figure 7.2** on page **196,** when you inhale, the diaphragm contracts and moves downward. The chest cavity enlarges, allowing air into the lungs. When you exhale, the reverse happens.

Like your pulse, your breathing rate increases during vigorous physical activity. If your lungs are healthy, you can breathe about 6 liters of air per minute at rest and up to 100 liters of air per minute during vigorous exercise. The muscles involved in breathing become conditioned to make your breathing more efficient. This allows more oxygen to reach the heart, enabling it to pump more blood to the muscles and to remove carbon dioxide from your body more effectively.

FITNESS Online

Gather information about asthma and fitness at **fitness.glencoe.com.**

Activity Investigate the site to find asthma triggers and treatments. Create a poster or brochure using information from the site.

Lesson 1 Your Heart, Lungs, and Circulation **195**

Curriculum CONNECTIONS

PHYSICS *Pascal's principle* states: Any change in pressure applied to a fluid in a confined space is sent unchanged through that fluid. The force of blood flowing through the circulatory system puts pressure on the walls of all the blood vessels. The pressure lessens as the blood travels from the aorta through the arteries and veins to the right atrium, where pressure is almost zero.

Assign students in groups to demonstrate Pascal's principle in the circulatory system. Students may choose to design an experiment, write a dramatization, etc.

Figure 7.2 Display *Transparency 41* and discuss the process involved in respiration. Point out that the diaphragm is involved mainly in breathing as the lungs fill with oxygen. *Caption answer: The lungs breathe more air, providing more oxygen.* **L2**

Activity

To help students understand the effect of asthma on the lungs, give each student a straw. Have them pinch their noses and breathe through the straw. Then have students walk briskly while breathing through the straw. Explain that this is much like the sensation asthmatics have when they feel restriction of the air passages. **L2**

Cooperative Learning

Have students work in groups to create posters that outline the benefits of aerobic activity to a person's overall health and fitness. Their posters should include lists as well as visuals that emphasize all of the benefits. Encourage students to brainstorm to come up with other benefits not mentioned in the student text. **L2**

FIGURE 7.2

THE PROCESS OF RESPIRATION

Your lungs bring in oxygen from the environment and send out carbon dioxide. *Explain how the lungs aid the circulatory system during strenuous activity.*

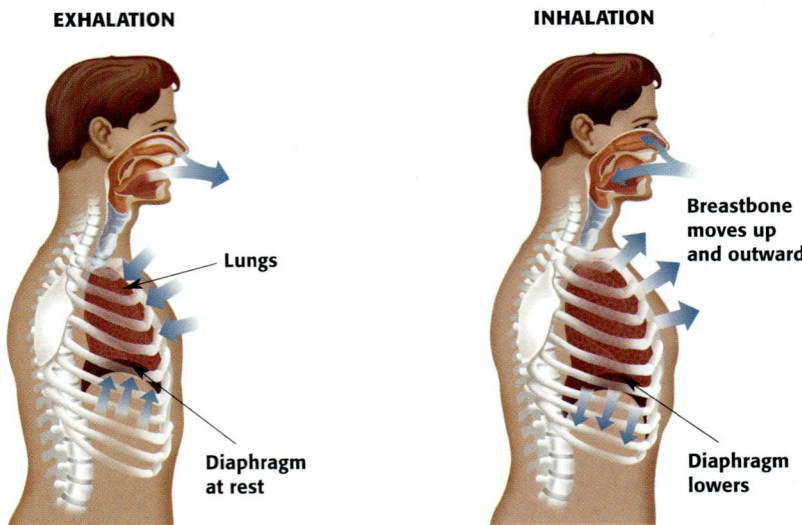

EXHALATION

INHALATION

Lungs

Breastbone moves up and outward

Diaphragm at rest

Diaphragm lowers

Benefits of Aerobic Activity

Regular aerobic activity strengthens the body in several ways. It increases stroke volume and lowers your resting heart rate. This means your heart is working more efficiently, resulting in a more effective delivery of oxygen to your body.

Aerobic activity also conditions the muscles used in breathing to function more efficiently. Such day-to-day tasks as climbing stairs require less effort because your muscles are more efficient. One of the most important benefits of aerobic activity is that it builds on itself. In other words, the more you condition aerobically, the more strenuous physical activity you are able to do.

▶ Jogging regularly is one great way to increase your stamina. *How can increased stamina benefit you in your daily life?*

Teacher-Coach Tips

Breathing Technique The best way for athletes, or those exercising at high intensity, to move large amounts of air is to breathe through both the nose and mouth. Many individuals try to breathe deeply only through their nose during exercise. However, this method does not allow the lungs to move as much air and to deliver the amount of oxygen required to meet their exercise demands. Encourage students to try both ways and determine which breathing technique is more efficient.

Evaluating Cardiorespiratory Endurance

In this activity, you will participate in one of two tests of cardiorespiratory fitness. The first is a 3-minute step test. The second is a 1.5-mile (2.5-k) run and/or walk. Warm up before you start either test. Stop if you feel dizzy or become overheated. After completing the test of your choice, allow between 5 and 10 minutes to cool down.

3-Minute Step Test

Procedure:
1. Begin stepping up and down on a 12-inch step at a rate of approximately 24 steps per minute.
2. At the end of 3 minutes, stop. Immediately take your pulse.
3. Use the Fitness Ratings Chart for the 3-Minute Step Test to determine your level of cardiorespiratory fitness.

Fitness Ratings: 3-Minute Step Test

Pulse Rate	Score
84 or less	High
85 to 95	Good
120 or higher	Low

1.5-Mile (2.5-k) Run/Walk Test

Procedure:
1. Go to a local indoor or outdoor track or other flat course in your community. Select a day when the temperature is moderate—between 50 and 75 degrees F (11 and 25 degrees C)—and winds are calm.
2. Complete 6 laps or a distance of 1.5 miles (2.5 k) in as short a time as possible. You may walk, jog, or use a combination of both.
3. Use the Fitness Ratings Chart for the 1.5-Mile (2.5-k) Run/Walk to determine your level of cardiorespiratory fitness.

Fitness Ratings: 1.5-Mile (2.5-k) Run/Walk

Males	Females	Score
9 min or less	11 min or less	High
9 to 14:30 min	11 to 15:30 min	Good
14:30 min or more	15:30 min or more	Low

TECHNOLOGY FILE

Cardiorespiratory Heart Monitors

Have students wear heart monitors while performing the 3-minute step test. At the end of the test, students can see their current heart rate on their watch receivers. If the heart monitors download to a computer, transfer and print out the data. Have students review the printout, noting their heart rate during the test and at the conclusion of the test. Students may wear the heart monitors during a variety of physical activities in order to determine whether the activity is aerobic or anaerobic.

Evaluating Cardio-respiratory Endurance

OBJECTIVES
- Participate in aerobic activities that develop health-related fitness. **TEKS C4B**
- Evaluate current levels of cardiorespiratory endurance.

TEACHING STRATEGIES

3-Minute Step Test
1. Make sure students are wearing appropriate nonskid footwear. **TEKS C3A**
2. Demonstrate the test before students begin.
3. This test can be administered to the entire class all at once.
4. When counting, use "up down" commands equal to 24 per minute.
5. Have students sit down immediately and count their pulse for one minute. Then have students apply cooldown. **TEKS C1A2**
6. Distribute *Fitness Check Worksheet 7-1* and have students record their pulse and find their scores on the Fitness Ratings chart. 📁

1.5-Mile Run/Walk Test
1. Students should prepare for the evaluation by working out for a period of five to eight weeks before the test and practice before the day of the test.
2. Create testing teams to time each other.
3. Have students record their results and find their scores on the Fitness Ratings chart.

Reading Check

Short term: lower resting heart rate, higher lung capacity. Long-term: lower risks for disease, less stress, more energy.

3 ASSESS

EVALUATING THE LESSON

Assign and discuss the Lesson 1 Review.

Name _____ Date _____ Class Period _____

Lesson Quiz | 7-1

Fill in the Blanks

Directions: *Fill in the spaces with the correct answers.*

1. Done regularly, aerobic activities strengthen two organs, the heart and _____.
2. The circulatory system consists of the _____, blood, and blood vessels.
3. During strenuous physical activity your pulse increases and the amount of _____ pumped per beat of the heart increases.
4. There are three types of blood vessels: arteries, capillaries, and _____.
5. The body system that exchanges gases between your body and the environment is the _____ system.
6. The principal organ of the respiratory system is the _____.
7. Because the lungs are not a muscle, they get their power from the _____.
8. Healthy lungs breathe up to _____ liters of air during vigorous exercise.

RETEACHING

Ask students to write two test questions based on the lesson content. Use them as a basis for a class discussion. Then assign *Reteaching Activity 7-1.*

ENRICHMENT

Have students make a poster of the circulatory and respiratory system.

4 CLOSE

Divide the class into groups and ask them to write a paragraph that summarizes the lesson and incorporates every vocabulary term from the lesson.

 **Mind OVER Matter**

Making Positive Choices

For many people, the hardest part of starting a program of aerobic conditioning is overcoming "inertia." A regular routine of inactivity can be a hard habit to break. But breaking out of such a routine yields great benefits to your cardiovascular system.

If you aren't physically active, make up your mind to take charge and begin a program of lifelong training today. There's no time like the present!

Long-Term Benefits of Aerobic Activity

One long-term result of regular aerobic activity is **cardiorespiratory endurance.** This is *the ability of the body to work continuously for extended periods of time.* Also known as *cardiovascular fitness,* cardiorespiratory endurance offers many benefits. People who have a high level of cardiorespiratory fitness have lowered risks of adult lifestyle diseases, such as cardiovascular disease, type 2 diabetes, and obesity. They also

- have increased energy.
- have less stress in their lives.
- look and feel better.

An Aerobic Lifestyle

Cardiorespiratory endurance increases your chances for living a longer and healthier life. The death rate from cardiovascular and other lifestyle diseases is much higher among adults who are inactive, or have low levels of cardiorespiratory endurance, than it is for those with higher levels.

As a teen, you may think that "heart health" is an adult concern. However, your adult years are just around the corner. A high level of fitness and health will be easier to maintain as an adult if you develop positive fitness behaviors and attitudes now. By engaging in regular aerobic activity now, you can reduce your risk of developing lifestyle diseases later.

 Reading Check

Summarize Make a list of both the immediate and long-term benefits of aerobic activity.

Lesson 1 Review

Using complete sentences, answer the following questions on a sheet of paper.

Reviewing Facts and Vocabulary

1. **Vocabulary** Define *aerobic activity.*
2. **Recall** What two body systems are most immediately involved in aerobic conditioning?

Thinking Critically

3. **Analyze** What is one benefit of aerobic activity to the heart? to the lungs?
4. **Synthesize** At what age do you think people should be encouraged to begin aerobic conditioning? At what age do you think people should be encouraged to stop? Explain your answers.

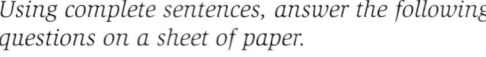 **Personal Fitness Planning**

Planning a Workout Design a walking or jogging course in or around your neighborhood that allows you to cover 2 miles in 20 to 30 minutes. When choosing your course, you should consider all safety issues and factors that will affect your intensity (hills, bridges, type of surface, and so on).

Lesson 1 Review

Answers to Lesson 1 Review

1. Continuous activity that requires large amounts of oxygen.
2. Circulatory and respiratory systems.
3. Answers will vary, but may include: makes the heart pump blood more efficiently; increases lung capacity.
4. Because of the long-term benefits, aerobic activity should be a lifelong behavior. Students should use facts from the text to support their answers.

Problems and Care of Your Heart and Lungs

Yஒu do not have to think about your heart beating because the process is automatic. So is the action of your lungs as you breathe. What is *not* automatic is care of these two organs and their body systems. Maintaining the health of these two systems requires both an awareness of health risk factors and a lifestyle that reduces your risks.

Risk Factors and Lifestyle Disease

Rolf and Ray are identical twins, although you might not know it to look at them. Rolf looks about 10 years older than his brother. He spends most of his time in front of the TV with a bowl of snacks. Ray, by contrast, works out at the gym regularly and maintains a healthful eating plan.

The more important difference between Rolf and Ray is one that is not plainly visible. That is because it is on the inside. The arteries leading to Rolf's heart have begun to close up, as a result of his unhealthful lifestyle. He is in the early stages of heart disease.

Heart disease, lung cancer, and other illnesses of the circulatory and respiratory systems are sometimes referred to as **lifestyle diseases.** These are *diseases that are the result of certain lifestyle choices.* Some lifestyles involve risk factors. Risk factors increase a person's

What You Will Do

- Identify changeable risk factors that can lead to diseases of the heart and lungs.
- Explain diseases that can result from certain lifestyles.
- Apply healthy behaviors that can reduce the risk of developing lifestyle diseases.

Terms to Know

lifestyle diseases
cardiovascular disease (CVD)
atherosclerosis
stroke
peripheral vascular disease
hypertension
emphysema
blood pressure

◄ Your lifestyle can affect your chances of developing certain diseases. *How does aerobic activity help to improve the health of your heart and lungs?*

Lesson 2 Problems and Care of Your Heart and Lungs **199**

Problems and Care of Your Heart and Lungs

1 MOTIVATE

GETTING STARTED

- Ask students to name as many diseases associated with the cardiovascular system as they can.
- Distribute copies of *Guided Practice Activity 7-2* for students to use while studying this lesson. 📁

IN THIS LESSON

- **Any Body Can**
  "Lance Armstrong: The Champion Who Wouldn't Quit," page 205

INTRODUCING VOCABULARY

- Ask students to start a chart, listing the diseases from the vocabulary list down the left side. Across the top, ask students to write *Causes, Symptoms,* and *Results.* As they read the chapter, have them fill in the chart.
- Have students use *Vocabulary Worksheet 7* or the PuzzleMaker software to practice vocabulary terms for this lesson. ELL 📁 💿

Photo Follow-up

Caption answer: Aerobic activity builds cardiorespiratory endurance.

Student Edition TEKS

Page 199: C5G

LESSON 2 RESOURCES

Teacher Classroom Resources
- 📁 Guided Practice Activity 7-2
- 📁 Reteaching Activity 7-2
- 📁 Lesson Quiz 7-2

Reproducible Charts and Graphs
- 📁 Reproducible Masters 7-1, 7-2

Multimedia
- 💿 Vocabulary PuzzleMaker
- 📥 Transparencies 42, 43

2 TEACH

Discussing

Discuss with students diseases of the heart and lungs. Explain to students that many of these diseases can be prevented through a healthy physically active lifestyle. **L1**

Ask students to discuss the statistics presented. Which of these facts do they find surprising? Have students research more facts about cardiovascular disease.

✓ Reading Check

A lifestyle disease is brought on by behavior. Any two: inactivity, being overweight, smoking, fatty foods.

Community Involvement

Encourage students to become involved with an organization such as the American Heart Association. They could join or initiate a fundraising campaign (such as a walk-a-thon). Have them consider involving other classrooms, schools, neighborhoods or the PTA. **L1**

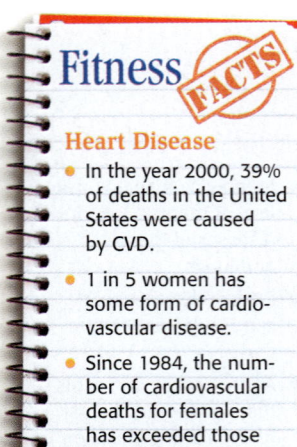

Fitness FACTS

Heart Disease
- In the year 2000, 39% of deaths in the United States were caused by CVD.
- 1 in 5 women has some form of cardiovascular disease.
- Since 1984, the number of cardiovascular deaths for females has exceeded those for males.

Source: American Heart Association, 2002.[1]

hotlink

cholesterol
For more on LDL and HDL cholesterol, see Chapter 4, page **120**.

► Being physically active helps reduce your risk of developing a lifestyle disease. *What other measures can you take?*

chances of developing disease. Some risk factors for heart and lung disease are

- inactivity.
- being overweight.
- smoking and using other forms of tobacco.
- eating foods high in fat and cholesterol.

✓ Reading Check

Explain In your own words, tell what a lifestyle disease is, and name two behaviors that can lead to such a disease.

Cardiovascular Disease (CVD)

In addition to being a lifestyle disease, heart disease is also considered a **cardiovascular disease**, or **CVD**. This is *any medical disorder that affects the heart or blood vessels.* CVD is the leading cause of death in the United States, claiming some 950,000 lives each year.

One health condition that is present in virtually all individuals diagnosed with CVD is **atherosclerosis** (ath-uh-roh-skluh-ROH-suhs). This is *a condition in which a fatty deposit called plaque (PLAK) builds up inside arteries, restricting or cutting off blood flow.* **Figure 7.3** shows the progression of atherosclerosis. The cause of atherosclerosis is not known for sure, although it is linked to a person's cholesterol levels. Regular aerobic activity lowers LDL **cholesterol** and raises HDL cholesterol and helps to reduce the risk of developing atherosclerosis.

200 Chapter 7 Basics of Cardiorespiratory Endurance

Myths & Realities

Myth 1 Only older people have heart attacks.

Fact 1 Congenital heart defects, diseases, and use of drugs can cause heart attacks at an early age.

Myth 2 Cigarette smokers do not have a higher death rate than nonsmokers.

Fact 2 Smoking does increase the risk of heart attack. It causes the blood vessels to constrict, decreasing blood flow to the cells. It increases blood pressure and strains the heart. It releases carbon monoxide into the blood, decreasing the oxygen supply in the blood.

FIGURE 7.3

THE PROGRESSION OF ATHEROSCLEROSIS

As fatty deposits build up, the blood flow to the heart lessens.

Which of the artery cross-sections shown most likely belongs to someone who is physically active?

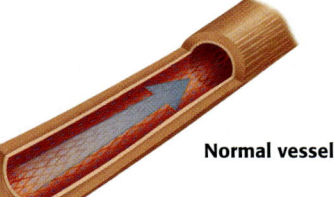

Normal vessel

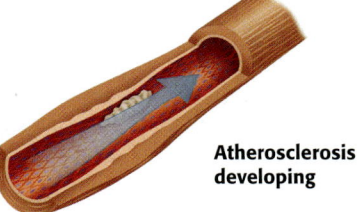

Atherosclerosis developing

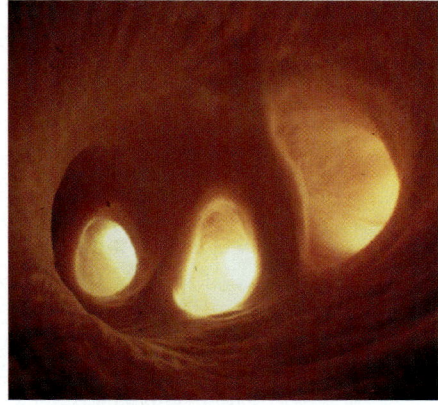

A healthy artery provides an open passageway for the flow of blood.

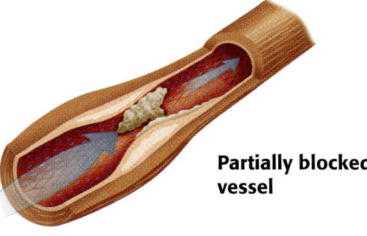

Partially blocked vessel

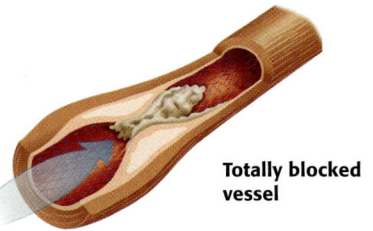

Totally blocked vessel

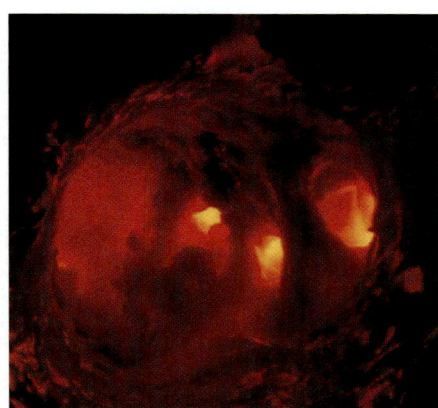

Plaques along an artery narrow its diameter and interfere with blood flow. Clots can form, making the problem worse.

Heart Attack

Each year 1 million people in the United States suffer heart attacks. Half of these people die. A heart attack results from blockage of a blood vessel that feeds the heart muscle. This causes damage to the heart muscle. Symptoms of heart attack include tightness in the chest, tingling or pain in the left arm, sweating, nausea, and

---

Chapter 7, Lesson 2

Figure 7.3 Using *Transparency 42*, discuss the process of atherosclerosis, which is the most common cause of CVD. Explain that the development of atherosclerosis is a complex process that is not completely understood. Atherosclerosis begins in many individuals during childhood or adolescence, and therefore it is important to control, if possible, the risks one has for developing cardiovascular disease. *Caption answer: The top picture, because the artery is unobstructed.* **L2**

Discussing

One major factor involved in atherosclerosis is cholesterol level. Tell students that they can lower LDL (bad) cholesterol by losing weight. Also tell students that they can raise their levels of HDL (good) cholesterol up to 5 units by jogging 10–12 miles per week at a pace of 10–12 minutes per mile. **L1**

Service Learning

Organize students into groups and have them contact a local hospital, the American Red Cross, or the American Heart Association for information about CPR. Have them share their findings with the class in the form of a demonstration or visual aid. **L3**

COOPERATIVE Learning

VITAMIN E Have students work in pairs to conduct research to evaluate studies on how Vitamin E has been correlated with lower incidence of heart disease. Then assign one partner to plan a day's meals that supply the recommended dietary intake of Vitamin E without exceeding the recommended dietary guidelines for fat. The other partner is to plan a day's meals that supply the recommended amount of Vitamin E without exceeding dietary fat guidelines. Is a Vitamin E supplement advisable?

Student Edition TEKS

Page 200: C4A, C5G
Page 201: C4A

Guest Speaker

Invite a cardiologist or other healthcare professional that specializes in the field of cardiopulmonary health to speak to the class about cardiovascular disease. What diseases does he or she typically treat? Why is cardiovascular disease important for teens to learn? What steps can be taken to prevent cardiovascular disease? What are some of the latest developments in treating patients? Have students summarize the presentation in a paragraph. **L1**

Goal: To improve the quality of life through early detection and treatment of heart attack and strokes. Discuss the importance of this goal with students. Review other goals of *Healthy People 2010* in Appendix B, page 384.

Helping Others

Would you recognize the signs of heart attack and cardiac arrest in others? Knowing them could save a life. They include:

- Tightness in the chest.
- Tingling or pain in the left arm.
- Abnormal or labored breathing.
- Loss of responsiveness.
- No signs of circulation.
- No movement or coughing.

If this occurs, call 911. Begin CPR immediately if you have been trained to do so.

---

shortness of breath. Anyone with these symptoms should get to a doctor or hospital quickly.

The loss of blood supply to the heart muscle during a heart attack may cause the heart to stop beating, referred to as cardiac arrest. However, all heart attacks are not fatal and a person who participates in regular aerobic activity has a reduced risk of suffering a fatal heart attack.

Sudden Cardiac Death

You may have read or heard stories about young athletes suffering cardiac arrest and dying suddenly during practice or a game. Sudden death from cardiac arrest is referred to as *sudden cardiac death.* Sudden cardiac death can occur in young and older people during strenuous activity.

Sudden cardiac death in people under age 35 is rare and usually is the result of a congenital (kuhn-JEN-ih-tuhl) heart defect (one occurring at birth). In the cases of people 35 and older, sudden cardiac death is usually associated with atherosclerosis. (**See Figure 7.4.**)

The best way to prevent this fatal CVD is to know the symptoms that precede it: a tight sensation in the chest, nausea, profuse sweating, and difficulty breathing. Another safeguard is to have a complete physical checkup before beginning a program of strenuous physical activity or exercise.

Stroke

The building up of deposits in the arteries poses a risk not only to the heart but to the brain. *When blood flow to a person's brain is interrupted or cut off entirely by the blockage of an artery, the individual is said to have suffered a* **stroke**. Some warning signs of a stroke include:

- Sudden numbness or weakness of the face, arm, or leg, especially on one side of the body
- Sudden confusion, trouble speaking or understanding
- Sudden trouble seeing in one or both eyes
- Sudden trouble walking, dizziness, loss of balance or coordination
- Sudden, severe headache with no known cause

A stroke, like a heart attack, can be minor or more major. A stroke usually results in damage to the brain and can leave a person partially or totally paralyzed. Sometimes when the damage from a stroke is minor, a person may be paralyzed only temporarily. However, a major stroke often results in death. If you perform regular aerobic activity or exercise, you will significantly reduce your risk for stroke.

Peripheral Vascular Disease

Peripheral (puhr-IF-uhr-uhl) **vascular disease** is *a CVD that occurs mainly in the legs and, less frequently, the arms.* It causes pain during physical activity or exercise. Primary risk factors for peripheral vascular disease include cigarette smoking and type 2 diabetes, which frequently occurs in overweight individuals.

More About . . .

STROKE Due to improving diagnosis and treatment of strokes, the survival rate has increased by more than 50 percent in the last 20 years. As with heart attacks, early recognition and medical intervention are keys to surviving a stroke. With increasing survival rates, stroke victims are requiring more rehabilitative assistance. When speech is lost, a stroke victim requires speech therapy to relearn spoken language. When muscle strength and coordination are lost, a stroke victim requires physical therapy. When job skills are lost, occupational therapy is needed to learn new job skills.

FIGURE 7.4

CAUSES OF SUDDEN CARDIAC DEATH

The causes of sudden cardiac death vary with age. *Compare the percentage of individuals under 35 who died of enlarged heart with the percentage 35 and over who died of the same CVD.*

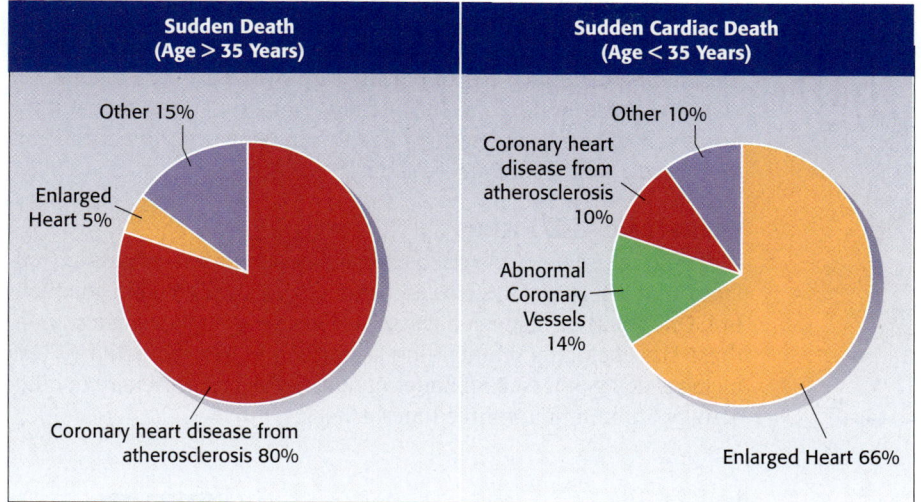

Sudden Death (Age > 35 Years)
- Other 15%
- Enlarged Heart 5%
- Coronary heart disease from atherosclerosis 80%

Sudden Cardiac Death (Age < 35 Years)
- Other 10%
- Coronary heart disease from atherosclerosis 10%
- Abnormal Coronary Vessels 14%
- Enlarged Heart 66%

Hypertension

High blood pressure, or **hypertension,** is a key risk factor in heart attacks, stroke, and heart failure. Because this CVD presents no symptoms, it is sometimes referred to as the "silent killer."

In 90 to 95 percent of all cases, the cause of hypertension is unknown. In fact, you can have the CVD for years without knowing it. Fortunately, hypertension can be treated effectively and safely under a doctor's supervision.

 Reading Check

Identify Select and describe one of the cardiovascular diseases mentioned in the previous sections.

Diseases of the Lung

Two lifestyle diseases of the respiratory system that deserve specific mention are lung cancer and emphysema (em-fuh-ZEE-muh). Of the 200,000 deaths from lung cancer each year, approximately half are directly linked to cigarette smoking. In fact, the American Cancer Society has singled out this deadly habit as the single most preventable cause of death in our society.

▼ Smoking is a dangerous habit—it kills more Americans each year than all other listed causes combined. *What are some other reasons people should avoid smoking?*

Smoking—*400,000*
Car accidents—*42,000*
Alcohol—*36,000*
Suicide—*30,000*
Homicides—*20,000*
Illicit Drugs—*20,000*
HIV/AIDS—*16,000*
Fires—*3,600*

Source: Centers for Disease Control and Prevention, 2003.²

Lesson 2 Problems and Care of Your Heart and Lungs **203**

COOPERATIVE Learning

EXERCISE AND DEEP BREATHING Professionals such as voice teachers, yoga practitioners, and exercise coaches say most people breathe too shallowly. They recommend deep breathing from the diaphragm or abdomen. Assign groups of students to study a system of breathing techniques and exercises taken from a class or book on one of the following: yoga, speech therapy, voice training, or stress management. Have them examine the benefits of deep breathing. Have each group share their findings with the class. **ELL**

Understanding Risks

Ask students to list other factors, besides smoking, that can affect proper functioning of their lungs and cardiorespiratory endurance. Lists may include smog, pollution, allergies, drug abuse, infectious diseases, and genetic diseases. Have them research and find out more about the effect of these on the lungs, and how they can be avoided or treated. **TEKS C3D**

Activity

Have students identify examples of how smoking is a changeable risk factor that affects physical performance and health. Have students interview someone who has quit smoking. They should find out how long the person smoked, what motivated them to quit, and how, specifically, has quitting smoking affected the way they feel physically. Ask them to identify positive changes in their health. Students should share their findings with the class. **L1** **TEKS C3D, C5G**

Cross-Curriculum Activity

Language Arts Have students write an essay persuading the audience to properly care for their hearts and lungs. Have students explain the relationship between physical fitness and health. They should focus both on the problems associated with poor health habits, as well as encourage positive behaviors. **L2** **TEKS C4A**

Understanding Risks

People who smoke do serious damage not only to their lungs, but to their desire and ability to become aerobically fit. They are less likely to take part in aerobic activities because they have reduced lung capacity. This makes it harder for them to sustain aerobic activity. This begins a vicious circle.

The best way to avoid this circle is to make a decision to avoid cigarettes and other harmful substances, and focus on fitness!

204

Emphysema is *a disease in which the small airways of the lungs lose their normal elasticity, making them less efficient in helping to move air in and out of the lungs*. Once the lung tissues have been damaged, they can never be restored. People with emphysema have difficulty breathing and develop a chronic cough. In nearly all cases, the disease is caused by cigarette smoking.

Care of the Circulatory and Respiratory Systems

The diseases discussed in this lesson can be serious and even life threatening. The best treatment for cardiovascular and respiratory diseases is prevention and fortunately, there are steps you can take to prevent many of the serious health problems that affect the cardiovascular and respiratory systems.

Changeable Risk Factors

Although some of the risk factors related to problems of the circulatory and respiratory systems are inherited, many are within your control. One behavior that you have already learned about that can counter these risk factors is maintaining a program of aerobic activity. This includes doing at least 20 minutes of nonstop vigorous exercise or other activity a minimum of three times a week.

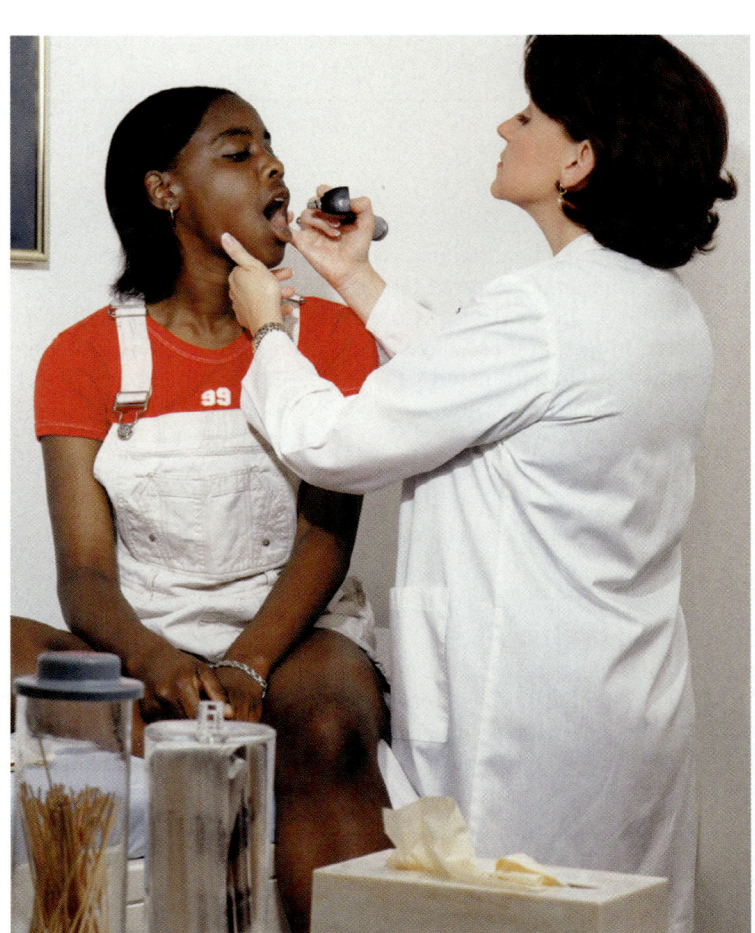

► Regular medical checkups are important for monitoring your risk factors for developing cardiovascular disease. *What is involved in a regular medical checkup?*

INCLUSION STRATEGIES

HEART DEFECTS Congenital heart conditions are often defects in the structure of the heart that can be repaired by surgery. Students with these types of congenital problems should maintain a healthy, active lifestyle to avoid future problems. Generally there are no restrictions after successful surgery. Students with chromosomal disorders (i.e., Down Syndrome) have a 40 to 60 percent prevalence of congenital heart defects. Contact a physician and parents before planning a physical activity program for these students. They will need to be restricted from any strenuous exercise.

Any Body Can

Lance Armstrong
The Champion Who Wouldn't Quit

Imagine receiving the news that you had cancer. What would you do? For an athlete named Lance Armstrong, the answer to this question was to work harder than ever.

Lance Armstrong was born on September 18, 1971, in Plano, Texas. At age 13, Lance won the Iron Kids Triathlon—a grueling athletic contest that combines swimming, bicycling, and running. After graduating from high school, Lance competed in national and international cycling competitions, including the 1992 Olympic Games.

Then in October of 1996, Lance was told he had advanced testicular cancer. Although he was given a 50-50 chance of surviving, Lance made up his mind he would not give in to his disease. After undergoing cancer treatment, he began to train again. He worked at improving his cardiorespiratory fitness until he was able to ride up to six hours (360 minutes) at a time.

In 1999, against all odds, Lance entered the ultimate bicycle race, the Tour de France, and came in first. He has since gone on to claim four more Tour de France titles.

Not everyone can win the Tour de France. However, anyone can regularly engage in aerobic activities for 150 minutes per week to improve his or her fitness. When it comes to improving cardiorespiratory endurance, Any Body Can!

Research

Lance Armstrong survived cancer and has won five Tour de France titles. Research another person who has overcome disease or poor health to lead a physically active life. Share your findings in a brief report.

Other activities that can keep your heart and lungs healthy include:

- **Avoiding tobacco.** Smoking puts added stress on the heart and lungs, and smokeless tobacco contains nicotine, a drug that increases blood pressure and heart rate. Exposure to secondhand smoke is also harmful.
- **Maintaining a healthy weight.** Being overweight has been linked to hypertension and heart disease.
- **Eating right.** This includes limiting your intake of foods high in fat and cholesterol. It also means eating foods high in **fiber**, which helps keep the arteries of the bloodstream clear.
- **Having regular medical checkups.** Seeing a health professional periodically for a **checkup** allows you to monitor the health of your circulatory and respiratory systems.

hot link

fiber
For more on fiber, see Chapter 4, page **117.**

medical checkups
For more on medical screenings, see Chapter 2, page **37.**

More About . . .

BLOOD PRESSURE Blood pressure is measured in two steps, using an instrument called a sphygmomanometer. First, the blood pressure cuff is applied to the right arm and the bulb is squeezed. Next, with the cuff still inflated, the nurse (or other health professional) releases the pressure slowly from the cuff and listens with a stethoscope for a tapping sound. The number on the dial when the first tapping sound is heard is the systolic pressure. The number on the dial when the tapping sound stops is the diastolic pressure.

Any Body Can

Ask students to share an experience they or someone they know has had with overcoming a physical setback to accomplish a goal. Ask them to write a brief paragraph explaining how they can apply stories, like that of Lance Armstrong, to their own fitness goals.

Discussing

Discuss with students the importance of going to the doctor for regular medical checkups. Explain that a basic evaluation is fairly simple, and is nothing to be afraid of. For teens, it can help detect problems of the circulatory and respiratory systems while they are young. The sooner they find out about potential problems with their health, the sooner they can adjust their lifestyle. **L1**

Activity

Have students ask the school nurse or other trained health professional to take their blood pressure. You may want to invite this person to class or have students do it on their own. Have students find out what else might be included in a regular medical checkup. **L1**

hot link

Reinforce the importance of nutrition and medical screenings in the health of the cardiovascular system. Have students review the facts in Chapter 2 and Chapter 4.

Reading Check

Any three: be physically active, avoid tobacco, eat right, maintain healthy weight, have medical checkups.

3 ASSESS

EVALUATING THE LESSON

Assign and discuss the Lesson 2 Review.

Name _____ Date _____ Class Period _____

Lesson Quiz | 7-2

True or False

I. **Directions:** *Place a "T" in the space if the statement is true; place an "F" in the space if the statement is false.*

_____ 1. Watching TV instead of going to the gym is a lifestyle choice that can lead to disease.
_____ 2. Heart disease is both a lifestyle disease and a cardiovascular disease.
_____ 3. If you have cardiovascular disease, it is likely that you also have atherosclerosis.
_____ 4. Half of all people who have a heart attack die.
_____ 5. Hypertension is also known as peripheral vascular disease.
_____ 6. When reading blood pressure, systolic blood pressure is the top number and diastolic blood pressure is the bottom number.

Multiple Choice

II. **Directions:** *Circle the letter of the correct answer.*

7. Which of the following are lifestyle diseases of the respiratory system?
a. stroke, hypertension   b. lung cancer, emphysema

RETEACHING

Ask students to chart the problems of the cardiovascular system and lungs, and include risk factors. Then assign *Reteaching Activity 7-2.* 📁

ENRICHMENT

Ask students to research one medication used to treat hypertension. Have them share their findings with the class.

4 CLOSE

Have students explain the proper way to care for the cardiovascular system and lungs.

Reducing Risks

While some stress can be a useful motivator, too much stress can impair good health. It can raise your blood pressure and heart rate. Some experts believe this changeable risk factor can increase your risk for CVD.

When the stresses of daily life get to be too great, try relaxing. Try one of the following options:

- Listen to music.
- Take a warm bath.
- Go for a walk.

What do you do to relax when you are feeling tense or stressed out?

Blood Pressure

As part of a regular checkup, your health care professional checks your **blood pressure.** This is *the force of the blood in the main arteries.* Your blood pressure rises and falls as the heart and muscles of your body cope with varying demands, including stress and vigorous physical activity.

Each time the heart muscles contract, blood surges through the arteries with such force that the artery walls bulge. The pressure in the arteries, which is at its greatest at this point, is called *systolic* (sis-TOL-ik) *pressure.* As the muscles of the heart relax to refill with blood, pressure in the arteries drops to its lowest point. This is called *diastolic* (dy-uh-STOL-ik) *pressure.*

Blood pressure is reported as two numbers, such as 120 over 80, which is written 120/80. Your systolic blood pressure is the top number. Your diastolic blood pressure is the bottom number. Normal blood pressure should fall below values of 140/90 on average, when measured on a regular basis.

Reading Check

Identify Describe three behaviors that contribute to a healthy heart and lungs.

Lesson 2 Review

Using complete sentences, answer the following questions on a sheet of paper.

Reviewing Facts and Vocabulary

1. **Vocabulary** What is *blood pressure*? Explain *systolic* and *diastolic pressure.*
2. **Recall** What are some symptoms of a heart attack?
3. **Recall** Explain sudden cardiac death from exercise. What can cause it in individuals under age 35? In those over age 35?

Thinking Critically

4. **Compare and Contrast** Compare the risk factors for CVD with the strategies for avoiding these illnesses. Make a list of five *do's* and five *don'ts* for healthy, disease-free living.

5. **Synthesize** How might you respond to the following argument? "So what if I smoke? I watch what I eat, and I get some exercise."

Personal Fitness Planning

Investigating Heart Disease Speak with a physician or learn through print or online resources about kinds of physical activity that are appropriate for someone recovering from a heart attack. Identify ways that inactivity is a changeable risk factor affecting health. Then design a walking/stationary cycling program for such a person. Include a description of precautions that should be taken and of differences between this program and one for a completely healthy individual.

Lesson 2 Review

Answers to Lesson 2 Review

1. The force of blood in the arteries.
2. Tightness in the chest, tingling or pain in the left arm, sweating, nausea, and shortness of breath.
3. Death from cardiac arrest; under 35: congenital defects. Over 35: atherosclerosis.
4. Answers should reflect an understanding of the importance of healthy behaviors.
5. Answers should reflect an understanding of controlling all risk factors, and the effects of smoking on the heart and lungs.

Influences on Cardiorespiratory Endurance

Dorothy, who is 81 years old, just completed her fourth marathon, a run of over 26 miles. Do you know any remarkable older adults like Dorothy? What permits some people to stay fit well into their later years? What are the advantages of staying aerobically fit? In this lesson, you will find answers to both these questions.

Measuring Cardiorespiratory Endurance

As noted in Lesson 1, cardiorespiratory endurance is the ability of the body to work continuously for extended periods of time. Fitness experts generally measure cardiorespiratory endurance in terms of **maximal oxygen consumption,** or **VO$_{2max}$.** This is *the largest amount of oxygen your body is able to process during strenuous aerobic exercise.* Specifically, **VO$_{2max}$** measures the amount of oxygen (or O$_2$) in milliliters (ml) per kilogram (kg) of body weight per minute. In general, the more aerobically fit you are, the higher your VO$_{2max}$ will be and vice versa.

◀ It is possible to maintain high levels of cardiorespiratory endurance, regardless of age. *Why might a physically fit older person seem younger than his or her age?*

What You Will Do
- Describe how cardiorespiratory endurance is measured.
- Identify factors that influence cardiorespiratory endurance.
- Evaluate the effect of added weight on aerobic performance.
- Explain the physical, mental, and emotional benefits of cardiorespiratory endurance.

Terms to Know
maximal oxygen consumption (VO$_{2max}$)
fast-twitch muscle fibers
slow-twitch muscle fibers

hotlink

VO$_{2max}$
For more on VO$_{2max}$ and how to estimate it, see Chapter 8, page **221.**

Lesson 3 Influences on Cardiorespiratory Endurance **207**

Influences on Cardiorespiratory Endurance

1 MOTIVATE

GETTING STARTED
- Discuss the following with students: *How do you think your age, gender, and heredity might influence your aerobic fitness?*
- Distribute copies of *Guided Practice Activity 7-3* for students to use while studying this lesson. ☞

IN THIS LESSON
- **Active Mind—Active Body** *"The Effect of Added Weight on Aerobic Performance,"* page 209

INTRODUCING VOCABULARY
- Have students examine the phrase *maximal oxygen consumption* and then write a sentence explaining what this might mean.
- Have students use *Vocabulary Worksheet 7* or the PuzzleMaker software to practice vocabulary terms for this lesson. ELL ☞ ◉

Photo Follow-up
Emphasize the importance of maintaining fitness as you grow older. *Caption answer: Older adults can raise fitness levels by participating in regular aerobic activity.*

Student Edition TEKS
Page 206: C5G
Page 207: C5G

LESSON 3 RESOURCES

Teacher Classroom Resources
☞ Guided Practice Activity 7-3
☞ Active Mind—Active Body Worksheet 7-3
☞ Reteaching Activity 7-3
☞ Lesson Quiz 7-3

Reproducible Charts and Graphs
☞ Reproducible Master 7-3
Multimedia
◉ Vocabulary PuzzleMaker

2 TEACH

Discussing

Explain to students that their cardiorespiratory endurance is affected by some factors they cannot control. However, one factor they can control is their level of physical activity. The more active they are, the more aerobically fit they will be. **L1**

Cross-Curriculum Activity

Biology Have students choose a particular congenital disease of the heart or lungs and write a brief report on it. They should research and include information about how a person with such a disease should approach developing cardiorespiratory endurance. **L3**

Explaining

Remind students that evaluating health-related fitness is not meant to be competitive. By working to achieve higher levels of conditioning, they will experience the health benefits, even if they don't go on to set the world-record for long-distance running. **L1**

> ✓ **Reading Check**
>
> Slow-twitch fibers increase ability to do aerobic activity; fast-twitch increase muscular strength.

Photo Follow-up

Caption answer: The runner in the top photo probably has a higher slow- to fast-twitch because running requires cardiorespiratory fitness.

Factors Affecting Cardiorespiratory Endurance

Although Dorothy has managed to maintain a high level of fitness, her husband Arthur has fared less well. Even though Arthur is a year younger than Dorothy, he has suffered a stroke and is now confined to a wheelchair. Some people believe that such differences are a matter simply of genetics. Yet, there are other factors besides heredity at work. Among these are age, gender, body composition, and level of conditioning.

Age

As a person ages, he or she loses cardiorespiratory fitness. Generally, one's fitness level begins a gradual decline after age 25. The typical rate of decline in VO_{2max} is about 0.5 ml/kg/min. per year or 5 ml/kg/min. per decade. Part of this decline is due to a decrease in the heart's ability to work as efficiently as it once did.

Heredity

Your genetic makeup affects both your initial levels of cardiorespiratory endurance and your capacity to improve it. The amount of blood your heart can pump per beat is determined by your genetic makeup. Also, some people develop higher levels of cardiorespiratory fitness than others because they are born with a greater proportion of slow-twitch to fast-twitch muscle fibers.

- **Slow-twitch muscle fibers** are *muscle fibers that contract at a slow rate,* thus allowing for greater muscle endurance. Found in higher proportion in long-distance runners, these fibers are associated with an increased ability to do aerobic work.
- **Fast-twitch muscle fibers,** in contrast, *contract rapidly, thus allowing for greater muscle strength.* These muscle fibers, found in greater proportion in weight lifters, have little bearing on aerobic levels.

The skeletal muscles of young adults tend to consist of about 50 percent slow-twitch and 50 percent fast-twitch fibers. Adults who perform well at aerobic activity and have high levels of cardiorespiratory fitness have closer to 70 or 80 percent slow-twitch fibers.

Gender. After puberty, males on average retain higher cardiorespiratory fitness levels than females. The chief reasons for this difference is that males generally have higher hemoglobin levels and carry less body fat than females.

▲ The individual's ratio of slow- to fast-twitch muscle fibers can make a difference in his or her fitness level. *Which of the teens pictured likely has a higher proportion of slow- to fast-twitch muscle fiber? Explain.*

> ✓ **Reading Check**
>
> **Describe** What is the difference between slow- and fast-twitch muscle fibers?

What Teens *Want* to Know

What's the difference between conditioning and training? Conditioning involves physical activity to improve health-related fitness. It combines aerobic exercises, such as running, with anaerobic exercises, such as diving. Conditioning aims to improve overall health. Training usually focuses on skill-related fitness. In a training program one learns skills like pitching, batting, or swinging a golf club. Team sports and physical education classes combine both conditioning and training to help students achieve peak health and performance.

Active Mind Active Body

The Effect of Added Weight on Aerobic Performance

Have you ever wondered what carrying excess weight or being obese does to your exercise heart rate? In this activity, you'll find out. You'll determine for yourself what effect added weight has on your heart rate and RPE (rating of perceived exertion) during aerobic training.

What You Will Need
- Backpack
- Textbooks or small weights
- 12-inch high step
- Stopwatch, clock, or wristwatch

What You Will Do
1. Fill a backpack with textbooks or small weights. The total weight of the loaded pack should be 20 lbs (9 kg).
2. Strap the backpack to your shoulders.
3. Begin stepping up and down on a 12-inch step at a rate of approximately 24 steps per minute. Continue for three minutes.
4. Stop and measure your heart rate for one minute and record your rating of perceived exertion using the RPE scale to the right.

20	Maximum exertion
19	Extremely hard
18	
17	
16	Vigorous
15	Hard/heavy
14	
13	Somewhat hard (moderate)
12	
11	Light
10	
9	Very light
8	
7	Extremely light
6	No exertion at all

Source: Borg's Perceived Exertion and Pain Scales, 2002.[3]

Apply and Conclude

How did your heart rate and RPE with the backpack compare to the results in the Fitness Check in Lesson 1? Why do you think the results were different? How do you think gaining weight influences cardiorespiratory endurance?

Body Composition

Your percentage of body fat also influences your cardiorespiratory endurance. Carrying high amounts of **body fat** reduces aerobic capacity because fat is just "extra baggage" that does not help you burn calories. By controlling your body composition—reducing body fat and increasing lean muscle mass—you can improve your fitness level.

Level of Conditioning

Your level of conditioning can affect your cardiorespiratory endurance. If you are currently doing no aerobic activity at all, you can improve your fitness level by beginning a personal fitness program that includes aerobic exercises. Your potential for fitness depends not only on your initial fitness level but also on genetics, trainability, your application of FITT principles, and your specific goals.

✔ **Reading Check**

Identify Name five factors that affect your cardiorespiratory endurance.

hotlink

body fat
For more on body fat see Chapter 5, page **151**.

COOPERATIVE Learning

COMPARING HEART RATES Let students work in small groups to check, compare, and graph their pulse rates. Have each member take and record his or her own pulse three times: while at rest, after performing the step test, and after performing the step test with added weight.

Encourage students to discuss how their pulse rates compare in each situation. What do the differences indicate? Then have group members work together to plan and draw a multiline graph that shows the pulse rates of all group members in all three situations. **ELL**

Active Mind Active Body

The Effect of Added Weight on Aerobic Performance

This activity shows how extra body weight affects students' heart rate and cardiorespiratory endurance.

Teaching Tips

- Have students review their score from the 3-minute step test performed in Lesson 1.
- If students did not perform the 3-minute step test, have them do it before this activity. Allow ten minutes for students to rest between activities.
- Review the concept of *perceived exertion* first introduced in Chapter 3.
- Make sure students have an appropriate amount of weight in their backpacks.
- Have students take their heart rate immediately.
- Distribute *Active Mind–Active Body Worksheet 7-3* for students to record their results. 📂
- Ask students to demonstrate the skill-related components of coordination and balance during this activity. How was their coordination and balance affected? **TEKS C4C2,3**

Apply and Conclude

Ask students to identify ways that nutrition is a changeable risk factor that affects physical activity and health. How can good nutrition benefit their cardiorespiratory endurance? **TEKS C5G**

209

Figure 7.5 Use *Reproducible Master 7-3* as a handout or overhead transparency. Ask students to look at the benefits of aerobic activity. How does this figure reinforce what they have already learned about the relationship between aerobic activity and health? ☞ **L1**

Cooperative Learning

Have students work in pairs to create a role-play in which one student offers several reasons for not improving his or her cardiorespiratory fitness, while the other student tries to persuade him or her to start a program of aerobic activity. Have them perform these for the class and ask students which arguments they found to be the most persuasive. **L2**

Review with students the VO$_{2\text{ max}}$ for different individuals listed in **Figure 7.6**. Discuss the ways students can have some controls over their own levels of fitness.

✓ **Reading Check**
Answers should reflect an understanding of emotional and physical benefits.

Student Edition TEKS

Page 210: C4A, C5G
Page 211: C4A, C4G, C5G

FIGURE 7.5

BENEFITS OF AEROBIC ACTIVITY

Heart and Lungs:	• Lower resting heart rate • Increases in stroke volume at rest and maximal exercise • Decreases in heart rate at moderate levels of aerobic activity • Lower blood pressure during sub-maximal aerobic exercise • Better ability to maintain high breathing rates for longer periods of time	**Muscle Cells and Bones:**	• Increased ability to use oxygen in cells • Increased ability to store (energy) glycogen • Increased ability to use fat as a fuel • Increase number of red blood cells and capillaries • Can help increase bone strength which helps prevent osteoporosis
Blood and Arteries:	• Higher HDL "good" cholesterol • Lower LDL cholesterol and other "bad" blood fats • Higher hemoglobin levels • Decrease in blood stickiness • Lowered risk of atherosclerosis • Better blood flow • Lower blood pressure at rest • Improved ability to deliver oxygen to tissues and organs	**Body Composition:**	• Helps burn calories and control body weight • Helps increase muscle mass
		Emotions:	• Reduces stress levels • Improves regulation of stress hormones
		Image and Lifestyle:	• Improves self-image • Improves personal appearance with weight control • Increases functional health and functional fitness as you age and can increase your longevity

Benefits of Cardiorespiratory Fitness

The physical and emotional benefits of aerobic activity are listed in **Figure 7.5**. Participation in regular aerobic activities can reduce your anxiety and improve your concentration and alertness. Working toward your fitness goals can provide you with positive feedback that can improve your self-image. In addition, regular physical activity and exercise are associated with better regulation of stress hormones. Regular aerobic workouts help you decrease the production of these hormones and reduce daily tensions. They enhance your ability to deal with daily challenges.

Extended aerobic activity promotes the brain's release of mood-elevating substances called *endorphins* (en-DOR-fuhnz). These chemicals produce a feeling of pleasure. The person experiences less fatigue and a sense of renewed energy.

Aerobic exercise reduces the risk of certain preventable cancers, including cancer of the colon and rectum. There is also evidence that exercise can lower the risk of breast and reproductive cancer in women.

Promoting Coordinated School Health

INVOLVING PARENTS Have students plan a parent night of aerobic activities. They should include: a presentation, a short aerobic workout program, and refreshments. The presentation should highlight the benefits and importance of aerobic activity. The workout should include a warm-up/cooldown, as well as a variety of aerobic activities. Students should plan a play list of music for the workout. This raises awareness about physical activity, and brings students, family, and school together in a fun and educational environment.

Making the Most of What You Have

Several of the factors described in the previous sections are beyond your control. Among these are age, gender, and heredity. However, anyone can sustain a relatively high level of fitness, regardless of age, gender, and heredity. The strategy for doing so includes the following steps.

- **Start while you're young.** As a teen, your potential for cardiorespiratory fitness is greater than it will be at any time in your future. Begin a program of regular activity.
- **Stay active.** As **Figure 7.6** shows, an active 45-year-old female can achieve a VO_{2max} nearly as high as a less-active 15-year-old male. Highly trained female distance runners or cross-country skiers often have a VO_{2max} twice that of untrained males.
- **Pay attention to fitness factors you can control.** This includes your level of conditioning, your weight, and your body composition.
- **Make your body work *for* you, rather than *against* you.** A major source of muscle fuel is fat, and most body fat is lost by burning it in the muscle. Aerobic exercise conditions your muscles and burns more fat, helping to control your blood fat levels.

Reading Check

Describe Explain in detail one of the benefits of maintaining a high level of cardiorespiratory fitness.

FIGURE 7.6

VO₂MAX

Activity level, gender, and age are all factors that affect VO_{2max}. *Over which factors do you have some control?*

Group	VO2MAX (ml/kg/min)
Inactive Female	35
Inactive Male	40
Active/Fit Female	45
Active/Fit Male	55
Elite Trained Female	70
Elite Trained Male	80
Inactive Female (Age 45)	32
Inactive Male (Age 45)	35
Active/Fit Female (Age 45)	38
Active/Fit Male (Age 45)	42
Cardiac Patient (Male or Female)	20

Lesson 3 Review

Using complete sentences, answer the following questions on a sheet of paper.

Reviewing Facts and Vocabulary

1. **Vocabulary** What is VO_{2max}?
2. **Recall** Explain why males on average have higher VO_{2max} levels than females.
3. **Recall** Name two factors that influence a person's cardiorespiratory endurance level. Name two benefits of maintaining a high cardiorespiratory endurance level.

Thinking Critically

4. **Compare and Contrast** How do slow-twitch fibers differ from fast-twitch fibers?

5. **Synthesize** Wilbur is 15 and has a VO_{2max} of 30 ml/kg/min. What does this reveal about him?

Personal Fitness Planning

Evaluating Your Environment Make a list of environmental factors in your community that might be used to build your cardiorespiratory endurance level. Possibilities might include a long flight of stairs or hill that you could climb without stopping. Try implementing this challenge with your personal fitness program. Note your pulse rate before and after the challenge in your Fitness Journal.

Lesson 3 Influences on Cardiorespiratory Endurance **211**

Lesson 3 Review

Answers to Lesson 3 Review

1. The largest amount of oxygen your body is able to process during aerobic exercise.
2. Males often retain higher cardiorespiratory levels due to higher blood levels and less body fat.
3. Heredity, gender, age, body composition, level of conditioning, and lifestyle. Benefits include: concentration, self image, less stress.
4. Slow-twitch: greater endurance and aerobic work; fast twitch: more strength.
5. He is not aerobically fit.

EVALUATING THE LESSON

Assign and discuss the Lesson 3 Review.

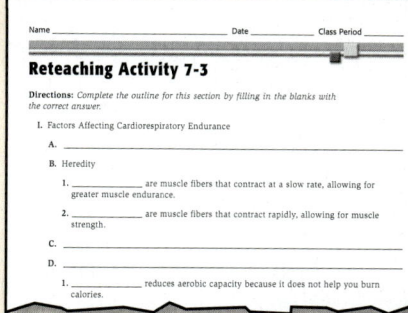

RETEACHING

Ask students to explain five factors that influence cardiorespiratory endurance.

ENRICHMENT

Have students research more about endorphins and how they affect mood.

4 CLOSE

Have students make a two-column chart titled, *Factors That Influence Cardiorespiratory Endurance* and determine which factors affect their own endurance. Which are controllable? Which are not?

Aerobic vs. Anaerobic Physical Activities

GETTING STARTED

- Ask students to discuss which would feel less strenuous on your body—sprinting 40 yards or jogging for twenty minutes?
- Distribute copies of *Guided Practice Activity 7-4* for students to use while studying this lesson. 📁

IN THIS LESSON

- **Active Mind—Active Body** *"Are You Working Aerobically or Anaerobically?"* page 213

INTRODUCING VOCABULARY

- Remind students that the word *aerobic* means "with oxygen." Ask them what the prefix "an" means.
- Have students use *Vocabulary Worksheet 7* or the PuzzleMaker software to practice vocabulary terms for this lesson. **ELL** 📁 💿

Photo Follow-up

Compare anaerobic and aerobic fitness. *Caption answer: You need all three for the demands of the sport.*

What You Will Do

- Compare aerobic and anaerobic fitness.
- Identify examples of anaerobic activities.
- Explain the benefits of interval training.

Terms to Know

anaerobic activity
anaerobic fitness
interval training

Lesson 4

Aerobic vs. Anaerobic Physical Activities

Total fitness is like a coin. That is, it has two sides. In the previous lessons of this chapter, you learned about one of these sides, cardiorespiratory fitness. In this lesson, you will learn about the other—*anaerobic fitness.*

What Is Anaerobic Fitness?

Cardiorespiratory fitness, as noted earlier, is developed by engaging in aerobic activities. Remember, *aerobic* means "with oxygen" and oxygen plays a key role in helping the heart pump blood to the large muscle groups of the body. In order to do its job, aerobic activity must occur over a sustained period of time.

Anaerobic activity works differently. It is *activity that requires high levels of energy and is done for only a few seconds or minutes at a high level of intensity.* The term *anaerobic* itself means "without oxygen" because the energy produced in such exercises does not depend on oxygen. Participation in anaerobic activities leads to anaerobic fitness, which may be defined as *higher levels of muscular strength, muscular endurance, and flexibility.*

▶ Anaerobic fitness is defined by muscular strength, muscular endurance, and flexibility. *How are these three elements of health-related fitness necessary in kickboxing?*

LESSON 4 RESOURCES

Teacher Classroom Resources
📁 Guided Practice Activity 7-4
📁 Active Mind—Active Body Worksheet 7-4
📁 Reteaching Activity 7-4
📁 Lesson Quiz 7-4

Multimedia
💿 Vocabulary PuzzleMaker

Active Mind Active Body

Are You Working Aerobically or Anaerobically?

Is the physical work you do more aerobic than anaerobic? Is it the other way around? This activity will help you find out.

What You Will Need

- Weight room access
- Stopwatch, wristwatch, or clock
- Access to football or soccer field
- 1-mile (1.6-km) track or walking course

What You Will Do

1. Go to a weight room, warm up, and then do a bench press with a weight you can press six to seven times. Write down your RPE (rating of perceived exertion) score for the lift. *(Note: Make sure you have appropriate weight training, including a spotter, before attempting the bench press.)*
2. Warm up, and then do two hard 40-yard (38-meter) sprints. Have a classmate time you and record your RPE. Record the average of the two trials.
3. Finally, warm up and then walk one mile. Again, record your time and your RPE after five minutes.

Apply and Conclude

Which of the activities you performed were aerobic? Which ones were anaerobic? Did monitoring your RPE help you understand which was which? Explain.

Anaerobic Activities

Examples of anaerobic activities include running up two flights of stairs, sprinting 40 yards, doing a fast break in basketball, or swimming 100 meters as fast as you can. These activities require large amounts of energy—a requirement that your body cannot meet for very long. This is because your heart cannot supply enough oxygen-rich blood to your tissues and organs to meet the high demand. Therefore, your ability to work anaerobically depends on the ability of your tissues and organs to function with limited amounts of oxygen.

 **Reading Check**

Explain Tell the difference between aerobic and anaerobic activities.

Active Mind Active Body

Are You Working Aerobically or Anaerobically?

This activity will allow students to participate in both aerobic and anaerobic activities, as well as ask them to evaluate how their bodies respond to each.
TEKS C4B

Teaching Tips

- This activity should be performed over two to three class periods, or in one block period, to allow students enough rest time between activities.

- Have volunteers demonstrate proper spotting techniques (see Chapter 9) and apply weight lifting procedures (see Chapter 10).
TEKS C2A2, C3A

- Distribute *Active Mind–Active Body Worksheet 7-4* for students to record their results. 📁

Apply and Conclude

Ask students to write down their responses to the questions at the end of the activity. Also ask: Which activities did they prefer and why? Which activities did they find the easiest to perform?

Dealing with Sensitive Issues

SHOWING SUPPORT Because students have varying levels of fitness and physical ability, it is important that the evaluations performed in class are in a supportive, noncompetitive environment. Emphasize to each student that the evaluations are intended to raise their own awareness about their own personal fitness. Be sensitive to students who may prefer to work alone (if possible) and who may not want to share in class discussions. Offer praise to all students who participate with a positive attitude and put forth their best efforts.

Reading Check
Aerobic activity requires oxygen; anaerobic depends on muscular strength, endurance, and flexibility.

2 TEACH

Explaining

Explain that anaerobic activities, such as sprinting, do not depend on aerobic fitness, but rather strength and power supplied to the body in relatively short bursts.

Encourage students to perform the fitness evaluations, such as the talk test in Chapter 3 and the step test in Lesson 1, periodically during the course. Students can continue to monitor their fitness levels and track their own progress.

Cooperative Learning

In groups, have students make a chart with two columns. In one column, students should list as many aerobic activities as they can. In the other, they should list as many anaerobic activities as they can. **L1**

Activity

Ask students to observe a sporting event, paying close attention to which components of the sport require aerobic work and which depend on the body to work anaerobically. Ask them to create a chart, diagram, or drawing that shows the various aerobic and anaerobic components of the sport. **L2**

✓ Reading Check

High-intensity activity alternating with low-intensity recovery.

hotlink

talk test
For more on the talk test and scoring, see Chapter 3, page **86**.

Aerobic versus Anaerobic Work

When you can meet your energy needs by supplying large amounts of oxygen to your body, you are working primarily in an aerobic mode. If you cannot meet the oxygen demands of a high-intensity physical activity, your body is more conditioned to working anaerobically. To determine which mode your body operates in, try the **talk test** on page **86**, if you have not already done so. This test involves carrying on a conversation while working steadily. If you are unable to pass the talk test because you are breathless at a high work intensity, you are working anaerobically.

Many physical activities and sports are part aerobic and part anaerobic. For, example, tennis is played more or less continuously over a sustained period of time, which works the heart and lungs (aerobic). The sport also involves short bursts of intense activity—for example, sprinting and hitting the ball hard—mixed in with short rest periods (anaerobic).

▲ These people are engaging in fitness activities. *Which of the activities shown is anaerobic? Explain.*

Promoting Coordinated School Health

COMMUNITY FITNESS Have students explore free or low-cost exercise options in their community. Do schools, recreation parks or churches offer workout facilities? Do many large apartment buildings provide swimming pools or gyms? Does the local YMCA or YWCA have a gym? Are safe bike paths or lanes provided in their area? Do appropriate jogging paths exist? Is walking, jogging, or cycling safe? Are they near a body of water appropriate for water sports? Encourage students to create a fitness directory based on their findings.

Interval Training

One way of achieving the best of both types of activity at once is through interval training. This is *a program in which high-intensity physical activities alternate with low-intensity recovery bouts for several minutes at a time.* Sprinting along the straight-aways on a track and walking or jogging around the curves for several laps is an example of interval training.

Advantages of Interval Training

For individuals just starting out, interval training has several advantages over activities and exercises that are exclusively aerobic or anaerobic. First, such training allows you to work at higher intensities for longer periods of time than you otherwise could in a continuous manner. By increasing intensity level for short periods during your workout you enable your body to burn more calories than it would working at a constant intensity level. It also increases your ability to work at higher intensities. In addition, interval training improves skill-related fitness and health-related fitness simultaneously.

 **Reading Check**

Explain What is interval training?

▲ Interval training can allow you to work aerobically and anaerobically in the same workout. *Why might interval training be a good way to start an overall fitness program?*

Lesson 4 Review

Using complete sentences, answer the following questions on a sheet of paper.

Reviewing Facts and Vocabulary

1. **Vocabulary** What is *anaerobic activity*?
2. **Recall** What is *interval training*?

Thinking Critically

3. **Analyze** Explain how a physical activity such as handball might be classified as both aerobic and anaerobic.
4. **Synthesize** Karen is interested in improving her anaerobic fitness level in order to participate in soccer. Is soccer primarily an aerobic

or anaerobic sport? List three activities Karen can do to improve her anaerobic fitness level.

Personal Fitness Planning

Participating in Aerobic Activity Determine whether you can jump rope for three minutes at a rate of 120 skips per minute. If you can, you are working primarily in an aerobic mode. If not then you are working primarily in an anaerobic mode. Find two activities that will help you improve or maintain your cardiorespiratory endurance.

Lesson 4 Aerobic vs. Anaerobic Physical Activities **215**

---

3 ASSESS

EVALUATING THE LESSON

Assign and discuss the Lesson 4 Review.

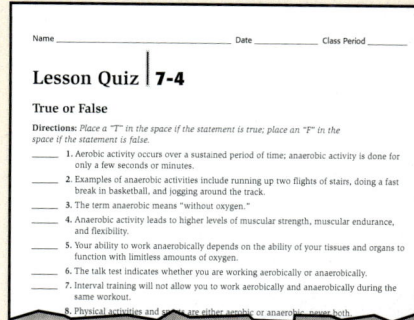

RETEACHING

Ask: What is required of the body in performing an aerobic activity well? An anaerobic activity?

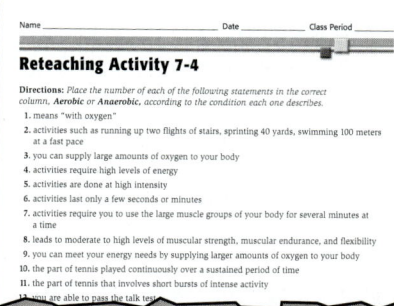

ENRICHMENT

Have students create a puppet show intended for elementary students that describes and demonstrates aerobic and anaerobic exercise.

Lesson 4 Review

Answers to Lesson 4 Review

1. Activity that is done for a few seconds at high intensity.
2. A program of high-intensity workouts and low-intensity recovery bouts.
3. Running is aerobic; hitting the ball is anaerobic.
4. Soccer is both aerobic and anaerobic. She can practice by sprinting, swimming, or lifting weights.

4 CLOSE

Discuss how interval training can be used by athletes in training as well as by individuals with injuries.

CHAPTER 7 Review

CHECKING COMPREHENSION

- Assign and discuss the chapter review.
- Use the Puzzlemaker CD-ROM to review vocabulary. 💿

CHAPTER 7 REVIEW ANSWERS

True/False

1. False
2. True
3. True
4. False
5. False
6. True
7. False
8. True
9. True
10. True

Multiple Choice

11. b
12. c
13. a
14. c
15. d
16. a
17. b
18. d
19. d
20. b

Discussion

21. Answers will vary, but might include: walking, doing alternating intervals of jogging and brisk walking, swimming laps, riding a bike, or stair-stepping.
22. Answers will vary but might include lower resting heart rate, more blood pumped per beat, better ability to maintain high breathing rates, lower LDL cholesterol, reduced stress.
23. Increased muscular strength, muscular endurance, and flexibility.

Vocabulary

24. g
25. c
26. e
27. b
28. a
29. d
30. f

TRUE/FALSE

On a sheet of paper, write the numbers 1–10. Write True or False for each statement below.

1. The main organ of the circulatory system is the lungs.
2. The heart beats at different rates depending upon whether your body is at rest or at work.
3. Atherosclerosis is a condition in which a fatty deposit called plaque builds up inside arteries.
4. When blood flow to a person's heart is cut off by a blocked artery, the person has suffered a stroke.
5. Hypertension is a disease in which the small airways of the lungs lose normal elasticity.
6. VO_{2max} is the largest amount of oxygen your body is able to process during strenuous aerobic exercise.
7. Slow-twitch muscle fibers are associated with your ability to do anaerobic work.
8. One benefit of regular aerobic activity is reduced anxiety and improved concentration.
9. Anaerobic activity requires high levels of energy and is done very briefly at a high level of intensity.
10. Interval training is a program in which high-intensity physical activities alternate with low-intensity recovery bouts for several minutes at a time.

MULTIPLE CHOICE

On a sheet of paper, write the letter of the word or phrase that best completes each statement.

11. Of the following, the organ that is NOT part of the circulatory system is
    a. the heart.
    b. the diaphragm.
    c. the capillaries.
    d. the arteries.

12. Done regularly, aerobic activity does all of the following EXCEPT
    a. strengthen the heart.
    b. strengthen the lungs.
    c. strengthen the arm muscles.
    d. raise the heart rate.
13. The diaphragm is
    a. a muscle.
    b. part of the heart.
    c. part of the circulatory system.
    d. all of the above.
14. Of the following, the one that is NOT a benefit of regular aerobic activity is
    a. increased energy.
    b. less stress.
    c. immunity from disease.
    d. looking and feeling better.
15. Of the following, the one that is NOT a risk factor for heart and lung disease is
    a. inactivity.
    b. being overweight.
    c. smoking.
    d. avoiding foods high in fat.
16. A CVD is
    a. a disease of the circulatory system.
    b. a device for measuring cardiorespiratory fitness.
    c. a machine that increases anaerobic fitness.
    d. none of the above.
17. Another name for hypertension is
    a. cardiorespiratory fitness.
    b. high blood pressure.
    c. heart attack.
    d. cardiorespiratory endurance.
18. Factors affecting cardiorespiratory endurance include
    a. age.   c. heredity.
    b. gender.   d. all of the above.
19. All of the following are anaerobic activities EXCEPT
    a. running up a flight of stairs.
    b. sprinting 40 yards.
    c. swimming 100 meters.
    d. 30 minutes on a treadmill.
20. Interval training may best be defined as
    a. exercising on different days.
    b. alternating high-intensity work with low-intensity work.
    c. alternating high-intensity work with rest periods.
    d. exercising different body parts.

Critical Thinking

31. You can reduce your risk by developing and maintaining a cardiovascular workout program and avoiding tobacco, maintaining a healthy weight, eating right, and having medical checkups.
32. Interval training can be designed so that you are combining moderate to vigorous exercise periods with short recovery periods. It can be used by athletes, students in personal fitness classes, or individuals in rehabilitation programs.

DISCUSSION

Using complete sentences, answer the following questions on a sheet of paper.

21. List and identify five different physical activities or exercises that will help you improve or maintain your cardiorespiratory fitness level.
22. List and describe five benefits of cardiorespiratory conditioning that a previously inactive young adult might realize after 8 to 30 weeks of training.
23. What are the benefits of anaerobic fitness?

VOCABULARY

On a sheet of paper, write the letter of the term from Column B that best fits the definition in Column A.

Column A

24. A disease in which the small airways of the lungs lose their normal elasticity.
25. The muscle between the chest cavity and the abdomen.
26. Arteries, veins, and capillaries.
27. Sprinting the straight-aways on a track and walking/jogging the curves for several laps.
28. An iron-rich compound in the blood.
29. The force of the blood in the main arteries.
30. Higher levels of muscular strength, muscular endurance, and flexibility.

Column B

a. hemoglobin
b. interval
c. diaphragm
d. blood pressure
e. circulatory system
f. anaerobic
g. emphysema

CRITICAL THINKING

Using complete sentences, answer the following questions on a sheet of paper.

31. **Explain** How can you reduce your risk of cardiovascular disease?

32. **Discuss** How can you use interval training in your personal cardiorespiratory fitness plan? Explain your answer.

CASE STUDY

DIANE'S FITNESS LEVEL

Diane, who is now seventeen, was very active earlier in her teens. She participated regularly in aerobic dance, walking, and swimming. However, in the past year she has become very inactive because she works at a part-time job after school and is taking several honors courses, which keeps her busy much of the time. Lately, Diane has begun feeling tired and has low levels of energy. Because she has never had a class that educated her in personal fitness, she needs the help of someone knowledgeable to design and implement a fitness program. That someone is you!

HERE IS YOUR ASSIGNMENT:

Organize a list of factors Diane should consider before beginning a moderate-to-vigorous personal cardiovascular fitness program. Then list the recommendations you would make for the first two weeks of her conditioning. Use the following keys to help you:

KEYS TO HELP YOU

- Consider Diane's history of personal aerobic activity and exercise.
- Consider how she should evaluate her current cardiorespiratory fitness level.
- Consider her needs and goals (for example, how she will find time to do physical activity or exercise).
- Determine a reasonable plan for Diane that covers the concepts of overload and FITT factors.

EVALUATE

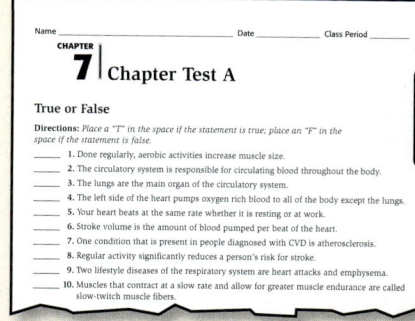

ENRICHMENT

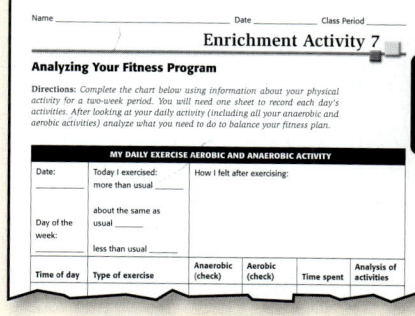

CASE STUDY

ANSWERS

Answers will vary but might include: Diane should complete the PAR-Q questionnaire in Chapter 2 before beginning her program, just to be safe. If she can answer "no" to the seven questions, she can begin conditioning by following a 20-minute walk/jog conditioning program, or 30-minute walking conditioning program. Following an initial conditioning period, she can assess her progress by taking a cardiovascular fitness evaluation of her choice from Chapter 7.

Student Edition TEKS
Page 217: C4G

CHAPTER 8

Lesson 1 Evaluating Your Cardiorespiratory Endurance

Lesson 2 Aerobic Activities

Lesson 3 Applying FITT to Cardiorespiratory Workouts

Lesson 4 Selecting Fitness Equipment

CHAPTER RESOURCES

- **Chapter Study Guide 8**
- **Vocabulary Worksheet 8**
- **Enrichment Activity 8**
- **Chapter 8 Test A**
- **Chapter 8 Test B**
- **Parent Letter and Activities 8 (English/Spanish)**

FITNESS *Online*

Ask students to take the STEP Personal Inventory for Chapter 8. Have them record their responses to the statements in their notebooks. Remind students that responses are private and for their use only.

FITNESS *Online*

Did you take either of the endurance tests presented in Chapter 7? How did you do? Tests like these measure your cardiorespiratory endurance. To learn more about your level of cardiorespiratory fitness, take the STEP Personal Inventory for Chapter 8. Find it at **fitness.glencoe.com**.

218

INCLUSION STRATEGIES

LANGUAGE DIVERSITY *Use the following suggestions to help students who have difficulty with English:*

- Pair English-language learners with native speakers of English who can restate key points in language that helps students comprehend important concepts.

- Direct Spanish-speaking students to the written summaries of this chapter in the *Foundations of Personal Fitness* Spanish Resources Booklet.

- Encourage Spanish-speaking students to use the Glosario provided in the back of the student text. **ELL**

Evaluating Your Cardiorespiratory Endurance

In Chapter 7 you learned about the basics of cardiorespiratory fitness. In this chapter, you will apply your knowledge. You will learn how to build and maintain healthful, lifelong levels of cardiorespiratory fitness. In this first lesson, you will learn how to evaluate your current fitness levels using a variety of physical activities, including running, swimming, and cycling.

Cardiorespiratory Fitness Tests

Several tests can be used to evaluate cardiorespiratory fitness. Two of these—the 3-minute step test and 1.5-mile run/walk test—were featured in the "Fitness Check" in Chapter 7 (page **197**). These tests, like the three that follow, measure cardiorespiratory endurance over time, distance, or both. They are:

- **Steady-state walk test.** This is *a test that requires you to pace yourself steadily as you briskly walk for 30 minutes and try to achieve a specific goal distance.*
- **Cooper's 1.5-mile run test.** This is *a test that requires you to jog/run as fast as you can to cover the distance of 1.5 miles.*
- **Steady-state jog test.** This is *a test that requires you to pace yourself steadily as you jog for 20 minutes and try to achieve a specific goal distance.*

▶ Some cardiorespiratory-endurance evaluations involve running or jogging for a specific amount of time. *What other aerobic activities can be used to evaluate cardiorespiratory endurance?*

What You Will Do

- Participate in aerobic exercises that develop cardiorespiratory endurance.
- Describe Cooper's 1.5-mile run and other methods of evaluating cardiorespiratory endurance.
- Evaluate your cardiorespiratory-fitness levels.

Terms to Know

steady-state walk test
Cooper's 1.5-mile run test
steady-state jog test
steady-state cycle test
steady-state swim test
exercise stress test

LESSON 1 RESOURCES

Teacher Classroom Resources
- Guided Practice Activity 8-1
- Fitness Check Worksheet 8-1
- Reteaching Activity 8-1
- Lesson Quiz 8-1

Reproducible Charts and Graphs
- Reproducible Master 8-1

Multimedia
- Vocabulary PuzzleMaker
- Transparencies 44, 45, 46

Evaluating Your Cardiorespiratory Endurance

1 MOTIVATE

GETTING STARTED

- Ask students whether they have ever participated in a walk, jog, or run to test their cardiorespiratory endurance.
- Distribute copies of *Guided Practice 8-1* for students to use while studying this lesson. ☞

IN THIS LESSON

- **Fitness Check** *Estimating Percentage of* $VO_{2\ max}$, *page 221*

INTRODUCING VOCABULARY

- Explain to students that *Cooper's 1.5 mile run test* originated when Dr. Kenneth Cooper developed a 12-minute run test to evaluate the cardiorespiratory endurance of Air Force personnel at Brooks Air Force Base in San Antonio, Texas.
- Have students use *Vocabulary Worksheet 8-1* or the PuzzleMaker software to practice vocabulary terms for this lesson. ELL ☞ ◉

Photo Follow-up

Explain that the treadmill is an effective measure of cardiorespiratory endurance. *Caption answers will vary but may include those listed in the vocabulary terms.*

2 TEACH

USING VISUALS

Figure 8.1 Discuss the figure and caption on this page. Have students think about their walking speeds as they walk between classes and during sports or leisure time. Then demonstrate various speeds by walking, jogging, and running a few steps in front of the classroom.
Caption answer: You should walk at a speed to reach the specific goal.

LIFELINE

Becoming a Fitness Mentor

Explain to students that in this course they are learning the basics of personal training. Point out that if they become familiar with the topics presented here, they can become personal fitness mentors for those around them, including friends and family. Encourage students to investigate positive and negative attitudes toward exercise and physical activity. As they recognize the attitudes of their friends and family, remind them to find opportunities to mentor others, particularly when they can use what they have learned to correct misinformation or prevent common injuries.
TEKS C5A

Student Edition TEKS

Page 220: C4C
Page 221: C4B

FIGURE 8.1

AVERAGE SPEEDS FOR ADULTS AND TEENS
At what speed should you walk when completing the steady-state walk test? Explain.

Test	Average Speed (Miles per Hour)
Walking	2 to 4 mph (30 to 15 minutes per mile)
Jogging	4 to 5 mph (15 to 12 minutes per mile)
Running	5 to 7 mph (12 to 8.5 minutes per mile)
Swimming	1.5 to 2 mph (30 to 40 minutes per mile)
Cycling	7 to 8 mph (8.5 to 7.5 minutes per mile)

The chart in **Figure 8.1** provides average rates of speed for performing these tests.

Your initial cardiorespiratory-fitness goal should be to complete these tests at good-to-better ratings for your age and gender. You will learn more about these ratings in the pages ahead. If you cannot meet the standards of these evaluations at first, keep trying. Your functional health and functional fitness depend on it. Once you achieve the goals, try to maintain or improve your levels of cardiorespiratory fitness.

Alternative Evaluations

Some people may have difficulty performing the tests described above. Among these are people with physical disabilities or injuries that prevent them from running, jogging, or walking. Two alternative tests for such individuals are as follows:

- **Steady-state cycle test.** This is *a test that requires you to pace yourself steadily as you pedal for 20 minutes on a stationary cycle.*
- **Steady-state swim test.** This is *a test that requires you to pace yourself steadily as you swim for 20 minutes.*

Others who may experience difficulty are individuals who are sedentary and/or obese. In this case, cardiorespiratory fitness is assessed by means of an **exercise stress test.** This is *an evaluation in which you walk on a treadmill or ride a stationary bicycle under medical supervision.* This method is also used when a medical screening suggests the possibility of a health problem.

220   Chapter 8   Developing Cardiorespiratory Endurance

LIFELINE

Becoming a Fitness Mentor

Do you have younger brothers or sisters? Maybe there are younger children in your neighborhood that you know. If so, there is no time like the present to get them involved in their personal fitness.

Becoming a *mentor* (a teacher or adviser) is a way of sharing the information you are learning in this program. It is also a great way to reinforce your knowledge and practice the skills you have learned in this course.

More About . . .

CALORIC EXPENDITURE Several equations are used to estimate the energy cost of walking or jogging in calories per minute. One resource for these equations is the *American College of Sports Medicine (ACSM) Guidelines for Exercise Testing and Exercise Prescription*, by Lippincott/Williams & Wilkins Publishers (6th ed., 2000). The ACSM equations allow you to use the speed of walking or jogging and the grade of the surface to calculate the estimated amount of energy required. These equations are often built into the microprocessors of exercise equipment that display the energy cost (in calories).

Estimating Percentage of VO$_{2 max}$

Cardiorespiratory fitness can be evaluated by measuring **VO$_{2 max}$**. As discussed in Chapter 7, VO$_{2 max}$ is the largest amount of oxygen your body is able to process during strenuous aerobic exercise. Remember, the more aerobically fit you are, the higher your VO$_{2 max}$ will be. Participate in a variety of activities that develop your health-related fitness, including cardiovascular efficiency. VO$_{2 max}$ can be measured directly with the *maximal exercise test*. This test requires specialized equipment and is performed under the supervision of a health care professional, such as a doctor or exercise physiologist.

However, you can assess your cardiorespiratory fitness on your own by performing one of the tests described in this lesson and calculating your *estimated percentage of VO$_{2 max}$*. In this activity, you will do 20 to 30 minutes of walking or jogging and try to work at between 50 and 85 percent of your VO$_{2 max}$.

Procedure:

1. Choose one of the following tests: the steady-state jog test or the steady-state walk test.
2. Before doing the test, make sure you are properly prepared. Use the checklist for cardiorespiratory testing (see "Preparing for Cardiorespiratory Fitness Testing" on page **222**).
3. Do the test you have chosen. (See **Figure 8.2**, page **223** or **Figure 8.3**, page **224**.)
4. If a heart rate monitor is available, use this to measure your heart rate during and after the test. Otherwise, take your pulse (as you learned in Chapter 3) immediately after you complete the test.
5. Record your pulse.

6. Use the formula that follows to determine if you were able to work at between 50 and 85 percent of your maximum estimated VO$_{2max}$. (*Note that the value of k in this equation is 61 for a male and 73 for a female.*)
7. Use the Fitness Ratings Chart for Estimated percentage of VO$_{2 max}$ to assess your performance.
   - If your estimated percentage of VO$_{2 max}$ for the steady-state jog test or the steady-state walk test was between 50 and 85 percent, you are at a good-to-better level of cardiorespiratory fitness.
   - If you do not work at least at 50 percent of your VO$_{2 max}$, you should continue to condition until you can achieve this aerobic fitness goal.

$$\text{Estimated percentage of VO}_{2 max} = \frac{(\text{Heart Rate} - k) \times 100}{(220 - \text{Age} - k)}$$

Fitness Ratings

Predicted %VO$_{2 max}$	Rating
50–85%	Good
Greater than 85%	Jogged or ran too fast—needs work
Less than 50%	Needs work

OBJECTIVES

- Identify what percentage of their estimated VO$_{2 max}$ students can work at for 20 or 30 minutes.
- Practice measuring heart rate, predicting maximum heart rate, and calculating estimated percentage of VO$_{2 max}$.

TEACHING STRATEGIES

1. Be sure students adhere to the five criteria listed on page 222 before beginning the evaluation.
2. Demonstrate each of the activities.
3. This activity requires a warm-up. Remind students to avoid working on a slick surface and to use nonskid footwear. **TEKS C3A**
4. Observe students during the exercise to make sure they perform the activities safely.
5. Have students record results on *Fitness Check Worksheet 8-1.*
6. Encourage students to develop and maintain a good-to-better level of cardiorespiratory fitness by participating in a variety of activities that develop health-related fitness. Teens and adults should be able to reach the good-to-better range on the 20-minute steady-state jog or 30-minute steady-state walk and also work for 20 to 30 minutes at between 50 and 85 percent of their estimated VO$_{2 max}$. **TEKS C4B**

Promoting Coordinated School Health

ON-SITE HEALTH SERVICES One characteristic of a successful coordinated school health program is an adequate level of staffing, with personnel committed to screening, surveillance, and management of health problems. Traditionally, the school nurse serves as the primary source of health information both inside and outside the classroom, with support from administration, parents, and community members. The nurse addresses the specific health needs of students and reinforces positive health concepts. Physical education teachers can benefit from this information.

Activity

A variety of activities can be used to develop cardiorespiratory efficiency. Students should be evaluated on at least one of the cardiorespiratory tests presented in this lesson (1.5-mile run, 20-minute steady-state jog, 30-minute steady-state walk, 20-minute steady-state stationary cycle or swim). Allow students to choose between the run, jog, or walk tests so that they will enjoy the conditioning program.

The 20-minute cycle and swim tests are best suited for students with physical challenges that restrict their ability to walk, jog, or run.

In some cases you may have to choose one test for the whole class based on time, facilities, or other classroom management issues. **L2**

Discussing

Emphasize the importance of preparing for cardiorespiratory fitness testing. Students should practice the conditioning protocols, listed on page 222, for at least five weeks before they are tested. **L1**

Reading Check

Students should participate in a minimum of five to six weeks of conditioning before taking one of the recommended cardiorespiratory tests.

Preparing for Cardiorespiratory Fitness Testing

To ensure an accurate reading on any endurance test, you need to prime your body. You can accomplish this through regular aerobic conditioning for at least five weeks. **Figure 8.2** provides a sample conditioning routine for the steady-state walk test. **Figure 8.3** on page **224** provides a conditioning routine for Cooper's 1.5-mile run and the steady-state jog tests. **Figure 8.4** on page **225** provides routines for the steady-state cycle and swim tests.

The checklist that follows offers other recommendations that will help you further prepare.

- **Verify the distance.** Make sure the distance you cover is accurate. For all tests except cycling or swimming, it is best to use a regulation track. The distance around a regulation track is exactly 400 meters—about 440 yards.
- **Pace yourself.** For example, by slowing down as needed—until you are able to go the whole distance without stopping. Gradually work at improving your rate of speed.
- **Practice.** Try covering the distance once or twice before the day of the actual test.
- **Consider weather.** Test yourself only when the weather is fair. It should not be too hot, too cold, or too windy.
- **Warm-up and cooldown.** Always perform a proper warm-up before each aerobic workout and the test itself. Do a proper cooldown afterward.

Reading Check

Explain What is the minimum amount of weeks needed to condition one's self for a cardiorespiratory fitness test?

Activities to Develop Cardiorespiratory Efficiency

This lesson provides you with the opportunity to participate in any of the several testing programs for cardiorespiratory fitness. It also provides you with information about conditioning before the test, and evaluating your performance after the test. Any one of these tests can be used to evaluate, develop, and maintain your cardiorespiratory fitness.

The 30-Minute Steady-State Walk Test

The six-week conditioning program, test, and ratings for the steady-state walk test are provided in **Figure 8.2.** For example, if Elena completed the 30-minute walk and covered 1.85 miles, she would be at a good level of cardiorespiratory fitness. A distance of 2.0 miles would be even better for her. Elena could then maintain her performance by following the maintenance program also shown in **Figure 8.2.**

Teacher-Coach Tips

Interval Training Students first learned about interval training in Chapter 7. Figures 8.2, 8.3, and 8.4 illustrate examples of interval-type training programs for walking, jogging, running, cycling, and swimming. Interval training has been used by coaches for many years to train athletes in a variety of sports to improve their aerobic and anaerobic fitness levels. Coaches usually use high-intensity intervals to optimize physical conditioning. To improve or maintain the cardiorespiratory fitness levels of students, teachers and coaches can use modified interval training as illustrated in this lesson.

FIGURE 8.2

30-MINUTE STEADY-STATE WALK TEST

	Day 1	Day 2	Day 3
	Minutes of Brisk Walking/Minutes of Slow Walking		
Week #1	3 minutes/1 minute–3/1–3/1	3/1–3/1–3/1	4/1–3/1–3/1
Week #2	5/1–5/1–4/1	7/1–4/1–3/1	9/1–9/1, or 15 minutes nonstop brisk walk
Week #3	10/1–10/1, or 17 minutes nonstop brisk walk	11/1–10/1, or 18 minutes nonstop brisk walk	12/1–11/1, or 19 minutes nonstop brisk walk
Week #4	14/1–9/1, or 20 minutes nonstop brisk walk	15/1–10/1, or 22 minutes nonstop brisk walk	18/1–9/1, or 24 minutes nonstop brisk walk
Week #5	**Perform the test and evaluate yourself** (see box below). If your rating is within the good-to-better range, begin the maintenance program found below. If not, continue conditioning for weeks 5 and 6.	22/1–8/1, or 26 minutes nonstop walk test	24/1–8/1, or 25 minutes nonstop walk test

EVALUATE YOURSELF. *The good-to-better ratings for teens ages 13 to 17 are as follows:*

Males: Walking 2.0 to 2.2 miles in 30 minutes.
Females: Walking 1.8 to 2.0 miles in 30 minutes.

| Week #6 | 25/1–6/1, or 26 minutes nonstop walk test | 26/1–4/1, or 28 minutes nonstop walk test | **Retest.** Those who successfully complete the test can move on to the maintenance program. All others restart conditioning on the Week #5 Program and continue for two additional weeks, then retest on day three of the second additional week. |

Maintenance Walking Program
- **For Moderate Fitness:** Walk 2 miles in 30 minutes, 3 times per week, or accumulate 225 minutes of aerobic activity per week.
- **For High Fitness:** Walk 2 miles in 30 minutes, 5 or more times per week, or accumulate up to 300+ minutes of aerobic activity per week.

Source: Medicine and Science in Sports and Exercise, 1999.[1,2]

Cooper's 1.5-Mile Run/20-Minute Steady-State Jog

Figure 8.3 on page **224** provides a six-week conditioning program for Cooper's 1.5-mile run and the steady-state jog tests. It also provides a way to rate test performance at week 5. For example, if Joe finished between 9:41 and 10:48 minutes for the 1.5-mile distance, he would be at a good level of cardiorespiratory fitness. A time of 9:40 or faster would place him at a better—or higher—level of fitness.

USING VISUALS

Figure 8.2 Display *Transparency 44* to introduce the 30-minute steady-state walk test and read through the table with students. Guide them in interpreting the figure by asking a volunteer to read aloud the steps for Day 1 of Week 1: *Begin with three minutes of brisk walking, followed by one minute of slow walking. Repeat three times.*

Discussing

Ask students to keep a daily log for one week to calculate the amount of time they spend watching TV, playing video games, or sitting at the computer. At the end of the week, ask them if they were surprised at the number of hours. Ask: What effect does this have on time spent doing physical activities? Discuss ways to replace sedentary activity with physical activity. **L2 TEKS C5G**

Activity

Present the following scenario: Two teens decide to increase their physical activity. Kristy begins walking to school, in-line skating, and swimming. Darryl decides to lift weights every night. After a week, Darryl gives up. Kristy, however, continues to be physically active. Ask students: Why did Kristy's plan work better than Darryl's? **L2**

Student Edition TEKS
Page 222: C4B
Page 223: C4E

QUOTES FOR LIFE

"Ability is what you're capable of doing. Motivation determines what you do. Attitude determines how well you do it."

—Lou Holtz
Football Coach, (1937–)

FIGURE 8.3

COOPER'S 1.5-MILE RUN AND 20-MINUTE STEADY-STATE JOG TESTS

USING VISUALS

Figure 8.3 Use *Transparency 45* for Figure 8.3 to help students evaluate their 20-minute jogging/ running cardiovascular performance. Ask students to describe how this activity is one method of evaluating health-related fitness. The main difference between Cooper's 1.5-mile run test and the 20-minute steady-state jog test is the fact that the 20-minute test involves continuous physical activity for at least 20 minutes. However, both are valid and reliable tests of cardiorespiratory fitness and require conditioning and pacing to successfully meet the time and distance goals. **TEKS C4E**

	Day 1	Day 2	Day 3
	Minutes of Jogging or Running/Minutes of Walking		
Week #1	2 minutes/1 minute–2/1–2/1	2/1–2/1–2/1	3/1–2/1–2/1
Week #2	3/1–3/1–3/1	4/1–4/1–2/1	5/1–4/1–4/1
Week #3	7/1–6/2, or 11 minutes steady jog or run	8/1–5/1, or 11 minutes steady jog or run	8/1–6/1, or 13 minutes steady jog or run
Week #4	9/1–6/1, or 13 minutes steady jog or run	10/1–4/1–3/1, or 15 minutes steady jog or run	10/1–8/1, or 16 minutes steady jog or run
Week #5	**Perform the test and evaluate yourself** (see box below). If your rating is within the good-to-better range, begin the maintenance program found below. If not, continue conditioning for weeks 5 and 6.	12/1–7/1, or 15 minutes steady jog or run	13/1–7/1, or 16 minutes steady jog or run

EVALUATE YOURSELF. *The good-to-better ratings for teens ages 13 to 17 are as follows:*

Cooper's 1.5-Mile Run
Males: Jogging or running 1.5 miles in 10:48–9:41.
Females: Jogging or running 1.5 miles in 14:30–12:30.

20-Minute Steady-State Jog (Ages 14–17)
Males: Jogging 1.8 to 2.0 miles in 20 minutes.
Females: Jogging 1.6 to 1.8 miles in 20 minutes.

Week #6	14/1–6/1, or 17 minutes steady jog or run	16/1–4/1, or 18 minutes steady jog or run	**Retest.** Those who successfully complete the test can move on to the maintenance program. All others restart conditioning on the Week #5 Program and continue for two additional weeks, then retest on day three of the second additional week.

Maintenance Walk/Jog/Run Program

- **For Moderate Fitness:** Walk/jog/run 2 miles in 30 minutes, 3 times per week, or accumulate 225 minutes of aerobic activity per week.
- **For High Fitness:** Walk/jog/run 2 miles in 20–24 minutes, 5 or more times per week, or accumulate up to 300+ minutes of aerobic activity per week.

Source: The Aerobics Program for Total Well-Being: Exercise, Diet, Emotional Balance, 1985.[3] Medicine and Science in Sports and Exercise, 1999.[1,4]

Explaining

Explain to students that these tests are based on authentic research gathered from teens their own age, and are part of the national effort to reduce the risks of disease and obesity. The 20-minute steady-state jog was originally developed in 1986 by a subcommittee of the Texas Governor's Commission for Physical Fitness. This test was adapted as an alternative to running and jogging tests by the authors and Dr. John Walker from Southwest Texas State University. The walk test is based on research conducted at Marcus High School in Lewisville, Texas. The authors have modified the original distance goals in cooperation with Dr. Walker.

L1

Similarly, if Lisa covered 1.6 miles in the 20-minute jog, she would be at a good level of cardiorespiratory fitness. A distance of 1.8 miles would place her at a high level. If she was unable to cover at least 1.6 miles, she would need to continue conditioning for two weeks and retest. Once Joe and Lisa are ready, they can begin a maintenance program, provided in **Figure 8.3.**

More About . . .

COOPER'S 1.5-MILE RUN Dr. Kenneth Cooper is a leader in promoting aerobic exercise. He became interested in the study of aerobic exercise when he was in the United States Air Force. He completed a study showing that aerobic fitness could be accurately measured with distance-run tests such as the 12-minute run and 1.5-mile run. In 1970, he founded the Cooper Aerobic Center in Dallas, Texas. Today, the center is known worldwide as a leading center for demonstrating how physical activity and exercise help improve and maintain functional health and fitness.

FIGURE 8.4

20-Minute Steady-State Stationary Cycle/ 20-Minute Steady-State Swim Tests

	Day 1	Day 2	Day 3
	2 minutes of cycling at moderate level of resistance/1 minute of cycling at 0 resistance *or* 2 minutes of moderate forward crawl lap swimming /1 minute of slow swimming		
Week #1	2 minutes/1 minute—2/1–2/1	2/1–2/1–2/1	3/1–2/1–2/1
Week #2	3/1–3/1–3/1	4/1–4/1–3/1	6/1–6/1, or 10 minutes steady cycling with moderate resistance/ moderate forward crawl lap swimming
Week #3	7/1–6/2, or 11 minutes steady cycling with moderate resistance/ moderate forward crawl lap swimming	8/1–5/1, or 11 minutes steady cycling with moderate resistance/moderate forward crawl lap swimming	8/1–6/1, or 13 minutes steady cycling with moderate resistance/ moderate forward crawl lap swimming
Week #4	9/1–6/1, or 13 minutes steady cycling with moderate resistance moderate forward crawl lap swimming	10/1–4/1–3/1, or 15 minutes steady cycling with moderate resistance/moderate forward crawl lap swimming	10/1–8/1, or 16 minutes steady cycling with moderate resistance/ moderate forward crawl lap swimming
Week #5	**Perform the test and evaluate yourself** (see box below). If your rating is within the good-to-better range, begin the maintenance program found below. If not, continue conditioning for weeks 5 and 6.	12/1–7/1, or 15 minutes steady cycling with moderate resistance/moderate forward crawl lap swimming	13/1–7/1, or 16 minutes steady cycling with moderate resistance/ moderate forward crawl lap swimming

EVALUATE YOURSELF. *The good-to-better ratings for teens ages 13 to 17 are as follows:*

Males: Cycling 5 miles or more in 20 minutes.
Females: Cycling 4.5 miles or more in 20 minutes.

Males and Females: Swimming 3/8 mile or more in 20 minutes.

| Week #6 | 14/1–6/1, or 17 minutes steady cycling with moderate resistance/ moderate forward crawl lap swimming | 16/1–4/1, or 18 minutes steady cycling with moderate resistance/moderate forward crawl lap swimming | **Retest.** Those who successfully complete the test can move on to the maintenance program. All others restart conditioning on the Week #5 Program and continue for two additional weeks, then retest on day three of the second additional week. |

Maintenance Cycling Program
- **For Moderate Fitness:** Cycle 6–7 miles in 30 minutes, 3 times per week, or accumulate 225 minutes of aerobic activity per week.
- **For High Fitness:** Cycle 6–7 miles in 30 minutes, 5 or more times per week, or accumulate up to 300+ minutes of aerobic activity per week.

Maintenance Swimming Program
- **For Moderate Fitness:** Swim 1/2 to 3/4 miles in 30 minutes, 3 times per week, or accumulate 150 minutes of aerobic activity per week.
- **For High Fitness:** Swim 1/2 to 3/4 miles in 30 minutes, 5 or more times per week, or accumulate 200 to 300+ minutes of aerobic activity per week.

Source: Medicine and Science in Sports and Exercise, *1999.*[5]

USING VISUALS

Figure 8.4 Display *Transparency 46* and discuss the stationary cycle test. Explain to students that this and the swim test can be useful for those who are injured or excessively overweight, or for those with other disabilities that prevent them from successfully meeting the good-to-better cardiorespiratory fitness levels for the walk, jog, or run tests. The 20-minute steady-state stationary cycle test is a new test developed by the authors, who based it on the work of the Human Performance Laboratory at Southwest Texas State University and their own review of the research literature.

Activity

As an alternative, you can choose to have students test their cardiorespiratory endurance with the outdoor 12-minute cycling test or the 12-minute swimming test, both of which can be found in Dr. Cooper's book *The Aerobics Way*, published by Bantam Books, 1977. **L3**

Teacher-Coach Tips

Swimming Efficiency Before administrating the 30-minute steady-state swim test, you should observe individually each student who is going to swim. Be aware that even students who claim to be good swimmers may have poor swim-stroke skills, which can cause them to be inefficient, burning more calories than necessary. Students should be allowed to practice the six-week interval swimming program to improve their stroke efficiency. This will allow them to swim at a steady pace and achieve good-to-better levels of cardiorespiratory fitness on the test.

Student Edition TEKS

Page 224: C4E

EVALUATING THE LESSON

Assign and discuss the Lesson 1 Review.

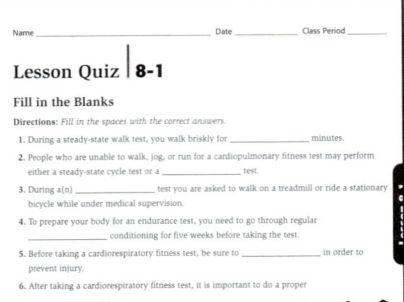

RETEACHING

Ask students to describe one of the tests they learned about in this lesson for evaluating cardiorespiratory endurance.

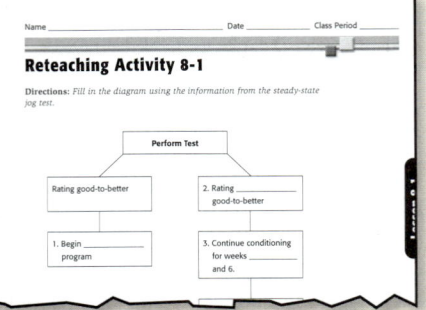

ENRICHMENT

Have students complete more than one of the cardiorespiratory tests and compare their results for each test.

Have students keep track of their adherence to their cardiorespiratory maintenance program for six weeks. **TEKS C4B**

226

Steady-State Cycle and Swim Tests

For people who are unable to walk, jog, or run, due to disability or injury, they may perform either the cycle test or swim test as described in **Figure 8.4** on page **225,** which provides appropriate conditioning, testing, ratings, and maintenance for both tests.

The cycle test should be performed on a stationary cycle, alternating periods of cycling at moderate resistance, with periods of cycling using no resistance. As in the steady-state jog test, fitness levels are determined by the distance covered in 20 minutes. For example, if Greg, who is unable to jog, completed the cycle test and covered 5.0 miles in 20 minutes, he would be at a good level of cardiorespiratory fitness. A distance of 6.0 miles would place him at a higher level.

The swim test alternates periods of swimming a forward crawl at moderate intensity with periods of slow swimming. As in the cycle and jog tests, fitness levels are also evaluated based on the distance covered in 20 minutes. For example, if Jamie completed the swim test and covered 0.5 miles in 20 minutes, she would be at a good level of cardiorespiratory fitness. Covering a distance of 0.6 miles in the same time period would put her at a high fitness level. Both Greg and Jamie can maintain their performance by following the appropriate maintenance program shown in **Figure 8.4.**

Lesson 1 Review

Using complete sentences, answer the following questions on a sheet of paper.

Reviewing Facts and Vocabulary

1. **Recall** Describe two alternate evaluations that are used for people who may have difficulty performing the run/walk evaluations.
2. **Recall** Describe the procedure for performing Cooper's 1.5-mile run test.
3. **Vocabulary** Define *steady-state walk test.*

Thinking Critically

4. **Compare and Contrast** Explain the difference between the walking maintenance program for moderate versus high cardiorespiratory fitness.

5. **Evaluate** If a 14-year-old female can walk 2 miles in 30 minutes, how would you rate her cardiorespiratory fitness? Explain your answer.

Personal Fitness Planning

Implementing a Plan Design a maintenance walk/jog/run program to help you maintain a moderate level of cardiorespiratory fitness. Make a walk/jog/run schedule for the next 30 days, and then implement your program by following your schedule. Then evaluate your cardiorespiratory fitness level once more, using one of the tests described in this lesson.

Lesson 1 Review

Answers to Lesson 1 Review

1. The 20-minute steady-state cycle test and 20-minute steady-state swim test.
2. Students should jog or run as fast as they can for 1.5 miles.
3. Walk briskly for 30 minutes for a specific distance.
4. The maintenance program for moderate fitness requires walking 2 miles in 30 minutes, 3 times per week; for high fitness, walk 2 miles in 30 minutes, 5 or more times per week.
5. She would rate good to better, based on her score.

Aerobic Activities

Arthur loves swimming. Beth enjoys jogging. Charlene likes dancing. What do these three teens have in common? All enjoy some form of aerobic activity. Regular aerobic activity promotes moderate-to-high levels of cardiorespiratory fitness. Many aerobic activities require little or no equipment, making them inexpensive to do. Best of all, they are fun.

In this lesson, you'll learn about some popular aerobic activities. These can be done alone, in a group, at home, or at a fitness facility.

Walking

Walking is the simplest and most basic aerobic activity. All you really need for a walking program is a pair of comfortable walking or running shoes and appropriate clothing. You can walk (or jog and run) indoors on a treadmill or outdoors on a track or measured course. You can also get a variation of walking and jogging movements by working out indoors on an **elliptical motion trainer.** This is *an exercise machine that mimics the natural motions of running but without placing stress on the joints.*

 Walking is a convenient way to improve your cardiorespiratory fitness. It requires little more than a good pair of shoes. *Do you recall the basics of selecting athletic shoes?*

What You Will Do

- Identify common aerobic activities and exercises.
- Investigate the benefits of various aerobic activities and exercises.
- Identify the purpose of cardiorespiratory-fitness equipment and accessories.

Terms to Know

elliptical motion trainer
pedometer
heart rate monitor

---

1 MOTIVATE

GETTING STARTED

- Ask students to list cardio-respiratory fitness activities they participated in regularly for the past month. Ask them why they have or have not engaged in aerobic activities regularly for the past month. Explain that they will learn more about aerobic activities in this lesson.
- Distribute copies of *Guided Practice 8-2* for students to use while studying this lesson. ☞

IN THIS LESSON

- **Active Mind— Active Body** *Researching Aerobic Activities,* page 231

INTRODUCING VOCABULARY

- Ask whether anyone can explain the meaning of the prefix *ped* in *pedometer.* Answer: *ped* is Latin for "foot." Then have students look up the definition of *pedometer.*
- Have students use *Vocabulary Worksheet 8* or the PuzzleMaker software to practice vocabulary terms for this lesson. **ELL** ☞ ⊙

Photo Follow-up

Ask students to consider the convenience and benefits of walking. *Caption answers will vary but should rely on information from Lesson 3 in Chapter 2.*

LESSON 2 RESOURCES

Teacher Classroom Resources
☞ Guided Practice Activity 8-2
☞ Active Mind—Active Body Worksheet 8-2
☞ Reteaching Activity 8-2
☞ Lesson Quiz 8-2

Multimedia
⊙ Vocabulary PuzzleMaker

2 TEACH

Fitness FACTS

Have students read the *Fitness Facts* feature on this page. Then ask them to research more fitness facts on conditioned athletes in other endurance sports such as cycling, swimming, or triathlons.

✓ **Reading Check**

Brisk walking is a moderately intense aerobic activity done at a pace of 3.5 to 4 mph; race walking is a vigorous activity with a pace of at least 5 mph.

hot link

Remind students that biomechanics, pronation, and supination are important concepts that can be applied to develop and maintain proper form for many aerobic activities. Have students review Chapter 2 for more on these topics.

Student Edition TEKS

Page 228: C1B
Page 229: C1B

Fitness FACTS

Conditioned Runners

● Elite marathon runners—those at the peak of performance—often train by running 100 miles or more per week.

● Elite women marathon runners often have a VO_{2max} of 70 or more, which is nearly twice that of an average 15-year-old female teen.

hot link

biomechanics
For more on biomechanics, see Chapter 2, page **54**.

pronation and supination
For more on pronation and supination and proper footwear, see Chapter 2, page **49**.

There are several kinds of walking programs that you can participate in. These include:

● **Brisk walking.** At a pace of 3.5 to 4 miles per hour, brisk walking is moderately intense aerobic activity.
● **Power walking.** Power walking is done at a speed of 4 to 5 miles per hour. The intensity level is moderate to vigorous.
● **Race walking.** Race walking is done mainly by competitive athletes. The pace is greater than 5 miles per hour, and the intensity level is vigorous.
● **Water walking.** Water walking is done primarily by people who are injured or in rehabilitation. It is also often prescribed for people who are severely overweight, because it avoids placing excessive stress on the legs and back. Water walking is performed in a pool in chest-deep or deeper water at low, moderate, or vigorous intensity, depending upon the person's needs.

Pedometers

An easy way of monitoring your progress and staying motivated is by using a **pedometer** (puh-DOM-uh-tuhr). This is *a device that measures the number of steps you take and records the distance you travel on foot*. Pedometers are worn on a belt. They cost about $15 to $20 and can be purchased at sporting-goods stores or department stores. A general cardiorespiratory fitness goal when walking with a pedometer is to try to accumulate 10,000 steps per day, or 4 miles. (Most pedometers require 2,000 steps for each mile for adults and about 2,500 steps for adolescents.)

 Reading Check

Compare Identify the differences between brisk walking and race walking.

Jogging and Running

Two related aerobic activities—jogging and running—are ideal for controlling body weight and maintaining higher levels of cardiorespiratory fitness. The difference between jogging and running is speed. Joggers move at between 4 and 5 miles per hour. Runners move at speeds of 5 to 7 miles per hour or faster. When starting a jogging or running program, progress slowly. (Review **Figure 8.3** in Lesson 1 on page **224** for a sample conditioning program for running or jogging.)

By starting your jogging and running programs slowly and with proper footwear, you can help prevent common injuries. For example, beginning joggers and runners often get shinsplints (pain in the front of the lower leg) due to wearing improper footwear or using improper **biomechanics.** Give your body plenty of time to adjust to the forces of **pronation** and **supination.** This will help you avoid knee and ankle problems that often occur if you begin your program too aggressively.

More About . . .

PEDOMETERS The invention of the pedometer has been attributed to Thomas Jefferson. However, in the fifteenth century Leonardo da Vinci developed a design that was gear-driven and would swing back and forth as one walked. Pedometer research in America has only recently been used to encourage people to become more physically active. The first brands of pedometers were considered too unreliable to be used effectively. However, newer brands of electronic pedometers provide more accurate measurement, and some can even record up to 24 hours of step information.

Heart Rate Monitors

A good way to monitor the intensity of your jogging or running program is to use a **heart rate monitor**. This is *a device that records your heart beat by means of a chest transmitter and wrist monitor.* There are many types of heart rate monitors. These can cost between $50 and $100, while more sophisticated models can cost even more. Many heart rate monitors have a function that allows you to set a beeper at a low and higher heart rate zone. You can use this feature to help you jog or run at moderate-to-high intensity without the risk of overtraining.

Bicycling

Bicycling is another way to develop and maintain your cardiorespiratory-fitness levels. It is a low-impact activity and is an excellent activity for overweight individuals because the body weight is supported. There is less of a risk of the types of injuries that can occur from jogging.

It is important to use good biomechanical form while cycling. You will need to make sure the seat is adjusted to a height that gives you good leg extension. (Your leg should remain slightly bent as you push one pedal completely downward.) When bicycling, be sure to wear a safety helmet.

Stationary Cycling

An alternative to conventional bicycling is riding a stationary bicycle. You and your family can purchase a good stationary bicycle for home use. Your school may also have stationary cycles. Some stationary bicycles allow you to monitor your heart rate and the number of calories you are burning.

Many health and fitness clubs offer "spinning" classes. These classes consist of alternating low-intensity stationary cycling with high-intensity cycling. The sessions are often set to music and conducted by a fitness trainer. This type of aerobic activity may be best for those who find that they are getting bored with their personal fitness program. It may help those individuals avoid reaching the relapse stage of the behavioral-change stairway.

✓ **Reading Check**

Analyze Why might stationary cycling be a more convenient alternative to cycling outdoors?

▲ A heart rate monitor is a useful tool in fitness assessments. *Under what other circumstances might you wear a heart rate monitor?*

FITNESS Online

Use online tools to help keep your heart healthy at **fitness.glencoe.com**.

Activity Download information sheets on lifestyle activities and risk reduction. Keep records of your progress to stay fit.

Photo Follow-up

Ask for a volunteer to explain the function of a heart rate monitor. *Caption answer: It could be used during conditioning to help monitor an individual's physical activity or exercise intensity.*

Explaining

Explain to students that they should evaluate marketing claims when buying fitness equipment, for example, when choosing a bicycle for outdoor riding. Encourage them to do comparison shopping for the bike that best meets their needs. For example, students should compare racing road bikes (usually very light with thin tires), mountain bikes (usually heavier with knobby tires for off-road riding), and hybrid bikes (moderate weight with tires designed for roads and lighter off-road riding). **L2 TEKS C4H**

✓ **Reading Check**

Stationary cycles are safer and are equipped with monitors for measuring heart rate and calories burned. Stationary cycling can be done in a class with a fitness trainer.

FITNESS Online

Help students recognize the relationship between physical fitness and a healthy heart. Direct them to Web Links at **fitness.glencoe.com** to track their heart health.

TECHNOLOGY FILE

Heart Rate Monitor Analysis

Have students wear heart monitors while performing a variety of aerobic activities, including jogging, walking, cycling, swimming, in-line skating, skateboarding, aerobic dance, stair-stepping, and kickboxing. If the heart monitors download to a computer, transfer and print out the data at the conclusion of the workout. Otherwise, have students stop every five minutes to record their heart rates. Instruct students to evaluate their results and explain the differences in heart rate between different activities and between different points in time within each workout.

▶ In-line skating is popular in many communities. *What are some safety precautions a person should take when skating?*

hot link

aerobic dance and stair-stepping
For more on aerobic dance and stair-stepping and how to perform these activities, see Chapter 12, page **366.**

Fitness FACTS

Dance

• Any dance—ballet, modern dance, tap, square dancing, ballroom dancing—can be aerobic if it is done nonstop over a period of minutes.

• To be safe and effective, you will probably need to take dance lessons to master the steps for a particular form of dance.

Other Aerobic Activities on Wheels

Other aerobic activities to increase cardiorespiratory endurance include in-line skating and skateboarding. To perform these activities safely, you need to wear protective equipment, including a helmet, knee pads, elbow pads, and wrist pads.

You will need to practice your balancing and coordination skills to be able to work several minutes at a time at these aerobic activities. When skating or skateboarding, you should avoid hills and congested traffic areas, and always keep your safety and the safety of others a top priority.

Aerobic Dance and Stair-Stepping

Aerobic dance and **stair stepping** are aerobic activities that allow you to exercise and socialize at the same time. Often the two activities are combined, which helps keep participants' interest levels high.

Stair-stepping involves stepping up and down on a single step (usually 6 inches high), or steps stacked on top of one another. This exercise may involve different upper-body movements or routines as well.

Usually aerobic dance is performed in a group and is set to music. The dancing can be done at low, moderate, or high intensities. Most aerobic dance routines last for approximately 45 to 60 minutes. Many beginners find that it takes several weeks before they can complete a full routine. If you participate in aerobic dance, make sure to wear appropriate clothing. Wear supportive footwear to prevent injuries.

Kickboxing

Kickboxing is a popular new aerobic activity. Like aerobic dance, it is usually performed in a group with high-energy or rhythmic music.

230 **Chapter 8** Developing Cardiorespiratory Endurance

Active Mind Active Body

Researching Aerobic Activities

In order to begin an aerobic workout program, you need to research and choose an activity that's right for you. This activity will help you find out more about the many activities discussed in this chapter.

What You Will Need

- Pen or pencil
- Paper
- Access to research materials, such as books, periodicals, or catalogues.

What You Will Do

1. Choose one of the aerobic activities discussed in this lesson.
2. Read about the activity.
3. Make a list of equipment, materials, and skills needed to start the activity.
4. Visit a local sporting-goods store, look at a sporting-goods catalogue, or check advertisements to research the price of equipment and supplies.
5. Research the type of lessons necessary to learn appropriate skills for the activity, and check the availability and cost of such lessons in your community.

Apply and Conclude

Share your findings with your classmates. What skills are necessary for your activity? Are there lessons or classes in your area? Compare costs and availability for specific equipment and items needed for your activity. What is the best overall source of supplies and equipment? Share your findings with the class.

It is commonly done with a group in a gym. Kickboxing requires your body to work both aerobically and anaerobically because the routines involve kicks and punches. You may need to practice your program before you can finish the usual 45-to-60 minute class. Make sure you have a knowledgeable instructor and practice appropriate safety measures to avoid injuries.

Cross-Country Skiing

Cross-country skiing is one of the best types of cardiorespiratory-fitness conditioning because it requires the use of both your arms and legs in a continuous activity. Cross-country skiing can be done indoors, on a stationary trainer, or outdoors. For outdoor cross-country skiing, most beginners will need to take lessons. Make sure to wear layers of clothing that can be removed or added as the body heats up or cools down. Cross-country skiing is a low-impact aerobic activity, meaning it puts less stress on your joints than running or jogging.

▲ Kickboxing is a popular aerobic activity. *How is kickboxing similar to aerobic dance?*

What Teens *Want* to Know

Which sports and physical activities are most popular?
Share these figures with the class and ask which of these activities are popular with your students.

Source: National Sporting Goods Association

Sport or Physical Activity	2002	1997
	Number of participants (in millions)	
Snowboarding	5.6	2.8
Skateboarding	9.7	6.3
Soccer	14.5	13.7
Running/jogging	24.7	21.7
Aerobic exercising	29.0	26.3
Exercising with equipment	50.2	47.9

Photo Follow-up

Discuss with students the aerobic benefits of kickboxing. *Caption answer: Both are done in a group with high-energy music.*

Active Mind Active Body

Researching Aerobic Activities

This activity will help students better understand aerobic activities and help them identify the ones they might participate in on a regular basis.

Teaching Tips

- Have students use *Active Mind–Active Body Worksheet 8-2* to record their information. 📁
- Remind students to keep a list of the items required for the activity.
- Have students bring examples of their findings back to class to share.

Apply and Conclude

After students have completed the activity, discuss the importance of researching aerobic activities before attempting a new endeavor. Then ask how they would mentor someone else who is inactive but wants to participate regularly in an aerobic activity.

Student Edition TEKS

Page 231: C4H
Page 233: C1A, C4G

Reading Check

Cross-country skiing, bicycling, and swimming are considered low-impact aerobic activities.

3 ASSESS

EVALUATING THE LESSON

Assign and discuss the Lesson 2 Review.

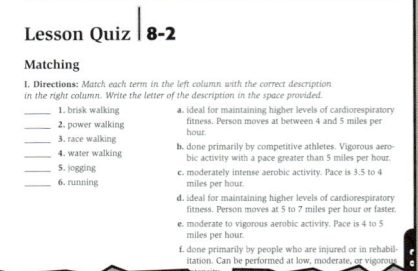

Name _____ Date _____ Class Period _____

Lesson Quiz | 8-2

Matching

I. Directions: *Match each term in the left column with the correct description in the right column. Write the letter of the description in the space provided.*

_____ 1. brisk walking
_____ 2. power walking
_____ 3. race walking
_____ 4. water walking
_____ 5. jogging
_____ 6. running

a. ideal for maintaining higher levels of cardiorespiratory fitness. Person moves at between 4 and 5 miles per hour.
b. done primarily by competitive athletes. Vigorous aerobic activity with a pace greater than 5 miles per hour.
c. moderately intense aerobic activity. Pace is 3.5 to 4 miles per hour.
d. ideal for maintaining higher levels of cardiorespiratory fitness. Person moves at 5 to 7 miles per hour or faster.
e. moderate to vigorous aerobic activity. Pace is 4 to 5 miles per hour.
f. done primarily by people who are injured or in rehabilitation. Can be performed at low, moderate, or vigorous intensity.

RETEACHING

Ask students to list and describe two aerobic activities and explain how these activities help develop cardiorespiratory endurance. Assign *Reteaching 8-2.* 🗂

ENRICHMENT

Have students identify one aerobic activity they might use for cross-training if they suffer a minor injury. **TEKS C4B**

4 CLOSE

Have students visit a local sporting-goods store or use catalogues to investigate heart rate monitors. Have them compare each item by price and features. **TEKS C4H**

Water Activities

Exercising in the water is a low-impact activity that improves not only cardiovascular fitness, but also muscular strength and endurance. Aerobic activities in water include lap swimming, aquatic aerobics, aquatic step training, and aquatic line dancing. Swimming laps is a great way to develop and maintain your cardiorespiratory fitness and help control your body composition. It helps to control body fat while improving and maintaining muscle tone. If you choose lap swimming as a regular aerobic activity, you may need to take lessons to master a variety of swim strokes and to improve your efficiency or biomechanics.

Aquatic aerobics and aquatic line dancing incorporate rhythmic movements and dance steps performed in the water. These workouts are often performed to music. Aquatic step training is a cardiovascular workout that involves stepping on weighted steps on the bottom of the pool. Many fitness facilities offer classes in aquatic aerobics for beginner to advanced levels. Because they place less stress on the body than regular aerobics, they are an excellent option for people with arthritis, neck and back problems, and obesity.

 Reading Check

Evaluate Of the aerobic activities discussed, which is considered low-impact?

Lesson 2 Review

Using complete sentences, answer the following questions on a sheet of paper.

Reviewing Facts and Vocabulary

1. **Vocabulary** What is a *pedometer*?
2. **Recall** How many steps per day should you try to accumulate if you use a pedometer when you walk for cardiorespiratory fitness?
3. **Recall** How can you prevent shinsplints and knee and ankle problems when beginning a walking/jogging program?

Thinking Critically

4. **Compare and Contrast** Explain the differences between indoor and outdoor cross-country skiing. What are the advantages and disadvantages of each?
5. **Analyze** How might using a pedometer motivate you in your walking/jogging program?

Personal Fitness Planning

Planning for Individual Needs If you became injured or disabled and could not use your legs, how would you design a cardiorespiratory-fitness program for yourself? Design a program that could meet your needs for participation in regular moderate-to-vigorous aerobic activities, using as wide a variety of activities as possible.

232 **Chapter 8** Developing Cardiorespiratory Endurance

Lesson 2 Review

Answers to Lesson 2 Review

1. A pedometer is a device that measures the number of steps you take and records the distance you travel on foot.
2. Approximately 10,000 steps per day.
3. Start slowly and use proper footwear.
4. Primary differences would be that for outdoor cross-country skiing, students would need lessons and warm clothing.
5. They can help you keep track of your walking steps and help motivate you to get your 10,000 steps each day.

Applying FITT to Cardiorespiratory Workouts

A s with any physical activity or exercise, what you get out of an aerobic activity depends on what you put into it. That is, aerobic activities, like other types of exercise, are governed by FITT principles.

Cardiorespiratory FITT and Overload

The physiological principle of *overload* is applied to your cardiorespiratory workout by increasing the amount of aerobic activity that you do. This will overload the main muscle of your cardiovascular system, the heart.

As with any other fitness goal, your cardiorespiratory FITT must be designed to achieve the principle of overload. If the workload is too light, you will not reach your fitness goal. If it is too heavy, you risk serious injury.

Frequency

How frequently should you do aerobic exercise or activity? The answer to that question depends on your current fitness level and age. As a teen, you should try to

- be aerobically active every day.
- accumulate 60 minutes of aerobic activity or exercise per day, or at least 225 minutes per week.

▶ No matter what type of aerobic activities you include in your workout, always apply FITT factors. *What do the letters in FITT stand for?*

What You Will Do

- Apply the physiological principles of overload, progression, and FITT to your cardiorespiratory workout.
- Determine your target heart rate range.
- Evaluate consumer issues and marketing claims promoting fitness products and services.

Terms to Know

target heart rate range
deconditioned

Lesson 3   Applying FITT to Cardiorespiratory Workouts   **233**

---

1 MOTIVATE

GETTING STARTED

- Ask how often students participate in aerobic activities and how many minutes of aerobic activity they are getting each week.
- Distribute copies of *Guided Practice 8-3* for students to use while studying this lesson. 📁

IN THIS LESSON

- **Consumer Corner** *Selling Fitness: Misleading Claims, page 235*

INTRODUCING VOCABULARY

- Explain to students that the term *target heart rate range* is often referred to as the "Karvonen Formula," after Dr. Robert Karvonen, who researched the optimal ranges of intensity to gain the maximum benefits of cardiorespiratory conditioning.
- Have students use *Vocabulary Worksheet 8* or the PuzzleMaker software to practice vocabulary terms for this lesson. ELL 📁 💿

Photo Follow-up

Emphasize the variety of aerobic activities students can use to improve cardiorespiratory fitness. *Caption answer: Frequency, intensity, time, and type.* **TEKS C4F**

LESSON 3 RESOURCES

Teacher Classroom Resources
📁 Guided Practice Activity 8–3
📁 Reteaching Activity 8–3
📁 Lesson Quiz 8–3

Reproducible Charts and Graphs
📁 Reproducible Master 8-3

Multimedia
💿 Vocabulary PuzzleMaker
💾 Transparencies 47, 48

2 TEACH

USING VISUALS

Figure 8.5 Ask students why applying the physiological principle of frequency to training and exercise for aerobic conditioning is often a good way to start a program. Explain to them that an every-other-day schedule allows them to recover on their days off, which decreases the risk of overtraining. **TEKS C1A4**

hotlink

Reinforce to students that it's important to understand the concept of maximum heart rate in order to safely and effectively develop their FITT for aerobic exercise.

USING VISUALS

Figure 8.6 Explain that teens and adults can use the target heart rate range formula to calculate their heart rate intensities for optimal aerobic conditioning. Display *Transparency 47* and discuss how to determine target heart rate range.

✓ Reading Check

First subtract your age from 220 for your maximum heart rate. Then take 60 percent and 90 percent of that number to get the bottom and top of your target heart range.

234

FIGURE 8.5

FREQUENCY OF AEROBIC ACTIVITY

Aerobic Fitness Level	Frequency of Conditioning
Beginner	3 to 5 days per week
Moderate-to-High	5 to 7 days per week

hotlink

maximum heart rate
For more on maximum heart rate and the formula for computing it, see Chapter 3, page **85**.

FIGURE 8.6

INTENSITY OF AEROBIC ACTIVITY

Aerobic Fitness Level	Intensity (Target Heart Range)
Beginner	120 to 145 beats per minute
Moderate-to-High	145 to 185 beats per minute

If you are just starting out, you can safely begin with three days a week of aerobic activity. Then, as your cardiorespiratory fitness levels increase, gradually add one day at a time. This advice is summed up in **Figure 8.5.**

Intensity

As noted in Chapter 3, the level of intensity in aerobic conditioning can be expressed as a measure of **maximum heart rate.** Most teens are advised to work at between 60 and 90 percent of their target heart rate range. This is *the range your heart rate should be in during aerobic exercise or activity for maximum cardiorespiratory endurance.* Teens that have long been sedentary may need to start out at lower intensities (40 to 50 percent of their target heart rate range). They can then gradually progress to 60 to 90 percent.

To calculate your target heart rate range, first compute your maximum heart rate (220 – *age*). Then determine 60 and 90 percent of that number to get your target heart rate range. Thus, the target heart rate range for a 15-year-old teen would be between 123 and 184 beats per minute.

Note that the lower number in the range represents moderate intensity. If you work at intensity levels lower than this number, you would derive some health benefit. You would not, however, see much change in your physical-fitness levels. If you worked at greater intensity levels than the high-end number (which represents vigorous intensity), you would place yourself at increased risk for overtraining and overuse injuries. **Figure 8.6** shows typical target heart ranges for teens at different levels of cardiorespiratory fitness. For good-to-better cardiorespiratory fitness levels, you do not have to work above the high-end number. However, it is not uncommon to go over the high-end number for short periods when doing anaerobic activities.

✓ Reading Check

Explain How do you calculate target heart rate range?

Time

Figure 8.7 offers guidelines for how much time you should devote to aerobic activity or exercise sessions. It depends, once again, on your current levels of fitness. If you are just starting cardiorespiratory conditioning, your goal should be 20 to 30 minutes per session. If you are unable to accumulate 20 or 30 minutes continuously, you may have to accumulate 20 or 30 minutes each day in two or three separate aerobic sessions of 10 to 15 minutes each. This may also apply if you are **deconditioned,** meaning *having been out of training for a significant period after achieving at least a moderate level of fitness.* You could also do an *interval workout* at low intensity to accumulate your 20 or 30 minutes. Such a workout might involve jogging for two minutes at 60 percent of your maximum heart rate, then walking for

---

INCLUSION STRATEGIES

THRESHOLD LEVEL OF MHR For students with disabilities, oxygen intake differs depending on the disability. The greater the damage to the central nervous system, the less efficient oxygen transport can be. A 40 to 70 percent threshold level is appropriate for persons with health impairments. It is better and safer to start too low than too high. Gradually increase intensity until the 60 to 90 percent range can be tolerated. Some students with disabilities who have limited large muscle use may be unable to maintain their MHR long enough to improve cardiorespiratory endurance.

one minute to recover. This routine would be repeated ten times for a total of 30 minutes.

Individuals at good-to-better levels of cardiorespiratory fitness should work at 25 to 40 minutes per session. It should be noted that low intensity for longer durations of time often works best for weight loss and control compared to shorter duration at high intensities.

Type

To maintain or improve your cardiorespiratory endurance, you should choose aerobic activities that elevate your heart rate 60 to 90 percent of its target range, for 20 to 30 minutes at a time whenever possible. Remember, aerobic activities are those that are rhythmic, continuous, and use large muscle groups. Some common examples include, but are not limited to: walking, jogging, running, in-line skating, dance, stair-stepping, kickboxing, cross-country skiing, racquetball, and water activities. Try to think of one you would like to do.

✓ **Reading Check**

Explain How long should a cardiorespiratory workout last for a person who is just beginning?

FIGURE 8.7
LENGTH OF AEROBIC ACTIVITY

Aerobic Fitness Level	Time (per Workout)
Beginner	20 to 30 minutes
Moderate-to-High	30 to 60 minutes

Chapter 8, Lesson 3

USING VISUALS

Figure 8.7 Use *Transparency 48* to remind students to apply the physiological principles of frequency, intensity, time, and type to their exercise and training to develop cardiorespiratory fitness. Students should set a goal of being aerobically active every day and accumulating 225 minutes of aerobic and exercise activities every week. **TEKS C1A**

✓ **Reading Check**
Beginners should start at 20 to 30 minutes per session.

Consumer CORNER

Selling Fitness: Misleading Claims

Have students read the *Consumer Corner* feature and complete the Evaluate activity to create an advertisement advocating aerobic activity. Have volunteers share their results with the class. **TEKS C4H**

✓ **Reading Check**
(page 236)
Adjust FITT factors gradually when applying progression to workouts.

Student Edition TEKS

Page 234: C1A
Page 235: C1A, C4H

Consumer CORNER

Selling Fitness: Misleading Claims

As with other areas of health and fitness, people look for shortcuts or easy ways out. Although no quick fixes exist, promoters and advertisers suggest that they do. They have come up with a number of products and claims that should be approached with caution. Here are some to watch out for:

- **Promises of quick results.** Unless you already achieved good-to-better levels of fitness, don't expect miracles. A realistic estimate of when you should expect results is between 8 and 30 weeks. The more unhealthy your eating plan and the longer you have been sedentary, the longer it will take to get results.
- **Equipment that does the work for you.** These include motorized exercise machines, belts, and massagers. These do not overload the heart, lungs, or blood vessels. Without

that overload, you cannot improve your cardiorespiratory endurance.

- **Pills and foods.** Contrary to what the ads promise, there are no pills or foods that exercise the heart. Some chemicals may speed up the heart rate, but these do not improve heart and lung function. In fact, some can be dangerous.

Evaluate

Analyze advertisements for fitness products. Then, create your own commercial or written advertisement to encourage people to participate in an aerobic activity discussed in this lesson. Your advertisement should be persuasive and highlight the benefits of the activity you are "selling." Share your ad with the class.

Lesson 3 Applying FITT to Cardiorespiratory Workouts **235**

More About . . .

ADVERTISING AND HEALTHY BEHAVIORS

Popular media and advertising can affect consumer choices. For example, advertising may encourage consumption of high-fat convenience foods. Much of this advertising is directed at children and teens. Balancing the messages in these ads with pro-nutrition messages could have a powerful impact on health and fitness. In recent years, widespread public education programs that include antismoking messages have reduced cigarette smoking. Ads featuring celebrity endorsements are credited with a 30-percent increase in milk consumption.

3 ASSESS

EVALUATING THE LESSON

Assign and discuss the Lesson 3 Review.

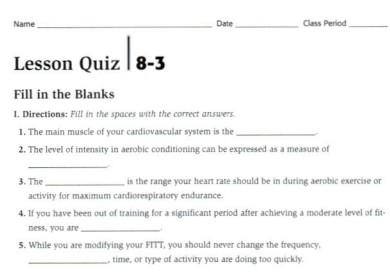

RETEACHING

Ask students to summarize how FITT can be applied to cardiorespiratory workouts.

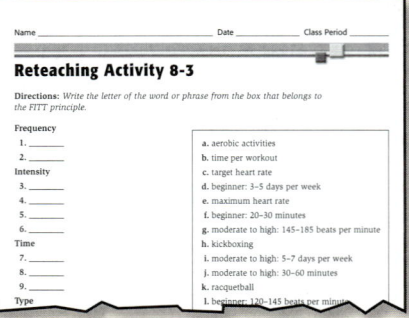

ENRICHMENT

Have students determine the target heart rate range for two adult family members or friends and compare the results to their own.

4 CLOSE

Have students use their *Consumer Corner* evaluation results to develop a campaign using posters or flyers about misleading claims found in fitness advertising.

Everyone can improve their levels of cardiorespiratory fitness. *What are some ways in which people with disabilities can achieve levels of cardiorespiratory fitness?*

Progression Principle

The rate at which you modify your FITT should be based on your personal fitness goals and your changing levels of cardiorespiratory fitness. To achieve progression, you should adjust FITT factors gradually. Never change your frequency, intensity, time, or the type of activity you are doing all at once or too quickly. Be patient, adjust FITT factors individually, and allow for gradual improvements.

Special Situations

The guidelines for FITT and cardiorespiratory conditioning need to be modified for some people. This includes people with physical disabilities or debilitating injuries. Such people need to consult with a health or fitness professional before participating in a cardiorespiratory program. The same is true for individuals who are obese.

The following are possible activities for people with special needs:

- Water exercises (for individuals unable to walk or jog)
- Arm work (for individuals with lower-body limitations)
- Upper-body cycling (for individuals to reduce weight-bearing exercise)
- Other special modifications that can be made to the aerobic activities described in Lesson 1.

 Reading Check

Identify How should you apply the physiological principle of progression to your cardiorespiratory workout?

Lesson 3 Review

Using complete sentences, answer the following questions on a sheet of paper.

Reviewing Facts and Vocabulary

1. **Vocabulary** What is *target heart rate range*? How does it apply to the intensity of a workout?

2. **Recall** When applying the physiological principle of overload to a cardiorespiratory workout, what muscle should you target?

3. **Recall** How should you apply frequency to your cardiorespiratory workouts?

Thinking Critically

4. **Analyze** Marla is 16 and has not worked out for several months. Compute Marla's target heart rate range. Review **Figure 8.6** and identify (in beats per minute) the intensity level at which she should work to achieve moderate cardiorespiratory fitness.

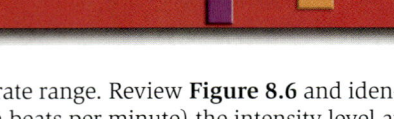

Researching Activities Do some research in your local community and determine if you can find a health and fitness facility that is offering a new aerobic-fitness activity you would like to try. Find out how much it costs to participate and determine if they have special classes for teens.

Lesson 3 Review

Answers to Lesson 3 Review

1. Target heart rate range is the range in which your heart rate should fall during aerobic activity for maximum cardiorespiratory endurance. It helps you determine your aerobic workout intensity.

2. The heart.

3. You should participate in aerobic activity daily and accumulate 225 minutes of aerobic activity or exercise per week.

4. 124 to 185 beats/min. She should start at 60 percent of her maximum heart rate and work up to 70–75 percent for moderate cardiorespiratory fitness.

Selecting Fitness Equipment

The sale of home exercise equipment has become a big business. Since 1990, the number of people who have bought this type of equipment for the home has tripled. Some people prefer the convenience, while others are more comfortable working out in the privacy of their own homes.

Would you like to have an in-home fitness center? In this lesson you will find out how to go about selecting this equipment. You will also learn the costs involved.

Personal Fitness Equipment

There are a number of factors to consider before setting up a home fitness center and buying equipment. These include the following:

- **Intended use.** How many people will be using the equipment? How flexible is it? What type of exercise is planned? Some machines and devices are designed for cardiorespiratory work, others for resistance, or weight training. It is critical to know which area of fitness will be focused on before making a purchase.
- **Cost.** How much money can you afford to invest in the equipment?

▶ Some people prefer to work out at home. *What are the advantages and disadvantages of having an in-home fitness center?*

What You Will Do

- Identify the factors to consider when choosing home fitness equipment.
- Evaluate the purpose and cost of common types of cardiorespiratory-exercise equipment.

Terms to Know

warranty
recumbent cycles

Selecting Fitness Equipment

1 MOTIVATE

GETTING STARTED

- Ask students what types of home fitness centers they have seen. Then ask them what kinds of equipment they think should be in a home fitness center. Explain that they will learn more about developing a home fitness center in this lesson.
- Distribute copies of *Guided Practice 8-4* for students to use while studying this lesson. 📁

IN THIS LESSON

- **Active Mind—Active Body** *Designing Your Personal Fitness Center,* page 238

INTRODUCING VOCABULARY

- Explain to students that the term *warranty* comes from the root *warrant,* which implies authorization or assurance.
- Have students use *Vocabulary Worksheet 8* or the PuzzleMaker software to practice vocabulary terms for this lesson. ELL 📁 💿

Photo Follow-up

Discuss what types of fitness equipment can be used in home fitness centers. *Caption answer: In-home fitness centers offer convenience and comfort.*

LESSON 4 RESOURCES

Teacher Classroom Resources
- 📁 Guided Practice Activity 8-4
- 📁 Active Mind—Active Body Worksheet 8-4
- 📁 Reteaching Activity 8-4
- 📁 Lesson Quiz 8-4

Multimedia
- 💿 Vocabulary PuzzleMaker

2 TEACH

Active Mind Active Body
Designing Your Personal Fitness Center

This activity will help students better understand how to develop or design a personal fitness center. They will develop techniques for becoming wise fitness consumers.

Teaching Tips

- Make copies of the *Active Mind–Active Body Worksheet 8-4* and distribute them to students to use in designing their personal fitness centers.
- Remind students to create a comprehensive list of the items they will research in this activity.
- Have students bring examples of their findings back to class to share.

Apply and Conclude

After students have completed the activity, discuss the benefits and importance of conducting consumer research to evaluate marketing claims promoting fitness products and services. Students should always research products before buying any fitness equipment or developing a home fitness center.
TEKS C4G, C4H

Active Mind Active Body
Designing Your Personal Fitness Center

In this activity, you will evaluate your home or apartment setting in terms of a personal fitness center. You will use this information to design a center that will allow your family to maintain its cardiorespiratory-fitness levels.

What You Will Need

- Pen or pencil
- Paper
- Measuring tape

What You Will Do

- Decide where you could set up a fitness center. Consider all possibilities, such as a spare room or den, bedroom, basement area, or garage.
- Review with adults in your family the fitness equipment options described in this lesson. Explain what each piece of equipment does.
- Discuss which type or types would best meet the needs of all members.
- Measure the available space in the areas of your home that you have isolated as possible spots for a fitness center.
- Research the size and cost of the equipment you are considering by visiting local sporting-goods stores, or looking at catalogues. Get size dimensions and costs of the equipment you are considering.
- Rule out items that would not fit the available space or that would be beyond your family's budget.
- Determine which store has the best price for a given item.
- Calculate how much your home fitness center will cost.

Apply and Conclude

What area of your home or apartment seemed to be the most suitable location? Why? Were you able to find equipment that fit this area? What was the cost? Did you include the cost of shipping? How does the cost of this equipment compare with the cost of a year's dues at a health club?

- **Space.** How much space will you need for the equipment? Does such space exist in your home or apartment?
- **Accessibility.** The center must be in a convenient location. At the same time, it must also be out of the way of small children, who could be injured.
- **Safety.** Is the equipment sturdy and built to last? Are there moving parts in which clothing or limbs could accidentally become entangled?
- **Service.** Many brands of fitness equipment are sold. Does the brand under consideration have a **warranty?** A warranty is *a guarantee on the part of the manufacturer or representative of the manufacturer to repair or replace parts for a predetermined time period.* Also, is the equipment easy to get serviced and repaired? Is the price of labor included in the warranty?

A good starting point for many families is to make a working draft of what the fitness center will look like. This should be based on the dimensions of the home or apartment and the equipment you plan to purchase.

238 **Chapter 8** Developing Cardiorespiratory Endurance

EQUIPMENT OPTIONS

PERSONAL FITNESS EQUIPMENT Many types of cardiorespiratory conditioning equipment give exercisers feedback about how they are performing. Some equipment, including stationary cycles, has heart rate monitors that require you to hold on to a pulse bar with both hands for 10 seconds. The display provides you with an estimate of your exercise heart rate. Other pieces of equipment, including treadmills and stair-steppers, often give feedback about estimated calories burned per minute or per hour. Be sure to read and follow the manufacturer's instructions.

Cardiorespiratory Fitness Equipment

As you learned in Lesson 2, there are many sports, activities, and exercises that develop cardiorespiratory fitness. It should come as no surprise, therefore, that there are many choices for equipment geared to this area. Among these are treadmills, bicycles, stair-steppers, ski machines, elliptical motion trainers, and swimming pools.

Treadmills. Treadmills are the most popular aerobic machines for personal use. You can purchase a good treadmill for as little as $300. The price for state-of-the-art health-club grade models runs as high as $2,000. Most treadmills have basic programming panels for variable speeds, grades (incline), time, and calories expended. If your family can afford one, treadmills are an excellent option for indoor walk/jog/run fitness programs.

Stationary Bicycles. Stationary bicycles are another popular choice for fitness centers. There are two main types of exercise cycles: upright cycles, which function like outdoor bicycles, and **recumbent cycles,** *bicycles used in a reclining position.* One advantage of the recumbent type is that it offers better lower-back support.

Either type of cycle is easy to use, low-impact, and great for weight control. Most stationary cycles have digital displays that provide you with feedback about the number of calories you are burning. Some also come equipped with levers that you can use to work your upper body at the same time you are cycling.

A less expensive alternative to buying a dedicated stationary bicycle is to attach resistance rollers to a standard bike. These run anywhere from $125 to $250. One downside to rollers is that some models require you to maintain your balance. A solution to this problem is to place the cycle in a doorway. That way, the door frame can be grasped while cycling.

Exercise Options

Many new types of exercise classes are gaining popularity in health clubs across the country. The emphasis is shifting away from the repetition of traditional exercise and toward motivational routines that help participants enjoy working out.

One example is firefighter training, an advanced cardiorespiratory conditioning class that teaches activities similar to those done by firefighters.

◀ Stationary cycles may be either upright or recumbent. *What are some advantages to using a recumbent stationary exercise bicycle?*

TECHNOLOGY FILE

Video Games as Exercise

Teens need physical activity, but many prefer to spend their time in sedentary activities, playing video games instead of exercising. Technology-based games that make use of dance routines or virtual bicycling programs marry these two types of activities. Have individual students participate in these specialized programs while wearing a heart monitor in order to determine whether they can stay in their target heart rate zone while playing these games. Encourage those students who have participated to share their experiences.

Photo Follow-up

Identify and discuss the type of cycling equipment shown in the photo. *Caption answer: One advantage is that recumbent cycles provide lower-back support.* Ask: Which cycle do you think would be easier to ride—an upright stationary cycle or a recumbent cycle? *Possible answer: The recumbent cycle would most likely be easier, but you would not expend as many calories per minute because the recumbent cycle involves less muscle mass than the upright cycle.*

Exercise Options

Have students work in small groups to read and discuss the Mind Over Matter feature. Have groups conduct research and identify two other new types of motivational exercise routines. Ask one student from each group to share the results with the class.

Quick Demo

Ask volunteers to bring to class a picture or illustration of a piece of sporting equipment that offers good value and provides an effective aerobic workout. Have them present the item to the class and discuss the reasons for their choices. **L3**

Student Edition TEKS

Page 238: C4G, C4H
Page 239: C4G

Photo Follow-up

Explain to students that elliptical trainers also produce little muscle soreness, even for beginners. This can help individuals adhere to their fitness program because no one really enjoys getting very sore after they exercise. *Caption answer: They are also very effective for weight control when the appropriate FITT formula is applied for aerobic conditioning.*

Explaining

Discuss the following statement with students: "Try out equipment before you buy it." Explain to students that trying out a piece of cardiorespiratory fitness equipment will help them evaluate whether it is comfortable and easy to use. Remind them that even the fanciest equipment will not improve their cardiorespiratory fitness if they do not use it regularly. **L2 TEKS C4H**

Activity

Ask students to research an extreme sport (bicycle stunt riding, snowboarding, or kite skiing) in which safety is a major concern. Have them find out what special safety equipment is used and describe examples of unsafe or harmful situations that may occur. **L3 TEKS C3B**

✓ Reading Check

Students may say that stationary bicycles, inexpensive treadmills, or stair-steppers are most practical, and their reasons should be based on information in the text.

Stair-Steppers. Stair-steppers are machines that simulate the action of walking up a flight of stairs. On some models, you step up and down (usually with a 6-inch stepping action). On others, you walk on escalator-like stairs in a continuous manner, as on an elliptical motion trainer. Stair-steppers do not require much space. Basic steppers cost about $100. More advanced models, which have added features such as calorie counters, can run up to $3,000. Many steppers have levers that you can use to work your upper body at the same time you are stepping.

Cross-Country Ski Machines. Cross-country ski machines provide a low-impact solution to the cardiorespiratory workout. There are two types of ski machines, dependent and independent. On dependent models, the motion of the skis is linked; when you move one ski forward, the other ski moves backward. On independent models, each ski can be moved independently. Independent models are harder to master but can offer a more vigorous workout. They also better simulate the motion of real cross-country skiing.

These machines cost between $200 and $700. It takes some practice to get started on your cross-country ski machine. You will have to learn to adjust the machine to your size and fitness level.

Elliptical Motion Trainer. A recent innovation in cardiorespiratory-exercise equipment is the elliptical motion trainer. Elliptical trainers (like stationary cycles) are easy to use, low-impact, and great for weight control. Many of these machines allow you to train the upper and lower body simultaneously. Reliable elliptical exercisers cost between $100 and $1,200 depending on the features.

Swimming Pool. Some people, especially in hotter parts of the country, have swimming pools at their homes. Others may have access to a swimming pool at school, a local park, or other facility. As discussed in Lesson 2, a swimming pool can provide you with an excellent type of cardiorespiratory training. However, swimming pools will require daily maintenance, and weather conditions may prohibit safe swimming.

◀ Elliptical trainers are easy to use and low-impact. *What's another advantage of these machines?*

COOPERATIVE Learning

COMMUNITY TRAINING FACILITIES Have students work in small groups to research training and recreational opportunities in their community. They should identify facilities such as recreation centers, parks, swimming pools, tennis courts, skating rinks, and ski slopes. They should also include organized activity programs such as sports teams, classes, and activity clubs. Have all groups combine their information with illustrations to create a brochure for people who have recently moved to the community. Display the brochures in the classroom. **ELL**

Care of Fitness Equipment

If you have home fitness equipment, it is important to maintain this equipment to ensure that it is working safely and effectively. The following tips will help you keep your equipment in top condition.

- Read the operating manual or instructions thoroughly before using the equipment.
- Inspect all equipment regularly.
- Lubricate and repair equipment as advised by the operating manual.
- Use equipment safely and appropriately, as advised by the operating manual.
- Clean equipment, including the benches and work surfaces, before and after each use. Wipe down surfaces with a towel and a disinfectant or 1-percent bleach solution. This will control the spread of germs.
- For safety reasons, pick up and store all loose equipment after use. Keep workout areas free of clutter.
- Know what your warranty covers in the event your machine requires repair.

 Reading Check

Evaluate Which item discussed do you think is the most practical to have in a home? Why?

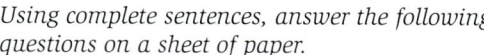
Lesson 4 Review

Using complete sentences, answer the following questions on a sheet of paper.

Reviewing Facts and Vocabulary

1. **Recall** What are two factors to consider in setting up a home fitness center?
2. **Vocabulary** Explain the difference between a *recumbent* and upright exercise cycle.

Thinking Critically

3. **Compare and Contrast** Compare the costs of the following types of cardiorespiratory home exercise equipment: treadmills and stair-steppers.

4. **Analyze** Explain the sentence "Taking care of your home fitness equipment is like taking out an insurance policy on your investment."

Personal Fitness Planning

Investigating Products Visit a local health and fitness club. Learn what the various cardiorespiratory-fitness machines and equipment do. Decide which items you would include in your own dream-home fitness center, and tell why. Finally, investigate whether it would be possible to build your dream fitness center if you had a budget of $2,000.

Answers to Lesson 4 Review

1. Answers will vary but could include intended use, cost, space, accessibility, safety, and service.
2. On a recumbent cycle the person is reclining, which offers better lower-back support than the upright cycle.
3. Treadmills would be more expensive than the basic stair-steppers.
4. Answers should include the fact that it will cost less and be safer if maintained.

3 ASSESS

EVALUATING THE LESSON

Assign and discuss the Lesson 4 Review.

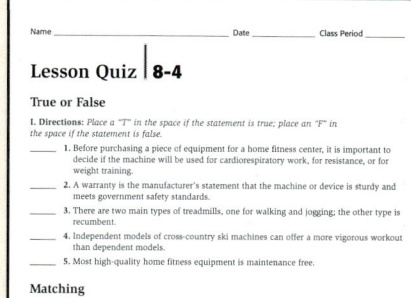

RETEACHING

Ask students to create a quiz summarizing the main points in the lesson.

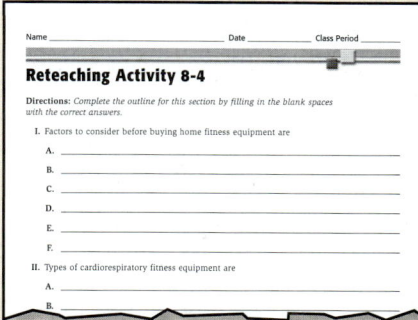

ENRICHMENT

Have students pretend that they own a commercial fitness center and need a plan to purchase cardiorespiratory equipment with a $10,000 budget. What would they buy?

4 CLOSE

Have students use what they have learned to design a cardiorespiratory fitness program for a family member.
TEKS C4F, C4G

CHECKING COMPREHENSION

- Assign and discuss the chapter review.
- Use the PuzzleMaker software to review vocabulary. 🔘

CHAPTER 8 REVIEW ANSWERS

True/False

1. False   6. True
2. False   7. True
3. False   8. True
4. False   9. True
5. False   10. True

Multiple Choice

11. d   15. a
12. d   16. c
13. c   17. b
14. d

Discussion

18. Answers will vary but might include Cooper's 1.5 mile run test, the 20-minute steady-state jog test, the 30-minute steady-state walk test, the 20-minute steady-state cycle test, and the 20-minute steady-state swim test.
19. Any five: walking, jogging, swimming, cycling, aerobic dance, stair-stepping, kickboxing.
20. Answers will vary but might include intended use, cost, space, accessibility, safety, and service.

Vocabulary

21. b
22. a
23. d
24. e
25. c

TRUE/FALSE

On a sheet of paper, write the numbers 1–10. Write True or False for each statement.

1. To achieve a good-to-better score on the Cooper's 1.5-mile run test, a female teen would need to cover the distance in under 1.6 minutes.
2. The exercise stress test is an alternative test for people who are sedentary and/or obese.
3. To achieve accurate results on an endurance test, you should avoid doing any exercise in the weeks leading up to the test.
4. Race walking is done at a pace of 3.5 to 4 miles per hour.
5. A typical kickboxing class lasts between 20 and 30 minutes.
6. Cross-country skiing is a low-impact aerobic sport.
7. Teens who have long been sedentary may need to start out at lower percentages of their target heart rate range than active teens.
8. For moderate-to-high cardiorespiratory fitness levels, you should achieve a time of 30 to 60 minutes per session.
9. Treadmills are the most popular aerobic machines for home exercise use.
10. You can buy a basic fitness stepping bench for $100.

MULTIPLE CHOICE

On a sheet of paper, write the letter of the word or phrase that best completes each statement.

11. The cardiorespiratory evaluation most likely to be done if a medical screening suggests a health problem is
    a. steady-state jog test.
    b. Cooper's 1.5-mile run test.
    c. steady-state swim test.
    d. exercise stress test.

12. To evaluate your cardiorespiratory fitness using estimated $VO_{2\,max}$, you need to do 20 to 30 minutes of aerobic activity at
    a. 30 to 65 percent of your estimated $VO_{2\,max}$.
    b. 40 to 75 percent of your estimated $VO_{2\,max}$.
    c. 60 to 95 percent of your estimated $VO_{2\,max}$.
    d. 50 to 85 percent of your estimated $VO_{2\,max}$.
13. The device used to measure the number of steps you take and estimate the distance you walk is a(n)
    a. heart-rate monitor.
    b. waist/hip pouch.
    c. pedometer.
    d. elliptical motion trainer.
14. Of the following statements about jogging and running, all are true EXCEPT that
    a. the difference between the two is a matter of speed.
    b. a good way to monitor the intensity of either is by using a heart-rate monitor.
    c. both involve the forces of pronation and supination.
    d. neither contributes to cardiorespiratory fitness.
15. Teens who are at least moderately active and in good health are advised to work at
    a. between 60 and 90 percent of their target heart rate range.
    b. 45 percent of their target heart rate range.
    c. between 60 and 90 percent of their estimated $VO_{2\,max}$.
    d. 45 percent of their estimated $VO_{2\,max}$.
16. Of the following, the intensity range recommended for beginners to cardiorespiratory conditioning is
    a. 100 to 110 beats per minute.
    b. 115 to 120 beats per minute.
    c. 120 to 145 beats per minute.
    d. 140 to 170 beats per minute.
17. A person who is deconditioned might BEST be described as
    a. having been kicked off the team for failing to observe training requirements.
    b. having been away from training for a period after achieving at least moderate levels of fitness.
    c. having gained so much weight from years of sedentary living as to be at serious risk.
    d. none of the above.

DISCUSSION

Using complete sentences, answer the following questions on a sheet of paper.

18. **Explain** Describe three ways you can evaluate your cardiorespiratory fitness levels.
19. **Identify** List and describe five different aerobic activities or exercises that will help you improve or maintain your cardiorespiratory-fitness level.
20. **Identify** List and explain four factors to consider when purchasing home exercise equipment.

VOCABULARY

On a sheet of paper, write the letter of the term in Column B that best fits the definition in Column A.

Column A

21. Test that requires you to pace yourself steadily as you walk for a prescribed time.
22. An evaluation in which you walk on a treadmill or ride a stationary bicycle under medical supervision.
23. Numerical range your heart rate should be in during aerobic activity.
24. Test that requires you to pace yourself steadily as you swim for a prescribed time.
25. Device that records your heart beats by means of a chest transmitter and wrist monitor.

Column B

a. exercise stress test
b. steady-state walk
c. heart rate monitor
d. target heart rate range
e. steady-state swim

CRITICAL THINKING

Using complete sentences, answer the following questions on a sheet of paper.

26. **Evaluate** Which method of evaluating cardiorespiratory fitness would you recommend to a friend who was very sedentary and 20 pounds overweight? Describe what is involved in performing the evaluation.

27. **Compare and Contrast** What tips could you give a friend who was considering buying a treadmill for home use? Give the pros and cons of such a purchase.

CASE STUDY

DENISE'S FITNESS PLAN

Denise, who is 16 years old, is physically active and lives in a large city. Her family is going to relocate to a rural community situated several miles from the nearest town. Denise is concerned that she will become less active because she will not have as many resources and opportunities for working out. She has considered asking her parents to convert a room in their new home into a home fitness center. Denise could use some help from a friend who is knowledgeable about setting up a home fitness facility—someone like you.

HERE IS YOUR ASSIGNMENT:

Assume Denise has asked you for help with her plans for designing a personal fitness facility. Organize a list of things Denise should consider and do before purchasing exercise equipment. Use the following keys to help you:

KEYS TO HELP YOU

- Guide Denise in methods to improve her cardiorespiratory fitness.
- Provide her with a list of factors to consider when selecting home fitness equipment.
- Explain the equipment options available.
- Determine a reasonable plan to give Denise that helps her to be successful in developing a fitness facility.

Chapter 8 Review 243

Critical Thinking

26. Answers will vary but should include reasons why the student chose a particular evaluation method for someone who may not be able to perform a more strenuous test. Descriptions should include the steps involved in the evaluation.
27. Answers will vary, but students should recommend that the person consider cost, space, accessibility, safety, and service.

EVALUATE

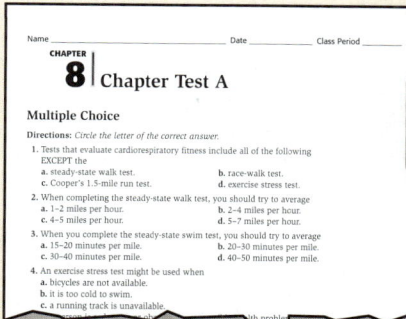

ENRICHMENT

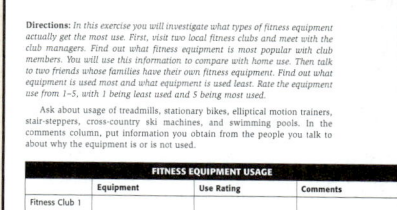

CASE STUDY

ANSWERS

Answers will vary but should include information from Lesson 4 about setting up a home fitness center, as well as the experience gained from completing the *Active Mind—Active Body* feature on page 238.

Student Edition TEKS

Page 243: C4E, C4G, C4H

243

CHAPTER 9

Basics of Resistance Training

CHAPTER 9

Lesson 1 Benefits of Resistance Training

Lesson 2 Your Muscles and Their Functions

Lesson 3 Resistance-Training Myths

Lesson 4 Resistance-Training Equipment and Gear

CHAPTER RESOURCES

- **Chapter Study Guide 9**
- **Vocabulary Worksheet 9**
- **Enrichment Activity 9**
- **Chapter 9 Test A**
- **Chapter 9 Test B**
- **Parent Letter and Activities 9 (English and Spanish)**

FITNESS *Online*

Ask students to take the STEP Personal Inventory for Chapter 9. Have them record their responses to the statements in their notebooks. Remind students that responses are private and for their use only.

FITNESS *Online*

Regular training to build muscular strength and endurance, such as working out with weights, should be part of everyone's fitness plan. How do you rate in this area of fitness? Find out by taking the STEP Personal Inventory for Chapter 9. Find it at **fitness.glencoe.com**.

244

INCLUSION STRATEGIES

LANGUAGE DIVERSITY *Use the following suggestions to help students who have difficulty with English:*

- Pair English-language learners with native speakers of English who can restate key points in language that helps students comprehend important concepts.

- Direct Spanish-speaking students to the written summaries of this chapter in the *Foundations of Personal Fitness* Spanish Resources Booklet.

- Encourage Spanish-speaking students to use the Glosario provided in the back of the student text. **ELL**

Benefits of Resistance Training

I t was not too long ago that the term *weight lifting* brought to mind an image of body builders with bulging muscles. However, that has changed. Working out with weights is popular among males and females of all ages. In this lesson you will learn more about this trend. You will also discover the many benefits of this form of exercise and of other ways to build muscular strength and endurance.

What is Resistance Training?

The best way to build and tone your muscles is through a program of resistance training. **Resistance training,** or strength training, is *a systematic program of exercises designed to increase an individual's ability to resist or exert force.* Resistance training may involve weights,

What You Will Do

- Define resistance training and identify its importance to your health and fitness.
- Identify the role of muscular strength and muscular endurance in resistance training.
- Explain the benefits of resistance training.

Terms to Know

resistance training
muscular strength
absolute muscular strength
relative muscular strength
muscular endurance
relative muscular endurance
progressive resistance

◀ Resistance training builds muscular endurance through use of free weights, weight machines, or elastic bands. *Why do you think it is important to include resistance training in a fitness program?*

Benefits of Resistance Training

1 MOTIVATE

GETTING STARTED

- Ask the class to think about the following questions: What pictures come to your mind when you think of someone who has been lifting weights for a long time? What would this person look like?
- Distribute copies of *Guided Practice 9-1* for students to use with this lesson. 📁

IN THIS LESSON

Mind Over Matter, *p. 247*

INTRODUCING VOCABULARY

- Explain to students that *resistance* is a force that tends to oppose or retard motion or movement. When you apply this force against a muscle, the strength of that muscle increases.
- Have students use *Vocabulary Worksheet 9* or the PuzzleMaker software to practice vocabulary terms for this lesson. 📁 💿 ELL

Photo Follow-up

Ask whether students have used any of the equipment shown in the photos.

Caption answer: There are many benefits to be gained from resistance training. It builds and tones muscle, improves metabolism, strengthens tendons, ligaments, and bones. It reduces the possibilities of injury.

LESSON 1 RESOURCES

Teacher Classroom Resources
📁 Guided Practice Activity 9-1
📁 Reteaching Activity 9-1
📁 Lesson Quiz 9-1

Multimedia
💿 Vocabulary PuzzleMaker
 Transparency 49

2 TEACH

Discussing

Ask students: How many of you have ever been involved in a weight-training program? Have students explain why they started lifting, how long they lifted, and whether they are still lifting. **L2**

USING VISUALS

Figure 9.1 Use *Transparency 49* to discuss each of the primary and secondary benefits of resistance training. Ask students to give examples of how these benefits might improve their lives today and in the future.

Activity

Have students make a list of any concerns or fears they may have about the weight-training unit. They should identify medical factors that would cause concern about participating in the activities in this unit. **L1**

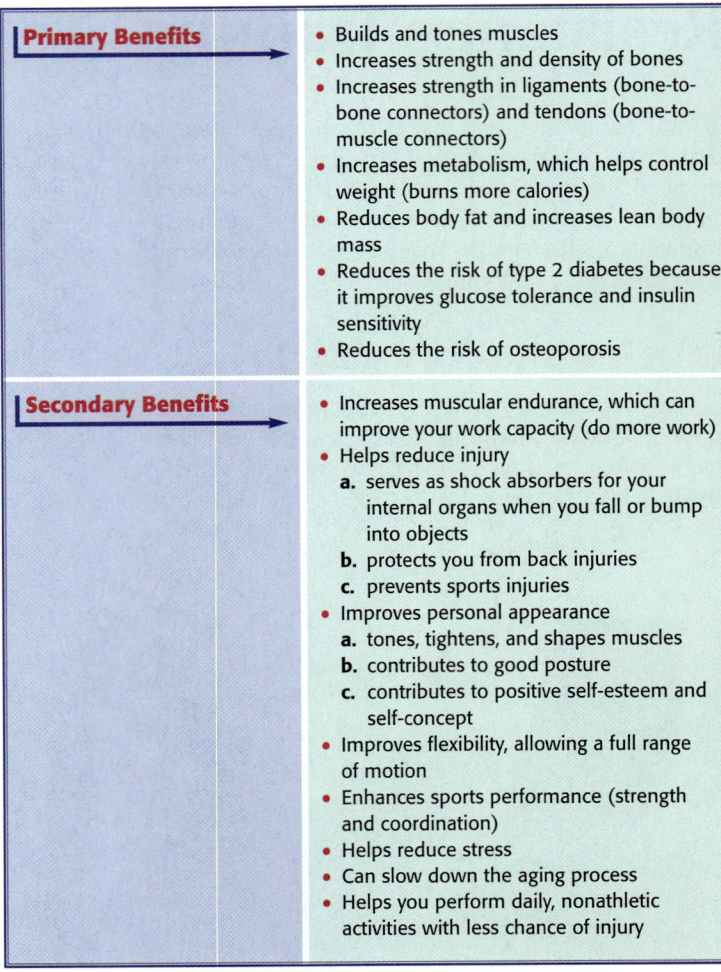

FIGURE 9.1

BENEFITS OF RESISTANCE TRAINING
A resistance-training program benefits more than just your muscles. *What other parts of your body can benefit from resistance training?*

Primary Benefits
- Builds and tones muscles
- Increases strength and density of bones
- Increases strength in ligaments (bone-to-bone connectors) and tendons (bone-to-muscle connectors)
- Increases metabolism, which helps control weight (burns more calories)
- Reduces body fat and increases lean body mass
- Reduces the risk of type 2 diabetes because it improves glucose tolerance and insulin sensitivity
- Reduces the risk of osteoporosis

Secondary Benefits
- Increases muscular endurance, which can improve your work capacity (do more work)
- Helps reduce injury
  a. serves as shock absorbers for your internal organs when you fall or bump into objects
  b. protects you from back injuries
  c. prevents sports injuries
- Improves personal appearance
  a. tones, tightens, and shapes muscles
  b. contributes to good posture
  c. contributes to positive self-esteem and self-concept
- Improves flexibility, allowing a full range of motion
- Enhances sports performance (strength and coordination)
- Helps reduce stress
- Can slow down the aging process
- Helps you perform daily, nonathletic activities with less chance of injury

weight machines, elastic bands, or simply the weight of your own body. Because it often includes weights, it is sometimes called weight training.

Resistance training has many benefits. It builds and tones muscles. It improves metabolism and increases the strength of tendons, ligaments, and bones, which may help to prevent injuries. For other benefits of resistance training, see **Figure 9.1.**

246 **Chapter 9** Basics of Resistance Training

More About . . .

BENEFITS OF RESISTANCE TRAINING The National Strength and Conditioning Association (NSCA) states that a well-designed resistance-training program can enhance cardiovascular health by reducing risk factors associated with disease. Such changes include decreased resting blood pressure, decreased exercise heart rate, improvements in glucose tolerance, and improvements in hemoglobin in patients with diabetes mellitus. Other improvements are seen in body composition and bone mineral density. Also, resistance training reduces anxiety, depression, and sport-related injuries.

Muscular Strength and Endurance

Building muscular strength and endurance is an integral part of personal fitness for teens and adults of all ages and genders. People with high levels of muscular strength and endurance are able to perform daily tasks more efficiently. This helps them conserve energy and accomplish more in a typical day. They also have better posture and fewer back problems.

Muscular Strength

Muscular strength is *the maximum amount of force a muscle or muscle group can exert against an opposing force.* There are two measures of muscular strength:

- **Absolute muscular strength.** This is *the maximum force you are able to exert regardless of size, age, or weight.* For example, a person able to lift 100 pounds is stronger in an absolute sense than a person able to lift only 80 pounds. The person lifting the 100 pounds generates 20 more pounds of muscular force. Note that females overall have lower percentages of absolute muscular strength than males.
- **Relative muscular strength.** This is *the maximum force you are able to exert in relation to your body weight.* For example, Jim weighs 125 pounds and can lift 130 pounds during a weight training exercise. Tom weighs 160 pounds and can lift 150 pounds on the same exercise. Tom clearly is stronger in an absolute sense, but which of the two teens is the stronger pound for pound? The answer, shown in **Figure 9.2,** can be determined by dividing the amount of weight lifted by the body weight of the individual. The individual with the higher number is exerting more strength per pound of body weight. Thus, in this example, Jim has more relative muscular strength.

From a fitness standpoint, relative muscular strength is more important than absolute muscular strength. In Chapter 10, you will be asked to determine your relative muscular strength for a variety of weight-training exercises.

FIGURE 9.2

RELATIVE MUSCULAR STRENGTH
Below is the formula for calculating relative muscular strength.

	Weight Lifted ÷ Body Weight = Relative Muscular Strength
Jim	130 lbs ÷ 125 lbs = 1.04
Tom	150 lbs ÷ 160 lbs = 0.93

Lesson 1   Benefits of Resistance Training   **247**

Mind OVER Matter

Developing Muscular Strength

The strongest person may not be the fittest. Try not to worry about your maximum strength and how it compares to others. Where fitness is concerned, it is your strength in relation to your body weight that matters.

By developing your relative muscular strength, you will have more of the physical energy you need to perform day-to-day physical tasks as well as a more positive outlook.

Mind OVER Matter

Developing Muscular Strength

The largest student in class is often the strongest—but not necessarily the healthiest and most fit—student. Be sure students understand that large individuals who lack the strength to carry their bodies correctly and efficiently are not as healthy as someone who has the appropriate relative muscular strength appropriate for their body weight.

Discussing

Ask the following questions: How strong does a person need to be for good health? How strong should a person be when participating in organized sports? Is there a difference? Emphasize to students that being strong enough to handle your body weight is important to your total health. **L1** TEKS C4A

USING VISUALS

Figure 9.2 Have students use the formula to determine their personal relative strength in a variety of muscle groups. They can estimate their personal relative strength on the bench press. Later, when they actually participate in the weight room, they can recalculate their relative strength.

Student Edition TEKS

Page 246: C1B, C4A

Enrichment

Muscular Fitness for Work Students should consider how muscular fitness relates directly to the ability to perform tasks in certain occupations. Have students interview professionals, homemakers, construction workers, salespeople, and school staff. During their interviews, students should gather information about actual physical movement relating to each job. Students can then analyze ways to maintain a certain level of muscular fitness within each occupation. Have students develop creative workouts to improve workers' basic muscular fitness.

Photo Follow-up

Everyone can benefit from regular resistance-training workouts. These workouts benefit your personal appearance as well as your physical and mental health.

Discussing

Discuss and explain each of the possibilities for resistance training listed on page 249. Have students compare and contrast the skill-related and health-related fitness benefits of each form. Which of the forms are adults most likely to choose for maintaining a lifetime of health and fitness? *Weight training is appropriate for lifetime health and fitness.*
L1 TEKS C4D

✓ Reading Check

Absolute muscular strength is the maximum force you are able to exert, while relative muscular strength is the maximum force you can exert in relation to your body weight.

hotlink

In Chapter 10, students can find out more about the role of repetitions in resistance training. Have them review the overload principle in Chapter 3.

✓ Reading Check

Five types of progressive resistance that can be included in an exercise prescription are weight training, weight lifting, bodybuilding, strength training, and rehabilitation.
TEKS C4F

▶ Improving your muscular strength and endurance can improve the way you look and feel.

hotlink

repetitions (reps)
For more on repetitions and their role in resistance training, see Chapter 10, page **296.**

hotlink

overload principle
For more on the overload principle, see Chapter 3, page **83.**

Muscular Endurance

Muscular endurance is *the ability of the same muscle or muscle group to contract for an extended period of time without undue fatigue.* Muscle endurance is measured by two numbers: the amount of resistance (or weight) and the number of **repetitions** (or "reps"). A person who can properly lift 75 pounds for 15 reps, for example, has greater muscular endurance than a person (of the same gender) who can only do 10 reps with the same amount of weight.

As with muscular strength, good health and fitness depend more on relative muscular endurance than on absolute endurance. **Relative muscular endurance** is *the maximum number of times you can repeatedly perform a resistance activity in relation to your body weight.*

✓ Reading Check

Compare How is absolute muscular strength different from relative muscular strength?

Resistance Training and Overload

According to the **overload principle,** to improve a muscle's strength or endurance, you must first overload that muscle. In resistance training, *overloading* means putting more stress, in the form of weight or resistance, on a muscle than it is accustomed to handling. The extra stress load takes the form of weight or some similar force.

Progressive Resistance

As your muscles gradually adjust to the increased stress, you need to increase the workload further. This causes the muscles to become stronger. **Progressive resistance** is *the continued systematic increase of muscle workload by the addition of more weight or resistance.*

INCLUSION STRATEGIES

OVERLOAD PRINCIPLE The overload principle needs to be carefully studied and modified for those students with neuro- and progressive muscular disorders. Overloading already weak muscles can cause permanent loss of muscle fiber and function. Progressive resistance programs often need to be conducted at a slower rate of progression than the rate used with able-bodied students. Review the value of weight training for students with muscular disorders. No weight-training program should be developed for students with disabilities without input from a qualified physician.

There are many forms of progressive resistance that training can take. Each has its own specific goal. They include:

- **Weight training.** This is a general term that refers to the use of weights to improve general fitness, health, and appearance. Weight training can be done with barbells, dumbbells, and weight machines. It can also be done with a combination of machines and free weights.
- **Weight lifting.** This term refers to a competitive sport done by athletes who follow very specific training programs. Weight lifting is designed to build power and strength.
- **Bodybuilding.** This term refers to a competitive sport in which muscle size and shape are more important than strength. Like weight lifting, bodybuilders follow very specific programs and do many different resistance exercises.
- **Strength training or muscle conditioning.** This term refers to training done by athletes in competitive sports *other than* weight lifting or bodybuilding. Basketball, baseball, and football players all do strength training. Their common goal is to improve performance in their sport and reduce the chance of sports-related injury.
- **Rehabilitation.** This term refers to the use of resistance exercises to recover from a muscle or bone injury. Rehabilitative conditioning usually uses low levels of resistance.

 **Reading Check**

Summarize List the five components of progressive resistance training.

Lesson 1 Review

Using complete sentences, answer the following questions on a sheet of paper.

Reviewing Facts and Vocabulary

1. **Vocabulary** What is *resistance training*?
2. **Recall** Why is relative muscular strength more important to personal fitness than absolute muscular strength?
3. **Recall** What is *muscular endurance*?

Thinking Critically

4. **Compare and Contrast** Explain the difference between weight training and bodybuilding.
5. **Evaluate** Cory and Troy are both 15. Cory weighs 135 pounds and lifts 150 pounds on the bench press exercise. Troy weighs 142 pounds and lifts 165 pounds on the bench press. What is each teen's relative muscular strength? Which teen has the higher absolute strength? Which teen is more fit, generally speaking?

Personal Fitness Planning

Identifying Benefits Review the benefits of resistance training listed in **Figure 9.1.** Consider your personal fitness and choose five benefits that are most important to you. List them in order of importance, and briefly explain why they are important to you.

Lesson 1 Review

Answers to Lesson 1 Review

1. Exercises that increase a person's ability to resist or exert force.
2. Higher fitness is related to strength ability in relation to body weight. Strength pound for pound is related to your fitness.
3. When muscles can contract for an extended period without undue fatigue.
4. Weight training is the use of weights to improve fitness and appearance. Bodybuilding is a competitive sport to increase muscle size and shape.
5. Cory—1.11, Troy—1.16. Troy is more fit.

3 ASSESS

EVALUATING THE LESSON

Assign and discuss the Lesson 1 Review.

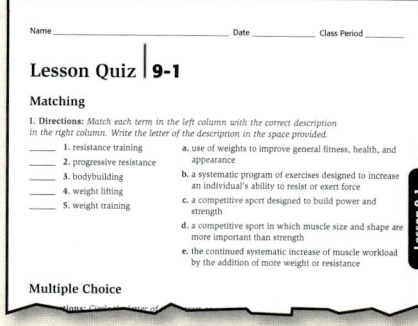

RETEACHING

Divide the class into five groups and have each group explain one of the five areas of resistance training.

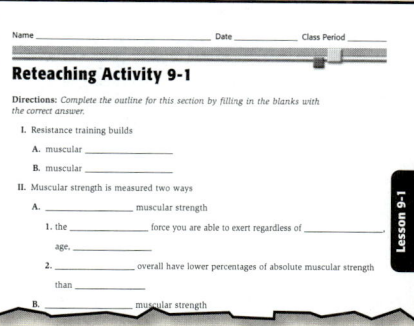

ENRICHMENT

Encourage students to use their personal journals to record their resistance-training program and the benefits they derive from weight training.

4 CLOSE

Ask students to consider whether their muscular strength and endurance are at acceptable physical fitness levels.

Your Muscles and Their Functions

1 MOTIVATE

GETTING STARTED

- Have students respond to the statement "Use it or lose it" with respect to the use of muscles. Ask: What are some of the most important muscles in the body? Why?

- Distribute copies of *Guided Practice 9-2* for students to use with this lesson. ☞

IN THIS LESSON

- **Lifeline,** *Understanding Rules,* page 255

INTRODUCING VOCABULARY

- Have a volunteer read the definition of *cardiac muscle* on this page. Then have students work in small groups to discuss why it is important for cardiac muscle to contract involuntarily.

- Have students use Vocabulary 9 or the PuzzleMaker software to practice vocabulary terms for this lesson. ELL ☞ ◎

Photo Follow-up

Have students identify daily activities that would be enhanced by increased skeletal muscular strength and endurance. *Caption answer: Stronger muscles are less likely to tear and fatigue during everyday tasks.*

What You Will Do

- Identify the different types of muscles and explain how muscles work.
- Apply the biomechanical principle of type of contraction to resistance training.
- Identify the role nerves play in muscle function and strength.
- Describe how muscles grow and become stronger.

Terms to Know

cardiac muscle
smooth muscles
skeletal muscles
contraction
extension
dynamic contraction
static contraction
nerves
muscle fiber
muscle hyperplasia
hypertrophy
microtears

Your Muscles and Their Functions

Most of the routine movements you make in a typical day, such as standing and walking, require little conscious thought. Yet, each of these movements involves the complex interaction of many different muscles and muscle groups. Muscles are elastic, stretching to allow a wide range of motion. In this lesson, you will learn about these biomechanical principles and the muscles that make them possible.

Types of Muscles

All body movements depend on muscles. Each muscle is grouped into one of three categories, depending on its function:

- **Cardiac muscle.** This is *a special type of striated tissue that forms the walls of the heart.* Your heart is the most important muscle in your body. Its unique properties enable it to contract rhythmically about 100,000 times a day to pump blood throughout the body. Contraction of cardiac muscle is involuntary.

  - **Smooth muscles.** These are *muscles responsible for the movements of the internal organs, such as the intestines, the bronchi of the lungs, and the bladder.* Also involuntary, they work without a person's conscious control.
  - **Skeletal muscles.** These are *muscles attached to bones that cause body movement.* There are more than 600 such muscles. Unlike the cardiac and smooth muscles, skeletal muscles are voluntary—that is, you consciously control their movement. The major skeletal muscles are shown in **Figure 9.3.**

◀ Resistance training will improve your ability to perform daily tasks. *How can increased muscular strength and endurance reduce your risk of injury when performing daily tasks?*

LESSON 2 RESOURCES

Teacher Classroom Resources
☞ Guided Practice Activity 9-2
☞ Reteaching Activity 9-2
☞ Lesson Quiz 9-2

Reproducible Charts and Graphs
☞ Reproducible Masters 9-1, 9-2

Multimedia
◎ Vocabulary PuzzleMaker
♨ Transparencies 50, 51, 52

Resistance training has little effect on involuntary muscles. The remainder of this lesson will focus mainly on skeletal muscles and how resistance training influences them.

Skeletal Muscles

Approximately two-thirds of the muscles in your body are skeletal muscles. They account for 40 percent of your body weight. Skeletal

Explaining

Discuss the three types of muscle tissue. Explain to students that this section focuses on the components and development of skeletal muscle tissue. **L1**

USING VISUALS

Figure 9.3 Use *Transparency 50* on the Skeletal Muscles to give students an idea of the location and function of the different muscle tissues and to discuss the way bones and muscles are attached. You may wish to display *Transparency 51*, showing the skeletal system, to discuss how muscles and bones work together. *Caption answer: Skeletal muscles will respond the most to resistance-training activities.*

FIGURE 9.3

THE SKELETAL MUSCLES

Muscles are grouped into three categories: cardiac, smooth, and skeletal. *Which of the three muscle types is most affected by weight training?*

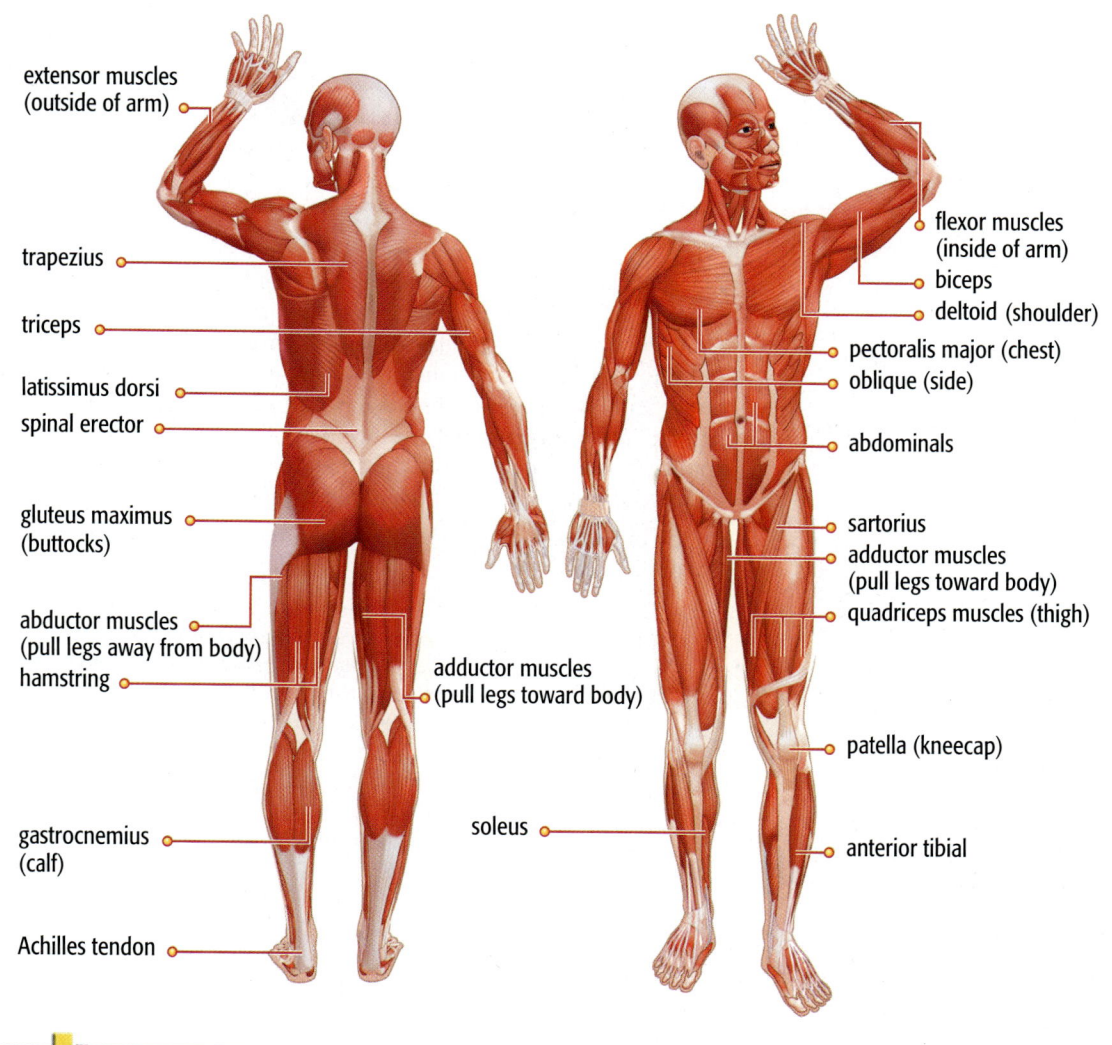

- extensor muscles (outside of arm)
- trapezius
- triceps
- latissimus dorsi
- spinal erector
- gluteus maximus (buttocks)
- abductor muscles (pull legs away from body)
- hamstring
- gastrocnemius (calf)
- Achilles tendon
- adductor muscles (pull legs toward body)
- soleus
- flexor muscles (inside of arm)
- biceps
- deltoid (shoulder)
- pectoralis major (chest)
- oblique (side)
- abdominals
- sartorius
- adductor muscles (pull legs toward body)
- quadriceps muscles (thigh)
- patella (kneecap)
- anterior tibial

Quick Demo

As you discuss the location of each skeletal muscle, show how the specific muscles move and demonstrate the potential range of motion for each area. Students can apply biomechanical principles to exercise and training by identifying the type of contraction. Have students simulate your movements and pronounce the name of the muscle correctly. **L2** **ELL**
TEKS C1B3

More About . . .

ANAEROBIC AND AEROBIC PROCESSES IN MUSCLES
Adenosine triphosphate (ATP) is a molecule that results in the breakdown of glucose. ATP is stored in a limited way as energy in cells. When ATP is broken down chemically in muscle tissue, energy is released. When glucose or glycogen is broken down without the presence of oxygen (*anaerobic*), energy is released. However, when glucose or glycogen is broken down in the presence of oxygen (*aerobic*), 18 to 20 times more ATP is produced than in the anaerobic process. This results in a higher yield of energy.

Student Edition TEKS

Page 250: C1B

Figure 9.4 Opposite muscles work by opposing each other to move the bones through their range of motion. Show *Transparency 51* and have volunteers demonstrate the process. All muscles at joints must have opposing muscles so that joints can be flexed and extended. Have students apply these biomechanical principles to exercise and training by explaining the use of force, leverage, and type of contraction in their demonstration. *Caption answer: The triceps will begin to relax from the contraction and stretch completely.* **TEKS C1B3**

Explaining

Point out to students that the six major muscle groups include the arms, legs, back, abdominals, shoulders, and chest. **L1**

Activity

While discussing the concept of muscle contraction, have students move specific joints and identify which muscles are contracting and which are extending. Then have them experience the three types of contraction (concentric, eccentric, and isometric). *Note: it will be difficult to experience the eccentric contraction since no resistance is being used.* **L1** **TEKS C1B**

FIGURE 9.4

MUSCLE CONTRACTION

The biceps and triceps are opposing muscles of the arm. Place the fingers of one hand on the triceps of your other arm and flex your biceps. *What do you feel happening to your triceps?*

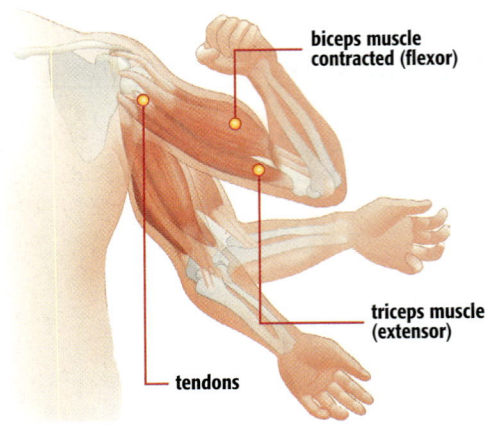

biceps muscle contracted (flexor)

triceps muscle (extensor)

tendons

---

muscles work together to produce two *complementary,* or opposing, actions. These are **contraction,** *the shortening of a muscle,* and **extension,** *the stretching of a muscle.* See this process at work for yourself right now by "making a muscle." When you flex the muscle in your upper arm (your biceps), the bulge you see is caused by the muscle's contraction (see **Figure 9.4**). Notice that as your biceps shortens and compacts, the large muscle on the other side of your arm becomes rigid and stretched tight. This muscle (your triceps) is extending.

Types of Contractions. There are two main types of muscle contractions. These are:

● **Dynamic contraction.** Also sometimes called *isotonic contraction,* this is *a type of muscle contraction that occurs when the resistance force is movable,* such as a barbell. Dynamic contraction has two phases. In the *concentric phase,* the muscle shortens and exerts force in a direction opposite the pull of gravity. In the *eccentric phase,* the muscle should slowly and smoothly release its contraction and become longer. Arm curls with a dumbbell are an example of an exercise that uses dynamic muscle contraction. If the muscle were simply to relax rather than slowly lengthen, gravity would quickly pull the arm down. This would not allow for any muscle work to be done during the eccentric contraction. Muscle work during the eccentric contractions is necessary for development of muscle strength and growth.

252 **Chapter 9** Basics of Resistance Training

More About . . .

ISOMETRIC WORKOUTS Guide students in discussing ways to involve different muscle groups to produce isometric contractions. Explain ways to apply biomechanical principles such as force and leverage when concentrating on these types of contractions. Then divide the class into two or three work groups to design and prepare a variety of isometric workout stations. Encourage each group to include the use of towels, ropes, and doorways in their plan. Be sure each work station is set up safely. Have students work with partners, and be sure they use different parts of their bodies. **ELL** **TEKS C1B**

- **Static contraction.** Also sometimes called *isometric contraction*, this is *a type of muscle contraction that occurs absent of any significant movement.* Flexing the muscle in your upper arm is an example of a static contraction. So is pushing against a wall or other immovable object. Pushing your fist with all your might into the palm of your other hand is also a static contraction.

Nerves and Muscle Fibers

For a muscle to contract, it must receive a signal from the brain. This signal is carried by **nerves**. These are *pathways that deliver messages from the brain to other body parts.* The **muscle fiber** is *the specific structure in the muscle that receives this signal.* This is a long, thin strand no wider than a human hair. Bundles of such fibers account for most of a muscle's mass. Blood provides oxygen, energy, and a waste removal system for each muscle fiber.

Connective Tissues

Skeletal muscles are connected to the bones by means of fibrous cords of tissue called tendons. These bind the two together while allowing the muscles to move efficiently. Bones are connected to one another by bands of tissue called *ligaments*.

 **Reading Check**

Compare What is the difference between a dynamic contraction and a static contraction?

How and Why Muscles Grow

Scientists do not fully understand exactly how and why resistance training builds muscles. However, several theories have emerged.

Muscle Hyperplasia

Some experts believe that muscles get larger during weight training due to **muscle hyperplasia** (hy-per-PLAY-zhuh), *an increase in the number of muscle fibers.* As yet, muscle hyperplasia has been seen only in some animals, such as cats and dogs.

Muscle Hypertrophy

Other researchers contend that a person is born with his or her full number of muscle fibers. According to this view, muscle growth is due to **hypertrophy** (hy-PER-truh-fee), *a thickening of existing muscle fibers,* not to an increase in their number.

During resistance training, chemical and physical changes occur inside the muscle fiber that can cause hypertrophy. If each of the hundreds of thousands of fibers within a muscle slightly increases in size, the entire muscle will become larger.

Fitness FACTS

Muscles at Work

- The concentric phase of a contraction is also known as *positive work,* the eccentric phase as *negative work.*
- The majority of weight-training activities and exercises make use of both positive and negative muscle work.

Fitness FACTS

Have students read the Fitness Facts, and emphasize to them the importance of eccentric contractions. Concentric and eccentric contractions contribute equally to the development of skeletal muscle.

Activity

- Have students do arm curls with a light dumbbell to feel the concentric and eccentric contractions. Explain how the eccentric is working against the resistance of the weight, not against the pull of the contracting triceps.
- Have students place their left palm in their right palm. Instruct them to push with the left hand and pull with the right hand as they apply force. They should push as hard as they can. Explain that this movement represents an isometric contraction.
L2 TEKS C1B

✓ **Reading Check**

A dynamic contraction occurs when resistance force is movable; static contraction occurs without any significant movement.

Student Edition TEKS

Page 252: C1B
Page 253: C1B

RESISTANCE TRAINING Isokinetic resistance machines are exercise machines that provide resistance (positive only) to movement at a given speed. In recent years isokinetic machines have become one option in the rehabilitation of injured athletes. Isotonic exercises, on the other hand, use several different forms of resistance, including gravity, and the speed of movement is controlled by the athlete. Finally, there are free weights, which involve constant balancing and thus a greater recruitment of surrounding muscles to better simulate the real-world movement of athletics and exercise.

Discussing

Ask: What happens to your muscles when a cast has been placed around a broken bone for a number of weeks? Explain that the loss of muscle mass is called *atrophy*. Then ask what happens to the muscles after the cast is removed and you use weights or other resistance devices for a period of time. Point out that the increase in muscle mass is called *hypertrophy*. **L1**

hotlink

Slow- and fast-twitch muscle fiber is primarily a result of heredity. See Chapter 7 for more information.

USING VISUALS

Figure 9.5 Using *Reproducible Master 9-2*, point out that some of the activities listed require both kinds of muscle fiber. This is an indication that both speed and endurance are involved in the activity. *Caption answers will vary. Students may be better at certain activities depending on their personal ratio of slow- to fast-twitch muscle fibers. Remind students that athletes—regardless of their heredity—need to work hard at their chosen activity to acquire a high degree of proficiency.*

hotlink

slow- and fast-twitch muscle fibers
For more on the ratio of slow-twitch to fast-twitch muscle fibers, see Chapter 7, page **208.**

How and Why Muscles Get Stronger

Increased strength is usually the main goal of individuals who begin a resistance-training program. With proper training and good nutrition, weight training can and will improve muscle strength. However, many other factors affect muscle strength. Among these are heredity, muscle size, and nerve function.

Heredity

Heredity is the total of physical and mental traits that you inherit from your biological parents. One inherited trait that directly affects your potential for building muscle strength is your muscle fiber ratio. Specifically, everyone is born with two types of fiber—**slow-twitch** and **fast-twitch.** As noted in Chapter 7, fast-twitch fibers are better suited to anaerobic work than slow-twitch fibers. They also have a greater capacity to increase in size. The greater the proportion of fast-twitch to slow-twitch muscle fibers a person inherits, the greater his or her increase in muscular strength is likely to be. **Figure 9.5** shows the role of slow- and fast-twitch muscle fibers in specific activities.

Muscle Size

The larger the muscle, the greater its potential for strength. Strength, in other words, is directly related to a muscle's size. Researchers have found that muscle fibers are capable of developing

FIGURE 9.5

FAST-TWITCH AND SLOW-TWITCH MUSCLE FIBERS

This chart shows the relative involvement of fast-twitch and slow-twitch muscle fibers in sport events. *Which of these activities do you do best? What does this suggest about your ratio of slow-twitch to fast-twitch muscles?*

Event	Involvement of Fast-Twitch Fibers	Involvement of Slow-Twitch Fibers
100-yard dash	High	Low
Marathon	Low	High
Olympic weight lifting	High	Low
Barbell squat	High	High
Soccer	High	High
Basketball	High	Low
Distance cycling	Low	High

More About . . .

MUSCLE STRENGTH AND WEIGHT TRAINING Two concepts are important to understand with regard to muscular strength and weight training: specificity and symmetry. The principle of specificity states that a weight-training program can focus on a particular muscle or group of muscles. If you are weight training to improve performance in a particular sport or activity, then your weight-training program should exercise the muscle groups actually used in that sport or activity. For example, a bodybuilder who wants to develop size and definition in the lower a maximal force of 3.5 kg (7.7 lb) per square centimeter (0.4 in²) of muscle area on average. Supposing, for example, that Kyle increases his muscle size by 50 percent (from 100 to 150 cm²). Then the maximal force Kyle could exert (his strength) would be increased from 350 kg (770 lb) to 525 kg (1,155 lb).

Nerve Function

Before a muscle can contract, it must receive a message from the brain. That message is carried by nerves. Regular resistance training improves the ability of nerves to carry messages to a muscle. The messages will then arrive faster and cause more muscle fibers to contract. The result is improved strength. A person just beginning weight training can attribute most early gains in strength to improved nerve function.

Other Factors Associated with Muscle Strength

Several other lesser factors can influence the development of muscular strength. These include:

- **Consistent training habits.** People who work out regularly will see more improvement than those who do not.
- **Level of strength.** Beginning lifters will see a more rapid strength improvement than experienced weight trainees.
- **Training intensity.** This includes how hard you work, the kind of program you follow, the number of sets and repetitions, and which muscles you are working. You will learn more about factors associated with weight-training intensity in Chapter 10.
- **Length of your program.** The longer you work, whether it is weeks, months, or years, the more you can improve your strength.

✔ Reading Check

Summarize Name three major factors that influence muscular strength.

Why Muscles Get Sore

Everyone has experienced some muscle soreness at one time or another. This is especially common in the beginning stages of resistance training. This soreness usually occurs within twenty-four to forty-eight hours of the workout.

There are several theories about why muscles get sore. One theory is that microtears—*microscopic rips in the muscle fiber and/or surrounding tissues*—occur during greater-than-normal resistance. These tears are most likely to happen during the negative, or eccentric, phase of an activity or exercise. This is especially true when you come down too fast and stop quickly when lowering a heavy weight.

LIFELINE

Understanding Rules

Apart from the physical dangers and illegality of steroid use, there are other issues potential users need to consider:

- Steroid use violates school rules. Players who use steroids may be barred from all future competition.
- Any performance advantage gained from using steroids is unfair. By taking *any* performance-enhancing drug, you cheat the other team, your team, and yourself.

  Avoid steroid use, and encourage others to do the same. Steer clear of steroids.

**FITNESS** *Online*

Learn more about muscles and their function at **fitness.glencoe.com**.

Activity Click on the interactive buttons and test your knowledge of each muscle in the body.

LIFELINE

Understanding Rules

Lead a discussion on the legal and ethical issues involved with steroid use. Remind students that all steroid use, other than that prescribed by a licensed physician, is illegal and dangerous. Ask students to consider what they value in being part of a team. Then ask: How would using steroids contradict those values? How can you apply these rules during physical activities? **TEKS C2A1**

Discussing

Discuss the following statement: "Anybody who works hard enough and long enough can become a world-class bodybuilder or power lifter." **L2**

✔ Reading Check

Muscle strength is influenced by heredity, muscle size, and nerve function.

Photo Follow-up

Discuss the photo on page 256. *Caption answer: The bending of the knee to slow down the pitcher's momentum is an example of an eccentric contraction.*

leg would focus his or her efforts on the gastrocnemius, soleus, and tibialis anterior muscles. Symmetry, on the other hand, refers to the interrelation of muscles to form an aesthetically pleasing and properly functioning whole. It's important to maintain a degree of symmetry within the muscle groups. If one particular group becomes hypertrophied, meaning excessively developed, there may be an increased likelihood of injury due to this muscle imbalance. Also, a body that is extremely asymmetrical in muscular development appears unbalanced.

Student Edition TEKS

Page 254: C1B
Page 255: C1B, C2A, C3D

3 ASSESS

EVALUATING THE LESSON

Assign and discuss the Lesson 2 Review.

Name _____ Date _____ Class Period _____

Lesson Quiz | 9-2

Multiple Choice

I. **Directions:** *Circle the letter of the correct answer.*

1. The three different muscle categories are
   a. dynamic, static, and skeletal.   b. cardiac, smooth, and skeletal.
   c. abductor, adductor, and flexor.   d. none of the above.
2. Skeletal muscles work together to produce complementary actions known as
   a. hyperplasia and hypertrophy.   b. dumbbell and barbell.
   c. contraction and extension.   d. fast-twitch and slow-twitch.
3. A factor associated with muscle strength is
   a. heredity.   b. muscle size.
   c. nerve function.   d. all of the above.
4. Hypertrophy is
   a. an increase in the number of muscle fibers.
   b. a specific structure in the muscle.
   c. the pathway that delivers messages from the brain to other body parts.
   d. a thickening of existing muscle fibers.
5. To prevent muscle soreness

RETEACHING

Have students work in small groups to develop a concentric and eccentric movement for the leg, arm, and shoulder. Have volunteers demonstrate these movements. Then assign *Reteaching Activity 9-2.* 📁

ENRICHMENT

Have students design and implement a personal resistance-training program that works all the major muscles with concentric and eccentric contractions. **TEKS C4G**

4 CLOSE

Have student groups discuss activities that can be used in resistance training.

256

▲ Baseball pitchers often experience soreness in the leg muscles from "braking" too abruptly at the completion of their pitching motion. *What phase of a dynamic muscle contraction is occurring at this point?*

Another theory suggests that during intense exercise, a muscle may not receive all the oxygen it needs. Even though this oxygen shortage is temporary, it may still contribute to soreness.

A third explanation is that waste products build up around the muscles during intense exercise. This accumulation is believed to increase pressure on sensory nerves. The result is muscle pain.

Treating Muscle Soreness

Regardless of the cause of exercise-related muscle soreness, this soreness is not a serious problem. In fact, it is quite normal. With proper training technique and time, the soreness will go away.

In the meantime, there are several steps you can take to help relieve muscle soreness.

- Be sure to perform a proper warm-up and cooldown.
- If the pain is excessive, you are lifting too much. Reduce the amount of weight, and do a lighter workout.
- Drink plenty of water—before, during, and after working out. Eat meals on a regular basis and choose nutritious foods.
- Give the muscles time to repair themselves before reworking them. After two to three days, most soreness is usually gone.

 Reading Check

Explain How can you prevent muscle soreness?

Lesson 2 Review

Using complete sentences, answer the following questions on a sheet of paper.

Reviewing Facts and Vocabulary

1. **Vocabulary** What is *muscle hypertrophy?* What causes it?
2. **Recall** List and explain the two main types of muscle contraction.
3. **Recall** What is one explanation of why and how muscles get stronger?

Thinking Critically

4. **Analyze** Name a sport or activity that you enjoy doing or would like to begin doing. Identify aspects of this sport that involve concentric muscle contractions and aspects that involve eccentric muscle contractions.

256   Chapter 9   Basics of Resistance Training

5. **Evaluate** What advice would you give a friend who is experiencing muscle soreness after beginning a program of resistance training?

Personal Fitness Planning

Designing a Program Devise a plan for a regular program of resistance training for your upper body, shoulders, arms, and legs. Your plan should not use any additional weights; use only the weight of your body. Start slowly, no more than three days a week. This will allow your muscles time to adapt gradually and begin the strengthening process. Begin your program, and keep a log of your progress.

Lesson 2 Review

Answers to Lesson 2 Review

1. A thickening or enlargement of muscle fibers in a muscle. Performing weight training or resistance training.
2. Dynamic: shortening and slow release; Static: absent of any significant movement.
3. Heredity can determine your potential for muscle growth. The intensity and consistency of workouts plays a role.
4. Answers will vary.
5. Provide the muscle with two or three days of rest or reduced activity and include some light stretching.

Resistance-Training Myths

More and more people are recognizing the benefits of resistance training. However, there are several myths about resistance training that may prevent some from making it part of their workout. In this lesson, you will explore some of these myths and understand the reality of resistance training and its benefits.

Resistance-Training Myths Associated with Females

Many of the most widespread and lasting myths about resistance training involve women. The two that follow are among the most commonly repeated.

Myth 1: Bulky Muscles

Females who lift weights will develop big, bulky muscles. The average female has a smaller and lighter skeleton, has narrower shoulders, and is 30 to 40 pounds lighter than the average male. She also has less muscle mass. The total number of muscle fibers tends to be lower in women. Also, there is a difference in testosterone levels between the genders. **Testosterone** is *a chemical produced by the body that plays an important role in building muscles.* Although

▶ Contrary to one myth, resistance training can improve athletic performance and skill-related fitness. *What specific advantages does resistance training offer to these volleyball players?*

Lesson 3 Resistance-Training Myths **257**

What You Will Do

- Compare differences between the muscles of males and females.
- Identify the age at which a program of resistance training can safely be started.
- Recognize how resistance training can benefit older adults.

Terms to Know

testosterone
osteoporosis
muscle tone

Resistance-Training Myths

1 MOTIVATE

GETTING STARTED

- Before you begin roll call, ask the class to think about the following: Are there reasons why males or females should not be involved in a resistance-training program?
- Distribute copies of *Guided Practice 9-3* for students to use with this lesson. 📁

IN THIS LESSON

- **Fitness Facts**, *p. 259*

INTRODUCING VOCABULARY

- Explain that osteo is from the Greek *osteon*, meaning "bone," and *porosis* means "porous." The term *osteoporosis* literally means "porous bone."
- Have students use *Vocabulary Worksheet 9* or the PuzzleMaker software to practice vocabulary terms for this lesson. **ELL** 📁 💿

Photo Follow-up

Discuss the photo and caption with students. *Caption answer: Resistance training provides increased performance in the sport and a reduction of potential injury and severity of injury should one occur.*

LESSON 3 RESOURCES

Teacher Classroom Resources
📁 Guided Practice Activity 9-3
📁 Reteaching Activity 9-3
📁 Lesson Quiz 9-3

Multimedia
💿 Vocabulary PuzzleMaker

Student Edition TEKS
Page 256: C1B, C4G
Page 257: C5E

257

2 TEACH

Discussing

Discuss Myth 1 and list reasons why the females in your class will not develop large muscles during the next few weeks of resistance training. The list should include the following: Females have considerably less testosterone; the intensity in this class and in weight training in general is not high enough; females have fewer and smaller muscle fibers, and on average have about 8 percent higher body fat and less total body weight than males; strict diets and long, hard workouts are required to achieve the look associated with female bodybuilders.

L1 **TEKS C5G**

Photo Follow-up

Ask the class to think about the professional female athletes they have seen on TV. Are those athletes built like the female bodybuilders you have seen? Why do the bodybuilders look different? *Caption answers may vary, but could include that females will not gain strength or it may make them less feminine. It was once believed that weight training would reduce flexibility in women, increase their risk for disease, or even reduce their potential for athletic performance.*

✓ **Reading Check**

Resistance training offers added strength and reduces the risk of osteoporosis in females.

---

the female body does produce some testosterone, the level is 1/10 to 1/20 that of males. These factors provide assurance that females who engage in strength training will not develop big, bulky muscles.

Myth 2: Strength

Female muscles will not develop increased strength. Although females typically have less muscular strength than males, this does not mean lesser strength gains. When placed in similar resistance-training programs, females may enjoy *greater* strength improvements than males. This is because of the lower level at which they started. Also, although they may have less muscular strength than males, females who follow regular programs of weight training have a reduced risk of osteoporosis (os-tee-oh-pur-OH-sis). This is *a bone disease that causes decreased bone mass and density,* especially in older women. It is especially important for females during the teen years to build bone mass to reduce the risk of osteoporosis. This can be done through weight-bearing activities and a diet that includes calcium-rich foods.

✓ **Reading Check**

Explain Name two benefits of resistance training for females.

► The fear of developing big, bulky muscles has been exposed as a myth. *Can you name another myth about resistance training involving females?*

INCLUSION STRATEGIES

MUSCLE STRENGTH AND DISABILITIES
Some students with disabilities may have disorders that directly affect muscular strength and endurance. These conditions may result from actual involvement of the muscles (e.g., muscular dystrophy) or may be a result of faulty nerve transmission (e.g., myasthenia gravis). Care must be taken when developing weight-training programs for these individuals. Muscular strength and endurance in the mentally retarded population is generally poor due to inactivity. Weight training is an excellent activity for the higher-functioning.

Other Resistance-Training Myths

Some of the remaining popular myths about resistance training relate to the age of the lifter. Others relate to the lifter's expectations of results.

Myth 3: Children and Teens

Weight training is harmful to the growth and development of children and teens. A recent study by the American Academy of Pediatrics suggests that, with proper supervision, weight training can be done by children as young as age 5. Teens can obtain many of the same benefits as adults through a specially designed program of weight training. Weight training also offers the additional benefit of maximizing bone development during adolescence. This can help reduce your risk of osteoporosis later in life. It also improves glucose tolerance, reducing your risks of obesity and type 2 diabetes.

Serious injury can occur if weight lifting is not done properly. However, if teens observe proper technique and safety precautions when lifting weights, they can avoid injury. Proper supervision and training under a certified fitness trainer or a coach is important. Done correctly, resistance training is not dangerous for teens.

Myth 4: Older Adults

Older adults should avoid weight training. More and more older adults recognize the benefits of resistance training. Medical professionals advise them to participate in a fitness program throughout the life span that includes strength training. The results include improved ability to walk, lift things, climb stairs, and stay active and healthy. Moreover, since older adults rapidly acquire strength gains, they can practice weight training for a lifetime.

Myth 5: Bodybuilders

With enough time and effort, anybody can be a world-class bodybuilder or power weight lifter. Although anyone can expect some strength and size improvements with regular weight training, not everyone will obtain the same results. You are limited by your heredity. This does not mean that you should not work at reaching your maximum potential in the weight room. Resistance training will lead to health and fitness benefits, even if it doesn't make you a world-class bodybuilder.

Myth 6: Muscle and Fat

Muscle can turn to fat if a person stops lifting weights. Muscle and fat are different kinds of tissue. They are not interchangeable. Strength training improves lean body mass and tones muscles. People who stop lifting may see a decrease in muscle size and **muscle tone.** This refers to *a muscle's firmness and definition.* They will not, however, see an increase in body fat unless they discontinue all forms of physical activity while taking in the same number of **calories.**

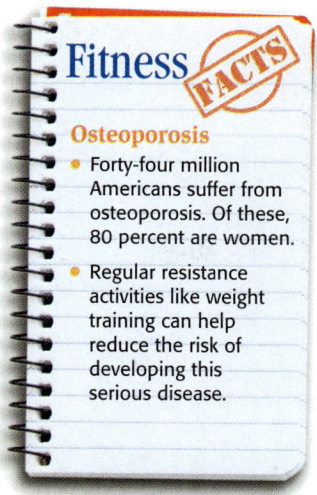

Fitness FACTS

Osteoporosis
- Forty-four million Americans suffer from osteoporosis. Of these, 80 percent are women.
- Regular resistance activities like weight training can help reduce the risk of developing this serious disease.

Source: National Osteoporosis Foundation, 2003.[1]

hotlink

calories
For more on the relationship between calories and physical activity, see Chapter 4, page **115.**

Explaining

Resistance training offers many benefits that can be enjoyed by people of all ages. Resistance training, if done safely and correctly, is very beneficial to children's health. Children should not lift more than 50 percent of their body weight on any lifts and should never be forced to participate in a program. Older adults can maintain good muscular strength throughout their lives if they regularly practice lifting. **L3**

Fitness FACTS

Discuss the facts about osteoporosis with students. Remind them that getting enough calcium during the teen years, along with regular physical activity, will help reduce the risks of developing osteoporosis later in life. Explain that teens need at least 1,300 mg of calcium daily. **TEKS C5G**

Reading Check
(page 260)

Students should discuss the myths and facts for children, teens, or older adults. **TEKS C5E**

The overload principle needs to be carefully studied and modified for those students with neuromuscular disorders. Overloading already weak muscles can cause permanent loss of muscle fiber and function. Progressive resistance programs often need to be conducted at a slower rate of progression than the rate used with able-bodied students. The value of weight training for disabled students with muscular weakness disorders needs to be carefully reviewed. No weight training program should be developed for any student with muscular disorders without input from a qualified physician.

3 ASSESS

EVALUATING THE LESSON

Assign and discuss the Lesson 3 Review.

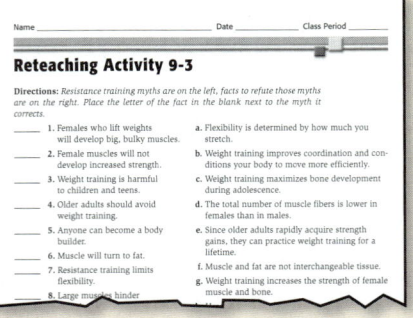

Name _____ Date _____ Class Period _____

Lesson Quiz | 9-3

Matching

I. Directions: *Match each term in the left column with the correct definition in the right column. Write the letter of the definition in the space provided.*

_____ 1. testosterone
_____ 2. osteoporosis
_____ 3. muscle tone

a. a bone disease that causes decreased bone mass and density
b. muscle firmness and definition
c. a chemical produced by the body that plays an important role in building muscles

Fill in the Blanks

II. Directions: *Fill in the spaces with correct answers.*

4. Females have less muscle mass than males, and the total number of _____ tends to be lower in females.

5. The female body produces _____ at 1/10 to 1/20 the level produced by males.

RETEACHING

Have students identify the differences between body builders and endurance-event athletes.

Name _____ Date _____ Class Period _____

Reteaching Activity 9-3

Directions: *Resistance training myths are on the left, facts to refute those myths are on the right. Place the letter of the fact in the blank next to the myth it corrects.*

_____ 1. Females who lift weights will develop big, bulky muscles.
_____ 2. Female muscles will not develop increased strength.
_____ 3. Weight training is harmful to children and teens.
_____ 4. Older adults should avoid weight training.
_____ 5. Anyone can become a body builder.
_____ 6. Muscle will turn to fat.
_____ 7. Resistance training limits flexibility.
_____ 8. Large muscles hinder

a. Flexibility is determined by how much you stretch.
b. Weight training improves coordination and conditions your body to move more efficiently.
c. Weight training maximizes bone development during adolescence.
d. The total number of muscle fibers is lower in females than in males.
e. Since older adults rapidly acquire strength gains, they can practice weight training for a lifetime.
f. Muscle and fat are not interchangeable tissue.
g. Weight training increases the strength of female muscle and bone.

ENRICHMENT

Have students survey students in the school to determine which myths in this lesson are thought to be true. Have them report the results to the class.

4 CLOSE

Discuss how weight training is a vital part of a sound fitness program for everyone.

Myth 7: Muscles and Flexibility

Resistance training will limit my flexibility. Some people believe that increasing muscular strength and endurance means limiting or reducing flexibility. However, weight training will not negatively affect a person's flexibility. Your flexibility is determined primarily by how much you stretch. Proper weight lifting will help you maintain and improve your level of flexibility, as long as your fitness program includes proper stretching. You will learn more about the relationship between muscular strength and flexibility in Chapter 11.

Myth 8: Muscles and Skill-Related Fitness

Larger muscles will hinder athletic performance. Because resistance training increases muscle size, some believe that it decreases certain skills, such as speed and coordination. However, the increased strength those muscles provide allows your body to move *more* quickly. Similarly, because many weight-training exercises involve the coordination of several muscles, resistance training improves coordination and conditions your body to move *more* efficiently.

 Reading Check

Explain Identify and explain a resistance-training myth that is related to physical activity and age. Then give the facts.

Lesson 3 Review

Using complete sentences, answer the following questions on a sheet of paper.

Reviewing Facts and Vocabulary

1. **Recall** Why are females unlikely to develop large, bulky muscles?
2. **Recall** How can weight training help prevent *osteoporosis*?
3. **Vocabulary** What is *muscle tone*?

Thinking Critically

4. **Analyze** What role does weight training play in bone development? In body composition?
5. **Synthesize** Karen is interested in toning and improving the muscular strength of her legs but is afraid bigger muscles will one day turn to fat. What reassurances about weight training could you give her?

Personal Fitness Planning

Identifying Goals List your goals for incorporating resistance activities into your own personal fitness plan. Write them down so they can be used to assist you in the development of your personal fitness program in the future. Keep your goals and review them as you learn more about resistance activities and exercises.

Lesson 3 Review

Answers to Lesson 3 Review

1. Females have fewer and smaller muscle fibers, higher body fat, and less total body weight than males.
2. Resistance-training programs help a growing person increase bone mass and help an aging person reduce the loss of bone.
3. A muscle's firmness and definition.
4. Muscles that are worked through a resistance-training program will develop stronger and healthier muscle fibers.
5. A well-designed program will help her reach her goal and maintain strength. Muscles cannot turn to fat.

Resistance-Training Equipment and Gear

Jorge had read all about the benefits of resistance training. He couldn't wait to put his knowledge to use. After an hour of lifting, he felt a stinging sensation in his right shoulder. By nightfall, the sting had become a searing pain. Jorge could have avoided his misery by learning some key safety facts about weight-training equipment and gear.

What You Will Do

- Evaluate the advantages and disadvantages of various weight-training devices.
- Identify different pieces of equipment in resistance-training areas.
- Evaluate consumer issues related to weight-training equipment.
- Participate in activities to evaluate and develop muscular strength.

Terms to Know

free weights
spotter
weight machines
exercise bands
plyometric exercises
calisthenic exercises
weight-training gloves
weight-training belts

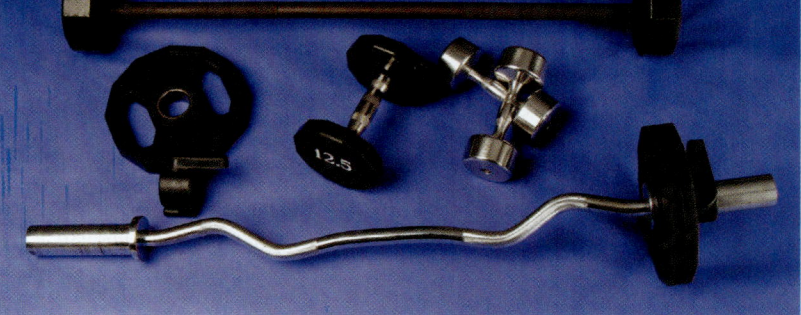

▲ Using equipment correctly is an important aspect of safety in the weight room. *What other precautions can you take to avoid injury and ensure a safe workout?*

LESSON 4 RESOURCES

Teacher Classroom Resources
- 📁 Guided Practice Activity 9-4
- 📁 Active Mind—Active Body Worksheet 9-4
- 📁 Fitness Check Worksheet 9-4
- 📁 Reteaching Activity 9-4
- 📁 Lesson Quiz 9-4

Multimedia
- 💿 Vocabulary PuzzleMaker
- 🖲 Transparency 53

---

1 MOTIVATE

GETTING STARTED
- Introduce this lesson to students in a weight room. Ask them to look at all the equipment and recall equipment they have seen or used in the past.
- Distribute copies of *Guided Practice Activity 9-4* for students to use with this lesson. 📁

IN THIS LESSON
- **Active Mind—Active Body** *What Is in Your Weight Room? p. 262*
- **Consumer Corner** *Purchasing Weight-Training Equipment, p. 265*
- **Fitness Check** *Evaluating Muscular Endurance, p. 267*

INTRODUCING VOCABULARY
- Go over the vocabulary terms in class. Invite volunteers to share what they know about each term.
- Have students use the *Vocabulary Worksheet 9* or the PuzzleMaker software to practice vocabulary terms for this lesson. **ELL** 📁 💿

Photo Follow-up
Free weights and weight machines are two types of resistance-training equipment. *Caption answer: Always use proper lifting technique; have a partner* **TEKS C2A1**

2 TEACH

Active Mind Active Body
What Is in Your Weight Room?

This activity will help you identify and better understand the types of equipment in your resistance-training facility.

Teaching Tips

- Have students meet in the weight room of your school. Have them work in cooperative groups to complete this project. **ELL**

- Remind students that they are not to actually use the equipment, but are to simply observe it and the facility.

- Copy and distribute *Active Mind–Active Body Worksheet 9-4* for students to complete when doing this activity. 📁

- Have students observe all parts of the facility and answer the questions on the worksheet.

- Have students seek help if they are not sure of any items.

Apply and Conclude

Ask students to evaluate any pieces of equipment that are new to them. Which pieces of equipment are they most familiar with?

Resistance-Training Equipment

Resistance training is performed using a variety of methods with equipment described in **Figure 9.6**. These include free weights, weight machines, exercise bands, plyometric exercise, and calisthenics. Each approach has its pros and cons.

Free Weights

Free weights is *a term applied collectively to dumbbells and barbells, as well as plates and clips.* A *dumbbell* is a short bar with weights at both ends, designed to be held and lifted with one hand. A *barbell* is a long, metal bar with weights at both ends, lifted with both hands at once. The weights placed on a barbell or dumbbell are often referred to as *plates*. They come in a variety of weights and are fastened to the bar using *clips* and *collars*. The reason they are called "free" weights is because of the unlimited direction and movement capabilities of this equipment. Free weights offer the advantage of being more versatile and less expensive than weight machines.

One notable disadvantage of free weights is that their use requires more balance and coordination than machines. The risk of unintentional injury is also greater. When using this equipment, it is vital to have a **spotter.** This is *a partner who can assist with the safe handling of weights and offer encouragement during a training session.*

Active Mind Active Body
What Is in Your Weight Room?

Every weight room is different. Some facilities have mostly machines—others, free weights. Still others have a combination of the two. In this activity, you will get to know the weight-training equipment at your school, a local branch of the YMCA, or another club to which you have access.

What You Will Need
- Pen or pencil
- Paper

What You Will Do

1. Visit the facility you will be using for your resistance training. Refer to the equipment checklist in **Figure 9.6** to identify all the equipment. Place a check mark in the appropriate boxes.
2. If you are unable to identify a particular machine or piece of equipment, speak with a manager or personal trainer. Add categories to your checklist as needed.
3. Complete your inventory by identifying the type(s) of resistance-training equipment available.

Apply and Conclude

Based on your training needs and current level of training (beginning, intermediate, and so on), identify which types of equipment you will work with. State how these will help you achieve your training goals.

262   **Chapter 9**   Basics of Resistance Training

More About . . .

STRENGTH AND CONDITIONING FACILITIES

Fitness instructors are often charged with improving and reorganizing their facilities. Before any changes are made, examine the following questions: How many people will be using the facility? What is the age and experience of those people? What is the status of the equipment? There are two generally accepted methods for organizing a facility. The first is to create areas that emphasize different body parts. The second is to arrange the facility according to the types of equipment (free weight, machines, plyometric, or stretching mats).

FIGURE 9.6

FITNESS FACILITY EQUIPMENT CHECKLIST

Knowing which types of resistance training are available to you is important for planning your workout.

Types of Bars	Types of Benches	
• Olympic	• Flat	• Abdominal
• Standard	• Incline	• Dipping Bar
• Cambered/Straight	• Hyper extension	• Chin-up bar
	• Preacher	

Types of Plates	Types of Machines	
• Olympic	• Leg press	• Leg abduction
• Standard	• Back squat	• Leg adduction

Types of Dumbbells		
• Dumbbell rack	• Leg extension	• Seated calf
• Hex style	• Leg curl	• Standing calf
• Pro style	• Lat pull down	
• Adjustable		

Weight Machines

Weight machines are *mechanical devices that move weights up and down using a system of cables and pulleys.* Some machines have an electronic component that digitally tracks resistance, workout time, and the like. Most machines require little or no balance on the part of the user. Spotters are not required because the weights are connected to the machine and have a predetermined path of movement. Varying the resistance is also easy, in most cases requiring the simple movement of a pin from one weight setting to another.

Anyone planning to buy a weight machine should be mindful of this equipment's expense, which can run into the thousands of dollars. Another problem is that weight machines require large amounts of space. Finally, most machines are targeted at a single muscle area, unlike free weights, which can be used for a multitude of tasks. The chart in **Figure 9.7** on page **264** compares other aspects of weight machines and free weights.

✓ Reading Check

Explain Give one advantage and one disadvantage of using weight machines.

Other concerns include traffic flow and the distance between machines and free weights. Environmental conditions can help to create a place in which students feel motivated to work out. A well-lighted facility can help prevent injuries and create a positive environment. A recommended temperature range is 72 to 78 degrees, with a relative humidity of 60 percent or less. Sound systems are encouraged but should not exceed 90 decibels. Items such as mirrors, drinking fountains, helpful signs, and bulletin boards are highly recommended.

USING VISUALS

Figure 9.6 Have students read the equipment checklist in Figure 9.6. Students may refer to this list as they complete the *Active Mind—Active Body* feature on page 262.

Activity

Have students visit their local YMCA, community recreation center, or private facility to evaluate consumer issues related to fitness services. Have them examine the many different types of equipment available. Have them pay particular attention to how machines can be adjusted for the different sizes of users. This is an important safety consideration. Using an incorrect setting can injure muscles or joints. **L3 TEKS C4H**

✓ Reading Check

Weight machines require no spotters, thus reducing risk of injury. Machines require only the movement of a pin to change resistance, which saves time. The disadvantage is their increased cost and their lack of versatility. Free weights are very versatile and cost less money. They require spotters and a great deal more balance, which makes free-weight lifting harder to learn.

Student Edition TEKS

Page 262: C4H

FIGURE 9.7

USING VISUALS

Figure 9.7 Display *Transparency 53* and discuss the pros and cons of free weights and weight machines. Allow students to discuss each of the factors being evaluated in the figure. Ask students to consider the following questions in their discussion: Have you been to professional facilities to see the many types of weight machines? Do they have resistance equipment? Was it costly, and does it take up a lot of space? How often is it used? Why do you think most schools have free weights and not machines? Which kind of equipment is more likely to motivate you to work out?

Discussing

Students should begin, as early as possible, their introduction to weight-training safety and proper exercise techniques. Students will be asked to perform strength evaluations both before and after their exercise program. It is important that students prepare for these evaluations over a reasonable period of time. This will allow students to perform their best as well as meet guidelines for adolescent activity levels. You may wish to combine the concepts in Chapters 9 and 10, but be sure students are actively involved in resistance-training exercises at least three times per week. **L3**

FREE WEIGHTS VS. WEIGHT MACHINES

Understanding the advantages and disadvantages of both free weights and machines is helpful in planning your program.

Name one advantage and disadvantage of both free weights and machines.

Factor	Free Weights	Machines	Advantage
Cost	Less expensive, $200 can buy a complete set	Very costly to purchase and maintain, need a variety of machines	Free weights
Space	Take minimal space and may be moved easily	Large, bulky, and heavy; difficult to move	Free weights
Safety	Require a spotter, require balance, greater chance of injury, can cause accidents if not stored in a safe place	Weights are secured, requires no balance or spotters to lift	Machine
Variety	Allow for many different exercises with the same equipment, prevents boredom, works all parts of the body	Usually only one exercise can be done on a machine, many machines are necessary to provide variety	Free weights
Technique/Balance	Difficult to learn, much more complicated technique, balance is a necessity	Much easier to learn, no balance required	Machine
Time	Require a spotter, takes more time to change weight plates	Less total time, can work out alone, easier to change amount of resistance	Machine
Beginning Lifter	Require a spotter, harder technique to learn, balance	Safer, quicker, spotter is unnecessary, easier to learn technique	Machine
Athletic Power and Coordination	Improve coordination and balance of many muscles at the same time	Isolates single muscle and reduces need for balance	Free weights
Motivation	Easier to determine and see strength improvement	More difficult to understand strength improvement	Free weights

EQUIPMENT·OPTIONS

PURCHASING NEW WEIGHT-LIFTING EQUIPMENT What do you look for when it's time to purchase new weight-lifting equipment, and how do you decide what you need? These are two questions often considered by the physical education teacher. There are three major categories for weight-lifting equipment: free weights, universal systems, and hydraulic systems. The most durable equipment are free weights, which are virtually indestructible because they have few breakable parts and are forged from steel. The problem with this system is safety. Free weights need to be used under supervision.

Less Expensive Alternatives

Even though free weights are less expensive than weight machines, a complete set can still be quite costly. Certain progressive resistance exercises will call for an adjustable bench, which can cost even more. Fortunately, there are lower-cost and even no-cost alternatives. These include:

- **Exercise bands.** These are *elastic bands or tubing made of latex that are used to develop muscular strength and endurance.* The bands are color-coded to identify the level of resistance. Although the strips come in set lengths, usually three feet, they may be modified to meet your specific needs.

◀ Using the correct colored exercise band can provide a great strength workout. *What is another advantage of exercise bands?*

Consumer CORNER

Purchasing Weight-Training Equipment

When shopping for weight-training equipment, you need to be a wise consumer. Although equipment may look the same, it may not perform equally well once you get it home. Here are some other points to consider:

- **Quality.** When purchasing free weights, be aware that you get what you pay for. Plastic weights filled with sand, for example, may be less expensive than metal weights. However, they will not last as long.
- **Space.** All weight-training equipment takes up space. Before making a purchase, be sure you have a place where you can work out and, if necessary, store your equipment when you are done.
- **Expense.** Exercising at home with weight machines has become popular. Many different models are available. Before deciding to purchase a weight machine for home use,

you need to consider how much you can afford to spend.

- **Features.** Some weight-training equipment comes with added features that increase the expense of the machine. Determine if the extra features are worth the extra cost.

One last point to consider is whether the equipment lives up to its promise. Many worthless items are sold nowadays. Among these are crude machines that claim to work the abdominal muscles and pills that claim to burn fat.

Evaluate

Find an ad for a weight-training product. Make a list of the features offered, the manufacturer's claims, warranties, and the costs, including hidden costs such as inflated shipping charges. Share your findings in an in-class roundtable discussion of such products.

Lesson 4 Resistance-Training Equipment and Gear **265**

Consumer CORNER

Purchasing Weight-Training Equipment

After you have discussed the Consumer Corner feature with students and completed the *Active Mind—Active Body* feature on page 262, have students conduct a survey of equipment and cost. Students should evaluate consumer issues related to physical fitness products and services. Either by phone or personal visits, have students investigate the cost of home equipment. Possible sites of investigation would include sporting goods stores, discount stores, specialty stores, and resale stores.
TEKS C4H

Photo Follow-up

Remind students that resistance training involves more than just weights. There are many options. The photo identifies exercise bands, which have become popular to use in aerobic activities or by themselves. *Caption answer: Exercise bands are useful on vacations or trips, when time is limited and facilities are not available.*

Universal systems will fit in tight areas and are designed for the most popular exercises. These systems are much safer than free-weight systems; however, the range of motion for given exercises is limited. Hydraulic machines are the safest to use because rather than creating force, they react to force. The discouraging factors are their cost and repair rates. When choosing equipment, determine the exact space available for the weight-lifting equipment. Remember, space will be your most limiting factor.

Student Edition TEKS

Page 264: C4H
Page 265: C4H

Cooperative Learning

Have students work in groups and provide them with a variety of elastic bands. Their task is to design and demonstrate a variety of resistance exercises that will work the six major muscle groups. Have them demonstrate their exercises to the class. Which colors did they use for their exercises, and why? `L2` `ELL`

Photo Follow-up

Discuss with students the appropriate use of plyometrics. *Caption answer: Plyometric training is recommended for improved athletic performance, and is not meant for beginners because of the increased stress on the tendons.*

Activity

Have interested students form groups and provide them with a variety of equipment that can be used to design a plyometric exercise (e.g., boxes, medicine balls, and cones). Their task is to design and demonstrate a variety of plyometric exercises that will work legs and arms. Have them demonstrate their exercises to the class. Remember to stress warm-ups and safety when doing plyometrics, and do not allow students to use very tall boxes because of the increased stress on the tendons and ligaments. `L3`

✓ **Reading Check**

Calisthenics require only the use of your body weight and no other equipment, making this the most convenient choice.

▶ Proper plyometric technique and adequate strength can provide the athlete with improved muscular force and power. *Who should participate in plyometric training? Explain your answer.*

- **Plyometric exercise.** This is *a quick, powerful muscular movement that requires the muscle to be prestretched just before a quick contraction.* Many such exercises require jumping, leaping, and bounding. Common equipment includes boxes of different heights. When used properly, plyometric training can improve muscle force and power. One downside of plyometric exercises is the stress they can place on tendons. This type of training, furthermore, is not recommended for beginners and is most often associated with the improvement of athletic performance.
- **Calisthenic exercises.** These are *exercises that create resistance by using your body weight.* They include such well-known exercises as pull-ups, push-ups, abdominal curl-ups, and jumping jacks. They have been used for many years and were once the main source of fitness training. Calisthenics are low-level resistance activities and provide opportunities for increasing muscular endurance.

Reading Check

Analyze Which of the less expensive alternatives requires no equipment?

266 **Chapter 9** Basics of Resistance Training

Evaluating Muscular Endurance

In this activity, you will test two aspects of your muscular strength through resistance exercises. You will test your upper-body endurance by doing push-ups. You will then test your lower-body endurance by doing squats. Remember to warm up before you start. Breathe in a normal pattern and control your speed of movement for each exercise.

Upper-Body Endurance: Push-Ups

- *Primary muscles worked*: chest (pectoralis major), back of upper arm (triceps), shoulder (deltoid)
- *Beginning position*: Begin with your body lying facedown on a mat, legs straight and close together, hands placed palms-down next to your shoulders with fingers facing forward.

Technique:

1. Extend the elbows and push your body up to a fully extended arm position. Keep your back straight at all times.
2. Gradually lower your body to the point where your chest almost touches the ground.
3. Repeat this motion as many times as you can. *Individuals with advanced strength may want to elevate their feet on a box or step at a height of 6 to 24 inches.*
4. Use the Fitness Ratings Chart for Push-ups to assess your performance.

Fitness Ratings: Push-ups

Age/Number of Push-ups	Rating
Males:	
Age 13: 10–25	Acceptable
Age 14: 15–30	Acceptable
Age 15: 15–35	Acceptable
Age 16+: 20–35	Acceptable
Females:	
Age 13–16: 5–15	Acceptable

Lower-Body Endurance: Squats

- *Primary muscles worked*: thighs (quadriceps), buttocks (gluteals), back of upper leg (hamstring).
- *Beginning position*: Begin in a standing position with your feet shoulder width apart. Keep your back straight and your head facing forward with arms at your side.

Technique:

1. Slowly bend your knees, lowering your body to a position where your thighs are parallel to the floor. Avoid bending at the waist as much as possible.
2. Return to the starting position.
3. Repeat this motion as many times as you can.
4. Use the Fitness Ratings Chart for Squats to assess your performance.

Fitness Ratings: Squats

Number of Squats	Rating
Males: 25–50	Acceptable
Females: 20–40	Acceptable

TECHNOLOGY FILE

Electronic Monitoring of Workouts

Have students maintain a record of their workouts in a database or spreadsheet on a desktop, notebook, or—ideally—handheld computer. For each lift, students should record the date, name of the exercise, muscles worked, amount of weight lifted, number of repetitions, and sets. These variables become column headings in a spreadsheet or the field names in a database. Weight-lifting software programs are available that can be used for this task. Encourage students to maintain records on their fitness workouts to evaluate their progress.

Evaluating Muscular Endurance

OBJECTIVES

- Participate in resistance activities that develop health-related fitness. **TEKS C4B1**
- Evaluate current levels of muscular endurance.

TEACHING STRATEGIES

Have students properly warm up before each exercise. Demonstrate each test before students begin. Copy and distribute *Fitness Check Worksheet 9-4*. 📁

Upper-Body Endurance: Push-ups

1. Have students control the speed of each push-up and breathe in a normal fashion. Make sure they do not hold their breath.
2. Provide equipment for students with advanced strength. Allow modified bent-knee push-ups for students unable to do straight-leg type.
3. Have students also note they are demonstrating the skill-related component of power during this activity. **TEKS C4C4**

Lower-Body Endurance: Squat

1. Have students control the speed of each squat and breathe in a normal fashion.
2. Check for proper technique: depth of squat and position of back.
3. Have students use the Fitness Ratings chart to evaluate their health-related fitness and record their results. **TEKS C4E**

Discussing

Ask: What kinds of clothes are commonly worn in gyms and health clubs? Encourage students to evaluate consumer issues and marketing of fitness-related clothing. **L1 TEKS C4H**

Quick Demo

Bring a pair of weight-training gloves to class and demonstrate how they can be worn and used to aid in lifting. Have students try lifting with gloves and without gloves. What was the difference? **L2**

Activity

Have each student put on a correct-size weight belt and tighten it snugly. Make sure they have it positioned around the abdominal muscles near the navel. Point out that their main purpose is to increase back support. Have them use the belt anytime they do squats or any exercise that needs additional support for the back. **L1**

Photo Follow-up

Caption answer: Weight-training gloves prevent blisters; weight belt for back protection; straps to support wrist joints.

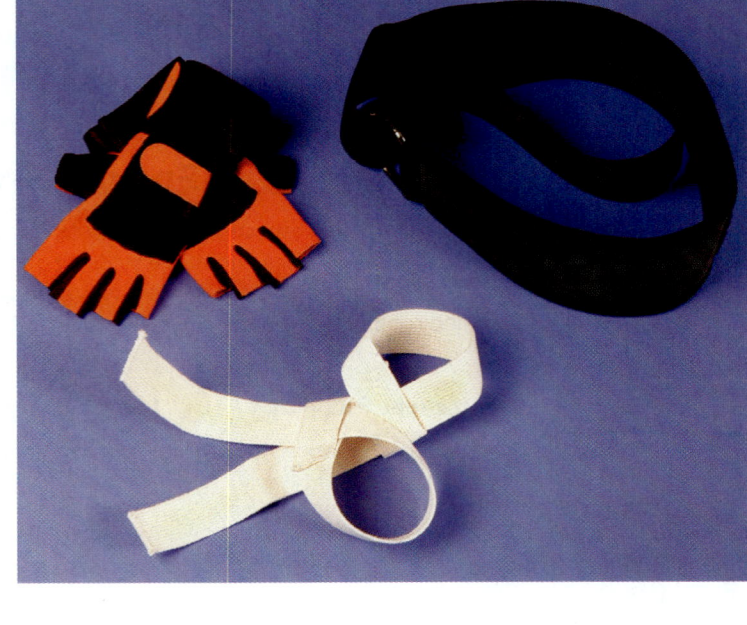

► Pictured is an assortment of weight-training gear. *Identify each item and describe its function.*

Resistance-Training Gear

A well-designed program of resistance training begins not just with a decision on which equipment you will use. Careful thought must be given as well to the right clothing and other workout gear. These items, too, will affect the safety, comfort, and cost of your training.

Clothing and Footwear

There are a variety of fabrics to choose from when selecting appropriate clothing for strength training. Everything from nylon to breathable synthetic fabrics to plain old cotton is available. Regardless of which style or color you choose, keep comfort, performance, and safety in mind. Remember these tips.

- Weight-training clothing should be nonbinding to allow full range of motion.
- Your outfit should keep you warm or cool, depending on the temperature of your workout facility. Wearing layers can help you control your body temperature.
- Avoid wearing any item that could easily become tangled or caught on the equipment.

Always wear properly fitted **footwear.** It should be designed to give you good arch support and provide traction. A cross-training shoe is probably the best style because it provides ankle support. Wearing a pair of absorbent socks can also help prevent blisters.

hot link

footwear
For more on choosing appropriate footwear, see Chapter 2, page **48.**

Student Edition TEKS

Page 266: C4H
Page 267: C4B

More About . . .

WEIGHT TRAINING AND SOCIAL DEVELOPMENT The weight room is a great environment to develop and encourage self-esteem. You can lift alone, with a single partner, or with a group. Positive social qualities such as sharing, caring, encouraging, and helping can all be developed through weight training with others. A good weight-training program allows people to train at their own level. It can be an excellent activity for family members or friends because everyone can be together while training. People who do difficult activities together often develop strong bonds of friendship.

Other Gear

The number of accessories available to weight trainees is almost limitless. Many of these are useful and inexpensive, though none are absolutely essential. Here are a few of the more useful items:

- **Weight-training gloves.** Similar to the gloves worn by athletes in some sports, these are designed to *prevent blisters and calluses from forming on your palms.* The most popular styles will have padding on the palms and open fingers. If you have sensitive skin or you want to avoid rough hands, wear gloves. Gloves will also improve your grip.
- **Weight-training belts.** These are used primarily to *protect your lower back and stomach when you lift heavy weights.* The belt is worn tightly around the waist to give the stomach muscles something to push against. As a result, pressure builds up in the abdomen, which in turn pushes against and stabilizes the lower spine. This protects the lower back.
- **Straps and wraps.** These 1½-inch-wide strips of a canvas-like material are wrapped around your wrist and then twisted around a bar. They are used for very heavy lifts when your grip cannot support the weight. Wraps or elastic bandages are used to give additional support to joints. They are most often used during heavy leg exercises. They can provide support, but they also restrict your range of motion.

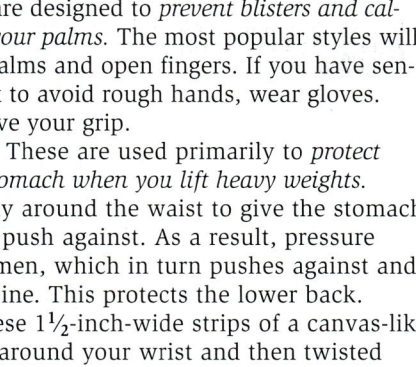

Fitness FACTS

Safety and Weight Belts

Use caution when wearing a weight belt. Weight belts

- cause an increase in blood pressure.
- should be worn only during specific lifting exercises.
- should be loosened when you rest between lifting exercises.

✓ **Reading Check**

Explain What is the purpose of a weight-training belt?

Lesson 4 Review

Using complete sentences, answer the following questions on a sheet of paper.

Reviewing Facts and Vocabulary

1. **Vocabulary** What is the collective name by which dumbbells and barbells are known?
2. **Recall** What are *plyometric exercises*? Who should do them?
3. **Recall** What are the advantages of wearing weight-training gloves while lifting?

Thinking Critically

4. **Compare and Contrast** Explain why it is important to consider the advantages and disadvantages of free weights and machines before starting a weight-training program.

Personal Fitness Planning

Assessing Equipment Make a list of the resistance equipment and gear you might use to meet the goals you stated in Lesson 3. Use the Fitness Check evaluations to better design your resistance goals. Chapter 10 will discuss weight-training exercises and their proper technique as well as programs for the entire body. You may want to consider a variety of exercises that can be used to work on your specific goals.

✓ **Reading Check**
Weight belts protect the lower back and stomach.

3 ASSESS

EVALUATING THE LESSON

Assign and discuss the Lesson 4 Review.

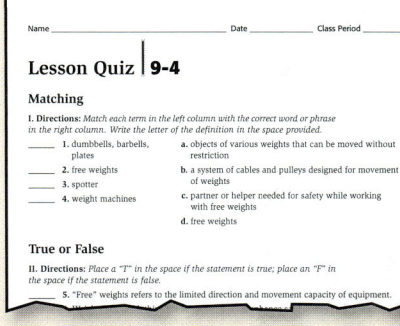

RETEACHING

Point out specific equipment (e.g., barbells, dumbbells, plates, straps, gloves, belts, and machines) and have the class correctly identify each piece. Then assign *Reteaching Activity 9-4.* 🗁

ENRICHMENT

Have interested students research safety information on resistance training and equipment and report their findings to the class.

4 CLOSE

Ask students to summarize the most important concepts in this lesson.

Student Edition TEKS

Page 268: C3A
Page 269: C4G

269

Lesson 4 Review

Answers to Lesson 4 Review

1. Free weights.
2. A quick, powerful muscular movement that requires the muscle to be pre-stretched—not for beginners.
3. They reduce the development of calluses and prevent bars from slipping.
4. The cost of equipment is a consideration, and the right choices will ensure safety and effectiveness.

CHECKING COMPREHENSION

- Assign and discuss the chapter review.
- Use the PuzzleMaker software CD-ROM to review vocabulary. 💿

CHAPTER 9 REVIEW ANSWERS

True/False

1. True	6. True
2. True	7. True
3. False	8. False
4. False	9. True
5. True	10. False

Multiple Choice

11. b	16. a
12. a	17. b
13. c	18. d
14. d	19. b
15. d	20. c

Discussion

21. Answers will vary, but relative muscular endurance is how many times you can lift a given weight in relation to your body weight and gender. Example: Jane has a maximum lift of 65 pounds on the shoulder press. Susan has a lift of 50 pounds on the shoulder press. If they are asked to do 50 percent of their maximum shoulder press as many times as possible, Susan might do more lifts than Jane. Even though Susan is not the strongest, she has higher relative muscular endurance than Jane.

22. Answers will vary but may include bench presses and push-ups for the upper body and squats for the lower body.

TRUE/FALSE

On a sheet of paper, write the numbers 1–10. Write True or False for each statement.

1. The maximum amount of force a muscle can exert against a resistance is muscular strength.
2. Relative muscular strength takes into consideration your body weight and your strength.
3. Putting greater stress on a muscle than it is accustomed to is the principle of specificity.
4. Body builders, athletes, and power lifters use the same kind of weight-training programs.
5. A primary benefit of weight training is the prevention of a bone disease called osteoporosis.
6. Tendons and ligaments are forms of connective tissue.
7. Testosterone is a male hormone also found in females that plays a role in building muscles.
8. Isometric contractions start by lengthening and then getting shorter.
9. The term *hypertrophy* is used to describe how muscle fibers get thicker and cause muscles to grow.
10. Most experts believe that weight training and good nutrition will increase the number of a person's muscle fibers.

MULTIPLE CHOICE

On a sheet of paper, write the letter of the word or phrase that best completes each statement.

11. Which of the following is an example of muscular endurance?
    a. Five arm curl reps with 20 pounds
    b. Fifteen bench press reps with 75 pounds
    c. Ten sit-ups
    d. A fifteen-second isometric contraction
12. Which of the following is not a benefit of weight training?
    a. Significant increase in cardiovascular efficiency
    b. Increased bone strength and density
    c. Reduction in stress
    d. Faster metabolism and better self-esteem

---

13. What term describes the use of barbells, dumbbells, and machines to improve fitness, health, and appearance?
    a. Body building
    b. Strength and conditioning
    c. Weight training
    d. Weight lifting
14. When Bob started weight lifting, he shoulder pressed 50 pounds, eight times. Later, he was able to press the same weight twelve times. He increased the weight to 60 pounds and pressed it eight times. Which of the following exercise principles is Bob using?
    a. Overload
    b. Specificity
    c. Intensity
    d. Progressive resistance
15. Skeletal muscles
    a. move bones and joints.
    b. protect against injury.
    c. burn up calories.
    d. all of the above.
16. Which of the following exercises is done mainly by athletes, involves quick, powerful muscular movements and little equipment?
    a. Plyometric   c. Calisthenics
    b. Isometric   d. Aerobic
17. When the muscle becomes shorter, what kind of a contraction is it?
    a. Eccentric   c. Isometric
    b. Concentric   d. Isotonic
18. Which of the following is a result of steroid use?
    a. violates school rules
    b. is illegal
    c. damages team spirit
    d. all of the above
19. What is the main reason that females do not grow muscles as large as males do?
    a. Females do not lift hard enough.
    b. Females do not have as much testosterone as men.
    c. The female body is not capable of lifting heavy weights.
    d. Females do not spend enough time in the weight room.
20. Which of the following is not an advantage of free weights?
    a. They cost less.
    b. They take up less space.
    c. They are less dangerous.
    d. They require more balance.

---

23. Answers will vary but should include any five of the eight myths covered in Lesson 3.

Vocabulary

24. e
25. b
26. a
27. c
28. d

Critical Thinking

29. Weight lifting is the use of barbells, dumbbells, and weight machines to improve general fitness, health, and appearance. Strength training improves performance.

DISCUSSION

Using complete sentences, answer the following questions on a sheet of paper.

21. **Explain** Define and give an example of relative muscular endurance.
22. **Describe** What is one method of evaluating upper-body strength and one method of evaluating lower-body strength?
23. **Identify** List and explain five myths associated with weight training.

VOCABULARY

On a sheet of paper, write the letter of the term in Column B that best fits the definition in Column A.

Column A

24. The amount of force a muscle or muscle group can exert in one maximum effort.
25. Applying greater stress to a muscle than it is normally accustomed to.
26. Your strength in relation to your weight.
27. An increase in the size of a muscle.
28. An inherited limitation.

Column B

a. relative muscular strength
b. overload principle
c. hypertrophy
d. genetic potential
e. muscular strength

CRITICAL THINKING

Using complete sentences, answer the following questions on a sheet of paper.

29. **Describe** Explain the difference between weight lifting and strength training.
30. **Evaluate** Respond to the statement, "Resistance training is going to be harmful for me because my body has not finished growing."
31. **Identify** List and explain reasons why females can benefit from weight training.

CASE STUDY

THE TRUTH ABOUT RESISTANCE TRAINING

Terri, who is a softball pitcher, would like to improve her arm strength. A friend recommended resistance training. However, Terri has heard many conflicting claims about this type of training. She isn't sure what to believe. She needs the help of someone knowledgeable to inform her about the benefits and mistruths of resistance training. That someone is you!

HERE IS YOUR ASSIGNMENT

Organize a list of statements that will correct the common misconceptions Terri has about weight training. Then list the recommendations you would make for her to get started in a resistance-training program. Use the following keys to help you prepare your list:

KEYS TO HELP YOU

- Explain the benefits of resistance training.
- Explain the truth behind myths that may be confusing Terri.
- Identify the many different types of equipment and resistance-training exercises.
- Explain the advantages and disadvantages associated with free weights and weight machines.
- Inform Terri of the need for proper gear and how to go about selecting what she may need.

---

30. Answers will vary, but teens can obtain many of the same benefits as adults through a specially designed program. Resistance training also offers the additional benefits of maximizing bone development during adolescence and improving glucose tolerance.
31. Benefits include muscle toning, muscle shaping, weight control, stronger muscles, improved athletic performance, reduction of injury and disease, and a greater capacity to handle daily tasks.

EVALUATE

Name _____ Date _____ Class Period _____

CHAPTER
9 Chapter Test A

Fill in the Blanks

Directions: *Fill in the spaces with the correct answers.*

1. The best way to build and tone your muscles is through a program of _____.
2. The two measures of muscular strength are _____ and _____.
3. Muscular endurance is measured by the amount of resistance and the number of _____.
4. In resistance training, _____ means putting more stress on a muscle than it is accustomed to handling.
5. Training done by athletes in competitive sports other than weight lifting or bodybuilding is called _____.
6. The term that refers to the use of resistance exercises to recover from a muscle or bone injury is _____.

Chapter 9

ENRICHMENT

Name _____ Date _____ Class Period _____

Enrichment Activity 9

Directions: *Use the information contained in your text, and conduct additional research to discover if the following statements are myth or fact. If a statement is a myth, explain why.*

1. You can use weights to spot reduce, or lose weight in particular areas of your body.
   Facts: _____

2. Protein supplements will increase muscle size and strength.
   Facts: _____

Chapter 9

CASE STUDY

ANSWERS

Answers will vary but might include: Terri should know that a well-designed resistance-training program can improve her pitching performance and reduce her chances of injury. The program could improve her muscle strength and endurance and provide her body with many other health benefits. Weight training is the most popular, with the use of free weights or machines, but exercise bands, calisthenics, and plyometrics are all acceptable forms of training. Terri should also use gloves.

CHAPTER 10 Developing Muscular Fitness

CHAPTER 10

Lesson 1 Beginning a Resistance-Training Program

Lesson 2 Planning Your Resistance-Training Workout

Lesson 3 Applying FITT to Resistance Training

Lesson 4 Achieving Muscular Fitness

CHAPTER RESOURCES

- **Chapter Study Guide 10**
- **Vocabulary Worksheet 10**
- **Enrichment Activity 10**
- **Chapter 10 Test A**
- **Chapter 10 Test B**
- **Parent Letter and Activities 10 (English/Spanish)**

FITNESS *Online*

Ask students to take the STEP Personal Inventory for Chapter 10. Have them record their responses to the statements in their notebooks. Remind students that responses are private and for their use only.

FITNESS *Online*

Do you have resistance-training goals? Are these goals reasonable? Do you know the correct and safe way to use weights and other equipment? Find out by taking the STEP Personal Inventory for Chapter 10. Find it at **fitness.glencoe.com**.

272

INCLUSION STRATEGIES

LANGUAGE DIVERSITY *Use the following suggestions to help students who have difficulty with English:*

- Pair English-language learners with native speakers of English who can restate key points in language that helps students comprehend important concepts.

- Direct Spanish-speaking students to the written summaries of this chapter in the *Foundations of Personal Fitness* Spanish Resources Booklet.

- Encourage Spanish-speaking students to use the Glosario provided in the back of the student text. **ELL**

Beginning a Resistance-Training Program

Setting goals is essential to the success of any endeavor. It is especially important when improving your muscular strength and endurance. In this lesson, you will learn how to set resistance training goals. You will also learn how to avoid injury when using free weights and resistance-training equipment.

Short- and Long-Term Goals

In Chapter 3, you learned about short- and long-term goals. Improving your muscular strength and endurance requires short-term goals that can be used as stepping stones to achieving long-term goals. Some short-term goals may include:

- Increasing your fluid intake
- Getting adequate rest—at least 8–10 hours of sleep each night

Long-term goals may be more complex and require considerable planning, discipline, and patience to achieve them. These may include:

- Increasing your strength by 10 percent
- Toning selected muscles
- Developing leaner body mass

▶ Part of setting a reasonable goal involves setting a reasonable time frame for achieving it. *Why is it important to include this information?*

What You Will Do

- Identify the importance of setting resistance-training goals.
- Demonstrate safety procedures, such as spotting.
- Apply rules, procedures, and etiquette to your workout.
- Identify a variety of resistance-training exercises that build muscular strength and endurance.

Terms to Know

clips
overhand grip
underhand grip
alternated grip

Beginning a
Resistance-Training
Program

1 MOTIVATE

GETTING STARTED

- Before you begin roll call, ask the class to think about the following question: *What are some reasonable long-term goals you would like to see as a result of weight training?*
- Distribute copies of *Guided Practice 10-1* for students to use while studying this lesson. 🗁

IN THIS LESSON

- **Fitness Facts** *Goal Setting,* p. 274
- **Lifeline** *Protecting a Friend's Health,* p. 276
- **Fitness Facts,** p. 277

INTRODUCING VOCABULARY

- Divide the class into four groups and assign each group one of the vocabulary terms. Have groups read and discuss the definitions for their assigned term.
- Have students use *Vocabulary Worksheet 10* or the PuzzleMaker software to practice vocabulary terms for this lesson. **ELL** 🗁 ⊙

LESSON 1 RESOURCES

Teacher Classroom Resources
🗁 Guided Practice Activity 10-1
🗁 Reteaching Activity 10-1
🗁 Lesson Quiz 10-1

Multimedia
⊙ Vocabulary PuzzleMaker

2 TEACH

Photo Follow-up
(page 273)

Be sure students recognize the difference between long- and short-term goals. *Caption answer: Goals should be attainable, so you should allow reasonable time for short-term and long-term goals you can achieve.*

Fitness instructors should help students to set reasonable goals. If their goals are too difficult, they will not succeed and will quickly become uninterested in their program. If their goals are too easily reached, they will become bored and lose interest.

✓ Reading Check

Short-term goals help motivate you to reach your long-term goals.

In Chapter 1, you were introduced to the behavioral-change stairway. This is a step-by-step approach for achieving personal fitness goals. This lesson will provide you with additional tips for planning your resistance-training program.

Setting Your Goals

Plan carefully before you begin your resistance-training program, and write down your goals and how you plan to achieve them. Refer to your plan periodically to stay focused and assess your progress. Consider the following steps as you write your goals.

- **Set reasonable goals.** Your goals should be specific and realistic. They should be goals that are challenging, but that you are capable of attaining.
- **Establish short- and long-term goals.** The short-term goals act as motivators to keep you going and as steps toward reaching your long-term goals. For example, your long-term goal might be to increase your absolute strength from lifting 100 pounds to lifting 135 pounds on the bench press in four months. Your short-term goals could be to lift 110 pounds the first month, then 120 pounds the second month, then 130 pounds the third month, and finally 135 pounds the fourth month.
- **Identify a variety of short-term goals.** Short-term goals enable you to reach your long-term goals. It is important to think of a variety of short-term goals that will help you along the way. Some examples include: strength training three to four hours a week, improving eating habits, drinking plenty of water, and getting adequate rest.
- **Keep written records.** After each workout, record the number of sets and repetitions you performed for each exercise. Periodically, review your progress. This will motivate you to keep going.
- **Revise goals.** Be prepared to accept setbacks. It is not uncommon to have "off" days during resistance training. Learn to accept these days and move on. The same is true of illness or minor injuries, which may cause a delay in training. Don't give up. Revise your goals or end date if necessary. The important thing is to get right back into your workout routine as soon as you can.
- **Think positively.** Believe in yourself and focus on the positive, not the negative. Read your goals aloud each day immediately before and after workouts. Have fun and enjoy the process.

✓ Reading Check

Explain Why is it important to set short-term goals as well as long-term goals?

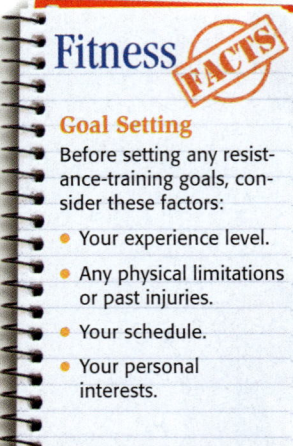

Goal Setting
Before setting any resistance-training goals, consider these factors:
- Your experience level.
- Any physical limitations or past injuries.
- Your schedule.
- Your personal interests.

QUOTES FOR LIFE

"Nothing ever comes to one that is worth having except as a result of hard work."

—Booker T. Washington
Author, educator (1856–1915)

Applying Safety Rules and Procedures

Proper resistance training can improve your fitness, but if done improperly, it can also lead to serious injury. Before beginning your first workout, you need to learn some basic safety guidelines for the proper use of weight machines and free weights.

- **Familiarize yourself with the training facility.** Know where various pieces of equipment can be found.
- **Warm up before each session.** Do a combination of aerobic exercise and stretches of the muscle groups to be worked.
- **Learn and use proper technique on any exercise.** Shortcuts or improper use can minimize your lifting leverage and lead to injury.
- **Use spotters.** When using free weights, have a partner who can support and assist you.
- **Wear a safety belt.** When doing heavy lifting that requires the use of abdominal or back muscles, consider wearing a safety belt.
- **Use clips when adding weights to barbells.** Clips are *clamp-like devices that secure the weights in place.*
- **Practice all lifts.** Practice with very light weights before attempting heavier weight.
- **Control the speed of the resistance movement at all times.** If you find that it is difficult to control the speed, you are probably attempting to lift too much. Reduce the weight.
- **Be alert and act responsibly.** Showing off or behaving irresponsibly can lead to unintentional injury.
- **Return equipment.** Put equipment in its proper place after using it.
- **Allow time for muscles to repair.** Between training sessions, give muscle tissues enough time to repair and renew themselves. For most people, forty-eight hours is enough time.
- **Cool down after each session.** As with the warm-up, combine aerobic exercise and stretches.

▶ A safe resistance-training workout includes safety belts. *Identify two other ways you can make your workout safe.*

Photo Follow-up

Applying safety rules should always be the number one concern in the weight room. Students should be properly instructed on when and how to use weight belts and safety clips. *Caption answers may vary but could include any of the guidelines from the list of safety procedures.* **TEKS C2A1**

Discussing

Point out that resistance-training facilities differ from one another and that it is important to notice these differences. Take the time to establish any specific guidelines in the facility and explain each of the suggested safety procedures. Identify all facility rules and the consequences of breaking them. Hang posters in the weight room that list safety guidelines. **L1**

Quick Demo

Demonstrate to the class the correct way to place weights onto the bar and how different clips are attached. Have students demonstrate this procedure for all types of bars and clips. **L2 TEKS C2A**

Activity

Have the class determine two or three activities that each class member should use prior to lifting. Have them list and describe the components of an exercise prescription before beginning a training program. **L2 TEKS C4F**

Student Edition TEKS

Page 274: C4G
Page 275: C2A, C3A

INCLUSION STRATEGIES

WEIGHT-TRAINING CAUTIONS Weight training may be contraindicated for students with certain disabilities. Any strength-training program must be consistent with the student's capacities. First, establish the focus of any weight-training program. Basic safety considerations for weight training for the disabled include getting medical evaluations and assessments, being aware of when muscle exhaustion sets in, and ceasing training when exhaustion occurs. A warm-up period is essential. Any program must be slow and carefully monitored. Constant supervision is essential.

LIFELINE

Protecting a Friend's Health

Many injuries occur each year as a result of lifters not having spotters to assist them. These injuries can be very serious and can sometimes result in death. Even experienced lifters are strongly advised to use spotters when lifting heavy weight. **TEKS C3B**

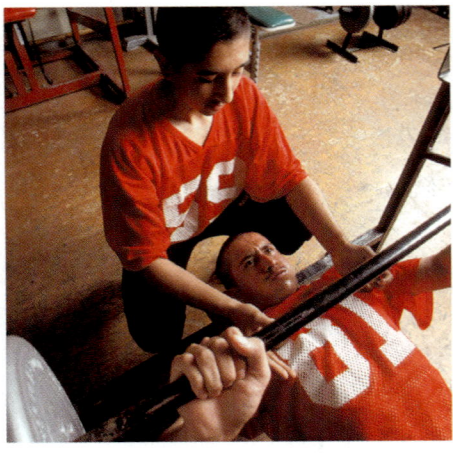

▲ A spotter can help ensure a safe workout. *What else can a spotter provide?*

LIFELINE

Protecting a Friend's Health

Having a spotter is more than just helpful—it is necessary for a safe workout.

If you have a friend who wants to lift weights alone, offer to spot for him or her. Explain that by having a spotter, he or she is cutting down the risk of injury as well as benefiting from the advice and motivation of a good spotter.

Spotting

When training with free weights, it is essential to have a spotter. As noted in Chapter 9, a spotter is a partner who can assist with the safe handling of weights and offer encouragement during a session. A spotter has three main jobs:

- Helping the lifter keep the weight moving in a smooth, steady motion
- Observing and pointing out any improper technique being used by the lifter
- Providing motivation and encouragement to the lifter

Spotting is a serious job that demands a high degree of personal responsibility. A good spotter can be the difference between serious injury and a safe, successful workout.

Other Duties of the Spotter. In addition to the three primary jobs just described, a spotter

- keeps the exercise area free of weights or other equipment that could be tripped over.
- puts the proper amount of weight on the bar and spaces it evenly.
- keeps his or her body and hands in a ready position at all times.
- communicates with the lifter. It is important that all verbal and nonverbal commands are understood.
- knows how many repetitions the lifter will be attempting.
- applies assistance without jerking the bar.
- is ready to assume all the weight, if necessary.

✓ **Reading Check**

List What are the three main duties of a spotter?

Proper Technique

In resistance training, technique is important. Using proper technique can help you make the most of your training sessions and achieve your goals more quickly. Remember these technique tips.

- Keep your back straight at all times.
- Adjust all weight machines for proper body alignment.
- When performing standing lifts, be sure to have a wide, stable base. Place your feet flat on the floor.
- When lifting objects, use your legs, not your back.
- Keep the weight close to your body to maintain proper leverage.
- All lifts should be done through a full range of motion. Your muscles should be flexed and extended completely.
- Concentrate on the muscles that should be doing the work.
- Make sure you keep your hands on the bar and maintain pressure until all weights are safely put back on the racks.

276   **Chapter 10**   Developing Muscular Fitness

COOPERATIVE Learning

SPOTTERS Spotting requires a great deal of cooperation between the spotter and the lifter. Spotters have many duties, the foremost of which is a commitment to the lifter's safety and success. The coordination and communication between the two cannot be overemphasized.

Spotters need to give special attention to any lifts that are over the lifter's head, neck, back, and chest. All dumbbell lifts should be spotted at the wrist near the dumbbell and not at the elbows. Spotters should always use an alternating grip to ensure that the bar does not slip.

Breath Control

Learning the proper technique for breathing is critical to the success of your workout. There are three steps involved in breath control.

- Slowly take two or three deep breaths, holding the last breath.
- Begin your lift, exhaling the air slowly.
- Return the weight to its starting position, inhaling as you do.

Getting used to breathing in this manner takes time. Some new lifters practice breath control in front of a mirror.

Proper Grips

One of the most important—and often overlooked—parts of proper lifting technique is gripping the bar correctly. There are three types of grips. The type used depends on the exercise. You will learn more about when to use each grip later in this chapter.

- **Overhand grip.** In the overhand grip, *the bar is grasped with the palms facing downward and the knuckles facing upward* (see **Figure 10.1a**).
- **Underhand grip.** In the underhand grip, *the bar is grasped with the palms facing upward and the knuckles facing downward* (see **Figure 10.1b**).
- **Alternated grip.** In the alternated grip, *the bar is grasped with one palm facing downward and the other palm facing upward* (see **Figure 10.1c**).

Regardless of how you grip the bar, always make sure your fingers are wrapped closely around it so that the thumb meets the index finger. This will ensure that the bar is firmly within your control.

FIGURE 10.1

PROPER GRIPS

Proper lifting technique involves using one of the three types of grips. *What are the names of each grip?*

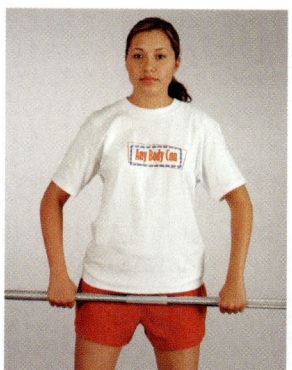  

| Figure 10.1a | Figure 10.1b | Figure 10.1c |

Communication is critical to the safety of all lifts. Spotters should know how many reps the lifter will attempt, as well as the commands for unracking (lifting off) and racking (returning) the weights. Simple commands of "up" or "one, two, three, lift" are common for unracking the weight. "Take it" or "help" can be used for successfully assisting the lifter at the end of a set. Experienced spotters know how to smoothly apply the minimal amount of assistance needed for the completion of a fatigue rep. It is not recommended for spotters to assist in power exercises. These exercises are too dangerous.

Fitness FACTS

Controlled Breathing
- Breathe out during the concentric (positive) phase of a contraction.
- Breathe in during the eccentric (negative) phase of a contraction.
- Never hold your breath during a lift. Doing so can reduce the flow of oxygen and cause dizziness or fainting.

Explaining

Explain to students how progression in both strength and hypertrophy are quicker and safer when proper lifting technique is strictly adhered to. Cheating on your form results in working muscles that the exercise was not intended to work. Emphasize that controlled speed of both concentric and eccentric movements will produce results faster and more safely. Rapid eccentric movements reduce your workout results by as much as one-half. **L1**
TEKS C4C6, C4F

Fitness FACTS

Holding your breath during the positive phase of lifting can increase the risk of injury. This is of even greater concern when lifting heavy weights or at the end of a set, when you are near fatigue. Have students practice their breathing patterns, and when you observe them lifting, remind them of the correct technique.

USING VISUALS

Figure 10.1 Tell students that all correct lifting techniques begin with the correct grip for the specific exercise to be performed. *Caption answer: From left to right overhand, underhand, and alternated.*

Student Edition TEKS

Page 276: C2A, C3A
Page 277: C3B

Figure 10.2 Most weight-training exercises will require a standard hand placement. It is important to use the correct hand placement for each specific exercise. *Caption answer: Hand placement is important to ensure that the bar remains balanced and the chance of injury is reduced.* TEKS C3B

Discussing

As the class works through the exercises in this lesson, guide each student in developing positive self-management and social skills. The weight room is an excellent place to apply these skills as students work independently and with others. Reinforce at all times the importance of applying rules, procedures, and etiquette as outlined here and in Chapter 1, page 7. **L2** **ELL** TEKS C2A

Explaining

Make sure students understand their etiquette responsibilities in the weight room. In most weight-training classes, students are given limited time to move through their workouts. With this in mind, students should not waste time and should adhere to established safety practices. Encourage students to use towels to wipe perspiration off equipment and to alert the instructor to any equipment that may need repair or adjustment. This takes only a few seconds and shows consideration for the next lifter. **L1** TEKS C2A3

FIGURE 10.2

HAND PLACEMENT

Whether you are using the wide, common, or narrow grip placement, your hands should always be evenly spaced from the ends of the bar. *Why is this important for your safety?*

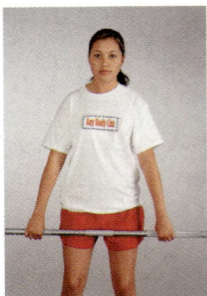  

Figure 10.2a   Figure 10.2b   Figure 10.2c

Hand Placement

Just as critical as *how* you hold the bar is *where* you hold it. **Figure 10.2** shows the three main grip placements, and the one you choose will depend on the specific exercise. In the common (or standard) grip, your hands are spaced about shoulder width apart (see **Figure 10.2a**). In the narrow grip, your hands are spaced closer together (see **Figure 10.2b**). In the wide grip, your hands are spaced farther apart than your shoulders (see **Figure 10.2c**). No matter which grip you are using, always make sure your hands are evenly spaced from the ends of the bar. This will ensure that the bar remains balanced and reduces the chance of injury. This will also ensure that the muscles on each side of the body receive the same workout.

Weight Room Etiquette

Whether you are working out in the school gym, the YMCA, the YWCA, or some other location, be courteous. Always consider the needs of others.

- Limit your time on a machine or at a work station. This is especially true at peak hours or when others are waiting to use the equipment.
- Use one machine or station at a time. If your training includes alternating between two exercises, choose a time when the facility is less crowded, such as early morning. Even then, be prepared to share.
- Put away free weights and other equipment at the end of your session. In addition to demonstrating courtesy, cleaning up after yourself helps ensure the safety of other users.
- Use a towel. If the facility does not provide towels, bring one from home. Spread the towel on the bench or other surface before your body comes into contact with it. Wipe down the equipment when you have finished using it.

Weight-Training Exercises for the Whole Body

There are many weight-training exercises that may be used to improve strength and fitness. You should choose a variety of exercises that will work all the major muscles and joints of the body.

As you learn and participate in the following exercises, always remember to practice all the resistance-training safety guidelines you have learned. It is especially important for you to strictly follow the lifting procedures described. Have your physical education teacher, trainer, or coach observe your technique to help reduce your chance of injury.

278 Chapter 10 **Developing Muscular Fitness**

More About . . .

WEIGHT ROOM ETIQUETTE Each gym or facility has its own customs and procedures. There are, however, general rules that everyone should follow to avoid offending others who are utilizing the facility. Return all weight plates, barbells, and dumbbells after you have used them. Weights left on the floor pose a serious risk of injury. Be willing to share machines and stations, ask other participants if you can "work in" the circuit, and move through your workout quickly to avoid dominating machines. Personal hygiene should be a consideration when working with others. TEKS C2A

Bench Press

Body area: *middle chest*
Muscles: *pectoralis, deltoid, triceps*
Variation: *dumbbells*
Caution: *Spotter required*

- Lie faceup on a bench. Position your back and buttocks flat on the bench.
- Position your eyes directly under the bar. Keep your head on the bench.
- Position your feet flat on the floor. If the bench is too high, use a chair or the end of the bench to lift your feet. (This prevents injury to your back from arching.) Your legs should remain relaxed.
- Grasp the bar with hands slightly farther apart than shoulder width.
- Your hands should be evenly spaced on each side from the center of the bar; use a wraparound thumb grip, and lock your wrists.
- Move the bar off the rack, and position it over your chest. (Spotter should assist.)
- Keep your elbows out, parallel to the bar.
- Stabilize the bar before lowering it. (Spotter should release the bar.)
- Lower the bar slowly to the middle of your chest. Maintain control and speed; touch, do not bounce the bar off your chest.
- Push upward to the starting position. Go through the full range of motion. (Spotter's hands should be in the ready position.)
- Exhale during the push stage. Do not hold your breath.
- Keep your back, head, and buttocks in contact with the bench at all times.
- When you are done, replace the bar on the rack. Never release your grip until the bar is safely in the rack. (Spotter should assist to replace the bar.)

▼ **Bench Press**

▶ **Variation of Bench Press—Flat Bench Dumbbell Press**

Lesson 1 Beginning a Resistance-Training Program **279**

Limit your personal items on the floor space to water jugs and towels. Avoid dominating the water fountain. If you carry your own bottle of water, be sure to wait for appropriate times to refill your bottle. Do not leave gym bags or other items in the way of other lifters. Keep your conversations at a low level to avoid distracting other lifters. When lifting, control the speed of your movements. Plates should not bang together, creating noise or potential damage to the machines. Finally, always keep the weight room area clean and tidy. Pick up trash and wipe off any sweat from the equipment you use.

Discussing

The Bench Press is one of the most popular weight-training exercises. This multi-joint exercise is valuable for developing overall upper-body strength. Have students explain how the physiological principle of overload can be applied to resistance training while using the bench press. **L1 TEKS C1A3**

Demonstrate

Demonstrate a stable body position on the bench. This will require lying face up with a five-point body contact:

- back of head
- upper back and shoulders
- lower back and buttocks
- both feet touching floor

If students' knees are below their hips when they lie on the bench, they probably need a stool.

● DO

- control speed of weights.
- maintain five-point contact.
- exhale during positive phase.
- maintain balanced bar.
- use full range of motion.

■ DON'T

- arch back at any time.
- wiggle or lean your body.
- raise shoulders off the bench.
- lock out elbows.
- count on spotters to lift all the weight.

Variations By adjusting the angle and direction of the bench, you can target specific areas of the chest. A decline bench press targets the bottom of the chest, while an incline targets the top of the chest.

Student Edition TEKS

Page 276: C2A, C3A
Page 277: C3B

Discussing

The Incline Bench Press is similar to the flat bench but is designed to target the upper part of the chest (upper pectoralis). It requires a bench that can be positioned at a variety of angles. The best angle for developing the upper chest is between 15 and 30 degrees. Students will not be as strong in this exercise as with the bench press, because they use more parts of their chest muscle in the bench press. **L1**

Demonstrate

Demonstrate a stable position with five-point body contact on the angled bench. If the bench is too high, students may need a stool for their feet. The path of the bar should make an arc toward the head during the positive phase, and touch the chest near the chin at the end of the negative phase. When dumbbells are used, emphasize the positioning of the spotter's hands on the lifter's wrists.

● DO

• control speed of weights.
• maintain five-point contact.
• exhale during positive phase.
• maintain balanced bar.
• use full range of motion.

● DON'T

• arch back at any time.
• wiggle or lean your body.
• raise shoulders off the bench.
• lock out elbows.
• count on spotters to lift all the weight.

Variations Barbells, dumbbells, or machines. By adjusting the angle of the bench, you can target specific areas of the chest and shoulders.

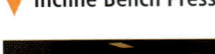
▼ Incline Bench Press

▲ Variation of Incline Bench Press—Dumbbells

Incline Bench Press
Body area: *upper chest*
Muscles: *upper pectoralis, deltoid, triceps*
Variation: *dumbbells*
Caution: *Spotter required*

• Lie faceup on an incline bench. Position your back and buttocks flat on the bench.
• Position your feet flat on the floor. If the bench is too high, use a chair or the end of the bench to lift your feet. Do not use your feet to lift your body. Your legs should remain relaxed.
• Grasp the bar with hands slightly farther apart than shoulder width.
• Your grip should be evenly spaced. Use a wraparound thumb grip, and lock your wrists.
• Move the bar off the rack, and position it over your chest. (Spotter should assist.)
• Keep your elbows out and parallel to the bar.
• Lower the bar slowly to the top of your chest, near your chin. Maintain control and speed. Touch the bar to your chest. Do not bounce it off your chest.
• Push the bar upward to the starting position. Go through the full range of motion. (Spotter's hands should be in a ready position.)
• Exhale during the push stage. Do not hold your breath.
• Your back, head, and buttocks must remain in contact with the bench at all times.
• At the completion of the reps, replace the bar on the rack. Never release your grip until the bar is safely in the rack. (Spotter should assist in replacing the bar on the rack.)

Enrichment

Personal Training Log Have students keep a training log that records the activities in their personal fitness program. For cardiovascular conditioning, they should record their exercise heart rate for each workout. For weight training, they should record the amount of weight they lift for each exercise. After each week, have students average their heart rate or weight lifted. For cardiovascular conditioning, beginners should exercise at 60 to 70 percent of their maximum heart rate. Beginning weight trainers should exercise at 50 to 60 percent of the maximum weight they can lift at one time.

Flat Bench Fly
Body area: *chest*
Muscles: *pectoralis*
Variation: *incline or decline bench*

- Lie faceup on a flat bench. Position your back and buttocks flat on the bench.
- Position your feet flat on the floor. If the bench is too high, use a chair or the end of the bench to lift your feet. Do not use your feet to lift your body. Your legs should remain relaxed.
- Grasp a dumbbell in each hand. Use a wraparound thumb grip.
- Raise your arms and hands to position the dumbbells together over your chest. Your arms should be extended, and your palms should face each other.
- Before you lower the dumbbells, slightly bend both elbows.
- Lower the dumbbells in a wide arc.
- Your elbows should remain slightly bent. Keep your arms in line with your shoulders and chest.
- Lower the dumbbells slowly, controlling their speed until they are level with your shoulders. (Spotter can assist).
- Return the dumbbells to the starting position. Keep your elbows slightly bent until you reach the top of the lift. Continue the reps.
- Exhale during the push stage. Do not hold your breath.

▲ Flat Bench Fly

Discussing

The Flat Bench Fly is a single-joint exercise used primarily to isolate the pectoralis muscles. The biceps are only lightly used, and the triceps not at all. It is not the best exercise for strength development, but it is great for defining and shaping the pectorals. By isolating this area, students can apply the biomechanical principle of specificity to training and exercise. This exercise should be done after the completion of the two-joint exercises for the chest. **L1** **TEKS C1A6**

Demonstrate

Demonstrate a stable position with five-point body contact on the flat bench. If the bench is too high, students may need a stool for their feet. The path of the dumbbells makes a smooth, continuous arching motion that simulates the hugging of a barrel. Emphasize that spotter's hands should be on the lifter's wrists, not the elbows.

🟢 DO
- control speed of weights.
- maintain five-point contact.
- exhale during positive phase.
- keep elbows slightly bent.
- keep elbows aligned with shoulders.
- use full range of motion.

🔴 DON'T
- arch back at any time.
- wiggle or lean your body.
- lower arms below shoulders.
- lock out elbows.
- bend wrists during the lift.
- touch dumbbells together.

Variations Can be performed on an incline bench or a decline bench to target specific areas of the chest. Machines are also available.

What Teens *Want* to Know

Does weight training cause a muscle-bound condition? The definition of "muscle-bound" is someone having a limited range of motion in a variety of joints. Incorrect weight-training can contribute to a muscle-bound condition. If you do not go through a full range of motion in all your exercises, you may lose some flexibility. Muscles should receive equal amounts of work to prevent one from overpowering the joint. A well-designed strength and conditioning program that is properly implemented will only serve to enhance the development of strength and flexibility.

Discussing

The Seated Shoulder Press, also known as the military press, is one of the best weight-training multijoint exercises for developing the upper back and shoulders. This exercise works both the triceps and the anterior and medial deltoids. Have students use this exercise to demonstrate strength improvement during the weight-training unit. **L1**

Demonstrate

Demonstrate a stable position with five-point body contact in a chair or appropriate bench. The path of the dumbbells or barbell makes a smooth, continuous motion from a position even with the shoulders to a position above the head. If the lifter is using dumbbells, emphasize that the spotter's hands should be on the lifter's wrists, not on the elbows.

● DO

- control speed of weights.
- maintain five-point contact.
- exhale during positive phase.
- keep elbows aligned with shoulders.
- use full range of motion.

● DON'T

- arch back at any time.
- wiggle or lean your body.
- lower arms below start position.
- lock out elbows.
- bend wrists.
- touch dumbbells together.

Variations Can be performed either standing or seated. Machines are also available.

▲ Seated Shoulder (Military) Press

▲ Standing Dumbbell Overhead (Military) Press

◄ Seated Dumbbell (Military) Press

Seated Shoulder (Military) Press
Body area: *shoulders*
Muscles: *deltoid and triceps*
Variations: *standing dumbbell press, seated dumbbell press, and machine (seated shoulder press, incline shoulder press)*
Caution: *spotter required*

- Sit on a bench or chair. Place your feet flat on the floor.
- Grasp the bar using a standard grip.
- Your grip should be evenly spaced. Use a wraparound thumb grip, and lock your wrists.
- Your elbows should be under the bar and parallel to the bar.
- Your back should be straight (not arched) and your head looking forward.
- The starting position for the bar is at shoulder height and close to the body. (Spotter can assist.)
- The bar is pushed upward to full arm extension.
- Exhale during the push stage. Do not hold your breath.
- Your elbows should remain under, and parallel to, the bar at all times, with your back flat.
- Lower the bar slowly to the top of your chest. Maintain control and speed. Do not let the bar bounce off your chest.
- At the completion of the reps, replace the bar on the rack. (Spotter can assist.)

282   Chapter 10 Developing Muscular Fitness

EQUIPMENT OPTIONS

TECHNOLOGY AND WEIGHT LIFTING EQUIPMENT New technological advancements in weight-lifting equipment include adjustable, hydraulic, counter-resistant weight-lifting machines. These machines resemble a Universal weight-lifting system, except the weight plates are replaced with hydraulic cylinders and the resistance exerted by the cylinders is controlled by an adjustable flow valve. These machines create a resistant force, but the force is unidirectional instead of constant. These machines were designed to increase safety, which they have done. The disadvantage of

Shoulder Shrug
Body area: *shoulders*
Muscles: *trapezius*
Variation: *dumbbell*

- To pick up the bar from the floor, assume a shoulder-width stance, with your feet flat.
- Bend your knees, not your waist. To place your hands on the bar, fully extend your arms.
- Your grip should be slightly wider than your shoulders and outside your knees.
- Your grip should be evenly spaced. Use a wraparound thumb grip.
- The bar should be close to your shins.
- Position your shoulders over the bar.
- Your back must stay flat. Keep your head up. Pull your shoulder blades together. Do not bend at the waist.
- Begin lifting by extending your legs, not your back.
- Move your hips forward, and raise your shoulders.
- Keep the bar close to your body, with your back and feet flat.
- Raise the bar until your knees are slightly bent and your arms are fully extended.
- Exhale during the lifting stage.
- Lift the bar by raising your shoulders toward your ears. Do not bend or pull with your arms.
- Hold this "shrug" position for two counts.
- Exhale during the lifting stage.
- Lower the bar slowly to your waist. Maintain control and speed. Keep your feet flat and your knees slightly bent.
- At the completion of the reps, return the bar to the floor. To protect your back, be sure that you use the same technique you used to pick up the bar to return the bar to the floor.

▶ **Variation on Shoulder Shrug (Dumbbell)**

Discussing

The Shoulder Shrug is a single-joint exercise that develops the muscles in the general area of the neck (trapezius and deltoids). This exercise benefits athletes who do contact sports in which head or neck injuries are common. **L1**

Demonstrate

Demonstrate the correct form for picking up weights from the floor and establish a stable standing position with the feet shoulder-width apart. Show how to move your shoulders smoothly upward toward your ears while squeezing the shoulder blades together.

Remind students to apply rules, procedures, and etiquette while performing these exercises and handling weights. **TEKS C2A**

● DO
- maintain correct stance with knees slightly bent.
- exhale during positive phase.
- keep elbows slightly bent.
- squeeze contraction for two counts.

● DON'T
- rock back and forth.
- roll shoulders backward.
- bend or tilt your head.

Variations Can be performed with dumbbells or a barbell. Barbells can be placed to the rear above the gluteals and lifted to target more of the upper back muscles. Machines are also available.

---

this new technology is twofold. The cost of these new machines is high, because each machine is designed for a specific muscle workout. The second disadvantage is the change in muscle dynamics. Due to the unidirectional resistive force, ordinary weight-training exercises may not provide the results seen with conventional weight sets. Physical education teachers thinking of buying this new equipment should first learn more about it. The Internet provides a vast amount of information about the most current weight-training technologies.

Discussing

The Upright Row is a multijoint exercise that develops the muscles in the general area of the upper back and shoulders (trapezius and deltoids) and the front upper arm (biceps).

L1

Demonstrate

Demonstrate the correct form for picking up weights from the floor and establish a stable standing position with the feet shoulder-width apart. Shoulders and elbows move smoothly upward toward your chin. At the top of the lift, the elbows should be level with the shoulders.

● DO

• maintain correct stance with knees slightly bent.
• exhale during positive phase.
• keep bar close to body.
• keep abdominal and back muscles tight and straight.

● DON'T

• rock back and forth.
• roll shoulders backward.
• bend or tilt your head.
• raise hands above elbows.

Variations Can be performed with dumbbells, a barbell, or an E-Z curl bar. Machines are also available.

Upright Row
Body area: *shoulders*
Muscles: *deltoids, trapezius, biceps*
Variation: *dumbbells*

• To pick up the bar from the floor, assume shoulder-width stance, with feet flat.
• Bend your knees, not your waist. To place your hands on the bar, fully extend your arms.
• Your hands will grip 8 to 10 inches apart and be placed inside your legs.
• Your hands should be evenly spaced in the grip. Use a wrap-around thumb grip.
• The bar should be close to your shins.
• Position your shoulders over the bar.
• Your back must stay flat. Keep your head up. Pull your shoulder blades together. Do not bend at the waist.
• Begin lifting by extending your legs, not your back.
• Move your hips forward, and raise your shoulders.
• Keep the bar close to your body, with your back and feet flat.

▼ Upright Row (Barbell)

  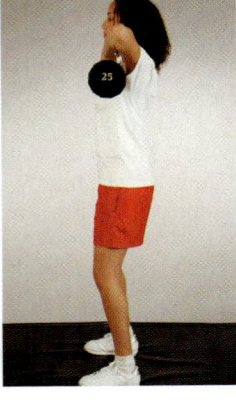

• Raise the bar until your knees are slightly bent and your arms are fully extended.
• Exhale during the lifting stage.
• Pull the bar upward along your stomach and chest toward your chin. Keep the bar close to your body.
• Continue to raise the bar until it is under your chin.
• Your elbows should be higher than your wrist and shoulders.
• Exhale during the lifting stage.
• Lower the bar slowly to your waist. Maintain control and speed. Keep your feet flat, with knees slightly bent.
• At the completion of the reps, return the bar to the floor. To protect your back, be sure to use the same technique you used to pick up the bar to return the bar to the floor.

▲ Upright Row (Dumbbells)

284   **Chapter 10**   Developing Muscular Fitness

Front Dumbbell Shoulder Raise

Body area: *shoulders*
Muscles: *front part of deltoids*
Variation: *sitting*

- Start in a standing position with feet shoulder width apart and head up.
- Hold a dumbbell in each hand, with arms hanging on each side of your body and elbows slightly bent.
- Slowly raise your arms in front of your body. Continue to raise your arms until your hands are level with your shoulders. Your arms must stay in front. (The exercise can be done by alternating arms or raising both arms at the same time.)
- Exhale during the lifting stage.
- Hold this position for two counts.
- Lower your arms slowly to the starting position. Maintain control and speed. Continue the reps.

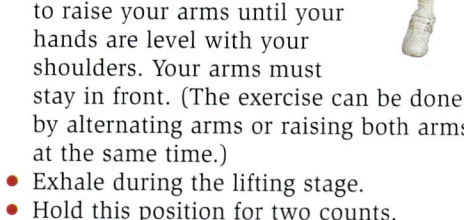

▲ **Front Dumbbell Shoulder Raise**

Side (Lateral) Dumbbell Shoulder Raise

Body area: *shoulders*
Muscles: *middle part of deltoids*
Variation: *sitting*

- Start in a standing position, with feet shoulder width apart and head up.
- Hold a dumbbell in each hand, with arms hanging on each side of your body and elbows slightly bent.
- Slowly raise your arms to the side of your body. Continue to raise your arms until your hands are level with your shoulders. Keep your elbows level with your hands.
- As you raise your arms, rotate your wrists down and elbows up, as if you were pouring water out of a glass. (This exercise may be done by alternating arms or raising both at the same time.)
- Exhale during the lifting stage.
- Hold the position for a count of two.
- Lower your arms slowly to the starting position. Maintain control and speed. Continue the reps.

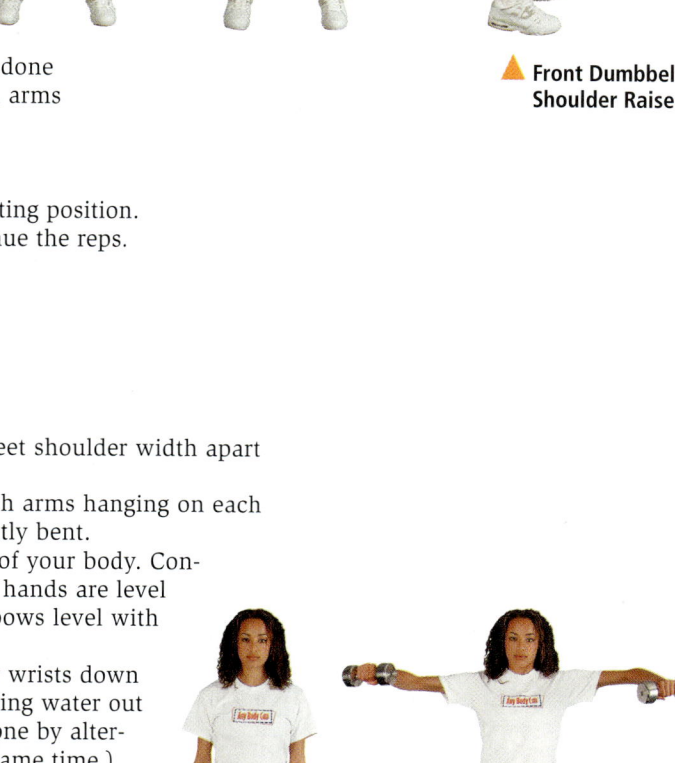

▲ **Side (Lateral) Dumbbell Shoulder Raise**

Discussing

The Front Shoulder Raise and Side (lateral) Shoulder Raise are single-joint exercises that develop the front and side shoulder muscles (anterior deltoids and medial deltoids, respectively). These exercises will increase your ability to lift objects from shelves and do daily tasks. **L1**

Demonstrate

Demonstrate the correct form for picking up weights from the floor and establish a stable standing position with the feet shoulder-width apart. Demonstrate a Front Raise by moving your arms slowly and smoothly upward to a position level with the shoulders. At the top of the lift, the elbows should be slightly bent, with the arms extended in front of the body, palms facing down. Side (lateral) Raises use the same movements, except the arms are extended to the side and not to the front.

🟢 DO

- maintain correct stance with knees slightly bent.
- keep elbows slightly bent.
- exhale during positive phase.
- keep abdominal and back muscles tight and straight.
- keep palms facing down.

🔴 DON'T

- rock back and forth.
- arch back.
- bend or tilt your head.
- raise arms above shoulders.

Variations Can be performed in a seated position. You can exercise one arm at a time. Machines are also available but not as common.

Teacher-Coach Tips

Grip Strength Many of the physical activities we perform for work or play require good grip strength. It is an important link in many athletic events and, if not properly worked, can prevent athletes from reaching full potential. Most skills are a combination of three types of grip strength: crushing is similar to what we do when we shake hands, pinching is done with straight fingers that sustain isometric or static force, and supporting is holding a semistatic load. Many exercises enhance grip strength. The key is to use variety to simulate the real world of physical activity.

Discussing

The Bent-Over Shoulder Raise is a single-joint exercise that develops the rear shoulder muscle and helps maintain muscle balance.

Demonstrate

Use the same starting techniques used in the Front and Side Raises. Bend at the waist to a point just short of parallel to the floor.

● DO

• keep your back straight and head up.

● DON'T

• raise your body from bent position.

Variations Commonly performed in a seated position.

Discussing

The Bent-Over Row is a multijoint exercise. It can be performed with a narrow grip and the elbows close to the body. When the grip is wide and the elbows are held away from the body, the trapezius and rear deltoids receive most of the stress. Secondary muscles include biceps and posterior deltoids. Have students use this exercise to demonstrate strength improvement. L1

Demonstrate

Demonstrate the correct form for picking up weights from the floor or rack and establish a stable standing position with the feet shoulder-width apart. The Bent-Over Row is done by bending at the hips to a 45-degree angle, with the arms fully extended. Slowly and smoothly pull the bar to the bottom of your chest.

▶ Bent-over Dumbbell Shoulder Raise

Bent-over Dumbbell Shoulder Raise
Body area: *shoulders*
Muscle: *back part of deltoid*
Variation: *sitting*

• Start in a standing position with feet shoulder width apart, knees slightly bent and head up.
• Hold a dumbbell in each hand with arms hanging on each side of your body.
• Bend at the waist. Your arms should be hanging straight down.
• Slowly raise your arms upward. Continue to raise your arms until your hands are almost level with your shoulders.
• Exhale during the lifting stage.
• Hold this position for 2 counts.
• Lower your arms slowly to a starting position. Maintain control and speed. Continue the reps.

Bent-over Row
Body area: *upper back*
Muscles: *latissimus dorsi, trapezius, biceps*
Variation: *one arm dumbbell*
Caution: *Weight belts may be necessary during maximum lifts.*

• To pick up the bar from the floor, assume shoulder-width stance, with feet flat.
• Bend your knees and waist to place your hands on the bar. Fully extend your arms.
• Your grip should be slightly wider than your shoulders.
• Your hands should be evenly spaced in the grip. Use a wrap-around thumb grip.
• The bar should be close to your shins.
• Position your shoulders over the bar.
• Your back must stay flat. Keep your head up, and pull your shoulder blades together.
• Begin lifting by extending your legs until your back is slightly above a parallel position in relation to the floor. Keep your knees flexed and your back flat. Hold this position.

286 **Chapter 10** Developing Muscular Fitness

More About . . .

MACHINES vs. FREE WEIGHTS The debate over the use of free weights or machines questions which is best for athletic performance. Early resistance-training machines incorporated pulleys, springs, wires, cables, and rubber elements. Some popular machines used a cam system to maintain resistance. Today, with the increased emphasis on exercising, the manufacturers of resistance machines have advanced their use and styles tremendously. The debate is centered around the fact that machines do not simulate the gravity-dominated world in which we live, work, and play.

◀ Bent-over Row
(Free Weight)

- With arms fully extended, pull the bar up and touch your lower chest or upper abdomen. Keep your elbows out.
- Exhale during the lifting stage.
- Keep your upper body and legs in a set position.
- Lower the bar slowly to the starting position. Maintain control and speed.
- At the completion of the reps, return the bar to the floor. Be sure to use the same technique you used to pick up the bar.

Lat Pulldown

Body area: *midback*
Muscles: *latissimus dorsi, trapezius, biceps*
Variation: *Pull bar to back of neck. (This exercise requires special apparatus.)*

- Grasp the bar with hands 7 to 8 inches wider apart than shoulder width.
- Your hands should be evenly spaced on the grip. Use the wraparound thumb grip, with arms fully extended.
- Pull the bar straight down until you reach a kneeling position, or sit in a chair.
- Your head and torso should remain in an upright position.
- Begin to pull the bar downward toward the top of the chest. Your back muscles, not your arms, should start the motion.
- Continue to pull the bar downward until it touches the top of your chest. Keep your head and torso up. (In an advanced variation, the bar would go to the back of the neck.)
- Exhale during the pulling stage.
- Allow the bar to return slowly to the starting position. Maintain control and speed. Continue the reps.

▼ Lat Pulldown
(Machine)

Bent-Over Row (continued)

● DO

- maintain correct stance.
- keep your back tight and flat.
- hold your head straight up.
- exhale during positive phase.

● DON'T

- rock back and forth.
- arch or roll back.
- lock knees.

Variations Can be performed using one arm at a time with dumbbells and the use of a bench. Machines are also available.

Discussing

The Lat (short for latissimus) Pull-Down develops the upper and lower back muscles (latissimus dorsi and trapezius). The biceps muscle is also involved. **L1**

Demonstrate

Demonstrate stable body form in a kneeling or chair-sitting position. Extend your arms to the bar and choose the appropriate grip to target the specific muscle area. Pull the bar slowly and smoothly to the top of your chest.

● DO

- control speed of weights.
- pull arms down and back.
- keep your back and head straight.
- use full range of motion.

● DON'T

- shrug shoulders.
- rock back.
- lock out elbows.
- lift off seat or floor.

Variations By adjusting grips and types of bars you use, you can target many areas of the back with this versatile exercise. Wider grips reduce stress on the biceps and place greater stress on the lats.

Free weights allow users to incorporate dynamic, free movement of multiple joints that translate to real-life activities. Free weights can use more muscle groups and create a larger training stimulus. They encourage proper lifting techniques that enlist the support of synergistic muscles, as in the real-world movements of sports. The use of free weights is very conducive to the development of power movements such as throwing or releasing maneuvers. Machines, however, can be safer and quicker to give results—particularly for beginners—and can satisfy the basic goals of fitness and health.

Discussing

The Straight-Back Good Morning is a single-joint exercise. It is designed to target the lower back muscles (spinal erectors). Lower back muscles can be quite weak and subject to injury. Be sure to closely monitor the amount of weight used in this exercise. **L1**

Demonstrate

Demonstrate the correct form for a stable standing position with feet shoulder-width apart. Spotters should lift the bar and correctly place it on the lifter's shoulders. Slowly and smoothly bend at the waist until your back is parallel with the floor, then return to the start position. **TEKS C3A**

● DO

- control speed of weights.
- exhale during positive phase.
- keep your back and head straight.
- keep knees flexed and aligned with toes.

● DON'T

- rock back on feet.
- round your back.
- place bar on your neck.

Variations None suggested.

Discussing

The popular Back Squat is one of the more dangerous exercises due to the heavy weight involved and the incorrect technique some lifters use. Explain to students that the biomechanical principle of intensity can be applied during this exercise. This multijoint exercise is designed to work the overall lower body (quadriceps, hamstrings, and gluteals). **L1 TEKS C1A5**

▲ **Straight-back Good Morning**

Straight-back Good Morning
Body area: *lower back*
Muscles: *spinal erectors*
Caution: *Spotters and light weights recommended*

- Assume shoulder-width stance, with feet flat and head and shoulders up.
- Spotters will lift and place the bar across the back of your shoulders, not your neck. (The lifter could use a weight rack to position the bar.)
- Grasp the bar with hands slightly farther apart than shoulder width.
- Your hands should be evenly spaced in the grip. Use a wrap-around thumb grip.
- Slightly bend your knees. Lean forward by bending at the waist.
- Continue downward. Bend until your back is parallel to the floor. Keep your back and feet flat.
- Slowly return to the starting position. Maintain control and speed.
- Continue the reps. Have spotters remove the bar at the completion of the reps.

Back Squat
Body area: *front upper leg*
Muscles: *quadriceps, gluteals, hamstrings*
Variation: *leg press (machine)*
Caution: *Spotters and squat rack recommended; weight belt required*

- The bar should be positioned on the rack about shoulder high.
- Your hands should be slightly farther apart than your shoulders.
- Your hands should be evenly spaced. Use a wraparound thumb grip.

More About . . .

SQUAT vs. LEG PRESS Which is safer? Which is the most effective at improving sport-specific strength and skills? The advantages of the squat include the fact that it requires a good athletic position at the bottom of the lift and a complete hip extension at the completion of the lift. Both of these movements are constantly required during athletic events. If the squat is taught correctly with light weight and an emphasis on proper technique, the results will be improved strength for the lower back, hips, and knees (a body's stabilizing core). Developing sport-specific strength and

▲ Back Squat

- Position your shoulders, hips, and feet under the bar.
- Place the bar across your shoulders (not on your neck).
- Pull your shoulders back. Straighten your back and raise your chest, with your head up.
- Begin the lift by straightening your legs. (Spotters assist in removing the weight.)
- Take one step away from the rack, and assume shoulder-width stance.
- Your feet should be lined up evenly. Your weight should be evenly distributed on your feet.
- Stabilize the bar before starting the downward motion. (Spotters should release the bar.)
- Slowly bend your knees and lower your hips. Keep your back flat. Do not lean forward.
- Continue to lower the bar until your thighs (quadriceps) are parallel to the floor. Do not bounce or hesitate at the bottom.
- Your knees must stay lined up with your feet. Do not let them point in or out.
- Your heels must stay on the floor. Do not lean forward on your toes.
- Lift the bar by straightening your legs and hips.
- Your head and eyes are up, your knees are aligned with your toes, and your back is flat.
- Your feet are flat, with weight slightly more on the heels.
- Exhale during the lifting stage near the top of the lift.
- Slowly return to the starting position. Maintain control and speed.
- Continue the reps. Replace the bar on the rack. Never release your grip until the bar is safely in the rack. (Spotters should assist in replacing the bar.)

▼ Leg Press (Machine)

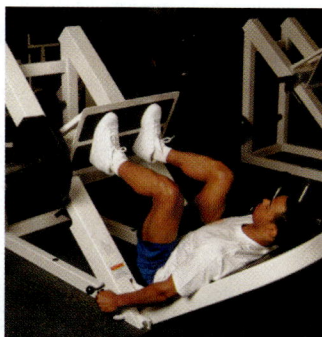

Back Squat (continued)

Demonstrate

Demonstrate a stable standing position in the squat rack. This will require a flat back and wide grip, with the head up and knees slightly bent. Weight belts should be properly used. Spotters should place the bar on the shoulders, not the neck. Begin the exercise by slowly bending your knees until the thighs are parallel to the floor. Return to the start position.

⬤ DO

- control speed of weights.
- keep back flat and head up.
- maintain balanced bar.
- use wide grip.
- keep knees aligned with toes.

⬤ DON'T

- over-arch back at any time.
- lean forward on toes or bend at waist.
- raise heels off floor.
- lock out knees.
- put chairs behind students to determine the depth of their squats.

Variations Dumbbells can replace barbells. Leg press machines are also available but do require a different technique.

Discussing

The Lunge (page 290) is a multijoint exercise designed to work the overall lower body (quadriceps, hamstrings, and gluteals). It can be used in conjunction with squats to develop the same muscles. The longer the stride, the greater the stress on the gluteus maximus. Shorter strides direct stress to the quadriceps. Use a nonslip surface. **L1**

balance in these areas will result in more efficient movement but may result in injury and prevent stability. Pros to consider for the leg press include its high safety factor. There is little risk of low-back injury because the back is supported against the seat. The legs are isolated and no spotters are involved. It is a good exercise for beginners. This exercise lacks balance skills and athletic movements involved in sports or everyday activities. Most machines do not produce full extension of the hips at the top of the movement, where much of the legs' power and speed come from.

Demonstrate

Establish a stable standing position. Place the dumbbells at your side and slowly bend, taking a large step forward. Bend your knee until the leg is parallel with the floor. Return to the start position.

🟢 DO

• keep back flat and head up.
• maintain balanced bar (if using barbell).
• have heel hit floor first.
• keep toes pointed straight.
• keep knees aligned with toes.

🔴 DON'T

• lean forward on toes or bend at waist.
• allow bent knee to extend past toes.

Variations You can use dumbbells, barbells, or just your body weight. Machines are not available.

Discussing

Leg Curls work the upper part of the back leg (hamstring). The hamstring muscles are usually much weaker than the quadriceps. Students should use less weight for these muscles. 🟥 L1

Demonstrate

Adjust the machine to your body dimensions. Slowly bend your knees and pull the heels toward the buttocks. Return to the start position.

🟢 DO

• maintain slow, controlled speed.
• keep toes pointed toward shins.

🔴 DON'T

• lift head or hips off bench.
• arch back.

Variations A standing variation of this machine is available.

▲ Lunge (Free Weight)

Lunge
Body area: *leg*
Muscles: *quadriceps, gluteals, hamstrings*
Variation: *straight bar*
Caution: *spotters recommended*

• Assume shoulder-width stance, with feet flat on the floor and back straight.
• Bend your knees and waist to place your hands on the dumbbells. Fully extend your arms and grasp the dumbbells with a wraparound grip.
• Your hands should be slightly farther apart than your shoulders.
• Return to a standing position.
• Take one big step directly forward with your right leg.
• Your right foot should hit heel first and go to a flat position.
• Bend your right knee slowly so your thigh is parallel to the floor. Your right knee should not go beyond your toes.
• Your left knee should bend slightly, but not touch the floor.
• Your back should remain straight. Do not lean forward or bend at the waist.
• Return to the starting position by pushing back with your right leg.
• Exhale during the push stage. Do not hold your breath.
• Hesitate at the starting position. Then repeat the same task with your left leg.
• At the completion of the reps, return the dumbbells to the rack.

Leg Curl (Machine)
Body area: *upper back leg*
Muscles: *hamstring*

• Lie facedown on the bench (machine).
• Keep your hips, legs, and chest flat on the bench.
• Your kneecaps should be past the end of the bench.
• Your hands should grasp the bench handles.
• Position the backs of your ankles on the roller pad.
• Begin the lift by flexing your knees. Raise the pad to your buttocks.
• Your hips must remain in contact with the bench.
• Exhale during the pull stage. Do not hold your breath.
• Slowly lower the roller pad to the starting position and continue the reps.

▶ Leg Curl (Machine)

290

Teacher-Coach Tips

Obesity in Teens Each year, more and more teenagers in the United States are overweight. It has become apparent that walking, jogging, and other aerobic activities have not been effective. Physical education teachers and coaches must seek out other methods to address this issue. Recently, professionals have begun using weight training as an alternative exercise to motivate overweight students to get active and stay active. Overweight students can realize all the usual benefits of weight training. Some of these benefits will have an immediate impact on their lives. A stronger musculoskeletal

◀ Leg Extension (Machine)

Leg Extension (Machine)
Body area: *front upper leg*
Muscles: *quadriceps*

- Sit in an upright position on the bench with your head up.
- Your back is flat, and your grip is on the handles.
- Place your upper ankles under the roller pad.
- Raise the roller pad by extending your legs at the knee.
- Extend your legs completely, and hold for 2 counts.
- Exhale during the push stage. Do not hold your breath.
- Slowly lower the pad to the starting position.
- Your back and buttocks must stay in contact with the bench.
- Continue the reps.

Standing Heel Raise
Body area: *lower leg*
Muscles: *gastrocnemius*

- The bar should be positioned on the rack about shoulder height.
- Your grip width should be slightly wider than your shoulder width.
- Your hands should be evenly spaced in the grip. Use a wraparound thumb grip.
- Place the bar across your shoulders (not on your neck).
- Your feet should be 8 to 10 inches apart. Place the balls of your feet on a raised surface 1½ to 2 inches high.
- Lock out your knees (straight not flexed).
- Push up on your toes to raise your heels to their highest position.
- Exhale during the push stage. Do not hold your breath.
- Slowly lower your heels until they touch the floor, and continue the reps.
- Replace the bar in the rack.

▼ Standing Heel Raise

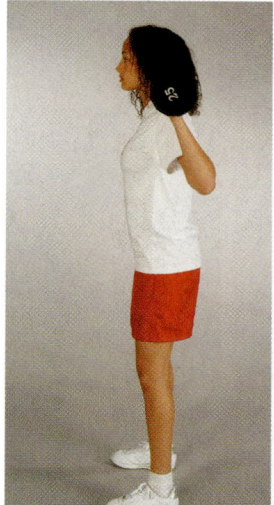
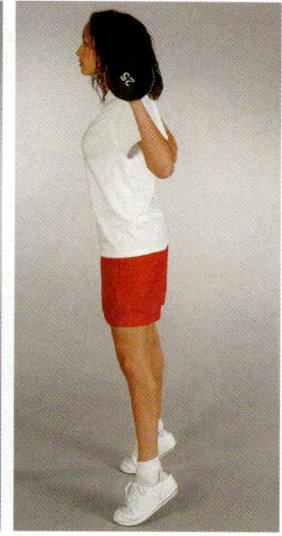

system will allow them to better conduct life's daily activities, as well as improve motor skills and sports participation. Unlike aerobic activities, in which overweight students are often unsuccessful, the weight room gives them an environment for success. In the weight room, these teens tend to be the strongest in their class, and they receive unsolicited praise from their peers. The psychological advantage of this environment makes it much more likely that they will continue to participate. Focus on factors such as skill improvement, fun, individual success, and improved confidence.

Discussing
The Leg Extension isolates the upper part of the front leg (quadriceps) and strengthens the knee joints. This exercise requires the use of a special apparatus. Most versions are done while seated. **L1**

Demonstrate
Demonstrate correct sitting position on the bench. Slowly extend knees until legs are straight. Return to start position.

DO
- maintain slow, controlled speed.
- keep toes straight up.

DON'T
- arch back.
- lift hips or back from bench.
- rub kneecaps on bench.

Variations A standing variation of this machine is available.

Discussing
The Standing Heel Raise is a single-joint exercise to strengthen and shape the back of the lower leg. **L1**

Demonstrate
Demonstrate the correct standing position with the balls of your feet on a two-inch raised surface. With the bar on your shoulders, raise your heels off the floor. Return to the start position.

DO
- maintain slow, controlled speed.
- keep knees straight.

DON'T
- roll back.
- bend hips.

Variations Single heel raises may be used.

Discussing

The Arm Curl is a single-joint exercise designed to strengthen and shape the front of the upper arm (biceps). **L1**

Demonstrate

Demonstrate the correct form for lifting weights from the floor or rack and establish a stable standing position with the feet shoulder-width apart. Fully extend the arms to waist level, then slowly raise the barbell by flexing the biceps. At the top of the lift, squeeze the biceps and return to the start position.

● DO
- maintain slow, controlled speed.
- keep knees flexed.
- keep elbows at your side.

● DON'T
- lean forward or backward.
- shrug shoulders.
- lock elbows at start position.

Variations Include various uses of dumbbells; different bars (such as E-Z curl); and Hammer, Concentration, and Preacher Curls. Machines are also available.

Discussing

The Triceps Extension is a single-joint exercise designed to strengthen and shape the back of the upper arm (triceps). A strong triceps helps you perform everyday activities like pushing and throwing. **L1**

Demonstrate

Extend your arms over your head, then slowly lower the barbell by bending the arm at the elbow. When the bar reaches the bottom of your neck, return to the start position.

▲ Arm Curl

Arm Curl
Body area: *front of upper arm*
Muscles: *biceps*
Variation: *dumbbells*

- Assume shoulder-width stance, with feet flat on the floor.
- Bend your knees, not your waist, to place your hands on the bar.
- Your grip should be the width of your hips.
- Your grip should be evenly spaced. Use a wraparound thumb grip, with palms up.
- Keep your back flat, and straighten your legs to stand up.
- In your starting position, your knees should be slightly bent and your arms fully extended in front.
- Keep your elbows in a stationary position at your side.
- Raise the bar by flexing your arms at the elbows. Raise the bar until your upper and lower arms are squeezed together.
- Keep your back flat and straight. Do not swing your body.
- Exhale during the lifting stage. Do not hold your breath.
- Slowly lower the bar to the starting position. Continue the reps.

▲ Triceps Extension

Triceps Extension
Body area: *back of upper arm*
Muscles: *triceps*
Variation: *dumbbells*

- Assume shoulder-width stance, with feet flat on the floor.
- Bend your knees, not your waist, to place your hands on the bar.
- Your grip should be 6 inches apart in the middle of the bar. Use a wraparound thumb grip.
- Keep your back flat, and straighten your legs to stand up.
- Raise the bar over your head, with arms fully extended and knees slightly bent.
- The area from the shoulder to the elbow should stay in this position throughout the exercise.

What Teens Want to Know

Which exercises may be dangerous, and what are some alternatives? Tell students that physical activity and exercise have many health benefits, but that some exercises may be harmful and should be avoided. Potentially dangerous exercises include straight-leg sit-ups, locked-knee toe touches, double leg lifts, full squats below parallel, ballistic stretching, neck circling, and hands-behind-the-head sit-ups. Alternatives include bent-leg sit-ups, bent-knee hand downs, raised leg crunches, partial squats, passive or static stretching, side neck stretches, and hands-crossed-on-chest sit-ups.

- Slowly lower the bar to the back of your neck by bending your arms at the elbows.
- Keep your elbows close to your head and near your ears.
- When the bar touches the back of your neck, return the bar to the overhead position by straightening your arms.
- Do not allow your elbows to move away from your ears.
- Exhale during the pushing stage. Do not hold your breath.
- Continue the reps.

Dumbbell Kickback

Body area: *back of upper arm*
Muscles: *triceps*

- Assume shoulder-width stance, with feet flat on the floor and knees slightly bent.
- Bend over at the waist until your upper body is parallel to the floor.
- Extend one arm, and place your hand on a bench or chair for balance.
- Place the dumbbell in your other hand. Use a wraparound thumb grip, with your palm facing your leg.
- Raise the dumbbell to your waist. Bend your arm at the elbow so that your upper arm is parallel to the floor and your lower arm is perpendicular to the floor.
- Straighten your elbow until your arm is straight. Do not move the position of your elbow in relation to your waist.
- Exhale during the lifting stage. Do not hold your breath.
- Slowly lower the dumbbell to the starting position. Do not swing your arm.
- Continue the reps, and then switch arms.

▲ **Variation of Triceps Extension (Dumbbells)**

▲ **Dumbbell Kickback**

Triceps Extension (continued)

🟢 DO
- maintain slow, controlled speed.
- keep knees flexed.
- keep elbows pointed up and near the ears.

🔴 DON'T
- lean forward or backward.
- shrug shoulders.
- lock elbows at start position.
- bend neck or head.

Variations Various dumbbells and ways to use them; different bars (such as E-Z curl); and a variety of machines.

Discussing

The Dumbbell Kickback is a single-joint exercise designed to strengthen and shape the back of the upper arm (triceps). **L1**

Demonstrate

Bend at the waist and hold on to a chair or bench for balance. Then extend the arm, holding the dumbbell to your side, and raise the elbow to your waist. Slowly extend the elbow until the arm is straight, then repeat the movement.

🟢 DO
- maintain slow, controlled speed.
- maintain support for back.
- keep knees flexed.
- keep elbow pointed up and in contact with waist.

🔴 DON'T
- lean forward or backward.
- shrug shoulders.
- swing arms.
- bend neck or head.

Variations
See French Press.

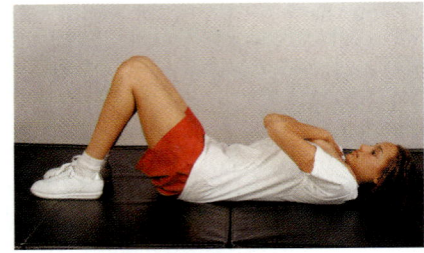 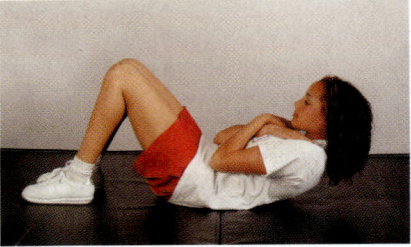

▶ **Abdominal Crunch**

Discussing

The Abdominal Crunch is the most popular exercise used to strengthen and shape the stomach (abdominals). Strong abdominals give support to the body in almost every movement we make. **L1**

Demonstrate

Demonstrate the correct form while lying on a mat. Bend the knees and fold the arms across the chest. Slowly raise your upper body to a point where the elbows can touch the stomach. Return to the start position and repeat.

🟢 DO

- maintain slow, controlled speed.
- maintain support for back.
- keep chin tucked to chest.
- keep knees bent.
- keep arms in contact with chest.
- keep feet flat on floor.

🔴 DON'T

- raise hips from floor.
- bend neck or head.
- let head touch floor.

Variations Many exercises can be used to work the abdominal area. These can be targeted for specific areas, such as the upper or lower abdominals.

Discussing

The Twisting Abdominal Crunch is very similar to the Abdominal Crunch. **L1**

Demonstrate

The beginning position is similar to the Abdominal Crunch. Begin by placing your bent legs on a chair or bench. Then raise and twist the torso at the top of the contraction.

Abdominal Crunch
Body area: *stomach*
Muscles: *abdominals*
Variations: *incline bench, raised feet, machines*

- Lie faceup on a mat or carpeted floor. Your back and buttocks should be flat on the surface.
- Your knees should be bent. Position your feet flat on the floor with your heels 12 to 18 inches from your buttocks.
- Place your hands and arms across your chest. Your hands should be placed near the opposite shoulders.
- Position your chin in a tucked position, allowing your chin to touch your chest.
- Contract your abdominal muscles and raise your torso until your elbows contact your upper thighs.
- Exhale when your elbows contact your thighs.
- Slowly return to the starting position. Do not let your chin lose contact with your chest. Your head should not touch the floor.
- Repeat the process until the reps are completed.

Twisting Abdominal Crunch
Body area: *stomach*
Muscles: *abdominals, obliques*
Variations: *incline bench, raised feet*

- Lie faceup on a mat or carpeted floor. Your back and buttocks should be flat on the surface.
- Your knees should be bent. Position your feet flat on the floor with your heels 12 to 18 inches from your buttocks.
- Place your hands and arms across your chest. Your hands should be placed near the opposite shoulders.
- Keep your chin in a tucked position, which allows your chin to touch your chest.
- Contract your abdominal muscles and raise your torso from the floor. Continue to raise your torso until your elbows are near your thighs.

Teacher-Coach Tips

Disease Prevention As students work with these exercises, remind them of the health concerns associated with obesity. Heart disease, high blood pressure, atherosclerosis, and stroke are more common in obese people. Liver disorders, respiratory problems, and diabetes also occur more frequently.

The burden of extra fat puts a strain on the skeletal system. Arthritis occurs in the hips, knees, and lower spine. The more weight a person carries, the greater the wear and tear on the joints. This can cause pain that results in even less physical activity and the risk of additional weight gain.

- Twist your torso to the left and touch your right elbow to your left thigh. If possible, extend your right elbow past the left thigh.
- Exhale when your elbow contacts your thigh.
- Slowly return to the starting position. Do not let your chin lose contact with your chest. Your head should not touch the floor.
- Start the process again, but twist the torso to the right side, touching your left elbow to your right thigh.
- Slowly return to the starting position.
- Repeat the process until the reps are completed.

◀ Twisting Abdominal Crunch

Lesson 1 Review

Using complete sentences, answer the following questions on a sheet of paper.

Reviewing Facts and Vocabulary

1. **Vocabulary** What is the purpose of *clips* in resistance-training safety? Name two other tips that ensure a safe workout.
2. **Recall** Why is proper grip important?

Thinking Critically

3. **Explain** Describe the proper etiquette for using a public weight room.
4. **Apply** Describe or demonstrate the proper procedure for gripping the bar when lifting weights.

5. **Demonstrate** Describe or demonstrate for classmates how to perform correct breathing and spotting techniques when lifting weights.

Personal Fitness Planning

Setting Goals Help a friend or family member determine and set his or her resistance-training goals. Remember to make the goals specific to the person's needs and to write them down. Then make a list of weight-lifting exercises you learned that will help him or her reach these goals. If you do not have access to weights, make a list of other resistance activities you could do together. Discuss how these activities can benefit your mutual health and fitness.

Lesson 1 Review

Answers to Lesson 1 Review

1. Keeps weights from slipping off the bar. Answers may vary but should include applying safety procedures.
2. To ensure that the bar is controlled.
3. Limit your time on a machine, put away equipment at the end of your session, and towel off any areas you use.
4. Wrap fingers around bar so that the thumbs meet the index fingers.
5. Correct breathing will ensure inhaling during the negative phase and exhaling during the positive phase.

3 ASSESS

EVALUATING THE LESSON

Assign and discuss the Lesson 1 Review.

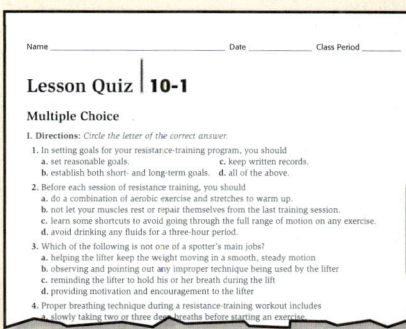

RETEACHING

Place note cards with questions throughout the weight room. Have students go to each station to answer the questions.

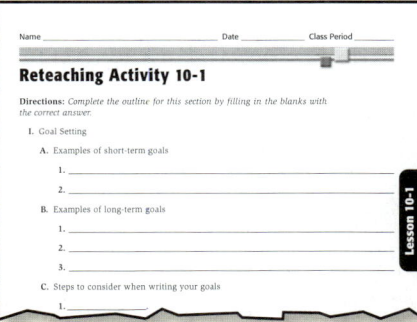

ENRICHMENT

Have students help a friend or family member identify goals and exercises that will help to develop and maintain his or her fitness goals.

4 CLOSE

Divide the class into groups and ask them to demonstrate proper technique for specific exercises.

295

Planning Your Resistance-Training Workout

Planning Your Resistance-Training Workout

1 MOTIVATE

GETTING STARTED

- Before you begin roll call, ask the class to think about the following question: *What is the difference between a set and a repetition? Can you identify other parts of a weight-training workout?*

- Distribute copies of *Guided Practice 10-2* for students to use while studying this lesson. 🗂

IN THIS LESSON

- **Active Mind—Active Body** *Participating in Strength-Training Exercises, p. 298*
- **Mind Over Matter** *Staying the Course, p. 302*
- **Fitness Facts,** p. 304

INTRODUCING VOCABULARY

- Explain how the word *circuit* refers to the act of moving or going around. In this lesson, *circuit* refers to moving from one exercise station to the next.

- Have students use *Vocabulary Worksheet 10* or the PuzzleMaker software to practice vocabulary terms for this lesson. ELL 🗂 💿

Photo Follow-up

Caption answer: Muscles in the upper body, including arms and shoulders.

What You Will Do

- Identify components of a resistance-training workout.
- Participate in a variety of exercises that build muscular strength and endurance.
- Describe the exercises that target major muscles.
- Identify various strength-training circuits and explain what each accomplishes.

Terms to Know

repetition (rep)
set
exercise
circuit training
large muscle group
small muscle group

I magine going into a weight room and choosing at random the exercises you will do and the equipment you will use. Probably, you would accomplish very little. To be effective, a workout needs to follow a careful plan. In this lesson, you will learn how to create a structured workout.

Components of the Workout

A successful weight-training workout consists of a number of components, or building blocks. These are shown in **Figure 10.3** and described below.

- **Repetition.** More commonly referred to simply as a **rep,** this is *one completion of an activity or exercise.* It is the most basic unit of a workout. A rep consists of lifting a weight and returning it to the starting position. So does doing the negative and positive phases of a push-up. The number of reps done for a particular exercise will vary, depending upon your goals.

- **Set.** A **set** is *a group of consecutive reps for any exercise.* If you do ten push-ups, one right after the other, you have done one set of ten reps. By repeating the process after a short rest of two minutes, you have completed a total of two sets. Like the number of repetitions, the number of sets will be determined by your goals.

◀ Resistance training exercises target a specific body area. *What body area and muscle group is this teen working?*

296   **Chapter 10**   **Developing Muscular Fitness**

LESSON 2 RESOURCES

Teacher Classroom Resources
🗂 Guided Practice Activity 10-2
🗂 Active Mind—Active Body Worksheet 10-2
🗂 Reteaching Activity 10-2
🗂 Lesson Quiz 10-2

Reproducible Charts and Graphs
🗂 Reproducible Master 10-1

Multimedia
💿 Vocabulary PuzzleMaker
🔦 Transparencies 54, 55

- **Exercise.** In a typical workout, you will do several sets of several different exercises. An *exercise,* as the term is used in resistance training, is *a series of repetitive muscle contractions that build strength and endurance.* When the resistance force is movable—the case with free weights and weight machines—the exercise is said to be dynamic. Some of the more common dynamic resistance-training exercises are the bench press, squat, and arm curl. Other examples of resistance-training exercises that do not require free weights or a machine are calisthenic exercises, such as push-ups and pull-ups, in which you apply biomechanical force.
- **Body area.** Every exercise has as its primary target a muscle group within one of the six specific weight-training "body areas," as shown in **Figure 10.4.** The bench press, for example, is targeted primarily at muscles within the chest. Squats work muscles within the leg. The "Active Mind—Active Body" activity on page **298** will give you practice identifying which exercises work which muscle groups.

You cannot expect noticeable results after a single workout. It is only by working out consistently over the course of weeks and months that you will begin to realize a difference.

 **Reading Check**

Identify List and describe the components of a resistance workout.

FIGURE 10.3

COMPONENTS OF A WORKOUT

The rep is the most basic component of a resistance-training program. *What is the term given to a series of consecutive reps?*

FIGURE 10.4

THE SIX MAJOR BODY AREAS

A workout will include exercises that work one or more of these body muscle areas. *Referring to Figure 9.3 on page 251, name one muscle in each body area.*

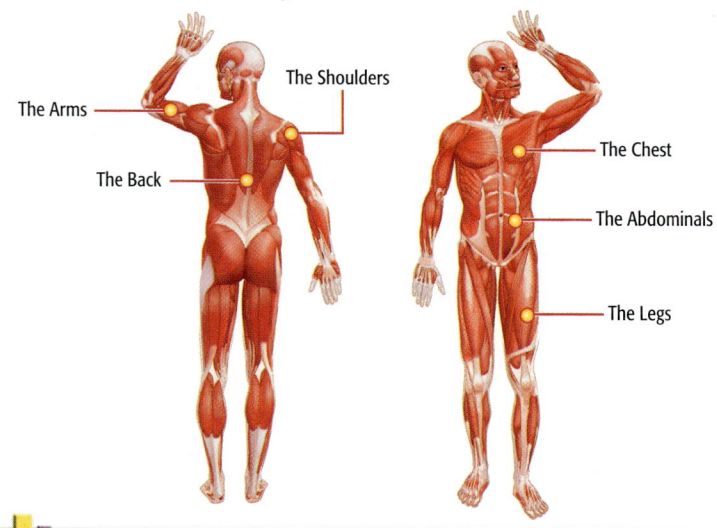

The Shoulders
The Arms
The Back
The Chest
The Abdominals
The Legs

Lesson 2   Planning Your Resistance-Training Workout   **297**

USING VISUALS

Figures 10.3 and 10.4
Components of a workout shown here include the rep, set, exercises, and body area. Use Figure 10.3 to teach the concept of the workout and how it is centered around the basic unit of repetitions. *Caption answer 10.3: Set is a series of reps.* Have volunteers name muscles and an exercise that targets each area.

Demonstrate

Use a dumbbell to demonstrate one rep of a biceps curl, then do eight reps to demonstrate one set of curls. Use the same dumbbell to execute the same procedure with a triceps kickback. This will show different muscle areas. **L2**

Activity

Have students work in groups to perform one set of eight reps for the bench press and one set of six reps for lunges. Check for correct lifting and spotting technique. Be sure students apply the biomechanical principle and correct use of leverage. Weights should be held close to the body. Other exercises can be substituted. **L2 ELL** TEKS C1B2, C3A

 **Reading Check**

A resistance workout includes reps, sets of reps, exercises, and the targeting of specific body areas.

TECHNOLOGY FILE

Digital Camera Muscle Project

Have students create their own muscle match game using a digital camera, clip art, and word processing or desktop publishing software. Arrange students in groups of four and assign each group five muscles. Have them create three task cards for each muscle: 1) name of the muscle, 2) clip-art picture of the muscle, and 3) photo of a weight lifting exercise that works the muscle. Completed cards from all groups can be shuffled and students match the exercise, muscle, and name. Include physical activity by having students correctly perform the lift.

Active Mind Active Body

Participating in Strength-Training Exercises

This activity will help students determine the location and name of the muscles worked by specific exercises. Divide these exercises into four or five subgroups. Use these subgroups throughout the unit to introduce students to new exercises.

Teaching Tips

- Use *Transparencies 54 and 55* showing muscle groups to introduce students to the activity.
- Have students demonstrate the weight-lifting exercises you have assigned. Use the exercise technique checklist on pages 279–295.
- Distribute *Active Mind– Active Body Worksheet 10-2* to record progress. 📁
- Be sure students use only the bars (with no added weight) to perform these exercises. You can substitute broomsticks to ensure safety at this early stage.
- Constantly monitor students and teach and reteach as necessary.

Apply and Conclude

Have students explain how they applied the biomechanical principle of force and demonstrated the skill-related component of power, as explained in Chapter 3. **TEKS C1B1, C4C4**

Active Mind Active Body

Participating in Strength-Training Exercises

Can you name an exercise that will strengthen muscles in the upper legs? In the back? After completing this activity, you will be able to identify several exercises and the muscles they work.

What You Will Need

- Pen or pencil
- Paper

What You Will Do

1. Take a moment to identify the major muscle groups shown in **Figure 10.5** on pages **299–300**.
2. Next, copy the following table (which lists some of the more common weight-training exercises) onto a separate sheet of paper.
3. For each exercise, write the muscle group and body area that it targets. You may want to refer to **Figures 10.6** on page **301**, **10.7** on page **302**, and **10.8** on page **303** as you complete the table.
4. Finally, attempt each of the exercises so you can feel in your own body

where the work is being done and how biomechanical force is applied. Follow the guidelines for weight-training exercises in Lesson 1 on pages **279–295** to help you prevent injuries.

Apply and Conclude

What similarities did you find among exercises that worked the same muscle groups? How did these activities differ from one another?

Exercise	Muscle Group	Body Area
1. bench press		
2. flat bench fly		
3. military press		
4. shoulder shrug		
5. upright row		
6. front, lateral, and bent-over shoulder raises		
7. bent-over row		
8. Lat pulldown		
9. straight-back good morning		
10. back squat		
11. lunge		
12. leg curl		
13. leg extension		
14. standing heel raise		
15. arm curl		
16. triceps extension		
17. abdominal crunch		

The Strength-Training Circuit

If you are a beginner to weight training, your goal should be to develop a well-designed resistance-training program for all areas of the body. The most efficient way of achieving this goal is through **circuit training.** Also known as following the strength-training circuit, this is *an approach to resistance training where you rotate from one exercise to the next in a particular sequence.* Training facilities that have a full set of weight machines often arrange these in a training circuit.

More About . . .

MUSCLE FIBER TYPES AND SPECIFIC TRAINING Before you can design programs that will work best for your students and athletes, you should understand at least some of the complexities of skeletal muscles. Slow-twitch (Type I) fibers are associated with a slow contraction time and a high degree of resistance to fatigue. As a result of their low threshold for contracting, they are the first muscle cells to contract during activity. Functionally, these fibers are used for most of our daily activities. Fast-twitch (Type II) fibers are associated with high-intensity, quick contraction time and a

FIGURE 10.5

BODY AREAS

Many different types of exercises can be used to develop the same muscle area. *Which will you be including in your workout?*

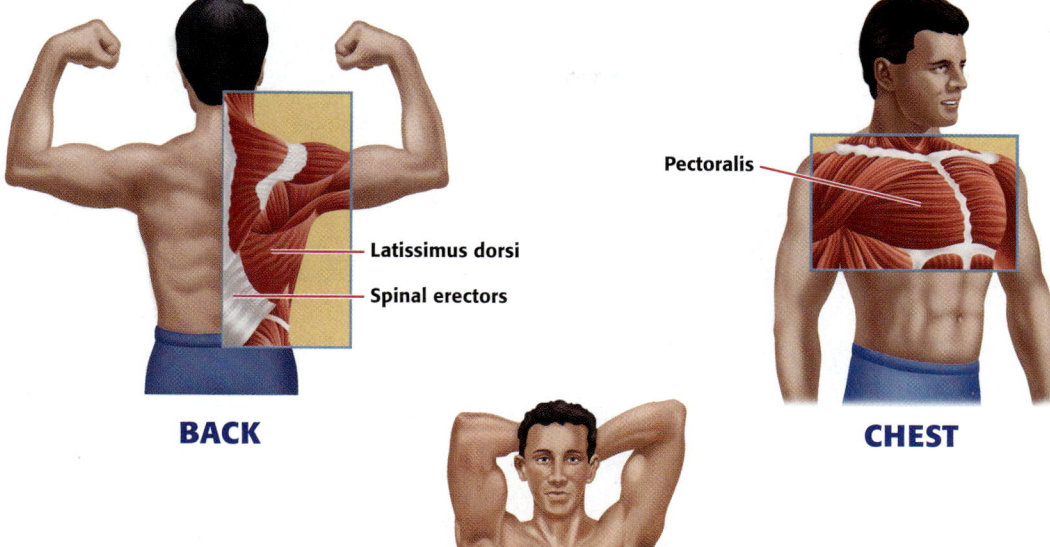

BACK
- Latissimus dorsi
- Spinal erectors

CHEST
- Pectoralis

ABDOMINALS
- External obliques
- Rectus abdominis

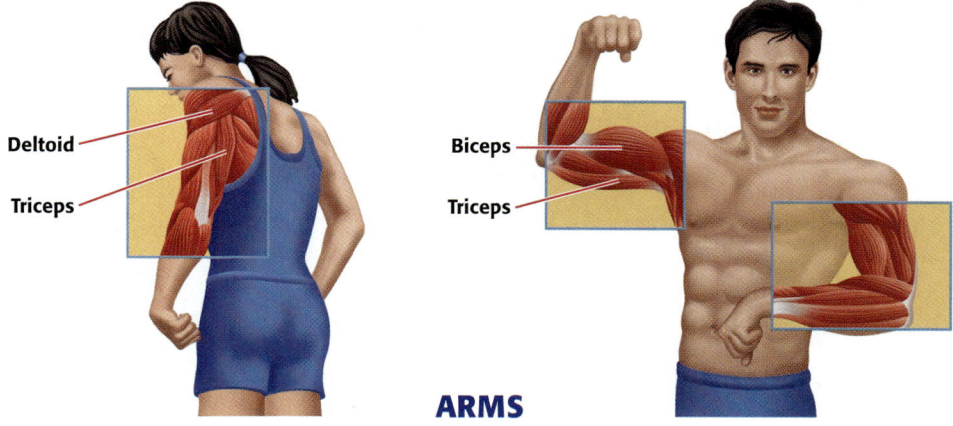

ARMS
- Deltoid
- Triceps
- Biceps
- Triceps

continued on next page

Lesson 2 Planning Your Resistance-Training Workout **299**

Discussing

Discuss the six areas of the body that are considered important to your workouts. They include the back, chest, abdominals, shoulders, and legs. Each area is important to a well-balanced muscular body. Remind students to properly apply the physiological principle of intensity. Explain that it is important to work all body parts with equal intensity to maintain high levels of health and fitness. Some athletic or performance-related activities may require higher intensities in some muscle areas. For example, gymnasts who do routines that work only the upper body (e.g., rings) will need more work on the arms and lats than the legs for effective application of progression. See Figure 10.6 on page 301 for examples of weight-training exercises that relate to specific activities. **L1** TEKS C1A5,7

USING VISUALS

Figure 10.5 Point out how many of the muscle groups shown on page 299 and 300 have more than one muscle and have numerous exercises to choose from. *Caption answers will vary for each student.*

low resistance to fatigue. They can further be divided into Type II-A and Type II-B. Type II-A fibers have a little more resistance to fatigue than II-B and are thus better for prolonged anaerobic activities. All athletes are not alike and will have a great difference in the number and type of muscle fibers. Those with a high percentage of slow-twitch fibers have a greater capacity for endurance activities. Those with a high percentage of fast-twitch fibers have a greater capacity for force and power activities.

Student Edition TEKS
Page 298: C4B

Discussing

Discuss the importance of knowing which primary and secondary muscles are involved during each weight-training exercise. For the primary muscle to fully function, it must have the help of secondary muscles bearing some of the load or acting as a stabilizer of the joint. Ask students to explain how the secondary muscles assist in applying the biomechanical principle of leverage during training. Secondary muscles are often referred to as *synergist* muscles, meaning they assist indirectly with the movement of the joint.

L1 **TEKS C1B**

Explaining

Explain what "putting your mind in the muscle" means. When exercises are done correctly, the primary muscle should be the one you feel working. You need to concentrate on proper technique in order to minimize the use of the secondary muscle and avoid using muscles that should not be used. **L2**

FIGURE 10.5 *continued*

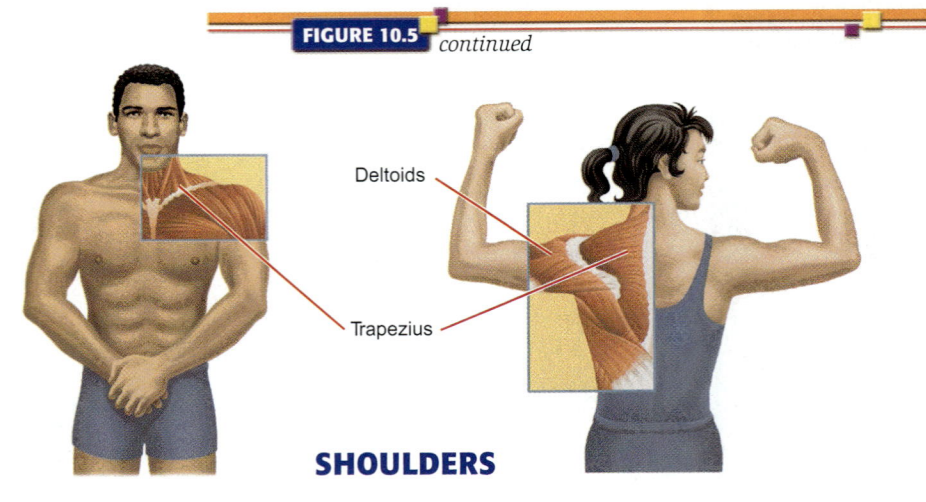

Deltoids

Trapezius

SHOULDERS

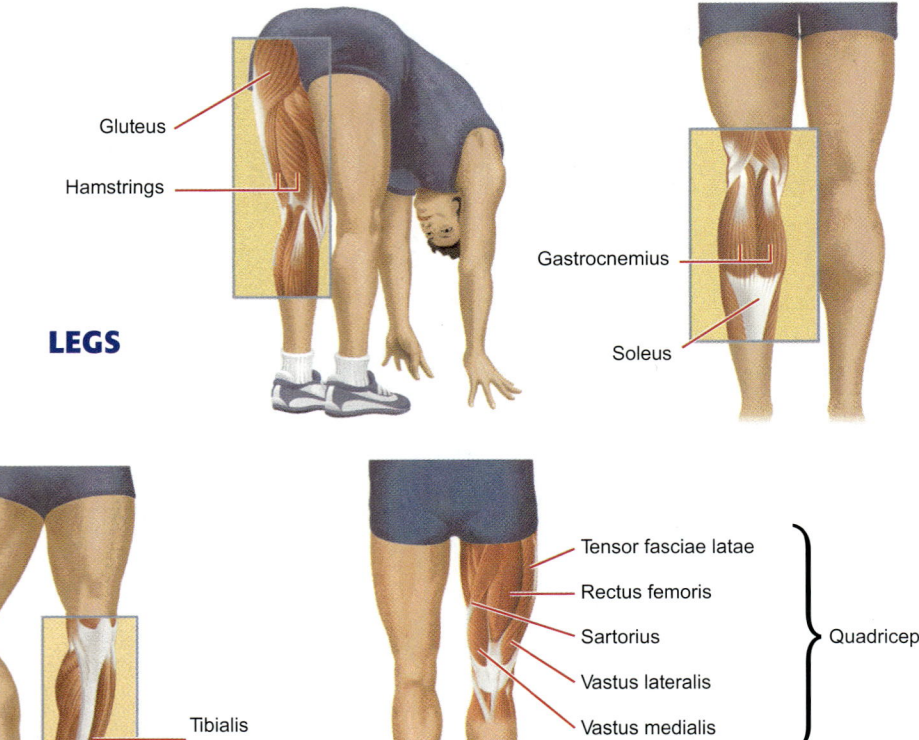

Gluteus

Hamstrings

LEGS

Gastrocnemius

Soleus

Tibialis anterior

Tensor fasciae latae

Rectus femoris

Sartorius

Vastus lateralis

Vastus medialis

Quadriceps

300   **Chapter 10**   Developing Muscular Fitness

Enrichment

Muscle Groups Introduce students to the major muscles and muscle groups that are used in exercise. These areas of the human body should be identified:

1. shoulders
2. chest
3. abdominals
4. upper back
5. lower back
6. upper legs
7. lower legs
8. arms
9. forearms
10. buttocks

FIGURE 10.6

EXERCISES, MUSCLE GROUPS, EQUIPMENT, AND ACTIVITIES

Exercise	Primary muscle group	Secondary muscle group	Equipment	Sport in which performance is enhanced
Leg extension	Quadriceps		Machine	All activities or sports
Leg curl	Hamstrings	Gastrocnemius	Machine	All activities or sports
Heel raise	Gastrocnemius, soleus		Machine, barbell	All activities or sports
Leg press	Quadriceps, gluteals	Hamstring	Machine	All activities or sports
Lunge	Quadriceps, gluteals	Hamstring	Barbell, dumbbells	All activities or sports
Squat	Quadriceps, gluteals	Hamstring	Barbell	All activities or sports
Sit-ups	Iliopsoas	Abdominals	Floor machine	All activities or sports
Bench press	Pectoralis major, anterior triceps, deltoid	Spinal erectors	Barbell, bench, machine, dumbbells	Football, basketball, wrestling, shot put
Incline press	Anterior pectoralis major, deltoid, triceps		Barbell, dumbbells, incline bench, machine	Football, basketball, wrestling, shot put
Fly (supine)	Pectoralis major	Deltoid	Dumbbells, machine	Football, tennis, discus throw, baseball, softball, wrestling, backstroke
Overhead press	Deltoid, triceps	Trapezius	Barbell, dumbbells, machine	Gymnastics, shot put
Bent-over rowing	Latissimus dorsi, rhomboids	Deltoid, biceps	Barbell, dumbbells, pulley machine	Wrestling, rowing, baseball, basketball
Upright rowing	Trapezius	Deltoid, biceps	Barbell, dumbbells, pulley machine	All activities or sports
Lat pull-down	Latissimus dorsi	Biceps	Pulley machine	Basketball, baseball, swimming, tennis, volleyball, wrestling
Good morning	Spinal erector		Barbell	All activities or sports
Front shoulder raise	Anterior deltoid		Barbell, dumbbells	All activities or sports
Bent-over lateral raise	Posterior deltoid	Rhomboids, latissimus dorsi	Dumbbells, machine	All activities or sports
Lateral shoulder raise	Deltoid	Trapezius	Dumbbells, machine	All activities or sports
Shoulder shrug	Trapezius		Barbell, dumbbells, machine	All activities or sports
Arm curl	Biceps	Forearm muscles	Barbell, dumbbells, pulley machine	All activities or sports
French press	Triceps		Barbell, dumbbells, pulley machine	All activities or sports

USING VISUALS

Figure 10.6 Discuss the relationship between exercises, muscle groups, equipment, and activities in this figure.

Explaining

You may wish to prepare a standard record sheet for students to use as soon as scheduled workouts begin. The record sheet should be used to note reps, sets, exercises, and the amount of weight used in each set. Over the course of the weight-training unit, provide well-designed workouts that utilize all the different circuits. As students gain experience with the variety of workout circuits, allow them to design their own. **L2**

Activity

Pair students into teams well suited as lifting partners. Each team should understand the daily routine for conducting the circuits. You might write the daily circuit on the board or explain it in a handout. As students enter the weight room they should acquire their record sheets, observe the circuit and begin their workouts with little needed extra instruction. **L2** **ELL**

Identification of muscle groups used during exercise enhances a student's ability to select proper strength-training exercises and routines. Have students list their favorite sport on a sheet of paper. Have them take one of the skills needed for that sport and do the following:

1. Analyze the skill, list muscles involved.
2. Develop a simple routine of two or three exercises used to strengthen the muscles. Two good examples to use for explaining this assignment: forearm tennis stroke and throwing a baseball.

Student Edition TEKS

Page 301: C1B

Staying the Course

Well-designed programs for weight-training will incorporate all three of these exercise principles. Be sure students recognize that by following the program, they will progress faster and be more likely to avoid injury.

USING VISUALS

Figure 10.7 Explain that the squat, bench press, and bent-over row require a great deal of energy as well as the use of smaller muscles. Ask students how applying the physiological principles of overload and progression correctly can help to keep smaller muscles from becoming fatigued too early. *Caption answer: The squat, because it uses large muscles.* **TEKS C1A3,7**

Explaining

Have students do a set of reps for a specific exercise using large muscles, rest, do another set, and continue this process until they have completed all sets for that specific exercise. Then have them describe the exercise prescription of specificity and choose a station that uses the smaller muscles from the previous sets. Proceed with the same type of sets and reps. The example in Figure 10.7 uses the bench press to target the large muscles (pectoralis), followed by the triceps extension to target the smaller triceps muscle. **L1 TEKS C4F8**

Staying the Course

You can avoid losing patience with your weight-training program by applying the physiological principles of:

- **Overload.** Increase your muscle intensity gradually over time by *overloading* your muscles.
- **Specificity.** Organize exercises to work *specific* muscle groups.
- **Progression.** Be prepared to *progress* gradually. Avoid overdoing and risking injury in order to see results.

FITNESS *Online*

Go to **fitness.glencoe.com** and click on Health Updates for informative articles on health and fitness.

Activity Read the update article on weight lifting. Answer the questions at the site, and then write an article on weight-lifting benefits and safety concerns for your school paper.

Variations on the Circuit

Today Brian and Jorge both worked on legs. Both used the same equipment during their sessions. However, Brian, who plays soccer, began his workout with squats to develop his thigh muscles. Jorge, who is on the school cross-country team, started with heel raises to build his calf muscles.

As Brian and Jorge's weight room preferences illustrate, circuit training can be customized to meet individual needs. Choosing a variation designed for your personal goals can help you maintain proper intensity for target muscles. It also helps you make the most of your workout time.

The following are three common variations used in circuit training. The remainder of this lesson will explore these approaches.

Training Large Muscle Groups Before Small Muscle Groups. Like Brian, many people who train with weights prefer to work large muscle groups—such as those in the upper leg—before small ones.

- **Large muscle group.** This term designates *any group of muscles of large size as well as any large number of muscles being used at one time.* Examples of large muscle groups are those of the upper legs, chest, and back.
- **Small muscle group.** This term designates *any group of muscles of small size as well as any small number of muscles being used at one time.* Examples of small muscle groups are those of the arms and lower legs.

One advantage of this approach is that large muscle groups require more strength, energy, and mental concentration. You have only limited amounts of each of these resources. Working the large muscles first allows you to make the most of them.

FIGURE 10.7

CIRCUIT TRAINING: LARGE MUSCLES BEFORE SMALL MUSCLES

A bench press, which works the chest muscle (pectoralis), uses the small muscle in the back of the upper arm (triceps). *Which exercise does the chart recommend doing first? Why?*

Exercise Order	Muscle Type	Muscle Groups
1. Squat	Large	Thigh and hips (quadriceps)
2. Heel raise	Small	Calf (gastrocnemius)
3. Bench press	Large	Chest (pectoralis)
4. Triceps extension	Small	Upper arm, back (triceps)
5. Bent-over row	Large	Back (latissimus dorsi)
6. Arm curl	Small	Upper arm, front (biceps)

INCLUSION STRATEGIES

TRAINING SEQUENCE For students with disabilities, the training sequence is critical to ensure that maximum benefit is gained from the workout. Lifts that work multiple muscle groups and joints should be utilized before work that involves individual muscles and joints. Each muscle group worked needs sufficient rest between sets. Testing to determine muscular fitness of a student with a disability is important in addressing his or her specific physical needs. Tests that can be used to assess muscular fitness will vary, depending on the specific disability.

FIGURE 10.8

CIRCUIT TRAINING: PUSH AND PULL EXERCISES

This chart shows one approach to alternating push- and pull-type exercises. *What is an advantage of following this strategy?*

Exercise Order	Exercise Type	Muscle Groups
1. Leg press	Push	Thigh-front (quadriceps)
2. Leg curl	Pull	Thigh-back (hamstring)
3. Bench press	Push	Chest (pectoralis)
4. Bent-over row	Pull	Back (latissimus dorsi)
5. Military press	Push	Shoulder (deltoid)
6. Arm curl	Pull	Upper arm, front (biceps)
7. Triceps extension	Push	Upper arm, back (triceps)

In addition, small muscle groups often play a supporting role in large muscle group exercises. If these small muscle groups become fatigued, completing the large muscle exercises will be more difficult.

Figure 10.7 shows a sample circuit in which large muscle-group exercises precede those for small muscle groups.

Alternating Push Exercises with Pull Exercises. A second variation on the training circuit is to alternate pulling motions (flexing) with pushing motions (extension). This approach gives the muscles extra time to recover between sets. Another benefit of this approach is that it keeps opposing muscles balanced.

Figure 10.8 shows a method for organizing the strength-training circuit in terms of push and pull exercises. **Figure 10.9** gives an example of how opposite muscles are worked in the push-pull model of the circuit.

Alternating Upper-Body Exercises with Lower-Body Exercises. A third variation of circuit training alternates exercises for the upper body (waist and above) with an exercise for the lower body (hips and below). This method allows muscles more recovery time, but it is more difficult than the other circuit-training options previously discussed.

Workouts alternating upper- and lower-body muscles require an equal number of upper- and lower-body exercises. This means doing two to three more leg exercises than in the two previous types of workouts. These additional leg exercises require more energy, making the workout more difficult. This type of alternating plan is, however, a suitable plan for the individual wanting to perform a higher-intensity leg workout. **Figure 10.10** shows an example of how to organize upper- and lower-body exercises in your workout.

FIGURE 10.9

THE ARM MUSCLES: PUSHING AND PULLING

The triceps create force by pushing and the biceps create force by pulling. *What other pairs of muscles could benefit from a push and pull circuit?*

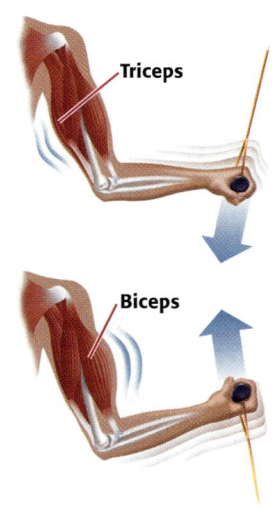

Triceps

Biceps

USING VISUALS

Figure 10.8 Use *Reproducible Master 10-1.* Have students identify specific push exercises and pull exercises. In push exercises, the joint is extended; in pull exercises, the joint is flexed. This is in keeping with the term *circuit.* **Caption answer: To allow more recovery time between sets.**

Activity

To have students complete a circuit, lifters will do one set of an exercise and then move to another exercise and do a set. Alternating the exercises keeps opposite muscles balanced and prevents muscle fatigue. **L1**

USING VISUALS

Figure 10.9 Have students explain how this motion applies the biomechanical principle of force to exercise and training. **TEKS C1B1, 2** *Caption answer: The quadriceps and hamstring benefit from a push-pull circuit.*

USING VISUALS

Figure 10.10 (page 304) This is similar to the push-pull, except that the exercises alternate upper-body lifts with lower-body lifts. *Caption answer: It requires many more leg exercises.*

QUOTES FOR LIFE

"Concentrate on finding your goal, then concentrate on reaching it."

—**Colonel Michael Friedsam** *Humanitarian, 1860–1931*

Student Edition TEKS

Page 302: C1B
Page 303: C1B

3 ASSESS

EVALUATING THE LESSON

Assign and discuss the Lesson 2 Review.

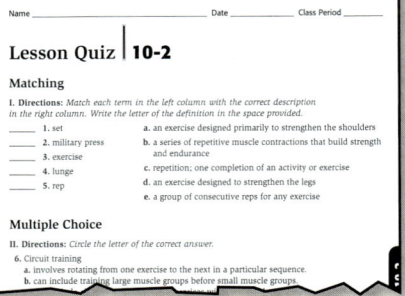

RETEACHING

Have students do examples of all three circuits. Be sure lifting and spotting technique is correct.

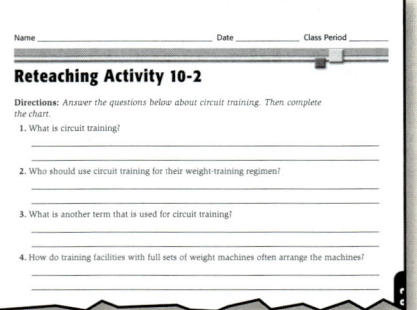

ENRICHMENT

Have students correctly design a circuit and use specific ones for class workouts.

4 CLOSE

Ask: Is it a good idea to change your circuits? Why?

Student Edition TEKS

Page 304: C4B, C4G
Page 305: C1A

304

Fitness FACTS

Muscle Mass

- A 3- to 4-pound increase in muscle mass in a year, resulting from weight training, will increase the amount of calories you burn in one day from 150 to 200.

- By their late twenties, people begin to lose 5 percent of their muscle mass per year on average.

FIGURE 10.10

UPPER-BODY AND LOWER-BODY EXERCISES

Alternating upper-body exercises with lower-body exercises allows muscles more recovery time. *Why is this more difficult than other training circuits?*

Exercise Order	Muscle Type	Muscle Groups
1. Military press	Upper	Shoulder (deltoid)
2. Leg extension	Lower	Thigh (quadriceps)
3. Back lat pull	Upper	Back (latissimus dorsi)
4. Lunge	Lower	Thigh and hip (quadriceps/gluteals)
5. Arm curl	Upper	Upper arm-front (biceps)
6. Leg press	Lower	Thigh-front (quadriceps)

Weakest Muscles Before Strongest Muscles. A final way to order your exercise regimen is to work the weakest muscle first. This approach is adopted commonly by athletes whose muscles have atrophied slightly following an injury. By working a weak muscle when your energy level is at its peak, you can get the muscle back in shape more quickly.

Lesson 2 Review

Using complete sentences, answer the following questions on a sheet of paper.

Reviewing Facts and Vocabulary

1. **Vocabulary** What is a group of *repetitions* called?
2. **Recall** What is *circuit training*?

Thinking Critically

3. **Recognize** Robert is concerned about the lack of muscular development in his legs. What small and large muscle-group exercises should he include in his workout?
4. **Synthesize** Melody, who is a dancer, would like to improve her muscle endurance. List the specific body areas you think she should work and identify the type of circuit you would recommend for her.

Personal Fitness Planning

Developing Muscular Strength Choose one of the strength-training circuits described in this lesson that best fits your training needs. Extend the circuit by adding at least two more exercises. Under the supervision of your coach or a professional trainer, try this circuit using light weights. Take note of how many sets and reps you did, indicating the weight used.

304 Chapter 10 Developing Muscular Fitness

Lesson 2 Review

Answers to Lesson 2 Review

1. A set.
2. Rotating from one resistance-training exercise to the next in a sequence.
3. Squats, leg extensions, lunges, leg press, leg curls, and heel raises.
4. She would benefit from doing a circuit that alternated upper body with lower body, since ballet emphasizes a greater leg endurance and this circuit requires more leg work. Her sets should be in the 15- to 20-rep category.

Applying FITT to Resistance Training

A carefully planned resistance-training program is necessary for building muscular strength and endurance. As you learned in Chapter 3, FITT factors must be properly adjusted in order to achieve your fitness goals. *FITT*, you will recall, stands for *frequency, intensity, time,* and *type.* In order to improve your muscular strength and endurance through a program of resistance training, you must first establish your resistance FITT.

Frequency

Frequency in weight training is how often you work out. For training to succeed, your time between workouts must be measured in days—not weeks. There are no easy shortcuts to muscular fitness. If, for example, you work out only once a week, you will not see any significant gains in your muscular fitness.

◀ Adjusting FITT factors is necessary to achieve resistance-training goals. *What does FITT stand for?*

Lesson 3   **Applying FITT to Resistance Training**   **305**

What You Will Do

- Apply the physiological principles of frequency, intensity, and time to resistance training.
- Apply intensity to your program by determining your training load.
- Keep accurate records detailing your resistance-training progress.

Terms to Know

total-body workout
split workout
training load
one-rep maximum (1RM)
recovery time
resistance-training cycles

Applying FITT to Resistance Training

1 MOTIVATE

GETTING STARTED

- Ask the class to consider the following: *How often should you work your muscles, and how much intensity is required to see results?*
- Distribute copies of *Guided Practice 10-3* for students to use while studying this lesson. ☞

IN THIS LESSON

- **Fitness Check** *One-Repetition Maximum and Relative Muscular Strength, p. 308*
- **Stress Break** *Varying Your Training, p. 311*
- **Fitness Facts,** *p. 312*
- **Any Body Can** *Arnold Schwarzenegger, p. 313*

INTRODUCING VOCABULARY

- Explain how *training load* should be determined by a percentage of the one-rep maximum (1RM) for each lift. In this lesson, each student will determine his or her 1RM for a variety of exercises.
- Have students use *Vocabulary Worksheet 10* or the PuzzleMaker software to practice vocabulary terms for this lesson. [ELL] ☞ ◉

Photo Follow-up

Caption answer: frequency, intensity, time, and type.

LESSON 3 RESOURCES

Teacher Classroom Resources
☞ Guided Practice Activity 10-3
☞ Fitness Check Worksheet 10-3
☞ Reteaching Activity 10-3
☞ Lesson Quiz 10-3

Reproducible Charts and Graphs
☞ Reproducible Master 10-2

Multimedia
◉ Vocabulary PuzzleMaker

2 TEACH

Explaining

The full-body workout is usually the choice of beginners and fitness weight-trainers. One reason is the reduced amount of time involved. This workout involves all six areas of the body with 8–10 exercises of 10–12 reps and no more than 2–3 sets per exercise. Total time in the gym should be between 35 and 45 minutes, 3 times a week. The goal is to maintain acceptable fitness levels at a moderate level of intensity. This concept is one way for students to apply the physiological principles of frequency and intensity to their training and exercise programs.
L1 **TEKS C1A4, 5**

USING VISUALS

Figure 10.11 There are a variety of three-days-a-week variations to meet your personal needs and schedules.
Caption answer: He could work out Tuesday, Thursday, and Saturday and take off the other four days.

✓ Reading Check

Answers will vary. Students should explain their own frequency and give reasons from the text. **TEKS C1A**

Student Edition TEKS

Page 306: C1A
Page 307: C1A

As with recovery time, workout frequency requires careful tracking. During an effective workout, your muscles become overloaded. Afterward, they need 48 to 72 hours of rest. Any less, and the muscles won't have a chance to repair themselves. Any more, and the strength training benefits start to diminish.

Most training authorities recommend working out three or four times a week on nonsuccessive days. The following are two popular strategies.

Three-Days-a-Week, Total-Body Workout

A total-body workout is *one in which all major muscle groups are worked three times a week, with at least one day off between workouts.* This is the most popular plan for beginners. It allows for all muscles to receive plenty of work, while at the same time allowing for plenty of rest. **Figure 10.11** shows a three-day, total-body workout.

Four-Days-a-Week, Split Workout

More advanced resistance training requires a split-workout schedule, shown in **Figure 10.12**. A split workout does not work every muscle group at every session. Instead, you *exercise three or four body areas at each session, working at much higher intensities.* You do three or four different exercises per body area and three or four sets for each exercise. Because this places greater demands on your muscles, more recovery time is needed before the same muscle group is worked again.

✓ Reading Check

Analyze Considering your experience with weights, how frequently should you work out?

FIGURE 10.11

SAMPLE—THREE DAYS, TOTAL BODY

Gill has band practice every Wednesday after school. *How could Gill adjust his workout schedule so that he could get his three sessions in?*

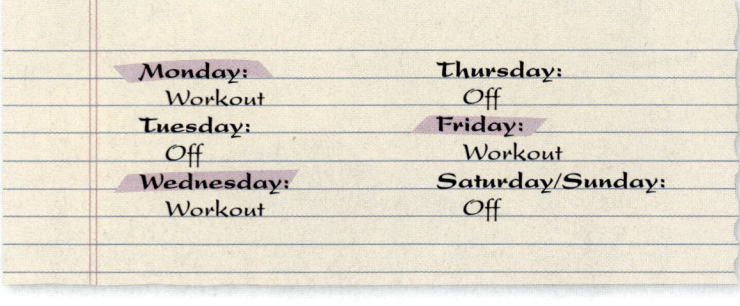

Monday:	Thursday:
Workout	Off
Tuesday:	Friday:
Off	Workout
Wednesday:	Saturday/Sunday:
Workout	Off

Teacher-Coach Tips

Guidelines for High School Programs There are many schools of thought on conducting your strength or conditioning program. Your facilities, staff, and athletes will play a role in your specific decisions. There are some general guidelines that apply to all effective programs. When starting or improving a program, use only one coaching-intensive exercise per workout. This practice will allow you to focus on one exercise and ensure that each rep by each athlete is done correctly. Do not have a squat station and power clean going on at the same time. An alternative is to do lunges on power-clean days. Do your

FIGURE 10.12

SAMPLE—FOUR DAYS, SPLIT WORKOUT

Examine this schedule. *How much rest time does each group of muscles receive before it is worked again?*

Monday:	**Thursday:**
Chest, Shoulders, Triceps, Abs	Repeat Monday's workout
Tuesday:	**Friday:**
Back, Legs, Biceps, Abs	Repeat Tuesday's workout
Wednesday:	**Saturday/Sunday:**
Rest!	Rest!

Intensity

Intensity, as the term is used in weight training, is the amount of exertion or tension placed on a muscle group. Several factors play a role in determining your training-intensity needs. These are:

- The amount of weight you will lift
- The number of reps and sets you will do
- How many different exercises you will perform per body area

The Amount of Weight

Training load refers to *how much weight you should lift for a given exercise.* This is the single most important factor in your *FITT.* To determine your training load, you must determine your **one-rep maximum (1RM)** for each exercise you plan to do. 1RM is *a measure of a lifter's **absolute muscular strength*** for any given exercise. There are several tests you can do to compute your 1RM. One involves doing one or two reps of the exercise, increasing the weight gradually until you "max out," or cannot complete the lift.

Inexperienced lifters who have not yet mastered proper technique are not advised to do 1RM tests. A safer alternative is finding your *estimated one-rep maximum.* The procedure for this is described in the Fitness Check on pages **308–309.**

Reasons for Testing. First, pretests can be used to determine your training load. Beginners should use 50 to 60 percent of their one-rep maximum, whereas conditioned weight trainers may want to use 75 to 85 percent of their maximum. (See **Figure 10.14** on page **310** to determine your training load). Second, muscular fitness tests help identify strengths and weaknesses, which you can then take into consideration when designing your weight-training program. Finally, these evaluations will help you keep track of your progress—a great motivator for your future workouts.

hot link

absolute muscular strength
For more on absolute muscular strength and what it represents, see Chapter 9, page **247.**

Chapter 10, Lesson 3

Explaining

As weight trainers advance, they will want to increase their workload, which requires more time. One method of dealing with this is the split routine. By working the upper body on Monday and Thursday and the lower body on Tuesday and Friday, you can increase the number of exercises and sets per exercise. The increased intensity of split workouts will require additional recovery time. Split workouts allow 72 hours between same-muscle exercises. Another option would be to do push exercises on Monday and Thursday and pull exercises on Tuesday and Friday. An option for advanced lifters is to do one-third of the workout on Monday and Thursday, another third on Tuesday and Friday, and the last third on Wednesday and Saturday.
L1 TEKS C1A

USING VISUALS

Figure 10.12 Ask students to design another possible split workout. It will require the use of one weekend day. *Caption answer: Total time is 72 hours of rest (3 days).*

hot link

Improving absolute muscular strength is a primary goal of most athletes. Strength is directly related to increased performance. In virtually all sports, the resistance program is a vital part of the total program. Have students review Chapter 9 for more on this topic.

coaching in the weight room—not at a desk or computer. Be focused and your athletes will be focused.

Never compromise technical proficiency. If you want parallel squats, then make sure they are not done any other way. During a bench press, lifters should not arch their backs or bounce the bar off their chests. Make it a practice not to count any reps done with incorrect technique. Once cheating gets started, it is hard to stop. Always test with strict guidelines and be there to observe all weights and lifts. Reward improvement and not strength.

Fitness Check

Determining Intensity: One-Repetition Maximum and Relative Muscular Strength

OBJECTIVES

- Determine students' estimated 1RM in a variety of weight-training exercises.
- Use a chart and 1RM to calculate students' relative muscular strength.
- Apply intensity to resistance training.

TEACHING STRATEGIES

Estimated 1RM Test

1. Explain to the class the reasons for testing the 1RM (absolute strength).
2. Tell students that they will apply the physiological principle of intensity in this exercise. With each repetition completed, students should feel the amount of tension on the muscle. **TEKS C1A**
3. Copy and distribute *Fitness Check Worksheet 10-3.* 📁
4. Encourage students to focus on improvement and not to be overly concerned with the scores of other students.
5. Have students do a warm-up and a stretching routine prior to any lifts. **TEKS C1A1**
6. Make sure all students have demonstrated correct lifting technique before they attempt this test. **TEKS C3A1**
7. Spotters should be in place and can assist in all exercises.

Determining Intensity: One-Repetition Maximum and Relative Muscular Strength

In this activity, you will learn how to compute an estimated one-rep maximum and then use that information to calculate your relative muscular strength.

One-Repetition Maximum

You will determine your estimated 1RM for these exercises: *bench press, squat, military press, biceps curl,* and *bent-over row.* Remember to warm up before you start. Have a spotter assist you with all lifts.

Procedure:

1. Divide a sheet of paper into four columns. In the first column write the name of each of the five exercises listed above. Leave a line or so of space after each exercise.
2. Starting with the bench press, choose a weight with which you can safely perform 6 to 10 repetitions. Write this weight on the appropriate line in the second column.
3. Complete as many full reps of the exercise as you can. Record the number of completed reps in the third column. *Do not count partial reps.*
4. Using **Figure 10.13,** find the column for the amount of reps you completed. Then look down the column to find the amount of weight you lifted. For example, if you completed 7–8 reps, you would use the second column.
5. Read across to the far right column and record the number. This is your estimated 1RM for the bench press. For example, if you lifted 105 pounds 7–8 times, your 1RM is 130.
6. Repeat this procedure for the remaining four exercises.

9-10 Reps Pounds Lifted (70% of Max.)	7–8 Reps Pounds Lifted (80% of Max.)	6 Reps Pounds Lifted (90% of Max.)	1RM Pounds Lifted (100% of Max.)
40	45	50	60
50	55	60	70
55	65	70	80
65	70	75	90
70	80	85	100
75	90	95	110
85	95	100	120
90	105	110	130
100	115	120	140
105	120	130	150
110	130	135	160
120	135	145	170
125	145	155	180
135	150	160	190
140	160	170	200
150	170	180	210
155	175	185	220
160	185	195	230
170	190	205	240
175	200	210	250

Figure 10.13

More About . . .

CORRECT LIFTING TECHNIQUE A common question associated with weight training is: Will I get a hernia from lifting? The definition of *hernia* is "the protrusion of an organ or tissue through a tear or rupture in its surrounding walls." This is most likely to occur in the abdominal or pelvic region. It can occur if lifters hold their breath while lifting, lift too much weight, or use incorrect technique. By holding your breath during a heavy lift, you increase the pressure in the abdominal cavity to unsafe levels, which could lead to a hernia. This can occur anywhere; for example, lifting a

Calculating Your Relative Muscular Strength

In this activity you will learn how to calculate your relative muscular strength by using your 1RM.

Procedure:

1. Divide a sheet of paper into five columns. In the first column write the name of each of the five exercises listed above.
2. Starting with the bench press, write the weight of your 1RM in the second column.
3. In the third column record your body weight.
4. In the fourth column record the number you get when you divide your body weight into your 1RM.
5. Use the number you got from step 4 and refer to the Fitness Ratings charts at right to determine your relative strength for the bench press. Example: if your number from step 4 was 1.14 and you are a male, your relative strength was average.
6. Repeat this procedure for the remaining four exercises.

Fitness Ratings: Relative Strength (Males)

Relative Strength Rating	Bench Press	Squat	Military Press	Biceps Curl	Bent-over Row
Outstanding	>1.29	>1.84	>.99	>.64	>.94
Good	1.15–1.29	1.65–1.84	.90–.99	.55–.64	.85–.94
Average	1.0–1.14	1.30–1.64	.75–.89	.45–.54	.75–.84
Below Average	.85–.99	1.0–1.29	.60–.74	.35–.44	.65–.74
Needs Work	<.85	<1.0	<.60	<.34	<.64

Fitness Ratings: Relative Strength (Females)

Relative Strength Rating	Bench Press	Squat	Military Press	Biceps Curl	Bent-over Row
Outstanding	>.85	>1.45	>.50	>.45	>.55
Good	.70–.84	1.30–1.44	.42–.49	.38–.44	.45–.54
Average	.60–.69	1.0–1.29	.32–.41	.32–.37	.35–.44
Below Average	.50–.59	.80–.99	.25–.31	.25–.31	.25–.34
Needs Work	<.50	<.80	<.25	<.25	<.25

Fitness Check

8. Allow students extra attempts if they desire.
9. These evaluations will take two to three days to complete. Allow for ample recovery time.

TEACHING STRATEGIES

Calculating Relative Strength

1. Explain relative strength and its importance to good health and fitness.
2. The goal is to see improvements during post-test evaluations.
3. Calculators will make this activity easier and more effective. (Check with the math department for availability.)
4. Explain the calculations.
5. Post examples of the calculations in the room.
6. Record all results in a record book.
7. Check the calculations for accuracy.
8. Have students identify any exercises that are below moderate. These will be used to design individual programs.
9. This activity can be used as a cross-curriculum activity with the math department.

heavy rock in your backyard or moving furniture in your house. The fact is, nonlifters experience many more hernias than lifters. A well-designed program will start individuals at appropriate levels and teach the proper progression. Using correct biomechanical technique, as well as properly exhaling during lifts, will greatly reduce the possibility of hernia injury. Consider also that the use of a weight-training belt may help prevent the abdominal muscles from being extended too far during certain heavy exercises.

Student Edition TEKS

Page 308: C1A
Page 309: C1A

Explaining

Explain why determining the correct training load is important to beginners and advanced lifters alike. Beginning lifters should use lighter weight (50 to 60 percent 1RM) in order to perform each exercise easily and correctly. Resistance can be gradually increased. Warn students not to rush into using heavy loads, as this only increases muscle soreness and risk of injury. Explain that using the correct training load will help them achieve their goals sooner and more safely. **L1**

USING VISUALS

Figure 10.14 This chart can be used to determine the correct training load for each exercise in this book and will meet the needs of most physical education students. *Caption answer: 35 to 42 pounds.*

Activity

Have students use their estimated 1RMs to determine what 50 to 60 percent of their training load will be for each of the five exercises they did in the Fitness Check on page 308. **L1**

Student Edition TEKS

Page 311: C5B

Training Load. When you have computed or estimated your 1RM, you can use the results to determine your training load. Training load is expressed as a percentage of your 1RM. Beginners should use 50 to 60 percent of their 1RM. Experienced and conditioned lifters will use a training load that is 75 to 85 percent of their 1RM. **Figure 10.14** shows training loads within this range. The chart covers lifts of up to 350 pounds.

FIGURE 10.14

TRAINING LOADS

Your training load is determined by your 1RM. Beginners should work at 50 to 60 percent of their 1RM. *What would the training load be for a beginning weight trainer with a one-rep maximum of 70?*

1RM	50%	60%	70%	75%	80%	85%	90%
30	15	18	21	23	24	26	27
40	20	24	28	30	32	34	36
50	25	30	35	38	40	43	45
60	30	36	42	45	48	51	54
70	35	42	49	52	56	60	63
80	40	48	56	60	64	68	72
90	45	54	63	68	72	77	81
100	50	60	70	75	80	85	90
110	55	66	77	83	88	94	99
120	60	72	84	90	96	102	108
130	65	78	91	98	104	111	117
140	70	84	98	105	112	119	125
150	75	90	105	113	120	128	135
160	80	96	112	120	128	136	144
170	85	102	119	128	136	145	153
180	90	108	126	135	144	153	162
190	95	114	133	143	152	162	171
200	100	120	140	150	160	170	180
210	105	126	147	158	168	179	189
220	110	132	154	165	176	187	198
230	115	138	161	173	184	196	207
240	120	144	168	180	192	204	216
250	125	150	175	188	200	213	225
260	130	156	182	195	208	221	234
270	135	162	189	203	216	230	243
280	140	168	196	210	224	238	252
290	145	174	203	218	232	247	261
300	150	180	210	225	240	255	270
310	155	186	217	233	248	264	279
320	160	192	224	240	256	272	288
330	165	198	231	248	264	281	297
340	170	204	238	255	272	289	306
350	175	210	245	263	280	298	316

More About . . .

SAFETY AND INJURY PREVENTION There are a variety of reasons for injuries in the weight room. Research suggests that the most common cause of strength-training injury in children and adolescents is loss of form when using excessive loads. These injuries occur most often during the aggressive use of free weights. This is where the coach can play an important role in injury prevention. Posture, alignment, and range of motion should be properly executed in all lifts but especially during lifts of excessive loads. Students tend to alter their posture to use additional muscle when lifting excessive

FIGURE 10.15

RECOMMENDATIONS FOR TRAINING GOALS: SETS AND REPS

Some fitness goals are more challenging than others. *Which of the goals shown do you think would be the most challenging?*

Training Goal	Number of Sets and Reps
➤ Fitness and Toning	1–3 Sets of 8–12 Reps
➤ Endurance	2–3 Sets of 12–20+ Reps
➤ Strength	3–5 Sets of 2–6 Reps
➤ Muscle Mass	3–5 Sets of 6–12 Reps

The Number of Reps and Sets

How many reps and sets you do is mainly a function of your fitness goals. Begin by asking yourself what you want to accomplish. Is your goal simply to develop basic muscle fitness? Is it to increase endurance? To add bulk? Maybe it is some combination of these. The chart in **Figure 10.15** shows different training goals and the recommended number of sets and reps for each.

The Variety of Exercises

The more exercises you do to work a body area, the greater the intensity of a workout. Again, your training goals should be the guiding factor. If your goal, for example, is maintaining muscle fitness and overall health, one or two different exercises per body area are enough. Athletes, power lifters, and body builders, by contrast, will do three or four different exercises per body area.

 **Reading Check**

Summarize Identify the three factors that shape your resistance-training intensity.

Time

The most important aspect of *time*, as a component of resistance training, is recovery time. This is *the duration of the rest periods taken between workout components.* In general, the greater the amount of resistance, the more time your muscles need to recover.

No rest should be taken between reps, which are done in a controlled, continuous fashion. The following are guidelines for recovery time between sets and exercises.

STRESS BREAK

Varying Your Training

A regular resistance-training program can help to reduce feelings of stress in your daily life. However, this benefit will be lost if you become bored with your routine. Varying your exercises, sets, and workout days can help you avoid boredom.

You can also make your program more interesting by adding other types of resistance exercises, such as push-ups, bar dips, chin-ups, or isometrics. Keep your workouts fresh. Don't be afraid to throw in some variety.

loads. An incomplete range of motion is another sign of excessive loads. However, in some cases a reduced range of motion may be encouraged for safety reasons. Students are often tempted to use excessive loads. Boys are more likely to sacrifice safety and effectiveness to lift more weight because it directly increases perceived competence. You need to provide a motivational environment in which form and technique are continually emphasized. The fastest and safest way to improve is to have students work at a level that is appropriate for them.

USING VISUALS

Figure 10.15 *Caption answer: Most students will find the strength or muscle-mass goals the most challenging because of the increased number of sets.*

Discussing

Have students compare the results of using heavy weights with few reps and light weights with many reps. Ask: Why does this make goal setting important? **L1**

STRESS BREAK

Varying Your Training

Changes in your physical appearance take time. Beginners usually see these changes faster than experienced lifters. After a couple of months the changes may not occur as quickly. This can lead to boredom and lack of regular participation. There are many ways to vary your workouts to keep them fresh and effective. Consider any of those listed in this lesson. When you make changes, give them time and try not to make more than two at once. **TEKS C5B**

 **Reading Check**

The three factors that determine your resistance-training intensity are the amount of weight you lift, the number of reps and sets, and the number of different exercises performed per body area. **TEKS C1A**

Discussing

Discuss the importance of recovery time in determining intensity and helping lifters achieve specific goals. Discuss the variety of ways recovery time can be implemented, and the reasons why rest is important to muscle growth. Refer to Chapter 9. **L1**

The effect of recovery time on muscle development is important to consider when designing a plan to meet your personal goals. The general rule is the heavier the load, the more recovery time needed between sets.

USING VISUALS

Figure 10.16 Students should begin the unit with fitness and toning as their training goals. *Caption answer: Larger muscles would need closer to two minutes, and smaller muscles one minute.*

Reading Check

Moving from large muscle exercises to small ones requires the longest rests between exercises (2 to 2½ minutes).

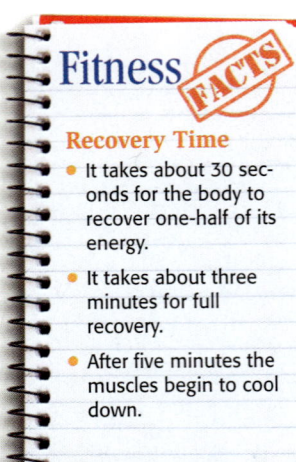

Recovery Time

- It takes about 30 seconds for the body to recover one-half of its energy.
- It takes about three minutes for full recovery.
- After five minutes the muscles begin to cool down.

- **Recovery time between reps.** There should be no time between reps. They should be continuous and controlled.
- **Recovery time between sets.** This depends on your weight-training goals. The chart in **Figure 10.16** will give you some specifics.
- **Recovery time between exercises.** This depends on the type of training circuit you are following. The alternating push-pull variation and upper-lower body variation requires 1½ to 2 minutes of recovery time. The large muscle/small muscle variation requires 2 to 2½ minutes.
- **Recovery time between cycles.** Athletes or competitive lifters do not train the same way year-round. Instead, they follow resistance-training cycles. These are *modified programs, designed to meet the needs of off-season, pre-season, and in-season.* Your personal health and fitness resistance-training routine will also require modifications (cycles) throughout the year. You should change your exercises, sets, and workout days to prevent boredom.

Always time your rest periods carefully. Never exceed five minutes. If you do, your muscles will begin to cool down. Allowing too little time will overtax your muscles. Either way you increase your risk of injury.

 Reading Check

Explain Which types of training require the longest rests between exercises? Which require the shortest rests?

FIGURE 10.16

RECOMMENDATIONS FOR TRAINING GOALS: RECOVERY TIME

Find your training goals in the chart. *How much recovery time should you allow between sets?*

Training Goal	Recovery Time
➤ Fitness and Toning	1½ to 2 minutes
➤ Endurance	30 seconds to 1 minute
➤ Strength	2 to 5 minutes
➤ Muscle Mass	30 seconds to 1½ minutes
➤ Power	3 to 5 minutes

Promoting Coordinated School Health

ADULTS AS MODELS You can use resources in the immediate school environment to stress the importance of lifelong responsibility for personal health and fitness. Since most school sites involve employees from a wide spectrum of age groups, students can witness how employees model healthful behaviors. For example, faculty and staff can be encouraged to participate in personal fitness programs or to plan team-sports events that involve students and adults. Above all, everyone of all ages should be encouraged to recognize their role in making the school community function positively.

Any Body Can

Arnold Schwarzenegger

A Fitness Role Model

In 1997 at age 49, Arnold Schwarzenegger's peers proclaimed him the greatest bodybuilder of the twentieth century. Schwarzenegger was pleased. Yet, as Arnold will be the first to tell you, there is more to being a big person than having big muscles.

Arnold was born in Austria in 1947. At age 15, he began weight training to strengthen his legs for soccer. He saw results quickly and spent even more time in the weight room. Arnold soon gave up soccer to become a bodybuilder. By 17, he had won his first of many titles.

In the early 1970s, Arnold entered a second career—movie actor. One of his first films, *Pumping Iron,* was the story of a bodybuilder. Audiences loved Arnold. His image began to have a profound impact on how people viewed the benefits of a healthy, fit body.

Off-screen, Arnold has followed up his actions with his words. He has been an outspoken advocate on the benefits of staying fit *and* staying in school. As Chairperson of the President's Council on Physical Fitness, he has delivered his message in all 50 states. He has also assisted in programs to encourage urban youth to stay off the street and to choose athletics as a positive alternative to drugs and violence.

Not everybody can be an award-winning bodybuilder or movie star like Arnold Schwarzenegger. However, Any Body Can learn to be a confident and goal-oriented advocate of physical activity and fitness.

Research

As Arnold Schwarzenegger's example shows, he believes in giving something back to the community. Using print or online resources, learn about the Special Olympics and its goals as well as Arnold's role in this important organization.

Type

Type or mode of resistance training, as it is often referred to, is the specific activities and equipment you might choose to use for your resistance program. This chapter has referred mainly to the use of free weights or weight machines. There are alternative resistance-training programs discussed in Chapter 9, Lesson 4.

Keeping a Workout Record

Today, Jared knows he is supposed to work out but can't remember which body area he should be exercising. Pitfalls like Jared's are easy to avoid. All it takes is keeping accurate records.

Lesson 3   Applying FITT to Resistance Training   **313**

More About . . .

IDENTIFYING ENDURANCE OR STRENGTH ATHLETES In addition to muscle biopsy tests, there are other ways to determine an approximate fiber composition. First step, establish the 1RM for a variety of exercises. Second, have students use 80 percent of their 1RM and perform as many reps as possible.

Students performing less than 7 reps are likely to have greater than 50 percent fast-twitch fibers. Students able to do more than 12 reps probably have 50 percent or more of slow-twitch fibers. If they perform between 7 to 12 reps, they are likely to have a 50-50 ratio of fast-twitch to slow-twitch.

Chapter 10, Lesson 3

Any Body Can

Arnold Schwarzenegger Ask students to explain what fitness accomplishments come to mind when they hear the name Arnold Schwarzenegger. Point out to students his work in promoting youth fitness. Even with the busy schedule of a state governor and entertainer, this 55-year-old superstar still maintains an active, fit lifestyle. What are some things you can do to ensure good fitness at age 55?

USING VISUALS

Figure 10.17 (page 314) *Caption answers will vary and may include any of the items listed in the record-keeping section of the text.*

Quick Demo

Demonstrate the correct use of the student record sheets. They should contain all the exercises and muscles the class will be responsible for knowing during the unit. Have students complete a record sheet each time they work out. Check the sheets regularly for accuracy. **L1**

ACTIVITY

Ask students to list and describe components of an exercise prescription related to resistance training. **TEKS C4F**

Student Edition TEKS

Page 312: C1A
Page 313: C1A

313

3 ASSESS

EVALUATING THE LESSON

Assign and discuss the Lesson 3 Review.

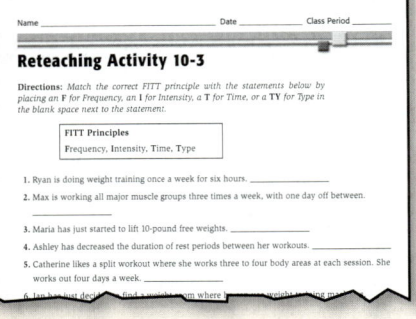

RETEACHING

Ask students to summarize the importance of establishing proper FITT factors for resistance training.

ENRICHMENT

Have students help each other develop a personal fitness record chart.

4 CLOSE

Ask: How can record keeping help you make decisions about the future?

Student Edition TEKS

Page 314: C4E
Page 315: C4G

FIGURE 10.17

SAMPLE WORKOUT RECORD

In this sample record, *S* stands for sets, *R* for reps, and *Wt* for weight.
What exercises would you include if this were your workout record?

	Date: 10/10			Date: 10/12			Date: 10/14			Date:		
	S	R	Wt	S	R	Wt	S	R	Wt	S	R	Wt
Bench Press	2	10	110	3	10	110	2	11	112			
Incline Press	1	10	90	1	10	90	2	11	90			
Military Press	2	10	40	2	10	40	2	8	50			

Your workout record might resemble the one shown in **Figure 10.17.** Regardless of how you organize your record, be sure to include the date and all the exercises you completed, including the sets and reps. Other items to consider might include:

- Rest between sets and exercise
- Order of exercises
- Illness and days missed
- Body weight changes
- Nutrition habits

Keeping a record of your workouts helps you avoid forgetting what you did earlier, but it also helps you determine which exercises and training methods work best for you. Also, noting the progress you have made is a great motivator.

Lesson 3 Review

Using complete sentences, answer the following questions on a sheet of paper.

Reviewing Facts and Vocabulary

1. **Vocabulary** What does *1RM* measure?
2. **Recall** What is *recovery time?*
3. **Recall** How does a split workout differ from a total-body workout?

Thinking Critically

4. **Evaluate** Eve's training goal is to improve her fitness and toning. Devise a program that will help her meet her goals. Include details about frequency, intensity, and time of workouts.
5. **Synthesize** Roberto has just begun lifting weights and wants to increase his intensity.

Describe the method he should use for evaluating his relative muscular strength and determining his training load.

Personal Fitness Planning

Keeping Records Design a personalized record-keeping chart. You may either use the model in **Figure 10.17** or create one of your own. If you have already begun a program of resistance training, complete the first entry of your chart for your most recent workout. If you have not begun training, set your chart aside so that you can begin completing it once you start.

Lesson 3 Review

Answers to Lesson 3 Review

1. The maximum amount of weight you can lift one time.
2. The duration of rest periods taken between workout components.
3. Split workouts work one-half of the muscles two times a week, and total-body workouts work all of the muscles three times a week.
4. Eve should use the total-body workout 3 days a week, 2–3 sets per exercise, and work at 50–60 percent of her maximum. Total time: 30–45 minutes.
5. Refer to the chart on page 309.

Achieving Muscular Fitness

So far, you have learned how to set resistance-training goals. You have also learned how to structure your workouts in a way that achieves your goals. Now it is time to put what you have learned into practice.

The remainder of this lesson will focus on specific training goals. It will also detail exercise programs that can be used to achieve each.

The Basic Resistance Fitness Program

If you have no previous resistance-training experience, your goals should be improving muscle tone and general fitness. Basic resistance-training goals are shown in **Figure 10.18**. A program, known as the "basic eight," can help you reach these goals. The eight exercises in the program work the entire body. They also take relatively little time and a minimum of equipment.

The most popular version of the basic eight is done three times a week, using free weights, one to three sets per exercise. However, variations of these exercises are acceptable as you progress. These are shown in **Figure 10.19**, page **316**.

FIGURE 10.18

TRAINING GOALS AT A GLANCE

This chart shows four main training goals, along with requirements in each category. *Which of these goals is closest to your own?*

Goals	Training Load	Reps	Sets	Recovery Time
Strength	85%–95%	2–6	3–5	2–4 minutes
Hypertrophy	70%–80%	6–12	3–6	30–90 seconds
Endurance	50%–70%	12–20+	2–3	30–60 seconds
Fitness and Toning	60%–80%	8–12	1–3	30–60 seconds

Lesson 4   Achieving Muscular Fitness   **315**

What You Will Do

- Identify the basic eight free-weight routine.
- Identify various programs designed for building strength and power.
- Design and implement resistance programs for strength, power, and muscle mass.

Terms to Know

pyramid training
multiple sets
negative reps
supersets
compound sets
multiple hypertrophy sets

---

1 MOTIVATE

GETTING STARTED

- Ask: *Do you have friends or family who use training methods different from those discussed in this class? What are these methods? Are they safe?*
- Distribute copies of *Guided Practice 10-4* for students to use while studying this lesson.

IN THIS LESSON

- **Active Mind—Active Body** *Designing a Weight-Training Program, p. 320*

INTRODUCING VOCABULARY

- Have students record in their logs each type of special weight-training program, and have them check off each one as they have the opportunity to experience the program.
- Have students use *Vocabulary Worksheet 10* or the PuzzleMaker software to practice vocabulary terms for this lesson. ELL

USING VISUALS

Figure 10.18 This figure identifies all the needed components for designing a resistance workout. *Caption answer: Answers may vary, but most beginners will train for fitness and toning.*

LESSON 4 RESOURCES

Teacher Classroom Resources
- Guided Practice Activity 10-4
- Active Mind—Active Body Worksheet 10-4
- Reteaching Activity 10-4
- Lesson Quiz 10-4

Multimedia
- Vocabulary PuzzleMaker
- Transparency 56

2 TEACH

Explaining

During the beginning weeks of the workout, students should do only one set of 10 to 15 reps per exercise. Each exercise will take less than one minute, and with one minute of recovery between exercises, the total time for the set will be 16 minutes. If they progress to two sets per exercise, the time is doubled to 32 minutes. Any variation of sets, reps, and exercises can be used to provide progression. Remind students to have some warm-up and cool-down time. **L1**

Activity

Have students work in groups to do the basic eight and see how long it takes for the class to complete the routine. **L2** **ELL**

USING VISUALS

Figure 10.19 Display *Transparency 56.* This program is simple, requires very little time, and is geared for fitness and toning. Dumbbells and a flat bench are the only equipment needed. *Caption answer: This program is suggested for fitness and toning and will be done three days a week. See Figure 10.15 in Lesson 3 for sets and reps. Determine your 1RM and use the 50–60 percent training loads for each exercise.*

FIGURE 10.19

BASIC EIGHT PROGRAM WITH FREE WEIGHTS

Note that these exercises can also be done with weight machines or exercise bands. *How would you go about determining the number of sets and reps of each exercise you would do?*

Body Area	Exercise/Technique	Variation/Technique	Equipment
Chest	Bench Press	Incline Press	Barbell/Dumbbell
Back	One-arm Dumbbell Row	Bent-over Row	Barbell/Dumbbell
Shoulder	Military Press	Seated or Standing	Barbell/Dumbbell
Biceps	Arm Curl	Seated or Standing	Barbell/Dumbbell
Triceps	Triceps Extension	Triceps Kickbacks	Barbell/Dumbbell
Thighs	Squats	Lunges	Barbell/Dumbbell
Calves	Heel Raises	One-leg or Two-leg	Barbell/Dumbbell
Abdominals	Crunch	Twisting Crunch	None

What Teens *Want* to Know

How can I make sure that my workout is safe? The American Academy of Pediatrics recommends the following guidelines for resistance training for teens:
- Use low-resistance exercises (little or no weight and few repetitions) until you learn proper techniques.
- Add weight only after 8 to 15 repetitions can be performed.
- Include all muscle groups in your routine, and perform each exercise through the full range of motion at each joint.
- Perform workouts for 20 to 30 minutes, three times a week.

Programs Designed for Strength and Power

There are several different programs that can be used to increase strength and power. All involve training loads that exceed 80 percent of the lifter's 1RM. These programs are not recommended for beginners. If you do not have adequate training experience, your risk of injury is high.

Pyramid Training

Pyramid training is *an approach to training that uses progressively heavier weights and fewer reps through successive sets of an exercise.* The first set uses relatively light weight. The amount of weight added for each following set is determined by increasing the percentage of the lifter's 1RM for that exercise. Note that each set is followed by a two- to three-minute rest.

Pyramid training is best suited for larger muscle groups, such as those in the chest, back, legs, and shoulders. Athletes frequently use this approach to improve their **skill-related fitness. Figure 10.20** shows a typical pyramid progression for the bench press done by a lifter with an 1RM of 130 pounds.

hot link

skill-related fitness
For more on skill-related fitness, see Chapter 3, page **71.**

FIGURE 10.20

PYRAMID TRAINING

Pyramid training is often used to improve skill-related fitness.
For which muscle group is pyramid training best suited?

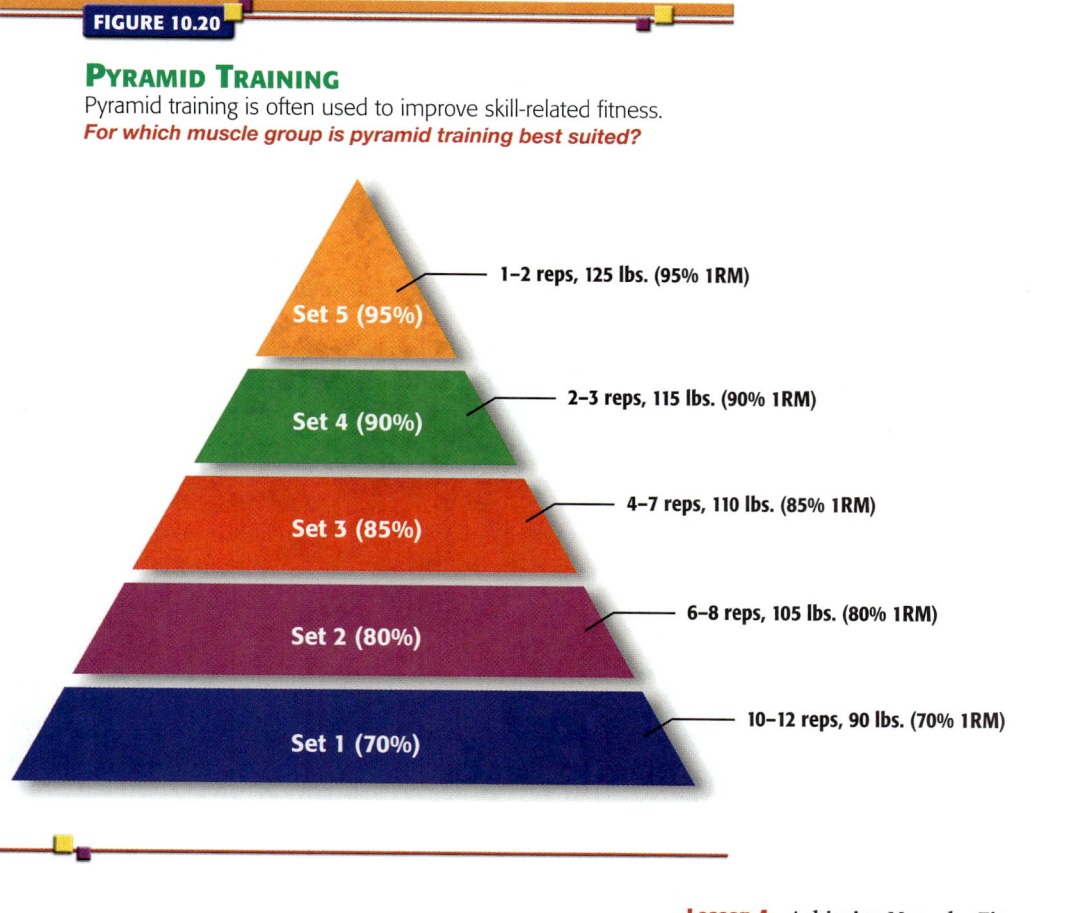

- Set 5 (95%) — 1–2 reps, 125 lbs. (95% 1RM)
- Set 4 (90%) — 2–3 reps, 115 lbs. (90% 1RM)
- Set 3 (85%) — 4–7 reps, 110 lbs. (85% 1RM)
- Set 2 (80%) — 6–8 reps, 105 lbs. (80% 1RM)
- Set 1 (70%) — 10–12 reps, 90 lbs. (70% 1RM)

Explaining

Explain to students how the pyramid technique works. You begin with a lighter weight that can be lifted for 10 to 12 reps. With each successive set, you increase the weight and decrease the reps. Beginners do three sets, the last of which has four to six reps with 85 percent of their 1RM. Advanced lifters can do five sets, with the last one having only one to two reps of 95 percent of their 1RM. This is a popular method of developing strength. Another version of the pyramid technique is to progress to the top and then return to the bottom, using the weight you started with. **L1**

USING VISUALS

Figure 10.20 Pyramid training can be used for ascending and descending the pyramid. This is a common strength-building program. Important note: Beginners should not use levels in sets 4 or 5 because of the heavier weight required. *Caption answer: Chest, back, legs, and shoulders. However, any exercise may use the pyramid routine.*

hot link

Because strength is a vital part of skill-related fitness, the pyramid program is used by many coaches for strength-building activities, both on- and off-season.

Teacher-Coach Tips

Improvement and Motivation The weight room is a great place for students to see how a well-designed, safe program can be effective in improving strength and endurance. During the first five to six weeks of a strength-training program, much of the improvement is due to the improved neuromuscular process that leads to the production of muscular forces. The actual strength of the muscle has improved very little, if any, but because more muscle fibers are being recruited, the muscle is able to lift more.

FIGURE 10.21

MULTIPLE SETS

This chart shows an example of a multiple-set training program for a lifter with a 1RM of 130 pounds. *How much weight should a person with a 1RM of 200 lift, using this same approach?*

Set	Reps	Weight (% of 1RM)
First	10–12	110 lbs (85% of 130 lbs.)
Second	6–8	110 lbs (85% of 130 lbs.)
Third	4–7	110 lbs (85% of 130 lbs.)

FIGURE 10.21

USING VISUALS

Figure 10.21 The multiple set utilizes the same workload for all sets. It is a popular program for strength development. *Caption answer: 170 lbs (85% of 200 lbs)*

Explaining

Negative workouts can be very effective in building strength and can help students become familiar with lifting heavy weights. Since this system involves heavy weight and the use of spotters, it is not recommended for beginners. This system should not be used more than once in a one- to two-week period.

The positive (concentric) and negative (eccentric) phases of all exercises are important. They should be done in a slow, controlled fashion at all times. Remind students of the effects of eccentric movements on muscle soreness.

Reading Check

Pyramids, multiple sets, and negatives.

eccentric and concentric
For more on eccentric and concentric muscle work and what occurs during each phase of a contraction, see Chapter 9, page **252.**

Multiple Sets

In the multiple-set approach, *the lifter uses the same amount of weight for three to five sets at a training load of 80 to 95 percent of his or her 1RM.* The number of reps will range from two to six and should be done to the point of fatigue. A recovery time of two to three minutes is allowed between sets. **Figure 10.21** shows multiple sets for the bench press done by a lifter with a 1RM of 130 pounds. A variation on the multiple-set approach, as you will see on page **321,** can be used to gain muscle mass. Unless you have been lifting for at least six to eight weeks, you should not use the higher maximum percentages.

Negative Reps

When doing negative reps, *you do the eccentric, or negative, phase of an exercise only, using a weight 10 to 15 percent greater than your 1RM.* The **concentric** phase is handled by one or more spotters. Spotters will raise the bar back to the starting position after you have slowly lowered the bar. Three to four reps per set is the recommended maximum for this exercise.

Negative reps are usually done at the end of a prescribed number of exercises for a particular muscle group. Athletes use these primarily for performance enhancement. Because this system uses eccentric movement, there will be a greater amount of soreness in your workout. Negative reps are an advanced exercise. They should not be done by beginners.

Reading Check

List What three programs are used for building strength and power?

More About . . .

WEIGHT TRAINING Manipulating the intensity and volume of your conditioning and training program throughout the year is the science of periodization. Even the beginning weight-trainer can take advantage of this technique. Simply changing the amount of sets and reps used with different exercises will often recharge your muscles and lead to new levels of progress. Periodization has become a vital part of yearly athletic programs. Most periodization programs are divided into four distinct divisions of the year. The first cycle is the Preparatory Period (off-season). The focus of this period is to

This teen is doing negative reps of the bench press. After he lowers the bar to his chest, the spotter raises it back to the starting position for one rep. *Describe the advantage of this type of workout.*

Photo Follow-up

Caption answer: Negative workouts are used for performance or skill-related activities. They are effective in developing strength but are not recommended for beginners.

Programs Designed for Building Muscle Mass

Several programs are available to lifters whose primary training goal is to increase muscle mass, also called hypertrophy. These approaches use training loads of approximately 70 percent of the lifter's 1RM. Again, these should not be attempted by individuals with little or no lifting experience.

Supersets

Doing supersets requires the lifter to *alternately perform sets of exercises that train opposing muscles, without resting between sets.* An example of this approach would be to do ten biceps curls followed immediately by ten triceps extensions to develop the arm muscles.

The main opposing muscle groups are biceps and triceps, quadriceps and hamstrings, chest and back, shoulders and back (latissimus dorsi). Examples of exercise combinations used for supersets include:

- Bench press and seated row for chest and back
- Squats and leg curls for quadriceps and hamstrings
- Shoulder press and lat pulldowns for shoulders and back (latissimus dorsi)
- Biceps and triceps for arms

Supersets are an effective way to keep opposite muscles balanced in strength. They are also extremely efficient, since they allow you to work two muscles at the same time.

Mind OVER Matter

Positive Training Procedures

One of your goals while training should be to make sure that your sessions are safe and injury-free. Be sure to apply rules, procedures, and etiquette while in the weight room. For example, check all equipment before use, take turns at workout stations, wipe down machines, and replace free weights after each use. Explain how these steps can help prevent injury to yourself and others.

Explaining

Remind students that hypertrophy is increased muscle mass and that specific programs can contribute to it. **L1**

Quick Demo

Demonstrate a superset by doing 10 reps of biceps curls, quickly followed by 10 triceps extensions. Ask students to apply physiological principles of progression and specificity to their exercise and training routines. Explain how using opposite muscles allows you to quickly perform reps of another muscle even after the first muscle group has fatigued.

One muscle is resting while the other is working. The recovery time between sets should be one to two minutes. This system is a great way to let students feel the "pump" when lifting weights. The intensity is high, and a great deal of blood flows to the muscles being used. **L2** **TEKS C1A5,7**

Activity

Have students perform two different types of supersets. Make sure they do not use heavy weight. **L2** **TEKS C4C**

improve the strength, power, hypertrophy, and endurance of the athletes. The next cycle, the Transition Period (preseason), lasting two to four weeks and continuing to the first contest, places a greater emphasis on skill development. The third cycle is the Competition Period (on-season). The focus is to reduce the volume of work while increasing the intensity and skill-specific activities. The last cycle is the Second Transition Period (postseason). The focus is to recover from the season with "Active Rest" activities.

Student Edition TEKS

Page 318: C4G
Page 319: C2A, C4G

Reading Check
They both use the same amount of weight.

Active Mind Active Body
Designing a Weight-Training Program

This activity will guide students in designing and implementing a resistance program geared to meet their personal needs and goals.

Teaching Tips

- Distribute *Active Mind–Active Body Worksheet 10-4.*
- Have students record their maximum scores and their goals as they design their workouts.
- Have students use each component suggested in the activity.
- Programs should include all the different exercises learned. **TEKS C4G**
- Identify any special programs for strength or hypertrophy.
- Check to see if normal progress is suggested in their plans.

Apply and Conclude

Encourage students to put their programs into practice and to evaluate their progress from week to week.

Student Edition TEKS

Page 320: C4G
Page 321: C4G

Compound Sets

Like supersets, **compound sets** require *doing alternate sets of exercises without allowing for rest between the sets.* Unlike supersets, compound sets train the same muscle group. An example of compound sets would be doing ten bench presses followed by ten flat bench flys.

The major muscle groups involved in compound sets are the chest, back, legs, and shoulders. Examples of common compound exercise combinations include:

- Bench press and flat bench fly for the chest
- Seated rows and lat pulldowns for the back
- Squats and leg press for the legs
- Military and side (lateral) dumbbell shoulder raise for the shoulders

Compound sets are most effective with large muscles or muscle groups and should be done once in a while—approximately every third workout—not every time.

Active Mind Active Body
Designing a Weight-Training Program

Weight training is an activity that you can do for the rest of your life. The skills and knowledge that you have gained in this chapter and Chapter 9 should provide you with the confidence and ability to establish and revise your own resistance program to fit your changing needs and goals.

Using your resistance goals and the results of your estimated 1RM, design a three-week resistance-training program that includes all of the necessary program components. You may record all of this information on the personalized training charts you developed in Lesson 3.

What You Will Need
- Pen or pencil
- Paper

What You Will Do

On a sheet of paper, note the following information:
1. Your goals (hypertrophy, strength, endurance, and so on).
2. Which days of the week you will work out (total body or split week).
3. Which exercises you will do (upper or lower body; big or small muscles).
4. The order of exercises (push-pull or big-small).
5. The weight arrangement (pyramid or same load).
6. Number of reps (based on intensity, such as 60, 75, or 85 percent of maximum).
7. Number of sets (1 to 3 or 4 to 5).
8. Length of rest periods between sets (20 to 30 seconds, 30 to 90 seconds, or 2 to 3 minutes).
9. How to vary the program from week to week (different systems, exercises).

Apply and Conclude

After you have made your list, implement your program. Take note of any changes you had to make to your plan once you put it into practice. What changes did you make and why?

QUOTES FOR LIFE

"The will to win is important, but the will to prepare is vital."

—**Joe Paterno**
Coach, 1926–

Multiple Hypertrophy Sets

Like the similarly named multiple sets for power, **multiple hypertrophy sets** require *using the same amount of weight throughout and to the point of fatigue.* Beyond this similarity, the two have several differences.

- The training load for multiple hypertrophy sets, for example, is significantly lower—between 65 to 80 percent of the lifter's 1RM.
- The number of reps per set is higher—between eight and ten.
- The rest period between sets is shorter—only 30 to 90 seconds.

 Reading Check

Compare How are multiple hypertrophy sets the same as multiple sets for power?

Lesson 4 Review

Using complete sentences, answer the following questions on a sheet of paper.

Reviewing Facts and Vocabulary

1. **Vocabulary** What is a *superset?*
2. **Recall** Explain how *pyramid training* works.
3. **Recall** Which approach to weight training works opposite muscles? Explain.

Thinking Critically

4. **Compare and Contrast** Compare the two different multiple set approaches. Tell how the two are similar and different in terms of their goals and how they are performed.
5. **Evaluate** Read and evaluate each of the following workout plans:
   a. Rudy is interested in adding muscle bulk. He does negative sets twice a week.

b. Ilana, who is on the volleyball team, wants to develop added power for her serves. Her plan is to do supersets daily, focusing specifically on her triceps and biceps. She has never done resistance training.

Personal Fitness Planning

Designing a Program Your family is planning a skiing vacation this winter. You have two months to get physically fit for the trip. What kind of strength training would be best for downhill skiing? Design the first two weeks of a program that could be used by the members of your family to get them ready for skiing the slopes. This program should provide fitness and injury prevention.

Lesson 4 Review

Answers to Lesson 4 Review

1. Alternately performing sets of exercises that train opposing muscles, without resting between sets.
2. A training program that uses progressively heavier weights and fewer reps through successive sets of an exercise.
3. The superset program works opposing muscles.
4. The multiple set and hypertrophy set use the same amount of weight but different 1RM and rest periods.
5. Answers should include information from the text.

---

3 ASSESS

EVALUATING THE LESSON

Assign and discuss the Lesson 4 Review.

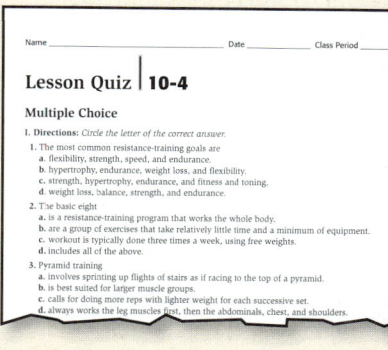

RETEACHING

Have students work in groups to demonstrate any of the programs for strength or hypertrophy that you name.

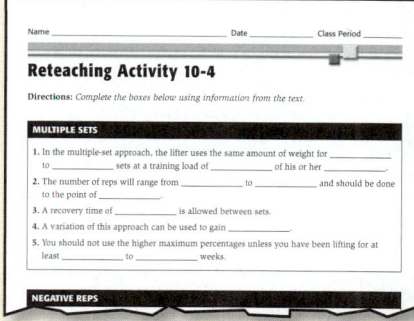

ENRICHMENT

Have students develop a strength-training program that will get the family ready for the ski slopes.

4 CLOSE

Ask students to describe one method of achieving muscular fitness.

CHECKING COMPREHENSION

- Assign and discuss the chapter review.
- Use the PuzzleMaker CD-ROM to review vocabulary. 💿

CHAPTER 10 REVIEW ANSWERS

True/False

1. True	6. True
2. True	7. True
3. False	8. False
4. True	9. True
5. True	10. True

Multiple Choice

11. b	16. d
12. d	17. a
13. a	18. d
14. c	19. a
15. d	20. c

Discussion

21. Common grip may include any of the following: arm curls, bench press, incline press, bent-over row, military press, and shrugs. Narrow grip may include any of the following: upright row and triceps extension.

22. **a.** Assist the lifters with the weight if needed.
    b. Correct improper lifting technique.
    c. Be a motivator.
    d. Keep weights put away for safety.
    e. Communicate with the lifter about the number of reps.
    f. Be alert at all times.
    All of these enhance safety and success in the weight room.

23. Answers will vary.

TRUE/FALSE

On a sheet of paper, write the numbers 1–10. Write True or False for each statement.

1. Increasing fluid intake is an example of a long-term goal to improve your muscular strength and endurance.
2. Weight room safety includes having a spotter.
3. An overhand grip should be used on all lifts.
4. Reps are the basic unit of any workout plan.
5. Working larger muscles before smaller muscles allows you to make the most of your strength, energy, and mental concentration.
6. Finding your 1RM can help you determine your training load.
7. Muscle strength can best be developed with heavy weights and low numbers of repetitions.
8. In negative reps, the lifter is responsible only for the concentric phase of the lift.
9. Supersets keep opposite muscles balanced in strength.
10. Compound sets require doing alternate sets of exercises without allowing for rest between the sets.

MULTIPLE CHOICE

On a sheet of paper, write the letter of the word or phrase that best completes each statement.

11. Which of the following exercises does not work the chest?
    a. Bench press
    b. Seated military press
    c. Incline bench press
    d. Flat bench fly

12. Kristin is considering a weight-training program. Which of the following should she consider before developing her goals?
    a. Her current level of strength
    b. Her daily schedule
    c. Past injuries
    d. All of the above

13. Which of the following are not main muscle areas of the body?
    a. Neck and abdominals
    b. Chest and shoulders
    c. Legs and arms
    d. Abdominals and arms

14. Bent-over dumbbell shoulder raises mainly work which muscle?
    a. Trapezius   c. Deltoids
    b. Biceps   d. Latissimus dorsi

15. Weight room safety includes which of the following rules?
    a. Familiarize yourself with the training facility
    b. Control the speed of weights at all times
    c. Practice all lifts before attempting them with heavier weights
    d. All of the above

16. Which of the following is not a responsibility of the spotter?
    a. Stay in a ready position at all times
    b. Motivate your partner
    c. Correct improper technique
    d. Fetching towels for all lifters in the area

17. If you do ten push-ups, one right after the other, you have done which of the following?
    a. One set of ten reps
    b. Ten sets of one rep each
    c. Ten sets of one exercise
    d. None of the above

18. Recovery time for muscles is important at which of the following times?
    a. Between reps   c. Between workouts
    b. Between exercises   d. Both b and c

19. In a total body workout, a person
    a. exercises all major muscle groups, five times a week.
    b. exercises all major muscle groups, three times a week.
    c. alternates the exercising of two major muscle groups, five days a week.
    d. exercises different muscle groups on each day, three days a week.

20. An approach to training that uses progressively heavier weights and fewer reps through successive sets of an exercise is known as which of the following?
    a. Negative reps
    b. Supersets
    c. Pyramid training
    d. All of the above

Vocabulary

24. b	
25. f	
26. d	
27. c	
28. a	
29. e	

Critical Thinking

30. **a.** Dates of workouts in a given week.
    b. How many sets and reps, and the amount of weight.
    c. Specific exercises.
    d. Order of exercises.
    e. Nutrition habits.
    f. Body weight changes.
    g. Illness and days missed.
    Weight-training records can show improvements and can help you plan future workouts.

DISCUSSION

Using complete sentences, answer the following questions on a sheet of paper.

21. Identify List three weight-training exercises that require the use of the common grip and three that require the use of the narrow grip.

22. Identify List and demonstrate six techniques used by spotters. Why are these techniques necessary in the weight room?

23. Design Plan and explain a five-set pyramid workout for the bench press and a three-set superset workout for the arms. Choose your own weight for each workout plan.

VOCABULARY

On a sheet of paper, write the letter of the term in Column B that best fits the definition in Column A.

Column A

24. Exercising three or four body areas at each session, working at much higher intensities.

25. A group of consecutive repetitions for any exercise.

26. The duration of the rest periods taken between workout components.

27. Alternately perform sets of exercises that train opposing muscles, without resting between sets.

28. One completion of an activity or exercise.

29. Doing the eccentric phase of an exercise only, using a weight 10 to 15 percent greater than your 1RM.

Column B

a. repetition
b. split workout
c. superset method
d. recovery time
e. negative workout method
f. set

CRITICAL THINKING

Using complete sentences, answer the following questions on a sheet of paper.

30. Analyze Identify five components of record keeping, and explain why keeping records is important to your weight-training program.

31. Evaluate Respond to the following statement: Megan is a 14-year-old who has never lifted weights and wants to start a weight-training program. She has had some instruction and wants to take a 1RM test to determine her workload. Explain why an estimated 1RM would be more beneficial to her at this stage of lifting.

CASE STUDY

BRET AND ALBERT'S SUMMER RESISTANCE-TRAINING PLAN

The school year is ending. Bret, a ninth grader, has decided to do weight training over the summer. His goal is to develop a program that will meet minimum health and fitness needs. His friend Albert also plans to train with weights. Albert, however, wants to try out for the varsity football team next year. His goal, thus, is to increase his muscle mass and strength.

Neither teen knows how to design a program to meet their specific needs. They need the help of someone knowledgeable about resistance programs. That someone could be you.

HERE IS YOUR ASSIGNMENT:

Organize a list of specific weight-training components for each teen. Then design a two-week sample weight-training program for each.

KEYS TO HELP YOU

- Consider each teen's specific needs and goals (for example, strength, power, or general fitness).
- Determine how to evaluate each teen's current strength.
- Which specific circuit should each teen use?
- Determine the number of reps, sets, and exercises.
- Determine training load.
- Determine frequency and recovery time.

31. Inexperienced lifters who have not yet mastered proper technique are not advised to do 1RM tests. A safer alternative is finding the estimated 1RM that allows a person to lift a lighter weight with more reps to obtain an estimated 1RM.

EVALUATE

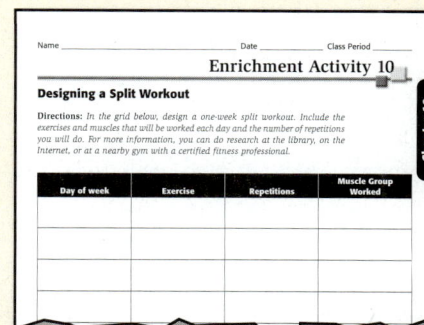

Name _____ Date _____ Class Period _____

CHAPTER 10 | Chapter Test A

Fill in the Blanks

Directions: *Fill in the spaces with the correct answer.*

1. Getting adequate rest every night is considered a _____ goal.
2. Developing leaner body mass is considered a _____ goal.
3. Every resistance-training workout should begin with a _____.
4. When training with _____, it is essential to have a spotter.
5. When lifting objects from the floor, use your _____.
6. One of the most important—and often overlooked—parts of proper lifting is the _____.
7. If you do ten push-ups, one right after the other, you have done one _____ of ten reps.
8. When the resistance force is movable, the exercise is said to be _____.
9. Resistance-training exercises that do not require free weights or a machine are _____.

ENRICHMENT

Name _____ Date _____ Class Period _____
Enrichment Activity 10

Designing a Split Workout

Directions: *In the grid below, design a one-week split workout. Include the exercises and muscles that will be worked each day and the number of repetitions you will do. For more information, you can do research at the library, on the Internet, or at a nearby gym with a certified fitness professional.*

Day of week	Exercise	Repetitions	Muscle Group Worked

CASE STUDY

ANSWERS

Answers may vary but might include: Both Bret and Albert are beginners and should start at lower levels of intensity to ensure safety. Both students should use the estimated 1RM to establish their workloads. They should begin their workloads with 50–60 percent of their 1RM. Bret can use the Basic Eight full-body program for the entire summer. Albert may use the hypertrophy program with full-body workout 3 days a week.

Student Edition TEKS
Page 323: C2A, C3A, C4G

CHAPTER 11

Basics of Flexibility

CHAPTER RESOURCES

- Chapter Study Guide 11
- Vocabulary Worksheet 11
- Enrichment Activity 11
- Chapter 11 Test A
- Chapter 11 Test B
- Parent Letter and Activities 11 (English and Spanish)

FITNESS Online

Ask students to take the STEP Personal Inventory for Chapter 11. Have them record their responses to the statements in their notebooks. Remind students that responses are private and for their use only.

FITNESS Online

Flexibility offers many benefits to your overall health and fitness. Regular flexibility training should be part of everyone's fitness plan. How do you rate in this area of fitness? Find out by taking the STEP Personal Inventory for Chapter 11. Find it at **fitness.glencoe.com**.

324

INCLUSION STRATEGIES

LANGUAGE DIVERSITY *Use the following suggestions to help students who have difficulty with English:*

- Pair English-language learners with native speakers of English who can restate key points in language that helps students comprehend important concepts.

- Direct Spanish-speaking students to the written summaries of this chapter in the *Foundations of Personal Fitness* Spanish Resources Booklet.

- Encourage Spanish-speaking students to use the Glosario provided in the back of the student text. **ELL**

Influences on Flexibility

Bending to tie your shoe or swinging a tennis racquet requires some degree of flexibility. So does twisting around to see who is calling your name. What exactly is flexibility? In this lesson, you will learn about flexibility and its role in functional health.

What Is Flexibility?

Flexibility refers to *a joint's ability to move through its full range of motion*. **Range of motion (ROM)** refers to *the degrees of motion allowed around a joint* (see **Figure 11.1**). ROM varies from joint to joint. Some joints allow a wide ROM. These include ball-and-socket joints, like those in the shoulders and hips. Other joints, such as the

What You Will Do

- Identify factors that can positively or negatively influence your flexibility.
- Apply the biomechanically correct use of leverage to lift objects.
- Explain how good posture may contribute to the prevention of lower-back problems.

Terms to Know

flexibility
range of motion (ROM)
elasticity
posture
static posture
dynamic posture

Flexibility is an important part of health-related fitness. *What sports or activities require a high level of flexibility?*

LESSON 1 RESOURCES

Teacher Classroom Resources
- Guided Practice Activity 11-1
- Reteaching Activity 11-1
- Lesson Quiz 11-1

Reproducible Charts and Graphs
- Reproducible Master 11-1

Multimedia
- Vocabulary PuzzleMaker
- Transparencies 57, 58, 59, 60

Influences on Flexibility

1 MOTIVATE

GETTING STARTED
- Ask students if they have ever tested their flexibility fitness. Explain to them why flexibility is important and how it contributes to the development and maintenance of moderate to high levels of personal fitness.
- Distribute copies of *Guided Practice Activity 11-1* for students to use while studying this lesson. 📁

IN THIS LESSON
- **Fitness Facts,** p. 329

INTRODUCING VOCABULARY
- Explain to students that the term *range of motion (ROM)* is based on moving joints between two points that are considered to be within normal limits (WNL). These flexibility limits have been established by exercise scientists and rehabilitation specialists over the past 50 years.
- Have students use *Vocabulary Worksheet 11* or the PuzzleMaker Software to practice vocabulary terms for this lesson. **ELL** 📁 💿

Photo Follow-up
Caption answers will vary, depending on students' experience, but should relate to flexibility activities rated high in Figure 11.6 on page 335.

2 TEACH

Figure 11.1 Have students perform the action described to see how high they can raise their legs. Display *Transparency 57* and describe full range of motion. Ask students how this motion relates to the physiological principle of specificity during exercise and training. Ask: Which muscles are being used? *Caption answer: Students should be able to raise both legs until they are perpendicular to the ground. Discuss with students ways they might maintain this minimum level of hip and leg flexibility.* **TEKS C1B6**

Activity

As students read about how flexibility affects joint movement, have them identify other examples of each joint. Then let students work in pairs to demonstrate and observe the functioning and flexibility of the wrist joint, called an *ellipsoidal* joint. **L2**

USING VISUALS

Figure 11.2 Using *Transparency 58,* discuss with students the different types of joints pictured. *Caption answers will vary, but students should recognize that some joints will allow more movement and ROM than others. For example, nodding your head "yes" involves the pivot joint of the head and neck, which has limited ROM.*

FIGURE 11.1

FULL RANGE OF MOTION
Range of motion refers to the degrees of motion allowed around a joint.
How high can you lift your leg?

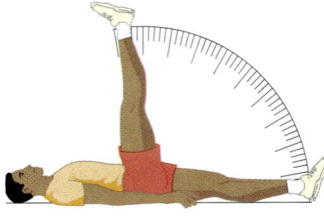

hinge-like joints in your knees, allow only forward and backward movement. Still others, such as those in the neck, allow pivoting and rotation. Yet a fourth type, the joints found in the wrists and ankles, allow bones to glide over one another. These joints and the type of movement allowed by each are shown in **Figure 11.2.**

Factors Affecting Flexibility

How flexible are you? Your answer to this question will be determined by one or more factors. These include:

- **Heredity.** Some people have more flexible joints, tendons, and ligaments than others because of their genetic makeup.
- **Gender.** In general, females are slightly more flexible than males, at least in some movements. For example, females usually have a greater ROM in their hip region. This allows them to touch their toes with greater ease.
- **Age.** Younger people are usually more flexible than older people, mainly because of a loss of elasticity that comes with aging. Elasticity is *the ability of the muscles and connective tissues to stretch and give.* You can maintain higher levels of elasticity as you age if you stretch regularly.
- **Body temperature.** Flexibility can change by as much as 20 percent with increases or decreases in muscular temperature. This is one reason why warming up before exercise or physical activity is especially important.

FIGURE 11.2

JOINTS OF THE BODY
Free and smooth range of motion is necessary for a healthy functional life. *What daily activities depend upon these joints?*

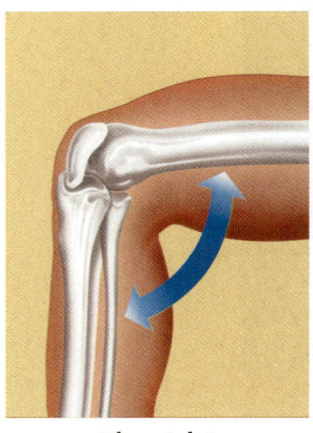 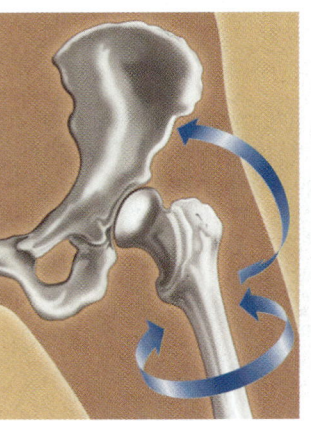 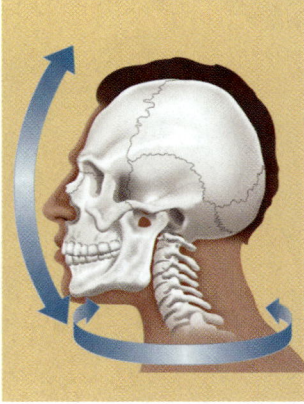

Hinge Joint **Ball-and-Socket Joint** **Pivot Joint**

EQUIPMENT OPTIONS

FLEXIBILITY You can measure static flexibility and ROM directly by using devices like goniometers, flexometers, or inclinometers. Goniometers are protractor-like devices that let you measure the ROM of the knee joint. Flexometers can be strapped to the body; as a joint is moved, the flexometer records the degree of arc or ROM. Inclinometers measure the angle between the long axis of the moving segment and the line of gravity. An inclinometer can be used to measure low back flexibility by holding the device on a person's back while standing erect and then bending forward at the waist.

- **Injuries.** Injuries to your muscles, skin, bones, or connective tissues may result in the loss of some flexibility. Scar tissue that forms when your body heals itself can limit your ROM. Flexibility exercises can help you regain normal ROM after many types of injury.
- **Percentage of body fat.** Excessive body fat can limit ROM. The excess fat restricts movement around the joints. Losing excess body fat can improve flexibility.
- **Activity level.** The most significant negative influence on your flexibility level is an inactive lifestyle. As you decrease your physical activity or exercise levels, your muscles and connective tissues lose elasticity. If you remain inactive, you will also add body fat, which further limits flexibility.

 **Reading Check**

Explain How does warming up affect your flexibility?

Staying Active, Staying Flexible

To prevent muscles and connective tissue from losing elasticity, you need to stretch your muscles regularly. By doing so, you move your joints through their full ROM. Remember the following guidelines.

- Participate in aerobic activities that do not strain your back to improve strength, endurance, and flexibility function. Options include swimming, walking, jogging, water activities, stationary biking, and hiking.
- Participate in resistance-training activities to condition abdominal and back muscles. These muscles work together to support the back.
- Do simple exercises on a regular basis to help support and align your back.
- Maintain proper body weight.
- Stay active.

Lower-Back Pain

Lower-back pain is often associated with inflexible and weak muscles that support the spine and pelvic girdle. This specific type of pain has become a major health problem in the United States. People with lower-back pain often end up with more serious chronic problems, such as lower-back injuries. The leading cause of back injury is lifting.

Even though back pain is common, simple measures can be taken to prevent it. By maintaining an appropriate amount of flexibility and muscular strength through a basic fitness program, you can condition your muscles to prevent injury. Learning proper lifting techniques and posture also reduces your chance of developing back pain or becoming injured. Later in the chapter, you will learn about exercises that can help prevent lower-back pain.

Lesson 1 Influences on Flexibility **327**

Quick Demo

Use a protractor or a goniometer (see Equipment Options on page 326) to measure the ROM of a student volunteer's wrist and ankle. (You may need to borrow a goniometer from an athletic trainer.) Have the student extend his or her wrist upward as far as possible. Align the protractor or goniometer with the student's forearm. Then, measure the difference between the forearm angle and the wrist extension angle. Do the same for the ankle in extension and flexion. **L2** **TEKS C1B**

✔ **Reading Check**
Warming up improves your flexibility by as much as 20 percent.

Discussing

Discuss the most common causes of lower back pain. Display or distribute copies of *Reproducible Master 11-1* and ask students to note the largest section of the graph. Then discuss proper and improper lifting techniques on page 328.

More About . . .

LOW BACK PAIN Low back pain is a major health problem in industrial societies. About 80 percent of adult Americans suffer from low back pain at some point during their lives. Back problems are most prevalent among workers employed in physically demanding occupations and are the most common reason for a worker's disability. Back problems are a common reason for reduced leisure time activity in Americans below age 45. Low back problems are usually not permanently disabling—the pain usually subsides within three weeks, but may periodically return.

Student Edition TEKS
Page 326: C1B
Page 327: C4A

FIGURE 11.3

USING VISUALS

Figure 11.3 Display *Transparency 59* and discuss the importance of applying rules for lifting objects correctly to avoid injury. Have students answer the photo caption. *Caption answer: Students who answer no should review and learn to follow the biomechanically correct lifting techniques listed at the bottom of this page and on page 329.* **TEKS C1B, C2A**

hot link

Reinforce to students that understanding the concepts of biomechanics can help them develop and maintain flexibility. Have students review Chapter 2 for more about biomechanics. **TEKS C1B**

Activity

Ask for volunteers to demonstrate the correct way to apply the biomechanical principle of leverage while lifting an object. Have them show how to keep the weight of the object close to the body while using their legs to lift. Applying this principle to exercise and training can help to prevent injury. **TEKS C1B2**

PROPER AND IMPROPER LIFTING

Improper lifting is a major cause of lower-back injury. *Do you practice proper lifting?*

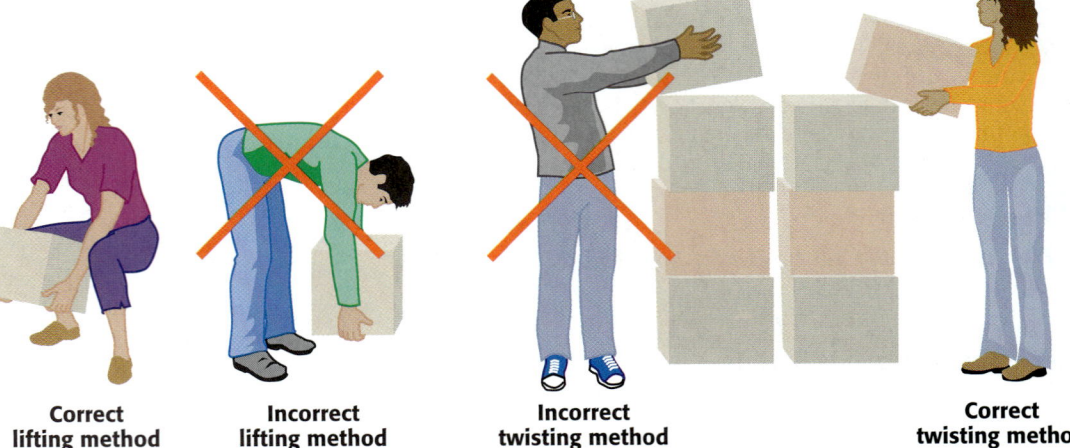

Correct lifting method   Incorrect lifting method   Incorrect twisting method   Correct twisting method

hot link

biomechanics
For more on biomechanics, see Chapter 2, page **54**.

Rules for Biomechanically Correct Lifting

As noted in Chapter 2, **biomechanics** is the application of principles of physics to human motion. By applying these principles to the lifting and carrying of heavy objects, you can help prevent lower-back injuries. Imagine you had to lift a heavy box the size of the one in **Figure 11.3.** Would you lean over at the waist and lift upward? If you did, you might hurt your back. When carrying heavy objects, balance the load so that there is equal stress on each of the joints involved. For example, when carrying two sacks of groceries, carry one in each hand, not both in one hand. Avoid excessive twisting, pulling, or pushing movements, which can strain your lower back.

The following are tips on lifting and moving objects of any weight and should be practiced regularly.

- When lifting bulky or heavy items, try to plan ahead. Get a partner to help with the lifting.
- Always position your body close to the object.
- Place your feet shoulder width apart to give yourself a solid base of support.
- Bend your knees when possible and tighten your stomach muscles.
- Use your legs to lift most of the load, keeping it close to your body to apply the correct leverage and prevent injury.

More About . . .

OCCUPATIONAL BACK INJURIES Dr. A. S. Jackson from the University of Houston and his colleagues have developed a series of simple isometric (or static) exercise tests to help predict which employees in physically demanding jobs may be at risk for back injuries and low back pain. Dr. Jackson has measured employees for static handgrip strength, static arm-curl strength, and static lower-body strength. He found that he can predict which employees are at higher risk of back injuries and low back pain by determining simple measures of individual strength.

- If only one hand is necessary to pick up the object, use the other hand to support your body weight.
- When walking with the object, try to keep knees slightly bent. Point your toes in the direction you want to move and pivot in that direction. Do not twist at the waist.
- Avoid side bending.
- Lift in a slow, controlled fashion.

✓ Reading Check

Summarize When lifting, which part of the body should be used to lift most of the load?

Posture and Lower-Back Pain

Has someone ever said to you, "Sit up straight" or "Don't slouch"? This is advice worth listening to. Good posture habits can reduce stress and strain on your spine and help prevent back injuries. Posture refers to *the alignment of the body's muscles and skeleton as they provide support for the total body.* Gravitational forces are at work on your joints, ligaments, and muscles at all times. This is true whether you are standing, sitting, moving, or lying. Good posture helps to distribute the force of gravity through your body. That way, no one structure is overstressed.

◀ Dynamic posture refers to how you position your body to perform movements. *What is static posture?*

Teens and Back Pain
- 30 to 50 percent of teens suffer back pain.
- Factors in this trend include long periods of inactivity, poor posture, and carrying backpacks that are improperly worn and weigh more than 15 percent of their body weight.

Fitness FACTS

Have students read the *Fitness Facts* feature. Ask how many of them have suffered low back pain from incorrect lifting or poor posture habits. Also ask them if they personally know any adults who suffer from these flexibility-related problems.

✓ Reading Check

Use your legs to lift most of the load while keeping it close to your body. Seek help with lifting if you know the object is heavy for you to lift.

Photo Follow-up

Have students examine the type of posture required for these dancers to maintain balance. *Caption answer: Static posture is the posture the body exhibits in a resting position.*

What Teens *Want* to Know

Are backpacks causing injury? In a survey conducted by the American Academy of Orthopædic Surgeons, 58 percent of the orthopedists reported seeing patients complaining of back and shoulder pain caused by heavy backpacks. More than 70 percent of the orthopedists surveyed indicated that heavy backpacks can become a clinical problem in school-age children if not enough attention is paid to decreasing the weight being carried in the packs. It is important for students to be aware that they may be contributing to their own back pain by overloading their backpacks.

Student Edition TEKS

Page 328: C1B
Page 329: C1B

Figure 11.4 Allow time for students to examine and compare each of the illustrations on this page, or display *Transparency 60* to open the discussion. After discussing the proper and improper positions for sleeping, sitting, standing, and walking, have students answer the caption. Emphasize that students who do not practice these proper posture recommendations should become more aware of their posture and practice better posture habits in order to develop and maintain a healthy spine and to prevent low back problems. Ask for ways you may become aware of poor posture. *Stiffness, pain, or ask someone to remind you to use good posture.* **Caption answers will vary.**

Discussing

Have students evaluate three different occupations and the types of work these occupations require. Have them consider the posture that an employee would have to maintain for eight hours a day. Then have them describe the potential problems associated with posture that the employees might face and how they might prevent them. **L3**

FIGURE 11.4

PROPER AND IMPROPER POSTURE

Improper posture can cause unnecessary stress to your body.
Which of these static posture habits do you practice? Which of the dynamic posture habits do you practice?

Sleeping

Do not lie flat on your back; this arches the spine too much.

Do not use a high pillow.

Do not sleep face down.

Lie on your back and support your knees.

Lie on your side with knees bent and pillow just high enough to keep your neck straight.

Sitting

Do not leave your lower back unsupported.

Sit straight with back support, knees higher than hips.

Standing

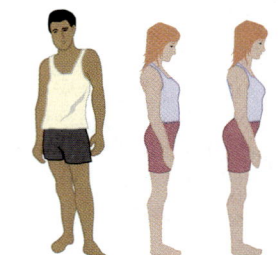

Do not let your back bend out of its natural curve.

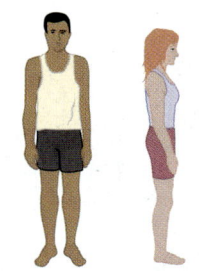

Stand upright, hips tucked, knees slightly bent.

Walking

Do not lean forward or wear high heels.

Lead with chest, toes forward.

More About . . .

POSTURAL CONTROL AND STABILITY Postural control and stability involve the abilities to predict, detect, and encode any change in posture so that your body can select a response and execute it within your biomechanical limitations. Three challenges to your normal postural control and stability occur (1) while moving against the force of gravity; (2) while lifting; and (3) while being thrown off-balance. Students can improve and maintain good to better levels of postural control and flexibility by participating regularly in strength and flexibility physical activities.

Most poor posture habits relate to **static posture**. This refers to *the posture your body exhibits while in a resting position*. Your body is in a state of static posture when you sit at a computer or stand in place. Good **dynamic posture**, however, is also important. Also known as "posture in motion," dynamic posture refers to *the posture your body exhibits while in motion or preparing to move*. This includes how you position your body to perform movements such as pushing, lifting, carrying, twisting, and swinging. The following tips can also help prevent lower-back pain and injury.

- When sitting, try to keep your back straight.
- When working at a computer, use a chair that provides built-in lower-back support.
- When you need to stand for extended periods, place one foot on a low footstool. Occasionally alternate feet. This will take some of the load off your back.
- When sleeping, use a firm mattress.
- When sleeping, use a pillow that provides support for your head.
- When sleeping on your side, place a pillow between your knees.

Figure 11.4 illustrates improper and proper posture habits. Practicing techniques of good posture will allow your body to work more efficiently. They will also ensure that less stress is placed on a single body part.

FITNESS Online

Go to **fitness.glencoe. com** for more accurate information about good posture.

Activity Evaluate your own posture with the self-test, then follow suggestions for improving your posture for a lifetime.

Lesson 1 Review

Using complete sentences, answer the following questions on a sheet of paper.

Reviewing Facts and Vocabulary

1. **Vocabulary** Define *flexibility*.
2. **Recall** What is the meaning of *ROM*?
3. **Recall** List and explain the two types of posture.

Thinking Critically

4. **Analyze** Describe an example of an unsafe lifting technique. Why is biomechanically correct lifting and use of leverage important?
5. **Evaluate** Respond to the following statement: "I am a well-conditioned 15-year-old, so I don't need to worry about my posture." What are the potential dangers of this attitude?

Personal Fitness Planning

Evaluating Fitness Make a list of the activities and chores that you do daily. Evaluate each in terms of your posture and flexibility habits. Which of these could be improved upon? How? How can you apply proper biomechanics to these activities? Is there a pattern regarding when and where you are most likely to exhibit poor posture habits? Attempt to correct any poor habits by becoming more aware of them. Keep a log of your progress.

Lesson 1   Influences on Flexibility   **331**

3 ASSESS

EVALUATING THE LESSON

Assign and discuss the Lesson 1 Review.

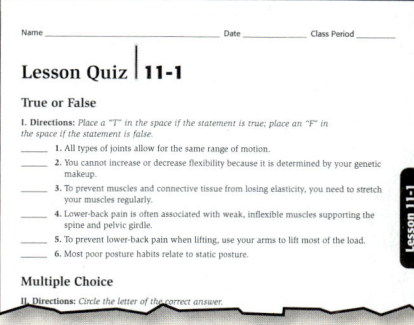

Lesson Quiz | 11-1

RETEACHING

Have students outline correct biomechanical lifting procedures.

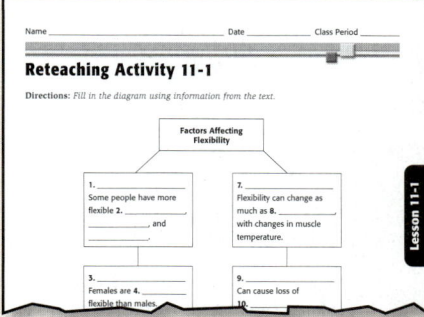

Reteaching Activity 11-1

ENRICHMENT

Have students make three columns in which they list (1) names of joints, (2) accidents that might diminish the ROM of a particular joint, and (3) preventive measures.

4 CLOSE

Have interested students talk to a physical therapist about treatments for low back pain caused by lifting injuries or poor posture.

Evaluating Your Flexibility

Lesson 2

1 MOTIVATE

GETTING STARTED

- Ask students if they have noticed being more or less flexible than other people they know. Have them explain the reasons for these differences.

- Distribute copies of *Guided Practice Activity 11-2* for students to use while studying this lesson. 📁

IN THIS LESSON

- **Active Mind—Active Body** *Which Activities Improve Flexibility?* p. 334
- **Fitness Facts,** *p. 335*
- **Fitness Check** *Evaluating Your Flexibility, p. 336*

INTRODUCING VOCABULARY

- Explain to students that the term *muscle imbalance* refers to one muscle group being stronger than another (e.g., the quadriceps vs. the hamstrings).

- Have students use *Vocabulary Worksheet 11* or the PuzzleMaker software to practice vocabulary terms for this lesson. **ELL** 📁 💿

Photo Follow-up

Caption answer: Students should note that they can improve or maintain the ROM of their major body joints by maintaining flexibility.

What You Will Do

- Identify sports and activities that promote flexibility.
- Explain why too much flexibility can be unsafe.
- Participate in activities to evaluate your flexibility.

Terms to Know

hyperflexibility
muscle imbalance
core stability

Evaluating Your Flexibility

How flexible are you? Do you participate in activities and exercises that benefit your flexibility? Can you think of ways your performance in certain activities might improve if you increased your flexibility level? How might flexibility benefit your health in other areas?

In the last lesson, you learned that flexibility is influenced by some factors you cannot control, such as heredity and gender, and several factors you can control, such as your level of activity. In this lesson, you will learn more about the role physical activities and sports play in improving flexibility. You will also learn about the many benefits that improved flexibility offer your overall functional health. In the "Fitness Check" on pages **336–337,** you have a chance to assess your current level of flexibility.

▶ Flexibility is important for your overall fitness. *What are the benefits of developing and maintaining your flexibility?*

LESSON 2 RESOURCES

Teacher Classroom Resources
- 📁 Guided Practice Activity 11-2
- 📁 Active Mind—Active Body Worksheet 11-2
- 📁 Fitness Check Worksheet 11-2
- 📁 Reteaching Activity 11-2
- 📁 Lesson Quiz 11-2

Reproducible Charts and Graphs
- 📁 Reproducible Master 11-2

Multimedia
- 💿 Vocabulary PuzzleMaker
- 🔦 Transparency 61

FIGURE 11.5

BENEFITS OF FLEXIBILITY CONDITIONING

The chart illustrates the benefits of 8 to 30 weeks of flexibility conditioning in a previously inactive teen. *How can flexibility improve more than just your physical health?*

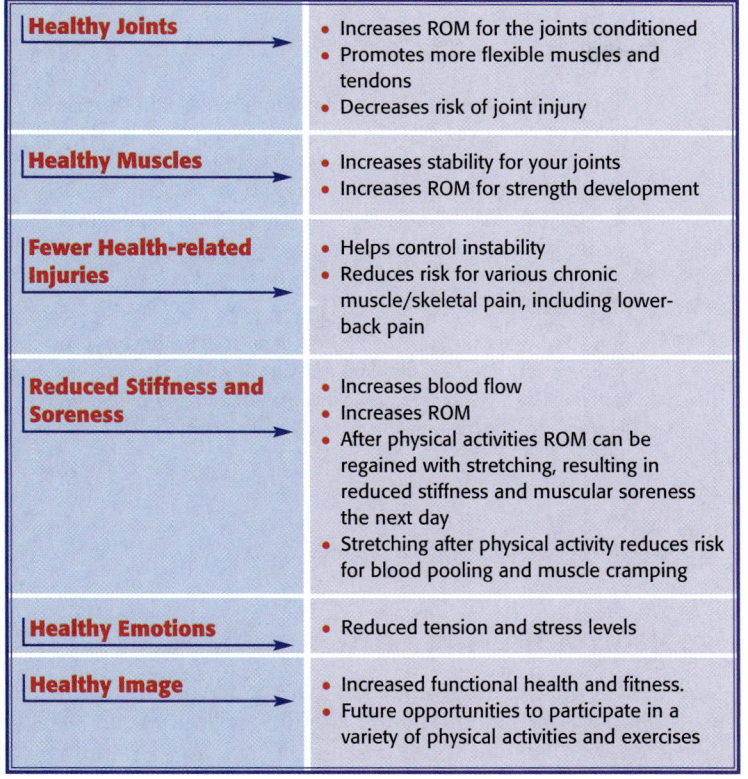

Healthy Joints	• Increases ROM for the joints conditioned • Promotes more flexible muscles and tendons • Decreases risk of joint injury
Healthy Muscles	• Increases stability for your joints • Increases ROM for strength development
Fewer Health-related Injuries	• Helps control instability • Reduces risk for various chronic muscle/skeletal pain, including lower-back pain
Reduced Stiffness and Soreness	• Increases blood flow • Increases ROM • After physical activities ROM can be regained with stretching, resulting in reduced stiffness and muscular soreness the next day • Stretching after physical activity reduces risk for blood pooling and muscle cramping
Healthy Emotions	• Reduced tension and stress levels
Healthy Image	• Increased functional health and fitness. • Future opportunities to participate in a variety of physical activities and exercises

Benefits of Flexibility

Figure 11.5 reveals how moderate-to-high flexibility contributes to several areas of health. It reduces stiffness and soreness and helps limit the risk of chronic back pain and similar health problems. Flexibility also prevents injury and improves athletic performance.

There are many physical activities that lead to improvements and maintenance of flexibility. There are also many that do not. The list in **Figure 11.6** on page **335** rates sports and activities according to their potential flexibility benefits. Which of these, if any, do you participate in on a regular basis?

Lesson 2   Evaluating Your Flexibility   **333**

2 TEACH

USING VISUALS

Figure 11.5 Display *Transparency 61*. Have volunteers read the benefits associated with each area of health in the figure. Have students use these benefits to compare and contrast health-related and skill-related fitness. Point out that flexibility activities done with soothing music in the background can also enhance one's mood and can be relaxing. *Caption answer: Flexibility can help reduce tension and stress.* TEKS C4D

Cooperative Learning

Divide the class into small groups and have them identify celebrities who depend on developing and maintaining high levels of flexibility in order to perform in their profession (examples might be celebrities from sports, music, or the movies). ELL L2

Explaining

Explain to students that a certain amount of elasticity in joints is important but that too much can create imbalances. Elasticity around joints is lost through the aging process, and individuals will suffer more loss of ROM if they do not maintain their flexibility. L1

Teacher-Coach Tips

Contraindications for Flexibility Conditioning
While there are many benefits to be gained from regular flexibility conditioning, a person may sometimes need to avoid participating in flexibility conditioning, at least temporarily. The reasons, or contraindications, for avoidance include the following:
• Limited ROM due to injury
• Recent unhealed fracture
• Infection and/or acute inflammation
• Sharp pain associated with stretching

Student Edition TEKS
Page 332: C3B, C4B
Page 333: C3B

Active Mind Active Body
Which Activities Improve Flexibility?

This activity will help students understand more about physical activities that improve their flexibility and identify those they might participate in on a regular basis.

Teaching Tips

- Have students use *Active Mind–Active Body Worksheet 11-2* to record their information. 📁
- Remind students to keep a list of the items required for the activity.
- Have students bring examples of their findings back to class to share.
- Ask students to show how the activities demonstrate the skill-related components of agility, balance, coordination, or reaction time they learned about in Chapter 3. **TEKS C4C1,2,3,5**

Apply and Conclude

After students have completed the activity, discuss with them the importance of researching flexibility activities before participating in them. Then ask how they might mentor someone who is inactive but wants to participate regularly in flexibility activities.

Active Mind Active Body
Which Activities Improve Flexibility?

Do you play sports or take part in some other form of regular physical activity? You may be surprised to know that many such activities provide minimal flexibility benefits. In this activity, you will determine how much flexibility conditioning your sports and activities provide.

What You Will Need
- Pen or pencil
- Paper

What You Will Do
1. Make a list of activities you do on a regular basis. Include sports and exercises.
2. Consult **Figure 11.6**. Write down the number of stars indicated next to each activity you identified.
3. Determine which activities are rated at least *Fair* (★★) in terms of the flexibility levels offered.
4. Add activities or sports to your daily activity routine that are rated *Fair, Good,* or *Better*.

Apply and Conclude

Based on your findings, tell whether your activities are providing adequate flexibility benefits. If they are not, what activities can you add to help you meet your flexibility needs? Note specific activities you would like to add to your personal fitness plan.

Hyperflexibility and Muscle Imbalances

You might think that the more flexibility a person has, the better. This is not necessarily true. A joint with too much ROM can become injured easily. This *excessive amount of flexibility* is known as **hyperflexibility.**

Hyperflexibility can occur when a joint has been stretched beyond its normal ROM or when weak muscles surround a joint (as can happen following a muscle injury). Hyperflexibility can also occur because of hereditary tendencies for "loose joints." A person with a hyperflexible shoulder joint, for example, may have stretched ligaments or tendons. This condition may, in turn, cause the shoulder to dislocate easily. Such a person can improve the stability of his or her shoulder by strengthening the muscles that control its movement. These muscles are the rotator cuff (the muscles that surround the shoulder joint) and the biceps (the muscles in the front of the upper arm).

When you strengthen muscles around a joint, you need to be sure to work the two opposing muscle groups involved. This will help you avoid a **muscle imbalance.** This is *a condition in which one muscle group becomes too strong in relation to a complementary group.* Muscle imbalances occur when one or more FITT factors are misapplied in

QUOTES FOR LIFE

"Don't be afraid to fail. Experience is just mistakes you don't make anymore."

–Joe Garagiola
Baseball Player and Broadcaster, 1926–

the training of opposing muscle groups. The underdeveloped muscles are at increased risk of becoming injured. This, in turn, can reduce your normal ROM and cause pain or injury.

 **Reading Check**

Analyze What is a muscle imbalance? What factors cause muscle imbalances?

FIGURE 11.6

ACTIVITIES THAT BENEFIT FLEXIBILITY
Not all sports will improve your flexibility. *Which sports or activities provide the most flexibility conditioning? The least?*

Sports or Activity	Flexibility Benefits	Sports or Activity	Flexibility Benefits
Archery	★★	Mountain Climbing	★
Backpacking	★★★	Racquetball	★★
Ballet	★★★★	Rhythmical Exercise	★★★
Badminton	★★		
Baseball	★★★	Rope Jumping	★★
Basketball	★★★	Rowing	★★
Bicycling	★★	Skating: Ice, Roller, or In-line	★★
Bowling	★		
Canoeing	★★		
Circuit Training	★★★	Skiing: Cross-Country or Downhill	★★★
Dance, aerobic	★★★		
Dance, line	★★		
Dance, social	★★	Soccer	★★
Fencing	★★	Softball	★★
Fitness: Calisthenics	★★★★	Surfing	★★★
		Swimming	★★★
Football	★★	Tennis	★★
Golf (walking)	★★★★	Volleyball	★★
Gymnastics	★★★★	Walking	★
Handball	★★★	Water Polo	★★
Hiking	★★	Waterskiing	★
Jogging	★	Weight Training	★★★
Martial Arts	★★★★	Yoga	★★★★

Better ★★★★ Good ★★★ Fair ★★ Low ★

Fitness FACTS

Resistance Training and Flexibility
- Done properly, lifting weights does not lead to muscle imbalances and reduced flexibility.
- Weight training can benefit flexibility.
- Stronger arms, legs, and abdominal muscles reduce the risks of falls, flexibility injuries, and back strain.

Fitness FACTS

Have students read the *Fitness Facts* feature. Ask how many of them have had to increase their flexibility or ROM to lift weights. Tell students that in Chapter 10 they will learn more about how weight lifting affects their ROM.

Reading Check
Muscle imbalance is a condition in which one muscle group becomes too strong relative to a complementary group. Muscle imbalances are related to hyperflexibility problems and underdeveloped opposing muscle groups.

USING VISUALS

Figure 11.6 Have students work in small groups and share ideas on how flexibility benefits each sport or activity listed. *Caption answers for most flexibility should include those activities coded with three to four stars; least flexibility should include activities coded with one to two stars.* **L2**

Enrichment

High Levels of Flexibility? Which sports demand very high levels of flexibility? Here is one top-ten list of sports or physical activities that require flexibility. Have students discuss whether they agree or disagree with this list: Yoga, Ballet, Gymnastics, Fitness Calisthenics, Cheerleading, Weight Training, Wrestling, Modern Dance, Social Dance, Pole Vaulting.

Fitness Check

Evaluating Your Flexibility

OBJECTIVES

- Determine each student's back-extension flexibility.
- Measure each student's arm and shoulder flexibility.
- Determine each student's back and hamstring flexibility.

TEACHING STRATEGIES

Trunk Lift

1. This activity requires some warm-up first.
2. Demonstrate the proper movements for the trunk lift test.
3. Observe students to make sure they perform the activities safely. Remind them to go slow to avoid ballistic (jerky) movements.
4. Have students record results on *Fitness Check Worksheet 11-2* to assess performance. 🗁
5. Encourage students to develop and maintain good-to-better levels of back-extension flexibility.
6. Ask students to apply this flexibility exercise to demonstrate the effect on the skill-related components of agility and speed, as in the Picking Up Lines activity on page 78. **TEKS C4C1,6**

Evaluating Your Flexibility

Having acceptable levels of flexibility in a variety of joints is an important health and fitness consideration. You may not be aware of your range of motion for various stretches. However, if they are below acceptable levels, you may be at risk for injury.

In this activity, you will work with one or more partners to identify your specific range of motion for three stretches. You may choose to perform any or all of the following evaluations: trunk lift, arm lift, or sit-and-reach test. You will need the following items: paper, pencil, a yardstick, tape, a broomstick (or wooden rod 3 feet long), a mat, and a box that is 12 × 14 × 16 inches. Be sure to do a light warm-up prior to all stretches.

Trunk Lift

Procedure:
1. Lie facedown on the mat with your toes pointed and your hands next to your thighs (see **Figure 11.7a**).
2. While a partner holds your legs, slowly lift your chin as high as possible. Hold this position for about three seconds (see **Figure 11.7b**).
3. A second partner should use a yardstick to measure how many inches above the floor your chin reaches.
4. Repeat twice.
5. Use the Fitness Ratings Chart for Trunk Lift to assess your performance.
6. Reverse roles with each partner and repeat steps 1 through 5.

Fitness Ratings: Trunk Lift	
Inches Lifted	**Rating**
9 to 12 inches	Healthy
Under 9 inches	Low

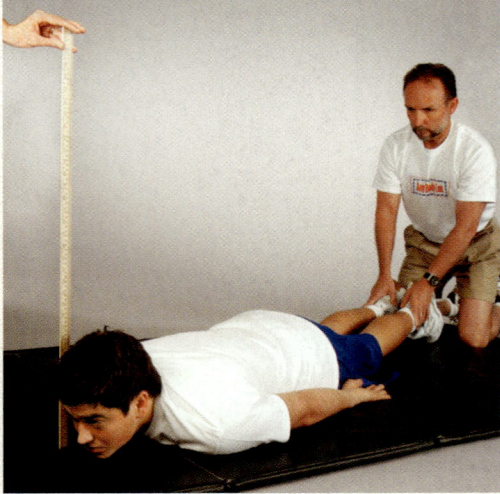
Figure 11.7a

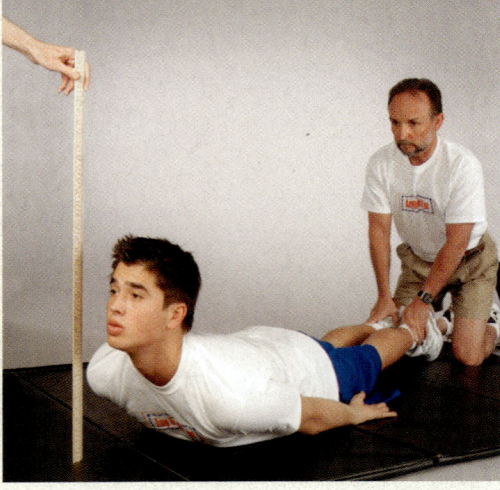
Figure 11.7b

More About . . .

TRUNK LIFT The Trunk Lift is a type of flexibility evaluation that tests back-extension capability. It is also used as an exercise by physical therapists to treat low back problems. This is based on the theory that patients who have back pain caused by the intervertebral disc, tears in the ligaments that surround the disc, or a herniated disc can reduce pressure on that disc by extending the spine and arching the back. As the extensor muscles become stronger, treatment helps to "centralize" the injured disc and reduce pain by decreasing the amount of pressure on the injured ligaments.

Study guide 11-2

1. List three contributions flexibility can make to your health: (p. 333, fig 11.5)
2. Explain hyper-flexibility and what can cause it to occur. (p. 334)
3. Explain what a muscle imbalance is and how to prevent it. (p. 334)
4. What can you do to develop core stability and what does this prevent? (p. 338)

Arm Lift

Procedure:

1. Lie face down on the mat (see **Figure 11.8**).
2. With your arms spread shoulder width apart, hold a broomstick or other light rod out in [front of you. Y]our palms should be face down, [your arm]s and wrists straight.
3. [With your] chin on the floor, raise your arms [as] high as possible. Hold the posi- [tion for ...] seconds.
4. [Have your partner] use a yardstick to measure how [far] the rod is above the floor. Repeat [...]
5. [Use the Fitne]ss Ratings Chart for Arm Lift to [assess your p]erformance.
6. [Reverse roles] with your partner and repeat [steps 1 throu]gh 5.

Fitness Ratings: Arm Lift	
Inches Lifted	**Rating**
11 to 14 inches	Healthy
Under 11 inches	Low

Figure 11.8

[Sit-and-Reac]h Test

[...] [yard]stick to the top of the box with [it prot]ruding beyond one end. [Remove your] shoes. Place the box in a station- [ary position] against a wall. Position yourself in [a sitting posi]tion with your legs straight and [the protrudin]g end of the yardstick facing you. [Put one foo]t flat against the side of the box [...] [B]end the other leg.

[Fitness Ratings: Si]t-and-Reach Test		
[...] ed		**Rating**
[...]		Healthy
[...]		Low
[...] 13–14):		
[...]		Healthy
[...]		Low
[...] 15 and up):		
[...]		Healthy
[...]		Low

4. Extend your arms over the yardstick, with your hands placed one on top of the other, palms down. Keep your hands together (see **Figure 11.9**).
5. Reach forward in this manner four times. The fourth time, hold this position for at least one second while a partner records how far you can reach.
6. Repeat with the other leg.
7. Use the Fitness Ratings Chart for the Sit-and-Reach Test to assess your performance.
8. Reverse roles with your partner and repeat steps 1 through 7.

Figure 11.9

Lesson 2   Evaluating Your Flexibility   **337**

[Co]ach Tips

[goo]d-to-better levels of core [...] [p]eople to condition the [...] [arms a]nd legs, as well as the [...] [...] to the pelvic bones and/or [...] trunk muscles are well [...] [...] will have optimal transfer [...] [la]rge to small muscles when

you sprint, twist, lift, jump, throw, or perform other movements. If the core is well trained, you are less likely to be injured. Athletes and others interested in high levels of performance fitness should perform exercises that improve and maintain their flexibility (See *Fitness Check* on pages 336–337).

TEACHING STRATEGIES

Arm Lift

1. This activity requires some warm-up.
2. Demonstrate the proper movements for the arm lift test.
3. Observe students to make sure they perform the activities safely and avoid ballistic (jerky) movements.
4. Encourage students to develop and maintain good-to-better levels of arm and shoulder flexibility.

Sit-and-Reach Test

- This activity requires some warm-up first.
- Demonstrate the proper movements for the back saver sit-and-reach test.
- Observe students to make sure they perform the activities safely. Remind students to perform the activity slowly to avoid ballistic (jerky) movements.
- Encourage students to develop and maintain good-to-better levels of back and hamstring flexibility.
- Ask students to demonstrate skill-related components of physical fitness such as balance and reaction time after performing this stretch.

TEKS C4C2,5

Student Edition TEKS

Page 336: C4B
Page 337: C4B

3 ASSESS

EVALUATING THE LESSON

Assign and discuss the Lesson 2 Review.

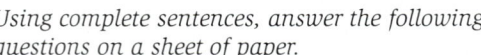

Lesson Quiz | 11-2

True or False

I. **Directions:** *Place a "T" in the blank if the statement is true; place an "F" in the blank if the statement is false.*

_____ 1. Flexibility prevents injury and improves athletic performance.

_____ 2. All physical activity improves flexibility.

Fill in the Blanks

II. **Directions:** *Fill in the spaces with the correct answers.*

3. An excessive amount of flexibility is known as _____.

4. When strengthening the muscles around a joint you can avoid _____ by working the two opposing muscle groups involved.

5. There are two components to core stability; strength training and _____.

6. When you stretch and strengthen the muscles around the spine and pelvis you develop _____.

RETEACHING

Ask students to explain one of the benefits of flexibility conditioning.

Name _____ Date _____ Class Period _____

Reteaching Activity 11-2

Directions: *Complete the outline for this section by filling in the blanks with the correct answers.*

I. Hyperflexibility

   A. Occurs when joint has been _____.

   B. Can also occur because of hereditary tendency for _____.

   C. Can be treated by developing _____.

II. Muscle Imbalance

   A. A condition in which one muscle group becomes too strong in relation to a _____.

   B. Occurs when one or more _____ factors are misapplied in the training of opposing muscle groups.

   C. Can reduce normal _____.

ENRICHMENT

Have students develop a plan to evaluate the flexibility levels of a school athlete in the following sports: football, soccer, and swimming.

4 CLOSE

Have students research and develop a half page of Fitness Facts on the benefits of flexibility.

Flexibility Training for Core Stability

One way to prevent and treat hyperflexibility and muscle imbalances is by developing core stability, *the stretching and strengthening of muscles around the spine and pelvic muscles.* Increasing core stability involves a combination of strength-training exercises and flexibility training. For example, basic abdominal crunches are a great way to strengthen the necessary muscles for core stability. In addition, many of the free-weight exercises discussed in Chapter 10, such as the incline press, bent-over row, and squats are great ways to increase the strength of one's back and pelvic muscles.

Flexibility training is the other component of developing core stability. You have already performed a few of these stretches in the "Fitness Check" on pages **336–337.** Several more stretches, introduced in Lesson 4, are also effective for this type of training. They include the single knee hug, reverse hurdler, wall slides, and leg raises.

▼ Core stability is developed by stretching and strengthening the back and pelvic muscles. *What aspects of performance fitness benefit from improving core stability?*

Core stability helps prevent injuries and low back pain. It is also essential for improving and maintaining your performance fitness. Core stability is an important element in developing balance, power, and coordination. When you participate in a variety of physical activities and competitive sports, you will benefit from increasing your core stability.

Lesson 2 Review

Using complete sentences, answer the following questions on a sheet of paper.

Reviewing Facts and Vocabulary

1. **Vocabulary**. What is *hyperflexibility*?
2. **Recall** Identify two sports that have high ratings for providing flexibility conditioning.

Thinking Critically

3. **Describe** Why might performing too many flexibility exercises or achieving too much flexibility be unsafe?

4. **Analyze** Explain why it is important to maintain adequate strength and flexibility in all the muscles around a joint.

Personal Fitness Planning

Improving Flexibility This activity examines your flexibility scores on the three evaluations you did for the "Fitness Check" activity. Over the next three weeks organize your daily schedule in such a way that allows time for you to practice the three stretches. At the end of the three weeks, retake the evaluations and make note of any improvements.

Lesson 2 Review

Answers to Lesson 2 Review

1. A joint that has an excessive amount of flexibility.
2. Answers will vary but might include ballet and weight lifting.
3. Too much flexibility is associated with hyperflexibility and muscle imbalances, which can have negative effects on your functional health and fitness.
4. To maintain the adequate flexibility and ROM of a joint and to prevent muscle imbalances.

Developing Your Flexibility

To develop flexibility, your personal fitness plan needs to include activities and exercises that will maintain or improve your ROM. One easy general approach to achieving this goal is to include stretching exercises in your warm-ups and cooldowns.

This lesson will help you apply physiological principles and develop the particulars of your flexibility program. It will help you determine your flexibility FITT.

FITT and the Principle of Overload

Determining your FITT for any fitness goal, as you have learned, begins with evaluations. For the present purposes, you will use your ratings from the three flexibility evaluations you performed in Lesson 2. If you achieved healthy levels of flexibility, you will design a stretching program that helps you maintain these levels. If your ratings were low, you will need to increase one or more FITT factors to achieve overload.

Remember, never change all four FITT factors at the same time. In addition, do not change any one factor too quickly. Be patient, and allow for gradual improvements.

What You Will Do

- Apply the physiological principles of overload, specificity, and progression to develop your flexibility.
- Apply the FITT formula to your flexibility plan.
- Describe types of stretches and what each type accomplishes.

Terms to Know

static stretching
ballistic stretching
reflexes
reflex-assisted stretching
passive stretching

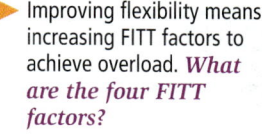 Improving flexibility means increasing FITT factors to achieve overload. *What are the four FITT factors?*

Lesson 3 Developing Your Flexibility **339**

LESSON 3 RESOURCES

Teacher Classroom Resources
- Guided Practice Activity 11-3
- Active Mind—Active Body Worksheet 11-3
- Reteaching Activity 11-3
- Lesson Quiz 11-3

Reproducible Charts and Graphs
- Reproducible Master 11-3

Multimedia
- Vocabulary PuzzleMaker

Developing Your Flexibility

1 MOTIVATE

GETTING STARTED

- Ask students whether they have ever actually conditioned to improve their flexibility or ROM. Explain that they will learn more about flexibility in this lesson.
- Distribute copies of *Guided Practice Activity 11-3* for students to use while studying this lesson.

IN THIS LESSON

- **Stress Break,** *p. 340*
- **Any Body Can** *Tiger Woods, p. 341*
- **Active Mind—Active Body** *Practicing Passive Stretching, p. 343*

INTRODUCING VOCABULARY

- Explain that the term *reflex-assisted stretching* refers to stretching muscles and then forcefully contracting them so that, over time, you can generate force quickly.
- Have students use *Vocabulary Worksheet 11* or the PuzzleMaker software to practice vocabulary terms for this lesson. **ELL**

Photo Follow-up

Caption answer: The FITT formula stands for frequency, intensity, time, and type. **TEKS C1A**

2 TEACH

STRESS BREAK

Stretching and Stress Relief
Ask students if they have ever stretched at their desks to relieve the stress of sitting in a classroom or taking an exam. Ask students to explain ways that stress is a change-able risk factor that affects their physical activity and health. Ask which stretches help reduce their stress levels. Then have the class work together to design three to four stretches that they could do at their desks to relieve stress. **TEKS C5B, C5G**

✓ Reading Check
Use the FITT formula and the ratings from flexibility evaluations to determine overload. **TEKS C1A, C4F**

Explaining
Explain to students that they will have to learn to per-ceive their *intensity*, or how hard they are stretching, to gain and maintain an effec-tive ROM in their joints. This will be similar to learning to use the perceived exertion scale explained in Chapter 3. Have students list compo-nents of an exercise prescrip-tion that includes progression, and ask them to explain this principle. **L1 TEKS C4D**

✓ Reading Check
Specificity applies to flexibility for specific muscle groups and joints involved with a stretch. **TEKS C1A, C4F**

STRESS BREAK

Stretching and Stress Relief

Stretching is an effective way to reduce stress. Stretch-ing reduces muscle tension and allows you to feel more relaxed. Stretching also allows you to sense which areas are tighter than others.

Without regular stretch-ing, your muscles tend to become tighter and feel tense, creating more dis-tress. Make time in your daily schedule for stretching opportunities.

Frequency
How often should you do your stretches? A minimum of three days per week is recommended. However, it is best to do some stretching daily. If you are just starting out, begin with three days per week. Then, during the improvement stage of progression, add more days per week.

Intensity
Because the risk of injury is great, you need to exercise care in establishing your intensity needs when stretching. Your goal should be to reach the point where a muscle or connective tissue is stretched just beyond its normal resting state. You have reached that point during the stretch if you feel slight discomfort but no real pain. Bouncing, jerking, or other sudden movements can increase your risk for injuries.

✓ Reading Check
Explain How can you achieve overload in your fitness program?

Time
How do you determine the duration of your stretches? For static stretching, begin by holding each stretch for 20 to 30 seconds. Repeat this three times for each static stretch you do. As your ROM increases, try to hold each stretch for 30 to 60 seconds, repeating three times per stretch.

Type and the Principle of Specificity
To improve the flexibility of a particular joint or body area, you need to apply specificity. That is, do stretches that affect the nerves, muscles, and connective tissues that control movement around a spe-cific joint or body part. To maintain or improve your overall flexibil-ity levels, do a variety of stretches that influence all your major body parts. Also, remember to work the two opposing muscle groups involved to avoid a muscle imbalance, as discussed in Lesson 2.

The "Active Mind—Active Body" feature in Chapter 3 (pages **104–105**) provides instruction on twelve basic stretches that could be included in warm-ups and cooldowns. In Lesson 4 of this chapter, you will learn several others.

The Principle of Progression
The rate at which you modify your FITT should be based on your overall fitness goals and changing levels of flexibility. Beginners should progress slowly with regard to time and intensity. It is fine, however, to stretch on a frequent basis.

✓ Reading Check
Describe How does specificity apply to a flexibility program?

More About . . .

STRESS AND YOGA Yoga is concerned with the development of flexibility, strength, and mental/emotional health. There are many types of Yoga. Seven basic types are Hatha Yoga, Laya Yoga, Mantra Yoga, Bhakti Yoga, Karma Yoga, Jnana Yoga, and Raja Yoga. Yoga originated in India many thousands of years ago and has undergone modifications and revisions by its many teachers and practitioners. For example, Hatha Yoga uses postures and breathing techniques to help bring the body into a state of peace and health.

Any Body Can

Tiger Woods

In the Swing of Fitness

Some people claim that sports is in their blood. In the case of Eldrick "Tiger" Woods, this claim is almost fact. As a toddler, Tiger was introduced by his parents to the sport of golf. By the age of 8, he had won his first of six international junior tournaments.

Tiger Woods was born on December 30, 1975, in Orlando, Florida. He grew up in Cypress, California. In 1996, he entered Stanford University on a golf scholarship. There he won the NCAA individual championship.

Since joining the professional golf tour, Tiger Woods has dominated the sport. He was named Player of the Year by the Professional Golf Association (PGA) in 1997, 1999, 2000, and 2001. With a win at the Masters Tournament on April 8, 2001, he became the first player in history to sweep all four major tournaments in a single year.

Tiger is physically active, on and off the golf course. He works out daily and enjoys weight training and flexibility exercises. Both help him maintain his remarkable golf skills.

Not everyone can be as great an athlete as Tiger Woods. However, anyone can learn to develop a personal-fitness plan and stick with it to improve the quality of his or her life. Yes, Any Body Can!

Research

Although flexibility may not seem important in some sports such as golf, a high level of flexibility has many benefits. Learn more about the role of flexibility in a particular sport by talking to a teacher, coach, or athlete about the type of flexibility exercises that are used in training, and how flexibility can positively impact an athlete's performance.

Types of Stretching and Your Flexibility

Four basic stretching techniques can help improve your flexibility levels. These include static stretching, ballistic stretching, reflex-assisted stretching, and passive stretching.

Static Stretching

Static stretching consists of *doing stretches slowly, smoothly, and in a sustained fashion.* You hold the stretch for 20 to 30 seconds until you feel slight discomfort but no real pain. Static stretching can also be done while sitting (see **Figure 11.10**) to stretch the hamstrings, by making slow circular motions with the arms or by slowly stretching the neck side-to-side. Static stretching, when done regularly, is safe and effective at increasing the ROM of the joints you work. Everyone should do some static stretching to help maintain or improve flexibility.

FIGURE 11.10

STATIC STRETCHING

Lesson 3   Developing Your Flexibility   **341**

What Teens *Want* to Know

How does Tiger Woods perform so well? The range of motion and rotational speed Woods is able to achieve during his swing are amazing. Genetics is partly responsible for Tiger's flexibility, but his work ethic and commitment to physical conditioning have enhanced his natural abilities. Studies show that greater amounts of force can be produced when a muscle is prestretched or lengthened before performing an activity. When a muscle is prestretched, it creates elastic recoil that applies additional force for a more powerful contraction. This procedure is known as preloading the muscle.

USING VISUALS

Figure 11.11 Ask for a volunteer to help you demonstrate the movement involved in ballistic stretching. After demonstrating with one student, have the class practice how to do correct quick up-and-down movements of ballistic stretching.

✓ Reading Check

Static stretching involves slow, smooth stretches in a sustained fashion, and ballistic stretching involves quick up-and-down bobbing movements in which the stretches are held briefly.

Explaining

Display *Reproducible Master 11-3.* Explain to students that plyometric training has become popular in many sports training but that the scientific results of such training are not as well understood as the research on other kinds of training, such as aerobic conditioning.
L3

hot link

Point out to students that plyometric exercise is recommended for specific sports training programs.

Student Edition TEKS

Page 342: C1A
Page 343: C1A

FIGURE 11.11

BALLISTIC STRETCHING

hot link

plyometric
For more on plyometric exercise and training, see Chapter 9, page **266.**

Ballistic Stretching

Ballistic stretching involves *quick up-and-down bobbing movements in which stretches are held very briefly* (see **Figure 11.11**). You may have seen athletes doing ballistic stretches in their warm-ups before a game.

Ballistic stretches are used primarily to build components of performance, or skill-related fitness. They are not necessary, or even recommended, for health-related fitness. The reason is that the short, quick motions involved can increase injury risks, particularly if you are not warmed up before you do them. An athlete doing ballistic stretching might do five to fifteen movements, repeating this three times per stretch. He or she may want to increase the number or sets of stretches over time, based on his or her performance needs.

✓ Reading Check

Evaluate What is the difference between static stretching and ballistic stretching?

Reflex-Assisted Stretching

Your muscle **reflexes** are *the automatic responses that your nerves and muscles provide to various movements.* An example of a reflex is a simple knee jerk. You have probably experienced this type of involuntary reaction as part of a medical checkup.

Your body performs a variety of reflex actions daily. These keep us from falling and help us maintain balance. Some reflex reactions are very sensitive, others dull. Your reflexes can dull as you age if you fail to remain active. Staying active and stretching regularly can help maintain or improve many of the normal reflex actions that dull with aging.

Reflex-assisted stretching includes *stretching movements that challenge the reflexes to adapt.* Such stretches allow your joints to move more quickly and with more explosive power. An example of reflex-assisted stretching is **plyometric** training (see **Figure 11.12**). Plyometric training includes bounding and jumping exercises. Such training is useful in sports such as basketball and some track events, which require jumping at maximal levels. Individuals interested in plyometric training are advised to seek out a certified strength and conditioning coach. A professional can help you develop a safe and effective program.

Like ballistic stretching, reflex-assisted stretching is not recommended for individuals seeking improvements in general fitness. Remember, reflex-assisted stretches are more hazardous than static stretching in regard to injury risk and, therefore, should be done with caution.

Passive Stretching

Passive stretching is *a type of stretching against a counterforce and in which there is little or no movement.* In passive stretching exercises, the counterforce offers resistance. This force may be provided by a partner or an inanimate object, such as a chair or towel.

Teacher-Coach Tips

Ballistic Stretching Ballistic stretching is often discouraged by health and fitness professionals because it can cause muscle tears in people who are not optimally fit or not used to the quick up-and-down bobbing movements. Ballistic stretching can cause a muscle to be stretched excessively, potentially injuring the muscle. Athletes, however, can see enhanced performance with ballistic stretching because their muscle reflexes can be reset to higher levels that allow them to increase their ROM and perform better. Remember, athletes should always warm up properly.

Active Mind Active Body

Practicing Passive Stretching

If done slowly and safely, passive stretching can yield considerable gains in your ROM. In this activity, you and a partner will take turns practicing this type of stretching. As you proceed, be sure to communicate about the speed of motion and amount of pressure being applied. The pressure should be stopped if there is significant discomfort.

What You Will Need

- Mat or other comfortable surface

What You Will Do

1. Sit on the mat with your legs together and extended.
2. Have your partner place his or her hands on your back near your shoulders.
3. Place your hands one on top of the other and slowly lean forward at the waist, with arms extended. Your partner should apply slight pressure to the point where you can no longer lean forward. The pressure will continue until you instruct the partner to stop.
4. Relax the exercise and repeat once more. Switch positions with your partner.
Note: This same procedure may be repeated with other flexibility exercises. You will learn about additional exercises in Lesson 4.

Apply and Conclude

Were you able to increase ROM as your partner applied pressure? How much additional distance was obtained? Was the second try easier or harder? Do you think this type of stretching will help you reach your goals sooner? Why is it important for your partner to exercise caution when doing this type of stretching? Explain your answer.

FIGURE 11.12

PLYOMETRIC TRAINING

Plyometric training is one type of reflex-assisted training. *In what sports is plyometric training helpful?*

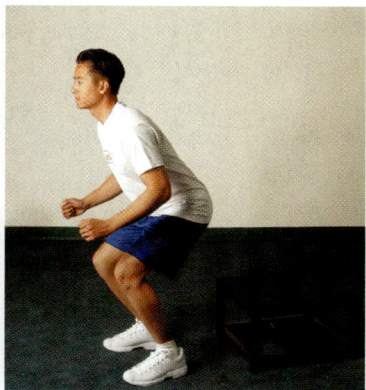

Lesson 3 Developing Your Flexibility **343**

More About . . .

PLYOMETRICS Another term used to describe plyometrics is "stretch-shortening cycle exercise." A stretch-shortening cycle occurs, for example, in walking: when your foot hits the ground, your muscles both lengthen and shorten against gravity. When the sequence of lengthening and shortening is performed quickly, your muscles store elastic energy and can then shorten more forcefully. For those interested in high levels of performance fitness, the main reason to engage in plyometric training is to help increase the rate of force development. This is important for success in many sports.

Active Mind Active Body

Practicing Passive Stretching

This activity will help students learn to safely and effectively perform static stretching. Performing such stretches regularly will improve or maintain their flexibility.

Teaching Tips

- Have students use the *Active Mind–Active Body Worksheet 11-3* to record their information.
- Demonstrate static stretching with volunteers from class before students perform on their own.

Apply and Conclude

After students have completed the activity, discuss how they can incorporate static stretching into their regular workouts or physical activities.

USING VISUALS

Figure 11.12 *Caption answers will vary but could include football, volleyball, track and field events.*

USING VISUALS

Figure 11.13 *(page 344)* Point out to students the correct methods for passive stretching. Have volunteers work in pairs to demonstrate.

3 ASSESS

EVALUATING THE LESSON

Assign and discuss the Lesson 3 Review.

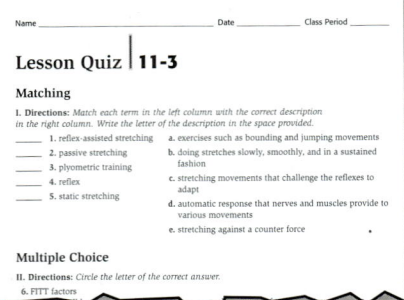

RETEACHING

Have students work in teams to demonstrate examples of each of the five types of stretches covered in this lesson.

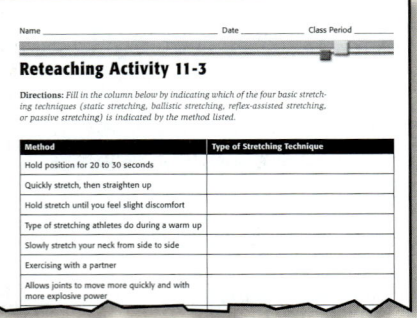

ENRICHMENT

Have students develop a list of strategies to help meet the *Healthy People 2010* adult objective for enhancing and maintaining flexibility.

4 CLOSE

Have students design a safe flexibility program for an older adult family member based on the FITT formula.

344

Two examples of passive stretching exercises are illustrated in **Figure 11.13.** In the example below on the right, the person sits on the floor and holds a towel around the heel of one foot. By pulling the towel toward herself while resisting with the foot, she is stretching the hamstring muscles.

Note that passive stretching carries some risks. If you or a partner pulls or pushes too hard, the target muscle or tissue may be overstretched. A muscle or connective tissue pull or tear may result. Passive stretching should thus be done with caution.

FIGURE 11.13

PASSIVE STRETCHING

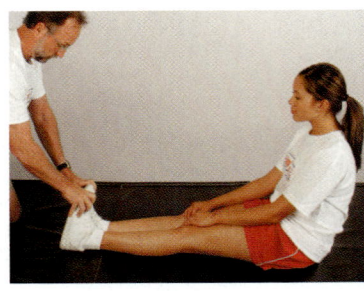 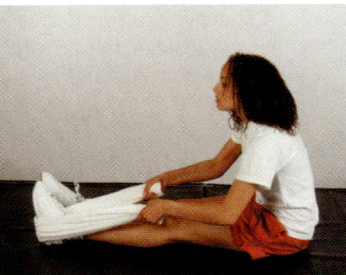

Lesson 3 Review

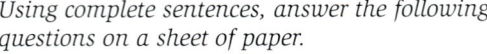

Using complete sentences, answer the following questions on a sheet of paper.

Reviewing Facts and Vocabulary

1. **Recall** How does frequency apply to your flexibility program?
2. **Vocabulary** What is *static stretching?*

Thinking Critically

3. **Synthesize** Robert has just started a beginner's tennis class and wants to develop some beneficial stretching habits. His level of flexibility is low, but he is eager to improve. How would you advise him to apply progression to his flexibility program, with regard to frequency, intensity, and time?

4. **Compare** What is the difference between ballistic stretching and passive stretching? How might you reduce the risks of these types of stretching?

Personal Fitness Planning

Designing Stretches Design a plan for using a towel as the counterforce in a passive stretching exercise. For example, you might sit on the floor with your legs extended. Place the middle of a towel around your toes, and gently pull the tops of your toes back and hold. Make a list of other ways to incorporate and practice passive stretching on your own.

344   **Chapter 11**   **Basics of Flexibility**

Lesson 3 Review

Answers to Lesson 3 Review
1. Stretching at least three days a week.
2. Static stretching includes smooth, slow, sustained stretches.
3. Robert should stretch more frequently and progress more slowly to increase his stretching time and intensity.

4. Ballistic stretching involves up-and-down bobbing movements, while passive stretching is a type of stretching against a counterforce, in which there is little or no movement. Both reduce injuries.

Flexibility Exercises and Activities

Jo is about to take her daily run in the park. Raul needs to get ready for his team's football game on Friday night. Although these teens have very different interests, they share a common need. Both need to stretch beforehand.

In this lesson, you will learn about many different stretches and the muscles and tissues that benefit from each. The "Active Mind— Active Body" feature on page **349** of this lesson will give you an opportunity to practice many of these stretches and safely introduce them into your flexibility program. You will also learn about some dangerous stretching practices that you should avoid, and alternative modifications of these stretches that are safe and beneficial.

What You Will Do

- Identify flexibility exercises for the whole body.
- Participate in exercises that develop flexibility.
- Identify exercises that are designed specifically to prevent lower-back pain.
- Describe potentially unsafe flexibility exercises.

Terms to Know

adductor muscles

◀ Stretching is an important part of any workout. *What types of stretches do you do as part of your workout routine?*

Lesson 4　Flexibility Exercises and Activities　**345**

LESSON 4 RESOURCES

Teacher Classroom Resources
- 📁 Guided Practice Activity 11-4
- 📁 Active Mind—Active Body Worksheet 11-4
- 📁 Reteaching Activity 11-4
- 📁 Lesson Quiz 11-4

Reproducible Charts and Graphs
- 📁 Reproducible Master 11-4

Multimedia
- 💿 Vocabulary PuzzleMaker
- 🔦 Transparencies 62, 63

---

1 MOTIVATE

GETTING STARTED

- Ask students whether they have ever strained a muscle when they were stretching. What kind of stretch caused the injury? Explain that they will learn more in this lesson about unsafe stretches and how to modify them.
- Distribute copies of *Guided Practice Activity 11-4* for students to use while studying this lesson. 📁

IN THIS LESSON

- **Active Mind—Active Body** *Participating in Flexibility Activities, p. 349*

INTRODUCING VOCABULARY

- Explain to students that *adduction* means "movement of an appendage toward the midline." Ask for volunteers to explain how this applies to the term *adductor muscles*.
- Have students use *Vocabulary Worksheet 11* or the PuzzleMaker software to practice vocabulary terms for this lesson. **ELL** 📁 💿

Photo Follow-up

Discuss the stretches shown in the photo. Explain that for safety, students should do mostly static stretches first before moving on to more aggressive stretching. *Caption answers will vary.*

2 TEACH

Explaining

Explain to students that the stretches on pages 346–349 are important for them to learn and practice regularly in order to improve or maintain their flexibility. **L1**

Discussing

Head Tilts and Turns, Shoulder Shrugs, Shoulder and Triceps Pull, Shoulder Pulls, and Towel Stretch are exercises designed to work the upper part of the neck, the shoulders, and the back of the arm (triceps). Side and Trunk Stretches work the obliques and latissimus dorsi. Performing these stretches does not require any special equipment. **L1**

Demonstrate

Demonstrate the correct methods to perform each of these stretches. Remind students to move slowly and use the components of their FITT formula for safe and effective stretching. Spread students out for stretching activities.

● DO

• Maintain slow, controlled speed while stretching.

● DON'T

• Jerk your head back and forth or rapidly to the side.

Variations May be performed while sitting.

Stretches for Flexibility

There are many stretches that may be used to improve flexibility. You should choose a variety of stretches and exercises that will work all the major muscles and joints of the body. You may want to review the stretches in Chapter 3, pages **104–105,** for other stretches that are useful for developing flexibility.

As you work through the stretches that follow, remember to
- perform all stretches and exercises slowly.
- always use the technique described.
- review FITT principles on stretching.

Neck

Head Tilts and Turns (neck flexors and extensors and ligaments of spine)

1. Turn your head to the right and hold. Repeat this motion, turning to the left.
2. Tilt your head down to your left shoulder and hold. Repeat this motion, tilting to the right.
3. Tilt your head forward and hold.
   Caution: Do not roll your head in a continuous motion.

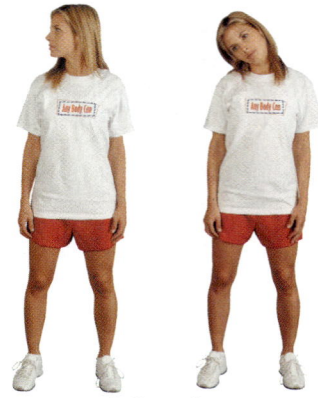
Head Tilts and Turns

Shoulders

Shoulder Shrugs (pectoralis and deltoid)

1. While standing or sitting, raise both shoulders toward your ears without lifting your arms.
2. Relax and repeat.

Shoulder and Triceps Pull (trapezius and triceps)

1. While standing or sitting, place the palm of either hand over the shoulder and on your back.
2. Position the opposite hand on the elbow of other arm. Push toward the back.
3. Repeat the process with the other shoulder.

Shoulder Pulls (trapezius and latissimus dorsi)

1. While standing or sitting, raise your arms to shoulder height.
2. Pull both shoulders toward your spine. Hold and repeat.

Shoulder Shrugs

Shoulder Pulls

Towel Stretch (triceps, shoulder, and chest)

1. Grasp a rolled-up towel with your hands spread shoulder width apart, palms down.
2. Slowly raise the towel from waist height to above your head with your arms extended.
3. Move toward your back as far as possible. Repeat.

Towel Stretch

EQUIPMENT OPTIONS

INCREASED FLEXIBILITY Before the 1980s, flexibility was measured as a pass or fail event. If you could touch the palms of your hands to the floor while bending over with straight legs, you were flexible; if you couldn't, you were like 98 percent of the population. Now that flexibility is considered an integral part of fitness, manufacturers are developing new equipment to improve and measure it. One of the most responsive and safe methods for increasing flexibility is a workout partner. Partners can increase the pressure of a stretching exercise and respond immediately to voice commands.

Side and Trunk

Trunk Stretches (obliques and latissimus dorsi)

1. While standing or sitting on a chair, place your feet shoulder width apart. If standing, bend your knees slightly.
2. Raise your left arm over your head, and bend to your right side. Do not bend forward. If standing, keep your lower body stationary.
3. Repeat this procedure, this time to the left side.

Trunk Stretches

Legs and Back

Single Knee Hug (hamstrings and lower back)

1. Lie flat on your back. Bend one knee toward your chest.
2. Place both hands behind the thigh, and gently pull the leg toward your chest.
3. Switch legs, and repeat. *Modification:* You may bring both knees to the chest at the same time.

Single Knee Hug

Lower-Leg Stretch (gastrocnemius and Achilles tendon)

1. From a standing position, lean toward a wall with your arms extended.
2. Place one foot in front of the other, and extend the back leg.
3. Keep both feet flat on the ground. Bend your elbows and push toward the wall.

Reverse Hurdler Stretch (hamstring and lower back)

1. Sitting on the floor, extend your left leg forward.
2. Bend your right leg, and place the bottom of the foot on the inside of the left thigh near the knee.
3. Bend at the waist. Extend your body and arms forward toward the toes.
4. Switch legs and repeat.

Lower-Leg Stretch

Reverse Hurdler Stretch

Discussing

The Trunk Stretch, Single Knee Hug, Lower Leg Stretch, and Reverse Hurdler Stretch are designed to work the lower part of the body, the low back, the front and back of the upper legs (quadriceps and hamstrings), and the lower part of the back of the legs (gastrocnemius and Achilles tendon). These stretches do not require any special equipment. **L1**

Demonstrate

Demonstrate the correct methods to perform each of these stretches. Remind students to move slowly and to use the components of their FITT formula for safe and effective stretching. Spread students out for stretching activities. Use gym mats if they are available.

● DO

- Maintain slow, controlled speed while stretching.

● DON'T

- Jerk your head or neck rapidly during the Single Knee Hug or Reverse Hurdler Stretch.
- Lean too forcefully into the wall for the Lower Leg Stretch.
- Turn out your bent leg like a hurdler when performing the Hurdler Stretch, as it can put too much stress on your knee.

Variations May be performed while leaning against a pole or other object.

Myths & Realities

Myth 1 Building muscles reduces flexibility.

Fact 1 If you strength-train without moving your joints through their full range of motion, you can indeed lose flexibility. But strength training can actually improve flexibility if you do move your joints fully. Stretch after a muscle-building workout to help keep yourself limber. (Stretch before as well as after an aerobic workout.)

Myth 2 Your ROM is influenced mostly by your heredity.

Fact 2 Heredity probably accounts for only 20 to 30 percent of your ROM and flexibility.

Student Edition TEKS

Page 346: C4B
Page 347: C4B

Discussing

The Modified Lotus or Adductor Stretch, the Quadriceps Stretch, and the Sit-and-Reach Stretch are designed to work the lower part of the body, the low back, the front of the upper legs (quadriceps) and the inside of the upper leg (adductors). Wall Slides and Rear Leg Raises are designed to work the middle front and back muscles (quadriceps and gluteals).

Demonstrate

Demonstrate the correct methods to perform each of the stretches. Use gym mats if they are available.

🟢 DO
• Maintain slow, controlled speed while stretching.

🔴 DON'T
• Bounce your legs too quickly while doing the Adductor Stretch.
• Pull your leg too forcefully during the Quadriceps Stretch.
• Move forward too quickly while doing the Sit-and-Reach.
• Go beyond the parallel position for Wall Slides.
• Strain or arch your neck during Rear Leg Raises.

Variations Leg and back stretches can be done using low resistance on weight-lifting machines (see Chapter 10).

Modified Lotus

Modified Lotus or Adductor Stretch (adductor muscles, lower back) (Your leg adductor muscles are *the muscles on the inside of the leg that pull the legs together.*)

1. Sitting on the floor, bend your knees and place the bottoms of your feet flat against each other.
2. Place your left hand on your right ankle and your right hand on your left ankle.
3. Keep your back straight. Press down on your knees with your elbows.
   Modification: You may grab both feet and pull your upper body toward your feet.

Quadriceps Stretch (quadriceps and knee)

1. From a standing position, bend your left leg toward your back.
2. Lean slightly forward, and balance against a wall or chair.
3. With your right hand, grab your foot and gently pull up and out.
4. Focus on pulling the quadriceps back, instead of compressing the knee. (See **Figure 11.14** on page **353.**)
5. Switch legs and arms and repeat.

Sit-and-Reach Stretch (hamstrings and lower back)

1. Sitting on the floor, extend your legs forward and together.
2. Bend at the waist, and extend your arms and upper body forward. (See **Figure 11.9** on page **337.**)
   Modification: This may be done while sitting in a chair with the knees bent.

Exercises for Prevention of Lower-Back Pain

As noted in Lesson 1, some exercises constitute a kind of insurance against the risk of lower-back pain. Among these are exercises that target the muscles of the back, stomach, hips, and thighs.

Wall Slides (hips, back, quadriceps)

1. Position your back against a wall with your feet shoulder width apart.
2. Slide downward into a bent-knee position. Your thighs should be parallel to the ground.
3. Count to 5 or 6. Return to the starting position.
4. Repeat these steps 6 or 7 times.

Rear Leg Raises (lower back and gluteal)

1. Lie facedown with your arms at your sides and your legs straight.
2. With your extended left leg, tighten the muscles of the leg and lift the leg from the floor.
3. Hold this position for 10 seconds, and return to the starting position.
4. Repeat the procedure with the other leg. Continue alternating legs until you have done five repetitions with each leg.

Wall Slides

Rear Leg Raises

Student Edition TEKS

Page 348: C3B, C4B
Page 349: C4B

Curriculum CONNECTIONS

MEDICAL TECHNOLOGY Technological advances in the field of medicine have enabled surgeons to use artificial body parts to replace hips, legs, and arms. Plastic and lightweight metal materials are used to make artificial joints and prostheses. Surgeons can restore mobility, ROM, and stability to many joints that have failed due to injury or disease. Discuss with students how knee or hip replacement surgery can benefit an older person as well as a younger one (restores mobility and ROM to the joint; increases independence; provides the opportunity to return to a physically active lifestyle).

Front Leg Raises (abdominal and hip adductors)

1. Lie on your back with your legs extended and your arms at your side.
2. Slightly bend the knee and raise your left leg straight above your waist.
3. Hold the position for 10 seconds, then return to the starting position.
4. Repeat the procedure with the other leg. Continue alternating legs until you have done five repetitions with each leg.

Front Leg Raises

Back Hyperextension Stretch (lower back)

1. Stand with your feet shoulder width apart.
2. Place your hands on your hips.
3. Keep your knees straight, and bend backward at the waist.
4. Hold the position for 2 to 3 seconds. Repeat the exercise 3 times.

Crunches (abdominal)

1. Lie on your back with your knees bent and your feet flat on the floor.
2. Raise your shoulders and head off the floor and extend your arms to your knees.
3. Hold for a 10-second count. Repeat 5 to 10 times.

Crunches

Discussing

The Front Leg Raise, Back Hyperextension Stretch and Crunches are designed to work the lower back and abdominals.

● DO

- Maintain slow, controlled speed while stretching.

● DON'T

- Hold your breath during front leg raises.
- Bounce when doing the Back Hyperextension Stretch.
- Bounce your head off the mat or floor when doing Crunches.
- Control neck movements.

Variations No variations needed for these stretches.

Active Mind Active Body
Participating in Flexibility Activities

Choosing the correct stretches for your program is important for your continued success. Equally important is ensuring that these exercises are done correctly. In this activity you will choose a variety of stretches. You will demonstrate how to perform each of them properly and in a safe fashion.

What You Will Need

- Mat or other comfortable surface

What You Will Do

1. Choose at least one stretch for each of the following body parts: neck, shoulders, trunk, lower back, quadriceps, hamstrings, adductors, and lower leg. Three of your choices should be modifications of hazardous stretches found in **Figure 11.14** on pages **350–353**.
2. Demonstrate the safe method for performing each stretch.

Apply and Conclude

Did you find that some stretches were easier to perform correctly than others? Which stretches were you able to demonstrate? Which stretches were you unable to perform correctly? What changes were suggested? Were you able to make the needed corrections? How will these changes improve your flexibility program?

Active Mind Active Body
Participating in Flexibility Activities

This activity will help students understand more about how to safely and effectively perform stretches.

Teaching Tips

- Have students use *Active Mind–Active Body Worksheet 11-4* to record their work. 📁

- Encourage students to work in pairs to ensure safe and correct stretching techniques.

Apply and Conclude

After students have completed the activity, ask them to explain the reasons for performing stretches safely and effectively as part of their personal fitness program.

More About . . .

JOINT SURGERY If joints become injured or diseased, there is an extreme loss of ROM. In extreme conditions there are various surgical procedures that may help relieve pain and increase ROM. Some of these include angioplasty (reconstruction of a damaged joint using a patient's own tissue); osteotomy (separation or cutting of a joint that has become fused or has shifted to an abnormal position); and anthrodesis (fusion of a damaged joint, usually done to relieve pain). Anthrodesis usually results in a decreased ROM, as does joint replacement (replacement or rebuilding of severely damaged joints).

Explaining

Emphasize to students that stretching exercises are valuable in preventing soreness and possible injury. All exercises must be done correctly or they may pose the risk of injury. Students with pre-existing muscle or joint injuries may need to avoid certain exercises. Ask volunteers to describe specific examples and exercises that may be harmful or unsafe. Discuss why these may cause injury. **L1 TEKS C3B**

✔ Reading Check

Hazardous stretches may cause strains, sprains, excess pressure on discs, and overstress of ligaments and muscles. **TEKS C3B**

USING VISUALS

Figure 11.14 Display *Transparencies 62 and 63* and discuss the risks involved with stretching incorrectly.

Caption answer: Some modifications have been developed to reduce the risk of injury.

HAZARDOUS STRETCH: *Bar Stretch.* Performing this stretch causes excessive strain on the lower back.

MODIFICATION: *Modified Bar Stretch.* Another alternative is to place the extended leg on a waist-high bench and bend forward. **TEKS C3B**

Hazardous Stretches and Their Modification

There are many flexibility stretches that have been practiced for years. A great number of these, including those demonstrated so far in this lesson, are beneficial. Some, however, have been identified by sports-medicine specialists to be high-risk. These hazardous stretches have been linked to a number of sports- and health-related injuries, including:

- **strains**
- sprains
- excess pressure on discs of the back
- overstress of ligaments and muscles

Modifications have been devised for some of these exercises that reduce injury risk. **Figure 11.14** illustrates both the unsafe and safe ways of performing these stretches. If you plan to do any of the following stretches, make sure you are doing the safe, modified version.

hotlink

strains
For more on strains, see Chapter 2, page **58**.

✔ Reading Check

Explain What are the risks of performing hazardous stretches? Describe examples that may be harmful.

FIGURE 11.14

UNSAFE STRETCHES WITH MODIFICATIONS
The stretches shown on the right provide a modified version of the stretch pictured on the left. *Why were these modified stretches developed?*

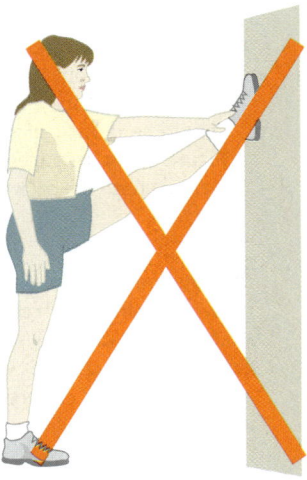

Bar Stretch

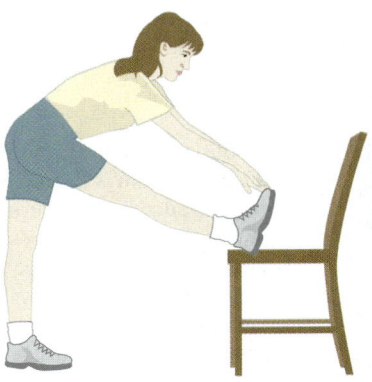

Modified Bar Stretch

Promoting Coordinated School Health

COMMUNITY SUPPORT Tapping into local resources is a key to effectively implementing a comprehensive school health plan. It is important to involve local health agencies, parents, churches, youth groups, and other organizations. By enlisting local groups and individuals, the Coordinated School Health committee can establish grassroots support. Community involvement provides the resources and support needed to reduce fragmentation of efforts or duplication of programs. Ongoing collaboration and cooperation between the team and other community members contribute to the program's success.

FIGURE 11.14 *continued*

Chapter 11, Lesson 4

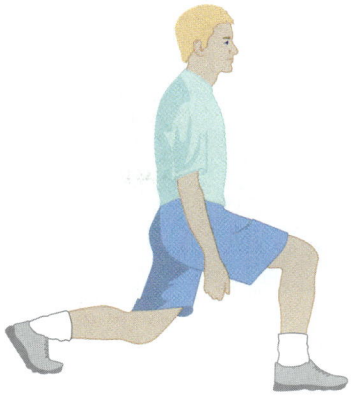

Deep Knee Bend

Forward Lunge

Hurdler Stretch

Reverse Hurdler Stretch

Stretch Neck Roll

Bent-Knee Neck Stretch

continued on next page

Lesson 4 Flexibility Exercises and Activities   **351**

Figure 11.14 *(continued)*
Point out that some stretching exercises are never recommended because of their high risk for injury. Flexibility exercises that may harm joints or muscles are called contraindicated exercises. These exercises should be avoided and replaced with the suggested alternatives. Remind students to perform exercises at an intensity that is mild but not painful. Students should not stretch to the point of pain, but should stop before pain occurs. **L1 TEKS C3B**

HAZARDOUS STRETCH: *Deep Knee Bend.* Knee bends cause excessive strain on the knees.
MODIFICATIONS: *Forward Lunge, Quad Stretch.*

HAZARDOUS STRETCH: *Hurdler Stretch.* This stretch places excessive strain on the knee joint.
MODIFICATIONS: *Reverse Hurdler Stretch or Sit-and-Reach Stretch.*

HAZARDOUS STRETCH: *Stretch Neck Roll.* Performing this stretch causes excessive strain on the neck discs and the lower back.
MODIFICATION: *Bent-Knee Neck Stretch.*

More About . . .

TESTING FLEXIBILITY Have students recruit parents and school staff members to test their flexibility. Ensure that as many different age groups as possible are represented. Students should select people that represent different occupations and lifestyles. Using three or four basic tests, have students measure the flexibility of these adults. Use the following tests: Sit and Reach, Trunk Lift, and the Arm Lift. Have students provide feedback to the adults as to how they performed. Then have them draw conclusions about how their own flexibility measures compare to their adult counterparts.

Student Edition TEKS
Page 350: C3B

FIGURE 11.14 *continued*

USING VISUALS

Figure 11.14 *(continued)*
Discuss each of the hazardous stretches on these pages. Explain to students why these stretches and positions are contraindicated and what types of stresses they can put on specific areas of the body. **L1**

HAZARDOUS STRETCH: *Prone Arch.* This position places excessive strain on the spine, knees, and shoulders.

MODIFICATION: *Modified Back Hyperextension.*

HAZARDOUS STRETCH: *Toe Touch.* This stretch causes excessive strain on the lower back and knees.

MODIFICATION: *Sit-and-Reach.*

HAZARDOUS STRETCH: *Yoga Plow.* This position places excessive strain on the spine, neck, and shoulders.

MODIFICATIONS: *Single-Leg Sit-and-Reach, Single-Knee Hug, Sit-and-Reach.*

HAZARDOUS STRETCH: *Quad Stretch.* This stretch can cause excessive strain on the knee joint due to compression.

MODIFICATION: *Modified Quad Stretch.* When done appropriately, this stretch is performed with the leg extended up and back.

Prone Arch

Modified Back Hyperextension

Toe Touch

Sit-and-Reach

Yoga Plow

Single-Leg Sit-and-Reach

Curriculum CONNECTIONS

T'AI CHI Traditionally, the Chinese use massage and gymnastics to strengthen the body. At dawn every day throughout China, people of all ages gather in public parks to practice t'ai chi, also called T'ai Chi Chuan or taijiquan. This fitness routine comprises fluid yet precise movements that demand both breath and muscle control. Elements of tai chi can also be used for self-defense. One-fourth of the world's people live in China, so space is a luxury. For this reason, table tennis, badminton, basketball, and gymnastics are popular. Bicycles are essential for transportation and provide good exercise.

FIGURE 11.14 *continued*

Quadriceps Stretch   Modified Quadriceps Stretch

Source: President's Council on Physical Fitness and Sports, 1999.[1]

Lesson 4 Review

Using complete sentences, answer the following questions on a sheet of paper.

Reviewing Facts and Vocabulary

1. **Recall** Name two stretches that benefit the shoulders.

2. **Recall** Describe two of the unsafe stretches illustrated in this lesson. What is the safe method of performing these stretches?

Thinking Critically

3. **Extend** Elma has been studying hard over the last few weeks and has noticed some tightness in her lower back while she sits at her desk. She is concerned that her muscles are not strong enough in the back and hip region. What exercises and stretches would help her solve this problem?

4. **Analyze** Why are head tilts and turns safer than doing the yoga plow stretch?

Personal Fitness Planning

Demonstrating Stretches Work with the adult members of your family to incorporate stretches and lower-back pain prevention exercises into their lifestyles. Caution them against improper stretching by explaining the unsafe versions of the stretches. Demonstrate the safe, modified versions of the exercises. Then observe their technique as family members perform the stretches.

Lesson 4   Flexibility Exercises and Activities   353

---

3 ASSESS

EVALUATING THE LESSON

Assign and discuss the Lesson 4 Review.

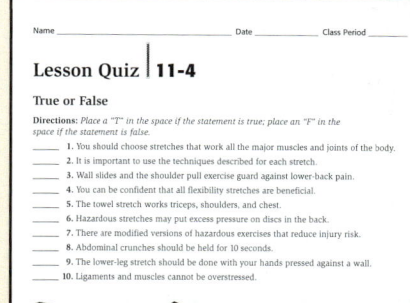

RETEACHING

Ask volunteers to demonstrate proper flexibility exercises and have the class identify correct safety measures.

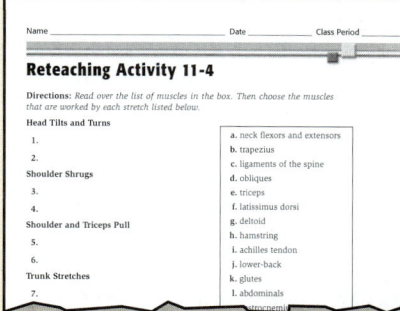

ENRICHMENT

Have students identify three hazardous stretches and describe why they think each might be hazardous if the stretches were performed incorrectly.

4 CLOSE

Divide the class into small groups to develop a stretching routine to share with the class.

Lesson 4 Review

Answers to Lesson 4 Review

1. Shoulder shrugs and shoulder pulls.
2. Answers may vary but may include quadriceps stretch and hurdler stretch. Students should modify these stretches as per the recommendations on pages 350–353.
3. Answers may vary, but students should use the exercises for prevention of lower-back pain as described on pages 350–353.
4. Answers may vary, but students should note that tilts and turns put less stress on the neck and lower back.

353

CHECKING COMPREHENSION

- Assign and discuss the chapter review.
- Use the PuzzleMaker CD-ROM to review vocabulary.

CHAPTER 11 REVIEW ANSWERS

True/False

1. False	6. True
2. True	7. False
3. True	8. False
4. False	9. True
5. True	10. False

Multiple Choice

11. a	16. c
12. a	17. d
13. c	18. b
14. a	19. a
15. d	20. d

Discussion

21. Answers may vary but might include: learn proper lifting techniques; avoid excessive bending, twisting, and pulling; strengthen the muscles of the lower back; and practice good posture habits.
22. Answers will vary but might include benefits listed in Figure 11.5.
23. Answers will vary but might include any of the stretches on pages 346–349.

Vocabulary

24. c
25. f
26. e
27. b
28. d
29. a
30. g

TRUE/FALSE

On a sheet of paper, write the numbers 1–10. Write True or False for each statement below.

1. ROM is the same for every joint.
2. Hinge-like joints allow you to move forward and backward.
3. Your risk of back injuries is increased if you have inflexible and weak muscles that support your spine and pelvic girdle.
4. Hyperflexibility is a positive trait found only in people with very high levels of flexibility.
5. Muscle imbalances occur when one muscle group is worked and its opposing group is not.
6. The minimum recommended frequency for stretching is three days per week.
7. Static stretches are unsafe and are not recommended.
8. Ballistic stretching is done very slowly without bouncing up and down.
9. Passive stretches require either a partner or a device that offers counterforce.
10. The yoga plow is a safe and effective stretch for hamstrings and lower back.

MULTIPLE CHOICE

On a sheet of paper, write the letter of the word or phrase that best completes each statement.

11. The condition of hyperflexibility is associated with
    a. loose joints.
    b. tight connective tissue.
    c. strong muscles.
    d. strong ligaments.
12. Of the following posture practices, the one that is NOT beneficial is
    a. using a soft mattress.
    b. maintaining a straight back when sitting.
    c. using computer chairs with lower-back support.
    d. using a footstool for one leg if standing for an extended period of time.

13. Your flexibility is influenced by all of the following EXCEPT
    a. heredity.
    b. age.
    c. height.
    d. physical-activity level.
14. The one factor that has the greatest negative influence on your flexibility levels is
    a. lack of physical activity.
    b. excess body fat.
    c. injured joints.
    d. your gender.
15. Biomechanical lifting
    a. includes twisting, pulling, or pushing movements.
    b. should be performed only by athletes.
    c. should be done only with a partner.
    d. can help prevent lower-back injuries.
16. Plyometric training is a type of
    a. static stretching.
    b. ballistic stretching.
    c. reflex-assisted stretching.
    d. passive stretching.
17. The type of stretching that requires a partner or device to help you complete a stretch is
    a. static stretching.
    b. ballistic stretching.
    c. reflex-assisted stretching.
    d. passive stretching.
18. When stretching, your goal should be to reach the point where
    a. a muscle or connective tissue is barely stretched.
    b. a muscle or connective tissue is stretched just beyond its normal resting state.
    c. a muscle or connective tissue is stretched well beyond its normal resting state.
    d. none of the above.
19. The stretch most associated with stretching the lower back is
    a. the knee hug.
    b. the wall slide.
    c. the quadriceps stretch.
    d. the reverse hurdler stretch.
20. Which of the following stretches is hazardous and may cause injury?
    a. the knee hug
    b. the calf stretch
    c. the adductor stretch
    d. the stretch neck roll

Critical Thinking

31. Some individuals can get hyperflexible joints due to injuries; thus, too much flexibility can sometimes be detrimental.

32. Participating in regular physical activity and exercise stimulates healthy changes to your muscles, tendons, and ligaments (see Figure 11.5) and therefore helps you maintain your flexibility.
33. Answers will vary but should include the tips (bullets) for biomechanically correct lifting on pages 328 and 329.

DISCUSSION

Using complete sentences, answer the following questions on a sheet of paper.

21. **Identify** Describe five ways you can help reduce your risk for lower-back pain and injuries.
22. **Explain** Give five benefits that typically follow 8 to 30 weeks of flexibility conditioning in a previously inactive teen.
23. **Identify** List five stretches that are safe and effective for increasing or maintaining your flexibility levels.

VOCABULARY

On a sheet of paper, write the letter of the term in Column B that best fits the definition in Column A.

Column A

24. A condition in which one muscle group becomes too strong in relation to a complementary group.
25. Stretching with bobbing movements.
26. The automatic responses that your nerves and muscles provide to various movements.
27. A type of stretching against a counterforce in which there is little or no movement.
28. Range of motion or varying degrees of movement.
29. The ability of the muscles and connective tissues to stretch and give.
30. Stretching movements that challenge the reflexes to adapt.

Column B

a. elasticity
b. passive stretching
c. muscle imbalance
d. ROM
e. reflexes
f. ballistic stretching
g. reflex-assisted stretching

CRITICAL THINKING

Using complete sentences, answer the following questions on a sheet of paper.

31. **Analyze** Respond to this statement: You can never have enough flexibility.

32. **Explain** Explain the relationship between physical fitness and health. How does maintaining an active lifestyle contribute to your flexibility?
33. **Synthesize** Most lower-back pain and injuries are preventable by practicing proper lifting and stretches. Identify enough examples of both to create a total program for the back.

CASE STUDY

CASE STUDY—BOB'S INJURY

Bob is a fifteen-year-old who is very active. He enjoys jogging 3 to 5 miles daily. However, in the past year he has noticed that his muscles feel very tight, his lower back hurts occasionally, and he feels like he has lost some flexibility. Bob does not like to stretch and really sees no benefit in it. However, he is concerned about his loss of flexibility, because he thinks it may increase his risk for injuries during jogging. He would like to improve his flexibility levels, but he is not sure how to do so. Therefore, he needs the help of someone knowledgeable about designing and implementing fitness programs—someone like you!

HERE IS YOUR ASSIGNMENT:

Assume that Bob has asked you for some assistance. Organize a list of factors Bob should consider before beginning flexibility conditioning. Then list the recommendations you would give Bob for his first two weeks of flexibility conditioning. Use these suggestions as a guide:

KEYS TO HELP YOU

- Consider Bob's history of flexibility conditioning.
- Consider how he should evaluate his current flexibility levels.
- Consider his needs and goals. (For example, how will he find time to do flexibility exercises?)
- Determine a reasonable plan for Bob that covers the concepts of overload, frequency, intensity, time, type, and progression.

EVALUATE

ENRICHMENT

CASE STUDY

ANSWERS

Bob should complete the PAR-Q in Chapter 2. If it is safe for him to start a personal fitness program, he should start by doing static stretching three times a week. He should do 10 stretches in each session. He can choose a variety of stretches from those presented in Chapter 11. He should read and learn tips to help reduce and prevent his lower back pain. He should also avoid hazardous stretches and recognize that he needs to be involved in personal fitness for long-term success.

Student Edition TEKS
Page 355: C1A

CHAPTER 12

Lesson 1 Fitness: A Lifetime Goal

Lesson 2 Your Changing Personal Fitness Goals

Lesson 3 Choosing Fitness Professionals

Lesson 4 Choosing Fitness Products

CHAPTER RESOURCES

- Chapter Study Guide 12
- Vocabulary Worksheet 12
- Enrichment Activity 12
- Chapter 12 Test A
- Chapter 12 Test B
- Parent Letters and Activities 12 (English/Spanish)

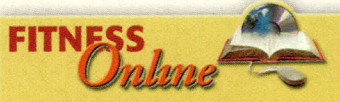

FITNESS Online

Ask students to take the STEP Personal Inventory for Chapter 12. Have them record responses to the statements in their notebooks. Remind students that responses are private and for their use only.

CHAPTER 12 Personal Fitness Throughout Life

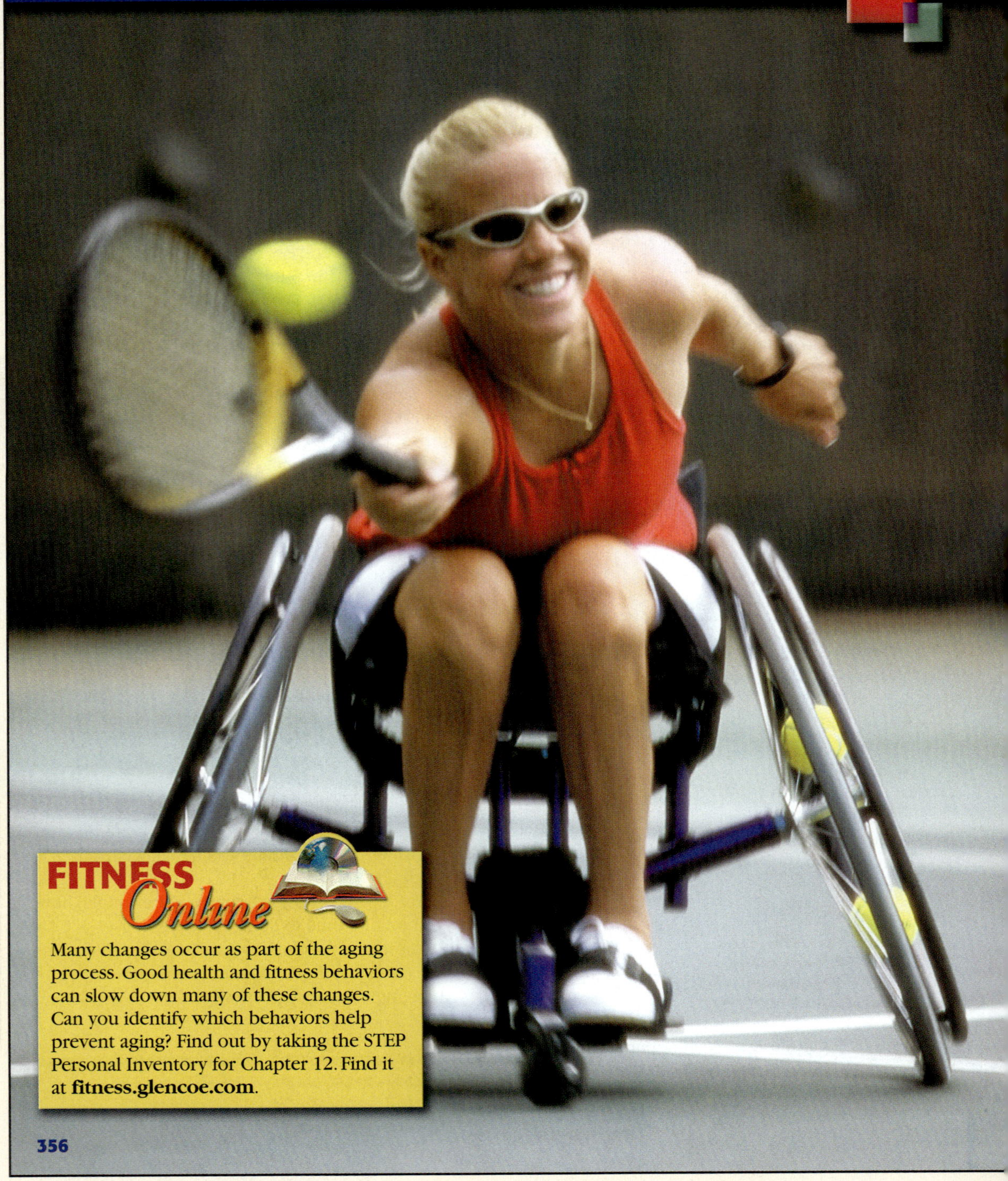

FITNESS Online

Many changes occur as part of the aging process. Good health and fitness behaviors can slow down many of these changes. Can you identify which behaviors help prevent aging? Find out by taking the STEP Personal Inventory for Chapter 12. Find it at **fitness.glencoe.com**.

356

INCLUSION STRATEGIES

LANGUAGE DIVERSITY *Use the following suggestions to help students who have difficulty with English:*

- Pair English-language learners with native speakers of English who can restate key points in language that helps students comprehend important concepts.
- Direct Spanish-speaking students to the written summaries of this chapter in the *Foundations of Personal Fitness* Spanish Resources Booklet.
- Encourage Spanish-speaking students to use the Glosario provided in the back of the student text. ELL

Fitness: A Lifetime Goal

Developing personal fitness during your teen years is essential to maintaining good health throughout your life. As an adult, you will benefit from the fitness habits you develop as a teen, and it is important to maintain a high level of fitness as you begin to age. Although you may need to adjust your personal fitness as you get older, personal fitness throughout your life is an achievable goal.

Understanding the Aging Process

The **aging process** is *the manner in which the body changes as a natural result of growing older.* Some aging-related changes, such as gray hair and wrinkled skin, are outwardly visible. Others are not. The line graph in **Figure 12.1** on page **358** illustrates four internal changes. All are declines in bodily functions of inactive individuals as they get older. Take a moment to examine this graph. Notice that these declines do not occur at the same rate. For example, compare the changes in resting metabolic rate (RMR) and lung capacity from ages 30 to 90. You find that RMR declines only about 10 percent, while lung capacity decreases 25 percent for nonsmokers. While these declines are to some degree inevitable, they do occur more slowly in physically active individuals.

What You Will Do

- Explain the body's natural aging process.
- Identify the physical changes that occur as people age.
- Recognize and explain the relationship between physical fitness and health throughout the lifespan.

Terms to Know

aging process

◀ Personal fitness is a lifetime goal. *Why is it important to remain physically active as an older adult?*

Fitness: A Lifetime Goal

1 MOTIVATE

GETTING STARTED

- Before you begin roll call, ask the class to think about the following question: *What kind of physical activities do you see yourself doing for recreation, health, and fitness?*
- Distribute copies of *Guided Practice Activity 12-1* for students to use while studying this lesson. 🗁

IN THIS LESSON

- **Stress Break,** *Stress and Aging, p. 358*

INTRODUCING VOCABULARY

- Students should understand the meaning of the word *process* and how it pertains to aging. A process is a series of actions, changes, or functions that—in the case of aging—achieve an end or result over time.
- Have students use *Vocabulary Worksheet 12* or the PuzzleMaker software to practice vocabulary terms for this lesson. **ELL** 🗁 ⊚

Photo Follow-up

Ask students how they react to the photos showing older people with active lifestyles. Ask whether they are concerned about how they will look and feel as they get older. *Caption answer: Remaining active as an older adult slows the aging process, helps you feel younger, and keeps you healthy.*

LESSON 1 RESOURCES

Teacher Classroom Resources
🗁 Guided Practice Activity 12-1
🗁 Reteaching Activity 12-1
🗁 Lesson Quiz 12-1

Reproducible Charts and Graphs
🗁 Reproducible Masters 12-1, 12-2, 12-3

Multimedia
⊚ Vocabulary PuzzleMaker

2 TEACH

Explaining

Explain that aging is a fact of life that cannot be avoided. With physical activity and healthy behaviors, however, we can slow the aging process and maintain functional health for a longer life. **L1**

Discussing

Ask students how they can maintain personal fitness as they age. This discussion should get them thinking about the future and help them explain the relationship between physical fitness and health of their parents and grandparents, older relatives, or other older adults. What are some of the physical activities their grandparents do to stay active and fit? **L1**
TEKS C4A

USING VISUALS

Figure 12.1 Discuss the aging process using *Reproducible Master 12-1.*
Caption answer: Lung capacity declines the fastest, while resting metabolic rate, heart pumping, and nerve conduction decline at about the same rate.

STRESS BREAK
Stress and Aging

As you age, you will have to deal with new and different stressors. To do so successfully requires learning and using stress-reduction strategies. These include relaxation techniques, breathing exercises, meditation, yoga, physical activity, and exercise. The last two of these not only reduce stress, but also benefit your physical health because they reduce heart rate and blood pressure.

The Aging Process and Health

Although the aging process cannot be reversed or halted, it can be slowed. You probably know some people who look and feel much younger than others their age. You may know people in their fifties, sixties, and seventies who are able to do more physical work than many younger people. For at least some of these people, the key to slowing down the clock is personal fitness. Many of them developed positive attitudes and behaviors early on, when they were your age.

Among these positive behaviors are an active lifestyle and proper nutrition. **Figure 12.2** shows their impact on a number of aging-related changes. As you can see, staying active and eating right will not necessarily keep you from getting gray hair or going bald. You can, however, make a positive impact on health areas such as levels of body fat, blood pressure, resting heart rate, and many other factors that will decrease your risk for diseases later in life.

Preventing or Slowing the Loss of Bone Mass

One physical change that occurs with age is a gradual loss of bone mass. When you are young, your bones are dense. As you progress into young adulthood, this density—or bone mass—will increase. Typically, peak bone mass occurs between the ages of 27 and 32. After this, bone density begins to decline.

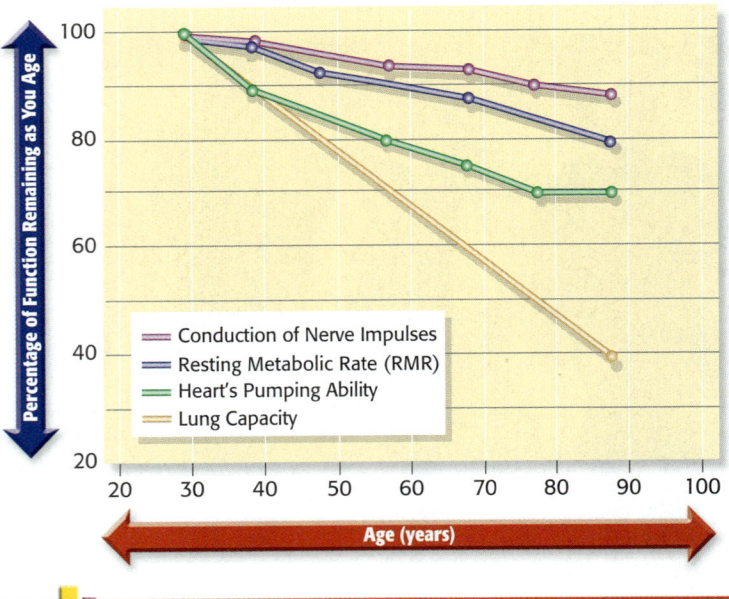

FIGURE 12.1

AGING AND PHYSICAL FUNCTIONS
The body's physical functions decline with age. *Which of these body processes declines the most rapidly? The most slowly?*

Percentage of Function Remaining as You Age

- Conduction of Nerve Impulses
- Resting Metabolic Rate (RMR)
- Heart's Pumping Ability
- Lung Capacity

Age (years)

Enrichment

Lifelong Fitness Have students create an activity time line spanning five decades. Ask them to record significant milestones on the right side of the time line. On the left side, they should indicate which physical activity they would like to participate in at every five-year interval. The time line might include college, graduating, becoming involved in a profession, marrying, having a child, retiring, and so on. When finished, ask students to share their long-term goals. What tools will be necessary to accomplish the goals? How might health behaviors and choices affect future plans?

FIGURE 12.2

EFFECT OF EXERCISE AND NUTRITION ON AGING

Staying physically active and eating healthfully will help you maintain your health as you age. *Which of these changes is related to mental/emotional health? To physical health?*

Aging-Related Change	Can (✓) Cannot (X) Make Positive Impact	
Graying of hair		X
Balding		X
Resting energy metabolism	✓	
Increased body fat	✓	
Increased blood pressure	✓	
Increased resting pulse	✓	
Elevated cholesterol levels	✓	
Decreased functional health	✓	
Inherited diseases		X
Hypokinetic diseases	✓	
Loss of elasticity of joints*		X
Loss of flexibility of joints**	✓	
Bone loss	✓	
Mental confusion	✓	
Reduced self-esteem	✓	
Depression	✓	

* elasticity = ability to return immediately to original size and shape
** flexibility = ability to bend without breaking

Source: Adapted with permission from Health: Making Life Choices, *1994.*[1]

Researchers have established a relationship between loss of bone mass and physical activity levels. **Figure 12.3** on page **360** shows this relationship. The graph reveals that more active people have greater bone mass than inactive people. This means that as active people age, they will be at a lower risk for **osteoporosis** than inactive people. Instead of developing brittle bones by age 65, they delay this onset into their seventies or eighties.

Proper nutrition is also important for preventing osteoporosis. Eating foods rich in the mineral calcium offsets some bone loss. Such foods include milk, yogurt, and canned salmon.

hotlink

osteoporosis
For more on osteoporosis and ways to slow this disease, see Chapter 9, page **258.**

Chapter 12, Lesson 1

USING VISUALS

Figure 12.2 Explain to students that many of the physical abilities they possess as adolescents will decline with age. Point out which ones are likely to decline the fastest. Also point out that while we cannot reverse or stop the aging process, we can do things to slow it down. *Caption answers related to emotional or mental state might include depression, low self-esteem, and confusion. Other answers will be related to physical changes.*

✓ Reading Check
(page 360)

Regular physical activity and proper nutrition can have an effect on the aging process. Physically active people have greater bone mass.
TEKS C4A

HEALTHY PEOPLE 2010

Goal: To reduce the amount of injury to vertebral and hip fractures due to low bone mass density (osteoporosis). These are the most common types of fractures for the elderly. Discuss the importance of physical activity in developing bone mass during the teen years. See Appendix B, page 384.

Student Edition TEKS

Page 359: C4A

TECHNOLOGY FILE

Multimedia-Based Fitness Plan

Have students create a multimedia project about their personal lifelong fitness plan. The plan should address specific fitness activities (along with the elements of time and intensity) for the decades of 20, 30, 40, 50, 60, 70, and 80 years of age. The project should include 2D and 3D graphics, animations, digital photographs, audio recordings, and data-driven charts. The software used for this project may include presentation, authoring/multimedia, or Web page design.

USING VISUALS

Figure 12.3 Use *Reproducible Master 12.3* to help students identify changeable risk factors of inactivity and nutrition. Emphasize the importance of adopting an active lifestyle during adolescence in order to develop as much bone mass as possible before their mid-20s. If adolescents remain inactive as teens, they will not develop as much bone mass and they will be at a higher risk for osteoporosis later in life. This is particularly important for adolescent females, who face a greater risk of losing bone density.
L1 TEKS C5G

Reinforce the importance of resistance training during bone-growth years. Have students review the benefits of resistance training and good nutrition in the reduction of osteoporosis. **TEKS C5G**

Review with students the importance of maintaining adherence to a physical activity program, as explained in Chapter 1.

✓ Reading Check
(page 361)

Moderate, everyday physical activities, such as walking a dog, form the base of the pyramid.

Student Edition TEKS

Page 360: C5G
Page 361: C4A

FIGURE 12.3

BONE MASS AND PHYSICAL ACTIVITY

Being physically active can increase peak bone mass and prevent osteoporosis. *At what age does bone become brittle in active people? In inactive people?*

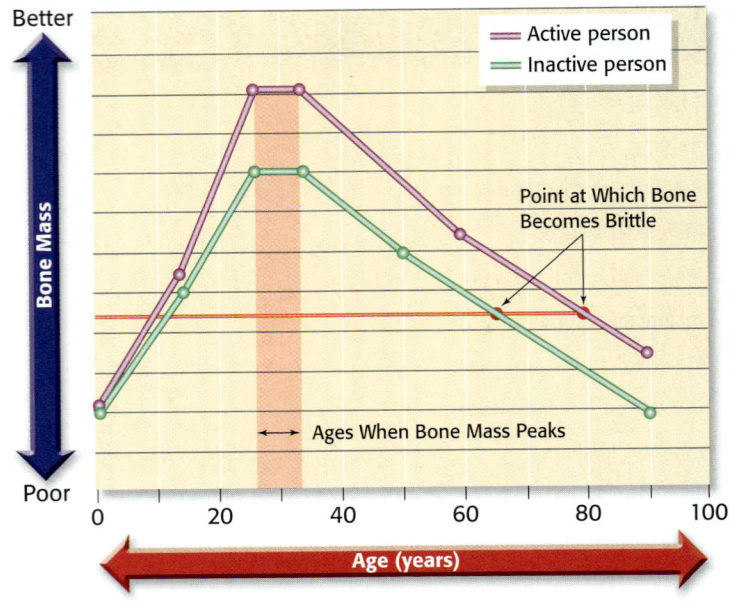

Source: Adapted with permission from New Horizons in Pediatric Exercise Science, *1995.[2]*

Modifying Your Activities

As you age, you will need to adjust your personal fitness program to meet your changing needs. For example, you may have to adjust your FITT for selected activities to enable you to recover more completely between workouts. You may find that you need to vary your exercise or activity routine or type to avoid boredom and to help maintain your **adherence.** You will need to understand your mental and physical limitations. Only then will you be able to meet special situations and needs effectively. By staying active throughout your life, you will learn to pay even closer attention to your body, which will help you recognize possible health problems. Then you will be able to maintain a healthy, active, and productive lifestyle throughout your life.

adherence
For more on adherence and strategies for maintaining it, see Chapter 1, page **21.**

✓ Reading Check

Evaluate What are two behaviors that can slow the aging process? How does physical activity affect bone mass?

COOPERATIVE Learning

LIFESTYLE RISKS FOR OSTEOPOROSIS A sedentary lifestyle and inadequate calcium intake can increase the risk of osteoporosis. Have students work in small groups to research other lifestyle factors that contribute to osteoporosis. For example, one group member might investigate the effects of dieting on bone density. Another might research the effects of alcohol, while a third examines caffeine effects. Have students conduct a panel discussion about risk factors and make lifestyle recommendations for preventing osteoporosis. **ELL**

The Physical Activity Pyramid: Fitness for Life

In Chapter 1 you learned about the Physical Activity Pyramid. It is a guide for developing and maintaining regular physical-activity patterns that will reduce your risks for chronic diseases as you age. The pyramid illustrates a sensible, step-by-step plan to becoming and staying active. If you currently maintain moderate-to-high levels of fitness, you are off to a good start. As you age, you may need to adjust the types of activities you do, but you can always maintain your overall fitness.

Remember that daily physical activities, such as walking the dog, form the base of the pyramid. The next level up includes aerobic exercise and leisure-time activities. The third level promotes the development and maintenance of strength and flexibility. The top step reminds you to cut down on your sedentary habits.

Sedentary
Infrequently

Muscular Strength/ Endurance
2–3 days

Flexibility
2 or more days

Aerobic Activities
3–5 days

Leisure Time Activities
2 or more days

Moderate Daily Activities
Every day

 **Reading Check**

Explain What type of activities form the base, or first step, of the Physical Activity Pyramid?

▲ The Physical Activity Pyramid can help you plan your physical activities. *What are some examples of each type of activity listed?*

Lesson 1 Review

Using complete sentences, answer the following questions on a sheet of paper.

Reviewing Facts and Vocabulary

1. **Vocabulary** What is the *aging process?*
2. **Recall** List and explain three examples of how your body changes as it ages.

Thinking Critically

3. **Analyze** What effect does physical activity have on health, as one ages?
4. **Evaluate** Explain the saying "Old age is a state of mind."

Personal Fitness Planning

Evaluating Physical Activities Review the Physical Activity Pyramid to determine if you are doing enough of the right activities. You may want to refer to **Figure 1.8** in Chapter 1 on page **10**. Make a list of the things you do daily at each level of the pyramid. Then make a list of the activities you hope to see yourself doing as an older adult. Which activities are the same? Which are different? Explain the relationship between physical fitness and health in your choices.

---

3 ASSESS

EVALUATING THE LESSON

Assign and discuss the Lesson 1 Review.

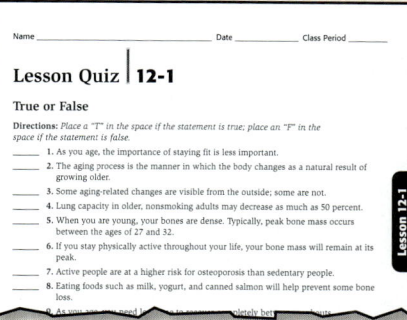

Lesson 12-1

RETEACHING

Have students work in groups to decide on the five main physical functions that decline with age.

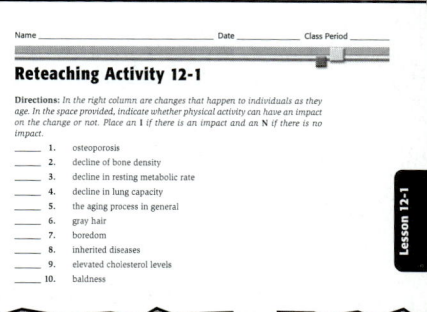

Lesson 12-1

ENRICHMENT

Ask students to describe stress management techniques they have used. **TEKS C5B**

4 CLOSE

Ask students to react to the statement, "A physically educated person *values* physical activity and its contributions to a healthful lifestyle." How does this connect to the aging process?

Lesson 1 Review

Answers to Lesson 1 Review

1. The manner in which the body changes as a natural result of growing older.
2. Answers may vary but can include any of the examples in Figure 12.2.
3. Slows the aging process while helping you feel younger and remain healthy.
4. Even though you may be advanced in actual years, your body and mind can still maintain many of the capabilities it had in your younger years. A positive mental attitude can help you view the world just as you did in your youth.

Your Changing Personal Fitness Goals

Your Changing Personal Fitness Goals

1 MOTIVATE

GETTING STARTED

- Before you begin roll call, ask the class to think about the following question: *What is the difference between leisure activities and competitive sports? Give five examples.*

- Distribute copies of *Guided Practice Activity 12-2* for students to use while studying this lesson. 📁

IN THIS LESSON

- **Fitness Check** *Designing an Aerobic Exercise Routine,* p. 365
- **Mind Over Matter** *Exercise You Can Enjoy,* p. 369

INTRODUCING VOCABULARY

- Point out that the word *leisure* means "free time." Have students identify two or three activities they do in their leisure time.

- Have students use *Vocabulary Worksheet 12* or the PuzzleMaker software to practice vocabulary terms for this lesson. **ELL** 📁 💿

Photo Follow-up

Introduce the photo and ask: How fit will you be 10 years from now? 20 years? What kind of activities will you be doing? *Caption answer: They reduce stress, encourage social interaction, burn calories, and build self-esteem.*

What You Will Do

- Discuss the health benefits of leisure-time activities.
- Identify leisure-time activities that meet your fitness goals.
- Recognize why people should vary their activity selection as they age.
- Design and implement an aerobic-workout routine.

Terms to Know

leisure-time activities
martial arts
t'ai chi

Your Changing Personal Fitness Goals

Throughout this text you have been encouraged to develop and maintain an active lifestyle. A broad spectrum of physical activities, exercises, and sports can help you achieve that goal. Many of these have appeared in earlier chapters. In this lesson, you will explore several others.

Leisure-Time Activities

Leisure-time activities include *sports and other action-oriented pursuits done for recreation.* Leisure-time activities do not focus on developing health-related or skill-related fitness the way other physical activities might, such as competitive sports. However, done regularly, leisure-time activities can improve some aspects of health-related or skill-related fitness. They also provide other benefits, such as

- reducing stress levels.
- providing an opportunity for social interaction.
- burning calories.
- developing and maintaining self-esteem.

As you continue to develop and refine your personal fitness program, you should experiment with and try a variety of leisure-time activities. Then you can select ones that you find enjoyable and, if possible, help you meet your personal fitness goals.

◀ A great way to maintain your personal fitness is by finding leisure-time activities that you enjoy. *What are some benefits of leisure-time activities?*

LESSON 2 RESOURCES

Teacher Classroom Resources
📁 Guided Practice Activity 12-2
📁 Fitness Check Worksheet 12-2
📁 Reteaching Activity 12-2
📁 Lesson Quiz 12-2

Reproducible Charts and Graphs
📁 Reproducible Master 12-4

Multimedia
💿 Vocabulary PuzzleMaker

▲ Many people enjoy resistance training as an aquatic activity. *What aspects of fitness do aquatic activities develop?*

Aquatic Activities

Many people enjoy swimming as a leisure-time activity. In Chapter 8, you learned about **lap swimming** as a way to develop and maintain your cardiorespiratory fitness. In addition to swimming laps, many people enjoy working out in the pool by doing exercises against the resistance provided by the water. For example, when you stand in a pool with water at chest level and move your arms back and forth through the water, you can feel the resistance of the water. Aquatic activities reduce the pounding that your body takes in weight-bearing activities (for example, walking or jogging) and can be modified in intensity by working in the shallow or deep ends of the pool. You can use aquatic activities to develop and maintain good to better levels of cardiorespiratory fitness, muscular endurance, and body composition.

Cycling

As noted in Chapter 8, **cycling** is excellent for developing balance and cardiorespiratory fitness and for controlling body composition. It is also a very popular form of exercise with all age groups. Tour cycling is usually done on roads with a light-framed bike that has thin tires. Mountain biking is done on trails with a bike that has a heavier frame and wider tires for better traction. These activities are made more enjoyable and safer when done in groups. Also for safety, always wear a helmet for touring or mountain bike cycling.

LIFELINE

Applying Etiquette

Choose two or three activities from this lesson, or identify some of your favorite activities. Share with the class specific etiquette involved with these activities. For example, you might discuss who has the right of way on trails shared by runners, hikers, and mountain bikers; or how skiers and snowboarders can share the slopes to avoid injury.

hotlink

lap swimming
For more on lap swimming and its benefits, see Chapter 8, page **232**.

cycling
For more on cycling, see Chapter 8, page **229**.

More About . . .

AQUATICS Aquatics classes are a popular way to meet your physical activity needs. Anybody can have fun and benefit from an aquatics class. Aquatics classes may also be called aqua aerobics, water aerobics, splash dance, and hydroaerobics, to list a few. This form of recreation and exercise can be performed by people of any age. When submerged to the neck, the pull of gravity on the body is reduced by as much as 90 percent, which in turn offers an excellent physical activity environment for almost anyone. All you need is the desire to participate in this beneficial environment.

2 TEACH

Explaining

Explain that it is important to identify physical activities that best meet your needs. By choosing the right activities, you are more likely to keep doing them as you get older. **L1**

Discussing

Point out to students that one of the best ways to improve their adherence to physical activity and exercise is to engage in leisure activities with family or friends. Have students identify specific times when family outings are more likely to happen. **L2**

Photo Follow-up

Point out how this photo reinforces what students have learned about cardiovascular efficiency and muscular strength, as well as endurance activities. Ask: Why would water be a great place for physical activity? *Caption answer: It helps maintain good-to-better levels of cardiorespiratory fitness, muscular endurance, and body composition.* **TEKS C4B**

hotlink

Emphasize that swimming may not increase heart rate as much as jogging would. Have students review the benefits of swimming and cycling in Chapter 8.

Student Edition TEKS

Page 362: C4G
Page 363: C2A

Photo Follow-up

Ask students how many have tried snow skiing or water skiing. How are they different in terms of muscle use and cardiovascular requirements? Remind them of the effects of altitude. *Caption answer: Skiing is an excellent way to develop and maintain cardiorespiratory fitness and body composition, as well as improving coordination and power.*

Explaining

Examine the many different types of dance and discuss how each one can provide an excellent opportunity to improve skill- and health-related fitness. Explain that the dance styles students choose now are likely to change as they get older. Dance can be a lifelong endeavor that enhances not only fitness, but also social interactions. **L1**

✔ Reading Check

Aerobic dance is a great way to improve all components of health-related fitness. Other forms of social dance can also contribute to your health-related fitness, as well as your skills of coordination, agility, and balance.

Have students review the benefits of cross-country skiing and aerobic dance in Chapter 8.

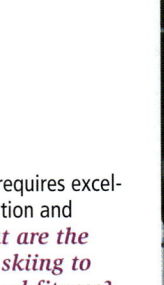

▶ Snow skiing requires excellent coordination and power. *What are the benefits of skiing to your personal fitness?*

cross-country skiing
For more on cross-country skiing, see Chapter 8, page **231**.

aerobic dance
For more on aerobic dance, see Chapter 8, page **230**.

Water and Snow Skiing

Whether you're on the water or the snow, skiing allows you to enjoy the great outdoors. The safest way to participate in skiing is to take lessons and purchase or rent quality equipment. Skiing of any type requires excellent coordination and power. As mentioned in Chapter 8, **cross-country skiing** is an excellent way to develop and maintain your cardiorespiratory fitness and body composition.

Dance

As discussed in Chapter 8, participating in **aerobic-dance** classes is an excellent way to improve your cardiorespiratory fitness. However, a fitness center is not the only place to experience the benefits of dance. There are many popular types of dance that are easy to do once you've had a few lessons. Dancing helps develop balance, coordination, and agility. Many forms of dance are also good for aerobic conditioning and weight control, provided they are done regularly and for long enough periods of time. (As you have learned, health-related fitness results depend on your FITT.) Dancing is also an excellent way to interact socially with others while achieving your fitness goals.

✔ Reading Check

Analyze Does dance improve health-related fitness, skill-related fitness, or both? Explain your answer.

INCLUSION STRATEGIES

SAFE AND EFFECTIVE PROGRAMS It can sometimes be difficult to develop a fitness program for disabled students that is both safe and effective. It takes a great deal of input from various sources (parents, physicians, physical therapists, adapted physical education specialists) as well as sufficient knowledge of disabling conditions. These students have the same need for recreation and leisure activities as do their nondisabled peers. Often, the need is even greater for disabled students since they tend to have more free time.

Designing an Aerobic-Exercise Routine

When planning your personal fitness program, you may decide to incorporate aerobic exercise as part of your plan. An aerobic workout is a convenient and enjoyable way to improve and maintain cardiorespiratory endurance.

In this activity, you will apply the physiological principle related to intensity to an aerobic-exercise routine by designing your own routine and evaluating its intensity, using your heart rate. Remember, for any fitness plan to be a success, you need to apply all FITT factors correctly. Once you have verified an appropriate intensity level for your aerobic-exercise routine, you may choose to integrate it as the cardiovascular component of your personal fitness program.

Procedure:

1. If possible, view two or three videotapes of aerobic workout routines. Determine the types of music used, intensities of the exercises done (low, moderate, or high), the types of warm-up and cooldown done, and the types of movements performed.
2. Design your own 12- to 15-minute aerobic-exercise routine.
3. Vary the routine intensity with low-impact and high-impact exercises.
4. Set the routine cadence to a count of 8.
5. Do not repeat any exercises for more than two sets of 8 counts.
6. Use correct exercise technique and develop smooth transitions from one exercise to the next.
7. Make sure your routine includes a warm-up (no longer than 2–3 minutes), aerobic activities that work the arms and shoulders, abdominals, and legs, followed by a cooldown (no longer than 2–3 minutes).
8. After you have practiced your routine, evaluate the intensity of your workout by taking your pulse a total of four times: before you begin, after the warm-up, after the main aerobic activities, and two minutes after the completion of the cooldown.

9. Copy the graph in **Figure 12.4** and chart your results. The shaded areas of the chart indicate an appropriate range of intensity for each phase of your routine. Take note of any areas where your results fall outside the shaded areas.
10. If the intensity was below moderate intensity or above vigorous intensity, plan how you can adjust the intensity level. If the intensity was within an appropriate range, incorporate the aerobic-exercise routine into your personal fitness plan and regularly assess your progress (every four to six weeks) by using one of the Cardiorespiratory Endurance evaluations from Chapter 7 or Chapter 8.

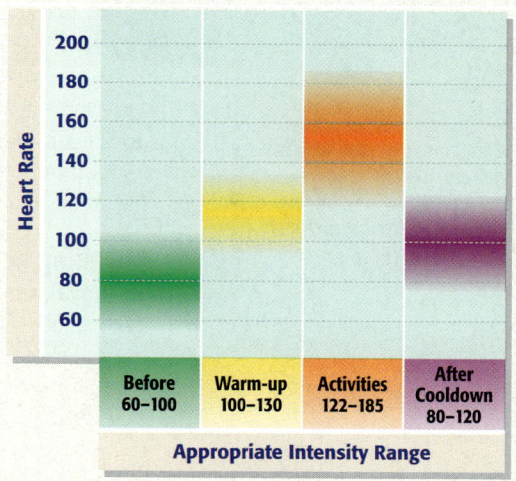

Figure 12.4 INTENSITY OF YOUR AEROBIC WORKOUT

	Before 60–100	Warm-up 100–130	Activities 122–185	After Cooldown 80–120

Appropriate Intensity Range

Fitness Check

Designing an Aerobic-Exercise Routine

OBJECTIVES

- Design and implement a complete aerobic exercise routine. **TEKS C4G**
- Assess and adjust your heart rate intensity for each stage of the exercise routine.

Teaching Tips

- This assignment is best done over five to seven class periods.
- For the first two to three classes, have students participate in a variety of aerobic videotapes.
- The next two to three classes can be allocated to designing and practicing the routines.
- Distribute *Fitness Check 12-2* for students to record their daily progress, identifying how long each part of their routines will take. 📁
- Have student groups make presentations of their routines.
- The rest of the class should participate in the guided exercise routine.
- Students should use pulse rates and the intensity chart to adjust exercise intensities.
- You may wish to videotape each group and have students critique the routines.

Participation in leisure activities, particularly within the community, tends to contribute to social acceptance of students with special needs in the sports setting. In addition, positive gains can be seen in the development of fitness, mobility, and self-image. It is often through recreational activities that students with disabilities are able to experience the success that they may not experience in other areas. Almost any leisure activity can be adapted or modified so that students with disabilities can successfully participate in physical activity.

Student Edition TEKS

Page 365: C4G

Photo Follow-up

Ask the class to discuss how the rules of volleyball can be changed so that it might be better suited for recreational play or backyard family gatherings. *Caption answer: All of the activities except hiking, backpacking, and calisthenics can be turned into a competitive endeavor.*

Discussing

Ask the class to identify different forms of martial arts. Ask students who have participated in martial arts to discuss the style they do and the benefits they gain from it. **L1**

Guest Speaker

Recruit a martial arts professional to demonstrate some of the varieties discussed in class (karate, judo, and t'ai chi). You may wish to show a videotape to generate student interest. **L2**

Photo Follow-up

Ask volunteers to share their kayaking or canoeing experiences with the class. Identify places in your area where students could do these activities. *Caption answer: to develop power, cardiorespiratory fitness, and muscular strength and endurance, as well as reduce stress.* **TEKS C5B**

▶ Volleyball is an activity that can be played at the recreational or competitive level. *What other activities mentioned in this lesson can also be competitive?*

▲ Canoeing is a good way to get outside and enjoy nature. *What are some other health benefits of this activity?*

Volleyball and Basketball

Basketball is excellent for developing coordination, reaction time, and power. They can also provide an excellent cardiovascular- and muscular-endurance workout. Two-person sand volleyball has become very popular. More and more communities are building sand courts to promote participation. Playing half-court or full-court basketball is a challenging activity, but many people are able to participate in it well into middle age by maintaining good-to-better fitness levels.

Racquetball and Tennis

Racquetball and tennis are excellent ways to develop cardiorespiratory endurance and body composition. They require high levels of coordination and agility. Racquetball is one of the most popular indoor leisure-time activities. If you like to compete, racquetball tournaments are regularly held at many fitness clubs and are designed to challenge players of all ages and abilities. If you prefer tennis, many city parks, recreation departments, and private tennis clubs offer lessons for people of all ages and abilities.

Kayaking and Canoeing

Kayaking and canoeing can be done recreationally or at competitive levels. These activities help develop your power. When done for long periods of time per session, they promote cardiorespiratory fitness, muscular strength, and muscular endurance. You will need to take time to develop the specific skills necessary for these activities to be done safely, but they are great ways to get outside, explore new areas, and help control stress levels.

366 **Chapter 12** *Personal Fitness Throughout Life*

More About . . .

T'AI CHI is gaining popularity in the United States. This physical activity from China is a set of slow, stylized movements and controlled, focused breathing. T'ai chi can contribute to improved circulation, flexibility, and stress reduction. The postures usually follow the same order, which makes it easy for strangers to meet and carry out the movements together in perfect unison. A typical round of t'ai chi lasts about 20 minutes, during which the arms and legs are in constant motion. The components of physical, mental, and social health can all be enhanced through the practice of t'ai chi.

Rowing

Rowing in all its different forms is an excellent activity to develop your coordination, power, cardiorespiratory fitness, and muscular endurance. It is also a great way to control your body composition. Rowing in a crew can be a great way to meet other people and be part of a team, even if it's just for recreation. Stationary rowing can be fun if you have access to a rowing machine with interactive video feedback to enhance your workout.

 **Reading Check**

Explain Which activities help to develop coordination? Power?

Martial Arts

The martial arts, which originated in Eastern Asia, are practiced by some 100 million people worldwide. The original purpose of the martial arts was self-defense. Today, martial arts are seen as *activities that combine exercise and relaxation techniques*. Many of these activities teach controlled breathing, which helps reduce stress.

There are approximately 200 separate martial arts. Karate and judo are two of the most well-known. Another popular form of martial arts is t'ai chi (DYE JEE). This is *a martial art that involves fluid, graceful movements, demanding precise muscular control*. Practicing t'ai chi provides excellent muscle tone.

Hiking and Backpacking

Hiking and backpacking are excellent ways to get outside and enjoy nature while developing muscular endurance and cardiorespiratory fitness. Most areas of the country provide numerous opportunities for these activities. For personal safety, you should hike with someone else, using well-marked trails. Carry a water supply to prevent dehydration. If you hike in an area you're not familiar with, make sure you carry a map and compass. These can help you avoid becoming lost. A good pair of hiking shoes or boots is also indispensable. It is a good idea to let someone know where you are going, or, if possible, carry a cellular phone.

Backpacking requires more planning than does a day of hiking. If you will be gone for several days, you will need a tent, food, and fluids. You also need to determine how much weight you are able to carry for extended periods of time.

Hiking and backpacking are useful for maintaining good levels of health-related fitness. However, you need to do some cardiovascular conditioning and muscular-endurance training prior to an extended hiking or backpacking trip.

You can increase your self-confidence and self-esteem by participating in the martial arts. *What are the other benefits of the martial arts?*

T'ai chi does not rely on strength or power, but on leverage. By leaning away from an attack, a skilled practitioner can throw an aggressor off balance, therefore making him or her vulnerable.

Photo Follow-up

Explain to students how martial arts demand a great deal of self-discipline and practice. *Caption answer: It is a great way to combine exercise and relaxation, thus improving muscle control and breath control, and reducing stress.*

Explaining

Remind students to be aware of their intensity levels. Any activity can be done anaerobically or at too high an intensity, which makes the activity less enjoyable and more difficult to sustain. Recreation activities are better suited for aerobic intensities.
L1 **TEKS C1A**

Reading Check
Volleyball, basketball, racquetball, tennis, kayaking, canoeing, and rowing all develop coordination and power.

Activity

Have students consider the activities on this page and share examples of ways to resolve conflicts. Have teams work together to choose one activity and identify conflicts that may arise when participating in that activity. How would they identify a conflict? Have them develop a strategy for resolving the conflict.
TEKS C2B

Student Edition TEKS
Page 366: C4D
Page 367: C4D

Mind OVER Matter

Place the class into groups and have them plan a hiking or backpacking trip. Have them determine the equipment they will need and how much of the equipment they already have available. What are some leisure activities they could do after they get to their destination?

Photo Follow-up

Explain that world-class runners can run each mile in under five minutes. Explain that an Iron Man Triathlon is a 2.5-mile swim followed by a 110-mile bike ride and completed with a full 26.2-mile marathon. The entire event takes the best athletes over 9 hours.

✓ Reading Check

Individuals must get professional advice and plan a sequential training program for proper conditioning.

anaerobic activity
For more on anaerobic activity and how it differs from aerobic activity, see Chapter 7, page **212.**

Rock Climbing

Rock climbing is a challenging activity that requires high levels of muscular strength and endurance. Excellent balance and coordination are also necessary. Though rock climbing is chiefly an **anaerobic activity,** longer climbs will also stress you aerobically. Although typically an outdoor activity, indoor facilities for rock climbing are becoming increasingly popular in many communities. No matter where you climb, you should practice safe climbing skills by always climbing with a partner and using your safety gear.

Calisthenics

Calisthenics are a convenient activity because they can be done in your own home, perhaps with the guidance of a workout video or television show. Doing regular calisthenics (push-ups, abdominal crunches, jumping jacks, and so on) can help you improve your muscular endurance and flexibility. If you do calisthenics in a continuous, rhythmic manner, you can also develop and maintain your cardiorespiratory fitness and control your body composition.

Triathlons, Biathlons, and Marathons

Triathlons are endurance competitions that include swimming, cycling, and running for various distances. Biathlons are endurance events that usually combine two activities—for example, running and cycling, swimming and running, or cross-country skiing and rifle shooting. Marathons are endurance competitions that include running distances of at least 26.2 miles. Triathlons, biathlons, and marathons require high levels of performance fitness, but they do have varied lengths and many participants can find a distance they can complete.

Most people will never try to complete a triathlon, biathlon, or marathon. However, you may want to challenge yourself to compete

► Running in a marathon requires at least several months of preparation.

More About . . .

ACTIVITIES OPTIONS Adults in the United States participate in a variety of physical activities for leisure and exercise. These include: walking for exercise, gardening, stretching exercises, strength-training exercises, jogging or running, aerobics, cycling, stair climbing, swimming, tennis, and basketball. The most common activities presented in physical education classes have included basketball, volleyball, softball, football, soccer, jogging, weights, and tennis. Physical education courses are beginning to focus on activities that can be developed as lifetime physical activities.

in one of these events just for your own satisfaction. If you decide to attempt one of these activities, make sure you seek out professional advice beforehand. You will need a sequential training program with periodic checkpoints for at least several months to condition yourself properly before the event.

 Reading Check

Extend What specific types of conditioning does a person need to do in preparation for a marathon?

Activities for a Lifetime

It is only natural that your interests will change as you age. So will your levels of health-related fitness. Your choice of leisure-time activities, thus, should change to reflect your changing needs. Your ultimate goal should be to make physical activity a lifetime habit.

Learn to analyze your lifetime activities to make sure they help you meet your personal needs for health-related fitness, skill-related fitness, stress reduction, and worthwhile leisure pursuits. Also, determine which lifetime activities are realistic for you based on the following:

- **Cost.** Can you afford to participate in the activity?
- **Your personality and attitude.** Does the activity fit your style?
- **Availability of equipment and facilities.** Where can you find equipment or facilities for the activity?
- **Your social needs.** Will you do the activity alone or with friends?
- **Environmental hazards.** Can you engage in the activity safely?

Mind OVER Matter

Exercise You Can Enjoy

Working out doesn't have to be work. Leisure-time activities are an enjoyable and effective way of staying physically fit throughout your life.

Whether you enjoy swimming, cycling, dancing, or another action-oriented pursuit, leisure-time activities are a great way of staying physically fit and having fun. Take time to find a leisure-time activity that works for you.

Lesson 2 Review

Using complete sentences, answer the following questions on a sheet of paper.

Reviewing Facts and Vocabulary

1. **Vocabulary** Define *leisure-time activities*.
2. **Recall** Name two activities that promote cardiorespiratory fitness.

Thinking Critically

3. **Compare and Contrast** In what ways are the benefits of hiking and backpacking similar to those of rock climbing? In what ways are they different?

4. **Extend** Jay has been an avid runner for the last five years. He has recently considered the possibility of entering a triathlon. What advice would you give him and why?

Personal Fitness Planning

Assessing Physical Activities Make a list of all the activities named in this lesson that you have personally participated in. Then make a list of those that you have not tried but would like to learn more about. What are the special considerations you need to examine before starting these activities?

3 ASSESS

EVALUATING THE LESSON

Assign and discuss the Lesson 2 Review.

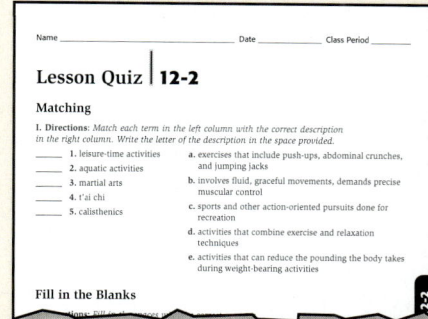

RETEACHING

Ask student groups to identify three favorite activities and which ones they will most likely participate in 10 or 20 years from now.

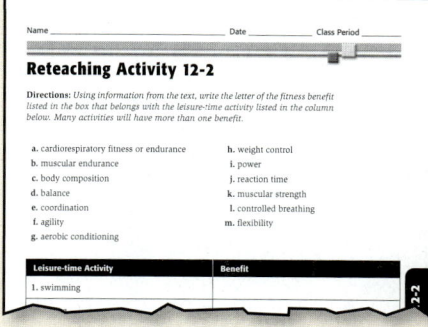

ENRICHMENT

Have students identify how many of the leisure or lifetime activities they have not done but would like to try.

4 CLOSE

Name two activities and have students identify the health and fitness benefits as well as equipment needed to perform them.

Lesson 2 Review

Answers to Lesson 2 Review

1. Sports and other recreation activities.
2. Answers might include aquatics, cycling, cross-country skiing, aerobic dance, rowing, triathlons, and marathons.
3. Both activities are beneficial in reducing stress and improving fitness. Rock climbing requires more muscular strength and endurance.
4. Get professional advice. He will need a well-designed training program with periodic checkpoints.

Choosing Fitness Professionals

1 MOTIVATE

GETTING STARTED

- Before you begin roll call, ask the class to think about the following question: *Who are the people you would most likely go to if you had a question or problem associated with fitness activities?*
- Distribute copies of *Guided Practice Activity 12-3* for students to use while studying this lesson. 📁

IN THIS LESSON

- **Any Body Can** *Dr. Sally Ride—When the Sky Is Not the Limit*, p. 373

INTRODUCING VOCABULARY

- Explain the meaning of the word *credentials* and have students prepare a list of credentials for each of the fitness experts in this lesson.
- Have students use *Vocabulary Worksheet 12* or the PuzzleMaker software to practice vocabulary terms for this lesson. **ELL** 📁 💿

Photo Follow-up

Ask students how this teen could have prevented back injury. *Caption answer: You might ask parents and friends, health care professionals, or local librarians.*

What You Will Do

- Discuss different types of health and fitness professionals.
- Identify the qualifications and requirements for careers in health- and fitness-related fields.
- Explain how to choose a fitness professional.

Terms to Know

credentials
orthopedics
podiatrist
physical therapists
athletic trainers
registered dietitians (RDs)
exercise physiologists

Choosing Fitness Professionals

Sheila had been lifting weights for only a short time when she began to experience back pain. She knew she needed to see someone who could tell her what was wrong. She also knew she needed future guidance about lifting techniques.

Would you know who to turn to if you were Sheila? After reading this lesson, you will learn about fitness professionals who are able to help you solve your health and fitness questions.

Finding Qualified Fitness Experts

If you feel you need expert advice in the areas of health and fitness during your teen years, it is always best to first seek the advice of your parents or guardian. As you reach adulthood, however, you will be increasingly responsible for your own health and well-being.

There are a number of professionals who can provide advice and counseling about nutrition, health, exercise, and more. All are required to complete specialized training and have appropriate licensing or certification. To ensure you are choosing a qualified professional, verify that they have the appropriate **credentials.** These are *a summary of the person's professional training and experience in a given field.*

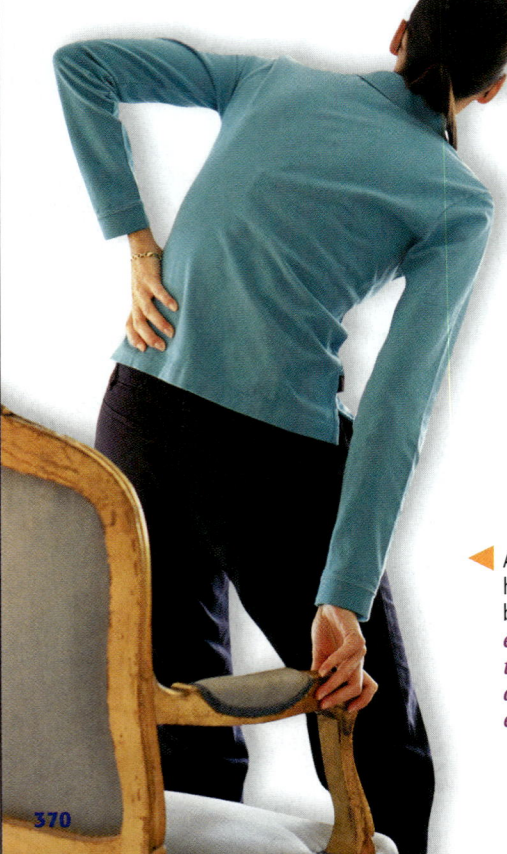

A qualified fitness professional can help with problems such as lower-back pain. *Aside from your parents, who is a good person to talk to if you think you need advice from a health or fitness expert?*

370

LESSON 3 RESOURCES

Teacher Classroom Resources
📁 Guided Practice Activity 12-3
📁 Reteaching Activity 12-3
📁 Lesson Quiz 12-3

Multimedia
💿 Vocabulary PuzzleMaker

When choosing a fitness or health expert, the following guidelines may be helpful.

- Ask friends or relatives for recommendations.
- Ask other health care professionals you know for a referral.
- Ask a local librarian or consumer protection agency if a directory of such professionals is available. A directory will provide information about their professional credentials and areas of specialization.

Physicians

This grouping includes doctors in general practice who treat day-to-day health problems or injuries. Although a general physician, such as your family doctor, may not specialize in fitness-related problems, he or she can help you determine if you have a fitness-related problem and refer you to the appropriate professional. If you have a specific concern about your health or fitness, a general physician is a great place to start.

Some doctors do have particular specialties. One specialty with particularly strong ties to fitness is **orthopedics.** This is *a branch of medicine that deals with bone and joint injuries and disorders.* Another physician who often treats fitness-related problems is a **podiatrist.** A podiatrist is *a physician trained specifically to treat disorders of the feet.* Typically, a family doctor will refer patients to see a specialist if necessary.

Reading Check

Summarize What do orthopedists do?

Physical Therapists

Physical therapists are *health professionals specially trained to work with people recovering from injuries.* They use a variety of treatments and techniques to help manage their patients' problems. Physical therapists undergo four to six years of academic and clinical training and must be licensed by the state. If you suffer an injury, your physician will most likely refer you to a physical therapist.

Athletic Trainers

Athletic trainers are *professionals who work with athletes undergoing rehabilitation.* Settings may include high schools, colleges, or traveling with professional sports teams. Athletic trainers undergo at least four years

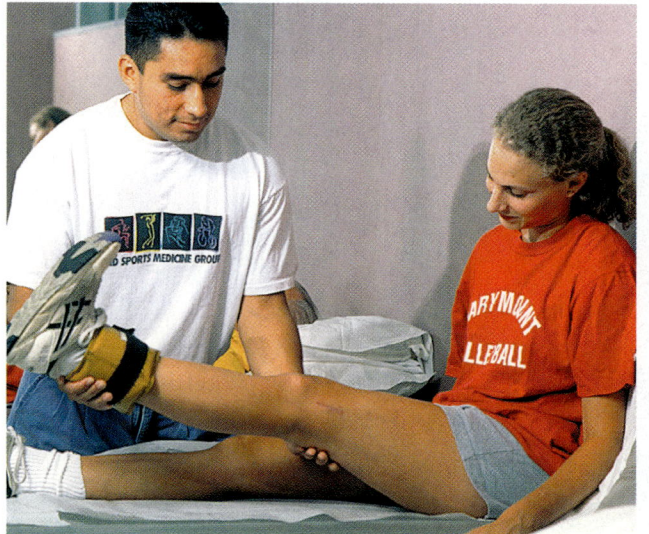

▼ Physical therapists are specially trained to work with people who are rehabilitating from injuries. *What type of personal skills do you think physical therapists need in their line of work?*

2 TEACH

Photo Follow-up

Tell students that physical therapists need to have an extensive knowledge of the functioning of the muscles and bones, as well as other systems of the body. They need to be well versed in the various treatments available for injuries and diseases. *Caption answer: They will need skills in working with the personalities of people trying to recover from injuries.*

Reading Check

Orthopedists treat bone and joint injuries and disorders.

Discussing

Remind students that there are many different types of health problems or injuries. Simple minor injuries may require only the attention of a family physician, while other problems may require the services of a specialist. Specialists may include cardiologists (for heart and blood vessel disease), chiropractors (for spine and joint problems), allergists and immunologists (for allergies and asthma), and orthopedic surgeons (to perform bone and joint surgery and rehabilitation). **L1**

More About . . .

AGING Physicians, exercise physiologists, and other groups are constantly searching for clues to better understand the aging process. Some theories include: The theory of *aging by program* states that every species of animal has its own longevity programmed into its body cells. The *cross-linkage* theory considers that proteins are made up of smaller molecules called peptides and that these chemical bonds can cause permanent changes. The *free radical* theory states that this process can lower your immune function. Free radicals produce chemical reactions that alter and damage body cells.

Photo Follow-up

Discuss with students the variety of tests performed by exercise physiologists to evaluate fitness levels and determine treatments. Which people are most likely in need of this type of testing? See Chapter 2 for medical screening and examinations.

Discussing

Have students describe the many roles of a registered dietitian. A dietitian can analyze an adolescent's diet and identify the common nutrient deficiencies that are associated with weight problems, cavities, acne, and other common concerns for adolescents. Have students consider how registered dietitians can help individuals develop appropriate methods of weight control. **L1** **TEKS C5F**

Activity

Point out that registered dietitians identify the leading factors associated with making poor food and behavioral choices. They can help teens make changes by asking simple questions, such as: Are you eating foods because you like them or because they are convenient? Do your friends have an impact on your eating habits? Have students work in teams to come up with three more questions they could ask a dietitian about their food choices. **L2** **ELL**

of academic and clinical training before they can practice. They work under the supervision of physicians and are often licensed by the state. If you would like advice from an athletic trainer, speak to your physical education instructor, coach, or doctor.

Registered Dietitians

Registered dietitians (RDs) are *professionals who specialize in providing nutritional advice and helping people control their weight.* Registered dietitians undergo at least four years of training and register with the American Dietetic Association before they can practice as a registered dietitian.

Be careful when choosing a professional to advise you about nutrition. Someone may call him- or herself a nutritionist, but they may not have the proper training. When choosing a dietitian, make sure he or she has the initials "RD" after his or her name. This ensures they have the appropriate qualifications.

Exercise Physiologists

Exercise physiologists are *specially trained to understand the body's physical reactions to exercise.* They must earn a college degree with an emphasis in exercise physiology. They are not licensed by the state but must be certified by a national organization. To do so, they must pass written tests and demonstrate their skill as leaders of physical activity.

Exercise physiologists work under the supervision of a doctor to administer medical tests to evaluate a person's fitness. They also develop, implement, and coordinate exercise programs. Often, they work with people who have physical problems, such as diabetes, obesity, or heart disease. Many also work with the general population to provide fitness evaluations and advice about physical activity and exercise.

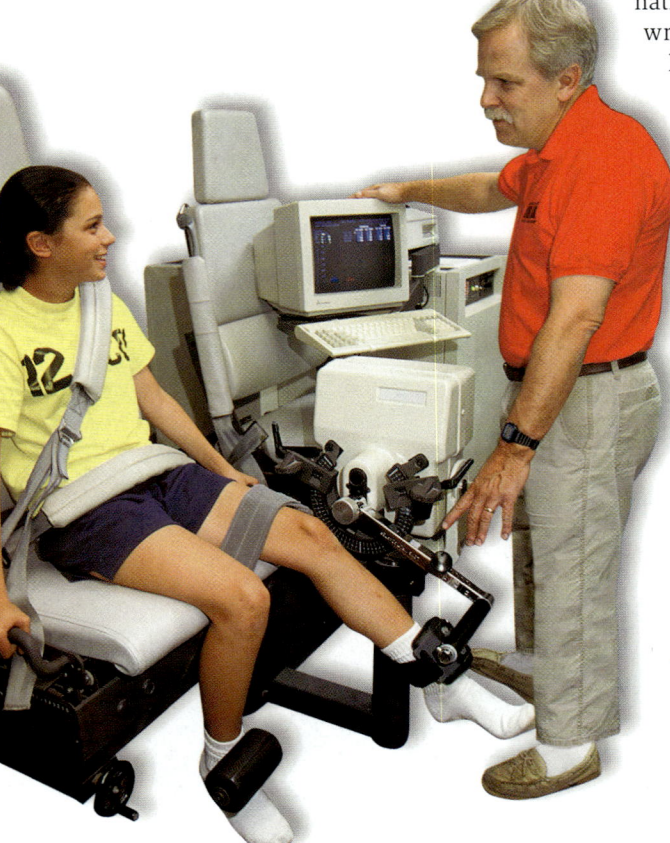

◄ Personal trainers, exercise physiologists, and athletic trainers are just a few of the health and fitness specialists who can advise you about your personal fitness.

More About . . .

SPACE FLIGHTS AND FITNESS During space flights, astronauts experience many physiological effects caused by the microgravity (weightless) environment, which results from the increased distance from earth and its gravitational pull. In the first three weeks of a space flight, astronauts may experience up to a 10-percent change in cardiovascular function, which reflects a deconditioning response. Within 14 days, a 10-percent change occurs in body fluid redistribution, contributing to high blood pressure. After three months, bone mass has declined by 5 percent and up to 15 percent after

Any Body Can

Dr. Sally Ride

When the Sky Is Not the Limit

Some people are willing to go far to achieve their goals. Astrophysicist and astronaut Sally Ride has indeed gone far, both scholastically and in physical miles. In 1983, she became the first American woman to go into space.

Sally Kristen Ride was born in Los Angeles, California, on May 26, 1951. She grew up dreaming of being a professional tennis player. She also developed a love for science. She attended Stanford University, where she eventually earned her doctorate in physics.

In 1978, Dr. Ride applied to become an astronaut with the National Aeronautics and Space Administration (NASA). She was one of 35 applicants selected out of a field of 8,000. She was selected partly on the basis of her ability to pass rigorous medical and physical tests. During her training, she mastered the extraordinarily high levels of fitness any person needs to travel in space.

After retiring from NASA, Dr. Ride returned to Stanford University as a professor. Currently she is director of the California Space Institute at the University of California at San Diego. She also continues to be physically active.

Not everyone can be a rocket scientist like Dr. Sally Ride. However, anyone can learn to optimize his or her functional health and fitness with age. Yes, Any Body Can!

Interview

What are other careers that demand high levels of health and fitness? Choose one such career. Interview a person in that field to find out more. Consider asking: What are the physical requirements of the job? How does one train for the tests? What do the physical tests and medical evaluations involve? Does the screening process involve any other types of testing?

Careers in Health and Fitness

Fitness-related professions include personal trainers, aerobic-dance instructors, and fitness specialists. All share a common interest in working with people, alone or in groups, whose goal is to achieve individual personal fitness. These professionals may or may not have formal academic or clinical training. Many organizations sponsor programs that provide professional health and fitness certification in these areas. Individuals must pass written and practical examinations.

✓ Reading Check

Extend Which health professional would you be most likely to see if you wanted to control your body composition? Explain.

five months. Loss of sufficient muscular strength is common and can exceed 25 percent after only 14 days in space. A variety of in-space exercises have been conducted and are still being studied. A typical program might include two daily one-hour ergometer cycling workouts, followed by 15 minutes of resistance exercises using bungee-cord devices. On missions that last over one month, passengers are expected to exercise twice daily for one hour on a passive (subject-driven) treadmill with a restraint system to simulate earth's gravitational pull.

✓ Reading Check

Physicians, registered dietitians, or exercise physiologists can help a person control his or her body composition.
TEKS C4H

Any Body Can

Dr. Sally Ride—When the Sky Is Not the Limit
The physical and medical standards for astronauts are very high. Each astronaut must meet minimum requirements. A complete medical history is obtained, followed by cardiovascular evaluations and tests of muscular strength and endurance, as well as psychological tests.

Discussing

The first American "Project Mercury" astronauts went through a number of grueling tests that have since been changed to better evaluate astronauts. A simple step test was given to determine physical fitness levels. A treadmill maximum workload was given for cardiovascular fitness. A cold foot plunge into ice was used to evaluate pulse and blood pressure. A 12-point reaction table was used to determine ability to process data. To measure reactions to heat stress, subjects were placed in a 130-degree chamber for three hours. **L1 TEKS C4E**

Student Edition TEKS

Page 373: C4H

3 ASSESS

EVALUATING THE LESSON

Assign and discuss the Lesson 3 Review.

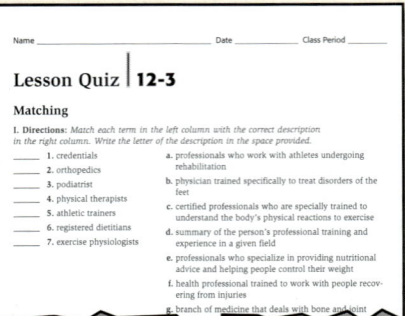

RETEACHING

Ask students to describe and discuss the roles of four fitness professionals.

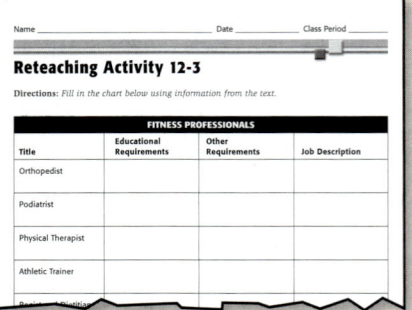

ENRICHMENT

Have students use the Personal Fitness Planning Activity to find professionals in their school and community.

4 CLOSE

Name specific responsibilities of fitness professionals and have the class identify which professionals you are describing.

374

▶ If you are interested in health and fitness, there are many careers you may want to consider. *What is required to become a high school physical educator?*

FITNESS Online

Learn more about careers in health and fitness by visiting **fitness.glencoe.com**.

Activity Visit the online Career Corner. Find careers under Fitness and Nutrition to determine what you can do to prepare for a career in fitness.

Health Educators and Physical Education Teachers

Do you enjoy sharing information with others? Are you interested in wellness, personal fitness, and possibly coaching? If so, a career in physical and/or health education might be right for you. Instructors in these areas must complete four to six years of college, earning degrees in health or physical education specialties. They are certified by the state to teach. The instructor for this class is most likely a health or physical educator or coach. He or she is a valuable resource when you are seeking personal fitness advice.

Lesson 3 Review

Using complete sentences, answer the following questions on a sheet of paper.

Reviewing Facts and Vocabulary

1. **Recall** What are two types of doctors who are likely to treat fitness-related problems?
2. **Vocabulary** Define *registered dietitian.*
3. **Vocabulary** Define *athletic trainer.*

Thinking Critically

4. **Compare and Contrast** Explain the differences between a physical therapist and an exercise physiologist.
5. **Synthesize** Imagine you felt a pain in the arch of your foot after playing basketball.

Which fitness professional would you most likely go to? Why would you select this person?

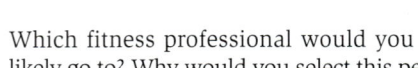

Identifying Fitness Professionals How available are fitness experts in your immediate community? Make a list of all the fitness experts in your school. Prepare another list for your local area. Lastly, identify types of fitness experts not available in your immediate area. Contact at least two people on your lists and ask about their credentials and certifications.

374 **Chapter 12** Personal Fitness Throughout Life

Lesson 3 Review

Answers to Lesson 3 Review

1. Orthopedic specialists and podiatrists.
2. Professionals who specialize in providing nutrition advice and helping people control their weight.
3. Professionals who work with athletes undergoing rehabilitation.
4. Physical therapists work primarily with people who are recovering from an injury or illness. Exercise physiologists evaluate a person's fitness and then develop and coordinate an exercise program.
5. Check with your coach or athletic trainer at school, or your family physician.

Choosing Fitness Products

There are a number of fitness products and facilities available for you to choose from. However, knowing whether a product is safe and effective can be a challenge. So can finding a gym or health club that will help you achieve your fitness goals.

In this lesson, you will learn how to evaluate fitness information related to fitness products and facilities. You will also learn questions to ask when choosing a health and fitness club.

Evaluating Health and Fitness Information

As consumers, we are bombarded by advertisements for health and fitness products. All carry claims that their product will make you fitter, look better, or feel better. While some of these claims are valid, many are false or misleading. The products that they sell are unsafe or ineffective. How can you separate fact from fiction when it comes to media ads, not to mention the countless fitness books and magazines that are available? Here are some guidelines that can help.

- Be suspicious of claims for quick and simple results.
- Beware of miracle breakthroughs that have not been reported by reputable sources.
- Beware of testimonials claiming great results with a product.
- When reading magazine articles or books, examine the writer's credentials. If no credentials are listed, there may be a good reason.
- Beware of mail-order sales or infomercials that promote products or services not endorsed by qualified health and fitness professionals.

In general, never spend money on a health or fitness product until you've had a chance to evaluate it. You'll practice your skills at doing just that in the "Active Mind—Active Body" activity on page **376**.

What You Will Do

- Analyze strategies for becoming a more informed fitness consumer.
- Evaluate consumer issues related to fitness, including health and fitness claims and services.
- Identify the characteristics of a reputable fitness center.

Terms to Know

commercial fitness centers
corporate fitness centers
sports medicine clinic centers

▼ When evaluating a fitness facility, it is a good idea to take notes on the equipment and features. This will enable you to compare options later.

LESSON 4 RESOURCES

Teacher Classroom Resources
- Guided Practice Activity 12-4
- Active Mind—Active Body Worksheet 12-4
- Reteaching Activity 12-4
- Lesson Quiz 12-4

Multimedia
- Vocabulary PuzzleMaker
- Transparency 64

Choosing Fitness Products

1 MOTIVATE

GETTING STARTED

- Before you begin roll call, ask the class to think about the following question: *What are some reasons someone might want to join a fitness facility and some reasons why someone might not want to join one?*
- Distribute copies of *Guided Practice Activity 12-4* for students to use while studying this lesson. 📁

IN THIS LESSON

- **Active Mind—Active Body** *Evaluating Health and Fitness Information, p. 376*

INTRODUCING VOCABULARY

- Place students in groups of two or three and have them develop a definition for *commercial fitness centers* and *corporate fitness centers*.
- Have students use *Vocabulary Worksheet 12* or the PuzzleMaker software to practice vocabulary terms for this lesson. **ELL** 📁 💿

Photo Follow-up

Ask how many students have visited fitness centers or commercial gyms in your area.

Student Edition TEKS
Page 375: C4H

2 TEACH

Activity

Once teens decide to start a physical activity program, they will need to determine whether they will work out at home, school, or a fitness facility. If they choose to join a facility, they will need to consider several factors before deciding which one is best for their needs. Have students work in groups to develop a list of factors to consider, adding to the list as they read this section. **L2**

TEKS C4H

Active Mind Active Body
Evaluating Health and Fitness Information

Have students work in groups to complete their evaluations.

Teaching Tips

- Distribute *Active Mind–Active Body Worksheet 12-4.*
- Discuss a health or fitness infomercial that students have seen on television. Ask them what it was about.
- Ask: How much did the product or service being promoted cost? Have students compare what types of experts were shown.

Apply and Conclude

Guide students in evaluating the validity of the advertisements they chose.

TEKS C4H

Health and Fitness Facilities

Many people choose health clubs and fitness facilities as a place to develop their personal fitness. As a teen, you will most likely need permission from your parents to join a fitness club. If you have access to a fitness facility, it can be a great place to focus on your fitness. You may not belong to any kind of club now, but you may decide to join one in the future. It is important to choose your fitness facility wisely.

Kinds of Facilities

The first thing you will need to know is that not all health and fitness facilities are alike. Despite some surface similarities, different clubs meet different needs. The services offered and the goals that members can realize also vary. **Figure 12.5** provides a listing of the types of health and fitness facilities described in the following sections. Advantages and disadvantages are also indicated.

Commercial Gyms. These health and fitness facilities are usually small in size and have relatively few members. These centers are geared toward the serious weight trainer or high-performance athlete. The exercise and activity opportunities may thus be limited.

Commercial Fitness Centers. These are *health and fitness facilities that offer a wide variety of resistance- and aerobic-training equipment.*

Active Mind Active Body
Evaluating Health and Fitness Information

This activity will give you and a small group of classmates some practice at evaluating claims for health and fitness products.

What You Will Need

- Pen or pencil
- Paper
- Recent newspapers
- Health and fitness magazines

What You Will Do

1. Each member of the group should select a different medium to investigate. One person should select TV, another magazines, another newspapers, and so on.
2. Look carefully through the examples of the medium you have chosen. Find advertisements for or articles on fitness products.
3. Carefully analyze the claims made in your source. To do this, apply the guidelines from page **375** of your textbook under the heading "Evaluating Health and Fitness Information."
4. Share your findings with your fellow group members.
5. Share these with the class in the form of a report or display (such as a bulletin board with clippings and critiques).

Apply and Conclude

Which of the claims analyzed turned out to be valid? What percentage of the total claims did this number represent? What did this activity teach you about the importance of evaluating health and fitness information?

Enrichment

Critical Assessment Have students locate an advertisement that promotes health and fitness. Then have them apply critical thinking skills to assess the truthfulness of the ad. Have volunteers show their advertisement, explain what product is being sold, tell the class whether they feel the advertisement is true or false, and explain the evidence on which they based their assessment. When the task is complete, advertisements can be placed on poster boards to create an advertising collage entitled "Fitness Fact or Fiction."

FIGURE 12.5

VARIOUS TYPES OF HEALTH AND FITNESS FACILITIES

Fitness facilities vary greatly. *What type of fitness facility would be the most convenient choice for you as a teen?*

Health and Fitness Facility	Advantages	Disadvantages
Commercial gym	Is good for high performance	Has limited facilities; members may be too serious for your needs
Commercial fitness center	Has a large variety of activities	May be expensive or too crowded
Commercial dance studio	Usually has certified instructors	Has a limited number of fitness activities
Hospital-based wellness center	Has medical supervision and highly trained personnel	Has a relatively higher cost
Corporate fitness center	Has a variety of recreational and fitness activities	Is limited to employees and family members
Community recreational center	Has a variety of recreational activities and is economical	May have limited health and fitness activities
College- or university-based fitness center	Has a wide variety of programs and trained personnel	To join, you must be associated with the school (student, faculty, or staff); it may be very expensive for others to join
Sports medicine clinic center	Has comprehensive programs and medical supervision; is research based	Is expensive

These centers cater to the general public. YMCAs and YWCAs are examples of facilities that are considered commercial fitness centers.

Commercial Dance Studios. As their name suggests, these are facilities targeted at individuals interested in aerobic dance and jazz forms of exercise. They usually have little in the way of exercise equipment, but offer a variety of dance and aerobic classes that develop cardiovascular fitness and flexibility.

Hospital-Based Wellness Centers. As strides are made in preventive medicine, some hospitals are adding wellness centers. These centers usually offer a variety of exercise and educational programs focusing on personal fitness. They primarily serve "special needs" individuals. These include people who require medical screening before beginning a fitness program and/or medical supervision during physical activity.

Corporate Fitness Centers. The cost of health care in this country has risen dramatically in recent years. Large corporations have borne

Lesson 4 Choosing Fitness Products **377**

QUOTES FOR LIFE

"You're not obligated to win. You're obligated to keep trying to do the best you can every day."

–Marian Wright Edelman
Educator, lawyer, activist (1939–)

USING VISUALS

Figure 12.5 Let students work in teams to discuss the advantages and disadvantages of the fitness facilities listed. *Caption answer: Students should identify areas that are convenient and cost-appropriate. The local community recreation center would be a great place to start.* TEKS C4H

Explaining

The list of health and fitness clubs or centers is designed to give students an overview of what they can expect. This industry is constantly changing to meet consumer needs. As health and fitness consumers become more knowledgeable, they will demand more service, flexibility, and convenience from their health and fitness clubs or centers. L1

Discussing

People who are shy or uncomfortable about exercising in public may find that public facilities are not for them. They may prefer the privacy of their own home. Advantages of home gyms include convenience, low cost, no waiting, and a personalized environment. For people who want to get out, however, discuss why a gym is a great place to meet people in a safe and highly motivated environment. L1

Student Edition TEKS
Page 376: C4H

Discussing

Point out to students that public facilities can offer a wide selection of machines that many people would not be able to afford at home. Boredom should not be a problem, since varying their exercises will keep students interested and motivated to stay on track with their fitness plan. Facilities often have added benefits such as swimming pools, saunas, and steam rooms to use at the end of a workout. **L1**

Guest Speaker

Have a manager or owner of a local facility attend your class to describe the facility and his or her job description. Encourage students to visit the local facility. **L3**

✓ Reading Check

Commercial gyms specialize in specific weight training or high-performance training. Commercial fitness centers are designed for developing general fitness.

Photo Follow-up

Caption answer: Answers will vary. Encourage students to discuss their strategies.

Activity

Direct students to evaluate consumer issues related to marketing claims promoting fitness services. Have students work in groups and contact local clubs to inquire about the cost of memberships and what they include. **L3** **TEKS C4H**

---

the burden of these expenses for their employees. Some have developed preventive strategies by featuring *on-site health and fitness facilities available to employees and their families.* At some larger companies, these corporate fitness centers rival local health clubs in the equipment and services offered.

College-Based Fitness Centers. Operated by state or private colleges and universities, these centers are available to students, faculty, and staff. Oftentimes, the centers are housed in the same campus building as the school's physical education department.

Sports Medicine Clinic Centers. Frequently associated with local universities and/or hospitals, sports medicine clinic centers are multipurpose facilities. They *focus on research promoting health and fitness, as well as on the development and operation of health, fitness, recreation, and educational programs.*

Community Recreational Centers. These health and fitness facilities are operated by city park and recreation departments. They offer a variety of recreational activities and programs to community members.

Reading Check

Explain Which fitness facilities are designed for specific types of exercises? Which are used for developing general fitness?

Choosing a Fitness Facility

Selecting a health and fitness club is a two-step process. First, you need to determine your fitness needs. Then you can explore facilities in your community that best meet those needs. It is also wise to visit several competing facilities to get an idea of what they offer. Here are some questions to ask yourself at each facility you visit:

Cost and Convenience.

- What are the prices? Does the club offer package deals or seasonal specials?
- Is it conveniently located?
- What time does it open and close? Is it open on holidays?
- Does it tend to be crowded at the time you plan to use it?
- Can you fit in and socialize easily with the other members?

Equipment and Facilities.

- Is the equipment well cared for and in top working condition?
- Does the facility have a variety of machines and free weights?
- Does the facility have a variety of aerobic conditioning activities (swimming, cycles, treadmills, stair-steppers, and so on)?
- Are aerobic-exercise classes offered?
- Are racquetball, basketball, or tennis courts available?
- Are there indoor and outdoor hiking and jogging tracks or trails?

INCLUSION STRATEGIES

ACCESSIBILITY The Americans with Disabilities Act (ADA) mandates accessibility to all facilities. Individuals with disabilities should be able to participate in the programs and activities of public facilities. When choosing a facility, keep in mind the following for students with disabilities: Does the facility have a pool that can be accessed by all? Can an individual in a wheelchair access the front door, elevators, bathrooms, showers, lockers, and equipment? Is there trained staff to help all abilities? As a class project, have students visit a local fitness facility and see how it measures up.

- Does the facility have a locker room? If so, are there towels and laundry service?
- Does it have enough showers, hot tubs, saunas, and steam rooms?
- Is there a system in place for evaluating your progress?
- Does the facility have computers to log or chart your progress?

Programs and Staff.

- Are the instructors or personal trainers certified and knowledgeable about resistance training?
- Are individual exercise programs available?
- Are educational programs available?

Safety and Cleanliness.

- Does the facility have a medical adviser for any special medical needs you have?
- Are the instructors certified in cardiopulmonary resuscitation (CPR) and first aid?
- Is the exercise area uncluttered and well monitored for safety?
- Is it clean and well maintained?

⚠️ If you join a health and fitness center or club, find one that meets your specific needs. *What are some strategies for achieving this goal?*

Lesson 4 Review

Using complete sentences, answer the following questions on a sheet of paper.

Reviewing Facts and Vocabulary

1. Vocabulary What is a *commercial fitness center?*

2. Recall What is the reason why corporate fitness centers have begun to appear?

Thinking Critically

3. Explain In what way do hospital-based wellness centers and corporate fitness centers share a similar outlook?

4. Evaluate Which of the questions used in choosing a fitness facility would be the most important to you? The least important? Why?

Personal Fitness Planning

Investigating Facilities Prepare a list of questions that may be used to survey the fitness facilities in your community. Use the questions suggested in this lesson to help you prepare your survey. Contact the fitness facilities in your community and see how they compare. Which one best meets your needs at present?

Lesson 4 Review

Answers to Lesson 4 Review

1. Health and fitness facilities that offer a wide variety of resistance- and aerobic-training equipment.
2. They provide their employees with on-site health and fitness facilities.
3. They both focus on strategies for preventive medicine.
4. Answers will vary and may include any of those listed under cost and convenience, equipment and facilities, programs and staff, or safety and cleanliness.

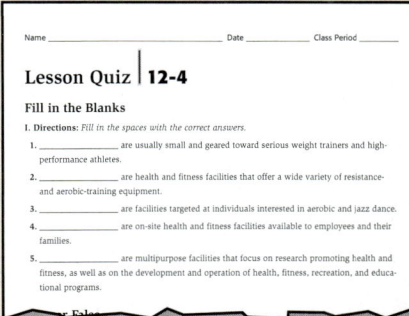
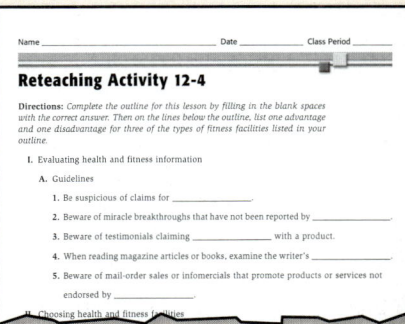
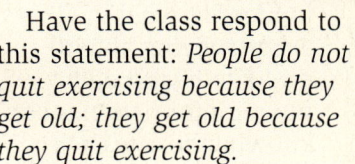

CHECKING COMPREHENSION

- Assign and discuss the chapter review.
- Use the PuzzleMaker CD-ROM to review vocabulary. 💿

CHAPTER 12 REVIEW ANSWERS

True/False

1. True	6. True
2. False	7. False
3. False	8. False
4. False	9. False
5. True	10. True

Multiple Choice

11. b	16. c
12. a	17. c
13. b	18. c
14. a	19. d
15. b	20. a

Discussion

21. Various mental and physical functions change with the aging process. Hair color can turn gray, bones become brittle, the conduction of nerve impulses slows, the resting metabolic rate decreases, reaction time slows, and so on. By living a physically active lifestyle and eating a healthy diet, you can prevent or slow some of these declines.

22. You can become a wiser health and fitness consumer by learning how to identify reliable fitness experts, being able to evaluate health and fitness information, and knowing how to pick and choose a reputable fitness facility.

TRUE/FALSE

On a sheet of paper, write the numbers 1–10. Write True or False for each statement.

1. You can have a positive impact on your risk for chronic diseases.
2. Your resting metabolic rate does not decrease with age.
3. Developing positive attitudes and behaviors while you age may speed up the aging process.
4. Leisure-time activities will not help you reduce your stress levels.
5. Rock climbing requires high levels of muscular strength and endurance.
6. Volleyball is a leisure-time activity that helps develop coordination.
7. Podiatrists are physicians who specialize in disorders of the heart and lungs.
8. Physicians do not require a state license to practice medicine.
9. Testimonials that a product yielded great results are usually proof that a fitness product claim is valid.
10. Not all health and fitness facilities are alike.

MULTIPLE CHOICE

On a sheet of paper, write the letter of the word or phrase that best completes each statement.

11. From ages 30 to 90, a person's lung capacity is likely to decrease by approximately
    a. 10 percent.   c. 40 percent.
    b. 25 percent.   d. 60 percent.
12. Of the following changes associated with aging, the one that can be controlled by being physically active and eating healthfully is
    a. increased body fat.   c. inherited diseases.
    b. graying of hair.   d. balding.
13. The statement that does NOT usually occur in people who remain sedentary as they age is:
    a. They get depressed.
    b. They maintain functional health.
    c. They lose self-esteem.
    d. They lose bone mass.

Vocabulary

23. a	26. c
24. e	27. f
25. b	28. d

Critical Thinking

29. Answers will vary but should include any of the activities from this chapter.

14. The top of the Physical Activity Pyramid consists of activities that you should
    a. cut down on.
    b. do 2 to 3 times a week.
    c. do every day.
    d. none of the above.
15. Leisure-time activities do all of the following EXCEPT
    a. provide an opportunity for social interaction.
    b. guarantee improvements in health-related or skill-related fitness.
    c. provide a source of recreation.
    d. burn calories.
16. Mountain biking should be done with all of the following EXCEPT
    a. a bike with a heavy frame.
    b. a bike with wide tires that provide better traction.
    c. a light-framed bike.
    d. a safety helmet.
17. Physical therapists primarily work with
    a. athletes.
    b. people who need to control their weight.
    c. people recovering from injuries.
    d. none of the above.
18. Podiatrists work with
    a. people who need to control their weight.
    b. people recovering from injuries.
    c. people with foot problems.
    d. none of the above.
19. When evaluating claims for fitness products you should be suspicious of all of the following EXCEPT
    a. claims of quick and simple results.
    b. miracle breakthroughs that have not been reported by reputable sources.
    c. mail-order sales or infomercials.
    d. writers of articles who have credentials.
20. All of the following are true of hospital-based wellness centers EXCEPT that they
    a. cater to patients recovering from serious injuries.
    b. are designed for people who require medical screening before beginning a fitness program.
    c. can be used by people who require medical supervision during physical activity.
    d. offer a variety of exercise and educational programs focusing on personal fitness.

DISCUSSION

Using complete sentences, answer the following questions on a sheet of paper.

21. **Identify** List the mental and physical functions that change with the aging process. Describe how you can control to some degree the rate at which these functions change.
22. **Describe** Explain how you can be a wiser health and fitness consumer.

VOCABULARY

On a sheet of paper, write the letter of the term in Column B that best fits the definition in Column A.

Column A

23. Professionals who specialize in providing nutritional advice and helping people control their weight.
24. Professionals specially trained to understand the body's physical reactions to exercise.
25. Sports and other action-oriented pursuits done for recreation.
26. Activities that combine exercise and relaxation techniques.
27. On-site health and fitness facilities available to employees and their families.
28. A branch of medicine that deals with bone and joint injuries and disorders.

Column B

a. registered dietitian
b. leisure-time activities
c. martial arts
d. orthopedics
e. exercise physiologists
f. corporate fitness centers

CRITICAL THINKING

Using complete sentences, answer the following questions on a sheet of paper.

29. **Identify** Develop a list of lifetime activities that you do now or would like to do now or in the future. Then explain why you enjoy these activities and how they can help you develop and maintain your personal fitness levels.

30. **Synthesize** React to this statement: Education can make you a better health and fitness consumer and can prevent you from being the victim of rip-offs.

CASE STUDY

MOLLY'S PROBLEM

Molly has just returned from a visit with her aunt, who is recovering from knee surgery. During their conversations, Molly's aunt talked about her concerns with getting older. She explained to Molly how she had begun to notice being out of breath while going up stairs and that she wanted to lose some weight. She further shared her concerns about fully recovering from her surgery.

HERE IS YOUR ASSIGNMENT:

Assume that you are Molly and you want to share with your aunt what you have learned about exercise and the aging process. Organize a list of benefits associated with exercise and nutrition and their relationship to the aging process. You should specifically address your aunt's concerns about her surgery and her desire to lose weight. Suggest specific professionals she should see.

KEYS TO HELP YOU

- Consider your aunt's current medical status.
- Consider your aunt's current fitness status and knowledge of fitness.
- Consider your aunt's needs and desires.
- Consider which fitness experts would be best for your aunt's fitness needs.
- Consider the types of fitness facilities that would be best for your aunt's fitness needs.

30. Answers will vary but might include: Evaluate any products before you buy them. Learn all you can about any products and services before you make a decision to buy or use them. The knowledge you gain can help you make the right decision.

EVALUATE

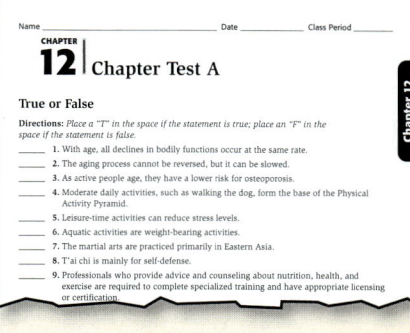

ENRICHMENT

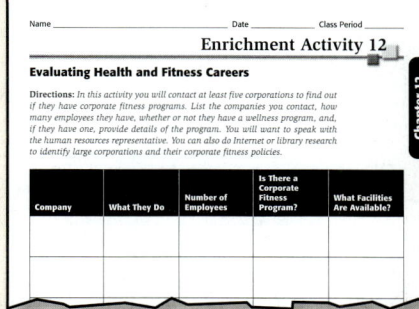

CASE STUDY

ANSWERS

Answers will vary but might include: Point out to your aunt that regular exercise and activity can lead to a healthier cardiovascular system, improved resting metabolism, weight control, decreased blood pressure, flexible joints and muscles, prevention of osteoporosis, and good mental health. She should see a physical therapist about an exercise program to ensure complete recovery. After recovering, she should find activities that she enjoys and begin a regular exercise program and good nutrition plan.

Student Edition TEKS

Page 379: C4H
Page 381: C4A, C5D

Contents

National Association for Sport and Physical Education (NASPE)

PHYSICAL EDUCATION STANDARDS

NASPE Content Standards for Grades K-12	A physically educated student:
Content Standard 1	Demonstrates competency in motor skills and movement patterns needed to perform a variety of physical activities.
Content Standard 2	Demonstrates understanding of movement concepts, principles, strategies, and tactics as they apply to the learning and performance of physical activities.
Content Standard 3	Participates regularly in physical activity.
Content Standard 4	Achieves and maintains a health-enhancing level of physical fitness.
Content Standard 5	Exhibits responsible personal and social behavior that respects self and others in physical activity settings.
Content Standard 6	Values physical activity for health, enjoyment, challenge, self-expression and/or social interaction.

Source: National Association for Sport and Physical Education Outcomes Committee Task Force, 2004.

Healthy People 2010

Healthy People 2010 is a set of 28 health objectives established for the nation to achieve over the first decade of the new century. The objectives, listed on these pages, were created after the Surgeon General's Report in 2000 identified specific National Health Promotion and Disease Prevention goals. The chapters in *Foundations of Personal Fitness* provide strategies for addressing many of these objectives.

1 **Access to Quality Health Services** Improve access to comprehensive, high-quality health care services.

2 **Arthritis, Osteoporosis, and Chronic Back Conditions** Prevent illness and disability related to arthritis and other rheumatic conditions, osteoporosis, and chronic back conditions.

3 **Cancer** Reduce the number of new cancer cases as well as the illness, disability, and death caused by cancer.

4 **Chronic Kidney Disease** Reduce new cases of chronic kidney disease and its complications, disability, death, and economic costs.

5 **Diabetes** Through prevention programs, reduce the disease and economic burden of diabetes, and improve the quality of life for all persons who have or are at risk for diabetes.

6 **Disability and Secondary Conditions** Promote the health of people with disabilities, prevent secondary conditions, and eliminate disparities between people with and without disabilities in the U.S. population.

7 **Educational and Community-Based Programs** Increase the quality, availability, and effectiveness of educational and community-based programs designed to prevent disease and improve health and quality of life.

8 **Environmental Health** Promote health for all through a healthy environment.

9 **Family Planning** Includes preventing unintended pregnancy.

10 **Food Safety** Reduce foodborne illnesses.

11 **Health Communication** Use communication strategically to improve health.

12 **Heart Disease and Stroke** Improve cardiovascular health and quality of life through the prevention, detection, and treatment of risk factors; early identification and treatment of heart attacks and strokes; and prevention of recurrent cardiovascular events.

13 **HIV** Prevent human immunodeficiency virus (HIV) infection and its related illness and death.

14 **Immunization and Infectious Diseases** Prevent disease, disability, and death from infectious diseases, including vaccine-preventable diseases.

15 **Injury and Violence Prevention** Reduce injuries, disabilities, and deaths due to unintentional injuries and violence.

16 **Maternal, Infant, and Child Health** Improve the health and well-being of women, infants, children, and families.

17 **Medical Product Safety** Ensure the safe and effective use of medical products.

18 **Mental Health and Mental Disorders** Improve mental health and ensure access to appropriate, quality mental health services.

19 **Nutrition and Overweight** Promote health and reduce chronic disease associated with diet and weight.

20 **Occupational Safety and Health** Promote the health and safety of people at work through prevention and early intervention.

21 **Oral Health** Prevent and control oral and craniofacial diseases, conditions, and injuries and improve access to related services.

22 **Physical Activity and Fitness** Improve health, fitness, and quality of life through daily physical activity.

23 **Public Health Infrastructure** Ensure that Federal, Tribal, State, and local health agencies have the infrastructure to provide essential public health services effectively.

24 **Respiratory Diseases** Promote respiratory health through better prevention, detection, treatment, and education efforts.

25 **Sexually Transmitted Diseases** Promote responsible sexual behaviors, strengthen community capacity, and increase access to quality services to prevent sexually transmitted diseases (STDs) and their complications.

26 **Substance Abuse** Reduce substance abuse to protect the health, safety, and quality of life for all, especially children.

27 **Tobacco** Reduce illness, disability, and death related to tobacco use and exposure to secondhand smoke.

28 **Vision and Hearing** Improve the visual and hearing health of the Nation through prevention, early detection, treatment, and rehabilitation.

The President's Challenge

Regular physical activity substantially reduces the risk of poor health. Physical activity need not be strenuous or very time-consuming to be beneficial, and all ages can benefit from modest physical activity. Every little bit of effort counts.

- **Adults, get at least 30 minutes of physical activity each day.** If it is too hard to set aside 30 minutes at one time, break it up into 10 or 15 minute segments. Developed by a panel of scientists under the leadership of the Department of Agriculture (USDA) and the Department of Health and Human Services (HHS) as a part of the *2000 Dietary Guidelines for Americans*, these recommendations for daily activity are based on the results of studies that examined the relationship between physical activity and health. If only 10 percent of American adults began regularly walking, $5.6 billion in health care costs associated with heart disease could be saved.

- **Children and teenagers, get at least 60 minutes of physical activity each day.** For children, setting aside time for physical activity should be easy. Unfortunately, even children have busy schedules today. According to the *Dietary Guidelines for Americans*, they can break activity up into segments. Regular activity for children is important. Normal childhood play or outdoor activity helps control blood pressure and manages weight while building and maintaining healthy bones, muscles, and joints.

- **Parents, commit to family activities that involve physical activity.** It can be easier to work physical activity into your daily routine if you combine it with family time.

PHYSICAL ACTIVITY AND FITNESS GUIDELINES

The Surgeon General's Report on Physical Activity and Health, along with the President's Council on Physical Fitness and Sports, identified fitness as a major public health concern. The Physical Fitness Objectives from *Healthy People 2010* for children and adolescents appear below.

Physical Activity in Children and Adolescents

- Increase the proportion of adolescents who engage in moderate physical activity for at least 30 minutes on 5 or more of the previous 7 days.

- Increase the proportion of adolescents who engage in vigorous physical activity that promotes cardiorespiratory fitness 3 or more days per week for 20 or more minutes per occasion.

- Increase the proportion of the Nation's public and private schools that require daily physical education for all students.
- Increase the proportion of adolescents who participate in daily school physical education.

- Increase the proportion of adolescents who spend at least 50 percent of school physical education class time being physically active.
- Increase the proportion of adolescents who view television 2 or fewer hours on a school day.

PHYSICAL FITNESS GUIDELINES

Regular physical activity performed on a daily basis reduces the risk of developing illness or disease. Moderate physical activity can be achieved in a variety of ways, and the Centers for Disease Control and Prevention (CDC) have developed this list of examples showing moderate amounts of activity that can contribute to an individual's health.

Physical Activities Arranged by Energy Level and Time

- Washing and waxing a car for 45–60 minutes
- Washing windows or floors for 45–60 minutes
- Playing volleyball for 45 minutes
- Playing touch football for 30–45 minutes
- Gardening for 30–45 minutes
- Wheeling self in wheelchair for 30–40 minutes
- Walking $1\frac{3}{4}$ miles in 35 minutes (20 min/mile)
- Basketball (shooting baskets) for 30 minutes
- Bicycling 5 miles in 30 minutes
- Dancing fast (social) for 30 minutes

- Pushing a stroller $1\frac{1}{2}$ miles in 30 minutes
- Raking leaves for 30 minutes
- Walking 2 miles in 30 minutes (15 min/mile)
- Water aerobics for 30 minutes
- Swimming laps for 20 minutes
- Wheelchair basketball for 20 minutes
- Basketball (playing a game) for 15–20 minutes
- Bicycling 4 miles in 15 minutes
- Jumping rope for 15 minutes
- Running $1\frac{1}{2}$ miles in 15 minutes (10 min/mile)
- Shoveling snow for 15 minutes
- Stair walking for 15 minutes

Source: CDC, Physical Activity and Health, A Report of the Surgeon General, 1999.

Obesity and Diabetes in the United States

More than one-third of students in grades 9–12 do not regularly engage in vigorous physical activity. Daily participation in high school physical education classes dropped from 42 percent in 1991 to 29 percent in 1999. The prevalence of obesity and diabetes among adults in the U.S. has increased significantly in the past decade, as shown in the maps below. The CDC reports that regular physical activity, healthy eating, and creating an environment that supports these behaviors are essential to reducing this epidemic of obesity and diabetes. A commitment to lifelong physical activity and fitness can help reduce these trends.

Percentage of Obese Adults: 1995 and 2001

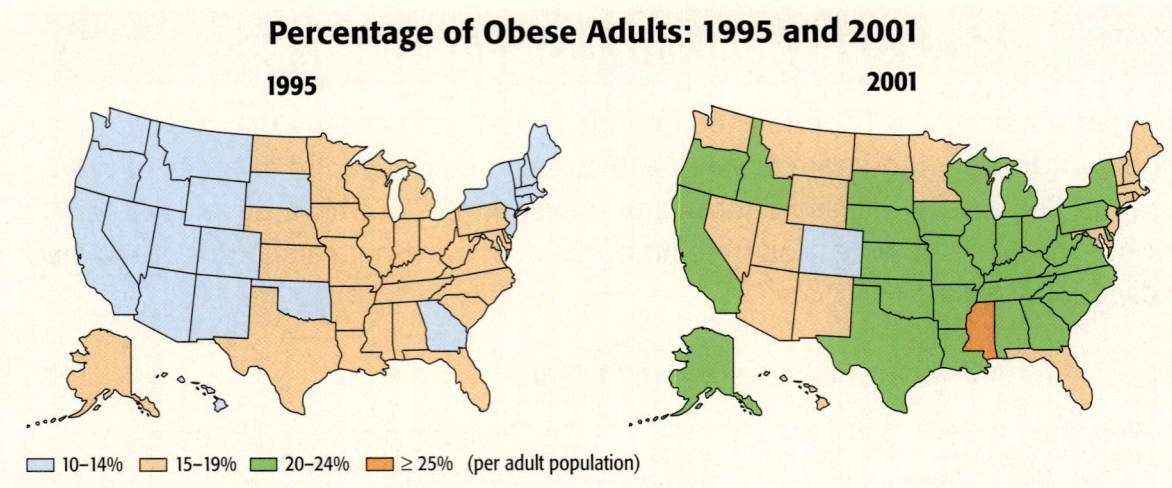

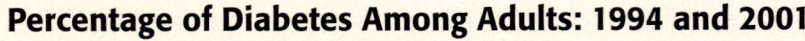

Percentage of Diabetes Among Adults: 1994 and 2001

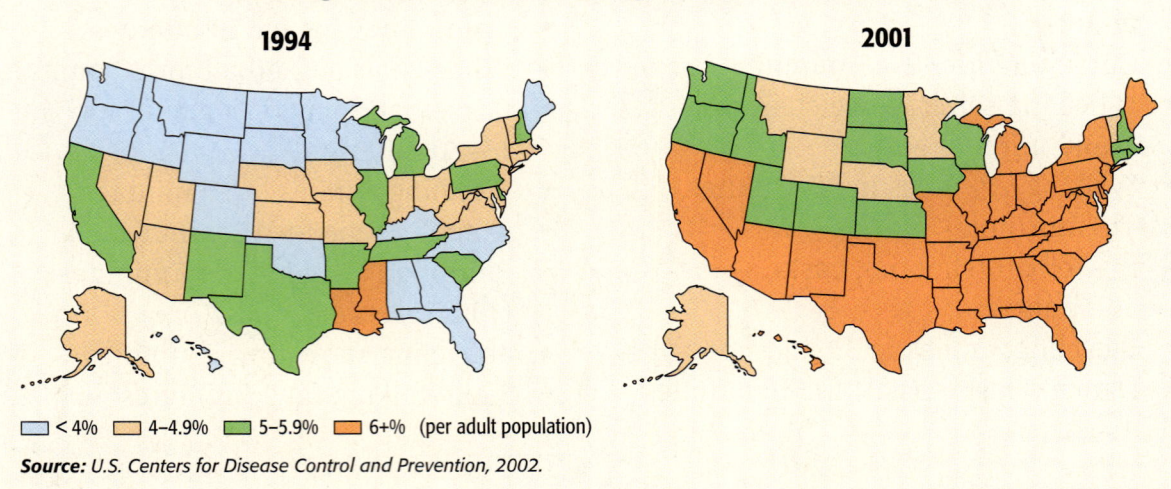

Source: U.S. Centers for Disease Control and Prevention, 2002.

Endnotes

Chapter 1

1. Centers for Disease Control and Prevention, Division of Nutrition and Physical Activity. "A Report of the Surgeon General, At-A-Glance, 1996." 14 Aug. 2003 < http://www.cdc.gov >
2. Adapted from U.S. Department of Health and Human Services; Centers for Disease Control and Prevention, National Center for Chronic Disease Prevention and Health Promotion, Division of Nutrition and Physical Activity. *Promoting Physical Activity: A Guide for Community Action.* Champaign, IL: Human Kinetics, 1999.
3. Reprinted with permission from Sizer, F.S., Whitney, E.N., Debuyne, L.K. *Health: Making Life Choices.* Lincolnwood: National Textbook Company, 2000. 236. Activity adapted from Russell Pate (University of South Carolina, Department of Exercise Science).

Chapter 2

1. U.S. Department of Health and Human Services. "The Surgeon General's Call to Action to Prevent and Decrease Overweight and Obesity." Rockville, MD, 2001.
2. Health Canada Online. "Canada's Physical Activity Guide to Healthy Active Living, Health Canada, 2002"©. Reproduced with permission of the Minister of Public Works and Government Services Canada, 2003. 14 Aug. 2003 < http://www.hc-sc.gc.ca >
3. Healthlink. Medical College of Wisconsin, 2001. 14 Aug. 2003 < http://healthlink.mcw.edu >
4. U.S. Consumer Product Safety Commission, 1999. 14 Aug. 2003 < http://www.cpsc.gov >
5. Modified from the *National Healthy People 2010 Objectives* as measured by the *National Youth Risk Behavior Survey,* 2001.

Chapter 3

1. Borg, Gunnar. *Borg's Perceived Exertion and Pain Scales.* Champaign, IL: Human Kinetics, 1998. 47.

Chapter 4

1. U.S. Department of Agriculture. "Dietary Guidelines for Americans, 2002." 14 Aug. 2003 < http://www.nal.usda.gov >
2. Jennings, D.S. and Steen, S.N. *Play Hard, Eat Right: A Parent's Guide to Sports Nutrition for Children.* New Jersey: John Wiley & Sons, ©1998. Reprinted by permission of John Wiley & Sons, Inc.
3. Jennings, D.S. and Steen, S.N. *Play Hard, Eat Right: A Parent's Guide to Sports Nutrition for Children.* New Jersey: John Wiley & Sons, ©1998. Reprinted by permission of John Wiley & Sons, Inc.
4. Jennings, D.S. and Steen, S.N. *Play Hard, Eat Right: A Parent's Guide to Sports Nutrition for Children.* New Jersey: John Wiley & Sons, ©1998. Reprinted by permission of John Wiley & Sons, Inc.

Chapter 5

1. Adapted from Jackson, A.S. and Ross, R.M. *Understanding Exercise for Health and Disease, 3rd Edition.* Dubuque, Iowa: Kendall Hunt Publishers, 1997.
2. McArdle, William D., Katch, Frank I., Katch, Victor L. *Exercise Physiology: Energy, Nutrition, and Human Performance, 5th Edition.* Philadelphia, PA: Lippincott Williams & Wilkins Publishers, 2001.
3. Town, G.P. and Wheeler, K.B. "Nutrition Concerns for the Endurance Athlete." *Dietetic Currents* 13 (1986): 7–12.

Chapter 6

1. Centers for Disease Control and Prevention, National Center for Health Statistics. "Prevalence of Overweight and Obesity Among Children and Adolescents: United States, 1999-2000." 16 Jul. 2003 < http://www.cdc.gov >
2. U.S. Department of Health and Human Services. "The Surgeon General's Call to Action to Prevent and Decrease Overweight and Obesity." Rockville, MD, 2001.

Chapter 7

1. American Heart Association, *Heart Disease and Stroke Statistics – 2003 Update.* Dallas, TX: American Heart Association, 2002.
2. Centers for Disease Control and Prevention, Tobacco Information and Prevention Source (TIPS), "Comparative Causes of Annual Deaths in the United States, 2003." 14 Aug. 2003 < http://www.cdc.gov >
3. Borg, Gunnar. *Borg's Perceived Exertion and Pain Scales.* Champaign, IL: Human Kinetics, 1998. 47.

Chapter 8

1. Walker, J.L., Murray, T.D., Jackson, A.S., Morrow, J.R., Michaud, T.D., Rainey, D.L. "The Energy Cost of Horizontal Walking and Running in Adolescents." *Medicine and Science in Sports and Exercise,* 31:2 (1999): 311–322.
2. Blair, S.N. and Brodney, S. "Effects of Physical Inactivity and Obesity on Morbidity and Mortality: Current Evidence and Research Issues." *Medicine and Science in Sports and Exercise,* 33:11 (1999): 646–662.
3. Cooper, Kenneth H. *The Aerobics Program for Total Well-Being.* ©1982 by Kenneth H. Cooper. Used by permission of Bantam Books, a division of Random House Inc.
4. Blair, S.N. and Brodney, S. "Effects of Physical Inactivity and Obesity on Morbidity and Mortality: Current Evidence and Research Issues." *Medicine and Science in Sports and Exercise,* 33:11 (1999): 646–662.
5. Blair, S.N. and Brodney, S. "Effects of Physical Inactivity and Obesity on Morbidity and Mortality: Current Evidence and Research Issues." *Medicine and Science in Sports and Exercise,* 33:11 (1999): 646–662.

Chapter 9

1. National Osteoporosis Foundation. "Disease Statistics: 'Fast Facts'." Updated 2003. 14 Aug. 2003 < http://www.nof.org >

Chapter 11

1. President's Council on Physical Fitness and Sports, "Questionable Exercises." *President's Council on Physical Fitness and Sports, Research Digest,* 3: 8 (1999). 14 Aug. 2003 < http://www.fitness.gov >

Chapter 12

1. Reprinted with permission from Sizer, F.S., Whitney, E.N., Debuyne, L.K. *Health: Making Life Choices.* Lincolnwood: National Textbook Company, 2000. 630.
2. Adapted with permission from Kemper and Niemeyer. "The Importance of a Physically Active Lifestyle during Youth for Peak Bone Mass." *New Horizons in Pediatric Exercise Science,* ed. C. Blimkie and B. Oded. Champaign, IL: Human Kinetics, 1995.

Chapter 5 (continued — from earlier column)

4. McArdle, William D., Katch, Frank I., Katch, Victor L. *Exercise Physiology: Energy, Nutrition, and Human Performance, 5th Edition.* Philadelphia, PA: Lippincott Williams & Wilkins Publishers, 2001.

Glossary

A

Absolute muscular strength The maximum force an individual is able to exert regardless of size, age, or weight (Ch. 9, p. 247)

Acclimatization The process of allowing the body to adapt slowly to weather conditions (Ch. 2, p. 42)

Active warm-up Exercises that raise body temperature by actively working the body systems centering on the muscles, skeleton, heart, and lungs (Ch. 3, p. 103)

Addiction Physical and mental dependence on a substance or activity (Ch. 2, p. 63)

Adductor muscles The muscles on the inside of the leg that pull the legs together (Ch. 11, p. 348)

Adherence The ability to stick to a plan of action (Ch. 1, p. 21)

Adipose tissue Body fat (Ch. 4, p. 117)

Aerobic activity Continuous activity that requires large amounts of oxygen (Ch. 7, p. 193)

Agility The ability to change and control the direction and position of the body while maintaining a constant, rapid motion (Ch. 3, p. 75)

Aging process The manner in which the body changes as a natural result of growing older (Ch. 12, p. 357)

Alternated grip A position in which a barbell is grasped with one palm facing downward and the other palm facing upward (Ch. 10, p. 277)

Amino acids The building blocks of proteins (Ch. 4, p. 118)

Anabolic steroids Chemicals similar in structure to the male hormone testosterone (Ch. 2, p. 66)

Anaerobic fitness High levels of muscular strength, muscular endurance, and flexibility (Ch. 7, p. 212)

Anaerobic activity Activity that requires high levels of energy and is done for only a few seconds or minutes at a high level of intensity (Ch. 7, p. 212)

Androstenedione A chemical agent that aids the body in its production of testosterone (Ch. 4, p. 143)

Anorexia nervosa An eating disorder in which a person abnormally restricts his or her calorie intake (Ch. 6, p. 177)

Antioxidants Substances that protect body cells, including those of the immune system, from damage (Ch. 4, p. 124)

Arteries Blood vessels that carry blood from the heart to the major extremities of the body (Ch. 7, p. 194)

Asthma A disease in which the small airways of the lungs become narrowed, making it difficult to breathe (Ch. 2, p. 36)

Atherosclerosis A condition in which a fatty deposit called plaque builds up inside arteries, restricting or cutting off blood flow (Ch. 7, p. 36)

Athletic trainers Professionals who work with athletes undergoing rehabilitation (Ch. 12, p. 371)

Attitude An individual's mindset or outlook toward a given topic or subject (Ch. 1, p. 18)

B

Balance The ability to control or stabilize the body while standing or moving (Ch. 3, p. 75)

Ballistic stretching Quick up-and-down movements in which stretches are held very briefly (Ch. 11, p. 342)

Behavioral-change stairway A step-by-step approach to setting and achieving fitness goals (Ch. 1, p. 26)

Bigorexia A disorder in which an individual falsely believes he or she is underweight or undersized (Ch. 6, p. 178)

Binge eating disorder An eating disorder where individuals eat more rapidly than normal until they cannot eat any more (Ch. 6, p. 178)

Biomechanics The study and application of the principles of physics to human motion (Ch. 2, p. 54)

Blood pooling A condition in which blood collects in the large veins of the legs and lower body (Ch. 3, p. 108)

Blood pressure The force of the blood in the main arteries (Ch. 7, p. 206)

Body composition The ratio of body fat to lean body tissue, including muscle, bone, water, and connective tissue (Ch. 5, p. 150)

Body image The way an individual sees his or her body (Ch. 6, p. 176)

Body mass index (BMI) A way to assess body size in relation to height and weight (Ch. 5, p. 149)

Bulimia nervosa An eating disorder in which people overeat and then force themselves to purge the food afterward (Ch. 6, p. 177)

C

Calipers A tweezer-like device used to pinch a fold of skin surrounding adipose tissue (Ch. 5, p. 161)

Calisthenic exercises Exercises that create resistance by using one's own body weight (Ch. 9, p. 266)

Calorie The amount of energy needed to raise the temperature of 1 kilogram (about a quart) of water 1 degree Celsius (Ch. 4, p. 115)

Calorie expenditure The total number of calories an individual burns or expends (Ch. 5, p. 154)

Calorie intake The total number of calories an individual takes in from food (Ch. 5, p. 154)

Capillaries Small blood vessels that deliver oxygen and other nutrients to individual cells (Ch. 7, p. 194)

Carbohydrates The starches and sugars found in food (Ch. 4, p. 115)

Cardiac muscle A special type of striated tissue that forms the walls of the heart (Ch. 9, p. 250)

Cardiorespiratory endurance The ability of the body to work continuously for extended periods of time (Ch. 7, p. 198)

Cardiovascular conditioning Exercises or activities that improve the efficiency of the heart, lungs, blood, and blood vessels (Ch. 3, p. 84)

Cardiovascular cooldown Moving about slowly and continuously for three to five minutes following physical activity or exercise (Ch. 3, p. 109)

Cardiovascular disease (CVD) A medical disorder that affects the heart or blood vessels (Ch. 7, p. 200)

Cartilage Tissue that surrounds the ends of bones at a joint to prevent the bones from rubbing against each other (Ch. 2, p. 57)

Cholesterol A fatlike substance that is produced in the liver and circulates in the blood (Ch. 4, p. 120)

Chronic disease A disease that is ongoing (Ch. 2, p. 36)

Circuit training An approach to resistance training that involves rotating from one exercise to the next in a particular sequence (Ch. 10, p. 298)

Circulatory system Consists of the heart, blood, and blood vessels (Ch. 7, p. 194)

Clips Clamp-like devices on a barbell that secure the weights in place (Ch. 10, p. 275)

Commercial fitness centers Health and fitness facilities that offer access to a wide variety of resistance- and aerobic-training equipment for a fee (Ch. 12, p. 376)

Commitment A pledge or promise (Ch. 1, p. 20)

Compound sets Alternate sets of exercises without rest between sets (Ch. 10, p. 320)

Conflicts Struggles or disagreements (Ch. 1, p. 7)

Contraction The shortening of a muscle (Ch. 9, p. 252)

Cooper's 1.5-mile run test A test that requires jogging or running 1.5 miles in as little time as possible (Ch. 8, p. 219)

Coordination The ability to use the senses to determine and direct the movement of your limbs and head (Ch. 3, p. 75)

Core stability The stretching and strengthening of muscles around the spine and pelvic muscles (Ch. 11, p. 338)

Corporate fitness centers On-site health and fitness facilities available to employees and their families (Ch. 12, p. 378)

Creatine A supplement that increases muscle size while enhancing the body's ability to use protein (Ch. 4, p. 143)

Credentials A summary of the person's professional training and experience in a given field (Ch. 12, p. 370)

Cross-contamination The spreading of bacteria or other pathogens from one food to another (Ch. 4, p. 136)

Cross-training Varying exercise or activity routine or type (Ch. 3, p. 98)

Culture The shared customs, traditions, and beliefs of a particular group (Ch. 4, p. 114)

D

Deconditioned Having been out of training for a significant period after achieving at least a moderate level of fitness (Ch. 8, p. 234)

Dehydration Body fluid loss (Ch. 2, p. 41)

Detraining The loss of functional fitness that occurs when one stops fitness conditioning (Ch. 3, p. 98)

Diaphragm A muscle found between the chest cavity and abdomen (Ch. 7, p. 194)

Dietary fiber A special subclass of complex carbohydrates that has several functions, including aiding the body in digestion (Ch. 4, p. 117)

Dietary Reference Intakes (DRI) Daily nutrient recommendations for healthy people of both genders and different age groups (Ch. 4, p. 130)

Dietary supplement A nonfood form of one or more nutrients (Ch. 4, p. 128)

Dynamic contraction A type of muscle contraction that occurs when the resistance force is movable (Ch. 9, p. 252)

Dynamic posture The posture of the body while in motion or preparing to move (Ch. 11, p. 331)

E

Eating disorders Psychological illnesses that cause people to undereat, overeat, or practice other dangerous nutrition-related behaviors (Ch. 6, p. 176)

Ectomorph A body type characterized by a low percentage of body fat, small bone size, and a small amount of muscle mass and size (Ch. 5, p. 147)

Elasticity The ability of the muscles and connective tissues to stretch and give (Ch. 11, p. 326)

Elliptical motion trainer An exercise machine that simulates the natural motions of running but without placing stress on the joints (Ch. 8, p. 227)

Emphysema A disease in which the small airways of the lungs lose their normal elasticity, making them less efficient in helping to move air in and out of the lungs (Ch. 7, p. 204)

Endomorph A body type characterized by a high percentage of body fat, large bone size, and a small amount of muscle mass and size (Ch. 5, p. 147)

Energy cost The amount of energy needed to perform physical activities or exercises (Ch. 3, p. 73)

Ephedrine A compound that increases the rate at which the body converts calories to energy (Ch. 4, p. 143)

Essential fat The minimum amount of body fat necessary for good health (Ch. 5, p. 151)

Excessive leanness Having a percentage of body fat that is below the acceptable range for an individual's age and gender (Ch. 5, p. 151)

Excessive weight disabilities Health problems and diseases linked to or resulting directly from long-term overweight or obesity (Ch. 6, p. 173)

Exercise Physical activity that is planned, structured, and repetitive, and that results in improvements in fitness (Ch. 1, p. 4)

Exercise bands Elastic bands or tubing made of latex that are used to develop muscular strength and endurance (Ch. 9, p. 265)

Exercise bulimia An eating disorder in which people purge calories by exercising excessively (Ch. 6, p. 177)

Exercise physiologists Specially trained professionals who understand the body's physical reactions to exercise and evaluate a person's fitness (Ch. 12, p. 372)

Exercise prescription A breakdown of a fitness program, based on the frequency, intensity, time, and type of physical activity or exercise (Ch. 3, p. 83)

Exercise stress test An evaluation of cardiovascular fitness that involves walking on a treadmill or riding a stationary bicycle under medical supervision (Ch. 8, p. 220)

Extension The stretching of a muscle (Ch. 9, p. 252)

F

Fad diets Weight-loss plans that are popular for only a short time (Ch. 6, p. 182)

Fast-twitch muscle fiber Muscle fiber that contracts rapidly, thus allowing for greater muscle strength (Ch. 7, p. 208)

Fatigue The feeling of being tired all the time (Ch. 3, p. 99)

Fats Substances that supply a concentrated form of energy and help transport other nutrients to locations in the body where they are needed (Ch. 4, p. 115)

Flexibility A joint's ability to move through its full range of motion (Ch. 11, p. 325)

Fluid balance The body's ability to balance the amounts of fluid taken in with the amounts lost through perspiration or excretion (Ch. 2, p. 41)

Food Guide Pyramid A visual guide to help make healthful food choices (Ch. 4, p. 130)

Foodborne illnesses Illnesses that result from consuming food contaminated with disease-causing organisms, the poisons they produce, or chemical contaminants (Ch. 4, p. 136)

Free weights A term applied collectively to dumbbells, barbells, plates, and clips (Ch. 9, p. 262)

Frequency The number of times per week an individual engages in physical activity or exercise (Ch. 3, p. 84)

Frostbite Damage to body tissue that results from freezing (Ch. 2, p .44)

Functional fitness A person's physical ability to function independently in life, without assistance (Ch. 1, p. 7)

Functional health The ability to maintain high levels of health and wellness by reducing the risks of developing health problems (Ch. 1, p. 7)

G

Girth The distance around a body part (Ch. 5, p. 159)

H

Health A combination of physical, mental/emotional, and social well-being (Ch. 1, p. 6)

Health-related fitness The ability to become and stay physically healthy (Ch. 1, p. 11)

Heart rate monitor A device that records the heart beat by means of a chest transmitter and wrist monitor (Ch. 8, p. 229)

Heart rate The number of times a person's heart beats per minute (Ch. 3, p. 85)

Heat cramps Muscle spasms resulting from the loss of large amounts of salt and water through perspiration (Ch. 2, p. 41)

Heat exhaustion An overheating of the body resulting in cold, clammy skin and symptoms of shock (Ch. 2, p. 41)

Heat stress index A scientific measure of the combined effects of heat and humidity on the body (Ch. 2, p. 43)

Heatstroke A condition in which the body can no longer rid itself of excessive heat through perspiration (Ch. 2, p. 41)

Hemoglobin An iron-rich compound in the blood that helps to carry oxygen from lungs to cells and tissues (Ch. 7, p. 194)

Heredity The sum of the physical and mental traits that are inherited from one's parents (Ch. 1, p. 13)

Hernia A condition that occurs when muscle fibers from the intestine protrude through the wall of the abdomen (Ch. 2, p. 37)

High-density lipoprotein (HDL) A type of compound that picks up excess cholesterol and returns it to the liver (Ch. 4, p. 121)

Hyperflexibility Excessive amount of flexibility (Ch. 11, p. 334)

Hypertension High blood pressure (Ch. 7, p. 203)

Hypertrophy A thickening of existing muscle fibers (Ch. 9, p. 253)

Hypothermia A condition in which the body temperature drops below normal (Ch. 2, p. 44)

I

Impaired glucose tolerance (IGT) A disorder in which blood glucose levels become elevated (Ch. 6, p. 173)

Insomnia Sleeplessness (Ch. 3, p. 99)

Insulin A hormone produced by the pancreas (Ch. 6, p. 173)

Intensity The difficulty or exertion level of a physical activity or exercise (Ch. 3, p. 85)

Interval training A program in which high-intensity physical activities alternate with low intensity recovery bouts for several minutes at a time (Ch. 7, p. 215)

L

Large muscle group Any group of muscles of large size or any large number of muscles being used at one time (Ch. 10, p. 302)

Lean body weight The combined weight of bone, muscle, and connective tissue (Ch. 5, p. 148)

Leisure-time activities Sports and other action-oriented pursuits done for recreation (Ch. 12, p. 362)

Lifestyle diseases Diseases that are the result of certain lifestyle choices, such as smoking, eating plan, and inactivity (Ch. 7, p. 199)

Ligament Bands of tissue that connect bone to bone and limit the movement of joints (Ch. 2, p. 57)

Long-term goal A goal that you plan to reach over an extended length of time (Ch. 3, p. 91)

Low-density lipoprotein (LDL) A type of compound that carries cholesterol from the liver to areas of the body where it is needed (Ch. 4, p. 120)

M

Martial arts Activities that combine exercise and relaxation techniques (Ch. 12, p. 367)

Maximal oxygen consumption (VO$_{2max}$) The largest amount of oxygen the body is able to process during strenuous aerobic exercise (Ch. 7, p. 207)

Media The collective forms of mass communication found within society at any given time (Ch. 1, p. 20)

Medical history A record of past health problems and illnesses (Ch. 2, p. 39)

Medical screening A basic assessment of a person's overall health and personal fitness (Ch. 2, p. 35)

Mesomorph A body type characterized by a low-to-medium percentage of body fat, medium-to-large bone size, and a large amount of muscle mass and size (Ch. 5, p. 147)

Metabolism The process by which the body converts calories from food to energy (Ch. 5, p. 155)

Microtear Microscopic rips in the muscle fiber and/or surrounding tissues (Ch. 9, p. 255)

Minerals Elements the body cannot manufacture but that help regulate the body's processes, such as the conversion of glucose to energy (Ch. 4, p. 125)

Moderate physical activity or exercise Any activity or exercise that ranges in intensity from light-to-borderline-heavy exertion (Ch. 1, p. 28)

Multiple hypertrophy sets Lifting the same amount of weight to the point of fatigue (Ch. 10, p. 321)

Multiple sets The lifter uses the same amount of weight for three to five sets at a training load of 80 to 95 percent of his or her 1RM (Ch. 10, p. 318)

Muscle fiber The specific structure in the muscle that receives signals from the nerves (Ch. 9, p. 253)

Muscle hyperplasia An increase in the number of muscle fibers (Ch. 9, p. 253)

Muscle imbalance A condition in which one muscle group becomes too strong in relation to a complementary group (Ch. 11, p. 334)

Muscle tone A muscle's firmness and definition (Ch. 9, p. 259)

Muscular endurance The ability of the same muscle or muscle group to contract for an extended period of time without undue fatigue (Ch. 9, p. 248)

Muscular strength The maximum amount of force a muscle or muscle group can exert against an opposing force (Ch. 9, p. 247)

N

Negative reps Performing the eccentric, or negative, phase of an exercise only, using a weight 10 to 15 percent greater than one's 1RM (Ch. 10, p. 318)

Nerves Pathways that deliver messages from the brain to other body parts (Ch. 9, p. 253)

Nutrient-dense foods Foods that are high in nutrients as compared with their calorie content (Ch. 5, p. 165)

Nutrients Substances in food that the body needs for energy, proper growth, body maintenance, and functioning (Ch. 4, p. 113)

Nutrition The study of food and how the body uses the substances in food (Ch. 4, p. 113)

Nutrition Facts panel A thumbnail analysis of a food's calories and nutrient content for one serving (Ch. 4, p. 132)

O

Obesity A medical condition in which a person's ratio of body fat to lean muscle mass is excessively high (Ch. 2, p. 36)

One-rep maximum (1RM) A measure of a lifter's absolute maximum strength for any given exercise (Ch. 10, p. 307)

Orthopedics A branch of medicine that deals with bone and joint injuries and disorders (Ch. 12, p. 371)

Osteoporosis A bone disease that causes decreased bone mass and density, especially in older women (Ch. 9, p. 258)

Overfat Carrying too much body fat for one's age and gender (Ch. 5, p. 151)

Overhand grip A position in which a barbell is grasped with the palms facing downward and the knuckles facing upward (Ch. 10, p. 277)

Overload principle A rule of exercise that states that in order to improve the level of fitness, one must increase the amount of regular activity or exercise he or she normally does (Ch. 3, p. 83)

Overtraining Exercising or being active to a point where it begins to have negative effects (Ch. 3, p. 99)

Overuse injury A muscular injury that results from overloading a muscle beyond a healthful point (Ch. 3, p. 95)

Overweight A condition in which a person is heavier than the standard weight range for his or her height (Ch. 5, p. 150)

P

Passive stretching A type of stretching against a counter force and in which there is little or no movement (Ch. 11, p. 342)

Passive warm-up Using outside heat sources to raise body temperature (Ch. 3, p. 103)

Pedometer A device that measures the number of steps a person takes and records the distance traveled (Ch. 8, p. 228)

Peers People the same age who share a common range of interests and beliefs (Ch. 1, p. 19)

Perceived exertion A measure of how intensely an individual feels he or she is working during physical activity or exercise (Ch. 3, p. 86)

Peripheral vascular disease A CVD that occurs mainly in the legs and, less frequently, in the arms (Ch. 7, p. 202)

Personal fitness Total, overall fitness achieved by maintaining acceptable levels of physical activity, a healthy eating plan, and avoiding harmful substances (Ch. 1, p. 4)

Physical activity Any movement that works the larger muscles of the body, such as arm, leg, and back muscles (Ch. 1, p. 4)

Physical fitness The body's ability to carry out daily tasks and still have enough reserve energy to respond to unexpected demands (Ch. 1, p. 4)

Physical therapists Health professionals specially trained to work with people recovering from injuries (Ch. 12, p. 371)

Phytonutrients Health-promoting substances found in plant foods (Ch. 4, p. 127)

Plyometric exercises Quick, powerful muscular movements that require the muscle to be pre-stretched just before a quick contraction (Ch. 9, p. 266)

Podiatrist Physician trained specifically to treat disorders of the feet (Ch. 12, p. 371)

Posture The alignment of the body's muscles and skeleton as they provide support for the total body (Ch. 11, p. 329)

Power The ability to move the body parts swiftly while simultaneously applying the maximum force of the muscles (Ch. 3, p. 76)

Pre-event meal The last full meal consumed prior to a practice session or the competitive event itself (Ch. 4, p. 139)

Progression principle A rule of exercise that states as fitness levels increase, so do the factors in FITT (Ch. 3, p. 95)

Progressive resistance Continued systematic increase of muscle workload by the addition of more weight or resistance (Ch. 9, p. 248)

Pronation The normal motion of the foot as one walks or runs, from the outside of the heel striking the ground through the normal inward roll of the foot (Ch. 2, p. 49)

Proteins Nutrients that help build, maintain, and repair body tissues (Ch. 4, p. 115)

Pyramid training An approach to training that uses progressively heavier weights and fewer reps through successive sets of an exercise (Ch. 10, p. 317)

R

Range of motion (ROM) The degrees of motion allowed around a joint (Ch. 11, p. 325)

Reaction time The ability to react or respond quickly to what you hear, see, or feel (Ch. 3, p. 76)

Recovery time The duration of the rest periods taken between workout components (Ch. 10, p. 311)

Recumbent cycles Reclining exercise cycles (Ch. 8, p. 239)

Reflex-assisted stretching Stretching movements that challenge the reflexes to adapt (Ch. 11, p. 342)

Reflexes The automatic responses that the nerves and muscles provide to various movements (Ch. 11, p. 342)

Registered dietitians (RDs) Professionals who specialize in providing nutritional advice and helping people control their weight (Ch. 12, p. 372)

Regular physical activity or exercise Any activity or exercise performed most days of the week, preferably daily (Ch. 1, p. 28)

Rehydrate To restore lost water (Ch. 2, p. 42)

Relative muscular endurance The maximum number of times an individual can repeatedly perform a resistance activity in relation to his or her body weight (Ch. 9, p. 248)

Relative muscular strength The maximum force an individual is able to exert in relation to his or her body weight (Ch. 9, p. 247)

Repetition (rep) One completion of an activity or exercise (Ch. 10, p. 296)

Resistance training A systematic program of exercises designed to increase an individual's ability to resist or exert force (Ch. 9, p. 245)

Resistance-training cycle Modified programs, designed to meet the needs of off-season, pre-season, and in-season (Ch. 10, p. 312)

Respiratory system The body system that exchanges gases between the body and the environment (Ch. 7, p. 194)

Resting metabolic rate (RMR) The amount of calories expended for body processes while at rest (Ch. 5, p. 155)

Restoration Ways in which an individual can optimize recovery from physical activity or exercise (Ch. 3, p. 100)

RICE (Rest, Ice, Compress, and Elevate) A first-aid procedure indicating proper treatment for strains and sprains that become swollen (Ch. 2, p. 58)

Risk factors Conditions and behaviors that represent a potential threat to an individual's well-being (Ch. 1, p. 12)

S

Saturated fatty acids Fats that come mainly from animal fats and are often solid at room temperature (Ch. 4, p. 119)

Sedentary Physically inactive (Ch. 1, p. 7)

Self-concept The view an individual has of his- or herself (Ch. 1, p. 22)

Self-esteem Feelings of self-confidence and personal worth (Ch. 1, p. 7)

Set A group of consecutive reps for any exercise (Ch. 10, p. 296)

Shinsplint Inflammation of a tendon or muscle in the leg (Ch. 2, p. 59)

Skeletal muscles Muscles attached to bones that cause body movement (Ch. 9, p. 250)

Skill-related fitness The ability to perform successfully in various games and sports (Ch. 1, p. 11)

Sleep apnea A condition in which a person stops breathing during sleep, due to obstructed or reduced air passages (Ch. 6, p. 173)

Slow-twitch muscle fiber Muscle fiber that contracts at a slow rate, allowing for greater muscle endurance (Ch. 7, p. 208)

Small muscle group Any group of muscles of small size or any small number of muscles being used at one time (Ch. 10, p. 302)

Smokeless tobacco Tobacco that is sniffed through the nose or chewed (Ch. 2, p. 64)

Smooth muscles Muscles responsible for the movements of the internal organs (Ch. 9, p. 250)

Specificity principle A rule of exercise that states overloading a particular component will lead to fitness improvements in that component alone (Ch. 3, p. 90)

Speed The ability to move the body or body parts swiftly (Ch. 3, p. 76)

Split workout A fitness program that exercises three or four body areas at each session, at a high intensity (Ch. 10, p. 306)

Sports medicine clinic Centers that focus on research promoting health and fitness, as well as on the development and operation of health, fitness, recreation, and educational programs (Ch. 12, p. 378)

Spotter A partner who can assist with the safe handling of weights and offer encouragement during a session (Ch. 9, p. 262)

Sprain A condition in which the ligaments that hold joints in position are stretched or torn (Ch. 2, p. 58)

Static contraction A type of muscle contraction that occurs absent of any significant movement (Ch. 9, p. 252)

Static posture The posture of the body while in a resting position (Ch. 11, p. 331)

Static stretching Exercises that stretch muscles slowly, smoothly, and in a sustained fashion for 20 to 30 seconds (Ch. 11, p. 341)

Steady-state cycle test A test that requires one to pedal for 20 minutes on a stationary cycle and try to achieve a specific goal distance (Ch. 8, p. 220)

Steady-state jog test A test that requires you to pace yourself steadily as you jog for 20 minutes and try to achieve a specific goal distance (Ch. 8, p. 219)

Steady-state swim test A test that requires one to swim for 20 minutes and try to achieve a specific goal distance (Ch. 8, p. 220)

Steady-state walk test A test that requires you to pace yourself steadily as you briskly walk for 30 minutes and try to achieve a specific goal distance (Ch. 8, p. 219)

Strain A pull in a muscle or tendon (Ch. 2, p. 58)

Stress fracture A break in the bone caused by overuse (Ch. 2, p. 59)

Stress The mind and body's response to the demands and threats of everyday life (Ch. 1, p. 16)

Stretching cooldown Three to five minutes of stretching following physical activity or exercise (Ch. 3, p. 109)

Stroke When blood flow to a person's brain is interrupted or cut off entirely by a blocked artery (Ch. 7, p. 202)

Stroke volume The amount of blood pumped per beat of the heart (Ch. 7, p. 194)

Substance abuse Any unnecessary or improper use of chemical substances for nonmedical purposes (Ch. 2, p. 63)

Supersets Alternately perform sets of exercises that train opposing muscles, without resting between sets (Ch. 10, p. 319)

Supination The normal outward roll of the foot as it hits the ground (Ch. 2, p. 49)

T

T'ai chi A martial art that involves fluid, graceful movements, demanding precise muscular control (Ch. 12, p. 367)

Talk test A measure of one's ability to carry on a conversation while engaged in physical activity or exercise (Ch. 3, p. 86)

Target heart rate range The range one's heart rate should be in during aerobic exercise or activity for maximum cardiorespiratory endurance (Ch. 8, p. 234)

Tendons Bands of tissue that connect muscles to bones (Ch. 2, p. 57)

Testosterone A chemical produced by the body that plays an important role in building muscles (Ch. 9, p. 257)

Time The duration of a single workout, measured in either minutes or hours (Ch. 3, p. 88)

Toe box The part of the shoe that surrounds the toes (Ch. 2, p. 50)

Total-body workout One in which all major muscle groups are worked three times a week, with at least one day off between workouts (Ch. 10, p. 306)

Trainability The rate at which an individual's fitness levels increase during fitness training (Ch. 3, p. 97)

Training load The amount of weight an individual should lift for a given exercise (Ch. 10, p. 307)

Training plateau A period of time during training when little, if any, fitness improvement occurs (Ch. 3, p. 98)

Trans fatty acids Fats that are formed when certain oils are processed into solids (Ch. 4, p. 119)

Type The particular type of physical activity or exercise you choose to do (Ch. 3, p. 89)

U

Underhand grip A position in which a barbell is grasped with the palms facing upward and the knuckles facing downward (Ch. 10, p. 277)

Underweight Having a Body Mass Index (BMI) that is below the 5th percentile for one's age (Ch. 6, p. 175)

Unsaturated fatty acids Fats that are usually liquid at room temperature and come mainly from plant sources (Ch. 4, p. 119)

V

Vegetarian A person who eats mostly or only foods that come from plant sources. (Ch. 4, p. 118)

Veins Blood vessels that deliver the blood back to the heart (Ch. 7, p. 194)

Vigorous physical activity or exercise Any activity or exercise that ranges in intensity from heavy-to-maximum exertion (Ch. 1, p. 29)

Vitamins Micronutrients that help control body processes and help the body release energy to do work (Ch. 4, p. 123)

W

Warm-up Portion of a complete workout that consists of a variety of low-intensity activities that prepare the body for physical work (Ch. 3, p. 102)

Warranty A guarantee on the part of the manufacturer or representative of the manufacturer to repair or replace parts for a predetermined time period (Ch. 8, p. 238)

Weight cycling The cycle of losing, regaining, losing and regaining weight (Ch. 6, p. 188)

Weight machines Mechanical devices that move weights up and down using a system of cables and pulleys (Ch. 9, p. 263)

Weight-training belts Belts that protect the lower back and stomach when lifting heavy weights (Ch. 9, p. 269)

Weight-training gloves Gloves that prevent blisters and calluses from forming on your palms (Ch. 9, p. 269)

Wellness Total health in the areas of physical well-being, mental/emotional well-being, and social well-being (Ch. 1, p. 6)

Wind-chill factor The combined influence of wind and temperature on the body (Ch. 2, p. 44)

A

Absolute muscular strength/Fuerza muscular absoluta La fuerza máxima que puede alcanzar un individuo, más allá del tamaño, el peso o la edad.

Acclimatization/Aclimatación Proceso que permite al cuerpo adaptarse lentamente a las condiciones del clima.

Active warm-up/Precalentamiento activo Ejercicios que elevan la temperatura del cuerpo al trabajar activamente los sistemas corporales, centrándose en músculos, esqueleto, corazón y pulmones.

Addiction/Adicción Dependencia física y mental a una substancia o actividad.

Adductor muscles/Músculos abductores Músculos de la parte interna de la pierna que controlan el cierre de las piernas.

Adherence/Adherencia Capacidad para atenerse a un plan de acción.

Adipose tissue/Tejido adiposo Grasa corporal.

Aerobic activity/Actividad aeróbica Actividad continua que exige gran cantidad de oxígeno.

Agility/Agilidad Capacidad para cambiar y controlar la dirección y posición del cuerpo mientras se mantiene un movimiento constante y rápido.

Aging process/Proceso de envejecimiento Modo en que cambia el cuerpo como resultado natural del paso de los años.

Alternated grip/Toma alternada Una posición en la cual la barra de pesas se toma con la palma de una mano hacia abajo y la otra palma hacia arriba.

Amino acids/Aminoácidos Los componentes básicos de las proteínas.

Anabolic steroids/Esteroides anabólicos Substancias químicas similares en estructura a la hormona masculina testosterona.

Anaerobic fitness/Buen estado físico anaeróbico Niveles elevados de fuerza muscular, resistencia muscular, y flexibilidad.

Anaerobic activity/Actividad anaeróbica Actividad que exige altos niveles de energía y se realiza sólo por pocos segundos o minutos a un elevado grado de intensidad.

Androstenedione/Androstenediona Agente químico que ayuda al cuerpo en la producción de testosterona.

Anorexia nervosa/Anorexia nerviosa Trastorno alimenticio en el que el individuo restringe en forma anormal su ingestión calórica.

Antioxidants/Antioxidantes Substancias que previenen el deterioro de las células corporales, incluyendo aquellas que pertenecen al sistema inmunológico.

Arteries/Arterias Vasos sanguíneos que transportan la sangre desde el corazón hacia las principales extremidades del cuerpo.

Asthma/Asma Enfermedad en la que las vías respiratorias inferiores de los pulmones se estrechan, provocando dificultades para respirar.

Atherosclerosis/Aterosclerosis Afección por la que un depósito graso denominado placa se acumula en el interior de las arterias, restringiendo o cortando el flujo sanguíneo.

Athletic trainers/Entrenadores atléticos Profesionales que trabajan con atletas en proceso de rehabilitación.

Attitude/Actitud La mentalidad de un individuo fija en un tópico o tema definido, o con una visión definida hacia ese tópico o tema.

B

Balance/Equilibrio Habilidad para controlar o estabilizar el cuerpo de pie o en movimiento.

Ballistic stretching/Estiramiento balístico Movimientos rápidos hacia arriba y abajo en los que el estiramiento se mantiene en forma muy breve.

Behavioral-change stairway/Cambio de conducta escalonado Método paso a paso, para establecer y alcanzar un objetivo personal para el logro de un buen estado físico.

Bigorexia/Bigorexia Trastorno por el que un individuo cree erróneamente ser de bajo peso, o tener un cuerpo subdesarrollado.

Binge eating disorder/Trastorno alimenticio por ingestión inmoderada Trastorno en la alimentación por el que un individuo come más rápido de lo normal, hasta que no puede seguir comiendo.

Biomechanics/Biomecánica Estudio y aplicación de principios de la física a la motricidad humana.

Blood pooling/Flebitis Afección por la que la sangre se acumula en las principales venas de las piernas, y en la parte inferior del cuerpo.

Blood pressure/Presión sanguínea Fuerza de la sangre en las principales arterias.

Body composition/Composición corporal Proporción entre grasa corporal y tejido corporal magro incluyendo músculo, hueso, agua y tejido conectivo.

Body image/Imagen corporal Forma en que un individuo ve su cuerpo.

Body mass index (BMI)/Índice de masa corporal Método de evaluación de las dimensiones del cuerpo con relación a altura y peso.

Bulimia nervosa/Bulimia nerviosa Trastorno en la alimentación a raíz del cual los individuos comen en exceso, y luego fuerzan la eliminación de lo ingerido.

C

Calipers/Calibrador Aparato con forma de tenaza, que se usa para pinzar un pliegue de piel que rodea tejido adiposo.

Calisthenic exercises/Ejercicios calisténicos Ejercicios que generan resistencia al utilizar el propio peso del cuerpo.

Calorie/Caloría Cantidad de energía necesaria para elevar 1 grado Celsius la temperatura de 1 kilogramo (aproximadamente un cuarto) de agua.

Calorie expenditure/Consumo calórico Número total de calorías que un individuo quema o consume.

Calorie intake/Ingestión calórica Número total de calorías que un individuo ingiere a través de los alimentos.

Capillaries/Capilares Pequeños vasos sanguíneos que proveen oxígeno y otros nutrientes a las células.

Carbohydrates/Carbohidratos Almidones y azúcares que aportan los alimentos.

Cardiac muscle/Músculo cardiaco Clase especial de tejido estriado que forma las paredes del corazón.

Cardiorespiratory endurance/Resistencia cardiorrespiratoria Capacidad del cuerpo para trabajar en forma continua durante prolongados períodos de tiempo.

Cardiovascular conditioning/Acondicionamiento cardiovascular Ejercicios o actividades que mejoran el rendimiento del corazón, los pulmones, la sangre, y los vasos sanguíneos.

Cardiovascular cooldown/Recuperación cardiovascular Consiste en moverse lenta y constantemente durante tres a cinco minutos, a continuación de la actividad física o el ejercicio.

Cardiovascular disease (CVD)/Enfermedad cardiovascular Término aplicado a todo trastorno que afecte al corazón o a los vasos sanguíneos.

Cartilage/Cartílago Tejido que rodea los extremos de los huesos en las articulaciones, y evita que friccionen entre sí.

Cholesterol/Colesterol Substancia de tipo graso que se produce en el hígado y circula por la sangre.

Chronic disease/Enfermedades crónico Enfermedades habitual o continuo.

Circuit training/Entrenamiento en circuitos Método de entrenamiento de resistencia, en el que se pasa de un ejercicio a otro en una secuencia determinada.

Circulatory system/Sistema circulatorio Comprende el corazón, la sangre y los vasos sanguíneos.

Clips/Topes o sujetadores Aparatos con forma de pinza—que a veces cargan peso—para mantener la barra de pesas en su lugar.

Commercial fitness centers/Centros comerciales de preparación física Instalaciones dedicadas a la salud y a la preparación física, que mediante el pago de una cuota, permiten el acceso a una amplia variedad de aparatos de resistencia y entrenamiento aeróbico.

Commitment/Compromiso Voto o promesa.

Compound sets/Series compuestas Series alternadas de ejercicios que se efectúan sin descanso entre las series.

Conflicts/Conflictos Luchas o desacuerdos.

Contraction/Contracción Acortamiento de un músculo.

Cooper's 1.5-mile run test/Test de Cooper de 1.5 millas Prueba que exige trotar/correr 1.5 millas tan rápido como sea posible.

Coordination/Coordinación Capacidad para utilizar los sentidos a fin de determinar y orientar los movimientos de las extremidades y la cabeza.

Core stability/Estabilidad central Estiramiento y fortalecimiento de los músculos que rodean la columna y los músculos pélvicos.

Corporate fitness centers/Centros empresariales de preparación física Instalaciones dedicadas a la salud y a la preparación física dentro de la propia empresa, a disposición de los empleados y sus familias.

Creatine/Creatina Suplemento que aumenta el tamaño de los músculos, al tiempo que potencia la capacidad del cuerpo para utilizar proteínas.

Credentials/Credenciales Resumen de la experiencia y el entrenamiento profesional de un individuo en determinada área.

Cross-contamination/Contaminación cruzada Propagación de bacterias u otros patógenos de un alimento a otro.

Cross-training/Entrenamiento cruzado Variación en el ejercicio, o en la rutina de la actividad, o bien, en el estilo.

Culture/Cultura Usos y costumbres, tradiciones y creencias que comparte un grupo determinado.

D

Deconditioned/Fuera de estado Carencia de entrenamiento durante un período significativo, que se produce tras haber alcanzado, al menos, un nivel moderado de preparación física.

Dehydration/Deshidratación Pérdida de líquido corporal.

Detraining/Desentrenamiento Pérdida en el nivel de funcionamiento físico, como resultado de un cese en el acondicionamiento del estado físico.

Diaphragm/Diafragma Músculo que se halla entre la cavidad toráxica y el abdomen.

Dietary fiber/Fibra dietética Subclase especial de carbohidratos complejos que posee varias funciones, entre otras la de asistir al cuerpo en la digestión.

Dietary Reference Intakes (DRI)/Referencia Dietética para la alimentación Recomendaciones de nutrientes diarios para individuos saludables de ambos sexos y diferentes grupos de edad.

Dietary supplement/Suplemento dietético Formula no alimenticia que consta de uno o más nutrientes.

Dynamic contraction/Contracción dinámica Tipo de contracción muscular que se produce cuando la fuerza de resistencia es móvil.

Dynamic posture/Postura dinámica Postura del cuerpo en movimiento o preparándose para moverse.

E

Eating disorders/Trastornos en la alimentación Enfermedades psicológicas que provocan que un individuo coma de menos o de más, o que ejerza una conducta peligrosa para su nutrición.

Ectomorph/Ectomorfo Tipo de cuerpo caracterizado por poseer un bajo porcentaje de grasa corporal, huesos pequeños, y reducida cantidad de masa y tamaño muscular.

Elasticity/Elasticidad Capacidad de los músculos y los tejidos conectivos para estirarse y dar de sí.

Elliptical motion trainer/Máquina de movimiento elíptico Aparato de ejercicios que simula el movimiento natural de correr, pero no genera tensión en las articulaciones.

Emphysema/Enfisema Enfermedad por la que las vías respiratorias inferiores de los pulmones pierden su elasticidad normal, haciéndolas menos eficientes en su función de facilitar la salida y entrada de aire a los pulmones.

Endomorph/Endomorfo Tipo de cuerpo caracterizado por poseer un alto porcentaje de grasa corporal, huesos grandes y cantidades reducidas de masa y tamaño muscular.

Energy cost/Consumo energético Cantidad de energía necesaria para realizar diferentes actividades físicas o ejercicios.

Ephedrine/Efedrina Compuesto que incrementa la proporción en que el cuerpo convierte calorías en energía.

Essential fat/Grasas esenciales Cantidad mínima de grasa corporal necesaria para gozar de buena salud.

Excessive leanness/Delgadez excesiva Poseer un nivel de grasa corporal por debajo de los valores aceptables según el sexo y la edad del individuo.

Excessive weight disabilities/Incapacidad por peso excesivo Problemas de salud y enfermedades relacionadas con o provocadas directamente por exceso de peso u obesidad prolongados.

Exercise/Ejercicio Una actividad física planeada, estructurada y repetitiva, que resulta en mejoras del estado físico.

Exercise bands/Bandas elásticas Bandas elásticas o tubulares de látex que se usan para desarrollar fuerza y resistencia muscular.

Exercise bulimia/Bulimia por ejercicio Trastorno en la alimentación por el que el individuo elimina calorías ejercitándose en exceso.

Exercise physiologists/Fisiólogos del ejercicio Especialistas entrenados para comprender las reacciones físicas del cuerpo hacia el ejercicio, y evaluar el estado físico de un individuo.

Exercise prescription/Plan de entrenamiento Información detallada de un programa de preparación física, basado en frecuencia, intensidad, tiempo y tipo de actividad física o ejercicio.

Exercise stress test/Test de stress por ejercicio Evaluación del estado cardiovascular de un individuo, que implica caminata en la cinta o pedaleo en la bicicleta fija, bajo supervisión médica.

Extension/Extensión Estiramiento del músculo.

F

Fad diets/Dietas de moda Planes para perder peso que se ponen de moda sólo por un breve período de tiempo.

Fast-twitch muscle fiber/Contracción de fibra muscular por espasmo rápido Contracción veloz, que permite una mayor fuerza muscular.

Fatigue/Fatiga Sentirse cansado todo el tiempo.

Fats/Reserva Provisión de una forma concentrada de energía, y asistencia en el transporte de otros nutrientes a los lugares donde el cuerpo los necesita.

Flexibility/Flexibilidad Capacidad de la articulación para moverse en la totalidad de su margen de movimiento.

Fluid balance/Equilibrio de líquidos Capacidad corporal para equilibrar la cantidad de líquido que se incorpora y que se pierde, por transpiración o excreciones.

Food Guide Pyramid/Pirámide nutricional Guía visual que orienta una elección saludable en la alimentación.

Foodborne illnesses/Intoxicación Enfermedad provocada por el consumo de alimentos que poseen organismos causantes de afecciones, los intoxicantes derivados de su mal estado, o contaminantes químicos.

Free weights/Pesas libres Término que se aplica en forma colectiva a mancuernas, barras de pesas, discos y topes de seguridad con sus cargas respectivas.

Frequency/Frecuencia Cantidad de veces por semana en que un individuo realiza actividad física o ejercicio.

Frostbite/Congelación Daño en el tejido corporal producido por congelamiento.

Functional fitness/Buen estado físico funcional Capacidad física de un individuo para funcionar independientemente en la vida, sin asistencia.

Functional health/Salud funcional Capacidad para mantener altos niveles de salud y bienestar, al reducir riesgos para desarrollar problemas de salud.

G

Girth/Contorno Medida alrededor de una parte del cuerpo.

H

Health/Salud Combinación de bienestar físico, mental/emocional, y social.

Health-related fitness/Buen estado físico conectado a la salud Resistencia cardiorrespiratoria, composición corporal, fuerza muscular, resistencia muscular y flexibilidad.

Heart rate monitor/Monitor de frecuencia cardiaca Aparato que registra los latidos del corazón por medio de un transmisor de pecho y de un monitor de pulsera.

Heart rate/Frecuencia cardiaca Cantidad de veces por minuto que late el corazón de un individuo.

Heat cramps/Calambres por calor Espasmos musculares resultantes de la pérdida de grandes cantidades de sal y agua a través de la transpiración.

Heat exhaustion/Agotamiento por calor Sobrecalentamiento corporal que se manifiesta por piel fría y húmeda, a la vez que conlleva síntomas de shock.

Heat stress index/Tabla de estrés por calor Medida científica que registra los efectos combinados del calor y la humedad sobre el cuerpo.

Heatstroke/Golpe de calor Afección por la cual el cuerpo ya no logra librarse del calor excesivo a través de la transpiración.

Hemoglobin/Hemoglobina Compuesto sanguíneo rico en hierro que ayuda a transportar oxígeno desde los pulmones a células y tejidos.

Heredity/Hereditario Suma de rasgos físicos y mentales que se heredan de los padres.

Hernia/Hernia Lesión que se produce cuando las fibras musculares del intestino sobresalen a través de las paredes del abdomen.

High-density lipoprotein (HDL)/Lipoproteína de alta densidad Tipo de compuesto que recoge el excedente de colesterol y lo devuelve al hígado.

Hyperflexibility/Hiperflexibilidad Excesiva cantidad de flexibilidad.

Hypertension/Hipertensión Alta presión sanguínea.

Hypertrophy/Hipertrofia Engrosamiento de fibras musculares preexistentes.

Hypothermia/Hipotermia Estado por el que la temperatura corporal desciende por debajo de lo normal.

I

Impaired glucose tolerance (IGT)/Deficiencia en la tolerancia a la glucosa Trastorno por el que se elevan los niveles de glucosa en sangre.

Insomnia/Insomnio Incapacidad para conciliar el sueño.

Insulin/Insulina Hormona producida por el páncreas.

Intensity/Intensidad Nivel de dificultad o esfuerzo en la actividad física o en el ejercicio.

Interval training/Entrenamiento por intervalos Programa en el que las actividades. físicas de alta intensidad, se alternan con tandas de recuperación de baja intensidad durante varios minutos por vez.

L

Large muscle group/Grupo grande de músculos Todo grupo de músculos de grandes. dimensiones, como así también, una cantidad grande de músculos utilizados al mismo tiempo.

Lean body weight/Peso corporal magro Peso combinado de hueso, músculo y tejido conectivo.

Leisure-time activities/Actividades recreativas Deportes y demás actividades orientadas al movimiento, con fines recreativos.

Lifestyle diseases/Enfermedades por estilo de vida Enfermedades resultantes de ciertas elecciones relacionadas con el estilo de vida, por ejemplo, el fumar, la inactividad o ciertos planes alimenticios.

Ligament/Ligamento Franjas de tejido que se extienden de un hueso a otro y limitan el movimiento de las articulaciones.

Long-term goal/meta a largo plazo Un objetivo que una persona trata de alcanzar durante un largo período de tiempo.

Low-density lipoprotein (LDL)/Lipoproteína de baja densidad Tipo de compuesto que transporta el colesterol desde el hígado hacia áreas del cuerpo donde se lo necesita.

M

Martial arts/Artes Marciales Actividades que combinan ejercicios físicos y técnicas de relajación.

Maximal oxygen consumption (VO_{2max})/Máximo consumo de oxígeno (VO_{2max}) Cantidad máxima de oxígeno que el cuerpo puede procesar durante ejercicios aeróbicos enérgicos.

Media/Medios Sistema colectivo de comunicación masiva, instalados en la sociedad en un momento dado.

Medical history/Historia clínica Registro de los antecedentes de enfermedades y problemas de salud de un individuo.

Medical screening/Chequeo médico Evaluación básica del estado de salud general y condición física personal de un individuo.

Mesomorph/Mesomorfo Tipo de cuerpo caracterizado por un bajo a mediano porcentaje de grasa corporal, huesos medianos a grandes, y gran cantidad y tamaño de masa muscular.

Metabolism/Metabolismo Proceso por el que el cuerpo convierte en energía las calorías aportadas por la alimentación.

Microtear/Micro desgarro Desgarro microscópico de fibras musculares y/o tejidos circundantes.

Minerals/Minerales Elementos que el cuerpo no puede generar, pero que ayudan a regular los procesos corporales, tales como la conversión de glucosa en energía.

Moderate physical activity or exercise/Actividad física o ejercicio moderados Toda actividad o ejercicio que varía en intensidad de leve al límite del esfuerzo máximo.

Multiple hypertrophy sets/Series múltiples de hipertrofia Levantamiento de igual carga de peso hasta el punto de fatiga.

Multiple sets/Serie múltiple Levantamiento de pesas en el que el individuo usa la misma cantidad de peso durante tres a cinco series, a una carga de entrenamiento del 80 al 95 por ciento de su 1RM.

Muscle fiber/Fibra muscular Estructura específica en el músculo que recibe la señal nerviosa.

Muscle hyperplasia/Hiperplasia muscular Aumento en la cantidad de fibras musculares.

Muscle imbalance/Desequilibrio muscular Estado en que un grupo de músculos se torna más fuerte, con relación a un grupo complementario.

Muscle tone/Tono muscular Definición y firmeza de un músculo.

Muscular endurance/Resistencia muscular Capacidad del propio músculo o grupo muscular para contraerse durante un período prolongado de tiempo, sin presentar fatiga excesiva.

Muscular strength/Fuerza muscular Máxima cantidad de fuerza que un músculo o grupo muscular puede ejercer contra una fuerza de oposición.

N

Negative reps/Repetición negativa Ejercitación que comprende sólo la fase excéntrica o negativa de un ejercicio, al utilizar un peso de un 10 o 15 por ciento superior al propio 1RM.

Nerves/Nervios Conductores que descargan mensajes desde el cerebro a otras partes del cuerpo.

Nutrient-dense foods/Alimentos de alta densidad nutritiva Alimentos que proporcionan altos valores nutritivos, en comparación con su contenido calórico

Nutrients/Nutrientes Substancias en los alimentos que aseguran al cuerpo energía, crecimiento apropiado, mantenimiento corporal y funcionamiento.

Nutrition/Nutrición Estudio de los alimentos y de la forma en que el cuerpo utiliza las substancias que estos aportan.

Nutrition Facts panel/Información nutricional Análisis condensado del valor calórico y nutritivo por porción de alimento.

O

Obesity/Obesidad Problema de salud en el que, la diferencia entre la grasa corporal y la masa muscular magra de un individuo, es extremadamente elevada.

One-rep maximum (1RM)/Máximo por ejercicio (1RM) Medida de levantamiento de pesas para fuerza máxima absoluta en cualquier ejercicio dado.

Orthopedics/Ortopedia Rama de la medicina que trata sobre esqueleto, lesiones y trastornos articulares.

Osteoporosis/Osteoporosis Enfermedad de los huesos que provoca disminución en la densidad y en la masa ósea, especialmente en mujeres mayores.

Overfat/Sobrepeso Exceso de grasa corporal en proporción a edad y sexo.

Overhand grip/Toma en prono Una posición en la cual la barra de pesas se toma con las palmas de las manos hacia abajo y los nudillos hacia arriba.

Overload principle/Principio de sobrecarga Regla de ejercitación que establece que, a fin de mejorar el nivel de preparación física, debe incrementarse la cantidad de actividad o ejercicio regular que se efectúa habitualmente.

Overtraining/Sobreentrenamiento Ejercitarse o entrenarse hasta un punto en el que comienzan a aparecer efectos negativos.

Overuse injury/Lesión por sobrecarga Lesión muscular ocasionada al sobrecargar un músculo más allá de un punto saludable.

Overweight /Sobrepeso Estado en el que un individuo pesa más que los valores establecidos según su altura.

P

Passive stretching/Estiramiento pasivo Tipo de estiramiento contra una contra fuerza en el que hay escaso o ningún movimiento.

Passive warm-up/Precalentamiento pasivo Utilización de fuentes de calor externas para elevar la temperatura corporal.

Pedometer/Podómetro Aparato que mide el número de pasos que da un individuo, y registra la distancia recorrida a pie.

Peers/Pares Individuos de la misma edad que comparten un marco común de intereses y creencias.

Perceived exertion/Percepción de esfuerzo Medida que denota en qué grado un individuo siente el trabajo durante la actividad o el ejercicio físico.

Peripheral vascular disease/Enfermedad vascular periférica Enfermedad cardiovascular que ocurre principalmente en las piernas y, con menor frecuencia, en los brazos.

Personal fitness/Buen estado físico personal Preparación física total y general, que se logra manteniendo niveles aceptables de actividad física, buena alimentación y evitando el consumo de sustancias perjudiciales.

Physical activity/Actividad física Todo movimiento que trabaja los músculos mayores del cuerpo, tales como los de brazos, piernas y músculos de la espalda.

Physical fitness/Buen estado físico Capacidad del cuerpo para llevar a cabo las tareas cotidianas, y aún conservar una suficiente reserva de energía para responder a exigencias inesperadas.

Physical therapists/Fisioterapeutas Profesionales de la salud especialmente entrenados para trabajar con individuos que se recuperan de lesiones.

Phytonutrients/Fitonutrientes Substancias aportadas por alimentos vegetales, que contribuyen a mantener la salud.

Plyometric exercises/Ejercicios pliométricos Movimientos musculares veloces y poderosos, que exigen un pre-estiramiento muscular exactamente antes de una rápida contracción.

Podiatrist/Podiatra Médico entrenado específicamente para tratar trastornos en los pies.

Posture/Postura Alineación de los músculos corporales y del esqueleto al sostener la totalidad del cuerpo.

Power/Fuerza Capacidad para mover las partes del cuerpo en forma veloz, mientras se aplica al mismo tiempo la fuerza máxima de los músculos.

Pre-event meal/Comida pre-evento La última comida completa consumida en forma previa a la sesión de ejercicios, o al propio evento competitivo.

Progression principle/Principio de progresión Regla de ejercitación que establece que, a medida que los niveles de acondicionamiento físico aumentan, se incrementan los factores en el FITT.

Progressive resistance/Resistencia progresiva Aumento de la carga del músculo, continuado y sistemático, al agregarse mayor peso o resistencia.

Pronation/Pronación Movimiento normal del pie al caminar o al correr, desde el talón hacia fuera al pisar el suelo, hasta la propulsión hacia adentro, normal en un pie.

Proteins/Proteínas Nutrientes que contribuyen a la construcción, mantenimiento y reparación de los tejidos del cuerpo.

Pyramid training/Entrenamiento piramidal Sistema de entrenamiento que recurre al incremento de peso progresivo en las pesas, y a una menor cantidad de repeticiones, a través de sucesivas series de ejercicios.

R

Range of motion (ROM)/Alcance de movilidad Grados de movimiento posibles alrededor de una articulación.

Reaction time/Tiempo de reacción Capacidad para reaccionar o responder velozmente a lo que se oye, se ve o se siente.

Recovery time/Tiempo de recuperación Duración del período de descanso que se toma entre los componentes del entrenamiento.

Recumbent cycles/Ciclos de reposo Ciclos de ejercicio en posición reclinada.

Reflex-assisted stretching/Estiramiento asistido por reflejos Movimientos de estiramiento que estimulan la adaptación de los reflejos.

Reflexes/Reflejos Respuesta automática que ofrecen nervios y músculos a variados movimientos.

Registered dietitians (RDs)/Dietólogos matriculados Profesionales que se especializan en proveer asesoraramiento nutricional a las personas, a la vez que los ayudan a controlar su peso.

Regular physical activity or exercise/Ejercicio o actividad física regular Toda actividad o ejercicio que se realiza la mayor parte de la semana, preferentemente, a diario.

Rehydrate/Rehidratación Reposición del agua perdida.

Relative muscular endurance/Resistencia muscular relativa Número máximo de veces que un individuo puede repetir una actividad de resistencia, en relación al peso corporal.

Relative muscular strength/Fuerza muscular relativa Máxima fuerza que un individuo es capaz de ejercer, con relación a su peso corporal.

Repetition (rep)/Repetición La ejecución completa de una actividad o ejercicio dado.

Resistance training/Entrenamiento de resistencia Programa sistemático de ejercicios, diseñado para incrementar la habilidad de un individuo para resistir o ejercer fuerza.

Resistance-training cycle/Ciclo de entrenamiento para resistencia Programas modificados, diseñados para cubrir las necesidades de pre temporada, temporada y fuera de temporada.

Respiratory system/Sistema respiratorio Sistema corporal de intercambio de gases entre el cuerpo y el medio ambiente.

Resting metabolic rate (RMR)/Tasa metabólica en reposo Cantidad de calorías que se gastan en los procesos corporales mientras se está en reposo.

Restoration/Recuperación Formas en que un individuo puede optimizar la recuperación por actividad física o ejercicios.

RICE (Rest, Ice, Compress, and Elevate)/Primeros auxilios deportivos (Reposo, Hielo, Compresión y Elevación) Procedimiento de primeros auxilios que establece el tratamiento indicado en caso de tirones y espasmos que se inflaman.

Risk factors/Factores de riesgo Condiciones y conductas que representan una amenaza potencial para el bienestar de un individuo.

S

Saturated fatty acids/Ácidos grasos saturados Grasas que provienen principalmente de grasas animales, y que generalmente son sólidas a temperatura ambiente.

Sedentary/Sedentario Físicamente inactivo.

Self-concept/Concepto personal La idea que se tiene de uno mismo.

Self-esteem/Estima personal Sentimiento de auto confianza y valor personal.

Set/Serie Grupo de repeticiones consecutivas de cualquier ejercicio.

Shinsplint/Herida a la espinilla Inflamación de un tendon o músculo de la canilla.

Skeletal muscles/Músculos del esqueleto Músculos adheridos al hueso que causan movimiento corporal.

Skill-related fitness/Buen estado físico relacionado con la habilidad Agilidad, equilibrio, fuerza, velocidad, coordinación y tiempo de reacción.

Sleep apnea/Apnea del sueño Afección por la que el individuo deja de respirar durante el sueño, debido a la obstrucción o reducción de los pasajes de aire.

Slow-twitch muscle fiber/Contracción lenta de fibra muscular Fibra muscular que se contrae a un ritmo bajo, permitiendo mayor resistencia muscular.

Small muscle group/Grupo de músculos pequeños Todo grupo de músculos de menor tamaño, o bien, una pequeña cantidad de músculos utilizados al mismo tiempo.

Smokeless tobacco/Tabaco sin humo Tabaco que se inhala por la nariz o se mastica.

Smooth muscles/Músculos lisos Músculos a cargo del movimiento de los órganos internos.

Specificity principle/Principio de especificidad Establece que, sobrecargar determinado componente derivará en mejoras del estado físico de dicho único componente.

Speed/Velocidad Capacidad para mover el cuerpo o partes del mismo rápidamente.

Split workout/Serie de ejercicios dividida Programa de preparación física en el que se ejercitan tres o cuatro áreas corporales por sesión, trabajando a una elevada intensidad.

Sports medicine clinic/Centros clínicos de medicina deportiva Centros que se concentran en la investigación, con el fin de promover la salud y el buen estado físico, como así también, el desarrollo y la operatividad de la salud, la preparación física, la recreación y los programas educativos.

Spotter/Compañero Compañero que puede, tanto asistir a un individuo en el manejo seguro de las pesas, como alentarlo durante la sesión.

Sprain/torcedura Una condición en que los ligamentos que mantienen las articulaciones en su lugar están distendidos o quebrados.

Static contraction/Contracción estática Tipo de contracción muscular que se produce en ausencia de cualquier movimiento considerable.

Static posture/Postura estática Postura del cuerpo en posición de reposo.

Static stretching/Estiramiento estático Ejercicios que estiran el músculo despacio, suavemente y en forma sostenida, entre 20 y 30 segundos.

Steady-state cycle test/Test de bicicleta a ritmo sostenido Prueba que exige pedalear durante 20 minutos en bicicleta fija, y tratar de alcanzar una distancia predeterminada.

Steady-state jog test/Test de trote a ritmo sostenido Prueba que exige mantener el ritmo del trote durante 20 minutos hasta alcanzar una distancia específicamente determinada.

Steady-state swim test/Test de natación a ritmo sostenido Prueba que exige nadar durante 20 minutos, y tratar de alcanzar una distancia predeterminada.

Steady-state walk test/Test de caminata a ritmo sostenido Prueba que exige sostener el ritmo a paso vivo durante 30 minutos, y tratar de alcanzar una distancia predeterminada.

Strain/Desgarro Desgarro de un músculo o tendón.

Stress fracture/Fractura por estrés Ruptura del hueso provocada por carga excesiva.

Stress/Estrés Respuesta del cuerpo y la mente a las exigencias y amenazas de la vida diaria.

Stretching cooldown/Estiramiento de enfriamiento Comprende entre tres y cinco minutos de estiramiento posterior a actividad física o ejercicio.

Stroke/Apoplejía Cuando el flujo sanguíneo al cerebro de un individuo se interrumpe, o cesa por completo, a causa de una arteria obstruida.

Stroke volume/Volumen por impulso La cantidad de sangre bombeada con cada latido del corazón.

Substance abuse/Consumo de drogas Todo uso inapropiado o innecesario de substancias químicas con fines no medicinales.

Supersets/Superseries La ejecución alternada de series de ejercicios para entrenar músculos opuestos, sin descanso entre series.

Supination/Supinación Giro normal del pie hacia afuera cuando toca el piso.

T

T'ai chi/T'ai chi Arte marcial que incluye movimientos fluidos y gráciles, que exigen un preciso control muscular.

Talk test/Test del habla Medida de la habilidad que se tiene para sostener una conversación, mientras se realizan ejercicios o actividad física.

Target heart rate range/Valores óptimos de frecuencia cardiaca Valores a los que el ritmo cardiaco debería instalarse durante el ejercicio aeróbico, o actividad física, para rendir una máxima resistencia cardiorrespiratoria.

Tendons/Tendones Bandas de tejidos que conectan músculo con hueso.

Testosterone/Testosterona Químico producido por el cuerpo, que juega un importante rol en la construcción del músculo.

Time/Tiempo Duración de una serie completa de ejercicios, generalmente medido en minutos u horas.

Toe box/Capellada Parte del zapato que recubre los dedos de los pies.

Total-body workout/Serie de ejercicios completa Aquélla en que los principales grupos musculares se trabajan tres veces por semana, dejando, al menos, un día libre entre cada preparación física.

Trainability/Entrenabilidad Valores a los que los niveles de estado físico se incrementan durante la preparación física.

Training load/Carga de entrenamiento Cantidad de peso que un individuo debe levantar en un ejercicio dado.

Training plateau/Entrenamiento mesetario Período de tiempo durante el entrenamiento, en el que se producen pocos o ningún avance en el estado físico.

Trans fatty acids/Ácidos trans grasos Grasas que se forman cuando ciertos aceites se convierten en sólidos.

Type/Tipo El tipo particular de actividad física o ejercitación que se elige realizar.

U

Underhand grip/Toma supino Una posición en la cual la barra de pesas se toma con las palmas de las manos hacia arriba y los nudillos hacia abajo.

Underweight/Bajo peso Tener un índice de masa corporal (IMC) que es menor a un quinto del percentil de la edad correspondiente.

Unsaturated fatty acids/Ácidos grasos no saturados Grasas que son generalmente líquidas a temperatura ambiente y provienen principalmente de fuentes vegetales.

V

Vegetarian/Vegetariano Una persona que come principalmente o solamente alimentos que provienen de las plantas.

Veins/Venas Vasos sanguíneos que devuelven la sangre al corazón.

Vigorous physical activity or exercise/ Ejercitación o actividad física vigorosa Toda actividad o ejercitación que varía en intensidad de fuerte a máximo esfuerzo.

Vitamins/Vitaminas Micronutrientes que ayudan a controlar los procesos corporales, y contribuyen a que el cuerpo libere energía para trabajar.

W

Warm-up/Precalentamiento Porción de un plan de ejercicios completo, que consiste en una variedad de actividades de baja intensidad para preparar el cuerpo para el trabajo físico.

Warranty/Garantía Aval por parte del fabricante o representante para reparar o proporcionar durante un período limitado de tiempo.

Weight cycling/Ciclo del peso Ciclo en el que se baja y se sube de peso, alternativamente.

Weight machines/Máquinas con pesas Aparatos mecánicos que mueven pesas de arriba hacia abajo, utilizando un sistema de cables y poleas.

Weight-training belts/Cinturón de levantamiento de pesas Faja para proteger la parte baja de la espalda y del estómago cuando se levantan pesas pesadas.

Weight-training gloves/Guantes de levantamiento de pesas Guantes que previenen la formación de ampollas y callos en las palmas de las manos.

Wellness/Bienestar Salud total en las áreas de bienestar físico, bienestar mental/emocional, y bienestar social.

Wind-chill factor/Factor de viento helado Influencia combinada de viento y temperatura en el cuerpo.

Index

Bent-over dumbbell shoulder raise, 286
Bent-over row, 286–287
Beta carotene, 127
Biathlons, 368–369
Biceps, *251, 252, 300, 334*
Bicycles, stationary, 229, 239
Bicycling, 229, 363
  stationary cycling, 229
  steady-state cycle test, 220, 225, 226
Bigorexia, 178
Binge eating disorder, 178
"Bingeing and purging," 177
Biomechanics, 54–56, 228
  for bicycling, 229
  for lifting, 328–329
Blind one-leg stand, 78
Blisters, 57, 268, 269
Blood
  benefits of aerobic activity to, *210*
  cholesterol in, 120–121
  circulation of, *195*
  as part of circulatory system, 184
Blood pooling, 108
Blood pressure, 37, 206
Blood vessels, 194
  and atherosclerosis, 200, *201*
  and cardiovascular disease, 200
  and stroke, 202
BMI. *See* Body Mass Index
Body areas, 297, *299–300*
Bodybuilding, 249, 259
Body circumference, 159–161
Body composition, 11, 72, 147–152
  of athletes, *166*
  benefits of aerobic activity to, 210
  and body circumference, 159–161
  and body fat, 151. *See also* Body fat
  and Body Mass Index, 149
  and body type, 147, *148*
  and body weight, 148–149
  and cardiorespiratory endurance, 209
  and energy equation, 154–157
  evaluating, 159–163
  Finger Pinch Test for, 8
  and functional health and fitness, 151
  influences on, 153–158
  and lifestyle behaviors, 154
  maintaining healthy, 164–167
  and risks for chronic diseases, *152*
  skinfold measures of, 161–163
Body fat, 117, 151
  and aerobic capacity, 209
  and aerobic exercise, 211
  and body composition, 151
  calculations for, *150*
  essential, 151
  and flexibility, 327
  and health rating, *161*
  influences on, 153
  and protein consumption, 118

and resistance training myths, 259
  skinfold measurements of, 161–163
Body fluid loss, 41
Body image, 176–179
  benefits of aerobic activity to, *210*
  distorted, 176
  and eating disorders, 176–178
Body Mass Index (BMI), 149
  for overweight, 171
  for underweight, 175
Body temperature
  and flexibility, 326
  warm-ups to increase, 102, 103
Body type, 147, *148*
Bone mass
  and physical activity, *360*
  presenting or slowing loss of, 358–360
Bones
  benefits of aerobic activity to, *210*
  injuries to, 59
  and overweight, 173
  stress fractures of, 58
  weight training for building, 258
Breakfast, 134–135
Breath control, 277
Breathing
  muscles used in, 194–195, *196*
  and overweight, 173
  and physical activity, 195
  with resistance training, 277
Brisk walking, 228
Bruises, 57
Bulimia nervosa, 177–178
Bush, George W., 16
Butterfly stretch, 105

C

Caffeine
  and rehydration, 43
  and stress, *127*
Calcium, *125, 126*
Calf stretch, 105
Calipers, 161
Calisthenics, 73, 266, 368
Calorie intake, 72, *115*, 154
Calories, 115
  burned during physical activity, *139*
  calculating, 134
  from carbohydrates, 116
  estimating expended, 142
  expenditure of, 154–156, *304*
  from fats, 121
  influences on burning of, 157
  intake of, 72, *115*, 154
  and muscle-fat ratio, 259
  per gram of nutrients, *155*
  from protein, 118
  and resting metabolic rate, 157
Cancers
  and aerobic exercise, 210
  colon, *13*

females' risk factors for, 210
  lung, 199, 203
  and overweight, 172
Canoeing, 366
Capillaries, 194
Carbohydrates, 115–117
  calories per gram of, *155*
  complex, 116
  simple, 116
Cardiac arrest, 202
Cardiac muscle, 250. *See also* Heart
Cardiorespiratory endurance, 72, 198
  and aerobic activities, 193, 196, 198, 227–232
  and aerobic vs. anaerobic activities, 212–215
  benefits of, 210
  and care of heart and lungs, 199–206
  and circulatory system, 194, *195*
  environmental factors in, 211
  equipment for, 237–241
  evaluating, 197, 219–226
  factors affecting, 208–209
  FITT principle in workouts for, 233–236
  measuring, 207
  and respiratory system, 194–196
Cardiorespiratory fitness, 208, 210. *See also* Cardiorespiratory endurance
Cardiovascular conditioning, 84
Cardiovascular cooldown, 109
Cardiovascular disease (CVD), 200–203
  and aerobic activity, 198
  and sleep apnea, 173
Cardiovascular fitness, 8, 11, 72, 73, 198
Cardiovascular phase
  of cooldowns, 109
  of warm-ups, 103
Cardiovascular system. *See* Circulatory system
Careers, health and fitness, 373–374
Cartilage, 58
Case studies
  Bob's injury, 355
  Bret and Albert's summer resistance-training plan, 323
  David's fitness program, 69
  Denise's fitness plan, 243
  Diane's fitness level, 217
  Gary's personal exercise, 111
  Jackie's activity level, 169
  Javier's weight goals, 145
  losing weight, 191
  Molly's problem, 381
  Raul's class cuts, 33
  truth about resistance training, 271
CBC (complete blood count), 37
Chamberlain Wilt, *75*

(continued from TM28)

5. Be aware that individuals with spinal cord injuries are prone to having abnormally low resting heart rates.

6. Developing upper body strength, flexibility, and endurance is particularly important for the paraplegic. It will not only assist them in propelling their wheelchair, but will also make transferring to and from the chair easier.

7. Exercises and activities that increase circulation to the lower limbs are important in alleviating some of the secondary complications that can occur.

8. If the students are able to transfer to and from the chair, encourage them to do so. This will not only enhance upper body development, but will also help to improve lower limb circulation.

9. All activities should allow for maximum participation with the students' peers.

10. Be aware that students with spinal cord injuries are unable to regulate heat dissipation from the injury site down.

11. Watch for the development of ulcers and/or pressure sores that may result from a particular exercise or activity.

12. Ask physical and occupational therapists for help in developing aids and assistive devices for students' wheelchairs to facilitate their participation in activities.

Muscular Dystrophy

Muscular dystrophy is a term that is used to describe a group of related degenerative muscle diseases. It is a chronic, progressive deterioration of the voluntary musculature, and remission does not occur. Although the exact cause of muscular dystrophy is unknown, it is known that muscle protein is lost, causing weakness and atrophy of the skeletal muscles. The protein is gradually replaced by fat and connective tissue.

Implications for Physical Education

Programs of physical activity for students with muscular dystrophy are critical in maintaining the best possible physical health. The more activities performed at an early age to maintain existing function, the more likely that the debilitating effects of the disease can be delayed. The adaptations and activities for individual students will depend on the type of muscular dystrophy they have and how far the disease has progressed.

Muscular dystrophy itself is not fatal, but the secondary complications of immobilization increase the effects of respiratory disorders and heart disease. The quandary facing the physical educator is how to increase or maintain cardiovascular fitness when muscle weakness makes endurance activities more difficult.

Instructional Strategies/Accommodations

1. Recommendations from students' physicians are critical when planning a program to ensure that the activities and modifications are not contraindicated.

2. Physicians may have outlined specific strengthening and stretching programs during each stage of the disease.

3. Due to progressive muscle weakness, respiratory and cardiac problems become evident. Encourage breathing exercises for students confined to wheelchairs.

4. Activities should focus on maintaining existing function.

5. Exercise of muscles involved in the activities of daily living to increase strength may permit greater functional use of the body.

6. When activities involve the affected muscle groups, no resistance other than gravity should be utilized.

7. Any exercise or activity that causes undue strain or fatigue should be avoided.

8. Activity periods should be frequent but short in duration. The students should be encouraged to participate to their fullest capacity. Include frequent rest periods.

9. Students should be encouraged to participate in as many different activities as possible.

10. Activities requiring locomotion should be performed for as long as possible to increase and prolong independent movement.

11. As the disease begins to progress, use adaptations and modifications that will allow students to successfully complete assigned tasks.

12. It is important to be particularly sensitive to the emotional needs of students with muscular dystrophy. Introduce dance activities, which can help students to express emotions.

13. Introduce sedentary recreational activities that will carry over when the students are in a wheelchair.

14. Individuals with muscular dystrophy must conserve their energy. Their diets should be closely monitored, as excess weight can cause greater fatigue.

Diabetes

Diabetes is a general term referring to a variety of disorders that are divided into two groups: diabetes mellitus and diabetes insipidus. Diabetes insipidus results from an inability to concentrate urine in the kidneys. Diabetes mellitus is a group of metabolic disorders resulting from insufficiency of insulin. Diabetes mellitus, the most common type, includes the following classifications:

- *Insulin-dependent diabetes (type I):* Usually diagnosed before 18 years of age. The pancreas stops producing insulin, which is needed to help the body use carbohydrates. Students manage diabetes by taking insulin, eating regular nutritional meals and snacks, exercising regularly, and monitoring blood sugars.

- *Non-insulin-dependent diabetes (type II):* Onset is gradual and frequently does not occur until after 30 years of age. Insulin therapy is usually not necessary because individuals with this type of diabetes usually retain some insulin secretion capabilities. Obesity usually accompanies type II diabetes.

Implication for Physical Education

Individuals with diabetes mellitus should be encouraged to exercise regularly because long-term exercise provides many benefits to help control the disease. However, unless strict food and insulin guidelines are followed, a single exercise activity can lead to negative responses. The negative exercise responses include:

- *Hyperglycemia (high blood sugar):* This is a problem for active individuals with type I or type II diabetes. It results when daily exercise volume is suddenly reduced without increasing insulin or oral agents used to control glucose levels. Symptoms of hyperglycemia are inattentiveness, lethargy, extreme thirst, and a frequent need to urinate.

- *Hypoglycemia (low blood sugar):* This is the greatest concern of the individual with type I diabetes. Hypoglycemia can occur quickly and needs immediate attention. Skipping or delaying meals or snacks, exercising, or having too much insulin can cause blood sugar to fall rapidly. The long list of symptoms includes shaking/trembling, irritability/mood swings, sweating, sleepiness, mental slowness, sudden hunger, inappropriate responses, sudden anger, sudden silence, double vision, slurred speech, headache, and numbness.

Instructional Strategies/Accommodations

If students' blood sugar is high, then let them rest if they are lethargic and let them exercise if they are hyperactive.

1. If students' blood sugar is low, then give some form of sugar immediately (a sugar tablet or 4 to 8 oz. of regular soft drink or fruit juice). If students do not improve after sugar intake, call for emergency assistance.

2. Determine physical activity tolerance levels through communication with students' parents or guardians and physician.

3. Help students schedule physical education within two hours of eating.

4. Avoid psychological stress caused by competitive or excitatory activities. Stress may influence students' metabolic rate, which in turn changes blood sugar levels.

5. Avoid having students walk barefoot.

6. Teach students to avoid wearing clothes that are too tight; this could cause circulatory restrictions.

7. Have students exercise with a peer who knows the signs of hyperglycemia and hypoglycemia.

8. Students should drink water before, during, and after exercise.

9. Encourage students to exercise.

10. Teach students how to keep a log book of blood sugar levels, dosage of insulin, amount and type of food eaten, and type of intensity of exercise.

11. Cleanliness and skin care are important, and any break in the skin needs to be promptly treated.

Mild Mental Retardation

Students with mild mental retardation (IQ 70-55) possess social and motoric skills that are similar to those of their nondisabled peers. Academic performance is the most apparent difference. Much of a student's academic difficulties originate from the inability to deal with higher cognitive functioning and abstract thinking.

Implications for Physical Education

Many students who are classified with mild mental retardation (MR) can, and do, participate in regular physical education activities without difficulty. They are much more like their "normal" peers in physical abilities and capabilities than in any other respect. Physical education classes and sports are often a primary opportunity for them to experience success and develop self-esteem.

It is important that students with mild MR receive a well-rounded physical education program that provides them with numerous opportunities to experience and practice a variety of skills in varied situations. It is critical that activities also provide ample opportunities for positive social interactions with nondisabled peers. This will ensure that younger students with mild MR have the chance to develop play skills that may not develop naturally. It also affords older students the opportunity to learn leisure skills that will enable them to successfully participate in community recreational activities.

Moderate Mental Retardation

The student who is classified with moderate mental retardation (IQ 54-40) generally experiences more pronounced deficits in social, emotional, mental, and motoric development than the student with mild mental retardation. As the student becomes older, these deviations from the norm become more apparent.

The student with moderate MR generally exhibits significant problems with attention span, memory, and recognition and generalizations of learned skills. Social behaviors are often rudimentary, necessitating frequent reminders of socially appropriate responses.

Implications for Physical Education

Motorically, the student with moderate MR demonstrates more pronounced deficits in psychomotor skills and performance. It is possible that some of the deficits may be a result of failure to understand the movement skill rather than an actual inability to perform the skill.

Increased deficits seem to exist in balance, fundamental locomotor skills, general body coordination, and fitness levels. These deficits necessitate a more individualized program of motor skill development in order for the student to receive maximum benefit from the program.

Severe and Profound Mental Retardation

Students with severe mental retardation (IQ 39-25) or profound mental retardation (IQ below 25) exhibit extreme developmental delays in all areas of growth and development. In addition to mental retardation, secondary disabling conditions such as cerebral palsy, visual deficits, hearing and speech problems, and delayed maturation often exist. Inappropriate social behaviors are often more pronounced in students with severe and profound MR. These behaviors tend to worsen if intervention does not occur. The most common behaviors that are seen are self-stimulating behaviors such as rocking and self-mutilation.

Implications for Physical Education

For students with severe and profound MR, even the most fundamental skills must be taught. The emphasis of physical education programming should be on motor skill development and activities of functional daily living. Tasks such as reaching and grasping, which normally develop automatically as children age, must be taught to students with severe and profound MR. Physical education activities, as well as the development of fundamental movement patterns and skills, must also be taught.

Specific Learning Disabilities

Students with specific learning disabilities compose the largest and perhaps the least understood group of students who experience learning difficulties.

Many students with specific learning disabilities exhibit average or above-average intellectual capabilities, but their achievement is delayed due to a breakdown in one or more of the information-processing steps. Normally, information processing is a continuous cycle that includes the following steps:

- *Receiving sensory input.* Stimuli are received through visual, auditory, kinesthetic, vestibular, and tactile systems.

- *Processing and decision-making.* The stimuli are sorted, organized, and synthesized.

- *Motor output.* The actual movement or action occurs.

- *Feedback.* The stimuli that result from the motor output are received through the sensory systems, and the process begins again.

Implications for Physical Education

Just as there is no single set of characteristics that describes a student with specific learning disabilities, there is also no clear profile of the motor performances of these students. Some students will exhibit average or above-average motor abilities and skills, while others will exhibit significant perceptual-motor deficits. Often, students with specific learning disabilities will experience the following motoric difficulties: inaccurate perceptions of sensory cues, general awkwardness or clumsiness, poor static and dynamic balance, delayed or immature motor patterns and skills, difficulty in sequencing and motor planning, difficulty with perseverance, and difficulty with fine motor tasks.

It is imperative when planning a physical education program for students with specific learning disabilities that the unique learning characteristics of each student be taken into consideration. Physical education activities that are carefully and individually designed for success can provide excellent opportunities for such students to develop their self-esteem.

Instructional Strategies/Accommodations

1. Be aware of and understand the nature of each student's specific learning difficulties.

2. Be aware of the students' medications and the side effects of them. Know when the students are supposed to take their medications, and make sure they do so.

3. Have consistent and clear stop and start signals for activities. This will help students who struggle with perseveration.

4. To eliminate frustration and failure, provide activities that are challenging but within the students' capabilities.

5. Make sure that each student experiences success during each activity and lesson by task-analyzing the activities and using progressions to teach skills.

6. Activities should proceed from simple to more complex in small increments.

7. Class routines should be highly structured and consistent from day to day.

8. Activities should concentrate on developing perceptual-motor abilities.

9. Instruction should be multisensory. Verbal directions need to be clear, concise, and accompanied by visual demonstrations. When appropriate, provide tactile assistance.

10. Highly competitive and elimination games should be avoided.

11. Allow students ample time to think through a task. Asking them to verbalize instructions may also prove to be beneficial.

12. Reinforce academic concepts through movement activities as frequently as possible.

13. When planning a sequence of activities, make sure each part of the activity is distinctly different from the others.

14. Carefully sequence movement activities so that each student experiences success and a sense of direction.

15. Eliminate as much extraneous stimuli from the learning environment as possible.

16. Utilize various group formations to enhance each student's role as a contributing member of a group.